Collected Works of Christian M.I.M. Matthiessen
Volume 2

Systemic Functional Linguistics
Part 2

Christian M.I.M. Matthiessen
Edited by Kazuhiro Teruya, Diana Slade, and Kaela Peijia Zhang

Collected Works of Christian M.I.M. Matthiessen

Editors

Kazuhiro Teruya
Academic Consultant

Diana Slade
Australian National University

Kaela Peijia Zhang
Hang Seng University of Hong Kong

The series is about the nature, the functions, and the structure of human language seen from a number of points of view within the framework of contemporary scientific thought. It covers about 35 years of work by one of the world's leading scholars in the field, Prof. Christian M.I.M. Matthiessen.

The series of volumes in the Collected Works of Christian M.I.M. Matthiessen are organized into a number of distinct topics. However, they all reinforce each other and together constitute a coherent body of theoretical and descriptive work.

Each volume consists of a series of chapters written by Matthiessen with a few coauthored chapters that are included so as to present Matthiessen's whole intellectual enterprise. Each volume also contains at least one new article written specifically for each volume. These reinforce the insights presented in each volume and further update the cutting- edge nature of the collective works.

Christian Matthiessen has taught and held visiting positions at various universities and research institutes in Australia, Germany, Japan, China, the US, and Hong Kong. He is currently Honorary Dean of The Language Studies Institute of Sun Yat-sen University, Honorary Professor of Beijing Normal University, Guest Professor of University of Science and Technology, Beijing, and Honorary President of the International Association for Hallidayan Linguistics. Matthiessen has broad linguistic expertise as a theoretician, descriptivist, educationist, and multilingual practitioner of enormous scope and importance, coupled with him being a prolific writer throughout his career.

Collected Works of Christian M.I.M. Matthiessen
Volume 2

Systemic Functional Linguistics
Part 2

Christian M.I.M. Matthiessen
Edited by Kazuhiro Teruya, Diana Slade, and Kaela Peijia Zhang

UNIVERSITY OF TORONTO PRESS
Toronto Buffalo London

Published by University of Toronto Press
Toronto Buffalo London
utppublishing.com
Printed in Canada

ISBN 978-1-0498-0004-2 (cloth)   ISBN 978-1-0498-0006-6 (EPUB)
                                 ISBN 978-1-0498-0005-9 (PDF)

Library and Archives Canada Cataloguing in Publication

Title: Collected works of Christian M.I.M. Matthiessen / Christian M.I.M. Matthiessen ;
    edited by Kazuhiro Teruya, Diana Slade, and Kaela Peijia Zhang.
Other titles: Works
Names: Matthiessen, Christian M. I. M., author | Teruya, Kazuhiro, editor |
    Slade, Diana, editor | Zhang, Kaela Peijia, editor.
Description: Includes bibliographical references and index. | Contents: Volume 2.
    Systemic functional linguistics, Part 2
Identifiers: Canadiana (print) 20250277034 | Canadiana (ebook) 20250277042 |
    ISBN 9781049800042 (v. 2 ; cloth) | ISBN 9781049800066 (v. 2 ; EPUB) |
    ISBN 9781049800059 (v. 2 ; PDF)
Subjects: LCSH: Functionalism (Linguistics) | LCSH: Systemic grammar. |
    LCSH: Structural linguistics.
Classification: LCC P147 .M38 2025 | DDC 410.1/833 – dc23

Cover design: Will Brown
Cover image: *Bymotiv (Village Motif)* by Martin Emond, Swedish painter, 1895–1965

We wish to acknowledge the land on which the University of Toronto Press operates. This land is the traditional territory of the Wendat, the Anishnaabeg, the Haudenosaunee, the Métis, and the Mississaugas of the Credit First Nation.

University of Toronto Press acknowledges the financial support of the Government of Canada, the Canada Council for the Arts, and the Ontario Arts Council, an agency of the Government of Ontario, for its publishing activities.

To the memory of Michio Sugeno (1940–2023)

As author and chief editor, we would like to dedicate this volume to the
memory of Michio Sugeno – world-class scholar in fuzzy theory and
mathematics, stimulating supporter and interpreter of systemic functional
linguistics (SFL) in computational modelling and neurolinguistics, and
wonderful friend and intellectual guide. We have many happy memories of
him in project meetings, excursions, and gourmet dinners around the
world – often together with Michael Halliday – and also with other systemic
functional linguists. Sugeno-sensei was a pioneer not only in fuzzy theory,
but also in computing with language informed by both fuzzy
theory and SFL – with an important additional intellectual ingredient
based on his deep expertise in the work by the post-Tractatus Wittgenstein.

Contents

List of figures

List of tables

Foreword

David Butt

There have been a number of remarkable intellectual troubadours – those who have followed the tantalizing threads of their thought and travelled to learn from luminaries and to experience different regions and cultures, all motivated on a yet-to-emerge "shape": the shape of a theory. A theory to the ancient Greeks – *theorein* – was a "way of looking" at the world. One can reasonably ask: how does such a motivation arise and stir the spirit of a person so moved to thought and action?

Christian Matthiessen knew early that he wished to follow an unusual trail of enquiry. But unlike the marine biology of Aristotle's field work (384–322 BCE) or the prolific mathematics of the wandering Paul Erdös (1913–1996), the subject of linguistics is a discipline that few study formally, or even meet, until university. Of course, there was the peripatetic career of the titanic linguist, Roman Jakobson (1896–1982), whose relocations were forced by politics and wars. And most linguists have travelled to understand cultures and languages that may be at a considerable semiotic distance from their own pattern of life. But Christian understood as a teenager that he wanted to know about languages as a human phenomenon, not just as a necessary activity. Consequently, he began by absorbing the theoretical expertise of Europe; then of theUS and the Americas; and so too, of East Asia and the Pacific. He sought the teachers who offered a framework for analysis of that phenomenon, a framework which would provide the most plausible accounts of language, and which would also assist in achieving practical outcomes for different language "users," namely, for all of us, since all of us are challenged by our communicative cosmos.

It may not have been the plan of the editors, but from this volume – Volume 2 of Christian's papers and his systemic functional "ways of seeing" – a chronological perspective emerges, the story of Matthiessonian semiotics. We have the evidence of Christian's earlier proposals on the representation of language for the purposes of computational modelling – the explicitness demanded by a computational model creates a "criterion of falsification." The success or not of such testing was the necessary bulwark against being "just an armchair philosopher" – one of Christian's most potent criticisms of those linguists (and philosophers or logicians) across the decades of his career who indulged in mere Platonic theorizing about language universals. In Chapter 8, we have an invaluable interview that sets out the "bildungsroman" more cogently: his semiotic development and the roles contributed by mentors and colleagues who helped to shape his practice.

In the early Chapters 1–4, aspects of Christian's developing "semiotic self" are set out. Having benefited from European teachers (Malmberg and Ellegård), he also witnessed the best trends from the West Coast of the US – not just in relation to the rigours of explicitness in AI and computational linguistics, but also from the sophisticated typological work centred around the universities of California. Particularly influential was the disciplinary and personal leadership of Bill Mann: such leadership allowed Christian's insights to be more fully expressed, and his connections out to other traditions of linguistics to be developed. Bill Mann was, by Christian's accounts, a thoughtful innovator and the acme of a research leader. And, through the PENMAN project, working with Michael Halliday, Christian Matthiessen and Bill Mann were able to set out a "Tektronic" map of the inter-relations between c. 1,200 "systems of choice" in English. This map is the network which both guides, and draws from, the fourth edition of *Halliday's introduction to functional grammar* (Halliday and Matthiessen 2014).

Like Matthiessen's work in that fourth edition of the *Halliday's introduction to functional grammar*, chapters 5–11 here are the axis of this volume of collected papers – consider, for instance, Chapter 9, "Halliday's conception of language as a probabilistic system." The chapters exemplify Christian's semiotics "in full stride." They are profound explorations of Halliday's *theorein*, his "way of looking at" the relation between *system* and *instance*. Matthiessen demonstrates how probabilities are crucial to Halliday's modelling: 1) the terms along the "cline of instantiation": system–register–text (instance); and 2) the cross-stratal realizations of systems, i.e. from semantics to lexicogrammar to phonology.

By contrast with the influential universalist models of language, Matthiessen followed Halliday in valuing the quantitative dimensions of what people actually say, as well as correlating acts of "saying" with the circumstances under which things are said. This includes a number of intra-systemic factors that needed to be distinguished – for example, the need to state: were the systems of choice between equal alternatives? or was there a skewing of meaning (for instance, towards *positive* in polarity, and towards *declarative* in mood)? Probabilities are a necessary step towards understanding language change.

Consequently, in Matthiessen's methods, corpus work, when directed by carefully structured linguistic questions and hypotheses, is an essential tool for linguists. Matthiessen always sought to motivate and develop his analysis through corpora, whether the questions arose in lexicogrammar, semantics (e.g. rhetorical structure or expressions of spatial meanings), or in register descriptions (e.g. reports of disease, or healthcare). A corpus not only draws on authentic data, it also lends what Christian called the all-important "industrial strength" to results. In Matthiessonian cartography, we are expected to "measure" ourselves against the methods and consequences of other branches of science, always noting, however, that in viewing the world other disciplines report what is "seen," whereas the linguist is examining the very medium of "seeing."

The final chapter deals with semiosis and the brain. Back in 1983, in discussing systemic functional linguistics, the computational scientist and developer of a computer program for understanding natural language, SHRDLU, Terry Winograd, emphasized that "the systemic mode of analysis has deep cognitive significance." The final chapter of this volume is a compilation of material that needs to be absorbed by all those who have thought that systemic functional linguists do not address the brain in the brain–language complex. Matthiessen has been an assiduous follower of social, evolutionary, and brain sciences: his studies followed a span of luminaries: for instance, the interdisciplinary career of Herb Simons (1916–2001, during which AI was partnered with the analysis of complex systems and economics) to the careers of Yorick Wilks, Margaret Masterton, Terry Winograd, Terrence Deacon, and Michael Arbib. With Halliday's emphasis on Darwinian theory, and with Ruqaiya Hasan's analysis of coding orientation (based on gender and class), Matthiessen has been a leader in arguing for the "semiotic brain." In Gerard Edelman's emphasis on the role of language in his neural Darwinism, in the writings of Antonio Damasio, of Susan Greenfield, and of Lisa Feldman Barrett, one can look to a future of brain sciences in which experience and emotion will be foregrounded (rather than isolating acts of "cognition" or IQ), and when the human brain will be studied for those particular channels by which it makes itself.

There are many volumes of Christian Matthiessen's papers to come. The ones presented here cover an interesting arc from early through to an emergent phase, as this internationalist scholar now lives in Spain. Given that is a country where Arabic and European cultures have coexisted, Christian may return to aspects of his early interests in Arabic and paintings. In this return to Europe, now along with his vibrant networks of collegial contacts around our globe, the only regret I can recall is his saying to me that he "missed a chance to hear Roman Jakobson speak." I can only say how much I would have been excited to hear these two troubadours of linguistics speak to each other. I must be grateful, however, that we all have better access to Christian's way of seeing languages through the efforts of the editors of this second volume of his "Works."

Acknowledgments

We are grateful to the original publishers for permission to reprint the articles and chapters in this volume. Original publication details are provided below.

"Semantics for a systemic grammar: the chooser and inquiry framework" from James D. Benson, Michael J. Cummings, and William S. Greaves (eds.), *Linguistics in a systemic perspective*, Amsterdam and Philadelphia: John Benjamins (Amsterdam studies in the theory and history of linguistic science. Series IV, Current issues in linguistic theory: v.39), 1988, pp. 221–42. Copyright © James D. Benson, Michael J. Cummings, and William S. Greaves. Reproduced with permission of John Benjamins Publishing. "Fuzziness construed in language: a linguistic perspective" from *Proceedings of 1995 IEEE International Conference on Fuzzy Systems*, vol.4, Yokohama, Japan, 20–24 March 1995, pp. 1871–8, https://doi.org/10.1109/FUZZY.1995.409935. Copyright © 1995, IEEE. Reproduced with permission of IEEE. "On the idea of theory-neutral descriptions" from Ruqaiya Hasan, Carmel Cloran, and David Butt (eds.), *Functional descriptions: theory in practice*, Amsterdam and Philadelphia: John Benjamins (Amsterdam studies in the theory and history of linguistic science. Series IV, Current issues in linguistic theory: v.121), 1996, pp. 39–83. Copyright © Ruqaiya Hasan, Carmel Cloran, and David Butt. Reproduced with permission of John Benjamins Publishing. "Interview with Christian Matthiessen (Liverpool 1998)" from Manuel A. Hernández Hernández, "Organising principles and expansion of the systemic functional model: A conversation with Christian Matthiessen," *Revista Canaria de Estudios Ingleses 40*, 2000, pp. 251–6. Copyright © Christian Matthiessen. Reproduced with permission of Servicio de Publicaciones, Universidad de La Laguna. "Halliday's conception of language as a probabilistic system" from Jonathan J. Webster (ed.), *The Bloomsbury companion to M.A.K. Halliday*, London and New York: Bloomsbury, 2015, pp. 203–41. Copyright © Jonathan J. Webster and contributors. Reproduced with permission of Bloomsbury Academic. "Systemic functional morphology: the lexicogrammar of the word" from Alina Villalva and Edson Rosa Francisco de Souza (eds.), *Estudos de Morfologia: Recortes e Abordagens Vol. 2*, Campinas: Mercado de Letras, 2019, pp. 15–78. Copyright © Christian Matthiessen. Reproduced with permission of Mercado de Letras. https://www.mercado-de-letras.com.br/livro-mway.php?codid=608

Editorial introduction

The second volume of the *Collected works of Christian M.I.M. Matthiessen: Systemic functional linguistics – Part 2* contains Matthiessen's papers on systemic functional linguistics (SFL) spanning forty years from 1981 to the present. During this period, Matthiessen has moved globally, starting from Sweden in northern Europe to the West Coast of the US to Sydney on the east coast of Australia and then from Hong Kong on China's southern coast to Costa del Sol on the southern coast of Spain. Throughout this period, Matthiessen maintains one of the underlying centres of gravity of his systemic functional research, i.e. modelling of language in various research contexts while he continues expanding his linguistic and interdisciplinary research agenda.

This volume thus covers a small fraction of his expanding research but addresses core aspects of SFL that help the reader discover the wealth of Matthiessen's systemic functional work. The volume is comprised of his earlier and more recent work on theoretically guided modelling of language in computational linguistic systems and on key aspects of systemic functional theory. It complements the first volume, which provides a comprehensive survey of the systemic functional architecture of language in context – treating it as a multidimensional semiotic space defined by intersecting semiotic dimensions such as rank, metafunction, and stratification, with key architectural features including indeterminacy and probability. It also includes a treatment of systemic functional metatheory – the theory of the nature and appliability of theory – concerned with linguistic modelling. That is, in this volume Matthiessen offers a sense of what we need to do to make our linguistic account explicit enough so that we can relate it to tasks that require explicit models, like the task of simulating language with computers, the task of relating the account of language to what we know about the brain in terms of processing of language by the brain.

Matthiessen's detailed comprehensive language description and theoretical modelling goes back to his earlier papers; Chapters 1 through 4 have been selected from work on text generation from the 1980s (except Chapter 4, published in 1990). They are concerned with a large-scale computational systemic functional grammar, Nigel, which was developed as part of the PENMAN text-generation system in projects led by Bill Mann at the University of Southern California (USC) Information Sciences Institute (ISI) in the US. Along the systemic functional theoretical dimensions of strata, metafunctions, instantiation, axis, delicacy, and rank, these chapters present computationally implementable representations and their computational architecture. Here the grammar, semantics, and their environments are represented explicitly to allow computational modelling for text generation. While these chapters are precursors to his more integrated subsequent theoretical and descriptive accounts (e.g. Matthiessen 1995), his accounts of systemic principles such as conflation, realization, and semantic interfaces should be of great interest to researchers who need to carry out or to understand detailed systemic functional analysis.

Apart from computational modelling and language description, Matthiessen has followed up a varied and broad range of interest from the start, including theoretical modelling. Chapters 5 through 7 reflect his theoretical research in the early 1990s.

In Chapter 5 Matthiessen discusses syntagmatic organization. Inspired by Halliday (1979) and Hasan (1984), he further advances the theoretical understanding of the structure of constituency that is often taken as the only mode of syntagmatic organization. He interprets the realization of "constituency" in terms of metafunctional modes of meaning and modes of expression across different strata. This brings out their complementarity and resonance in creating meaning and enrich, for example, the way in which different languages can be described systemic functionally (cf. Matthiessen 2004).

Matthiessen's extension and refinement of the theory has not only contributed to SFL but also helped establish a number of new interdisciplinary collaborations. Chapter 6 is one such example from 1995 where he collaborated with the fuzzy theorist and engineer Michio Sugeno and members of his labs. In this paper, Matthiessen characterizes the inherently indeterminate nature of language, "fuzziness," systemic functionally, based on Zadeh's conception of fuzzy set theory. Here distinct categories such as process types are seen as constituting fuzzy sets that reflect our way of construing our experience of a non-discrete world. Accordingly, he represents indeterminacy in language topologically, for example, the experience of quanta of change as regions on a cline, and class membership construed as a class in the network of different process types.

As a fine theorist and descriptivist of language, Matthiessen has dealt with many challenges placed upon the role, nature, and value of linguistic theory in the engagement with describing languages. In Chapter 7, first published in 1996, Matthiessen refutes traditional misconceptions about theory-neutral descriptions and metatheorizes linguistic theory as a semiotic resource in which the general theory of language and particular descriptions of language come to stand in a realizational relationship where one construes the other. Using Nesbitt's HyperGrammar as such a first step, he proposes a framework for reference grammars that would address the needs for the twenty-first century – a framework reflecting the wealth of theory as a resource in the description of particular languages.

In Chapters 8 through 11, Matthiessen continues addressing the principles and some of the theoretical dimensions of SFL.

His two papers mentioned above, one on fuzziness (Chapter 6) published in 1995 and the other on theory-neutral description (Chapter 7) in 1996 are both built on his earlier unpublished paper written in 1993 on instantiation and logogenesis, here included as Chapter 11. In the theory-neutral description paper, instantiation is seen as one dimension of the multidimensionality of description that helps linguists establish registerial profiles of systems in new variety of reference grammars, and in the fuzziness paper it brings about systemic probability of fuzzy classes in the system network of construing experience. His dynamic interpretation of the instantiations of an underlying potential in the unfolding text later comes to be formalized as logogenesis, one of the major processes of semogenic history (Halliday and Matthiessen 1999).

Chapter 8 takes a different format; it is an interview of Matthiessen in which he succinctly explicates the systemic functional approach and multidimensional aspects of SFL theory. He also provides his anecdotal accounts on its development at the time of his interview conducted in 1998.

Matthiessen's collaborative relationship with Halliday goes back to 1980. Since then they have published two coauthored books in 1999, reissued 2006, and 2004, revised 2014. It is no exaggeration, therefore, to say that he is the most fitting scholar to scrutinize Halliday's conception of language. In Chapter 9, which was commissioned for Halliday's companion book edited by Jonathan Webster, Matthiessen takes further Halliday's conception of language as a probabilistic system, the probabilistic nature of language Halliday took seriously as early as the 1950s. Matthiessen illuminates probabilistic properties of language by profiling different systems and registers variously in terms of not only conditional probabilities but also transitional probabilities as visualized as a text score.

Chapter 11 is also a commissioned paper. Matthiessen was asked to outline "morphology" systemic functionally based on seven set questions. Given that morphology is not a distinct module or component in the architecture of systemic functional theory, Matthiessen characterizes morphology, or word grammar, by locating it within the overall systemic functional architecture of language wherein non-systemic functional accounts on morphology are assigned relative value. This true scholarship provides a gateway into the richness of SFL theory, especially for those who are used to working with the notion of morphology and wish to be inspired by SFL, and those who wish to understand and/or describe languages systemic functionally.

The final chapter is a newly written paper from 2023. This chapter showcases another area of interdisciplinary research – a domain Matthiessen investigates here for the first time in print. It is concerned with bio-semiotic systems as interpreted in neurosemiotics and the role SFL can play in the development of neurosemiotics. He interprets bio-semiotic systems as the relationship between biological system and semiotic systems in relation to an ordered typology of systems. This means, among other things, that semantics is modelled as a stratal interface to bio-semiotic and socio-semiotic systems outside language. Using ideational semantics, he interprets the hub-and-spoke model in neurolinguistics systemic functionally and proposes that language serves an integrative role in relation to the modern language brain, and he offers a theoretical foundation for biologically implementable bio-semiotic systems.

The papers collected in this volume are not organized to be read necessarily in sequence. The reader may wish to read chapters of their interest in any sequence, while the first two chapters may help those who are unfamiliar with natural language processing by computer read the subsequent two chapters. This volume includes more than 120 intricately designed figures. They are given as a succinct summary, an expansion of discussion, theoretical modelling, etc., all of which should serve as scaffolding as one reads on Matthiessen's detailed and elegant semiotic accounts.

We have tried in this volume together with Volume 1 to contextualize Matthiessen's volume 3, *Discourse analysis and multisemiotic/multimodal studies*, and other volumes under preparation, in relation to his other contributions to systemic functional literature. Among those publications that we are unable to include in his collected works, there are at least two publications that we think should be very useful in engaging with and reading SFL: *Key terms in systemic functional linguistics* (Mattiessen, Teruya, and Lam 2010) and *Systemic functional linguistics: A complete guide* (Matthiessen and Teruya 2023). We highly recommend keeping them at one's elbows as resource books. We are very happy to be able to continue presenting Matthiessen's abundance of ideas in the study of language, or what David Butt calls "Matthessonian semiotics."

References

Halliday, M.A.K. 1979. Modes of meaning and modes of expression: Types of grammatical structure and their determination by different semantic functions. In D.J. Allerton, David Holdcroft, and Edward Carney (eds.), *Function and context in linguistic analysis: A festschrift for William Haas.* Cambridge: Cambridge University Press. 57–79.

Halliday, M.A.K. and Christian M.I.M. Matthiessen. 1999. *Construing experience through meaning: A language-based approach to cognition.* London: Cassell. Re-issued as: Halliday and Matthiessen, 2006, *Construing experience through meaning: A language-based approach to cognition.* London and New York: Continuum.

Halliday, M.A.K. and Christian M.I.M. Matthiessen. 2004/2014. *Halliday's introduction to functional grammar.* 3rd/4th edition. London: Routledge.

Hasan, Ruqaiya. 1984. The nursery tale as a genre. Nottingham Linguistic Circular 13. Reprinted in Ruqaiya Hasan, 1996, *Ways of saying: Ways of meaning: Selected papers of Ruqaiya Hasan,* edited by Carmel Cloran, David Butt, and Geoffrey Williams. London: Cassell. 51–72.

Matthiessen, Christian M.I.M. 1995. *Lexicogrammatical cartography: English systems.* Tokyo, Taipei, and Dallas: International Language Sciences Publishers.

Matthiessen, Christian M.I.M. 2004. Descriptive motifs and generalizations. In Alice Caffarel, J.R. Martin, and Christian M.I.M. Matthiessen (eds.). *Language typology: A functional perspective.* Amsterdam: Benjamins. 537–673.

Matthiessen, Christian M.I.M., Kazuhiro Teruya, and Marvin Lam. 2010. *Key terms in systemic functional linguistics.* London and New York: Continuum.

Matthiessen, Christian M.I.M. and Kazuhiro Teruya. 2023. *Systemic functional linguistics: A complete guide.* Abingdon and New York: Routledge.

Outline of Volume 2: Systemic functional linguistics – Part 2

Chapter 1 is concerned with designing a model where a grammar and a lexicon can be made to function as a text-production system, PENMAN. It discusses the sub-components that deal with semantic information and with syntactic information and identifies the problems of relating these two types of information to design strategies to meet the problems.

Chapter 2 illustrates how systemic functional linguistics makes contributions in the areas of grammar and choosers for grammar in computation to fulfil the demands placed upon a large-scale computational grammar in a text generator, Nigel, that was being developed as part of the PENMAN project. In particular it demonstrates the metafunctional organization of systemic grammar that leads naturally to a multifunctional factoring of the sentence-generation process. This process is then defined in terms of features of grammatical and semantic choice and their realization statements with realization operators for text generation.

Chapter 3 further expands the illustration of the text-generation system discussed in Chapter 2. It discusses the semantics of the NIGEL grammar, that is, the framework of a chooser and inquiry semantics that was developed to deal with the problem of making purposeful grammatical choices in response to a communicative situation. The whole chooser and inquiry framework is illustrated with respect to examples from the choosers of the MOOD TYPE and PRIMARY TENSE systems that are identified through a network of inquiries. The chapter suggests the compatibility of the framework with sociological semantics.

Chapter 4 deals with two semantic interfaces that are implemented in text-generation systems using systemic functional grammar, i.e. chooser and inquiry semantics, whose framework is discussed in Chapter 2, and situation-specific semantic systems. The former approaches from below with respect to lexicogrammar and the latter from above, from context. The chapter discusses each of these two complementary approaches to semantics and their relative merits in adopting these approaches in one generation system.

Chapter 5 sheds new light on the mono-modal treatment of constituency in linguistic theorizing as the default mode of syntagmatic organization by bringing out complementarity and resonance of different modes of organization in interpreting language. To this rule-based thesis of constituency, it presents an antithesis that there are different modes of meaning and that each of these modes of meaning engenders a different mode of expression. This contrast between the thesis and its antithesis expands the conception of grammatical organization to the point where grammatical structure is no longer insulated from its semiotic environment. It thus synthesizes in harmony metafunctional modes of meaning into simultaneous constituency structures of their complementary modes of expression, such as simulated waves and prosodies.

Chapter 6 interprets Zadeh's notion of fuzziness in terms of a constructivist view of the role of language in relation to human thinking and illustrates how fuzziness is constructed by language as an inherent property of how we construe our experience of the world as meaning organized into networks of fuzzy classes. The nature of fuzzy classes of meaning is illustrated typologically in terms of the system network of PROCESS TYPE in English that is complemented by fuzzy representations of topology. This illustrative example of a system network points to the overall potential of the grammar of English being instantiated in a given situation, accumulating relative frequencies to form probabilities of various features in the overall systemic potential of language.

Chapter 7 offers a solution to the problem of the disjunction between theory and description, which is to reconstrue theory and its role in description. Such solution construes linguistic theory as a semiotic resource to meet the unprecedented demands and technological possibilities for the new production of linguistic descriptions in the transition to the twenty-first century. After revealing how the complementary goals of theory and description have become polarized for some influential linguists and showing how some do not hold the notion of theory-neutral descriptions, this chapter further uses case marking systems as an example to indicate that theory is a resource for enriching description.

Chapter 8 features an interview held at the University of Liverpool, UK, in July 1998. Matthiessen's responses to seven questions provide his views on many issues related to systemic functional linguistics' theoretical backbones, including emphasizing its appliable strengths, nurturing the theory with various applications, affirming the importance of developing system networks, differentiating systemic functional approaches from other functional theories, listing some major areas of expansion within systemic functional linguistics, following the trinocular perspective to describe other semiotic systems, and valuing the typological work.

Chapter 9 gives an elaborate account for Halliday's conception of language as a probabilistic system. It conducts a holistic review of Halliday's work on probability, and the focus of this chapter is on the probability of choice in language. Halliday's characterization of probabilities in language are discussed as one continuous phenomenon extended along the cline of instantiation – systemic probabilities at the potential pole of the cline and their instantiation as relative frequencies in particular texts at the instance pole.

Chapter 10 explores two categories in the processing of text, i.e. instantial systems and logogenesis – the process of instantiation and the process of modifying an instantial system as a text unfolds. The nature of instantial systems and modification is illustrated with the REFERENCE system – as the meaning unfolds, the instantial system is continuously being modified between people in particular semiotic events. Instantial systems are exemplified from all three metafunctional vantage points to show that the logogenetic development of the instantial system is expansion – a cycle of modification throughout the semiotic event. After systematically explaining how such expansion is ordered, instantial systems and logogenesis are also located in the overall organizations of the system-process of language in context.

Chapter 11 presents a systematic overview of the systemic functional approach to the area of lexicogrammar which is traditionally called "morphology". Through defining the location of morphology in systemic functional theory, the grammar of words trinocularly is explicated in terms of the combination of the semiotic dimensions of rank, delicacy, stratification, and instantiation. This chapter shows to what extent this trinocular view in terms of the hierarchies of rank and stratification differs from other theoretical models with respect to the description of morphological phenomena, how the systemic functional approach analyses and/or classifies different morphological types of languages, and how this approach explains the lexical/grammatical distinction. Regarding the analysis of morphology issues, the main challenges of the systemic functional approach are discussed and its future research is also suggested.

Chapter 12 begins with Matthiessen's personal encounters with neurolinguistics, neuroscience, and related research fields from the 1970s to the 1990s. This chapter then approaches certain aspects of neurosemiotics informed by systemic functional linguistics, including locating the potential phenomenal realms of study of neurosemiotics in terms of an ordered typology of systems, identifying key properties of semiotic systems such as all strata of language in context, moving from internal strata to interface strata, and further concentrating on semantics as an interface stratum, especially in ideational semantics. This chapter goes into detail about neurosemiotics informed by systemic functional linguistics, which helps prepare scholars to develop "biologically implementable" linguistic accounts for neuroscience.

Kazuhiro Teruya, Diana Slade,
and Kaela Peijia Zhang

Introduction

Christian M.I.M. Matthiessen

The first volume of my collected works contains a number of overviews of systemic functional linguistics (SFL), e.g. on the systemic functional architecture of language, and one new chapter on systemic phonology. Most of the chapters in that volume were general overviews of (aspects) of SFL "commissioned" for various thematic volumes.

The papers in this second volume of my collected works, edited by Kazuhiro Teruya, Di Slade, and Kaela Zhang, span a period of forty years. Chapter 1 was written in 1981, and the final chapter, Chapter 12, was completed in 2023. It is an interesting experience to meet oneself four decades ago in writing, an encounter with a much younger semiotic self. It is also sometime a painful one, partly because of advances that have been made in different fields of linguistics over time and partly because I know or understand what I arguably should have realized four decades ago: Bill Mann used to say "hindsight is always wiser than foresight," and the previous president of The Hong Kong Polytechnic University, Timothy Tong, used a variant of that saying we often hear: "in hindsight, we all have 20/20 vision." Fortunately, one of my amazing teachers in the Department of Linguistics, Lund University – Sven Platzack – prepared me for the experience. He told me that once one has produced a paper, one will go through a succession of phases of hating it and loving it: hating it because in hindsight one feels or realizes one could have done so much better; loving it because in hindsight one feels compassion for the young scholar who tried his or her best at the time.

But it's not just that aspect of looking back, it is also the sense that one could have accomplished more, even so much more, and with respect to the papers addressing the area of computational SFL the realization that the field has changed considerably, in large part because of the significant developments of statistical natural language processing (NLP), machine learning techniques, and neural networks. (I will come back to this point since these developments are, while not informed by SFL, very resonant with systemic functional theory.) This all relates to the field of the research and writing; but the tenor aspect is equally important in my remembrance of things past – very prominently, naturally, of people lost (e.g. Matthiessen 2005). Going through several of the chapters in this book, I recall many conversations over the decades, prominently with Michael Halliday, of course.

Another aspect of this personal time travel is semiotic, more specifically my general sense of changes in my fashion of writing, or style of meaning (cf. Guerra-Lyons' 2021 pioneering study of longitudinal corpus of the academic writings by a range of linguists). I recall something Michael Halliday said to me in 1990, when he met with me after reading my draft contribution to the second issue of *Social semiotics* (Matthiessen 1991b): he pulled out a carefully and copiously annotated copy of my draft – marked up in different colours to distinguish different kinds of comment, and he said to me something along the lines of "at the risk of sounding too avuncular, your writing reminds me of how I wrote when I was your age." This was so characteristic of him, making a point I needed to reflect on but in a way designed to make me feel good about it. (To me, he was in fact never avuncular; he slotted into my tenor relations like an older brother – he was born in the same year as my half-brother Tryggve Emond. When they met, they got on very well.)

On another occasion, he gave me an important piece of advice about written output: he said that he had come to realize that to make sure the written text was accessible to readers, one should write it so that it could be read aloud, noting that he had written his *Introduction to functional grammar* to ensure that it could be read aloud. This approach would ensure that it would be possible to assign the information structures characteristic of spoken discourse to the written text, and thereby ensure that it was not too lexically dense. This made excellent sense to me because I had attended so many talks in linguistics where presenters read aloud from their manuscripts, but without being very effective because they were too experientially dense, not having adjusted their manuscripts to take information structure into account.

The papers in this volume can be categorized under four headings:

Computational modelling: Chapters 1 through 4
Modelling, theory, and metatheory: Chapters 5 through 7
Dimensions of systemic functional theory: Chapters 8 through 11
Theory, modelling, and neurosemiotics: Chapter 12

To contextualize this selection within systemic functional linguistics, I have presented them in Table I.1 together with related publications of mine not included in this volume and also related contributions by other systemic functional scholars:

Table I.1 Themes in Volume 2 and systemic functional publications

Heading	Chapters	Other CMIMM publications	Other SFL publications
Computational modelling	1 through 4	Matthiessen (1983a,c,d, 1987a, 1987b, 1988a, 1989, 1991a) Matthiessen and Bateman (1991); Matthiessen, O'Donnell, and Zeng (1991); Bateman and Matthiessen (1991); Matthiessen, Kobayashi, and Zeng (1995); Matthiessen et al. (1997, 1998); Bateman, Matthiessen, and Zeng (1999)	Mann (1982, 1983a, 1983b, 1983c, 1984); Mann and Matthiessen (1983, 1985); Halliday (2002a, 2004d); O'Donnell and Bateman (2005); Teich (2009); Bateman and O'Donnell (2015); Bateman et al. (2019)
Modelling, theory, and metatheory	5 through 7	Matthiessen et al. (2022); Matthiessen (2023)	Martin and Matthiessen (1992); Halliday (1995c, 1996, 2002a)
Dimensions of systemic functional theory	8 through 11	Matthiessen (2002a,b, 2006)	Martin (1985); Bateman (1989); Bednarek and Martin (2010)
Theory, modelling, and neurosemiotics	12	Matthiessen (1993b, 1998, 2020)	Halliday (1995b, 2001); Melrose (2005, 2006); Asp and de Villiers (2010, 2019); Asp (2013)

(In the area of computational modelling, there is also the work by Robin Fawcett, Gordon Tucker, and their group at Cardiff University, e.g. Fawcett and Tucker 1989; Fawcett, van der Mije, and van Wissen 1988; Fawcett and Weerasinghe 1993; Weerasinghe 1994; cf. Schulz and Fontaine 2019.)

The chapters in this volume start with a selection from my earliest papers, from the 1980s, and finish with a new paper on theory and modelling in the context of neurosemiotics. In this introduction, I will contextualize the chapters within the different sections, but first I will say something about the notion of **modelling language** in context.

The characterization of "model" in the Wikipedia can serve as a helpful starting point (links and footnotes omitted):

> A **model** is an informative representation of an object, person or system. The term originally denoted the plans of a building in late 16th-century English, and derived via French and Italian ultimately from Latin *modulus*, a measure.
>
> Models can be divided into physical models (e.g. a model plane) and abstract models (e.g. mathematical expressions describing behavioural patterns). Abstract or conceptual models are central to philosophy of science, as almost every scientific theory effectively embeds some kind of model of the physical or human sphere.
>
> [...]
>
> A **physical model** (most commonly referred to simply as a **model** but in this context distinguished from a conceptual model) is a smaller or larger physical copy of an object. The object being modelled may be small (for example, an atom) or large (for example, the Solar System). In some sense, a physical model "is always the reification of some conceptual model; the conceptual model is conceived ahead as the blueprint of the physical one", which is then constructed as conceived.
>
> [...]
>
> A **conceptual model** is a theoretical representation of a system, e.g. a set of equations attempting to describe the workings of the atmosphere for the purpose of weather forecasting. Conceptual models may be a representation of a system. It consists of concepts used to help people know, understand, or simulate a subject the model represents. The term may refer to models that are formed after a conceptualization or generalization process. Conceptual models are often abstractions of things in the real world, whether physical or social. Semantic studies are relevant to various stages of concept formation. Semantics

is basically about concepts, the meaning that thinking beings give to various elements of their experience.

(https://en.wikipedia.org/wiki/Model, accessed January 23, 2023)

As presented in the Wikipedia, models can be interpreted in terms of (i) the ordered typology of systems operating in different phenomenal realms, and (ii) the stratification of our metalanguage. I have set them out in Table I.2, together with types of models and examples of each type.

Table I.2 Types of model and systemic orders

(i) Systemic orders		(ii) Metalinguistic strata	Type of model		
Order/ matter	Realm		SFL	Examples	Wikipedia
immaterial	semiotic	theory > theoretical representation > computational representation > implementation	semiotic model	Text-generation system, text understanding system, translation system, summarization system	"conceptual model" (or "abstract model")
	social		social model	medical model, economic model	
material	biological		biological model	model organism, model brain, skeletons in closets; robot	"physical model"
	physical		physical model	model train, model house	

(i) There are four orders of systems operating in different phenomenal realms, of increasing complexity (see Section 12.2 for details and references): first-order systems: **physical** < second-order systems [physical + life]: **biological** < third-order systems [biological + value (social order)]: **social** < fourth-order systems [social + meaning]: **semiotic**. Among semiotic systems (which have alternatively been interpreted as cognitive systems), language is a higher-order semiotic system (with stratified content and expression planes, and simultaneous metafunctions). They have all been modelled at their own order: physical models such as model ships, biological models such as model brains, social models such as economic models and organizational models, and semiotic models such as machine translation systems. Biological and physical systems are both material systems and are modelled by "physical models"; but social and semiotic systems are both immaterial systems and are modelled by "conceptual (or abstract) models." (At the expression plane, language can of course be modelled by means of physical models, like models of our vocal apparatus; but "physical models" of aspects of the expression plane are symbolic, like different shapes of objects apprentice grammarians in primary school may use to differentiate processes, participants, and circumstances.)

Modelling is a key characteristic of bio-semiotic systems (Halliday and Matthiessen 1999; Chapter 12, this book). By emphasizing that our brains model our experience of the world, Barrett (2017: 13) also illuminates our general understanding of a model:

> The infant brain is missing most of the concepts that we have as adults. Babies don't know what telescopes are, or sea cucumbers, or picnics, let alone purely mental concepts like "Whimsy" or "Schadenfreude." A newborn is experientially blind to a great extent. Not surprisingly, the infant brain does not predict well. A grown-up brain is dominated by prediction, but an infant brain is awash in prediction error. So babies must learn about the world from sensory input before their brains can model the world.
> [...] p. 125:
> When the brain's predictions match the sensory input, this constitutes a model of the world in that instant, just like a scientist judges that a correct hypothesis is the path to scientific certainty.

(ii) Systems of any order can, of course, be modelled semiotically; for example, in building a house, one might go through stages from a blueprint (possibly rendered as a virtual image) to the builder's specification to the physical specification. The stages will depend on the nature of the semiotic system used in specifying the "object." In the case of language, we use a **metalanguage** to model the **object language** (see Section 11.10, and cf. Section 7.3). The metalanguage is stratified, the highest stratum being theory in context. These strata are all semiotic in nature, from the linguistic theory to the computational implementation in the case of computational modelling.

All theories are semiotic phenomena – folk theories, scientific theories, and educational versions of scientific theories across all subjects and disciplines. While language is central to all theories, the mixture of the contributing semiotic systems involved in theory creation will depend on the phenomena under investigation. For example, to develop his theory of motion, Newton needed to design a new branch of mathematics, viz. differential calculus. In the case of linguistic theories, there is considerable variation with respect to the extent to which semiotic systems other than language are used to represent the theories. In formal theories, linguists usually use some form of designed semiotic system like Boolean algebra, predicate logic, or categorial rules. Thus, the degree of formalization tends to be high, although as Emmon Bach (1989) shows in his book *Informal lectures on formal semantics*, it is possible to "delay" formalization to make key aspects of theory accessible to consumers who have not learned the formalized system of representation (cf. the theoretical notion of "model-theoretic semantics"). Here it is important to note that "formal" and "formalization" are independently variable; particularly in systemic functional computational modelling, there have been a number of contributions to the formalization of systemic functional grammar (see e.g. Patten and Ritchie 1987; Teich 1999) and also of other aspects of systemic functional linguistics.

What is special about linguistic theories in particular and semiotic theories in general is that the theories and the phenomena under investigation that are being theorized are of the same phenomenal order; they are both semiotic systems. In contrast, while social, biological, and physical theories are also semiotic constructs, their domains of investigation are of lower orders. In the case of linguistics, the fact that the phenomenon under investigation and the theory are both of the same order of phenomena, viz. semiotic phenomena, creates various special but interesting challenges (e.g. Halliday 1984a; Matthiessen 1988a, 1992) – challenges that will appear at various points in this book.

Computational modelling

The computational modelling of language has been developed within computational linguistics, NLP, and AI (for a recent overview, see Mitkov 2022). In the present book, the chapters on computational modelling are concerned with **text**

generation (for an overview, see Bateman and Zock 2022); they include two early ones on the Nigel **systemic functional generation grammar**, published in the early 1980s (Chapter 1, 1981; Chapter 2, 1983), an interesting and productive period in the development of grammatical frameworks.

During the 1980s, non-Chomskyan generative grammars came into prominence: generalized phrase structure grammar (GPSG; Gazdar et al. 1985), lexical functional grammar (LFG; Kaplan and Bresnan 1982), and, somewhat later, head-driven phrase structure grammar (HPSG; Pollard and Sag 1993) were just emerging from exploratory work in the late 1970s (cf. the range of "current approaches to syntax" represented in Moravcsik and Wirth's 1980, overview of "current approaches"[1]). Martin Kay's (1979) first presentation in print of his functional unification grammar had just appeared, and as I note in this book (see also Matthiessen et al. 2022: Chapter 5), it was the result of a project to develop a computational systemic functional grammar (SFG), one that would be reversible, and came to influence a number of "unification-based" framework that came into their own in the 1980s (cf. Shieber 1986), some of which were also influenced by developments in knowledge representation, referred to in Chapter 1 here. (Around a decade earlier, Richard Hudson was trying to develop a "generative" systemic functional grammar, documented in Hudson 1971. In one of my conversations with Martin Kay, he characterized this work as one of "wonderous complexity" [a wording that stuck in my brain!], saying that it suggested that the author did not know how to write a grammar. But for Hudson, this was of course only a stage; he went on to develop daughter dependency grammar and then word grammar. Michael Halliday had explained to me that while his own questions about language were quite different from Chomsky's, Hudson had accepted the challenge of Chomsky's questions and set out to develop an answer in the form of a non-transformational grammar.)

In 1981, Winograd's (1983) influential book on syntactic theories in a computational context had not yet appeared, but at some point before it was published, he sent us a draft, which was very helpful since it included SFG prominently and located it within other related approaches (in a chapter on "feature and function grammars"). And Martin Kay (1935–2021; Kaplan and Uszkoreit 2022) came to visit us at ISI in the early 1980s, and I visited him at Xerox PARC in Palo Alto, where he introduced me to Ron Kaplan, who developed LFG together with Joan Bresnan.

Around that time there were also recent new approaches to grammar within linguistics, developed without a focus on computational modelling: Dik's (1978) functional grammar (FG) and role and reference grammar (RRG; Van Valin and Foley 1980). A representative of the research team developing FG in Amsterdam came to visit us at ISI and drew on the computational modelling of SFG in similar work on FG. But at the time, one of the main concerns of FG and RRG seemed to be language typology rather than the development of comprehensive text-based and meaning-oriented descriptions of particular languages. (The addition of discourse to FG came later: Hengeveld and Mackenzie 2008.) I asked Simon Dik about the focus on language typology in relation to comprehensive descriptions of particular languages in Holland in 1986, and he responded that at the time there were no comprehensive descriptions of any language in FG. While he had clearly been influenced by the Prague School (perhaps in particular, Daneš 1964), from a systemic functional point of view the functionalism embodied in FG was not very far-reaching at the time. As in Daneš (1964), the hierarchy of stratification and the spectrum of metafunction were "conflated," and while the experiential and textual metafunctions can be located in their "architectures," the interpersonal one is not very prominent (an issue that has been taken up in functional discourse grammar).

The period from the late 1970s to the early 1980s was also an important transition in approaches to "knowledge representation," i.e. (in our systemic functional terms) theoretical representation for describing semantics. In the 1960s and through most of the 1970s, there had been a kind of Wild West frontier approach to the modelling of meaning ("concepts," "knowledge") by means of networks, often referred to as "semantic networks" (e.g. Charniak and Wilks 1976; cf. also the readings in Brachman and Levesque 1985). Woods (1975) problematized the fairly varied and informal approaches based on the network metaphor, and this led to more principled approaches in the 1980s, starting with Brachman (e.g. 1979). This line of development combined frame-based inheritance networks with (first-order) logic in order to cover both the systemic and instantial parts of semantics (a distinction known by different labels, including the T-box and the A-box). (For some discussion from a systemic functional point of view, see Halliday and Matthiessen 1999.)

The next two chapters in this computational modelling part are concerned with the **semantic interface** to a systemic text-generation grammar, first the **chooser-&-inquiry interface** that Bill Mann and I developed (Chapter 3, 1989) and a comparison between that grammar-based interface and one designed "from above" (Chapter 4, 1990). Quite naturally, the approach from below was general since it was organized in terms of the general grammar of English (or any other language being modelled in this way): choosers were assigned to each system in the grammatical system network; they were thus choice experts local to a particular grammatical choice point.

In contrast, the approach from above was semantics-based, but more specifically based on register-specific semantic systems operating in contexts with particular settings of field, tenor, and mode values – in particular situation types. This had been proposed by Halliday (1973) as a way of exploring semantics in a sociological frame of reference, relevant to the research being carried by Basil Bernstein and his group – for a retrospective, see also Turner (1987). Locating semantic networks within particular situation types made it possible to describe the semantic options as strategic, like the strategies available to a mother in controlling her young son to prevent him from playing again on a dangerous building site. This approach to semantics was picked up and developed by Terry Patten as part of the SLANG text-generation system he developed for his PhD at Edinburgh University (Patten 1986, 1988). He interpreted the register-specific approach to semantics in the light of work on **problem solving** in AI: a register-specific semantic system is like a solution compiled to address a recurrent problem, avoiding the need to solve the problem from first principle every time it occurs. (In terms of the cline of instantiation, this means that it is not necessary to move all the way up the cline from the instantial problem to the potential pole. Instead, one can select a register-specific solution from a "library" of pre-compiled solutions.)

The two approaches to the semantic interface are presented in Table I.3:

The chapters in this section dealing with computational modelling are perhaps mostly of historical interest since they only cover my publications from 1981 up through 1990, although Chapter 6 on fuzzy modelling represents explorations we were engaged with in the 1990s, and I sketched the context of this work in reference to our engagement with Professor Michio Sugeno in the 1990s, at the Tokyo Institute of Technology, and the 2000s, at the Brain Science Division of

Table I.3 Semantic interface seen from above and from below

Orientation of organization	General	Register-specific
"from above": charger		theory: Halliday (1973); text generation: Patten (1986, 1988)
"from below": chooser	text generation: chooser-&-inquiry framework: Mann (1982; 1983c); Matthiessen (1983c; 1983d; 1988b [Chapter 3, this volume])	

the RIKEN Institute in Tokyo. In the 'noughties," I was also involved in another computational linguistic project – **ScamSeek**, directed by Jon Patrick, a professor of information science at Sydney University (e.g. Whitelaw, Herke-Couchman and Patrick 2005; Patrick 2008); and I supervised a brilliant BA Honours thesis by Matthew Honnibal (2004). He took an approach to parsing that has become an important way of dealing with the challenge of a full-fledged systemic functional parse. This involved a two-level parse: based on the parses in the Penn T-bank produced by a dependency parser, he "parsed" the "trees" in order to produce more functional information such as the thematic structure of clauses.

However, the focus of the systemic functional engagement with computation had shifted from **computational modelling** – the theme in this first part of the book – to **computational tooling** of systemic functional work, anticipated in two insightful PhD theses I had the fortune to supervise, and learn from, in the 1990s: Nesbitt (1994) and Wu (2000). This shift is evident from the coverage of successive overviews of SFL and computation over a period of fifteen years: Wu (2000, 2009); O'Donnell and Bateman (2005); Teich (2009); Bateman and O'Donnell (2015); Bateman et al. (2019).

This shift towards computational tooling rather than computational modelling needs to be understood in the context of changes over the last three decades in computational linguistics/NLP in general: techniques based on statistical NLP, neural networks, and machine learning have become increasingly prevalent and successful (for an overview in the area of text generation, see Bateman and Zock 2022: 763–4), dramatically reducing the reliance on (and need for?) manual symbolic modelling. This development has, obviously, been very much in keeping with the systemic functional conception of language as a **probabilistic system** (and related to "statistical learning," briefly discussed in Chapter 12). The 1980s was in fact an important period in the early development of what has now been called the **deep learning revolution**, documented by one of the contributors, Terrence Sejnowksi, in Sejnowski (2018: x) – "a guide to the past, present, and future of deep learning."

The emphasis in NLP on statistical techniques does not mean that the tradition of computational modelling of linguistic accounts of (parts of) of language has disappeared. While systemic functional parsing as part of text understanding remains a challenging problem, there are a number of quite capable non-SFG parsers in active research use, like the Stanford Dependency Parser. However, the output of such a parse contains less lexicogrammatical information than a systemic functional (manual) analysis, as illustrated by Figure I.1, where a dependency parse taken from https://cl.lingfil.uu.se/~nivre/docs/ eacl3.pdf and a systemic functional analysis are compared. (In the British English version, the clause is taken to be agnate with *economic news had got little effect on financial markets, hadn't it?*.) As

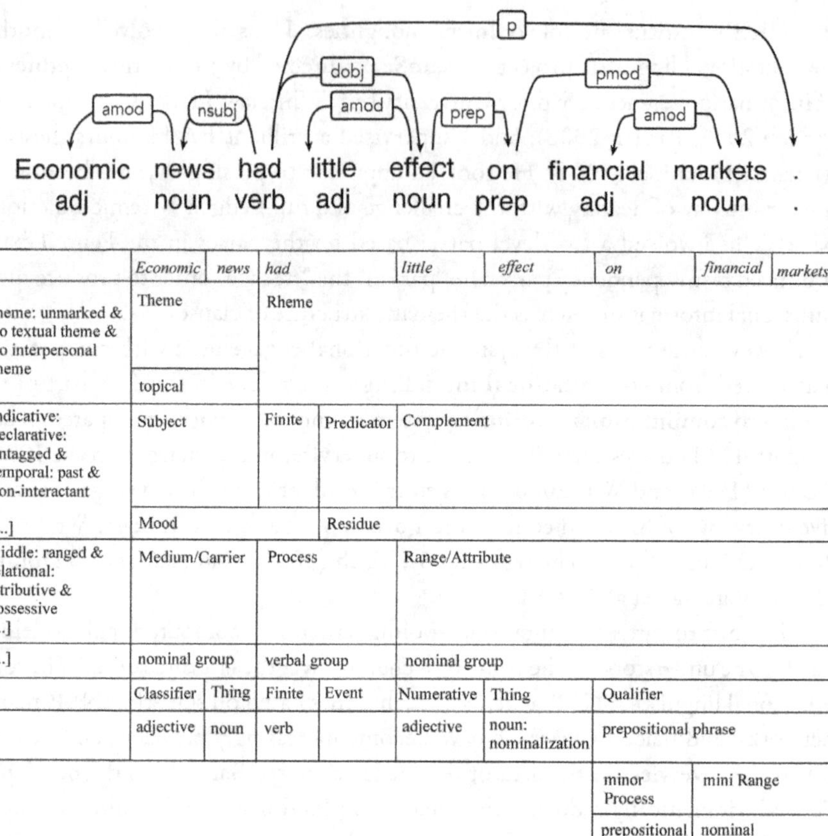

Figure I.1 Dependency grammar analysis of a clause, with a systemic functional analysis

can be seen, the systemic functional analysis includes information that is at best implicit in the dependency structure, viz. (i) the systemic analysis (shown in the leftmost column of the box diagram) and (ii) the metafunctional strands of the structure of the clause as a message (textual), as a move (interpersonal), and as a figure (experiential). In addition, in the systemic functional analysis, this example would be recognized as an instance of grammatical metaphor – an incongruent clause; a more congruent version would be *economic news affected financial markets little.* (And we might try to "unpack" the example further by asking how we would convey it to a pre-school child.)

The dependency parser makes an important contribution: it "chunks" the clause into segments, which is no mean achievement, especially since it has been argued that the systemic functional representation of function structures and their realizations as syntagms do not provide enough information for this "chunking" (cf. Bateman 2008). Researchers have tried different approaches to overcome this hurdle, the first one probably being Bob Kasper's (e.g. 1988a,b) use of a version of unification grammar during his time with us on the PENMAN project at ISI. See further O'Donnell and Bateman (2005). Since the turn of the century, researchers have experimented with using (the output of) dependency parsers, and then doing another "parse" based on SFG, an early example being Honnibal's (2004) use of the Treebank version of the Wall Street Journal corpus (see also Honnibal and Curran 2007).

The approach of first using non-SFG dependency parsers in the first phase of text understanding has also been adopted in a visionary new project undertaken by Applied General Intelligence (AGI: https://www.agi.live/), one informed by SFL and involving a few of us systemic functional linguists. One of the many innovative features of this project is to use multiple pre-systemic functional parsers so that their outputs can be compared and evaluated.

Chapter 1: A grammar and a lexicon for a text-production system (1981)

This was my first published paper, given at the annual conference of ACL (Association for Computational Linguistics) in 1981, hosted by Stanford University. Since the conference was a computational linguistics one rather than a linguistics conference, presenters used overhead slides rather than handouts, which was also a good way of preparing the talk, making sure that it was audience-oriented. It also made the transition to presentations using slide presentation programs such as PowerPoint and (in my case) Keynote much easier. As I was getting ready to present in what I recall as a huge auditorium, I didn't manage to attach the lapel mic to my shirt, so I had to use one hand to hold it and the other to change slides – a bit of a juggling act! The session chair was Bonnie Webber; she was very nice and helpful.

Again, unlike linguistics conferences, computational linguistics conferences were designed to come with published proceedings: the paper included here is from the volume of proceedings. I thought this was a productive way of ensuring that presentations would have a life beyond the ephemeral moment of the conference presentation, be accessible to a wider audience, and be recorded as a publication in people's CVs. Over the years, I suggested that this practice should be adopted for systemic functional conferences and congresses, but it wasn't until we ran the International Systemic Functional Congress (ISFC) 2008 at Macquarie University that this publication strategy was actually implemented, and then again for the next ISFC, hosted by Fang Yan at Tsinghua University. Computational linguistic papers would often appear as short papers in volumes of proceedings and also as extended journal articles, so researchers would get a good deal of publication mileage out of one quantum of research.

My paper turned out to be the first "report" on the NIGEL grammar. Bill Mann had also submitted a paper related to the PENMAN text-generation project he directed at ISI to the ACL conference, but it was not accepted. The model I presented in the paper was based on a plan for the PENMAN text-generation system, and it was in a sense a compromise between a systemic functional architecture and a computational linguistic one, for example with "grammar" and "lexicon" as separate modules. During my years working on the succession of PENMAN projects I suggested adopting the systemic functional architecture of lexicogrammar with grammar and lexis modelled as a continuum (cf. Matthiessen 1991a), but Bill Mann did not think this was a good way forward because that "taxonomic" organization of lexis was already being modelled based on the frame-based inheritance network organization of the "knowledge base" of the PENMAN system. In my own work after leaving ISI, I have continued to explore lexicogrammar as a unified continuum, approaching lexis as most delicate grammar (e.g. Matthiessen 1995a, 2014a).

The treatment of "semantics" as part of "conceptuals" in the paper was in a sense a sign of the times (i.e. early 1980s). It can be compared and contrasted with the account of (ideational) semantics that Michael Halliday and I developed starting in 1986, and reported in our book on "construing experience," Halliday and Matthiessen (1999). By then, we interpreted fourth-order systems as semiotic systems (systems of meaning) and a complement to the mainstream approach to them as cognitive systems (systems of knowledge). This meant, among other things, that we expanded the scope of semantics considerably: the ideational semantics, which we called the **ideation base**, now covered the whole (ideational) territory of "conceptuals" and "semantics."

Chapter 2: Systemic grammar in computation: the NIGEL case (1983b)

In this chapter, I set out to answer the question "What can systemic linguistic accounts of grammar and semantics offer computational linguistics in the area of text generation?" The answer is formulated in terms of two properties of the architecture of systemic functional grammar, viz. the **hierarchy of axis** (paradigmatic [systemic]/syntagmatic [structural]) and the **spectrum of metafunction**. It is, in part, an elaboration of what is covered in Matthiessen (1981), i.e. Chapter 1. The paper was presented at the first European Computational Linguistics Conference in Pisa in 1982 – hosted by a great team at the University of Pisa. Both Bill Mann and I took part in the conference. Initially, Bill had been reluctant, saying we should leave the conference to the Europeans; but I managed to convince him that it would be important and productive to engage with them, and the outcome was very positive.

The paper was thus written for computational linguistic readers, unlike three other papers of mine at around the same time: Matthiessen (1983a) on the computational modelling of systemic functional grammar addressed to systemic functional linguists, Matthiessen (1983c) on choosing primary tense addressed to linguists in general, and Matthiessen (1983d) addressed to linguists attending LACUS (Linguistic Association of Canada and the United States), centrally including tagmemic, stratificational, and systemic functional linguists. (LACUS had been formed to provide a venue in North America for non-Chomskyan linguists during a period when Chomskyan linguistics had become very dominant, the first conference having taken place in 1974. Now, almost fifty years later, it is perhaps difficult to imagine the challenges those linguists faced who were not part of the Chomskyan program.)

Since the participants in the conference were computational linguists and since text generation was still quite a recent new focus in computational linguistics, it made sense to foreground those aspects of SFG that made it a framework well suited to meeting the demands placed on a grammar that could be used in text generation (as opposed to the demands placed on a parsing grammar). At the LACUS conference at Université Laval the following year, I met Paul Garvin, whose work I was familiar with from his Prague School Reader (Garvin 1964). We were standing in a little group of people and he "confronted" me in a nice and engaging way, asking me to explain to him the advantages and strong points of systemic functional grammar. The "NIGEL case" paper had helped prepare me for such questions; they were "natural" during a period in linguistics when SFL was quite a marked choice. Highlighting the systemic and metafunctional organization, I think I managed to make the case for SFG. In the 1970s I had read, and been intrigued by, Halliday's (1964) paper "Syntax and the consumer," so it made sense to try to take on the role of a salesman in response to Garvin's probe (without worrying about the ominous title of one of Arthur Miller's plays).

The paper refers to the "environment" of the NIGEL grammar, which includes the "knowledge base" and "text plans" – aspects of the semantics. The environment was elaborated in Matthiessen (1987a), which I presented at a text-generation workshop in Nijmegen organized by Gerard Kempen (Kempen 1987; and cf. Kempen 1989); and we explored in much more detail in Halliday and Matthiessen (1999), where we interpreted the "knowledge base" as a **meaning base**, with three metafunctional "components": the **ideation base**, the **interaction base**, and the **text base.** Our account focusses on the ideation base, but we also outline the characteristics of the two other bases (for the text base, see also Bateman and Matthiessen 1993).

The description of English embodied in the NIGEL grammar was based originally on a specification of the clause grammar of English that Michael Halliday had developed for a project at UCI led by Benjamin Colby (see Halliday 2004d), consisting of around eighty to ninety systems. (Colby's project was based on the insight that it would be possible to describe cultures based on a volume of culturally significant text, an idea he had already explored in Colby 1966; and to do that, he needed a computational system for automatic text analysis.)

By the middle of 1982, we had expanded this original description very considerably, and Bill Mann suggested that we actually should have it plotted and printed on large tiles of paper. This task was carried out by a good friend of mine and fellow student in linguistics at UCLA, Yasu Fukumochi, who joined us for a year or two. He programmed the plotting program, and I remember Bill and I babysitting the (at the time) very advanced plotter for hours, waiting for it to produce large tiles of paper. We then taped these together into a very large display of the NIGEL grammar system network. Bill managed to persuade the ISI management that we needed a very large room to hang this immense display on the wall. They actually agreed to his request. We would walk up and down along this wall so that we could examine and reason about the connectivity of the system network. (Around that time, I had the opportunity to view the visualization resources available to researchers working on VLSI (Very Large Scale Integration) design. I was incredibly envious in the nicest sort of way, imagining what it would be like if we had such visualization resources.)

This "grammar on the wall" had been mounted before the first ISFC was hosted by the remarkable team at York University in Toronto. Once the papers we had submitted to ISFC had been accepted, Bill suggested that we should take the grammar on the wall with us to Toronto. So we rolled it up like a valuable painting. The hosts at York University were very welcoming and supportive, and found a room where we could mount it. However, somewhere in the middle of that wall, there was a fireplace, so from that time onwards, the grammar on the wall had the outlines of a fireplace imprinted on it.

Chapter 3: Semantics for a systemic grammar: the chooser and inquiry framework (1988b)

This chapter is concerned with the chooser-&-inquiry framework as the interface between the systemic functional generation grammar NIGEL and the "environment" (see also Mann 1982, 1983c; Matthiessen 1983c, d). Bill Mann and I had worked out this interface in the early 1980s, starting the task of specifying how grammatical choices could be made in an informed way, i.e. in such a way that the environment was consulted to identify the relevant factors. (I still remember the room we'd found at ISI, where we would not be interrupted, exploring the notion of a choice expert. Unlike our own offices, it had no windows; our offices had incredible views of the Pacific, where we were treated to inspirational sunsets – made more beautiful according to Bill by a combination of dust from the Southern California desert and LA pollution. One favourite activity at the sunset time was to try to catch a glimpse of the green light just as the sun disappears below the horizon.)

Each system in the systemic grammar had a chooser associated with it, an expert on how to make the appropriate selection among the terms of the system. Choosers took the form of decision trees consisting of inquiries – demands for information from the environment. Bill had introduced the framework to computational linguistics, and, in this paper, I took as my task to introduce it to systemic functional linguists.

Chapter 4: Two approaches to semantic interfaces in text generation (1990)

As I noted in the first part of this introduction, the semantics of a model of language can be approached "from below" or "from above." The approach "from below" is grammar-based, and the framework we developed was the chooser-&-inquiry framework. Here the interface is organized grammatically: choosers are parcelled out across the grammatical system networks, one chooser being assigned to each system. (This certainly made very good sense at the time since a key reason for choosing SFG as the framework for the grammar of the text-generation system was precisely that it was organized around systems of choice.) The approach "from above" is context-based (and thus, by another step, semantics-based), and the models that were around had been developed for particular contextual settings, particular situation types such as Halliday's (1973) example of the register-specific semantics of maternal strategies for controlling a young son's behaviour.

In reference to our work on the PENMAN system, Halliday suggested that the approach from above could be interpreted as a "charger" approach as opposed to a "chooser" approach. At one meeting with Bill Mann and me (at LACUS in Quebec City, I'm almost certain), he indicated that he would like to write this up, but it seemed to me that he was deterred by Bill's apparent lack of enthusiasm for the charger approach. It would have been a fascinating and valuable contribution – one outlining a more strategic kind of semantics sensitive to contextual variables and values. (One lesson I learned from this discussion was that it's crucially important to support people when they suggest new approaches, giving them space and time to develop them.)

However, meanwhile, Terry Patten had in fact taken note of Halliday's (1973) strategic, register-specific semantics and based the text-generation system that he designed for his PhD research, SLANG, on it (Patten 1986, turned into a book: Patten 1988). One of Terry's central points was that register-specific semantic systems could be interpreted in the light of AI problem-solving approaches: a register-specific semantic system is the compilation of solutions to a recurrent problem. In other words, instead of having to solve the problem from scratch each time they encounter it, language users can simply draw on the register-specific semantic system that has evolved in their communities. (In AI work on problem solving, starting in the 1970s, there was a tension between generalist accounts, like those drawing on the early work by Herb Simon and Alan Newell, and special case accounts, in particular the work on scripts by Schank and Abelson 1977. I thought and pointed out to anyone who'd listen to me that the gap between them could have been bridged with the help of SFL, since it had a general theory of context-based functional variation in language – register variation.)

In the paper reprinted here as Chapter 4, I set out to compare and contrast the two approaches, "from below" and "from above." It was accepted for presentation at COLING (International Conference on Computational Linguistics) 1990, but I couldn't get the funds in Sydney to attend myself since it was held in Helsinki, so John Bateman generously presented it for me and fielded questions.

Modelling, theory, and metatheory

The chapters on modelling, theory, and metatheory were certainly informed by my experience of research in the area of systemic functional computational linguistics, i.e. of research engaging with the computational modelling of language; but the chapters in this part of the volume are oriented more towards general theoretical concerns, not ones that are specific to computational modelling. Thus, in a way this group of contributions reflect and represent my transition from a(n apprentice) systemic functional linguist working on computational linguistic projects to a systemic functional linguist in general.

Chapter 5: Metafunctional complementarity and resonance in syntagmatic organization

This paper was, obviously, inspired by Halliday's (1979a) theory of the natural (iconic) relationship between the metafunctional modes of meaning and their modes of expression (cf. also Halliday 1981) – an insight further developed by Martin (1996). It also grew out of my analysis of representational challenges we encountered in the computational modelling of SFG as we developed the NIGEL grammar as part of the PENMAN text-generation system (Matthiessen 1988a). My diagnosis of the challenges ("representational issues") was guided by systemic functional theory; I wanted to show that the challenges were not simply an ad hoc list of difficulties but rather issues that could be illuminated by the difference in coverage between theory and theoretical representation in the systemic functional metalanguage.

I submitted the manuscript to a journal edited by Bernard Comrie, whom I knew from my studies at UCLA in the 1980s – in particular, from auditing his fascinating course on tense in different languages (later published as Comrie 1985), which was directly relevant to my MA research (cf. Matthiessen 1984, *Choosing tense in English*; cf. also Matthiessen 1983c, 1996). Comrie sent me a very nice letter of rejection – with certain suggestions, I think; but I was too busy with teaching, research, and publications at Sydney University to follow up (and also actually too daunted by the task of continuing to try to build a bridge between SFL and the functional typological literature – this seemed like yet another failed attempt). So while I circulated my manuscript among systemic functional linguists, I did not again attempt to get it published. (But the ideas continued to percolate in my brain, and in Matthiessen 2004b, I added another ingredient to the expression plane mix: medium of expression. Although I don't think it's been taken up by many researchers, I'm convinced my account is actually a very important part of the overall picture, and I've returned to it in Matthiessen, forthcoming b.)

Chapter 6: Fuzziness construed in language: a linguistic perspective

The insight that language is an inherently indeterminate system has been part of SFL from the start – or even before the start, as is clear from Halliday (1961) and also from his work on intonation. There are various ways to explore this indeterminate nature, a central one being fuzziness – more specifically, Lotfi Zadeh's fuzzy theory, originating with his conception of fuzzy set theory (Zadeh 1965). Although his line of research resonated with that of other scholars at his university, UCB – notably the research by the psychologist Eleanor Rosch on prototypes[2] (e.g. Rosch 1973), his work had more of an impact outside the US in the early stages, in particular in Japan.

One of the Japanese scholars who "imported" fuzzy set theory and developed and applied it was Michio Sugeno (following his teacher Toshiro Terano; see e.g. Kosko 1993). He applied it very successfully to various control systems – spectacularly to unmanned flying helicopters, which are incredibly unstable objects,[3] and also nurtured applications to language since the early 1990s, when he came across SFL and attended talks by Michael Halliday at the International Christian University (ICU) in Mitaka, Tokyo. He'd taken an interest in SFL after having been re-oriented philosophically in his thinking about the world by reading Wittgenstein (the later work, post-*Tractatus*), which meant moving away from the positivist and model-theoretic view of language concerned with truth towards an understanding of it as a central resource in human life based on use, one evolving through innumerable contexts of use. Bill Mann had also read Wittgenstein, and in both cases their reading seemed to prepare them for Halliday's SFL: Wittgenstein raised questions, Halliday provided answers. Interestingly, according to Monk (1991: 261), Wittgenstein characterized his new approach as "anthropological":

> Wittgenstein once remarked to Rush Rhees that the most important thing he gained from talking to Sraffa was an 'anthropological' way of looking at philosophical problems. This remark goes some way to explain why Sraffa is credited as having had such an important influence. One of the most striking ways in which Wittgenstein's later work differs from the *Tractatus* is in its "anthropological" approach. That is, whereas the *Tractatus* deals with language in isolation from the circumstances in which it is used, the *Investigations* repeatedly emphasizes the importance of the "stream of life" which gives linguistic utterances their meaning: a "language-game" cannot be described without mentioning their activities and the way of life of the "tribe" that plays it. If this change of perspective derives from Sraffa, then his influence on the later work is indeed of the most fundamental importance. But in this case, it must have taken a few years for that influence to bear fruit, for this "anthropological" feature of Wittgenstein's philosophical method does not begin to emerge until about 1932.

In Halliday's case – and also in Firth's, the anthropological orientation to the engagement with language – the emphasis on context, including both context of culture and context of use ("context of situation") – was grounded empirically in Malinowsky's pioneering fieldwork in the Trobriand Islands in the 1910s. Malinowski, Firth, and Halliday had always had the image of language as resource rather than as rule (Halliday 1977), with an orientation towards ethnography and rhetoric rather than towards philosophy and logic. Indeed, in his overview of schools of linguistics, Sampson (1980: 224) notes that Malinowski arrived at a key insight before Wittgenstein: "Words are tools, and the 'meaning' of a tool is its use: a view Ludwig Wittgenstein acquired a considerable reputation by restating long after Malinowski had argued the point at length." In the Malinowski–Firth–Halliday anthropological orientation towards language – language in context – language is inherently indeterminate and needs to be theorized as such by means of clines and continua (cf. Halliday's 1995a, review of Ellis 1993). So, fuzzy theory was an interesting candidate when we searched for ways of representing certain aspects of indeterminacy in language as construed by the theory.

The dialogue between Sugeno and his team and us in SFL (in particular, Halliday, Kazuhiro Teruya, and myself, and later also Wu Canzhong and David Butt) started when Sugeno was a professor at Tokyo Institute of Technology, where he was in charge of a fuzzy engineering laboratory, and directed PhD projects informed by SFL – importantly, Ichiro Kobayashi (1995), who spent a year with us in Sydney while working on his PhD project. This provided an opportunity to explore the use of fuzzy theory as a way of representing certain kinds of indeterminacy in systemic functional theory, and also to work on multimodal text generation (e.g. Cross and Matthiessen 1997; Matthiessen et al. 1997; Cross et al. 1998; Matthiessen et al. 1998).

My short paper reprinted here as Chapter 6 grew out of this dialogue during the 1990s. As part of FUZZ/IEEE, Anca Ralescu, a close friend of Michio Sugeno's, invited me to give a presentation at a workshop she had been asked to organize. At the same time, Michael Halliday had been invited as the keynote speaker at this huge conference (Halliday 1995c). I had intended to continue work on fuzzy set theory as a system of representation for systemic functional theory, but never had an opportunity to publish on it again.

The next phase of the dialogue with Sugeno took place during 2000–5, when he directed a lab at the Brain Science Institute of the RIKEN Institute. The overall goal of his lab was to explore intelligent, language-based computing, producing an example of a system that could serve as stimulation for further research and commercial applications. Intellectually, this project was very successful, producing new insights – like the logico-semantic organization of algorithms in programs, to cite just one example. But as far as I understand, it was too far ahead of the academic and commercial markets, so it proved difficult to find ways of extending the work beyond 2005. Still, the dialogue nurtured by Sugeno's project and his lab environment was very important even though it has arguably not been sufficiently recorded in publications outside of Japan. He brought together a powerful team – Japanese members who have gone on to do very valuable research and a privileged group of us from Australia (at the time): Michael Halliday, Kazuhiro Teruya, Wu Canzhong, David Butt, and myself. The insights produced by Sugeno's lab still need to be documented and taken further by us in the SFL community.

Chapter 7: On the idea of theory-neutral descriptions[4]

This chapter was "commissioned" by Ruqaiya Hasan for a book she edited together with Carmel Cloran and David Butt (Hasan, Cloran, and Butt 1996), which included important contributions from the ISFC she had organized with her team at Macquarie University, complementing other volumes based on that congress that she co-edited with various colleagues. For this volume, she felt a contribution dealing directly with the role of theory in the engagement with language and with the notion that descriptions of particular languages could be theory neutral would round out the volume.

So, Chris Nesbitt and I wrote this chapter, referring both to systemic functional work and to contributions from other traditions. The notion that descriptions could be theory neutral was around in certain areas of descriptive linguistics, but we could see that it was misleading: it simply meant that the theory was more covert and probably less well worked out as a coherent framework (eclecticism was already popular). While theory neutrality was an illusion, it was not hard to see why some descriptivists felt it was attractive. Some had done their PhD work in the 1960s and, not surprisingly, had come to see the increasingly prevailing Chomskyan theory as a straitjacket rather than as an empowering resource (which is how theory was seen by systemic functional linguists); and many descriptive linguists had experienced the successive fashions in that kind of theory (with much shorter lifespans than thirty years for each successive paradigm), so felt they needed to protect their descriptions from built-in obsolescence. But of course, throughout this period there were alternative ways of "doing theory" – theories that were designed as resources for doing linguistics, centrally for developing comprehensive text-based descriptions of a wide variety of languages, prime examples being tagmemic linguistics and systemic functional linguistics.

Since our chapter appeared in 1996, linguists have continued to take different positions on the role and nature and value of linguistic theory in the pursuit of different linguistic activities such as language description and text analysis. (i) On the one hand, eclecticism has continued to be seen as a Good Thing, a kind of ecumenical approach to the development of theoretical frameworks, importantly ones drawing on expertise from different disciplines. My own view is that this has often resulted in what I have uncharitably called Frankenstein's Monster theories (I was delighted to find recently that Barrett 2017: 161, has used the same notion to evoke the sense of ultimately incompatible parts, a "Frankenstein's monster of a theory"): frameworks stitched together from parts that do not actually fit together very well, thus making it very hard to illuminate the framework by means of systems thinking. Taking insights from different traditions within linguistics and from different disciplines is certainly both valuable and essential – a dialogic approach to theoretical advancement; but I have preferred to engage in metalinguistic engagement, i.e. to translate insights into SFL because then I can see how they fit together in an extensive multidimensional relational network.

(ii) On the other hand, the notion of theoretical neutrality – or even the limiting case of absence of theory – has manifested itself, since the mid-1990s, within linguistic research using "big data" in the form of corpora of texts. Here Tognini-Bonelli (2001) distinction between "corpus-based" and "corpus-driven" research has been cited frequently, and "corpus-driven" has come to be regarded as a more empirical approach (cf. Sinclair's, e.g. 1992, formulation "trust the text"). I think that although it seems to have been generally accepted, this dichotomy is incomplete, so even misleading. Halliday (e.g. 2002b) has emphasized that the corpus itself is a highly theoretical construct – so it is not one that is theory neutral. And I have argued (e.g. Matthiessen 2014c) that this dichotomy overlooks the critical importance of text analysis based on systemic descriptions. Briefly, corpus-based work = a **deductive** approach, corpus-driven work = an **inductive** approach, and system-based text analysis = an **abductive** approach.

At the same time as the implications of the dichotomy between "corpus-based" vs. "corpus-driven" approaches have been explored, computationally tooled and empowered analysis has progressed, using machine learning techniques (within SFL, e.g. Teich et al. 2016). Such techniques might be a twenty-first-century version of "discovery procedures" (cf. Longacre 1964), much maligned in early Chomskyan linguistics. However, we need to ask how much of the system can be "discovered" from instances without any guidance. For example, using sophisticated unsupervised learning techniques, Lee and Goldsmith (2016) report on the success of *Linguistica 5* (a descendent of Goldsmith's *Linguistica*) in learning linguistic structures in English morphology: "*Linguistica 5* opens new doors to reproducible, accessible, and extensible research in unsupervised learning of linguistic structure" (p. 25).They also explore this as a plausible model for "human morphological learning using child-directed speech data" (p. 24).

This is the inductive approach, but of course human learners will test their systemic generalizations in speaking and listening. And by the time they begin to learn the lexicogrammar of the mother tongue, they have already learned how to mean (Halliday 1975, 2003a) – although as work by Patricia Kuhl and her group has described, young children begin "taking statistics" on the sounds of the mother tongue spoken around them even during their protolinguistic stage. However, we need to take a few steps back to view the total system of a language in context, and ask how much of it might be learned by techniques such as unsupervised machine learning. In the case of young children, as already noted, they have already learned the basic principles of how to mean by the time they begin the transition into the mother tongue(s) spoken around them in earnest. (Cf. my remarks at the beginning of this Introduction on the "deep learning revolution.")

Dimensions of systemic functional theory

Chapters 8 through 11 are concerned with some of the semiotic dimensions that are part of the multidimensional "architecture" of language in context according to systemic functional theory. The first chapter in this set, Chapter 8, is fairly short. It is based on an interview conducted with me during the twenty-fifth ISFC, hosted by Robin Fawcett and his team in Cardiff – a very memorable congress. It serves to contextualize discussions of theoretical and metatheoretical issues in SFL, including also the metalinguistic comparison with other frameworks, in particular Dik's functional grammar (for an early account, see Dik 1978).

The other chapters are concerned with particular semiotic dimensions and the relations and processes that have them as their domain.

The cline of instantiation is the focus of Chapters 9 and 10. In Chapter 9, I discuss Halliday's conception of language as a probabilistic system – that is, systemic probabilities at the potential pole of the cline of instantiation and their instantiation as relative frequencies in texts at the potential pole of the cline.

The hierarchy of composition – the rank scale within lexicogrammar – is the focus of Chapter 11. Here I move down the grammatical rank scale from the two ranks that have so far been given the most attention in work on different languages – clause and group (or group/phrase) – and I examine the grammar of word ranks. This is "morphology," but in systemic functional theory, the grammar of clause and group, "syntax," and that of word, "morphology," are treated as unified rather than as distinct modules: it's up to the description of particular languages to bring out the division of grammatical labour across the ranks of a given language, and it's the task of language comparison and typology to show how the division of labour across ranks is one typological variable.

Chapter 8: Interview with Christian Matthiessen (Liverpool 1998)

This interview complements the interviews conducted with other systemic functional linguists for the same special issue on SFL (40) of *Revista Canaria de Estudios Ingleses*, an issue that provides a helpful overview of a number of aspects of SFL at the end of the twentieth century. As a consumer of texts in linguistics and other disciplines, I had come to appreciate the value of interviews in the 1970s, when I read the interviews Herman Parret (1974) conducted with an interesting group of leading linguists, including Michael Halliday: one of Parret's contributions was to ask the linguists questions about topics that they had not foregrounded in their own writing.

So it was a privilege to be interviewed for the special issue of the *Revista Canaria* on SFL, and to be "scaffolded" by the interviewer. The interview in Chapter 8 can be read together with other publications based on interviews with me – see Matthiessen et al. (2022), which is the first of a series of books based on interviews and contains references to journal articles also based on their interviews with me. And, very importantly, there is now the book of interviews with Michael Halliday compiled and edited by Jim Martin (Martin 2013). One important feature of such interviews, already hinted at, is that the interviewer or interviewers choose the topics that they want to explore; they are as it were in the dialogic driver's seat. Michael and I discussed such interviews on various occasions, and I realized that like him I prefer not to be given the questions in advance: it is actually quite productive to be stimulated and energized by unexpected questions. Of course, if such interviews are then turned into written publications, one is likely to need to revise one's own answers quite significantly, partly to recast them in a more written mode but also to expand on points with the benefit of hindsight. But the text is still interviewer-driven (rather than only interviewer-based).

Chapter 9: Halliday's conception of language as a probabilistic system

This chapter was in a sense commissioned. As the Halliday Bloomsbury companion was being planned by Jonathan Webster, there was a very productive meeting at Halliday and Hasan's home in Manly, Sydney. We were all invited, and gathered in their large living room, with spectacular views of the ocean and Sydney's natural harbour to discuss the exciting publication project. Most chapters had already been assigned to contributors, virtually all of whom were present at this very stimulating meeting. But the chapter on Halliday's probabilistic conception of language had not been; I offered to give it a try, and my offer was accepted.

I had to approach Halliday's conception of language as a probabilistic system as a linguist – as he himself had done, of course. My knowledge of probability theory and statistics really dated back to my high school days, when I had chosen to do the strand focussed on material sciences (physics, chemics, biology) and mathematics rather than on social sciences or the humanities. But I knew the systemic functional literature on language as a probabilistic system, in addition to Halliday's own contributions going back to the 1950s – importantly, the pioneering contribution by Nesbitt and Plum (1988) and also Plum and Cowling (1987); and I had kept counting relative frequencies of systemic terms in texts from different registers as a way of exploring the probabilistic nature of language (e.g. Matthiessen 1999, 2002b, 2006). Once I had drafted the chapter, I sent it to Michael to check if he was happy with it, and he was.

I had hoped that the chapter would serve as an invitation to systemic functional linguists to develop probabilistic profiles of particular languages and to advance the general theory of language as a probabilistic system; and I had also hoped that non-SFL linguists who had begun to explore language as probabilistic system would recognize Halliday's pioneering work and take an interest in it. Since the 1950s, Halliday had maintained this conception of language – even during the long period of Chomskyan dominance when this kind of conception of language was off the agenda, even ridiculed – but the situation began to change gradually in the late 1980s as corpus linguistics started to come into its own with corpora of increasing size and tools of increasing power and as statical NLP began to develop (Manning and Schütze 1999). (Cf. also references to statistical learning in Chapter 12.)

Chapter 10: Instantial systems and logogenesis

Like Chapter 9, this chapter is concerned with instantiation; and like Chapter 5, it has never been published before. I gave a version of it as a talk at a conference on discourse analysis hosted by Professor Ren Shaozeng at Hangzhou University in the early 1990s. In the 1990s, we were concerned with the creation of meaning as text unfolds as a central part of modelling text generation at the Information Sciences Institute in Los Angeles (see the chapters above on text generation and also e.g. Bateman 1989; Matthiessen and Bateman 1991). In Sydney, scholars and students were also concerned with the unfolding of text – interpreted as a dynamic view of semiotics, complementing the "unmarked" synoptic view, e.g. in accounts of exchanges in the unfolding of dialogue: see e.g. Martin (1985); Ventola (1987); Lemke (1991). These two strands were brought together in a thematic series of meetings we held at Sydney University around 1990 concerned with logogenesis, and participants produced a number of publications related to this theme, including O'Donnell (1990) and O'Donnell and Sefton (1995). There were also other systemic functional contributions foregrounding the dynamic view of text, e.g. Ravelli (1995).

My paper, published here as Chapter 10, was part of this discussion of dynamic interpretations. While I did not get it published (having missed the publication boat launched after Professor Ren's conference), I circulated it quite widely. In his account of "text as semantic choice in social contexts," Halliday (1977) had already introduced a dynamic view of text (cf. also his eventive interpretation of linguistic structure in Halliday 1961). In Halliday and Matthiessen (1999) we interpreted logogenesis as one kind of semogenesis, differentiating and relating the kinds in terms of time frames: logogenesis < ontogenesis < phylogenesis. In my paper, I explored logogenesis in particular, giving various examples; but at the same time, I made the point that the successive choices that create a text accumulate gradually to form an instantial system – a distillation of the accumulation of choices as system. This instantial system may of course remain purely instantial, but at the same time it constitutes a "moment" in the evolution of the overall meaning potential. (Here Halliday's notion of the "Hamlet factor" is relevant: if a text is valued in a community as significant artefact and it is not simply another specimen of the system, it may exercise more influence than would normally be expected of a single text, as in the case of Shakespeare's play *Hamlet*.)

While I didn't get my logogenesis paper published, I have continued to study the phenomenon of logogenesis, for example, in Matthiessen (2002a) I traced systemic selections in text, and visualized them as a text score (cf. also Matthiessen 1995a); and in Matthiessen (2023), I also discuss systemic text scores and systemic chords. (Visualization of logogenesis is also offered by Caldwell and Zappavigna 2011 and Zappavigna 2011.) Elsewhere I have related the instantial system that emerges from a text to ideology, as in Matthiessen (2015c): selections in text unit by unit (e.g. clause by clause) gradually form patterns that can be interpreted as instantial systems realizing some particular ideological setting of context and semantics. Their dynamic changes in patterns captured by systemic text scores can also be investigated under the heading of "phase portrait" – another way of bringing out trajectories of change in dynamic systems; but I like systemic scores because both language and music are semiotic systems, and it is helpful to highlight similarities across semiotic systems – and of course between semiotic systems and systems of lower orders, like physical systems analysed in terms of phase portraits.

Chapter 11: Systemic functional morphology: the lexicogrammar of the word

This chapter is concerned with a semiotic dimension other than the cline of instantiation, viz. the rank scale (a compositional hierarchy) – more specifically, the rank scale in descriptions of lexicogrammar at the rank of word. This is the grammar of words, or "morphology." While I had thought about the grammar of words in systemic functional theory and in relation to the description of various languages (including Akan: see Volume 3 of the *Collected works*), I had not produced a systematic overview. Fortunately for me, Edson Rosa de Souza invited me to contribute a chapter on systemic functional morphology to a book he was planning on a range of approaches to morphology. He sent us contributors a list of questions, so naturally I organized my chapter around those questions – an approach that ensured comparability across the chapters.

In the early 1990s, Halliday gave a talk on systemic functional morphology at ICU in Tokyo, and I found it fascinating and inspiring; but unfortunately, he never wrote it up. He illustrated theoretical points with examples from various languages, including Russian (which he knew). During the regular meetings he and I had after I had arrived in Sydney in 1988, we discussed morphology, and prepared notes on it for our two-volume manuscript *Outline of systemic functional linguistics*. When we worked on the third edition of his *Introduction to functional grammar*, we would have liked to include a sketch of English word grammar, but there was simply no space. However, in his book on complementarities, Halliday (2008) provides examples in particular of English derivational morphology. (There had been some work in earlier versions of systemic functional grammar, notably Hudson's (1973) description of Beja. He characterizes it as an item-and-paradigm approach – a nice echo of Robins' (1959) addition of word-and-paradigm as an approach to morphology to Hockett's (1954), comparison of item-and-arrangement and item-and-process approaches to grammatical description.)

In my chapter, I tried to characterize the systemic functional approach to the grammar of words, morphology, theoretically, making the point – Halliday's point going back to Halliday (1961) – that morphology and syntax are not separate modules of grammar (cf. the term "morphosyntax" in the descriptive and typological literature, designed to bring out the continuity of these domains of grammar) in the way that they have often been assumed to be, but rather simply reflect different ranks within the division of grammatical labour across the ranked units of a given language, a division of labour that is typologically variable (which was already recognized in nineteenth-century language typology, though not characterized in these terms). The domain of the grammar of words is simply another environment where general fractal principles are manifested. In fact, the fractal principles of axiality and of rank are manifested in all stratal subsystems of language in context. Thus, within the strata of form (lexicogrammar and phonology), morphological systems are the same type of systems as clause systems and group systems, but also as tone group systems, foot systems, and syllable systems.

In understanding and dealing with challenges that arise in accounts of morphology, I was greatly helped by the fact that I had started having to try to come to terms with the very awesome morphology of Arabic (Modern Standard Arabic [MSA]), as a learner of the language in the second half of the 1970s at Lund University but also as a linguist (including as the fortunate PhD supervisor of Bardi 2008). The template and overlay principle of MSA (and also of related languages) is in a sense an invitation to an approach that makes paradigmatic rather than syntagmatic organization primary – hence a systemic morphology, with word structures as realizations.

Theory, modelling, and neurosemiotics

Chapter 12: The architecture of language according to SFL: some reflections on implications for neurosemiotics

The last chapter of this volume is again concerned centrally with modelling. In the first instance, this is linguistic modelling for biological implementation rather than linguistic modelling for computational implementation; but a minor motif is also the analogy of the modelling undertaken by our brains by means of bio-semiotic systems, e.g. how our visual system construes visual "meaning" out of incomplete physical stimuli. This neurological modelling is fascinating – e.g. Barrett's (2017) account of the "conceptual cascade," which I refer to briefly in the chapter; and somebody with a grounding in neuroscience would be in an excellent position to develop the account of the brain's neurological modelling in bio-semiotic systems in such a way that the parallels with neurological modelling in language and other denotative semiotic systems are brought out, perhaps enabling us to explore bio-semiotic systems as paving the way for socio-semiotic systems.

At the beginning of Chapter 12, I give a brief account of how I came to write the original version of the chapter – thanks to Adolfo García.

Since the chapters in this volume of collected works span over four decades (1981 to 2023), Kazuhiro Teruya, as the chief editor, and I have had to deal with changes in conventions in the representation of different systemic functional categories and abstractions. I still remember clearly the attempts to sort out the conventions as computational linguistic, knowledge representation, and systemic functional conventions came face to face in the early 1980s. This involved terminology – in particular in the domain of the 'relational' clause grammar of English, since "attribute" and "value" were used in different senses across the disciplines involved; but it also involved spelling conventions. The systemic functional conventions were already well established:

Initial upper case: structural functionals, e.g. Theme, Subject, Actor; Finite, Event; Deictic, Thing;

All upper case (small capitals): names of systems, e.g. THEME, MOOD TYPE, AGENCY;

All lower case: names of terms in systems (features, options), often with single quotes, e.g. 'indicative'/'imperative'; 'middle'/'effective'; 'operative'/'receptive'

In the representation of "concepts" in various versions of frame-based inheritance networks, the convention was to use all caps, as in the chapters in the first part of this book.

Notes

1   When I came across this book in 1980, I was astonished that systemic functional grammar was not included; and I sketched an outline of an account of SFG that addressed the issues that were the focus for the approaches included in the book.

2   For a critical review of the notion of prototypes as a characterization of emotion concepts, see Barrett (2017: 89ff). Her account is quite interesting and important from a systemic functional point of view (see also Chapter 12), partly because she explains concepts in reference to what we would interpret as the cline

of instantiation: they are distillations of innumerable instances, created by categorization to suit different situations (types) – in her terms, they are goal-based concepts.

3   Kosko (1993: 191) writes of Sugeno: "Sugeno is aloof, parts his hair in the middle, and can do without Westerners. He was five in 1945 when the Allies bombed his city of Yokohama." We have actually always found him very engaging – and engaged; and the category of "Westerners" is far too broad. I remember one occasion with him, during a time I had been invited to LIFE, when we met with two high-ranking US Americans. They knew of his amazing success with controlling unmanned flying helicopters, and asked him if he would accept funding to include his unmanned flying helicopter as part of the opening ceremony of the 1996 Summer Olympics in Atlanta. He replied very crisply "I do not take American money," with such authority that two American men look stunned and did not pursue the topic. – Sugeno was very supportive of our work, and he was also a wonderful host. Just to set the record straight: it was Sugeno who introduced me to dry Martinis, not James Bond.

4   Chris Nesbitt and I co-authored this chapter, in part drawing on his PhD thesis, which he had completed under my supervision. Sadly, Chris passed away in June 2025; this is a tragedy: he had a great deal of life ahead of him. In the linguistics community, we owe him a huge debt for his many brilliant contributions across a full spectrum of academic activities, including his collegial support and friendship. He is remembered with warm affection in Nigeria, where the SFL community welcomed him in 2004. As Michael Halliday's student, Chris had absorbed Michael's deep understanding of language and built on it – encapsulating systemic functional grammar in his HyperGrammar application (see Chapter 7).

Chapter 1

A grammar and a lexicon for a text-production system

Abstract

In a text-production system high and special demands are placed on the grammar and the lexicon. This chapter will view these components in such a system (overview in Section 1.1). First, the subcomponents dealing with semantic information and with syntactic information will be presented separately (Section 1.2). The problems of relating these two types of information are then identified (Section 1.3). Finally, strategies designed to meet the problems are proposed and discussed (Section 1.4). One of the issues that will be illustrated is what happens when a systemic linguistic approach is combined with a KL-ONE-like knowledge representation – a novel and hitherto unexplored combination.[1]

1.1   The place of a grammar and a lexicon in PENMAN

This chapter will view a grammar and a lexicon as integral parts of a text-production system (PENMAN). This perspective leads to certain requirements on the form of the grammar and that of the subparts of the lexicon and on the strategies for integrating these components with each other and with other parts of the system. In the course of the presentation of the components, the subcomponents, and the integrating strategies, these requirements will be addressed. Here I will give a brief overview of the system.

PENMAN is a successor to KDS (Moore and Mann 1979; Mann and Moore 1980; Mann and Moore 1981) and is being created to produce multi-sentential natural English text. It has as some of its components a knowledge domain, encoded in a KL-ONE-like representation, a reader model, a text planner, a lexicon, and a sentence generator (called NIGEL). The grammar used in NIGEL is a systemic grammar of English of the type developed by Michael Halliday.

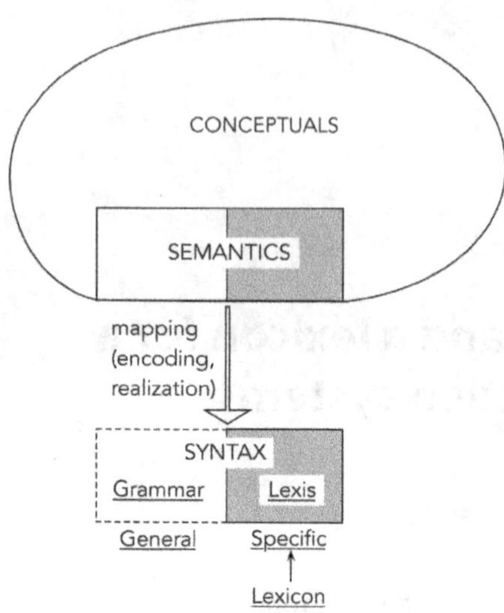

Figure 1.1 System overview

For present purposes the grammar, the lexicon, and their environment can be represented as shown in Figure 1.1.

The lines enclose sets; the boxes are the linguistic components. The dotted lines represent parts that have been developed independently of the present project, but which are being implemented, refined, and revised; the continuous lines represent components whose design is being developed within the project.

The box labelled *syntax* stands for syntactic information, both of the general kind that is needed to generate structures (the grammar, the left part of the box) and of the more specific kind that is needed for the syntactic definition of lexical items (the syntactic subentry of lexical items, to the right in the box – the term lexicogrammar can also be used to denote both ends of the box).

The other box (*semantics*) represents that part of semantics that has to do with our conceptualization of experience (distinct from the semantics of interaction – speech acts, etc. – and the semantics of presentation – theme structure, the distinction between given and new information, etc.). It is shown as one part of what is called *conceptuals* – our general conceptual organization of the world around us and our own inner world; it is the linguistic part of conceptuals. For the lexicon this means that lexical semantics is that part of conceptuals which has become lexicalized and thus enters into the structure of the vocabulary. There is also a correlation between conceptual organization and the organization of part of the grammar.

The arrow between the two boxes represents the mapping (realization or encoding) of semantics into syntax. For example, the concept SELL is mapped onto the verb *sold*.[2]

The *grammar* is the general part of the syntactic box, the part concerned with syntactic structures. *The lexicon* cuts across three levels: it has a semantic part, a syntactic part (lexis), and an orthographic part (or spelling; not present in the figure).[3] The lexicon consists entirely of independent lexical entries, each representing one lexical item (typically a word).

This figure, then, represents the part of the PENMAN text-production system that includes the grammar, the lexicon, and their immediate environment.

PENMAN is at the design stage; consequently, the discussion that follows is tentative and exploratory rather than definitive. The component that has advanced the farthest is the grammar. It has been implemented in NIGEL, the sentence generator mentioned above. It has been tested and is currently being revised and extended. None of the other components (those demarcated by continuous lines) have been implemented; they have been tested only by way of hand examples. This chapter will concentrate on the design features of the grammar rather than on the results of the implementation and testing of it.

1.2   The components

1.2.1   Knowledge representation and semantics

The knowledge representation

One of the fundamental properties of the KL-ONE-like knowledge representation (KR) is its intensional–extensional distinction, the distinction between a general conceptual taxonomy and a second part of the representation where we find individuals which can exist, states of affairs which may be true, etc. This is roughly a distinction between what is conceptualizable and actual conceptualizations (whether they are real or hypothetical). In the overview figure in Section 1.1, the two parts are together called conceptuals.

For instance, to use an example I will be using throughout this chapter, there is an intensional concept SELL, about which no existence or location in time is claimed. An intensional concept is related to extensional concepts by the relation

Individuates: intensional SELL is related by individual instances of extensional SELLs by the Individuates relation. If I know that Joan sold Arthur ice cream in the park, I have a SELL fixed in time which is part of an assertion about Joan, and it individuates intensional SELL.[4] A concept has internal structure: it is a configuration of roles. The concept SELL has an internal structure which comprises the three roles associated with it, viz. AGENT (the seller), RECIPIENT (the buyer), and OBJECT. These roles are slots which are filled by other concepts, and the domains over which these can vary are defined as value restrictions. The AGENT of SELL is a PERSON or a FRANCHISE, and so on.

In other words, a concept is defined by its relation to other concepts (much as in European structuralism). These relations are roles associated with the concept, roles whose fillers are other concepts. This gives rise to a large conceptual net.

There is another relation which helps define the place of a concept in the conceptual net, viz. SuperCategory, which gives the conceptual net a taxonomic (or hierarchic) structure in addition to the structure defined by the role relations. The concept SELL is defined by its place in the taxonomy by having TRANSACTION as a SuperCategory. If we want to, we can define a concept that will have SELL as a SuperCategory (i.e. bear the SuperCategory relation to SELL), for example SELLOB 'sell on the black market'. As a result, part of the taxonomy of events is TRANSACTION – SELL – SELLOB.

If TRANSACTION has a set of roles associated with it, this set may be inherited by SELL and by SELLOB – this is a general feature of the SuperCategory relation. In the examples involving SELL that follow, I will concentrate on this concept and not try to generalize to its supercategories.

The semantic subentry

In the overview in Figure 1.1, the semantics is shown as part of the conceptuals. The consequence of this is that the set of semantic entries in the lexicon is a subset of the set of concepts. The subset is proper if we assume that there are concepts which have not been lexicalized (the assumption indicated in the figure). The assumption is perfectly reasonable; I have already invented the concept SELLOB, for which there is no word in standard English: it is not surprising if we have formed concepts for which we have to create expressions rather than pick them ready-made from our lexicon. Furthermore, if we construct a conceptual component intended to support, say, a bilingual speaker, there will be a number of concepts which are lexicalized in only one of the two languages.

A semantic entry, then, is a concept in the conceptuals. For *sold*, we find *sold* with its associated roles, AGENT, RECIFIENT, and OBJECT. The right part of Figure 1.2 (marked "se:"; after a figure from Brachman 1978) gives a more detailed semantic entry for *sold*: a pointer identifies the relevant part in the KR, the concept that constitutes the semantic entry (here the concept SELL).

The concept that constitutes the semantic entry of a lexical item has a fairly rich structure. Roles are associated with the concept and the modality (necessary or optional); the cardinality of and restrictions on (value of) the fillers are given.

Through the value restriction the linguistic notion of selection restriction is captured. *The stone sold a carnation to the little girl* is odd because the AGENT role of SELL is value restricted to PERSON or FRANCHISE and the concept associated with *stone* falls into neither type.

The strategy of letting semantic entries be part of the KR would not have been possible in a notation designed to capture specific propositions only. However, since KL-ONE provides the distinction between intension and extension, the strategy is unproblematic in the present framework.

So what is the relationship between intensional–extensional and semantic entries? The working assumption is that for a large part of the vocabulary, it is the concepts of the intensional part of the KR that may be lexicalized and thus serve as semantic entries. We have words for intensional objects, actions, and states, but not for individual extensional objects, etc., with the exception of proper names. They have extensional concepts as their semantic entries. For instance, *Alex* denotes a particular individuated person and *The War of the Roses* a particular individuated war.

Both the SuperCategory relation and the Individuates relation provide ways of walking around in the KR to find expressions for concepts. If we are in the extensional part of the KR, looking at a particular individual, we can follow the individuates link up to an intensional concept. There may be a word for it, in which case the concept is part of a lexical entry. If there is no word for the concept, we will have to consider the various options the grammar gives us for forming an appropriate expression.

The general assumption is that all the intensional vocabulary can be used for extensional concepts in the way just described: expressability is inherited with the Individuates relation.

Expression candidates for concepts can also be located along the SuperCategory link by going from one concept to another one higher up in the taxonomy. Consider the following example: *Joan sold Arthur ice cream. The transaction took place in the park.* The SuperCategory link enables us to go from SELL to TRANSACTION, where we find the expression *transaction*.

Lexical semantic relations

The structure of the vocabulary is parasitic on the conceptual structure. In other words, lexicalized concepts are related not only to one another, but also to concepts for which there is no word-encoding in English (i.e. non-lexicalized concepts).

Crudely, the semantic structure of the lexicon can be described as being part of the hierarchy of intensional concepts – the intensional concepts that happen to be lexicalized in English. The structure of English vocabulary is thus not the only principle that is reflected in the KR, but it is reflected. Very general concepts like OBJECT, THING, and ACTION are at the top. In this hierarchy, roles are inherited. This corresponds to the semantic redundancy rules of a lexicon.

Considering the possibility of walking around in the KR and the integration of lexicalized and non-lexicalized concepts, the KR suggests itself as the natural place to state certain text-forming principles, some of which have been described under the terms lexical cohesion (Halliday and Hasan 1976) and thematic progression (Daneš 1974b).

I will now turn to the syntactic component in Figure 1.1, starting with a brief introduction to the framework (systemic linguistics) that does the same for that component as the notion of semantic net did for the component just discussed.

1.2.2 Lexicogrammar

Systemic linguistics stems from a British tradition and has been developed by its founder, Michael Halliday (e.g. 1961, 1976a) and other systemic linguists (see e.g. Fawcett 1973, 1980 for a presentation of Fawcett's interesting work on developing a systemic model within a cognitive model) for over twenty years, covering many areas of linguistic concern, including studies of text, lexicogrammar, language development, and computational applications. Systemic grammar was used in SHRDLU (Winograd 1972) and more recently in another important contribution, Davey's PROTEUS (Davey 1979).

The systemic tradition recognizes a fundamental principle in the organization of language: the distinction between *choice* and the *structures* that express (realize) choices. Choice is taken as primary and is given special recognition in the formalization of the systemic model of language. Consequently, a description is a specification of the choices a speaker can make together with statements about how he realizes a selection he has made. This realization of a set of choices is typically linear, e.g. a string of words. Each choice point is formalized as a *system* (hence the name systemic). The options open to the speaker are two or more *features* that constitute alternatives which can be chosen. The preconditions for the choice are *entry conditions* to the system. Entry conditions are logical expressions whose elementary terms are features.

All but one of the systems have non-empty entry conditions. This causes an interdependency among the systems with the result that the grammar of English forms one network of systems, which cluster when a feature in one system is (part of) the entry condition to another system. This dependency gives the network depth: it starts (at its "root") with very general choices. Other systems of choice depend on them (i.e. have a feature from one of these systems – or a combination of features from more than one system – as entry conditions) so that the systems of choice become less general (more *delicate*, to use the systemic term) as we move along in the network.

The network of systems is where the control of the grammar resides, its non-deterministic part. Systemic grammar thus contrasts with many other formalisms in that choice is given explicit representation and is captured in a single rule type (systems), not distributed over the grammar as, for example, optional rules of different types. This property of systemic grammar makes it a very useful component in a text-production system, especially in the interface with semantics and in ensuring accessibility of alternatives.

The rest of the grammar is deterministic – the consequences of features chosen in the network of systems. These consequences are formalized as feature *realization statements* whose task is to build the appropriate structure.

For example, in independent indicative sentences, English offers a choice between declarative and interrogative sentences. If interrogative is chosen, this leads to a dependent system with a choice between wh-interrogative and yes/no-interrogative. When the latter is chosen, it is realized by having the FINITE verb before the SUBJECT.

Since it is the general design of the grammar that is the focus of attention, I will not go through the algorithm for generating a sentence as it has been implemented in NIGEL. The general observation is that the results are very encouraging, although they are incomplete. The algorithm generates a wide range of English structures correctly. There have not been any serious problems in implementing a grammar written in the systemic notation.

Before turning to the lexico- part of lexicogrammar, I will give an example of the top-level structure of a sentence generated by the grammar in Figure 1.2. (I have left out the details of the internal structure of the constituents.)

The structure consists of three layers of function symbols, all of which are needed to get the result desired. The structure is not only functional (with function

[1]	Location	Actor	Process	Beneficiary	Goal
[2]	Subject	Finite			
[3]	Theme				
	In the park	Joan	sold	Arthur	ice cream

Figure 1.2 An example of top-level structure of a sentence generated by the grammar

symbols labelling the constituents instead of category names like Noun Phrase and Verb Phrase) but multifunctional.

Each layer of function symbols shows a particular perspective on the clause structure. Layer [1] gives the aspect of the sentence as a representation of our experience. The second layer structures the sentence as interaction between the speaker and the hearer; the fact that SUBJECT precedes FINITE signals that the speaker is giving the hearer information. Layer [3] represents a structuring of the clause as a message: the THEME is its starting point. The functions are called experiential, interpersonal, and textual, respectively, in the systemic framework: the function symbols are said to belong to three different metafunctions. In the rest of the chapter I will concentrate on the experiential metafunction, partly because it will turn out to be highly relevant to the lexicon.

The syntactic subentry

In the systemic tradition, the syntactic part of the lexicon is seen as a continuation of grammar (hence the term lexicogrammar for both of them): lexical choices are simply more detailed (delicate) than grammatical choices (cf. Halliday 1976a). The vocabulary of English can be seen as one huge taxonomy, with Roget's Thesaurus as a very rough model.

A taxonomic organization of the relevant part of the vocabulary of English is intended for PENMAN, but this organization is part of the conceptual organization mentioned above. There is at present no separate lexical taxonomy.

The syntactic subentry potentially consists of two parts. There is always the class specification – the lexical features. This is a statement of the grammatical potential of the lexical item, i.e. of how it can be used grammatically. For *sold* the class specification is the following:

verb
class 10
class 02
benefactive

where "benefactive" says that *sold* can occur in a sentence with a BENEFICIARY, "class 10" that it encodes a material process (contrasting with mental, verbal, and relational processes), and "class 02" that it is a transitive verb.

In addition, there is a provision for a configurational part, which is a fragment of a structure the grammar can generate, more specifically the experiential part of the grammar.[5] The structure corresponds to the top layer [1] in the example in Figure 1.2. In reference to this example, I can make more explicit what I mean by fragment. The general point is that (to take just one class as an example) the presence and character of functions like ACTOR, BENEFICIARY, and GOAL – direct participants in the event denoted by the verb – depend on the type of verb, whereas the more circumstantial functions like LOCATION remain unaffected and applicable to all types of verb. Consequently, the information about the possibility of having a LOCATION constituent is not the type of information that has to be stated for specific lexical items. The information given for them concerns only a fragment of the experiential functional structure.

The full syntactic entry for *sold* is:

Process	=	verb
		class 10
		class 02
		benefactive
Actor	=	
Goal	=	
Beneficiary	=	

This says that *sold* can occur in a fragment of a structure where it is PROCESS and there can be an ACTOR, a GOAL, and a BENEFICIARY. The usefulness of the structure fragment will be demonstrated in Section 1.4.

1.3   The problem

I will now turn to the fundamental problem of making a working system out of the parts that have been discussed.

The problem has two parts to it, viz.

1.   the design of the system as a system with integrated parts, and
2.   the implementation of the system.

I will only be concerned with the first aspect here.

The components of the system have been presented. What remains – and that is the problem – is to design the missing links; to find the strategies that will do the job of connecting the components.

Finding these strategies is a design problem in the following sense. The strategies do not come as accessories with the frameworks we have used (the systemic framework and the KL-ONE-inspired KR). Moreover, these two frameworks stem from two quite disparate traditions with different sets of goals, symbols, and terms.

I will state the problem for the grammar first and then for the lexicon. As it has been presented, *the grammar* runs wild and free. It is organized around choice, to be sure, but there is nothing to relate the choices to the rest of the system, in particular to what we can take to be semantics. In other words, although the grammar may have a part that faces semantics – the system network, which, in Halliday's words, is semantically relevant grammar – it does not make direct contact with semantics. And if we know what we want the system to encode in a sentence, how can we indicate what goes where, that is, what a constituent (e.g. the ACTOR) should encode?

The lexicon incorporates the problem of finding an appropriate strategy to link the components to each other, since it cuts across component boundaries. The semantic and syntactic subparts of a lexical entry have been outlined, but nothing has been said about how they should be matched up with one another. The reason why this match is not perfectly straightforward has to do with the fact that both entries may be structures (configurations) rather than single elements. In addition, there are lexical relations that have not been accounted for yet, especially synonymy and polysemy.

1.4   Looking for the solutions

1.4.1 *The grammar*

Choice experts and their domains

The control of the grammar resides in the network of systems. Choice experts can be developed to handle the choices in these systems.

The idea is that there is an expert for each system in the network and that this expert knows what it takes to make a meaningful choice – what the factors influencing its choice are. It has at its disposal a table which tells it how to find the relevant pieces of information, which are somewhere in the knowledge domain, the text plan, or the reader model.

In other words, the part of the grammar that is related to semantics is the part where the notion of choice is: the choice experts know about the semantic consequences of the various choices in the grammar and do the job of relating syntax to semantics.[6]

The recognition of different functional components of the grammar relates to the multifunctional character of a structure in systemic grammar I mentioned in relation to the example *in the park Joan sold Arthur ice cream* in Section 1.2.2. The organization of the sentence into PROCESS, ACTOR, BENEFICIARY, GOAL, and LOCATIVE is an organization the grammar imposes on our experience, and it is the aspect of the organization of the sentence that relates to the conceptual organization of the knowledge domain: it is in terms of this organization (and not e.g. SUBJECT, OBJECT, THEME, and NEW INFORMATION) that the mapping between syntax and semantics can be stated. The functional diversity Halliday has provided for systemic grammar is useful in a text-production system; the other functions find uses which space does not permit a discussion of here.

Pointers from constituents

In order for the choice experts to be able to work, they must know where to look. Assume that we are working on *in the park* in our example sentence *in the park Joan sold Arthur ice cream* and that an expert has to decide whether *park* should be definite or not. The information about the status in the mind of the reader of the concept corresponding to *park* in this sentence is located at this concept: the trick is to associate the concept with the constituent being built. In the example structure given earlier, *in the park* is both LOCATION and THEME, only the former of which is relevant to the present problem. The solution is to set a pointer to the relevant extensional concept when the function symbol LOCATION is inserted, so that LOCATION will carry the pointer and thus make the information attached to the concept accessible.

1.4.2   *The lexicon and the lexical entry*

I have already introduced the semantic subentry and the syntactic subentry. They are stated in a KL-ONE-like representation and a systemic notation, respectively. The question now is how to relate the two.

In the KR the internal structure of a concept is a configuration of roles, and these roles lead to new concepts to which the concept is related. A syntactic structure is seen as a configuration of function symbols; syntactic categories serve these functions – in the generation of a structure the functions lead to an entry of a part of the network. For example, the function ACTOR leads to a part of the network whose entry feature is Nominal Group just as the role AGENT (of SELL) leads to the concept that is the filler of it. The parallel between the two representations in this area is set out in Table 1.1.

(Where *exponent* denotes the entry feature into a part of the network [e.g. Nominal Group] that the function leads to.)

This parallel clears the path for a strategy for relating the semantic entry and the syntactic entry. The strategy is in keeping with current ideas in linguistics.[7] Consider the following crude entry for *sold*, given in Table 1.2 as an illustration.

Table 1.1 Correspondences between knowledge representation and syntactic representation

Knowledge representation	Syntactic representation
role	function
filler	exponent

Table 1.2 Lexical entry for the verb *sold*

Subentries				
semantic		syntactic		orthographic
		Functions		Lexical features
SELL-concept	=	PROCESS	=	verb class 10 class 02 benefactive	"sold"
AGENT	=	ACTOR		
OBJECT	=	GOAL		
RECIPIENT	=	BENEFICIARY		

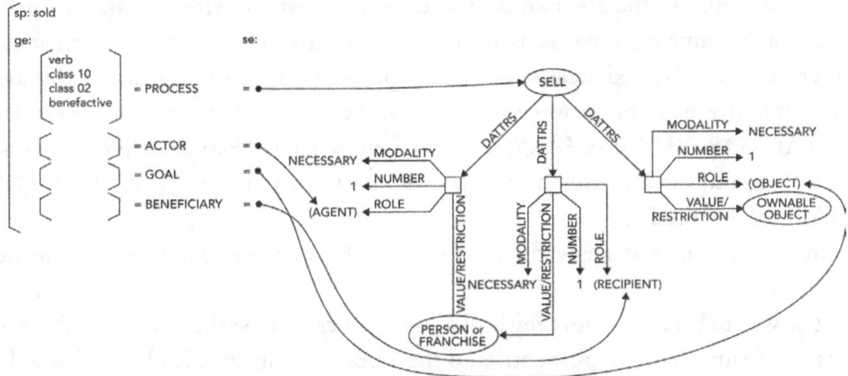

Figure 1.3 Lexical entry for *sold*

where the previously discussed semantic and syntactic subentries are repeated and paired off against each other.

This full lexical entry makes clear the usefulness of the second part of the syntactic entry – the fragment of the experiential functional structure in which *sold* can be the PROCESS.

Another piece of the total picture also falls into place now. The notion of a pointer from an experiential function like BENEFICIARY in the grammatical structure to a point in the conceptual net was introduced above. We can now see how this pointer may be set for individual lexical items: it is introduced as a simple relation between a grammatical function symbol and a conceptual role in the lexical entry of e.g. SELL. Since there is an individual link between this intensional concept and any extensional SELL, the extensional concept that is part of the particular proposition that is being encoded grammatically, the pointer is inherited and will point to a role in the extensional part of the knowledge domain.

At this point, I will refer again to Figure 1.3, whose right half I have already referred to as a full example of a semantic subentry ("se:"); "sp:" is the spelling or orthographic subentry, while "ge:" is the syntactic subentry.

We have two configurations in the lexical entry: in the semantic subentry the concept plus a number of roles, and in the syntactic subentry a number of grammatical functions. The match is represented in Figure 1.3 by the arrows.

All three roles of SELL have the modality "necessary." This does not dictate the grammatical possibilities. The grammar in NIGEL offers a choice between e.g. *They sold many books to their customers* and *The book sold well.* In the second example, the grammar only picks out a subset of the roles of SELL for expression. In other words, the grammar makes the adoption of different perspectives possible.[8]

I can now return to the observation that the functional diversity Halliday has provided for systemic grammar is useful for our purposes. The fact that grammatical structure is multilayered means that those aspects of grammatical structure that are relevant to the mapping between the two lexical entries are identified, made explicit (as ACTOR, BENEFICIARY, etc.), and kept separate from principles of grammatical structuring that are not directly relevant to this mapping (e.g. SUBJECT, NEW, and THEME).

In conclusion, a strategy for accounting for *synonymy* and *polysemy* can be mentioned.

The way to capture synonymy is to allow a concept to be the semantic subentry for two distinct orthographic entries. If the items are syntactically identical as well, they will also share a syntactic subentry. Polysemy works the other way: there may be more than one concept for the same syntactic subentry.

1.5   Conclusion

I have discussed a grammar and a lexicon for PENMAN in two steps. First, I looked at them as independent components – the semantic entry, the grammar, and the syntactic entry – and then, after identifying the problems of integrating them into a system, I turned to strategies for relating the grammar to the conceptual representation and the syntactic entry to the semantic one within the lexicon.

In the first step I introduced the KL-ONE-like KR and the systemic notation and indicated how their design features can be put to good use in PENMAN. For instance, the distinction between intension and extension in the KR makes it possible to let lexical semantics be part of the conceptuals. It was also suggested that the relations SuperCategory and Individuates can be used to find expressions for a particular concept.

The second step attempted to connect the grammar to semantics through the notion of the choice expert, making use of a design principle of systemic grammars where the notion of choice is taken as basic. I pointed out the correlation between the structure of a concept and the notion of structure in the systemic framework and showed how the two can be matched in a lexical entry and in the generation of a sentence, a strategy that could be adopted because of the multifunctional nature of structure in systemic grammars. This second step has been at the same time an attempt to start exploring the potential of a combination of a KL-ONE-like representation and a systemic grammar.

Although many aspects have had to be left out of the discussion, there are a number of issues that are of linguistic interest and significance. The most basic one is perhaps the task itself: designing a model where a grammar and a lexicon can actually be made to function as more than just structure generators. One issue related to this that has been brought up was that different parts external to the grammar find resonance in different parts of the grammar and that there is a partial correlation between the conceptual structure of the KR and the grammar and lexicon.

As was emphasized in the introduction, PENMAN is at the design stage: there is a working sentence generator, but the other aspects of what has been discussed have not been implemented and there is no commitment yet to a frozen design. Naturally, a large number of problems still await their solution, even at the level of design, and clearly, many of them will have to wait. For example, selectivity among terms, beyond referential adequacy, is not addressed.

In general, while noting correlations between linguistic organization and conceptual organization, we do not want the relation to be deterministic: part of being a good verbalizer is being able to adopt different viewpoints, to verbalize the same knowledge in different ways. This is clearly an area for future research. Hopefully, ideas such as grammars organized around choice and choice experts will prove useful tools in working out extensions.

Notes

1   This research was supported by the Air Force Office of Scientific Research, Contract No. F49620-79-c-0181. The views and conclusions contained in this chapter are those of the author and should not be interpreted as necessarily representing the official policies or endorsements, either expressed or implied, of the Air Force Office of Scientific Research of the US Government. The research represents a joint effort and so do the ideas stemming from it, which are the substance of this chapter. I would like to thank in particular William Mann, who has helped me think, given me many helpful ideas and suggestions, and commented extensively on drafts of the chapter; without him it would not be. I am also grateful to Yasutomo Fukumochi for helpful comments on a draft and to Michael Halliday, who has made clear to me many systemic principles and insights. Naturally, I am solely responsible for errors in the presentation and content.

2   I am using the general convention of capitalizing terms denoting semantic entries. Capitals will also be used for roles associated with concepts (like AGENT, RECIPIENT, and OBJECT) and initial capitals for grammatical functions (like Actor, Beneficiary, and Goal). These notions will be introduced later in the chapter.

3   This means that an entry for a lexical item consists of three subentries, viz. a semantic entry, a syntactic entry, and an orthographic entry. The lexicon box is shown as containing parts of both syntax and semantics in the figure (the shaded area) to emphasize the nature of the lexical entry.

4   It should be emphasized that calling the concept SELL says nothing whatever about the English expression for it; the reasons for giving it this name are purely mnemonic. The only way the concept can be associated with the word sold is through being part of a lexical entry.

5   This configurational part does not stem from the systemic tradition, but is an exploration in the present design.

6   A possible of the full semantics of the grammar is, as a result of this approach, "semantic = what the grammatical choice experts look at." In the present discussion, I have focussed on the knowledge domain only, partly because this is the area most relevant to lexical semantics.

7   The mechanism for mapping has much in common with one developed for lexical functional grammar (see e.g. Bresnan 1980), although the levels are not the same. The entry also resembles a lexical entry in the Pan-Lexicalism framework developed by Hudson (1984).

8   The strategy of letting the functional syntactic entry pick up different parts of a concept and adopt different perspective finds many uses, e.g. in the treatment of pairs like *buy vs. sell* and give vs. receive and in the account for nominalizations.

Chapter 2

Systemic grammar in computation: the NIGEL case

2.1   Introduction

Computational linguistics needs grammars for several different tasks, such as comprehension of text, machine translation, and text generation.[1] Clearly, any approach to grammar[2] has potentially something to offer computational linguistics, say for parsing or text generation (and, by the same token, there is a potential benefit from an application within computational linguistics for each approach [cf. Fawcett 1980]). However, it is equally clear that some approaches have much more to offer than others. Here I will take a look at systemic linguistics[3] in the service of computational linguistics tasks, concentrating on a large computational systemic grammar for text generation (NIGEL) that is currently being developed.

2.1.1   What can systemic linguistics offer?

The question I will try to answer in this chapter is what systemic linguistics can offer computational linguistics. Since the answer is, I think, far too long for a short discussion, I will let a more specific question represent the general question here: What can systemic linguistic accounts of grammar and semantics offer computational linguistics in the area of text generation? This question excludes, for example, the use of systemic grammar in parsing (see Winograd 1972) and the large systemic body of work on discourse organization (see in particular, Halliday and Hasan 1976; Hasan 1979; Halliday and Hasan 1980; Butler 1985; Martin 1985; Hasan 2014).

The text-generation task raises a number of demands on the grammatical component. Very roughly and generally stated, they amount to generating in conformity with diverse needs, such as the need for denotational appropriateness and the need for fluent text. There is no published general solution to the problem of controlling the grammar to generate in conformity with diverse needs. The discussion here continues and elaborates parts of Matthiessen (1981).

2.1.2 *Systemic functionalism as a contribution*

A cornerstone in systemic linguistics as developed by M.A.K. Halliday and others is systemic functionalism.[4] Grammar is to be investigated and interpreted in terms of the purposes it fulfils. Its organization is a function of these higher-level considerations. Apart from guiding research in systemic linguistics, this functionalism has been important in the design of systemic grammars. I will identify two design properties characteristic of systemic grammars that make them well suited to deal with the demands, better than grammars that are not designed to reflect the functionalism that the two properties stem from. The two properties have to do with the organization of grammar and with the process of sentence generation; they constitute factorings of the sentence-generation task. One is a factoring into a process of controlled choice and a process of structure specification as a consequence of choices made. This factoring is due to the need to represent the organization of grammar in its role as a resource for communicative needs. The other is a factoring of the grammatical resources into domains that serve different purposes (what will be called the metafunctional factoring). I will use NIGEL to illustrate how they work and what their value is in text-generation systems. I will also present a completely new addition to systemic grammar, the so-called chooser framework, developed in the context of the text-generation task.[5]

2.1.3 *Organization of the discussion*

First, I will sketch the steps in the process of text generation so that the role grammar has to play can be identified (Section 2.2). The rest of the chapter illustrates how systemic functionalism enables grammar to cope with tasks its role in the text-generation process entails. I will use the generation of a particular text realized by a single sentence, *Had Sir Christopher Wren been going to build a cathedral ever since his youth?* as a way of illustrating and organizing the discussion.

2.2   The text-generation process

In this presentation of text generation, I will follow an expository design by William Mann (see Mann 1983a). The model of text generation he gives an overview of is called PENMAN. It has been designed for monologue only, without, for example, any facilities for comprehension. However, although PENMAN cannot take part in a conversation, I will present an example that corresponds to a turn in a dialogue; PENMAN will be assigned the task of asking a question in this illustration. The reason for doing this is purely illustrative; the task of asking a question is a concise way of bringing out a number of features of the grammar.

Assume that a need for a text has arisen. In a conversation about Sir Christopher Wren, the need arises to know whether there was a plan for him to build a cathedral sometime after the time when he was still a youngster. The task of the text generator is to satisfy this need. (As we will see, one way of meeting this need is to ask *Had Sir Christopher Wren been going to build a cathedral ever since his youth?*) Three processes – Acquisition, Planning, and Sentence Generation – work in text generation towards meeting the need.

2.2.1   Steps in the text-generation process

Given the need for text, the text generator identifies the goals that the text should pursue and **acquires** the information necessary to pursue it. This process is supported by a knowledge base. The goal is roughly that the addressee should recognize that the information desired has been requested; in this case, we want to find out whether Sir Chris had been going to build a cathedral or not.

Next, there is a process of text planning. In response to the goal for the text and the information acquired, a plan to achieve the goal is created. The planning process uses a rhetoric of text organization to create the text plan.

The plan consists of (among other things) conceptual loci (at least one), each of which corresponds roughly to an independent clause.[6] In the present example, a text with one such locus is planned, a locus we can call CATHEDRAL-BUILDING. It is up to **sentence generation** to realize this plan, i.e. to find a wording for it. The process of sentence generation does this, relying on grammar as its resource. The remainder of the chapter deals with this part of the text-generation process. The grammar I will draw on for the rest of the discussion is the NIGEL grammar, the systemic text-generation grammar mentioned earlier.[7]

2.2.2   The task for sentence generation

The sentence-generation process can start when there is a fully specified local plan for CATHEDRAL-BUILDING in the text plan for an independent clause. Such a plan includes, among other things:

- A pointer to the process aspect of CATHEDRALBUILDING, called BUILDING in our example.
- A specification of the local speech act, here called BUILDING-QUESTION; see the discussion of MOOD below.
- A plan for temporal relations; cf. the discussion of TENSE below.

- Possibly a specification of a specific conceptual context defined temporally, spatially, in terms of purpose, or in some other way, to be indicated as a part of the organization of the text in terms of conceptual contexts. There is no such specification for the present example.
- Possibly a specification of a conjunctive relation (like contrast, enumeration, temporal sequence, disjunction, and cause) to be expressed. There is no such specification for the present example.

A list such as this represents expressive demands, all of which the grammar of the sentence-generation process has to cope with, but it *imposes no structuring or factoring* of this process. The task of the grammar and its semantics is to impose an organization of and find a wording for the material relevant to the local plan. Consequently, it is quite helpful if the grammar of the sentence-generation process is organized in such a way that the process can be decomposed into manageable subprocesses.

In what follows, I shall show how there is a natural factoring of the sentence-generation process that derives from the systemic organization of a grammar. As we will see, this factoring is due to the research program (a consequence of systemic functionalism) in systemic linguistics to uncover the functional organization of grammar and semantics and to reflect it in systemic notation.

2.3   Systemic factoring of sentence generation

The design of systemic grammar is the result of a long-term effort to create a grammatical framework that reflects the functional organization of grammar. The important point to note here is that the organization of systemic grammar leads naturally to a factoring of the sentence-generation process. In other words, the systemic factoring of the sentence-generation process is due to the organization of systemic grammar.

There are two simultaneous factorings that cross-cut:

1. The process of structure building is factored into two processes, each of which has its own notation: the process of **choosing** among grammatical alternatives (Section 2.4.1) and the process of **realizing**, or re-expressing, a particular choice as a specification of a fragment of grammatical structure (Section 2.4.2).
2. The statements of grammatical choice, realizations of choice, and resulting structure are factored into three fairly independent processes: an **ideational** process of representing the speaker's experience, an **interpersonal**

process of specifying the interaction between speaker and hearer (in terms of speech act and role assignments), and a **textual** process of enabling the two other processes. This is the metafunctional factoring (cf. Section 2.5).

The metafunctional factoring is possible because of the notations developed for choice and realization of choice into structure as a configuration of functions. Features originating in different metafunctions can be used to co-classify a grammatical unit and functions from different metafunctions can be conflated so that they apply to the same constituent in a structure.

2.4   Factoring into choice and realization

2.4.1   *The process of choosing*

The separation of statements of grammatical choice alternatives from structure specifications allows the grammar to have choice as its central organizing principle. The systemic network notation has been developed to make statements of minimal grammatical choice points and statements about the interdependencies among these choice points possible. The process of choice is itself factored into two parts: (i) grammatical choice: the statement of what the grammatical choice points and their interdependencies are – the systemic network notation just mentioned – and (ii) semantic choice: statements about how to select among the options of the grammatical choice points – a chooser semantics.

Grammatical choice

Each choice point is represented by a **system**. A system is a disjunction of two or more options (represented by grammatical **features** like Declarative, Past, and Passive)[8]. It has an entry condition, which is the condition under which the choice is available. As long as the condition has not been satisfied, no choice can be made. The condition is a Boolean combination of features (without negation, though) – minimally a single feature. When the entry condition is satisfied, one of the feature options must be chosen. An example of a system is given in Figure 2.1.

Together, the systems of the grammar constitute a **network of systems**: the features that are the output of one system are part of the entry conditions of other systems. The network as a whole represents the entire scope of the process of grammatical selection; the individual systems represent the decomposition of this process into minimal choice points. In Figure 2.2, the network fragment for mood is presented; see Section 2.6.

Semantic choice

The process of purposefully choosing among the feature options of a system is represented by a **chooser** or choice expert. The grammar supplies us with linguistically justified control points – the systems. Each system is assigned a chooser, which is a procedure composed of one or more steps leading to the determination of which grammatical feature to choose.

Where is the information relevant to the determination of which option should be chosen located? As we have seen, in addition to the grammar component, our text-generation system has a knowledge base and a text plan for the text to be generated. We can call these components and other possible sources of knowledge the environment of the grammar component. It is from this environment that a chooser demands the information it needs in order to be able to choose one of the features of its systems. It demands this information by presenting formal inquiries to the environment.[9] An inquiry is asked of one or more parameters. The parameters are variables like PROCESS, GOAL, $TEMPO_0$, and POLARITY, for which conceptual values are identified in the generation of every grammatical unit. As we will see presently in Section 2.4.2, grammatical structure is a specification of grammatical functions, and the variables correspond to those grammatical functions. The conceptual values are called **hubs**; they are concepts from which other concepts can be accessed. For instance, once a concept for a particular action has been identified, the participants in the action can be identified through the action concept. The inquiries are the only interaction between the choosers and the environment.

2.4.2   *The realization process*

There is a separate notation for the realization process. Grammatical structure is defined in terms of relations that can hold between grammatical **functions**; grammatical structure is a configuration of functions like subject, process, actor, and theme. The relations (conflation, expansion, ordering; see below) are introduced by realization statements. In the realization process, a function **structure** is specified step by step: A small number of realization operators operate on one grammatical function, a combination of grammatical functions,[10] or a grammatical function and a set of features.[11] A realization statement consisting of an operator and one or more operands is associated with a particular grammatical feature in a system; when that feature is chosen, the realization statement can be activated.

Among the important properties of the realization process, we find:

- The specification of structural presence (the insertion of a function into the structure being built) and the specification of constituency relations are separate from ordering specifications. For example, the specifications of the presence of FINITE, the finite verbal element of a clause, and SUBJECT are separate from specifications of their ordering. Either can be specified to follow the other, and there is no need for a transformation to invert an original ordering. This follows the general tendency in the grammar towards factoring the **realization** (i.e. structure-building) process into functionally motivated steps. It is typically the case that the presence of a **function** and its ordering with respect to other functions serve two different purposes.

- There is a "unification" operator on functions, called *Conflate*, that enables the grammar to reconcile function-structure fragments that are contributions from areas of the grammar serving different purposes. For example, SUBJECT is conflated with different functions depending on the voice of the clause – ACTOR, GOAL, RECIPIENT, etc.

- Collections of features that determine how each constituent of e.g. clause structure is further specified can be built up step by step. The features are associated with functions. Whenever two functions are declared to describe the same constituent, i.e. are conflated, their feature collections are merged. For instance, the auxiliary *had* has that form in our example because it serves both the function TEMPO_0, which constrains it to be a past form, and the function TEMPO_1, which constrains it to be a form of the auxiliary *have*.

Now I will show in some more detail how the sentence-generation process is organized. I will use the example already introduced and structure the discussion around the metafunctional factoring of sentence generation. We will see examples of all the characteristics of the choice process and the realization process identified above.

2.5   Metafunctional factoring

To see how the multifunctional factoring works, we will return to our CATHEDRAL-BUILDING example and look at it first in an interpersonal perspective, then in an ideational perspective, and finally in a textual perspective. Different perspectives draw on different types of information in the environment. The final wording the grammar will give us is *Had Sir Christopher Wren been going to build a cathedral ever since his youth?* We will consider the three metafunctions identified above; each corresponds to a different "event." There is the textual event itself, the event or process of creating a text for the addressee that enables the speaker to achieve his goals (the textual metafunction). In addition, we have (i) the speech event, an act of speaking involving speaker and addressee (the interpersonal metafunction), and (ii) an event in the speaker's experience (real or imagined, recalled or projected) (s)he wants to represent (the ideational metafunction).[12]

2.5.1 Interpersonal choices

When they explore the part of the grammar that deals with the clause as interaction between speaker and hearer, choosers ask questions that have to do with some aspect of the speech act, such as: (i) **MOOD**, i.e. a classification of the speech act: Is the speech act (BUILDING-QUESTION) a command? Is the speech act a question? I will use the mood area below to show in more detail how the grammar works; see Section 2.6. (ii) Identity of speaker/hearer: What is the identity of the hearer? Is the hearer included in the proposition? Here there is no involvement of speaker/hearer. (iii) The **POLARITY** of the speech act: Is the speech act a positive assertion or a denial? For polarity in our example, see Section 2.6.4. (iv) The sincerity of the act: Is the assurance of the speaker's sincerity to be expressed? Is a request for the hearer's sincerity to be expressed? Here we do not have a specification of a marking of sincerity.

2.5.2 Ideational choices

Second, consider the exploration of the clause as a representation of our experience. Chooser questions here concern the structure and character of the conceptual situation we are to represent. (i) **TRANSITIVITY**, i.e. the organization of our experience as a process with one or more participants and possibly attendant circumstances: here we choose to represent CATHEDRAL-BUILDING as an external process where one entity (SIR CHRIS) causes the building process, which effects (i.e. brings into existence) another entity (CATHEDRAL).

The function structure generated by realization statements that re-express our choices as structure has as functional constituents actor, process, and goal, all of which carry hub associations. actor is associated with SIR CHRIS, process with BUILDING, and goal with CATHEDRAL. In the final wording of the clause, *Sir Christopher Wren* is the actor of the clause, *built* is the process, and *this cathedral* is the goal.

(ii) **Tense**, i.e. the organization of our experience in terms of time relations: How is the event from our experience (here the CATHEDRAL-BUILDING event) to be related temporally to the speech event? This intricate question will be further examined in Section 2.7.

2.5.3 Textual choices

Finally, let us look at the clause as a message, the textual perspective. (i) **Voice:** Of two particular ideationally identified concepts, SIR CHRIS associated with ACTOR and CATHEDRAL with GOAL, which is conceptually closer to the topic of the paragraph being created? Is the causer of the event to be mentioned? In our example, the concept WREN is the paragraph topic and we get an active clause with a conflation of ACTOR and SUBJECT, i.e. actor/subject.

(iii) **Theme:** For a particular ideational function, we ask if it serves as a conceptual context for the rest of the clause? For example, it is determined that CATHEDRAL is not to serve this function, similarly, for interpersonal functions. Here, the conceptual context in relation to which the remainder is interpreted is finite, an indication that the clause expresses a question about polarity.

The different strands of functional reasoning hinted at above are unified into one structure as I will show in Section 2.8. Meanwhile, mood and tense will serve as representatives of the full range of choices sketched in this section.

2.6   Interpersonal choices: mood

Mood is the interpersonal part of clause grammar that expresses the role the speaker adopts and the role (s)he gives to the addressee in terms of speech act. I will present the choice organization of mood first, then the structural effects of different choices, and finally I will show how mood selections can be controlled.

2.6.1 Mood choices

In English there is a grammatical choice for clauses between imperative ones and indicative ones. This choice of the mood of a clause is represented by the mood system; the two options that constitute the choice are represented by the features Imperative and Indicative. Only clauses with a finite verb select for mood; infinitival and gerundial ones do not. This fact is captured through the entry condition of the system, which says that if the clause is Finite, the mood system can be entered. A diagrammatic representation of the system is given in Figure 2.1.

The feature Indicative is the entry condition to the system of IndicativeMood, where the options are Declarative and Interrogative. There is an additional step. The feature Interrogative is the input to the system InterrogativeType, where the options are Wh-Interrogative and Polarity-Interrogative. This network is represented diagrammatically in Figure 2.2. The boxes under the features in the diagram contain realization statements.

Our example can be represented as a path through the network for mood. The features Indicative, Interrogative, and Polarity-Interrogative are selected in that order. Each feature has structural consequences; the functional structure is built step by step.

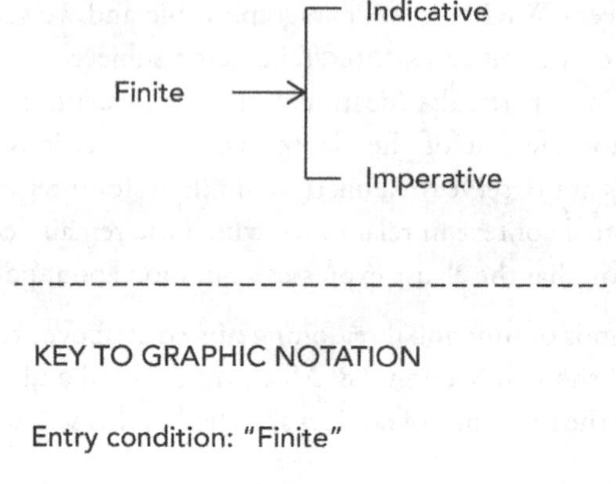

KEY TO GRAPHIC NOTATION

Entry condition: "Finite"

Feature options: "Indicative" and
"Imperative"

Figure 2.1 The mood system in English

2.6.2   Realizations and the structure of mood

The structural realization of mood is in the mood constituent, a function which embodies the mood or speech act aspect of the clause. The internal structure of mood expresses the mood selection of the clause.[13] The two principal daughters are subject and finite, the finite verbal element of the clause. In Declarative clauses, Subject precedes Finite; in Polarity-Interrogative clauses, finite precedes subject, as in our example.

In our example, the mood structure will be as diagrammed in Figure 2.3. The constituent organization is the result of the application of (Expand mood subject) and (Expand mood finite).

2.6.3   Semantic mood choices

Each system in the mood network is controlled by a chooser. For instance, the mood chooser of the mood system in Figure 2.1 asks questions that identify information about the speech act of the clause to be generated. Basically, if the intention is to command, the chooser chooses the feature Imperative, otherwise the feature Indicative.

For our mood system the chooser interaction with the environment proceeds as follows:

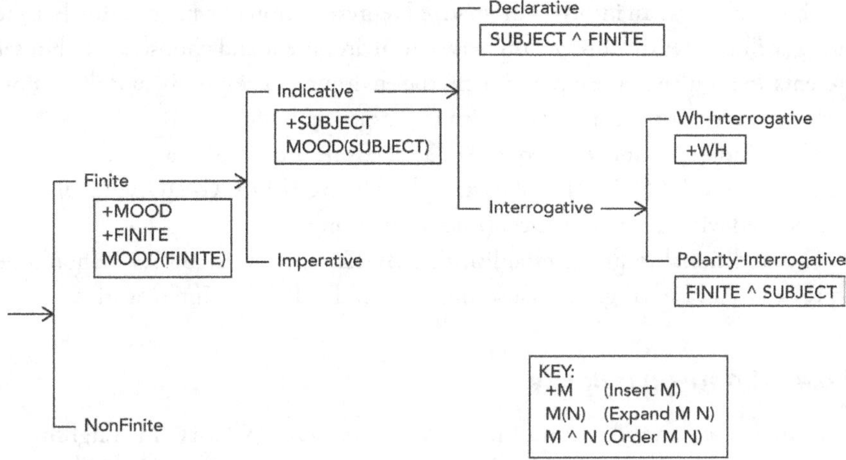

Figure 2.2 The grammar of mood: network representation

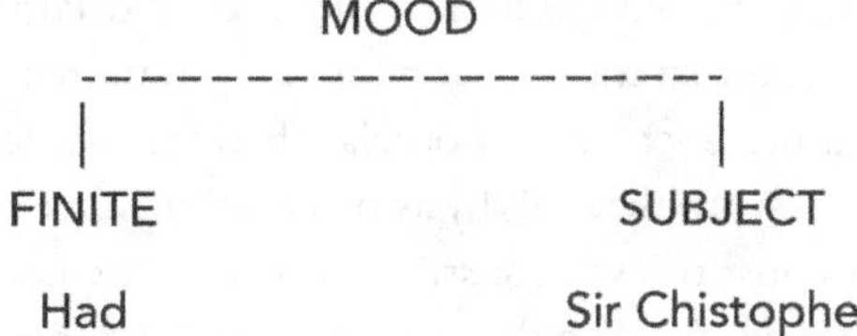

Figure 2.3 Mood structure in polarity-interrogative

Environment	Chooser
	Is the illocutionary point of the surface level speech act represented by BUILDING-QUESTION (Mood) a command. i.e. a request by the speaker of an action by the hearer?
It is not a command.	
	Then I choose feature Indicative.

This is of course an informal dramatized representation of what goes on, but the dialogue illustrates the interaction between environment and chooser: the chooser presents an inquiry to the environment, the environment responds, and the chooser chooses a feature in conformity with the response.

The inquiry above requests a classification of a hub, called BUILDING-QUESTION in the example. The BUILDING-QUESTION hub is associated with the grammatical (micro)function mood.

Two additional inquiries establish that BUILDING-QUESTION should be expressed by an Interrogative clause and that this is a Polarity-Interrogative.

2.6.4   A note on polarity

The choice of mood determines how we choose polarity in English. In Polarity-Interrogative clauses, the choice between Positive, as in *Had Sir Christopher Wren been going to build a cathedral?*, and Negative, as in *Hadn't Sir Christopher Wren been going to build a cathedral?*, is a choice that has to do with the bias in the reader's assumptions about which situation (s)he thinks obtains.

In our example, an unbiased question is intended and Positive is chosen. The realization of the choice is that the function finite is prohibited from being realized by a verb with the feature *negative*; it is outclassified for that feature: (Outclassify finite *negative*). We can symbolize this by associating "*negative*" with Finite. Notice that this realization constitutes a constraint on how the constituent described by finite can be expressed. As we will see in Section 2.7, other constraints on the constituent come from another part of the grammar (the functions $tempo_0$ and $tempo_1$).

2.7   Ideational choices: tense

Independent of and parallel with the grammar of mood is the grammar of tense. The two parts of the grammar originate from two different metafunctions, the interpersonal one and the ideational one.[14]

2.7.1   Grammar of tense

In English Indicative clauses (cf. the previous section), if they are non-modal, there is always a specification of at least one relation of precedence between two times, one of which is the time of speaking. This is the system of primary tense, whose options are Past vs. Present vs. Future. The realizations of these features are stated in terms of the tense function tempo$_0$. If Past is chosen, the realization is (Classify tempo$_0$ past); if Future is chosen, the realization is (Classify tempo$_0$ *will*). In the latter case, tempo$_0$ is a separate constituent, as in *will build*; in the former case tempo$_0$ is fused, i.e. conflated, with whatever verbal function follows to the right when Future is chosen – as in *built*. In English, the primary present tense is morphologically unmarked. It is possible to generate a more elaborate temporal verbal structure, with more than one tense function:

TEMPO$_0$	**TEMPO$_1$**	**TEMPO$_2$**
will	*have*	(jump)*ed*

This is possible because the grammar of tense does not just contain the system of primary tense, but also, in principle, indefinitely many systems of secondary tense (see especially Halliday 1976b). It is possible to iterate over tense options just as it is possible to iterate over tense operators in some tense logics. (cf. *will have been going to leave* and *FPFp*, where p is a proposition and F and P are tense operators.) The iteration defines tenses of different orders, starting, with first-order (or primary) tense, then second-order tense, third-order tense, and so on.

2.7.2 Tense choosers

Each selection of Past, Present, or Future corresponds to a specification of a precedence relation between two times, T_x and T_y. These times are concepts in NIGEL's environment. The task of each tense chooser is to establish what the current times to be related are, i.e. a current T_x and T_y pair, and what relationship obtains between them. This exploration proceeds in a step-by-step fashion, guided by the grammar.

In our example, there are four times: the time of speaking, called NOW, a time prior to that which falls within the period of Sir Chris's life under discussion, call it MATURE-TIME, a time prior to that which falls within the period of his youth, call it YOUTH-TIME, and the time of the building of a cathedral, call it BUILDING-TIME. The temporal relations are represented in Figure 2.4.

The tense functions receive hub associations. First, TEMPO$_0$ and TEMPO$_1$ are identified as NOW and MATURE-TIME respectively, then the following dialogue ensues:

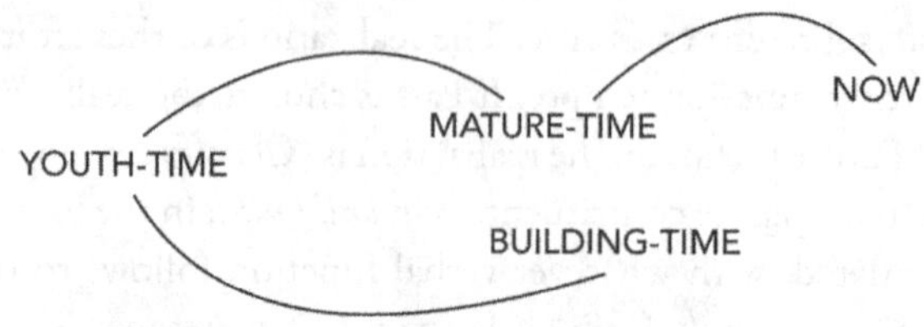

Figure 2.4 Temporal relations

Environment	Chooser
	Does MATURE-TIME (TEMPO$_1$) precede NOW (TEMPO$_0$)?
Yes, it does.	
	Then I choose Past.

This procedure illustrates the selection of primary or first-order tense. This type of activity is repeated for the pair MATURE-TIME (tempo$_1$) and YOUTH-TIME (tempo$_2$) where the choice is a second order, Past, and for the pair YOUTH-TIME (tempo$_2$) and BUILDING-TIME (tempo$_3$) where the choice is a third order, Future. As a result, we get three orders of tense, (i), (ii), and (iii), the realizations of which are:

(i)	Past	(Classify TEMPO$_0$ past)
(ii)	Past	(Classify TEMPO$_1$ have) (Classify TEMPO$_3$ en-participle)
(iii)	Future	(Classify TEMPO$_2$ be going) (Classify TEMPO$_3$ to-infinitive)

To sum up: Both the process of choosing tense and the process of specifying a tense structure are factored into steps that correspond to minimal temporal relations. The tense functions are ordered as a collection of tense functions: the sequence is iconic with the order of tense; increase in order of tense corresponds to the left-to-right sequence of tense functions. Since there are no more tense selections and no voice auxiliary, tempo$_3$ is conflated with process: (Conflate TEMPO$_3$ PROCESS) is activated.

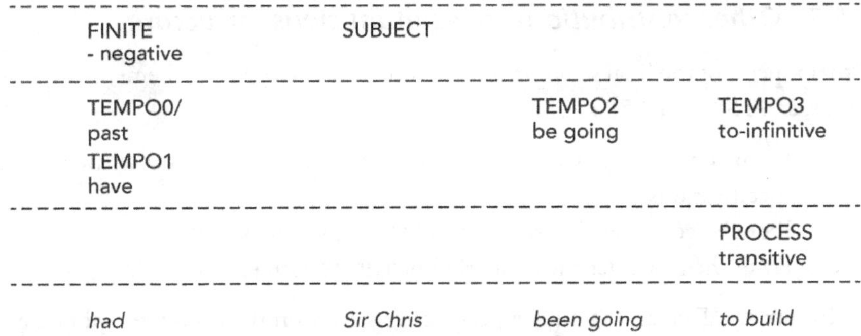

Figure 2.5 Mood and tense structures combined

2.8   Reconciliation on the metafunctions: structural result

2.8.1   Conflation of Finite and Tempo$_0$

The two function-structure fragments we have generated are mood (finite subject) and tempo$_0$/tempo$_1$ tempo$_2$ tempo$_3$. Typically, finite and tempo$_0$ conflate and the two fragments combine into the structure in Figure 2.5. Similarly, as already indicated, we have a conflation of tempo$_3$ with process. The latter function is a transitivity function and carries feature information about the transitivity type of the verb (i.e., constrains *build* in transitivity), symbolized by the feature *transitive*. Each one of the functions carries constraining feature information.

As the figure indicates, there are two consequences of the conflation of finite with tempo$_0$:

1. Feature constraints derived from independent choices are merged and co-constrain the final expression. In other words, for polarity reasons, *had* appears as *had* rather than *hadn't*, and for tense reasons, it appears in this form rather than for example *has*, *have*, *will*, or *was*.
2. The final sequence is a result of two independent ordering specifications, viz. the mood specification that FINITE comes before SUBJECT and the tense specification of the ordering of tense auxiliaries. In other words, as a tense auxiliary, *had* precedes *been going to build*, and as the FINITE element of the clause, it precedes the SUBJECT.

2.8.2   Other contributions to resultant clause structure

Other aspects of the final structure come from transitivity, voice, theme, etc. (as we have seen in Section 2.5):

- From transitivity we get ACTOR, PROCESS, and GOAL with feature specifications.
- From voice we get the conflation of SUBJECT with ACTOR.
- From theme we get the conflation of THEME with FINITE.

To sum up: Depending on the perspective we lay on the clause, the phrase *Sir Christopher Wren* will be SUBJECT (interpersonal perspective) or ACTOR (ideational perspective). We say that these functions are conflated (symbolized SUBJECT/ ACTOR). The conflation is the result of bringing independent lines of reasoning together. It is an operation that can only be performed on functions, not on categories like NP, N, and VP. The resultant structure is given in Figure 2.6 (associated features are left out).

Note that *had*, *Sir Chris*, etc. are not the result of equally many functions. Some constituents play a role only in one component (e.g. tense: *be going*), whereas others realize more than one function (*Sir Chris*, for example).

One important property of these conflations is that they could have been otherwise, if the choosers had received different responses from the environment and thus had made different choices. For instance, we could have SUBJECT/GOAL and get the clause *Had a cathedral been going to be built by Sir Christopher Wren*. Or, with a MODAL displacing $tempo_0$ in the conflation with FINITE: MODAL/FINITE followed by $TEMPO_0$ as in *may have* (instead of *had*).

2.8.3   A note on the development of the function constituents

The structure presented above represents clause structure; the terminal functions are functions of the clause. It is the solution to the problems that the clause has evolved to solve. For the development of each constituent, we have to go either to lexicon or (back) to grammar. The verbal elements have lexical features associated with them, and these features serve as constraints on what lexical items can be used. The ACTOR constituent and the GOAL constituent have to go through another round of development in the grammar, in the nominal group part of the grammar. Although I have not shown them, features are also associated with these two constituents. These features are grammatical and will serve as constraints on choices in the nominal group part of the network. This process is discussed in e.g. Matthiessen 1983a.

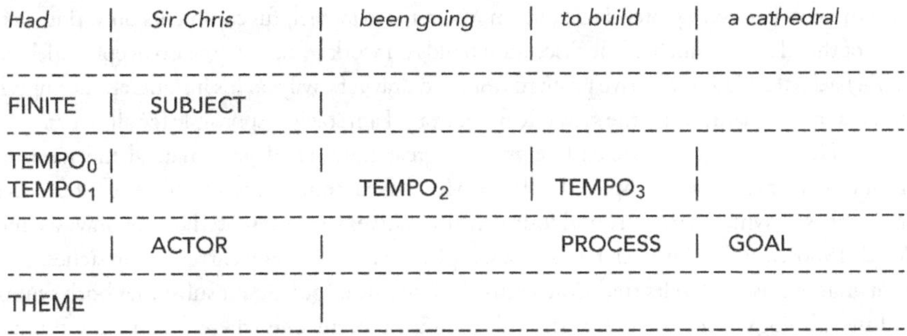

Figure 2.6 Clause structure

2.9   Conclusion

The first concise presentation of systemic suggestions was published when what came to be called ACL (Association for Computational Linguistics) was being formed. Now, roughly twenty years later, with the first meeting of the European chapter of ACL we can look back on substantial achievements in both computational linguistics and systemic linguistics, some of them in co-operation.

However, the most exciting developments are current and future. We can see the most ambitious applications of systemic linguistics to computational tasks to date. And we can see the growing interest in text generation, a task in the context of which systemic linguistics seems to have much to offer.

Here I have pointed to some properties and designs that come from the systemic tradition and which I think are of interest for the text-generation task. Systemic linguists have done and are still doing pioneering work on text organization, turning up insights that will most certainly be important to the design of text generators. However, here I have concentrated on contributions in the area of grammar and choosers for grammar with a view to showing how they help us fulfil the demands placed on a grammar in a text generator. I have focussed on the factoring of the sentence-generation process that systemic grammar supports.

Notes

1   This research was supported by the Air Force Office of Scientific Research, Contract No. F49620-79-C-0181. The views and conclusions contained in this chapter are those of the authors and should not be interpreted as necessarily representing the official policies or endorsements, either expressed or implied, of the Air Force Office of Scientific Research of the US

Government. I am very grateful to William Mann for many helpful comments on various versions of this chapter; much of the discussion builds on work by him. I am also deeply indebted to Michael A.K. Halliday; I have profited from and drawn heavily on his insights about English grammar and semantics and the systemic framework. I am solely responsible for all errors.

2   There are now in the early eighties a great number of grammatical mechanisms around – witness, for example, the 1979 Milwaukee conference on current alternative approaches to syntax where around fourteen alternatives were presented (see Moravcsik and Wirth 1980), a collection which is only a sample, leaving out many current approaches. The term grammar is used in its traditional sense in systemic linguistics: it subsumes both syntax and morphology. This use contrasts with the more recent one where grammar subsumes semantics, syntax, morphology, and phonology.

3   There are now in the early eighties a great number of grammatical mechanisms around – witness, for example, the 1979 Milwaukee conference on current alternative approaches to syntax where around fourteen alternatives were presented (see Moravcsik and Wirth 1980), a collection which is only a sample, leaving out many current approaches. The term grammar is used in its traditional sense in systemic linguistics: it subsumes both syntax and morphology. This use contrasts with the more recent one where grammar subsumes semantics, syntax, morphology, and phonology.

4   There are also strictly formal considerations having to do with the notation used. These have been more central in work on e.g. Lexical Functional Grammar, Functional Unification Grammar, and Generalized Phrase Structure Grammar. The results may or may not generalize to systemic grammar; that is a matter for future discussion.

5   Functionalism in linguistics will hopefully be reconciled with goal reasoning as it has developed in computational linguistics and AI. The term function has two related meanings in current linguistics in addition to its strictly mathematical sense. One is "metafunction," which can be defined as the purpose or goal–effect considerations that define a particular component of the grammar. The second meaning of function is what Halliday has called "micro-function." This type is the one that figures in traditional grammar – subject, object, etc – and more recently in, for example, Relational Grammar, Case Grammar, and Lexical Functional Grammar. Conceptually, micro-functions are very much like roles or slots used in semantic nets. (Micro vs. macro is here simply a distinction between small and big; meta means that the functions are on another plane, not part of the structure. In this way it is the same "meta" we find in, for example, "metalanguage.") For an interesting discussion of the development of metafunctions and micro-functions out of a set of macro-functions in early child language, see Halliday 1975. For some discussion of functional grammar: see e.g. Halliday 1969, 1974; Dik 1978; Fawcett 1980.

6   A traditional distinction between clause and sentence is maintained in systemic linguistics. A sentence can be defined simply as a complex of clauses, related by coordination or subordination.

7   Although the text-generation process can conveniently be factored into the three subprocesses identified above, these subprocesses are not necessarily serially arranged. There is one additional process, a process of improvement. For instance, the quality of the output of sentence generation is evaluated, and then, based on this evaluation, changes in the plan are proposed.

8   In systemic grammar, a distinction is usually (and always in work by Halliday) maintained between features and functions like Subject, Actor, and Theme. Features are the building blocks of the paradigmatic organization of grammar, i.e. of grammar as choice. Functions are the building blocks of the syntagmatic organization, i.e. of grammatical structure. The distinction is not maintained in Martin Kay's Functional Unification Grammar (cf. Kay 1979).

9   These formal inquiries have informal versions that are informal questions in English, used for purposes of discussion and presentation.

10   The realization operations include Insert, which inserts a function into the structure being built; Expand, which specifies a constituency relation between a function and one or more daughters; Order, which orders two grammatical functions; and Conflate, which states that two functions, say Subject and Agent, describe the same constituent. Two functions are not ordered until it is clear that the ordering imposed is the final one. There is thus no need for movement and formations. In fact, there are no transformations at all: a realization is only stated at a point where it is clear that it represents the final state.

11   This latter category of realization operator serves to state how the functionally defined constituents of a particular structure, say clause structure or prepositional phrase structure, are to be expressed grammatically or lexically. We will meet the operator Classify, which associates a lexical feature with a function; this feature is a constraint on what lexical items can realize the constituent that the function defines.

12   These two events may overlap in various ways, of course, as in so-called performative sentences.

13   Indicative clauses typically have a Subject in English, whereas imperative ones do not. Consequently, there is a realization statement which says "insert Subject" if the clause is indicative. This means that the grammatical function Subject is inserted into the grammatical structure being built. There is no need to delete Subject in imperative clauses; the function is never inserted unless it is actually expressed.

14   Note, however, that the full resources of tense are only at work in indicative clauses. For example, we cannot (in English) request of an addressee the past execution of an action.

Chapter 3

Semantics for a systemic grammar: the chooser and inquiry framework

3.1   The task of the chooser and inquiry framework

One of the current research areas involving systemic linguistics is **text generation** (discourse production). Text generation is one way of studying text. It is text study by synthesis rather than by analysis; deconstruction and then reconstruction.[1] The basic question is: given a communicative purpose (goal) in a natural context, how does the system of linguistic processes and resources work to produce a text? Or, how do we get from situation to text? The answer includes several levels (strata) of organization as well as the interaction between these levels: a specification of the goals (purposes) of the intended text, a specification of the relevant parts of the system's field of experience, text planning, grammatical expression, and so on. For an overview of some of the issues involved in text generation, see Mann et al. 1982 and McDonald 1983. For an early systemic text-generation system, see Davey 1979.[2] At the Information Sciences Institute in Southern California, one particular text-generation system, called **PENMAN**, is being designed and implemented (see Mann 1983a). The grammar of this system is a large systemic grammar of English, the **NIGEL grammar**. It is the result of a major ongoing research effort into systemic grammar in the context of text generation. First begun as a computational grammar in 1980, it is still being expanded and revised. (For introductions to NIGEL, see Mann 1983b, 1984; Matthiessen 1983d, 1985.)

The semantics of the NIGEL grammar is a **chooser and inquiry semantics**, which is a new development intended to deal with *the problem of making purposeful grammatical choices* in response to a communicative situation. (A presentation of the framework can also be found in Mann 1982, 1983c.) Given a system of options like middle[3] vs. effective, transitive vs. intransitive, or indicative vs. imperative, how is one option in the system to be chosen over another in a purposeful way?

The term *semantics* may suggest other tasks in addition to or instead of what is presented in this chapter. In Section 3.6, I will briefly discuss different approaches to semantics and different tasks for semantics.

The chooser and inquiry framework does not define a system network of semantic features at present. The framework addresses part of the task Robin Fawcett specifies for the Problem Solver of his model of communication.[4] Fawcett (1980: 63) describes the tasks of the Problem Solver as follows:

> The decisions as to which semantic features are to be selected are taken in the light of the relevant knowledge of the universe ... The problem solver therefore not only has the task of deciding on the best general tactics to help solve the problem, but also of helping in the selection of actual semantic features.[5]

3.2   The chooser of a system asks an inquiry

In a discussion of transitivity in English, Halliday (1970a) observes that there are two basic systems in English that "occur side by side," the transitive system (transitive vs. intransitive) and the ergative system (effective vs. middle). He characterizes the general semantic difference as follows, using questions:

> The transitive system asks "Does the action extend beyond the active participant or not?"; the ergative, "is the action caused by the affected participant or not?" (157–8)

In Halliday (1970a) the questions are used as a presentational technique. (For another illustration of the use of questions with systems, see Halliday 1985a: 58.) But in fact they illustrate the approach to the semantic task of making purposeful grammatical choices taken in the chooser and inquiry framework. An **inquiry** is the question asked, for example, "is the action caused by the affected participant or not?". It demands the information needed to make a choice. The answers to these questions are called **responses**. A **chooser** is the mechanism associated with a grammatical system that asks a question, i.e. presents an inquiry.[6] The chooser starts its work, presenting inquiries, when the system it is associated with has been entered.

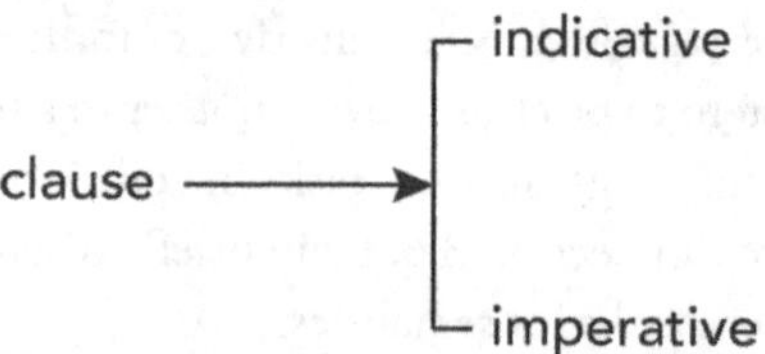

Figure 3.1 The mood type system

3.2.1 *Branching inquiries: commandQ*

I will illustrate the chooser and inquiry framework with examples from the mood region and systems such as primary tense that are affected by mood choices, since this region is well known and has been discussed elsewhere by systemic linguists. I will rely on Halliday's interpretation, and the examples can be read in the light of Halliday (1984b) and (1985b). The account encoded in the chooser and inquiry framework can be compared and contrasted with Butler's (1982) work, which could also have been encoded in the framework, in the way he and I have done with part of his account of modality in English. As an initial example, I will use the chooser of the mood type system. It has two options, indicative vs. imperative. The system is represented in Figure 3.1.

The inquiry used to obtain the information needed to choose between indicative and imperative asks whether the speech function is a command or not:

> Is the speech function of the clause a command or not? – set of responses: command, non-command

Notice that it defines two **branches**, one for each response. (There can be more than two branches, if the inquiry is an alternative question instead of a simple yes/no question. Moreover, a chooser may contain more than one inquiry.) In Figure 3.2 a graphic representation is given of this kind of **branching inquiry**.

We will call this inquiry CommandQ; the Q-tag is used in all branching inquiries. (Instead of simply calling the responses *yes* and *no*, we give them labels that indicate the content specific to their inquiry; they can be viewed as semantic features.)

3.2.2 *Identifying inquiries: MoodID*

In the inquiry *Is the speech function of the clause a command or not?*, there is one nominal group with specific reference, *the speech function of the clause*. It represents

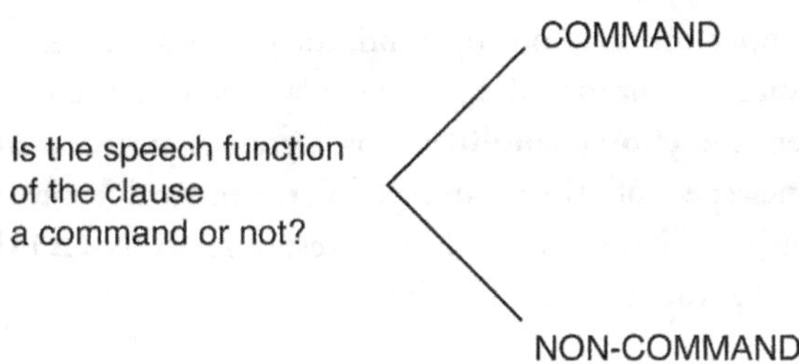

Figure 3.2 Branching inquiry in mood type chooser

the **parameter** of the inquiry whose referential identities change according to the context. Grammatically, the speech function will be expressed by the mood of the clause, and we can use the names of these grammatical functions as the names of the parameters: "is the speech function mood a command or not?".

We need a means of identifying the referents (values) of these parameters and we use **identifying inquiries** to accomplish this, one for each parameter that occurs in one of the inquiries. So, for example, mood can be identified by means of the following inquiry, called MoodID (all identifying inquiries are tagged-ID):

"What is the identity of the speech function of the clause?"

Identifying inquiries establish an identifying symbolic relation between a grammatical function like mood and a value. The value is defined at the stratum above the inquiry semantic stratum; cf. Section 3.3.1.

To sum up, there are two types of inquiry, branching inquiries, which are like yes/no questions (or alternative questions), and identifying inquiries, which are like wh-questions.

3.2.3 *The Choose operator: choice conditions*

I have noted that a branching inquiry like CommandQ is asked so that the chooser can act on the response and choose the appropriate grammatical feature. This choice is a kind of preselection from the chooser (at the chooser and inquiry stratum) that is activated whenever the response to an inquiry motivates the selection of a grammatical feature (at the grammatical stratum). We call the operator Choose and use it as illustrated in the following example:

[if] COMMAND [then] (Choose imperative)

The Choose operator takes one operand, the grammatical feature to be selected; and the choice is conditional upon the response to a branching inquiry.[7] A response is, then, the **choice condition** for a grammatical feature. One way of representing (one aspect of) the meaning of a grammatical feature is to specify its choice condition(s).[8] We can assume that the response NON-COMMAND is the choice condition for the selection of indicative:

[if] NON-COMMAND [then] (Choose indicative)

3.2.4   Choosers: the mood type chooser

I have introduced some of the most important abstractions of the chooser and inquiry framework; we are now in a position to discuss the full chooser of the mood type system.

First, let's return to CommandQ (the possible responses are given in parenthesis):

"Is the speech function MOOD a command or not?"
    (COMMAND, NON-COMMAND)

The mood type chooser contains only this inquiry, since the inquiry fully determines the possible choices in the system. If the response is COMMAND, the feature imperative is chosen, and if the response is NON-COMMAND, the feature indicative is chosen. We can abbreviate the inquiry as (CommandQ MOOD), which makes it easier to represent the chooser graphically, as in Figure 3.3.

3.2.5   Chooser-based typology of systems

Given the two choice conditions COMMAND and NON-COMMAND, we have a positive condition for choosing imperative and a negative one for choosing indicative, i.e. negative in the sense that we choose this latter feature when the response to CommandQ is the negative one.

The distinction between positive and negative responses as choice conditions gives us a basis for a typology of grammatical systems. For example, as characterized here, mood type is a privative system (to borrow Trubetzkoy's terminology for phonological oppositions). We could characterize it as equipollent, if the mood type chooser contained an inquiry or set of inquiries defining positive choice conditions for both features of the system. Space limitations prevent further discussion of the typology here, and I will just list the two types mentioned:[9]

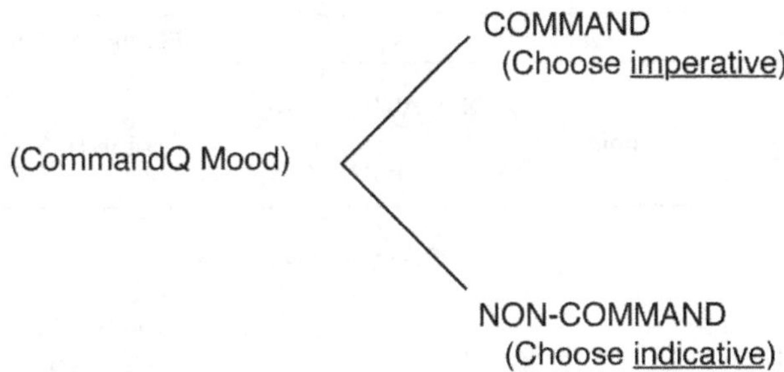

Figure 3.3 mood type chooser

1. **Privative systems**: A positive choice condition is defined only for one of the terms in a two-term system.
2. **Equipollent systems**: Positive choice conditions are defined for all the terms in the system.

3.2.6   Descriptive claims

Like all inquiries, CommandQ represents a claim about the semantics of the mood type system that we can test and argue about. We may want to elaborate on the inquiry and make the notion of command more detailed and specific.

The chooser as a whole also represents a descriptive claim. For example, we may want to argue that there should be two positive choice conditions rather than just one, or that the chooser should contain a disjunction of choice conditions for the choice of a feature (see below).

3.3   Inter-stratal organization: above and below inquiries

Figure 3.4 gives a diagrammatic summary of the mood type system and chooser as a pair in grammar and semantics, respectively. Note that only the system is part of a network. The inquiry CommandQ is part of the chooser of the mood type system, but it is not related to the inquiries of other choosers; see Section 3.4.

The stratum (level) below the inquiry stratum is the grammatical stratum. There is also a "stratum" above the semantic inquiry stratum, called Environment in the diagram. I will discuss it briefly below.

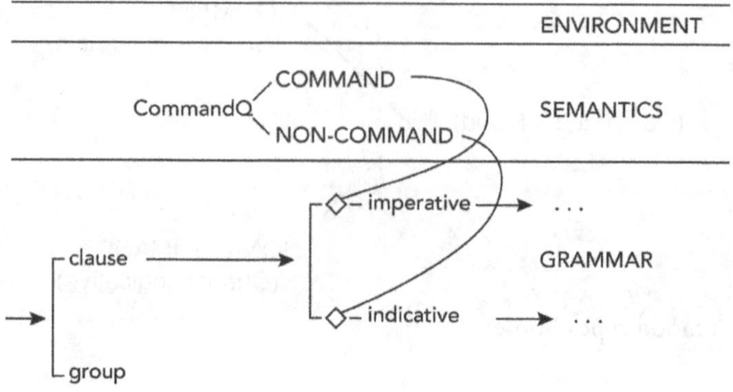

Figure 3.4 mood type: system and its chooser

3.3.1   Above – the environment: what inquiries are asked of

How do inquiries get answered; where do responses come from? What justifies the response COMMAND? There is a fairly short answer and a longer one. I will only sketch the short answer here.[10]

The NIGEL component, the grammar with its chooser and inquiry semantics, is embedded in a text-generation system. Among other things, the system contains a knowledge base representing the speaker's (i.e. the system's) domain/field of context[11] (relevant for the creation of any given text) and a detailed text plan (for any given text). These components are outside ('above') NIGEL and are thus part of NIGEL's environment. When NIGEL presents inquiries, we can think of these inquiries as being presented to NIGEL's environment. The knowledge base and the text plan are then the sources for the information used to determine the response the environment should return. For example, the level of social context Halliday identifies (see 1984b: 12) in his model of dialogue can be represented in the environment and used to determine the appropriate response to an inquiry like CommandQ. So, if the move is one of demanding goods-&-services, the response to CommandQ should be COMMAND.

Implemented inquiries. In the text-generation system, the environment is not represented in vernacular English. Rather, formal notations are used. An inquiry operator is said to be implemented if it is represented in terms of a formal notation in the environment rather than just glossed in English. What this means in practice is that the inquiry can be answered automatically from the environment rather than manually by somebody reading the English question.

For example, MoodID is implemented in such a way that it identifies a speech functional operator in a logical form. CommandQ can then be answered after an examination of the type for that operator.[12]

3.3.2   Below – grammar

The operator Choose relates the branch of a branching inquiry (at the inquiry stratum) to a grammatical feature in a system (at the grammatical stratum). It is represented by a vertical link in Figure 3.4 to show its role as an inter-stratal realization operator.[13] For example, COMMAND is linked to imperative.

There may be neutralization between the inquiry stratum and the grammar stratum. In particular, there may be different choice conditions for choosing one grammatical feature, a situation illustrated below for the primary tense chooser in Section 3.4.1.

3.4   Intra-stratal organization

I have only discussed an isolated inquiry, CommandQ. It is comparable to an isolated system. A system is just one part of the system network, the paradigmatic organization within the grammatical stratum. I will explore the paradigmatic organization of the inquiry stratum in two steps. First, I will take a look at the organization within the chooser of a system. I have only discussed a one-inquiry chooser so far, but choosers often contain more than one inquiry. I will use the PRIMARY TENSE chooser as an example. Then, I will discuss the possibility of inquiry organization beyond the single chooser, the possibility of a network of inquiries.

3.4.1   *Inquiry organization within a chooser: PRIMARY TENSE*

We can start by locating the PRIMARY TENSE system in the system network. The system can only be reached in indicative clauses and then only if the clause is temporal rather than modal, since a modal auxiliary does not normally show a primary tense distinction (see Halliday 1970b). The relevant part of the system network is shown in Figure 3.5.

The primary tense system has three options, past vs. present vs. future. Interpreting the system as a three-term one rather than as a two-term one has to

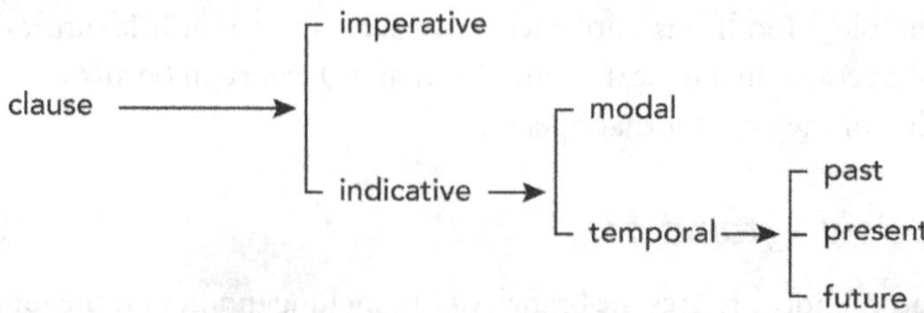

Figure 3.5 The PRIMARY TENSE system in the network

be justified. The inquiries to be presented also have to be justified. I have done that elsewhere (e.g. Matthiessen 1983c); here I will merely use the chooser as an illustration.

The selection of one of the PRIMARY TENSE features expresses the temporal relation between two times, T_0 and T_1. The first one is 'now', the time of speaking. The second one may or may not be the time of the PROCESS of the clause, depending on SECONDARY TENSE selections (cf. Halliday 1976b). If T_1 temporally precedes T_0, past is chosen.

If T_1 does not precede T_0, there are two possibilities depending on whether a logical/temporal condition is being expressed or not. If a condition is being expressed (resulting in, for example, a *when-* or an *if*-clause), the case in which T_1 does not precede T_0 leads to the selection of present (e.g. *When Henry gets a new job, we will all celebrate*).

If no condition is being expressed, a further distinction of temporal precedence must be made. If T_0 precedes T_1, future is chosen. If no precedence relation obtains between the two times, present is chosen.

How can we represent these cases in the chooser? We need one inquiry, call it PrecedeQ, that asks whether a precedence relation obtains between two times or not:

> PrecedeQ: Does TIME-X temporally precede TIME-Y or not?
> (PRECEDE, NON-PRECEDE)

PrecedeQ has two parameters, the two times whose temporal relation is under investigation. In the chooser we ask PrecedeQ twice, first for (T_1, T_0) and then (if the response is NON-PRECEDE) for (T_0, T_1).

We also need an inquiry to find out whether a logical/temporal condition is being expressed, call it ConditionQ:

ConditionQ: Does the situation to be expressed constitute a logical or temporal condition on some process, i.e. does it set up logically or temporally the possible world in which this process is instantiated? (CONDITION, NON-CONDITION)

For example, *when Henry gets a new job* is a temporal condition on the process of celebration in *we will all celebrate*. (The parameter ONUS represents all of the referent situation in Fawcett's terms.)

The organization of the PRIMARY TENSE chooser is set out in Figure 3.6. (I have turned the tree around simply for reasons of space.)

Inquiry presentation conditions. The response to (PrecedeQ T_1 T_0) is PRECEDE, the feature past is selected. If it is NON-PRECEDE, the chooser asks ConditionQ. We can say that this second inquiry is dependent upon (embedded under) the NON-PRECEDE response from the first inquiry; it is only asked under the condition that NON-PRECEDE is the response. We can think of NON- PRECEDE **as the inquiry presentation condition** for the second inquiry. It is comparable to an entry condition of a grammatical system consisting of a single feature.

When the response to ConditionQ is CONDITION, present is chosen. NON-CONDITION is the inquiry presentation condition for a third inquiry in the chooser. PrecedeQ is used again, this time with the time parameters reversed: (PrecedeQ T_0 T_1).

The positive response to this third inquiry, PRECEDE, leads to the selection of future. The response NON-PRECEDE also leads to a choice: present. How is this justified? Our assumption is that the choice condition for present is that no precedence relation obtains between T_0 and T_1, and at this point in the chooser that is precisely the information we have obtained. The inquiry presentation condition for the second inquiry is NON-PRECEDE (i.e. T_1 does not precede T_0) and the response under which present is chosen is also NON-PRECEDE (i.e. T_0 does not precede T_1). In other words, the information accumulated at the point at which present is chosen is that no precedence relation obtains between the two times. This illustrates the importance of the inquiry presentation condition of an inquiry.

Notice furthermore that the fact that (PrecedeQ T_1 T_0) is the first inquiry about precedence (rather than (PrecedeQ T_0 T_1)) is significant: the choice reasons for choosing past (the PRECEDE response) are unaffected by the further distinctions made in the chooser. In contrast, the reasons for choosing present and future are not. Consequently, we want the reason for choosing past to be branched off initially in the chooser.

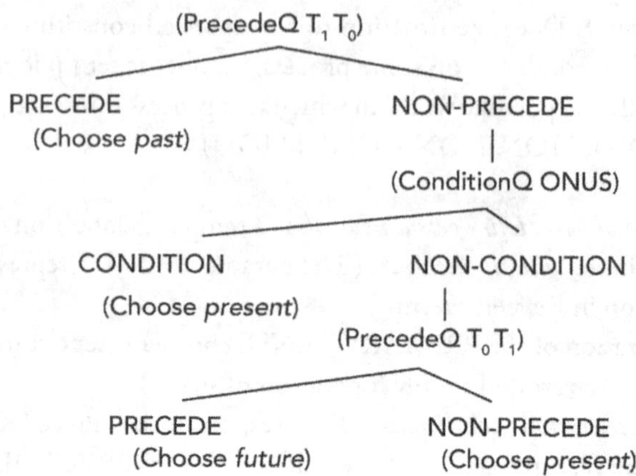

Figure 3.6 The chooser of the system of primary tense

There are no complex inquiry presentation conditions in the present version of the inquiry framework. In other words, there can be no conjunction or disjunction of branches before an inquiry is presented. Conjunction can be simulated by accumulating responses as the depth increases in the tree of inquiries. Disjunction can be simulated by using the same inquiry in more than one place. The same techniques have sometimes been used in so-called "displayed system networks" (see Fawcett 1988).

Neutralization. The primary tense chooser also illustrates how disjunctive choice conditions are handled. Notice that there are two "paths" leading to the choice of present. These are two alternative reasons for choosing the feature present. This disjunction of choice conditions is not represented explicitly in the chooser but can only be inferred from the repetition of "(Choose present)." In principle, this situation is comparable to an upward "or" in stratificational theory (cf. for example Lamb 1971).[14]

3.4.2 *Organization beyond the chooser – inquiries and the network: the mood region*

To explore some aspects of inquiry interaction beyond a single chooser like the primary tense chooser, we can consider the mood fragment of the clause system network in Figure 3.7. The interactions among inquiries I will point to are implicit rather than explicit, as in the chooser tree of the primary tense chooser.

First, consider the flow of information involving identifying inquiries as we move from left to right in the network. As soon as the feature clause can be chosen,

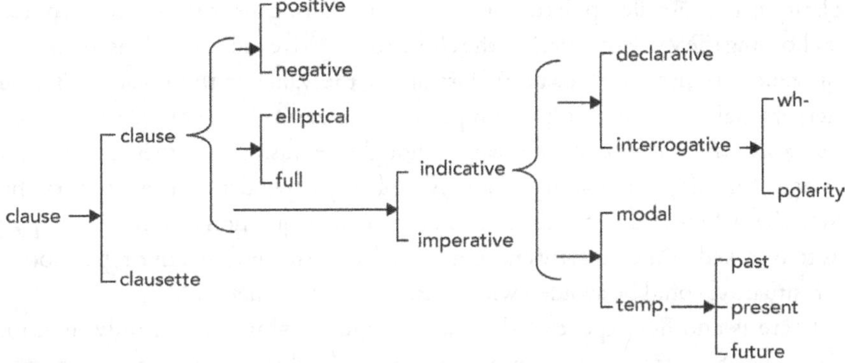

Figure 3.7 Mood grammar: network

MoodID is asked to identify mood. Consequently, the identity of mood has been established by the time the chooser of mood type is reached and (CommandQ MOOD) is asked.

Second, the branching inquiry of one chooser may set up the context in which the branching inquiry of the chooser of a more delicate system can be asked sensibly. For example, inquiries distinguishing between statements and questions are only asked after it has been established that the speech function is not a command. The system network takes care of this sequence of asking inquiries, since the system indicative type is dependent on the choice of indicative in the system mood type. Similarly, the organization of the system network ensures that no inquiries about temporal relations are asked if the speech function is a command, since the primary tense system is only entered in indicative clauses (more particularly, temporal clauses) and not in imperative clauses.

3.4.3 A network of inquiries?: polarity

To sum up, there is an implicit organization of the inquiries beyond the individual choosers. It follows from the system network organization in the grammar. Is this organization sufficient, or do we need an explicit inquiry network comparable to the explicit system network? I think there is reason to believe that an explicit inquiry network would be quite useful. For instance, the system polarity is simultaneous with the system mood type, which is quite justified in terms of the grammatical network. However, the conditions under which negative is chosen are not the same for all speech functions. In particular, questions concerned with the value of the polarity itself, so-called polarity or yes/no questions, constitute a special context for choosing the value of polarity: the choice of negative indicates a biased assumption/expectation on the speaker's part about the value of the polarity; it is an interpersonal comment about assumption/expectation. (For example *Isn't Henry coming over this afternoon?* can mean "I thought he was.") Since there is no way at present of making the polarity inquiries explicitly dependent on the inquiry that establishes whether the speech function is a polarity question or not, that inquiry has to be asked in the polarity chooser as well as in the interrogative type chooser. This situation could be avoided with an explicit inquiry network.[15]

There is another aspect of the use of inquiries which I will only mention in passing. Systemicists have used daggers and other symbols in system networks to indicate various dependencies between pairs of features that are not captured in the network organization itself. These conventions can be captured at the inquiry stratum, e.g. by asking the same branching inquiry twice in two different choosers and then choosing the appropriate features for a given response.

3.5   Factoring of the framework

I have now introduced the whole chooser and inquiry framework and will summarize it and relate it to other work on systemic semantics. To summarize the framework, I will factor it into five design assumptions:

1. **Semantic features** like EXTERNALLY CAUSED, STATEMENT, POSITIVE, PRECEDE, and so on can be used to specify the semantic distinctions correlating with grammatical distinctions.
2. Semantic feature labels are abbreviations of explicitly statable **choice conditions**, specified either in an informal English text or in a more formal notation.
3. Choice conditions can be viewed as the **responses to inquiries** presented to NIGEL's environment. An inquiry defines a minimal decision tree with two or more branches.
4. Not only grammatical choices can be associated with the response branches in this **tree**, but also additional branching inquiries, giving more tree organization.
5. Inquiries come in **chooser "parcels,"** one parcel for each system. The inquiries of a chooser may be embedded under one another, but they are not related to the inquiries of other choosers in this fashion. A chooser starts its

activity when its system is entered. As a result of the "chooser parcelling," choices are always local to the system whose chooser an inquiry is a part of.

The first design assumption shows how the chooser and inquiry framework is related to approaches that make use of **semantic features** or components, "componential semantics."

There are differences, some reflected in the subsequent design assumptions and some having to do with the domain the frameworks are applied to. Componential analysis has typically been used as a tool in lexical semantics.[16]

The notion of **choice condition** is similar to Robin Fawcett's procedural felicity conditions (cf. 1980: 253 and 1983). The explicit specification of choice conditions also suggests some relation to the notion of truth condition. The latter is, of course, a narrower notion, being grounded in truth, and is typically not part of a functional approach to semantics. Fawcett notes that linguists "are discovering that the specification of the meanings built into the code of language requires to be stated in complex terms of felicity conditions, truth conditions (which are really just a sub-category of felicity conditions), etc.; and moreover that these approaches to meaning can always be interpreted as a PROCEDURAL SEMANTICS that relates features of a language to knowledge of the universe" (1980: 253). The notion of choice condition is also related to the use of "semantic" conditions on the application of "syntactic rules" in various other approaches to generation; see. for example, Sowa (1983).

The third assumption, the view that choice conditions can be seen as **responses to inquiries**, determines the minimal organization of semantic features/choice conditions/responses into the paradigms defined by branching inquiries. This assumption brings out a similarity with the notion of the systemicization of features. The responses to a branching inquiry are disjunctive just as the output features of a system are disjunctive; in both cases the disjunction represents a minimal alternation.

The fourth assumption, that a branching inquiry can be **embedded** under the response to another inquiry, determines how inquiries can be organized into a decision tree with more than one branching point and thus more than minimal depth. It determines how inquiries can be related by dependency and vary in delicacy just as systems can. It also determines the current restrictions on inquiry organization (within a chooser), since trees do not have double motherhood (conjunction) or alternative motherhood (disjunction).

The fifth assumption, the **chooser parcel** assumption, defines a limit on how inquiries can be inter-related (at present), since only inquiries within the chooser of one system can be related by embedding. This assumption suggests how a collection of inquiries differs from a collection of systems: the latter collection forms a huge network; the former only fragments corresponding to choosers.

The factoring of the framework helps us see how it is composed. It also helps us see how we can create variants of it. For example, we can change the last assumption and let inquiries depend on one another across the boundaries defined by the chooser of a particular system. We can also change the fourth assumption so that we allow disjunction in the embedding of an inquiry (not presently allowed).

3.6   Semantics and the consumer

There have been different approaches to semantics in systemic linguistics. They differ, I think, mainly in terms of what questions they took as the starting point in the development of semantics.

3.6.1   Chooser–inquiry semantics and the consumer

The present design of the chooser and inquiry framework should be understood in the context of the task it was created to perform. A few years ago, we said to ourselves: we are developing a large computational systemic grammar of English as part of a text-generation system. One key issue for the success of the grammar is that grammatical choice must be made in a purposeful way, in response to a given communicative situation. How can we control grammatical selection in a purposeful way? This was a consumer demand on (systemic) linguistics. In response to this demand, the chooser and inquiry framework was developed. Since we already had a grammar that had been organized to be sensitive to semantic distinctions, we took it as our starting point and created choosers for the grammatical systems. This approach seems similar to the one Robin Fawcett envisions; cf. the remarks on his Problem Solver in the introduction.

3.6.2   Sociological semantics

An alternative strategy is to take communicative goals as a starting point and write a semantics that is a strategy or set of strategies for pursuing those goals. Turner's work (1973) can be described in that way. For example, if you are a mother and your goal is to control your child so that he or she does not do something undesirable, what are the meanings available to you to pursue this goal? This strategy for approaching semantics, let's call it sociological semantics (cf. Halliday 1973), differs from the chooser and inquiry framework in a number of ways. In particular, sociological semantics is situation specific and is designed to control grammatical generation from the semantic stratum, e.g. by using preselection.

3.6.3 Compatibility of chooser and inquiry semantics and sociological semantics

However, it is not incompatible with that framework; rather, the two approach the problem of interfacing context and grammar from different angles:

1   Sociological semantics takes purposes (goals) as a starting point; chooser and inquiry semantics takes the grammatical choices to be made in a purposeful way as a starting point.

2   As a result, it can be argued, the semantic unit of a sociological semantics is (a whole) text; the "domain" of chooser and inquiry semantics is whatever corresponds to a clause (complex) and so on down the grammatical rank scale.

3   Sociological semantics tends to be written for particular contexts; it is situation specific. As a result, the first step in the sociological semantics "program" would be a collection of various particular semantics rather than one generalized semantics. In contrast, the work on the chooser and inquiry framework has been carried out under the assumption that inquiries address general distinctions, not situation-specific distinctions. The result is one collection of choosers for the entire grammar, not different collections for different tasks.

There are obviously a number of ways to interpret these differences. I will not pursue them here, but will leave suggestions for another time. (See also Chapter 4.)

Both sociological semantics and the chooser and inquiry framework are attempts at creating a functional kind of semantics. Both have the task of an **interlevel**. In "Towards a sociological semantics," Halliday (1973: 64) writes that semantics is an interface which relates non-language to language: it "represents the coding of the 'input' to the linguistic system"; "it is the strategy that is available for entering the language system." In a similar way, it is the task of the chooser and inquiry framework to relate grammar to expressive demands in the environment.

There are other tasks that semantic frameworks have been created to deal with. For example, formal semantics addresses issues having to do with inference and interpretation in a model. The chooser and inquiry framework does not deal with (semantic) inference at all. We should not see this as a failing of the framework. It was developed to deal with a specific task, and inference is simply a different task. Inference is a different kind of "consumer need" and will lead to a different kind of semantics.

3.7   Conclusion

The fact that the chooser and inquiry framework was developed in the context of text generation explains its origins. However, it does not restrict its range of uses. (The reason for this is fairly obvious: text generation is a natural task, something speakers [and writers] always engage in.) For example, once the chooser and inquiry framework had been developed it was possible to make very definite statements about the choice conditions of grammatical features. As a result, it is also possible to argue from choosers to systems: arguments having to do with the content of inquiries and their arrangements in choosers are arguments "from above" about the organization of grammar. In practical work, it is useful to imagine the inquiries for a system that would lead to appropriate choices of its features. If it is not possible to word these inquiries, it is quite likely that the grammar should and could be reorganized.

As an additional example, consider the reliance in one inquiry of a particular chooser on the previous identification of one or more of its parameters in an earlier chooser. This reliance represents an interdependence in terms of the flow of information. Such interdependences can, I think, be used as strong indications of factoring into metafunctions; they are interdependences over and above the grammatical interdependences represented in the grammatical network.

Notes

1   Text generation is usually focussed on the system rather than reconstructions of particular instantiations of the system.

2   The computer has often been a tool in research on text generation. It is not a necessary component, but the computer makes the management of the various parts of the model (such as the grammar) much easier and also makes it possible to test the whole model of the text-generation system or parts of it. At the same time, the computer puts certain demands on the model. For example, all the details have to be made explicit; nothing can be left to the linguist to fill in.

3   Grammatical features will be marked by underlining.

4   Fawcett's Problem Solver also deals with tasks other than those handled by the chooser and inquiry framework. For example, it assembles the referent situations to be expressed by the semantics. In general, the tasks of the Problem Solver are decomposed and distributed across more than one process in our model of text generation; cf. for example Mann (1983a).

5   What Fawcett refers to as semantic features are grammatical features in Nigel.

6   Another term we have sometimes used is choice expert. It suggests a little process (procedure) with a very limited domain of expertise, viz. how to make a purposeful choice in one system by asking relevant questions. The choice experts are oblivious of one another but achieve the right result collectively. I will discuss the issue of what responds to the inquiries presently, but for now we can think of it simply as stratally above semantics. It is important to note in this context that the responses to inquiries are based on presentational considerations and not (directly) on an examination of the so-called real world. For instance, the inquiry "Is the action caused by the affected participant or not?" is not a question about the real world but a question about how a given (referent) situation is to be presented.

7   There is another choice operator, DefaultChoose, which is used in choosers of systems where one feature is to be chosen unless another feature has been preselected by the grammar. Choosers of this kind do not contain any inquiries, since the appropriate choice is a grammar-internal matter. For example, the chooser of the system pronoun case, nominative vs. oblique, only contains '(DefaultChooser oblique)', which is overridden when a Subject is preselected to be nominative.

8   Often the choice condition is a single response to one inquiry, but it is not uncommon for a choice condition to consist of a combination of responses to consecutively presented inquiries; see the discussion of the primary tense chooser in the following discussion and Mann (1983b).

9   The distinction between privative and equipollent systems based on chooser differences is often reflected in the feature names of the systems. Privative systems tend to have one term with non- in the name, e.g. *non-cause* vs. cause. The distinction is also reflected in realization statements. Privative systems usually only have a statement associated with the positive term. McCord gave graphic recognition to systems of this type in his revision of Hudson's systemic grammar (McCord 1975).

10   The longer answer to the question above would have to go into detail about exactly how the environment is organized (cf. Matthiessen 1987a), how the inquiries are interpreted by the environment, and how the appropriate responses are calculated. It would also have to address how the inquiries we have met in the shape of English questions are represented in a more formal inquiry notation.

11   The term *domain* is used in computational linguistics to mean something like the systemic notion of *field*.

12   Implementation is necessary for automatic text generation, but it also has other potential theoretical value. When I discuss inquiries here, I use English glosses; CommandQ means "Is the speech function MOOD a command or not?". These glosses are very helpful when we try to think about the inquiries, but there is a very real problem in using English as its own metalanguage. For example, if "command" is the inquiry gloss of the grammatical feature imperative, what is the gloss of "command"? Similarly, what is the gloss of the feature plural or the feature past? The problem we face has been discussed by Halliday in his paper on the *ineffability* of grammatical categories (Halliday 1984a).

There are various ways of approaching the problem of ineffability, and Halliday discusses several. For example, we can explore situation-specific semantics as well as highly generalized semantics. I will return to this topic briefly later in the chapter. Another possible approach is to use a semiotic system other than English for the glosses. (The two approaches are not mutually exclusive.) This is one way in which an implemented version of the "environment" in Figure 3.4 becomes relevant.

13   The comparable inter-rank operator is *Preselect* in Nigel.

14   The correlates of the inter-stratal connection types Lamb identifies are as follows:

Table 3.1 Inter-stratal connection types in stratificational theory and equivalents in the Nigel grammar

Inter-stratal relation	Strat. theory	Nigel
diversification	downward or	---
neutralization	upward or	Repetition of *Choose*-statement
portmanteau realization	upward and	succession of inquiries followed by *Choose*-statement
composite realization	downward and	same inquiry in different choosers leading to different choices

15   Notice that inquiry dependencies of this kind point to metafunctional organization that is not explicit in the system network since the mood type and polarity systems are simultaneous. In other words, the use of inquiries can be used as evidence of the metafunctional groupings in a language. In the case of polarity, the inquiry dependency is a piece of evidence in favour of interpreting it as an interpersonal region.

16   The chooser and inquiry framework is at present only used for what is called **grammatical semantics** in Halliday (1966a); lexical semantics is handled in a different way; cf. Matthiessen (1981).

Chapter 4

Two approaches to semantic interfaces in text generation

This chapter is a contribution towards the exploration of semantic interfaces in text-generation systems. It suggests a general interpretation of semantics for the purpose of text generation as an **interlevel** between lexicogrammar (the resources of grammar and vocabulary) and higher levels of organization (knowledge base, user model, text planning, and so on). Two approaches to the design of this interlevel that have been implemented in generation systems are then presented – chooser and inquiry semantics and situation-specific semantic systems. They are compared and contrasted to bring out their relative merits.

4.1   The role of semantics in text generation: semantics as an interlevel

Text generation is the creation of text, typically by means of a computer, in response to some well-specified need for text, such as the need to report on tomorrow's weather or to define a particular term for somebody (e.g. McKeown and Swartout 1987; Kempen 1989). That is, a text has to be created step by step from the initial specification of a need for a text to a final output, either in writing or in speech; minimally we can specify the initial need for text at one end and lexicogrammatical representation and orthographic representation at the other. The organization of the process of generating a text and of the resources that are activated in the course of this process can be seen as **stratification** or the arrangement into levels of successive orders of symbolic abstraction. So, given the task of text generation, the most productive interpretation of the semantic system is a stratal one, more specifically, semantics can be seen as the interlevel or interface between the linguistic resources of the system and the higher-level, non-linguistic ones. For instance, if there is a contextual specification that a service of some kind is needed, this can be addressed linguistically by choosing some semantic strategy such as pleading, requesting, or ordering; which strategy is selected will again depend on contextual factors such as the nature of the relationship between speaker and listener. The semantic selections are re-expressed lexicogrammatically and then again graphologically or phonologically.

While there are many possible conceptions of semantics, it is this interpretation of semantics as a strategic interlevel for accomplishing tasks linguistically that is central to text generation; and it is the conception of semantics that we find in systemic functional linguistics.[1] The strategies can be represented as a set of inter-related options by means of the system network of systemic theory. This corresponds to McDonald's (1980) characterization of text generation as being organized around the notion of **choice**. That is, generating a text is essentially a process of selecting among all the various alternatives available at different levels of abstraction. As Patten (1988) has pointed out, there is a significant parallel between Halliday's (e.g. 1973, 1978) emphasis on the process of choice and the organization of language as inter-related options in systemic linguistics and the paradigm of problem solving in artificial intelligence, involving the process of searching for solutions from among the options in a solution space.

4.2   Two approaches to the design of the semantic interlevel

Given that we interpret semantics as an interlevel, one central question is how we can explore the organization of this interlevel. Since semantics faces upwards, towards higher levels of organization, as well as downwards, towards lower levels within the linguistic system, there are two stratal approaches that can be adopted in exploring the organization and categories of semantics: 1. from below and 2. from above.[2]

1.   We can explore semantics from below, starting with lexicogrammar (the unified resource of grammar and vocabulary) – what might be called a **decoding** or **interpretive approach**, since it works by decoding or interpreting lexicogrammar in semantic terms.
2.   Alternatively, we can explore it from above, from outside the linguistic system – what might be called an **encoding approach**, since it looks at semantics as an encoding strategy and explores how contextual categories are encoded semantically.

Both of these approaches have been used in text-generation systems. I will discuss one example of the decoding approach in more detail in Section 4.3. chooser and inquiry semantics developed for and used in the PENMAN text-generation system (e.g. Mann 1982; Matthiessen 1989), and one example of the encoding approach in Section 4.4, the theory of situation-specific semantic systems (Halliday 1973) modelled in Patten's (1988) SLANG generator.[3] I should emphasize that the decoding and encoding approaches should not be seen as mutually exclusive alternatives. Rather, the assumption is that they can be reconciled into one account of the semantic interlevel that brings out how it relates its two interfaces.

4.3 Approaching semantics from below: chooser and inquiry semantics

Approaching semantics from below means taking lexicogrammar as the point of departure in modelling semantics.

4.3.1 *The organization of the level below: the grammatical system network*

The nature of the model of semantics that results from a lexicogrammatical point of departure will obviously be determined to a large extent by the nature of the theory of grammar. If the focus of the grammar is on structure, the semantics will essentially be a semantics of grammatical structure, possibly cast in some form of predicate logic. However, if the grammar is paradigmatically organized – i.e. if the theory takes choice as the basic organizing principle, as systemic theory does – the semantics will essentially be one of choice as well. We can call this model of meaning **choice semantics**. A number of generation systems have used systemic functional grammar (e.g. Davey 1979 [PROTEUS]; Mann and Matthiessen 1985 [NIGEL]; Bateman, Gen'ichirou, and Tabuchi 1987 [the Kyoto grammar] Patten 1988 [SLANG]; Fawcett and Tucker 1989; [COMMUNAL]). The central organizing principle is the system network; for example, the system network below is a fragment of the grammar of mood in English (the lower part of Figure 4.1).

4.3.2 *The semantic control of a system: choosers and inquiries*

Now, we can organize a semantic interface in terms of the system network, which is what Bill Mann and I did in the development of the chooser and inquiry framework for one particular systemic generation grammar – the NIGEL grammar developed at USC/Information Sciences Institute (Matthiessen 1981, 1989; Mann 1982); this framework was then adopted and extended for the systemic generator of

Japanese and Chinese by John Bateman and associates at Kyoto University (Bateman and Matthiessen 1993). Each system in the system network is equipped with a **chooser** – a semantic procedure for ascertaining the information needed to choose the appropriate feature in the system. The chooser achieves this by presenting one or more **inquiries** to the higher-level contextual systems above the grammar and its semantic interface.[4] Choosers can be added to the system network as shown schematically in the top layer of Figure 4.1 (choosers are represented by circles at the semantic level above the grammatical system network).

The mood fragment above is a simple taxonomy; but system networks in general allow for simultaneous systems and disjunctive entry conditions. The former property is important for multifunctionality and parallel generation algorithms; cf. Tung, Matthiessen, and Sondheimer (1988). An inquiry is simply a demand for information – e.g. "Is the current speech function a command, i.e. a demand on the addressee to perform a service or to provide goods?" (Command?); "Is the current speech function a question, i.e. a demand on the addressee to supply information?" (Question?); etc. – and the context has to return a response. The chooser then acts according to the response, either by presenting another inquiry if more information is needed or by selecting one of the grammatical features of its system if it has enough information. To take a very simple example, the chooser of the system indicative type has the task of choosing between "declarative" and "interrogative." It does this by presenting the inquiry Question? to the context – an inquiry asking whether the current speech function is a demand for information, i.e. a question, or not. If the response is positive, the chooser selects "interrogative"; if not, it selects "declarative." The chooser thus treats "declarative" as the default option of the system.

The inquiry has two or more possible responses; since these responses define branches in the organization of the chooser, this type of inquiry is called a **branching inquiry** (there is one other type, the so-called **identifying inquiry**, used to bind variables in inquiries to instantial values). This is an example of a minimal chooser: it consists of just one inquiry. However, a chooser may consist of more than one inquiry; if there is more than one, they are organized into a decision tree – an **inquiry tree** (for examples, see Mann 1982; Matthiessen 1983c, 1989). The response to one inquiry simply leads to another inquiry. During generation, an inquiry tree is simply stepped through one inquiry at a time until the process reaches a response that is a terminal branch in the tree and leads to the choice of one of the options the chooser is associated with.[5]

To sum up, as the grammatical system network is traversed, systems in the network are reached and their choosers are called into action. The chooser of a system has the task of making an appropriate selection in its system, and it does this

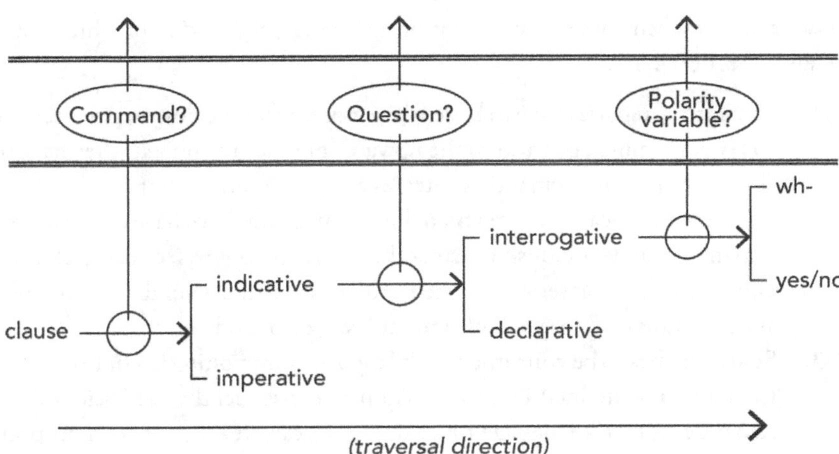

Figure 4.1 System network (grammar) with choosers (semantics)

by presenting one or more inquiries to the higher-level systems of the text generator. Consequently, the problem of controlling the grammatical resources in a purposeful way is decomposed into a number of very simple demands for information. These demands can be taken as the basis for specifying what kind of organization is needed to support the generation process: see Matthiessen (1987a) and Bateman and Matthiessen (1989, 1993). While there are considerable advantages in assuming that the semantic interface is simply a collection of choosers, the work on English and Japanese generation points towards an organization of inquiries that is more global than choosers local to grammatical systems: see Bateman and Matthiessen (1989).

4.4   Approaching semantics from above: context-based semantics

When we approach semantics from above, it is the interface between context and language that is highlighted. The role of semantics can be stated with respect to context as follows: semantics is the set of strategies for construing contextual meanings as linguistic meanings and thus moving into the linguistic system. Or, if we focus on the notion of goal in particular, semantics is the set of strategies for achieving some goal through symbolic activity. This is a functional approach to semantics: it interprets semantics in terms of the uses it has evolved to serve in different communicative contexts. This functional approach has a number of consequences for semantics; I will mention three here, the second of which I will pursue in Section 4.4.1:

1. Semantic categories have to be sensitive not only to the downward interface to lexicogrammar, but also to the upward interface to context; they have to show how it is that semantic strategies can play a role in context.
2. Since communicative contexts are highly diversified, we have to show how semantics can be responsible across these various contexts; one way of modelling this is to treat semantics itself as diversified into a number of semantic systems "tailored" to specific communicative demands.
3. Semantics has to be concerned with language functioning in context rather than any unit defined by lexicogrammar; consequently, the basic unit of semantics is text – language functioning in context – rather than propositions or predications.

4.4.1 Specificity of semantic categories – functional diversification of semantics

Since the approach from above takes context as its starting point, it is likely to yield **situation-specific semantic systems**: we project a variety of different uses onto semantics, giving us semantic interpretations of contextual categories; for example, "behavioural control of child" is semanticized as "appeal to authority figure," "threat of physical punishment," "threat of loss of privilege," and the like, whereas "behavioural control of student" is semanticized as "warning about fees," "threat of expulsion from program," and the like. The notion of function reflected in this kind of semantics is thus use in context, and there will be a large number of different uses.[6] There are at least two basic types of motivation for exploring and writing context-based semantic systems: **bridging** and **compilation**.

Bridging: the orientation towards context serves to bridge the gap between linguistic categories and higher-level categories. Within sociology, Halliday's concept of semantics is motivated partly because it can act as an interface between language and the rest of the social system. Turner (1973: 195) comments that Halliday's concept of meaning potential "should enable researchers to integrate sociological concepts and linguistic concepts. The sociological theory identifies the socially significant meanings. Once these are specified, their grammatical and lexical realizations are also capable of specification."

Within computational linguistics and AI, it is possible to make similar observations: situation-specific semantic systems may serve to relate non-linguistic categories to linguistic ones.

Compilation: furthermore, a situation-specific semantics can be seen as a set of strategies developed to deal efficiently with the specific, limited set of communication problems inherent in that context of situation. We can find this consideration in computational linguistics and AI. As noted earlier, Patten (1988) has shown that the approach of situation-specific semantics can be motivated in AI terms as well as in linguistic terms. Patten treats text generation as problem solving and shows that there is a striking similarity between the AI problem-solving framework and Halliday's systemic approach to language. The similarity is all the more interesting because the two traditions have developed independently of one another.

The lexicogrammatical system network can be seen as the space of inter-related alternatives for solving a communicative problem. There are different ways of searching the system network for appropriate feature selections. One way is to traverse the network from left to right and to reason about each systemic alternative by means of choosers (cf. Figure 4.1). Patten argues that it is potentially costly to do this kind of reasoning from basic principles. Another way is to rely on a strategy that has already been developed for a particular problem ("compiled knowledge"), and this is what Patten takes a situation-specific semantics to be. That is, for a given register there is a particular semantic strategy for traversing the lexicogrammatical system network. If we are faced with a novel generation task which does not correspond to a recognized register, we will have to revert to basic principles.

4.4.2 An example: a semantics of control in a regulatory context

Let's consider an example of the semantics of a particular register. Assume that we are building a generator for mother–child control, the situation Turner (1973) did sociological research on, which Halliday (1973) uses as an example of sociological semantics, and Patten (1988) takes over for text generation.[7] The situation is the following (Halliday 1973: 65):

> [A] small boy has been playing with the neighbourhood children on a building site, and has come home grasping some object which he has acquired in the process. His mother disapproves, and wishes both to express her disapproval and to prevent him from doing the same thing again.

The question is what her linguistic strategies are. The answer lies in the semantic system network; most generally, she can threaten, warn, or appeal to her son, issue a rule, etc. The semantic network consists of systems like threat/warning, physical

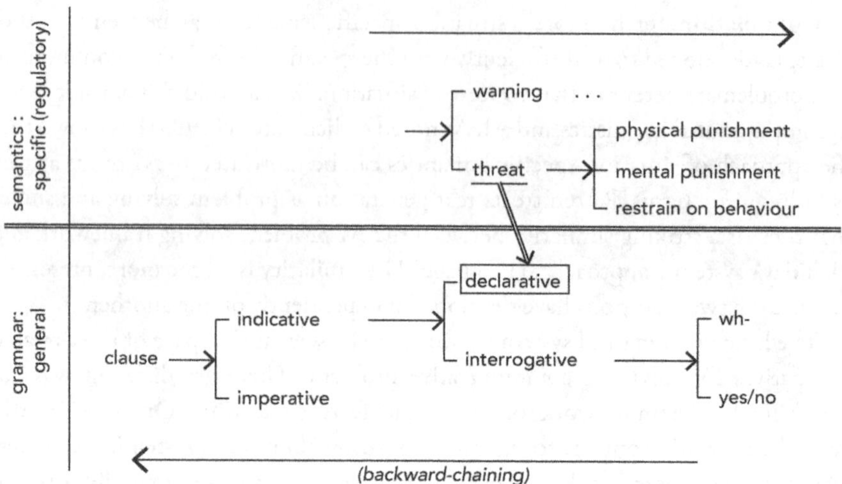

Figure 4.2 Generation with situation-specific semantics

punishment/mental punishment/restraint on behaviour, and so on. Semantic features are realized by preselections of grammatical features. For example, the semantic feature "threat" is realized by selection of the grammatical feature "declarative." In general, delicate grammatical features are preselected, and the less delicate features they presuppose can then be chosen automatically by moving from right to left by backward chaining in the system network rather than by explicit preselection. This method makes good use of the "logic" of the lexicogrammatical system network; see Figure 4.2.

As the diagram indicates, there is a tendency for the situation-specific semantics to be more delicate than the non-specific lexicogrammar. This is to be expected, particularly in the fairly restricted registers that have been attempted in text generation: only a restricted subset of the lexicogrammatical resources will be employed, and the semantics can simply "turn off" certain parts of the grammar by never preselecting grammatical features in these parts.

To extend Patten's line of research further within text generation, it is important to describe the semantic systems of a variety of situation types; for instance, Marilyn Cross, at Macquarie University, is currently working on descriptions of the water cycle for different addressees. There is good reason to think that the approach of situation-specific semantic systems will yield interesting results. The types of situation for which we can attempt to write semantic networks would also seem to be the types that can be addressed in text generation at present.

Now, the example of regulatory semantics has been discussed in terms of a network of semantic systems such as threat/warning. To relate these systems upwards, we can assume realizations of contextual features of interaction by means of pre-selections of semantic features. Alternatively, we can easily turn the systems into inquiries that demand information from context. For instance, the system threat/warning can be re-represented as an inquiry concerned with the basic strategy of control: is the child to be controlled by appealing to authority; by threatening him with punishment or restraint on behaviour if he carries on; or by appealing to the dangers of the world, warning him that his behaviour will harm him?

Although the systemic semantics used by Patten (1988) is context based, the texts that can be generated do not extend beyond the clause complex. There is, however, every reason to expect a **text semantics** rather than only a lexicogrammatical semantics – i.e. a semantics that is concerned with text as a semantic unit, the basic unit of communication. To develop the notion of text semantics further, we would need to examine proposals for how to organize text, since they would provide us with structures we can interpret as text semantic structures. The two types of approach that have been developed for text generation are McKeown's Rhetorical Schemas (McKeown 1982; Paris and McKeown 1987) and, within the PENMAN project, Rhetorical Structure Theory (see e.g. Mann and Thompson 1987; Matthiessen and Thompson 1988; Mann, Matthiessen, and Thompson 1992). McKeown's work is very similar to systemic work on generic structures by Hasan (1984a, 2014, etc.) and others. In either case, the structures they operate with can serve to realize semantic features in a text semantic system network.

4.5   Conclusion: the two approaches re-considered

To recapitulate, taking the basic systemic position that semantics is an interlevel between higher-level contextual systems and the purely language-internal level of lexicogrammar, I have suggested that we can approach it from either of the two semantic interfaces – from above, from context, or from below, from lexicogrammar – and that we find both approaches modelled in text-generation systems using systemic functional grammar. The chooser and inquiry interface, built from below, has the advantage that it is fairly easy to develop once there is a significant systemic functional grammar to base it on; it can be developed as "semantic glosses" on the organization already embodied in the grammatical system network. It does not change the basic principle of generation supported by the grammar: the grammatical system network guides the generation process, which is essentially a traversal of the network, and choosers are activated in the course of this process. The collection of inquiries can be used as design requirements in the development of the organization of the context of the generation system. The approach from above has other advantages. It enables the semantics to refer to different grammatical contexts in realization, as in the case of requests being realized both by selections in mood and selections in modality. Furthermore, it allows us to adapt the semantics to contextual requirements. This adaptation may take the form of a diversification of semantics into a range of situation-specific semantic systems. Such systems have the added advantage that they represent "compiled knowledge": they allow the generation system to take advantage of the semantic strategies that have evolved for a particular communication task rather than having to solve the problem from first principles. This means, among other things, that only those parts of the lexicogrammar that are relevant in that situation have to be explored, and others are simply "blocked off" by preselections from the semantics.

The two approaches have been used in different generation systems, but they have not been brought together into one system and I have not explored the question whether this would be possible or not. We can obviously say that one chooses one approach or the other depending on the nature of the generation task. For instance, more closed registers (specific sublanguages) might favour situation-specific semantic systems, whereas more open registers might favour the use of a general semantic system. However, in the long run, such a position would clearly be unsatisfactory since it would commit a generation system to one type of generation task or another. The two most clearly differentiated positions that are theoretically possible would thus be:

1. Situation-specific semantic systems are essentially based on different principles of organization, creating semantic potential for a given situation type, and cannot be drawn from one general semantic system.
2. Situation-specific systems are merely abbreviations of one general semantic system, "blocking off" semantic potential that is not needed in a given situation type.

This needs a long separate discussion, and I will leave the issues at this point for now; for further discussion, see Matthiessen (1988b) and cf. Bateman and Paris' (2011) approach to register by means of chooser and inquiry semantics.

Notes

1   Traditionally, semantics has tended to be modelled from the point of view of comprehension, by reference to rules for interpreting syntactic structures.

2   The two directions pertain to the *design* of the semantics, not to the direction in the flow of control. Encoding and decoding are thus not to be equated with generative and interpretive semantics. Both generative and interpretive semantics are essentially decoding in that they reflect the categories of grammar rather than contextual categories.

3   The survey here is thus not exhaustive; in text generators, we also find the use of parallel, coordinated taxonomies (as in Jacobs 1985), unification of semantic and grammatical information (cf. McKeown 1982), and augmented phrase structure rules (cf. Sowa 1983).

The system network guides the generation process. In the course of generation, the system network is traversed from left to right, that is, from more general options towards the more specific ones that become reachable once the more general ones have been chosen (see the "traversal direction" in Figure 4.1). Any feature may have a realization statement associated with it; that is, a statement that specifies how the choice of the feature is realized structurally (no realization statements are shown in the network in Figure 4.1). For instance, the feature "declarative" is realized (in English) by the relative ordering of Subject before Finite (*pigs can fly*), while "yes/no interrogative" is realized by the relative ordering of Finite before Subject (*can pigs fly*). As an option is chosen, any realization statements associated with it are executed, which means that a fragment is added to the grammatical structure being built as a realization of the selections. As the system network is traversed from left to right, structural specifications are accumulated until the network has been fully traversed and the structure fully specified by the realization statements that have been encountered and executed along the way.

4   If inquiries are interpreted as being concerned with choice conditions (cf. Matthiessen 1989), we can see that these choice conditions are comparable to Fawcett's (1983: section 4.3.2, 1984: 166) procedural felicity conditions in his systemic model.

5   I have glossed inquiries by using names such as Question? and Precede? and by using informal English questions, which is helpful in developing a design of a large system such as the Nigel generator. However, as part of an automatic text-generation system, inquiries are also **implemented**: the steps for testing an inquiry to see which response is appropriate are spelt out in the generation program (for more details on generation, see Nebel and Sondheimer 1986). Thus, for instance, the source of the response to "Posssesion? (Henry horse)" – "Is the relationship between Henry and horse one of generalized possession, i.e. one of ownership, meronymy, close social association, etc." – might be derived ultimately from a relation in a database. One important point here is that it is possible to specify different implementations of inquiries reflecting different types of representation of the

information that will be the basis of the responses. This information might be represented in, say, an extended predicate calculus notation or in terms of some kind of frame-based network. In the current version of the PENMAN system, of which the Nigel grammar and its chooser and inquiry interface form one part, there is a special simple notation for specifying the kinds of information the inquiries need (SPL, or sentence planning language).

6   This does not mean that the various situation-specific semantic systems cannot be derived from a generalized semantic system, but I won't discuss this important issue here.

7   We might undertake this project to test the model, possibly as a pilot for future work. The computer would simulate the mother. In other text-generation situations, such as expert system explanation, the computer's social role is more likely to be that of a computer.

Chapter 5

Metafunctional complementarity and resonance in syntagmatic organization

5.1 From mono-modal organization to pluri-modal organization

The hierarchic organization of constituency is typically taken as a fundamental property of language, and elaborate theories are based on it. It is a fundamental mode of organization, of course, but we have to ask what its role in the overall linguistic system is. We need to do this along at least two dimensions of linguistic organization. First, in terms of the paradigmatic/syntagmatic axis, what is the division of labour between constituency as a syntagmatic mode of organization and paradigmatic modes of organization? Second, in terms of functional diversification in language, what is the division between constituency and other possible modes of syntagmatic organization? In general, I think the answer is that constituency has been made to take over far too much of the descriptive burden. On the one hand, there is a very strong tendency to place features somewhere in constituency structures even when there is no a priori need to and they could be interpreted much more conveniently in paradigmatic terms. On the other hand, constituency is treated as the default mode of syntagmatic organization; the question of whether there are other complementary modes has not been raised very often. Here I will only be able to deal with the second issue.

In particular, I will be concerned with different aspects of the relationship between modes of meaning and modes of expression or syntagmatic organization. The primary sources of inspiration are Halliday (1979a) and Hasan (1984a). I will return to the significance of their work presently, but first let me organize the central issues of this chapter as a sequence of a thesis, an antithesis and a synthesis:

1. Thesis: there is only one mode of syntagmatic organization in grammar – constituency.
2. Antithesis: there are different modes of syntagmatic organization, each corresponding to a different metafunctional mode of meaning.
3. Synthesis: these different and complementary modes of organization resonate with one another.

5.1.1   Thesis: constituency is the only mode of syntagmatic organization

Structure typically means **constituency structure** in the interpretation of language; the explicit or implicit assumption in much linguistic theorizing is that constituency is the only mode of syntagmatic organization. We can thus call it the default mode of syntagmatic organization in linguistic theory in general. Most grammatical rule types proposed in the last thirty years or so have been concerned with constituency structure – phrase structure rules, base rules, transformational rules, and so on – and most structural relations have again been defined in terms of constituency – dominance, command, c-command, and so on. There have, of course, been different theories of constituency, taking up different options such as the following two:

1. The nature of the constituency labelling: class-based **or** function-based (sometimes both) – the contrast Halliday (1966b) called syntagm vs. structure, more recently called c- structure vs. f-structure within Lexical Functional Grammar.
2. The nature of the constituency bracketing: maximal or immediate constituency, as in American structuralism and the generative theory building on it, or minimal or rank-based constituency, as in systemic functional theory.

Whichever particular options are taken up in the theory of constituency, the important point in the present context is that constituency serves as the mode of expression for all types of meaning.[1] If we acknowledge that there are different modes of meaning, this means that these different modes of meaning are mapped onto the same mode of expression, constituency, as shown in Figure 5.1. Consequently, the differences among the modes of meaning are **neutralized** in the constituency mode of syntagmatic organization. As a result, syntagmatic organization is likely to appear largely autonomous and arbitrary relative to meaning (although it may still be clear that one particular mode of meaning is projected naturally through constituency).

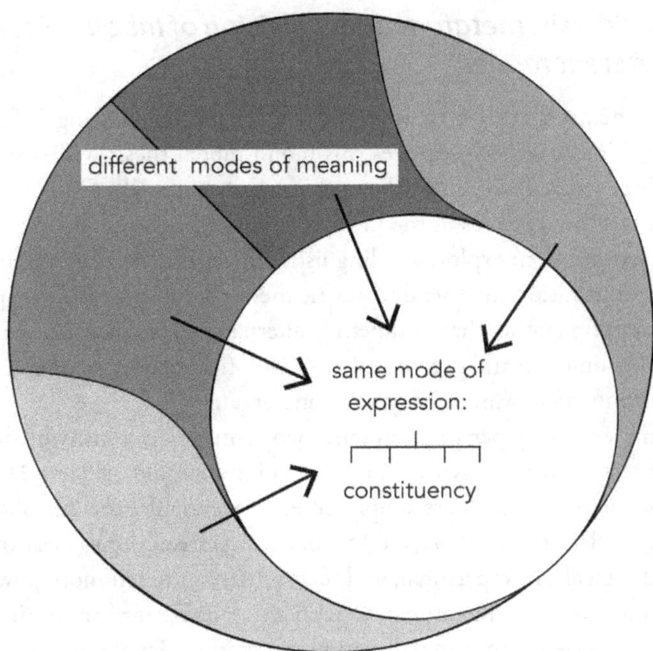

Figure 5.1 Different modes of meaning realized by the same mode of (syntagmatic) organization

This single mode of organization, constituency, then has to carry the whole burden of syntagmatic information (which is particularly heavy in theories that are syntagmatically based rather than paradigmatically based). As an alternative to constituency, **dependency** has been used by a number of dependency grammarians following Tesnière (1959), but it has the same segmental characteristics as constituency, which is the most fundamental issue in the present context.[2]

There is a very significant corollary to the single mode position: realizational categories are also identified and interpreted as in some sense unified phenomena. Thus, we speak of "word order," case marking, and so-called head marking as unified realizational categories to be accounted for. This is consonant with the traditional approach from "below" starting in Ancient Greece: grammar was explored on the one hand from the lower ranks – the word and its morphologically realized systems (case, person, number, tense, etc.) – and grammatical systems and functions were explored from their realizational categories. As we shall see below, it is important to recognize different kinds of "word order" and different kinds of case marking.

5.1.2   Antithesis: metafunctional division of labour among different modes

The Thesis, then, is that there is one mode of organization realizing different kinds of meaning. The Antithesis replaces this mono-modal thesis with a pluri-modal one. Pike (e.g. 1959, 1967, 1982) has suggested that particle, field, and wave are complementary perspectives in the interpretation of linguistic organization. This suggestion has not been explored in linguistics in general, but it is a tremendously important contribution to general linguistic theory because it raises the possibility of *complementary* (rather than competing, alternative) interpretations of the same linguistic phenomenon and provides alternatives (field and wave) to the dominant particulate constituency mode of syntagmatic organization.

The complementary perspectives raise two central questions: why do we have these three perspectives and what is the nature of the complementarity? One might assume that the perspectives are simply different views taken by the observer, but Halliday's (1968/8, 1973, 1979a, etc.) theory of **metafunctions** (ideational [experiential and logical], interpersonal, and textual) gives a much more powerful and explanatory answer. The metafunctions constitute **different modes of meaning**: meaning is dispersed into a metafunctional spectrum. Furthermore, each mode of meaning has its own **prototypical and iconic mode of expression** (Halliday 1978: 188, 1979a; Matthiessen 1989), such as particle, field, and wave. The particular correlations are depicted in Figure 5.2 (to be contrasted with Figure 5.1); they will be discussed in more detail in Section 5.2.2. Halliday's theory of metafunction thus gives us the basis not only for adopting different perspectives but also for explaining these by reference to different simultaneous functions inherent in the systems of semantics and lexicogrammar.

Since there is a metafunctional division of labour, constituency has to carry much less of a descriptive burden than it does in many formal approaches; and it is possible to see quite clearly that constituency and the other modes of organization are semantically **natural**. (In addition, systemic functional theory is paradigmatically based so the paradigmatic account carries a significant amount of what would be embodied in constituency in a formal grammar.)

Before turning to the Synthesis, I will just note that phonological theory has been one step ahead of grammatical theory in the exploration of different modes of organization. Within the approach that has come to be known as **prosodic analysis**, Firth and his students and colleagues made a strong case, starting in the 1940s, for the prosodic mode of organization within phonology as an alternative to the segmental, phonemic mode (e.g. Firth 1948a): see further Section 5.2.3. (Similar proposals emerged many years later from generative phonology, which had originally

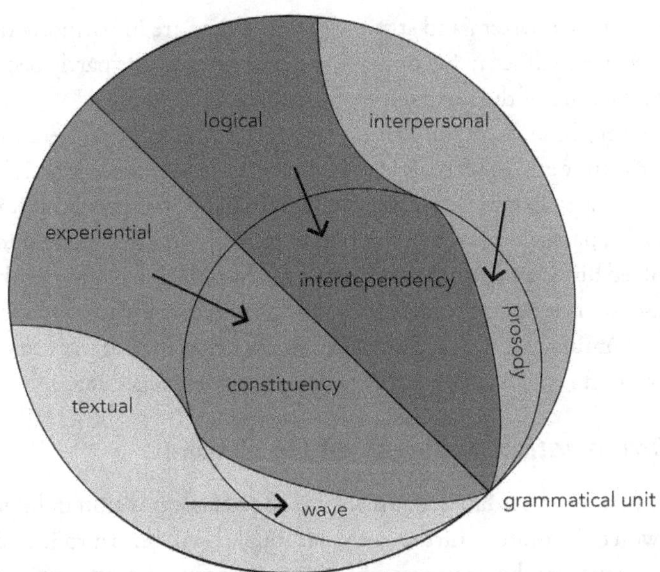

Figure 5.2 Different modes of meaning realized by different modes of (syntagmatic) organization

been based on American phonemic analysis and Jakobson's distinctive features – autosegmental phonology.) The important point here is precisely the exploration of **non-segmental** modes of organization. In addition to Pike's early work already mentioned, it is also important to note Firbas' (e.g. 1959; 1987) exploration of a non-segmental mode of organization in his work on **communicative dynamism**, where he represented degrees of textual prominence by means of numerical sequences (as in *She[11] did[20] not[32] want[31] him[12]*).

5.1.3   Synthesis: metafunctional complementarity but also resonance

The Antithesis says, then, that the different metafunctional modes of meaning are expressed by different modes of (syntagmatic) organization. Precisely because the metafunctions are different modes of meaning realized by different modes of expression, it is meaningful to ask how they interact. The interactions among the metafunctions can be explored in the light of Hasan's (1984b) theory of cohesive harmony in the organization of discourse. The answer seems to be that while they often point in different directions, creating points of tension in the linguistic system, they also *resonate* with one another in the unmarked case. That is, they conspire to organize system and structure so that they are in harmony rather than in conflict. As we shall see in Section 5.4, this is made possible partly because of the second-order nature of the textual metafunction.

To give a very brief example, participants and processes are differentiated both in experiential time and in textual time. Experientially, a phenomenon is likely to be construed as a participant if it persists through time but as a process if it unfolds in time. Textually, participants tend to persist as referents in a discourse, and languages have evolved different textual resources such as nominal deixis for tracking them; but processes do not persist (unless they are construed as if they were participants by means of nominalization), and while temporal deixis locates the occurrence of a process in time, it is not a resource for tracking that occurrence through a discourse.

5.1.4   Organization of the rest of the chapter

Since the Thesis discussed in Section 5.1.1 is the default position in linguistic theorizing, I won't elaborate it further here, although I will return to it at the end of the chapter to discuss the degree to which constituency misrepresents syntagmatic organization. I will begin with the Antithesis in Section 5.2, outlining the different modes of meaning and expression. I will then discuss them one by one in Section 5.3. Having done that, I will focus on the way in which they complement each other (still the position of the Antithesis) and how they also resonate with one another (the Synthesis) in Section 5.4.

5.2   Metafunctional modes of meaning and modes of expression

Many fundamental features of adult language are already anticipated in early child language, and we can understand the more complex adult system against the background of its ontogenetic roots since there is a significant functional continuity (alongside the discontinuity that is necessarily part of the child's move into the adult system). I will begin, then, with a very brief review of modes of meaning and expression in early child language in Section 5.2.1, drawing on Halliday's case study of one child, Nigel, learning how to mean, before turning to adult language in Section 5.2.2.

5.2.1   Modes in child language

In his first year, Nigel started his way into linguistic life with two modes of meaning, one reflective (e.g. "I'm curious about x") and one active (e.g. "I want x"). These were realized by two different modes of expression, vocal and gestural, respectively (see Halliday 1975, 1979b for an account of Nigel and of the nature of protolanguage; see also Painter 1984 for an extension of this line of research – in particular, pp. 129ff for the distinction between reflective and active meaning in various child language studies). Very significantly, the choice between the two modes of expression was a natural one – the gestural mode, that is, the mode most akin to non-symbolic action on the world, was adopted for the active mode of meaning. Furthermore, the gestures themselves were iconically related to non-symbolic actions (see Halliday 1979b).

While the semantic distinction between action and reflection remained, the distinction between the two expressive modes disappeared: Nigel opted for the vocal mode and generalized it across the different semantic domains.[3] However, Nigel had established a very important principle that anticipated later developments that took place as he moved from his early child tongue (protolanguage) into the mother tongue: different modes of meaning may correlate with different modes of expression. We can give the agency to either meaning or expression: different modes of meaning engender different modes of expression; different modes of expression construe different modes of meaning. In the bi-stratal system of protolanguage, this means that different domains of meaning are projected onto different domains of expression, as shown in Figure 5.3.

Since vocalization and gesture are different modes, they could, in theory, be employed simultaneously by the young child to realize reflective and active meanings at the same time; but the young child does not take up this semiotic potential for meaning more than one thing at the same time; reflection and action simply constitute an **opposition**. Protolanguage is **monofunctional** rather than plurifunctional or multifunctional: it is a system for engaging in one kind of meaning at a time. Like protolanguage, adult language allows us to make different kinds of meanings; but in contrast to protolanguage, it allows us to make these at the same time; adult language is **multifunctional** in this sense. That is, the different kinds of meaning can be unified in the same unit such as a clause or a nominal group. This is largely due to the different modes of expression; they are such that they can be integrated simultaneously. The distinction between the different modes is not so obvious as that between vocalization and gesture in protolanguage, but it as just as fundamental, and the semiotic potential for meaning more than one thing at the same time is taken up in adult language. For instance, an intonation contour can be deconstructed into (i) the direction of the pitch movement (falling, rising, etc.) and (ii) the location of the major pitch movement within the tone group; and these two different aspects of intonation serve to realize two different modes of meaning at the same time.

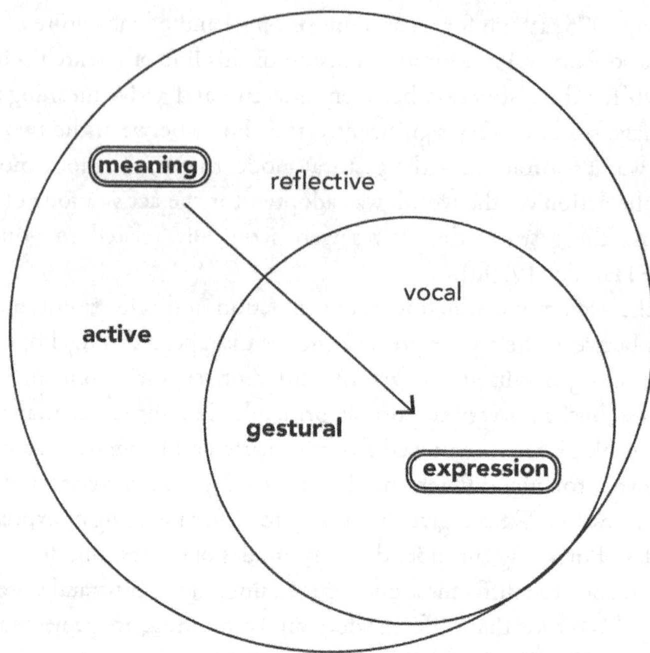

Figure 5.3 Different modes of meaning realized by different modes of expression in Nigel's early protolanguage

This principle of deconstructing the expression into different modes that can realize different modes of meaning simultaneously is very clear in the first step Nigel took towards a multifunctional semiotic as he was beginning the transition from protolanguage to adult language in his second year. He deconstructed his expression into prosodic and segmental organization so that they were independently variable, and this constituted the semiotic potential for making two kinds of meaning at the same time. He did this in the context of interacting with others; he created a system for personalized greetings that allowed him to identify the person ('Anna/Mummy/Daddy'), expressed segmentally, and to seek them ('where are you?') or find them ('there you are'), expressed prosodically by pitch. This interactional system is diagrammed in Figure 5.4. Note that the systems 'Anna/Mummy/Daddy' and 'seeking/finding' are not in opposition with one another; instead, they constitute the first move towards the introduction of a new dimension in the semiotic space, the dimension that organizes systems into simultaneous metafunctions.

In other semantic environments, segmental and prosodic expression were not independently variable at this stage in Nigel's development. Later in the transition towards adult language, Nigel adopted a general prosodic distinction between

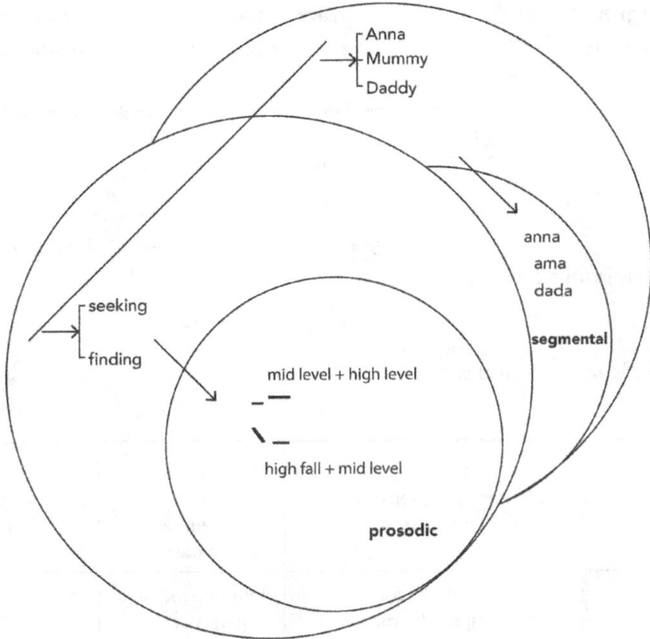

Figure 5.4 Beginning of simultaneous modes of meaning and expression, expanding the semiotic space

falling tone and rising tone to maintain a distinction between the reflective (or mathetic) and active (or pragmatic) modes of meaning. At first they were alternatives, but as he moved further into the adult system they turned into two of the three abstract metafunctions of adult language, the ideational and the interpersonal, and Nigel was able to reflect and interact at the same time. The third adult generalized function, the textual one, evolved a bit later. The developmental sequence is shown in Figure 5.5.

5.2.2   *The different modes of adult language*

For adult language, Halliday (1979a) has shown that different modes of meaning are realized by different modes of expression (cf. also Martin 1988, 1990; Bateman 1989; Matthiessen 1989, 1992; Bateman and Matthiessen 1993; Poynton 1996), and both meaning and expression are complementary so that they can be separated but also unified within the same clause, nominal group, or other grammatical unit. However, Halliday takes one very significant step further: he shows that the different modes of meaning are naturally related to the different modes of expression.

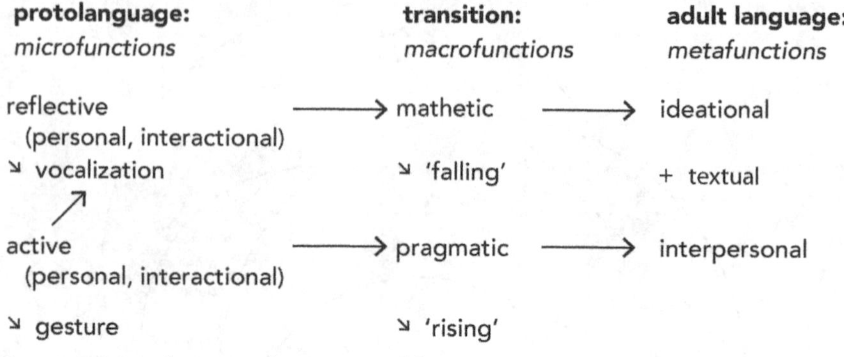

Figure 5.5 Developmental sequence of functions

experiential	deconstruction of phenomena into configurations of constituent parts	constituency *particle* (part–whole, segmental)	Actor Process Goal Recipient
logical	expansion of phenomena into complex by means of interdependency relations	interdependency (part–part, series, chain)	$1 \to 2 \to 3 \to ...$
interpersonal	colouring of phenomena according to interpersonal assessment and interaction	prosody *field*	[direction of pitch movement]
textual	creation of ideational and interpersonal meaning as text in context, with more or less prominent phases	pulse *wave*	[location of major pitch move]

Figure 5.6 Metafunctions, modes of meaning, and modes of expression

That is, given a particular mode of meaning, it will tend to favour one mode of expression rather than another, and vice versa. (This natural relationship was anticipated by Nigel very early on when he chose the gestural mode of active meanings and the vocal mode for reflective meanings, and then again later when he chose falling tone for mathetic meanings and rising tone for pragmatic ones.) The different modes of meaning and their favoured modes of expression are tabulated in Figure 5.6; the rightmost column gives a representative example.[4]

To review Halliday's proposal, let's first consider the different **modes of meaning** – the highly generalized functions or **metafunctions** of systemic functional theory (Halliday 1967/8; 1970a; 1973; 1985b/1994a; etc.). Linguistic content –

semantics and lexicogrammar – is organized according to three metafunctions: the **interpersonal**, **ideational**, and **textual**. The ideational embodies two types, the **experiential** and the **logical**. The metafunctions can be characterized briefly as follows:[5]

1. The **ideational** metafunction is concerned with "ideation" – with the interpretation and representation, with the construal of our experience of the phenomena in the world around us and the world of our consciousness. There are two ideational subtypes, (i) the experiential and (ii) the logical; these allow us to construe reality along different but complementary lines:

   (i) The **experiential** subtype construes our experience of the world by deconstructing phenomena into fairly particular categories such as processes, things, qualities, and circumstances, and it reconstructs these as parts configured in particular roles into unit wholes (sometimes called "frames" or "schemata"). The experiential resource of the English clause is the system of TRANSITIVITY; it is concerned with our experience of phenomena involving processes in particular, construed as configurations of a process, participants involved in it, and circumstances associated with it. Other ideational resources include those for representing things and circumstances. In general, the experiential mode of the ideational metafunction allows us to deconstruct a given phenomenon into constituent parts.

   (ii) The **logical** subtype is a highly generalized resource for expanding phenomena into complex phenomena, for relating all sorts of phenomena – processes, things, circumstances, times, and so on – into series (sequences) of phenomena. Examples of ideational resources within the logical subtype are those for serializing verbs into verb series, for chaining clauses into clause COMPLEXES, and for serializing time by means of TENSE. In general, the logical mode of the ideational metafunction allows us to expand a given phenomenon into a series (sequence) of such phenomena.

2. The **interpersonal** metafunction is concerned with establishing and maintaining the interaction between speaker and listener and the concomitant roles assigned by the speaker and accepted (or rejected) by the listener – stating, questioning, commanding, denying, refusing, requesting, and so on. This speech functional interaction characterizes the clause as a whole; it determines its particular dialogic value as a move contributing to an unfolding dialogue. It is grammaticalized as the system of MOOD in the clause, but the interpersonal metafunction includes resources for exchanging

comments by means of MODALITY and POLARITY and ATTITUDE and for defining PERSON (in relation to speaker and addressee).

3. The **textual** metafunction is concerned with the ongoing presentation of interpersonal and ideational information as text in context. It enables us to differentiate informational states of prominence along dimensions such as newsworthiness and identifiability. Major resources include THEME, INFORMATION, and REFERENCE.

These metafunctions are not extrinsic labels of language use; they are fundamental intrinsic principles organizing the linguistic system in its context (e.g. Halliday in Halliday and Hasan 1985 and Martin 1991).This can be seen in the first place in the internal organization of the semantic and lexicogrammatical system networks as clusterings of systems within each metafunction: within each metafunction, the systems show a high degree of interconnectivity, but across metafunctions there is a much lower degree of interconnectivity (cf. Halliday 1967/8), and this has strong implications for the way in which they are realized. We can look at this from a typological point of view as the likelihood of systems being independent of or dependent on one another in any given language, and the likelihood of terms from simultaneous systems being selected together. Hopper and Thompson's (1980) transitivity hypothesis illustrates (in non-systemic terms) how this works within the experiential metafunction, and we can explore similar hypotheses for the other metafunctions. For instance, certain configurations of the interpersonal systems of mood, person, deicticity (including modality), and politeness are much more likely than others; and certain configurations of the textual systems of theme, information (given/new), and specificity are also much more likely.

The metafunctions all create meaning; but they create different modes of meaning. These different modes of meaning are accommodated by different modes of expression; the differentiation into modes at both levels of abstraction allows the system to maintain the natural, iconic relationship between meaning and expression:

1. **Segmental modes of expression:** there are two segmental modes of expression; the difference is that one relates constituent parts to a whole (constituency), whereas the other relates parts to parts without presupposing a whole (interdependency).

    (i) **Constituency** is the familiar type of structure – the particle perspective, in Pike's (1959) discussion. It specifies elements of structure as parts of a unit whole (slots within a frame, or however we choose to characterize it); for example, a clause may have the experiential configurational structure Actor + Process + Goal as in (Actor:) *they* (Process:) *shoot* (Goal:) *horses, don't they?*

(ii) **Interdependency** defines elements of structure not as parts of a unit whole, but in relation to one another, and in this respect the structure is relational; any given element is defined as interdependent upon another element. An interdependency structure is strictly ordered by the interdependency relation. There are two types of interdependency: parataxis and hypotaxis.

2. **Prosody** runs through a unit across constituency boundaries within it – comparable to the field in Pike's work; from the point of view of constituency structure, it is thus "non-segmental." (As will be noted below, there are also boundary or juncture prosodies.)

3. **Pulse** operates by assigning varying degrees of prominence – the peaks and troughs of a wave or pulse of meaning.

Before discussing these different modes of meaning and expression in more detail, I will just illustrate them very briefly by means of a clause: *they shoot horses, don't they?*, taken from the screenplay of a film directed by Sydney Pollack, based on a novel by Horace McCoy (1935), both with the clause as their title. The story set during the Depression in the 1930s and evokes the sense of hopelessness through the depiction of a dance marathon "popular" at the time as possible way of earning some money, the last couple still dancing winning the prize. Gloria and Robert meet and agree to enter the competition, but after a long, gruelling experience they leave it, and, without any sense of purpose left, Gloria asks Robert to shoot her to put her out of her misery. He does, and two police officers arrive to arrest him:

Police officer 1: *Let's go.*
Police officer 2: *Why'd you do it, kid?*
Robert: *She asked me to.*
Police officer 1: *Obliging bastard.*
Police officer 1: *That the only reason you got, kid?*
Robert: *They shoot horses, don't they?*

Robert's last line is an allusion to a traumatic childhood experience Gloria shared with him. In the novel, she tells him:

When I was a little kid I used to spend the summers on my grandfather's farm in Arkansas. One day I was standing by the smokehouse watching my grandmother making lye soap in a big iron kettle when my grandfather came across the yard, very excited. "Nellie broke her leg," my grandfather said. My grandmother and I went over the stile into the garden where my grandfather had been ploughing. Old Nellie was on the ground whimpering, still hitched to the plough. We stood there looking at her, just looking at her. My grandfather came back with the gun he had carried at Chickamauga Ridge. "She stepped in a hole," he said, patting Nellie's head. My grandmother turned me around, facing the other way. I started crying. I heard a shot. I still hear that shot. I ran over and fell down on the ground, hugging her neck. I loved that horse. I hated my grandfather. I got up and went to him, beating his legs with my fists. Later that day he explained that he loved Nellie too, but that he had to shoot her. "It was the kindest thing to do," he said. "She was no more good. It was the only way to get her out of her misery."

Robert's clause *they shoot horses, don't they?* thus has a logogenetic history in the text that imbues it with considerable semantic and contextual significance in terms of all metafunctional modes of meaning (cf. Halliday 1992d). However, here I'm using it only as a specimen of English, not as an artefact in its own right.

The clause *they shoot horses, don't they?* is simultaneously organized experientially (constituency), interpersonally (prosody), and textually (pulse), as shown in Figure 5.7. (This example does not include the logical mode; while this mode organizes groups, it does not organize clauses in English.)

Experientially, the clause sorts out a quantum of experience of the flow of events as a configuration of three parts, a Process of a particular kind (material) and two participants involved in it, one bringing it about, Actor, and the other being impacted by it, Goal.

Interpersonally, the speaker locates the clause as a move in an exchange between himself and the listener; he gives information, but he also elicits an indication of agreement (or disagreement) from the listener and speaks the clause on a rising tone.

Textually, the clause is organized as a piece of discourse (within a larger discourse); two peaks of prominence fall within the domain of the clause, one peak of thematicity realized by sequential prominence (initial position) and one peak of newsworthiness realized by intonational prominence (location of the tonic). The thematic peak is followed by a trough of non-prominence, and the trough of non-sprominence as news builds up towards the peak of prominence (again followed by non-prominence). Sequence ("word order") and intonation are employed here specifically to achieve the differentiation of degrees of prominence, from high (peaks) to low (troughs); the pulse (or wave) is an abstract interpretation of these uses of sequence of intonation.

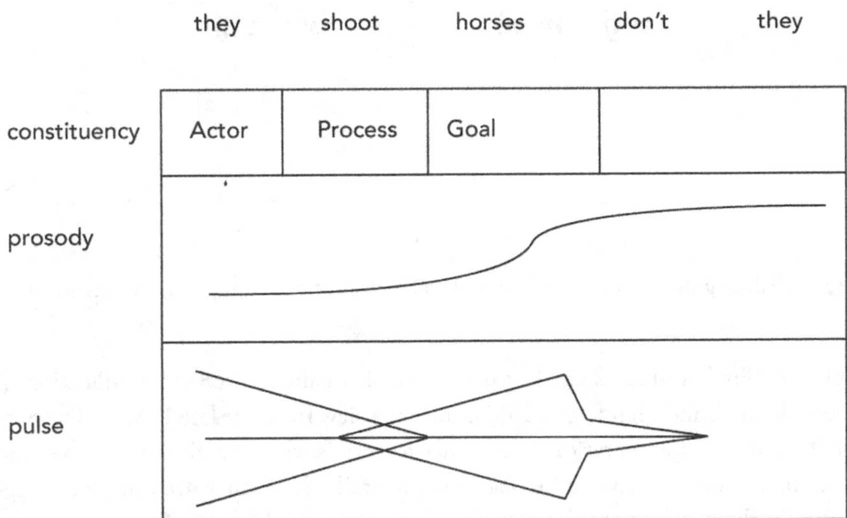

Figure 5.7 The three modes of organization of the clause

The non-experiential modes of organization are harder to represent than experiential constituency precisely because we have had most experience with the experiential mode: while we learn more about the other modes, we may use informal graphic representations or numeric sequences, as for the Prague School notion of communicative dynamism. The current lack of explicit forms of representation should not, of course, be taken as a reason for neglecting the other modes of organization. Similarly, we have to understand the implications of metaphors such as "wave" rather than reject them because they are metaphorical: new domains of experience are often interpreted by means of metaphorical systems.

5.2.3   *Trade-offs between different modes of organization*

We can learn from phonology about the trade-off between different modes of organization, in particular between segmental and prosodic organization. It is possible to represent prosodic phenomena in a segmental fashion – up to a point. This was the strategy adopted by American phonemics and "classical" generative phonology (i.e. pre-autosegmental phonology). The segmentation led to a number of problems, which were addressed by means of mutational rules. For instance, a particular phonemic segment is nasalized by means of a rule in the environment of a nasal within a syllable. Alternatively, a prosodic form of representation can be adopted as Firth and his colleagues did in prosodic analysis in Britain from the 1940s

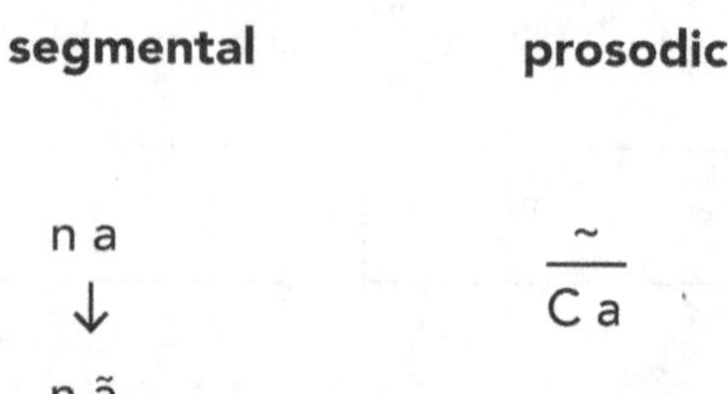

Figure 5.8 Segmental vs. prosodic representation of phonological organization

onwards (Firth 1948a, is the key paper; see also Palmer 1968 for a collection of prosodic work and Henderson 1987 for a brief view from the late 1980s). The prosodic mode of representation means that features such as nasality, rounding, and glottalicness do not have to be placed segmentally. Since they are not placed segmentally, there is no need for mutational rules to spread or alter features within a certain domain; for instance, a prosody of nasality can characterize a whole syllable (see further Matthiessen 2021a). The two treatments of syllabic nasality are shown schematically in Figure 5.8.

A similar grammatical example might be agreement between the Subject and the Finite verb of a clause; the segmental mode of representation would locate the number/person feature, say "singular," within the Subject, and this segmental representation would then have to be enhanced with a rule for spreading (copying) this feature to the Finite. In contrast, the prosodic representation would simply postulate a number/person prosody across Subject + Finite, thus making it unnecessary to add a rule for spreading (copying) it; see Figure 5.9.

Or, to take another example, the difference in function between *hopefully* in **Hopefully** *he looked at her* ('I hope') and *He looked at her* **hopefully** ('in a hopeful manner') can be characterized in constituency terms by analysing the first instance as a sentence adverbial and the second as a verb phrase adverbial. Alternatively, the first instance can be interpreted as a prosody of the clause as a whole and the second as a constituent within the (transitivity) constituency structure of the clause; see Figure 5.10.

The second approach is consonant with the potential positions of *hopefully* strung out prosodically throughout the clause, suggesting that it is not placed anywhere in particular relative to the constituency configuration of 'he + look + at her':

> Hopefully he looked at her;
> He, hopefully, looked at her;
> He looked, hopefully, at her;
> He looked at her, hopefully.

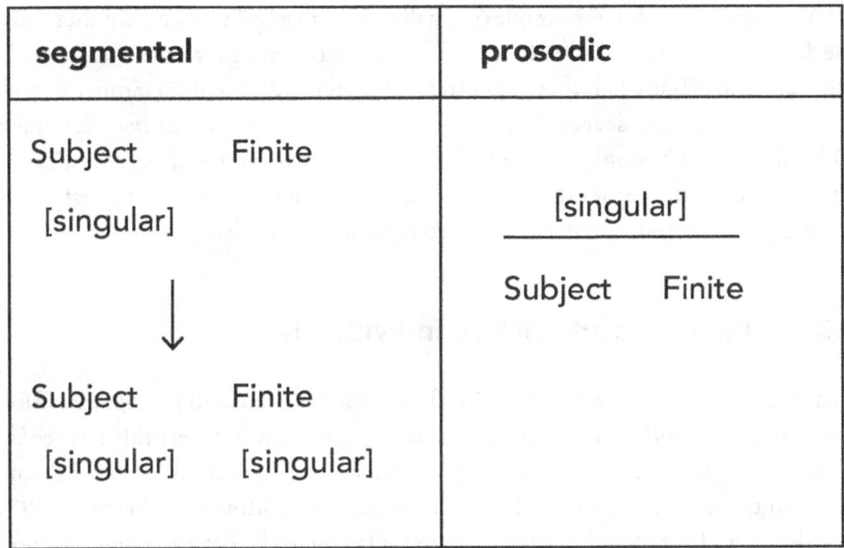

Figure 5.9 Segmental vs. prosodic representation of grammatical organization

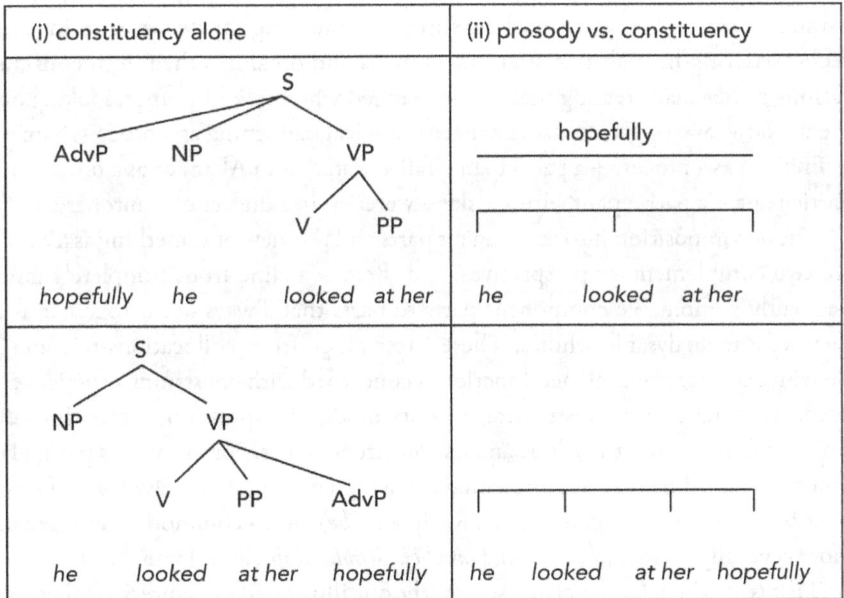

Figure 5.10 Constituency and prosody as modes of interpretation

As long as these different modes of analysis within grammar are only alternative mechanisms or notational variants, the choice between one or the other may be fairly arbitrary; but when they are correlated with the different metafunctions, we can begin to see the deeper functional significance in the choice between them. (This discussion has only touched on the syntagmatic modes of organization; in addition, many properties that are often placed segmentally in a syntagmatic constituency representation can be interpreted paradigmatically.)

5.3   The modes interpreted individually

I have reviewed and exemplified the different modes of meaning – the metafunctional modes – and their different modes of expression in brief; this has set the scene for a somewhat more detailed consideration of each mode. I won't discuss logical interdependency in any detail here; it has been addressed in Martin (1988), Matthiessen (1988a) and Bateman (1989). Having looked at the modes in more detail, I will then turn to the complementarity of the modes in Section 5.4.

5.3.1 Experiential ↘ constituency

The experiential metafunction is a resource for our construing experience of the world as meaning [i.e. as a model constituted in meaning] by **deconstructing and reconstructing** it: it abstracts out phenomena and organizes them into **configurations** rather than treating them as unanalysed wholes. For instance, looking out the window, one might construe a meteorological happening as a process, 'rain' as in English; as a process + a participant, 'fall + water' as in Akan; or as a process + a participant + a participant, 'drop + sky + water' as in a dialect of Cantonese.

The decomposition into component parts and the view of something as a whole are two complementary perspectives, and there is a cline from completely independently combinable component parts to parts that always occur together as if they were unanalysable wholes. These latter range from collocations to idioms. But since the experiential metafunction is concerned with construing experience – deconstructing and reconstructing it – its mode of expression is constituency, which embodies both the whole and its constituent parts. For instance, a particular process of awarding may be represented as having a temporal Locative (*in 1966*); an awardee or, in more general terms, a Recipient (*he*); and a commodity awarded or, more generally, a Goal (*a two-year Harkness Scholarship*), as in Figure 5.11.

That is, in a benefactive clause such as the one illustrated in Figure 5.11, there is a Process, three inherent participants – Actor, Goal, and Recipient – and potentially

(i) as box diagram

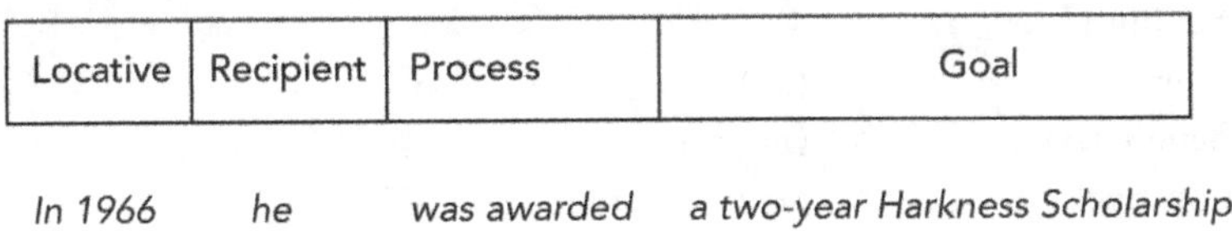

(ii) as tree diagram

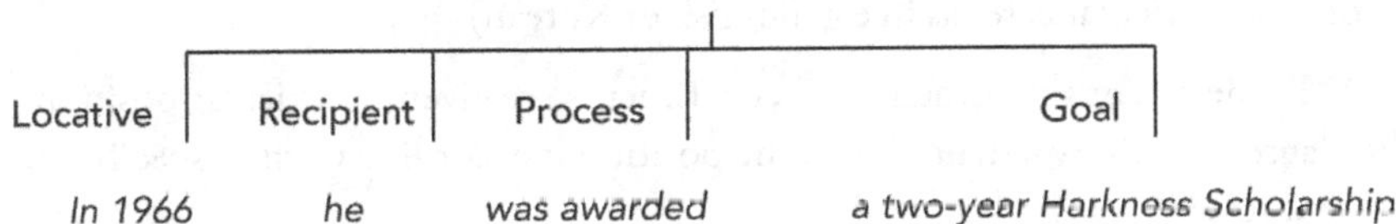

Figure 5.11 The transitivity structure of a clause

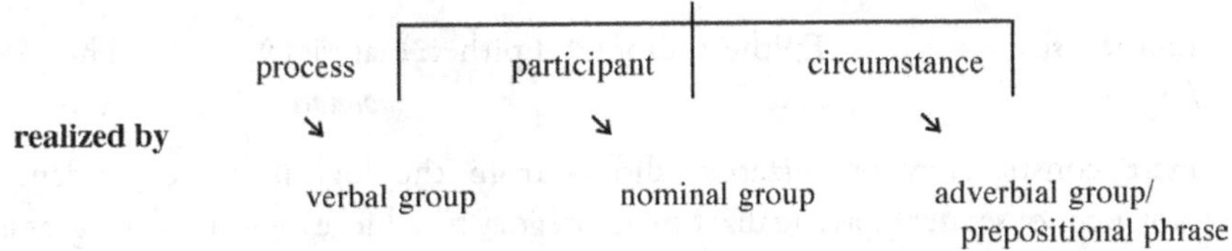

Figure 5.12 The types of experiential roles in the transitivity structure of the clause and their realizations by groups/phrases of different classes

also circumstances. The transitivity structure of a clause represents a composite configuration of a limited set of parts with unique values in relation to the whole configuration – Locative, Recipient, Process, and Goal in the example above.

Manifestations of experiential constituency

The constituency mode of organization is reflected in various ways; for example, we can see it 1. in the marking of constituents, 2. in the sequencing of constituents, 3. in the potential for serving as Subject, 4. in variation across languages in constituency, and 5. in "constraints" on constituent combinations.

1. The elements of experiential structure are marked as constituents playing a role in a configuration. (i) First of all, the classes of units realizing experiential elements indicate three generalized constituent functions: process, participants, and circumstance in English, as in the example in Figure 5.12.

(ii) Second, the particular role which a constituent plays in the whole is marked by a member of a set of adpositions, as in English with (sets of) prepositions:

Medium	–
Agent	(*by*)
Beneficiary	(*to*; *for*)
Locative	*at*, *on*, *in*, etc.
Cause	*because of*, *out of*, *for*, etc.
Role	*as*, *in the shape of*, etc.
Matter	*on*, *of*, *about*, *regarding*, *concerning*

or by a particular case (as in e.g. Finnish or Korean).

2. To the extent that experiential constituents are given a particular position in the clause in their experiential role, the position is according to their specific constituent role; for example:

Process ^ ... ^	Manner ^	Place ^	Time:
left	*quietly*	*from Victoria Station*	*at noon*

Epithet: size ^	Epithet: colour ^	Epithet: material ^	Thing:
large	*blue*	*wooden*	*table*

Here constituency organization differs from the logical interdependency employment of sequence as a realizational category to achieve logical ordering, as is shown in Matthiessen (1987a), as well as from the textual employment of sequence to achieve prominence.

3. The potential for serving as Subject in the clause is determined by the experiential value of a constituent. In general terms, participants can serve as Subject in English and circumstances cannot; but the likelihood that a given participant will serve as Subject depends on its specific experiential constituency role (cf. Halliday 1985b/1994a: 148), as is reflected in the notion of accessibility hierarchy proposed and discussed in descriptive and typological linguistics.

4. Within and across languages, differences within the experiential metafunction often concern constituency assignments – cf. meteorological processes (how many constituents), reflexive processes, mental processes (senser: whole conscious being or body part), etc.; for example, the phenomenon of 'rain' may be construed as a process, as a participant or as a combination of a participant ('water') and a process of movement ('falling, dropping'):

It's raining.	(English: process)
The rain has stopped.	(English: participant + process)
id-dunya ti-shti	(Palestinian Arabic: participant + process;
the-world 3sg.masc-rain	Givón 2001: 119)

'the world's raining'
nsuo retɔ   (Akan: participant + process)
water drop
'water's dropping'
xià yu le (Mandarin: participant + process;
'descend' 'rain' aspect: perf   Li and Thompson 1980: 91)

5. The combination of constituents as part of a whole is also reflected in grammatical 'constraints' and lexical 'constraints' (collocations) on particular constituent configurations such as Process + Medium, Process + Range, and Process + Manner (cf. Matthiessen 1991a). For instance, if the Range is a class of meal (*breakfast*, *lunch*, *dinner*, etc.) and the meaning of the Process is simply 'do,' the particular verb is likely to be *have*; but if the Range is *dance*, the Process will be *do*. Similarly, there are Process + Medium combinations such as *fall + temperature*; *decay + teeth*, *rot + orange*, *wilt + flower*; *decanter + wine*.

The solar-system nature of experiential constituency

The various properties just mentioned point towards a fundamental characteristic of experiential constituency (as opposed to constituency used in other metafunctional environments). One way of interpreting this is on the classic model of the solar system (or Rutherford's model of the atom) as diagrammed in Figure 5.13: the farther away from the sun-nucleus we get, the weaker the influence. The parts of a given configuration are a nuclear **process**, one to three different kinds of **participants** taking part in the process, and up to around seven different kinds of **circumstances** associated with it.[6] The difference between participants and circumstances is a cline (scale), reflecting the degree of involvement in the process. At one end of the cline, we find the nucleus of the process plus the most centrally involved participant, the Medium; these two represent the two complementary perspectives on a happening – a nominal perspective (changeless) and a verbal one (changing through time). At the other end we find "outer" circumstances such as temporal location. This cline is thus one of nuclearity/peripherality of involvement in the process.

While nuclearity is a cline, it is possible to recognize certain bands such as participants – inner and outer – and circumstances – again, inner and outer, although there will be significant variation across languages at this point since languages divide the labour between process and participants in different ways. Thus, English recognizes the difference between participants and circumstances in the different realizational classes: nominal groups and adverbial groups or prepositional phrases,

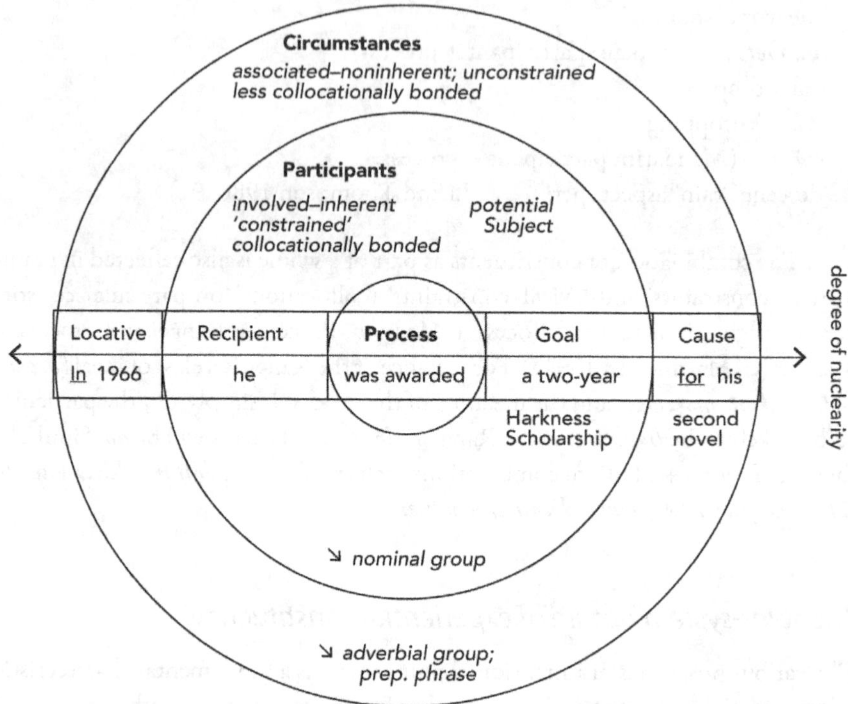

Figure 5.13 Transitivity as solar system

respectively. Indeed the preposition of the prepositional phrase symbolizes the less direct involvement of circumstances. Further, only participants are potential Subjects, circumstances are not, and the most nuclear or innermost participants are more likely to serve as Subject; and participants tend to be more constrained lexically and grammatically. There are, of course, departures from the general principle that participants and circumstances are distinct, but they do not invalidate the principle itself.

Since the Process can be interpreted as the nucleus of the configuration of process + participants + circumstances, it has often been taken as the "head" of the clause and the participants and circumstances as dependents (in particular since Tesnière (1959) and other dependency grammarians following him, but also more generally nowadays). Thus, dependency might seem an attractive alternative to constituency. If it is adopted as the canonical interpretation of the experiential mode of expression, it will still contrast with the other metafunctional modes of expression.[7] However, it is neither a necessary nor a desirable consequence of the solar-system model: we can note of the parts of a whole structure such as the solar system that they are more or less closely related to the nucleus without giving up the part–whole mode of organization, and there are strong reasons for preferring constituency over dependency as the mode of experiential organization. This choice needs a whole separate discussion; here I can only mention a few reasons for preferring constituency:

1. The Process is not, in fact, an obligatory part of the clause; in particular, it is very often absent in certain relational clauses in languages other than English (e.g. Arabic so-called nominal clauses, as in 'it's me' (Cantarino 1974: 19): [Identified:] ha:ða: 'this' [Identifier:] ʔana: 'I'). This is so because "relational" is a feature of the clause, not of the Process alone.

2. The transitivity potential of the clause is not determined by the verb alone – it is a feature of the clause rather than the verb and is influenced by participants as well. The difference between e.g. humans and natural forces as Agent in the potential for including a Means (instrument) in the clause is well known (e.g. *she felled the tree with an axe* but not *the wind felled the tree with a gust*); but the principle that the nature of a participant in combination with the process determines the transitivity options of the clause is a general one or even the nature of a(n inner) circumstance: cf. further *the tree fell : they felled the tree :: the economic indicators fell : * they felled the economic indicators; she opened the door : the door opened :: she opened the account : ?the account opened; she polished the piano : ?the piano polished : the piano polished easily*. This is so because instrumentality, causation, and so on are features of the clause, not of the Process alone.

3. Given a prototypical configuration of classes of participants, we can usually identify the class of verb serving as Process even if we find a new verb or invent one. Thus, *brilled* in *they brilled us the news* is very likely to be the class of verb that can serve in a verbal clause just like e.g. *tell*; in contrast, in the clause *the news brilled me*, it is likely to be the class of verb that can serve in an effective mental clause (the "please" type), just like *puzzle* or *please*.

4. While the "experiential content" associated with the process meaning is typically represented by the Process (e.g. *they danced*; *it matters*), it can also be represented by one of the participants, typically the Range or the Medium (Range as in *they did a dance*; *it is important*), with a highly generalized verb as Process (a so-called "light verb" or "vector verb"). This "redistributes" the "experiential content," but it does not change the primary transitivity type.

To sum up, since the experiential metafunction is concerned with the construal of experience – deconstruing phenomena into their parts and reconstruing parts into wholes, its mode of expression is constituency. The properties of constituency derive very clearly from the experiential metafunction. Specifications of experiential structure refer to the roles of constituent parts in relation to the whole (Process, Actor, Goal, Locative, Means, and so on). These are likely to be mutually constraining and also enter into lexical collocations – particularly the most nuclear roles. An element of experiential structure is realized as a constituent of a particular class; firstly according to its general role of process, participant, or circumstance as a verbal group, nominal group, or adverbial group/prepositional phrase; and secondly according to its more specific role in a clause of a particular transitivity type (as in the choice of preposition according to type of circumstance – Locative, Extent, Cause, and so on – and in the choice of verb class according to transitivity type).

5.3.2 *Interpersonal* ↘ *prosody*

The interpersonal metafunction is a resource for interaction; its mode of meaning is enactment, not construal: it provides the resources for interactants to enact their roles, relations, and values as meaning, prototypically in exchanges in dialogue. Unlike the experiential metafunction, is not concerned with sorting out experience – it is not a resource for the construal of our experience of phenomena. Consequently, we should not expect its mode of expression to be based on segmentation. The interpersonal metafunction assigns speech roles to the interactants in a dialogic exchange of a symbolic commodity and a dialogic value to this commodity itself as a contribution to the dialogue; and it establishes and maintains the sociosemiotic distance between them and between them (power, solidarity, familiarity; see e.g. the classic work by Brown and Gilman 1960 and the general theoretical work by Poynton 1984 and Martin 1992b) and the symbolic commodity they are exchanging (cognitively: "Do they think it's likely?", etc.; affectively: "Do they like it?", etc.).

Now, in the first instance, these interpersonal features concern the clause as a whole, giving it its dialogic value as a move contributing to the development of dialogue, so there is no reason why their syntagmatic realizations should be located anywhere in particular in relation to the experiential configuration of process + participants + circumstance. One way of avoiding the assignment of a location is to use a prosodic mode of expression rather than a segmental one, and this is indeed the interpersonal mode of expression; this mode of expression "colours" the whole clause as a dialogic move. The prosodic mode also makes it possible to express sociosemiotic "distance" iconically by varying the length of the prosody; an extended prosody can then mean increased distance along some dimension (as in the case of politeness in Japanese; cf. Bateman 1988, and in English examples such as *send me your manuscript by the 22nd* vs. ***I wonder if you could perhaps** send me your manuscript by the 22nd*). Prosody can thus serve as a horizontal expression of interpersonal intensity alongside vertical amplitude.

If prosody is the interpersonal mode of expression, we would predict that mood categories are expressed prosodically in English and in other languages as well, since mood is the major interpersonal system of the clause. This prediction is borne out: the resources of intonation – what has sometimes been called a sentence prosody – are used to realize different mood selections in English (Halliday 1967) as well as in many other languages (cf. Ultan 1978; Sadock and Zwicky 1986).

Types of prosody

The principle of prosodic realization includes not only obvious cases such as pitch contour. As was noted earlier, Firth, and his students and colleagues, demonstrated that prosodic analysis can be applied to a variety of phenomena that would be interpreted segmentally within phonemically based traditions. In the course of their research, they identified various types of prosody; Robins (1957: 193-4) identifies the following two cases:

1. **Prosodies realized continuously.** "In the first case a feature may be spread or realized phonetically over a structure, such as a syllable, as a whole; examples of this type of syllable prosody are stress, pitch, and length ..."
2. **Prosodies realized at boundaries.** "In the second case may be mentioned features which are not realized phonetically over the whole or large part of a structure, but which nevertheless serve to delimit it, wholly or partly, from preceding and following structures, thus entering into syntagmatic relations with what goes before or after in the stream of speech. By virtue of their syntagmatic relations in structures, such features may be treated as prosodies of the structures they help to mark or delimit."

The interpersonal metafunction employs both types of prosody as its mode of expression. This is to be expected since both characterize units as a whole; that is, both can express an interpersonal "colouring" of the clause as a whole.

(1) **Continuously realized prosodies.** I have already noted pitch contour as an example of the first type. We can consider one more example, taken from Halliday (1985b/1994a: 54); see Figure 5.14. The clause is a wh-interrogative one. The information unit selects for "certain" polarity and the tone group realizing it has tone 1 (falling tone), which is the unmarked tone in the context of wh-interrogatives.

tone 1 (falling):

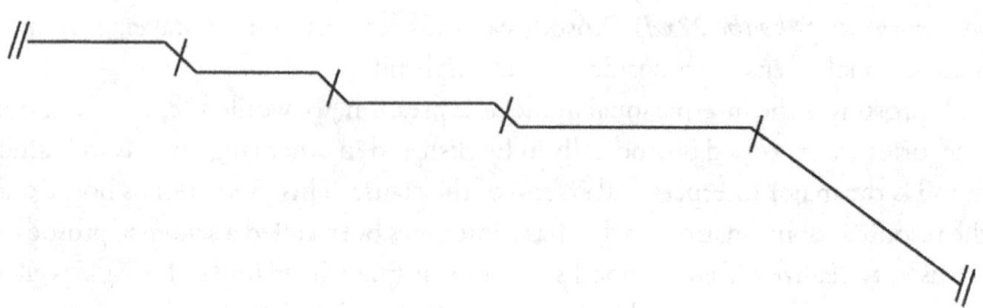

Figure 5.14 Pitch prosody expressing the interpersonal feature of certain polarity

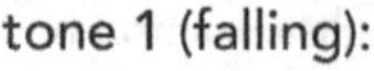

why	are	there	more floods	in houses	in the basement

Cause	Proc.		Existent	Locative	

Figure 5.15 Experiential constituency and interpersonal prosody

The melody runs throughout the tone group realizing the information unit; it is, in other words, a prosody. As a prosody, it contrasts with the experiential constituency of the clause, as shown in Figure 5.15. The prosody is represented as a continuous line. The location of the final fall (on basement) is not an interpersonal matter, but serves to realize a textual choice (see Section 5.3.3).

English thus uses pitch movement to realize interpersonal meanings. This is very common across the languages of the world, but languages may also use pitch level as an expression of mood selection.

(2) **Boundary prosodies.** A boundary prosody may indicate a point where there is a potential switch in the interaction between speakers. For instance, in Akan it seems that the presence of a glottal stop at the end of a clause realizes a combination of selections from the interpersonal systems of mood and polarity. Or, to take an example from writing, question marks serve as boundary prosodies either at the end of the clause only, as in English, or at the beginning and end of the clause, as in Spanish (e.g. Bejarano and Jörnving 1967: 16, *¿Cuándo van a comenzar las clases de fonética?*); for further discussion of graphological prosodies, see Sefton (1990).

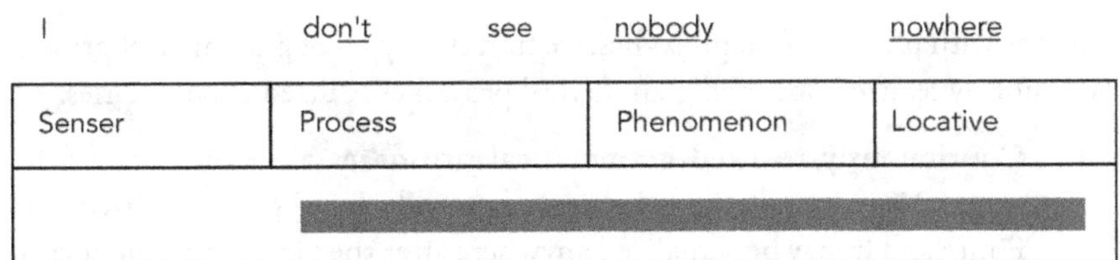

Figure 5.16 Grammatical prosody of negative polarity

If we take the phonological (or graphological) notion of a prosody as the starting point, these prosodies are all first-order prosodies: they apply to the first stratum of the linguistic system (starting "from below"). They are prosodies in the traditional sense, but we can generalize the notion of prosody (as Halliday [1979a] does) across the strata of the linguistic system so that it applies not only to phonology (graphology) but also to lexicogrammar and to semantics. This generalization is of fundamental importance for the following reason: a particular marker (such as *hal*, *ma*, *ka* etc.) may be phonologically segmental in the sense that it may consist of phonemic segments,[8] but it may still function prosodically at the stratum of lexicogrammar; and the same could be true of the relationship between lexicogrammar and semantics. We may thus recognize the following possibilities:

1. First-order or **phonological (graphological) prosody**: phonologically prosodic (as in early child language; cf. Section 5.2.1), e.g. pitch contour and punctuation marks used to express mood categories.
2. Second-order or **grammatical prosody**: phonologically segmental (i.e. with phonemic articulation), but grammatically prosodic, e.g. polarity and affect in English and mood markers in, for example, Arabic, Chinese, and Japanese.
3. Third-order or **semantic prosody**: phonologically segmental and grammatically prosodic or segmental, but prosodic at the stratum of discourse semantics. On this type, see Martin (1992a, 1992b).

The first type has already been discussed and illustrated; it is, as noted above, the traditional type of prosody. The second type, grammatical prosody, realizes interpersonal selections in the same way as phonological prosody does. Thus, *no*, *nobody*, and *nowhere* are phonologically segmental, but they can be strung out to form a grammatical prosody of negative polarity running through the experiential constituency structure, as in *I don't see **nobody nowhere***, where the negative prosody runs through Process + Phenomenon + Locative, diagrammatically as in Figure 5.16, or as in the song *She don't love me no more*.

Just as with phonological prosodies, we find two types of grammatical prosody: continuously realized ones and grammatical prosodies realized at boundaries.

1. **Continuously realized grammatical prosodies** are either potential or actual. Negative polarity is a potential prosody. It is typically realized in the Finite and it may be actualized anywhere after the Finite as the opportunity arises (i.e. in the environment of total, non-specific determination of a thing [nominal group] or a circumstance [adverbial group]). In an example such as *I don't see George in the garden* it is actualized only once, but in *I don't see **nobody nowhere*** (*I don't see anybody anywhere*), it is actualized three times. Further examples:

    "I **don't** want **never** to see him again, I **don't**." (G.B. Shaw, Pygmalion)
    "If there **wasn't no** Federal Government there **wouldn't** have been **no one** to fix up any problems that would have occurred in the community." (Student essay, quoted in Martin and Peters 1985)

Similarly, modality has to be actualized once, but the prosodic potential may be actualized again. For instance, alongside *I **might** have walked out too from all the accounts,* we could get *I think I **might perhaps** have walked out too from all the accounts*; similarly: *I shall **probably** go out to Ealing, I think.* Attitude is again the same; the prosodic realization gives it increased "amplitude":

    "**God damnation**, I'll crown that **bastard**" (CEC: A corpus of English conversation 47)
    "and I can't **bloody** remember where the address is" (CEC 267)

For a penetrating discussion of interpersonal attitudinal amplification in the nominal group, see Poynton (1996). Certain interpersonal features are typically only realized once in the clause, but their occurrence within the clause is still prosodic in the sense that their potential positions are strung out through the clause instead of being located constructively in relation to an element of the experiential constituency structure. Vocatives, for instance, have this prosodic potential:

    "In this job **Anne** we're working with silver." (Halliday 1985b)
    "Sorry to disturb you, **mum**." (G.B. Shaw, *The Devil's Disciple*)
    "**Anthony Anderson**: I arrest you in King George's name as a rebel." (G.B. Shaw, *The Devil's Disciple*)
    "I come, **sir**, on your invitation." (G.B. Shaw, *The Devil's Disciple*)

The same is true of interpersonal comments such as *unfortunately, surprisingly; honestly, frankly*: they apply to the clause as a whole, so their potential positions are strung out prosodically; cf. Section 5.2.3.

Grammatical boundary prosodies occur at the beginning or end of a clause. English does not actually make use of grammatical boundary prosodies as a mode of expression, but they are quite common across the languages of the world. They are typically interpersonal particles expressing a mood selection or some other interpersonal assessment corresponding to English modality or moodtagging, as with Japanese *ka, na,* and other clause-final particles expressing a range of interpersonal meanings including mood, modality, and attitudinal assessment (cf. S. Martin 1988: 914); Chinese *ma, ne,* and other clause-final particles realizing mood (yes/no-interrogative) and other interpersonal meanings; Arabic clause-initial *hal,* *ʔa* realizing the feature yes/no-interrogative; and French clause-initial *est-ce que* (interpreted as a particle).

Constituency in the interpersonal environment: prosodic constituency

It seems clear, then, that prosody is the favoured mode of interpersonal expression. However, outside systemic functional linguistics, systems such as polarity and modality have sometimes been interpreted in constituency terms as higher verbs (within an essentially syntactic analysis) or as higher predicates (within an essentially semantic analysis). While it is obviously possible to adopt such an approach, it fails to show how polarity and modality are different from experiential constituents such as Actor, Process, Goal, Locative, and Cause. For instance, it fails to show why polarity or modality does not enter into collocational patterns with other constituents along the same lines that Process does with participant functions such as Actor. One might argue that English grammar invites a constituency interpretation with examples such as *I don't think he's coming* as an alternative to *he's probably not coming.* However, on the one hand the relation between *I don't think* and *he's coming* is not a constituency one but rather an interdependency one (hypotactic projection, see Halliday 1985b/1994a: section 7.5) and, on the other hand, such examples have the status of being interpersonal metaphors in any case (see Halliday 1985b: section 10.4) as is indicated by the Moodtag (*I don't think he's coming, is he?*).[9]

Within systemic functional linguistics, constituency has been used in the environment of the interpersonal metafunction. Halliday (e.g. 1985b/1994a: ch. 4) has shown that the clause in English has an interpersonal structure of Mood + Residue (+ Moodtag), as in the example given in Figure 5.17.

This is a constituency structure; from an interpersonal point of view, the clause is interpreted as consisting of Mood, Residue, and Moodtag, which in turn have subconstituents (Subject, Finite, and so on). However, even if we accept Mood,

They	won't	shoot	the horses	will	they
Subject	Finite	Predicator	Complement	Finite	Subject
Mood		Residue		Moodtag	

Figure 5.17 Interpersonal constituency – the modal structure of the clause

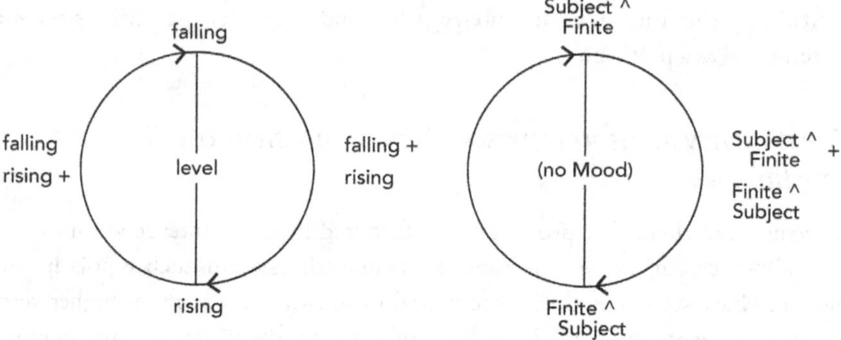

Figure 5.18 Analogy between expressive potential of pitch and Subject + Finite

Residue, and Moodtag as constituents, they differ from experiential constituents such as Actor, Process, Goal, and Cause in a number of fundamental respects; and these differences basically point towards prosodic properties. There is an important sense in which Mood, Residue, and Moodtag constitute a **constituency representation of interpersonal prosodies**. First, the combination of Mood and Moodtag achieve a prosodic effect as in the example in Figure 5.17 – *they won't … will they*; together they realize an interpersonal mood feature that characterizes the clause as a whole. Second, the internal organization of Mood and Moodtag, i.e. Subject + Finite, provide the same kind of expressive potential as pitch prosodies: there is a significant analogy between the opposition between Subject ^ Finite and Finite ^ Subject and the phonological opposition between falling and rising tone. The analogy can be brought out schematically as in Figure 5.18.

The interpersonal employment of the relative sequence of Finite and Subject is very different from the textual use of sequence as a way of achieving thematic prominence (see Section 5.3.3); this is an instance of the general principle that the metafunctions use realizational categories such as sequence ("word order") and "case marking" in fundamentally different ways (cf. Section 5.1.1).

Third, both Mood and Moodtag on the one hand and Residue on the other can be interpreted as **prosodic domains**. Mood and Moodtag are the domains of mood person and number within the clause: *he is … isn't he*; *I am … aren't I*; *they were … weren't they*. These are normally thought of as agreement or concord between Subject and Finite; but alternatively, they can simply be analysed as person and number prosodies as already suggested in Section 5.2.3 (Figure 5.9). Similarly, within Residue, reflexivization also seems to work as a prosody. Whenever appropriate, a constituent following the interpersonal function Subject of a clause is marked for identity of reference:

> [Mood:] ***Henry*** *would* [Residue:] *talk about **himself** to **himself** often in those days of intense loneliness.*

The particular value in the transitivity structure of the constituent reflexivized (Goal, Actor, Recipient, etc.) does not matter; what matters is whether the reflexive prosody runs through it or not and whether it can expound the reflexive prosody or not.[10] In this respect, it is like the prosodic potential of negative polarity in English.

We are now at a point where it's possible to suggest a prosodic re-interpretation of Subject – or at least a partial re-interpretation. Interpreted abstractly, the Subject is arguably a feature of the clause as a whole. This is very clearly the case with imperative clauses: the category imperative itself means that modal responsibility rests with the interactants (the addressee by default, but possibly the speaker instead or both together). We can also see evidence of this with indicative clauses. An indicative clause may realize an offer or a command. This speech functional value is a semantic feature of the clause as a whole and it typically means that the clause's modal responsibility is interactant (declarative: *I can*; *you should*; interrogative: *shall I*; *could you*). Furthermore, the traditional notion of Subject number and person is, as already suggested, interpretable as a prosody over Mood and Moodtag. In addition, as we have now seen, the Identity of the Subject – that is, of the modal responsibility – is a prosody of the clause as a whole, actualized first non-reflexively (within Mood) and then reflexively (within Residue) and then non-reflexively again (within Moodtag since the clause has returned to the Mood in the tag).

After this brief discussion of the interpersonal mode of expression, I will now turn to the textual metafunction.

5.3.3 Textual ⬃ wave (pulse)

The experiential metafunction is concerned with analysing out the component parts of a whole and representing them as constructional parts of this whole, and the interpersonal metafunction is concerned with assigning the clause as a whole a value in the dialogic exchange between speaker and addressee, a semantic value that pervades the clause. In contrast, the textual metafunction is concerned with giving prominence over non-prominence of experiential and textual meanings in the evolving discourse in context in which the clause occurs. We can characterize this control of prominence as foregrounding/backgrounding as long as we keep in mind that there are different kinds of grounds. Now, textual prominence is not expressed, in the first instance, through constituency or prosody.

The textual mode of expression can be characterized as a **wave** or **pulse**. Thus, the textual metafunction gives the clause a status as a "wave" in the ongoing development of text. The importance of the wave metaphor is (i) that it suggests a textual differentiation between prominence (the peak of the wave) and non-prominence (the trough), (ii) that it suggests a movement, and (iii) that it allows for the interaction of more than one wave. Like the movement of a wave, the textual metafunction is inherently dynamic. It's always in the process of creating its own history: what is the present peak will become a trough in the past-to-come.

Carriers of textual waves

The textual metafunction is **second order** in the sense that its meaning is oriented towards symbolic reality – the reality of ideational and interpersonal meanings (see further Matthiessen 1991b); it gives value to these meanings as text in context. Its mode of expression reflects its second-order status. The textual metafunction gives value to aspects of the expressive potential that are opened up by segmental and prosodic modes of organization but are not used by the experiential and interpersonal metafunctions.

The experiential metafunction creates constituency, but it does not assign any value to the relative order of the constituents; for example, Actor + Process + Goal and Goal + Process + Actor are experientially the same. This expressive potential is not taken up by the experiential metafunction, so the textual metafunction can draw on this constituency to give textual meaning to the relative ordering of the constituents (so-called "word order," which is really the order or sequence of elements of a grammatical unit).

The interpersonal metafunction creates a pitch prosody, deploying the contour of the prosody (its direction), but it does not assign any value to the location of the major pitch movement. This expressive potential is thus not taken up by the interpersonal metafunction, so the textual metafunction can draw on this prosody to give textual meaning to the placement of the major pitch movement (the tonic). The textual metafunction can thus achieve prominence through the use of

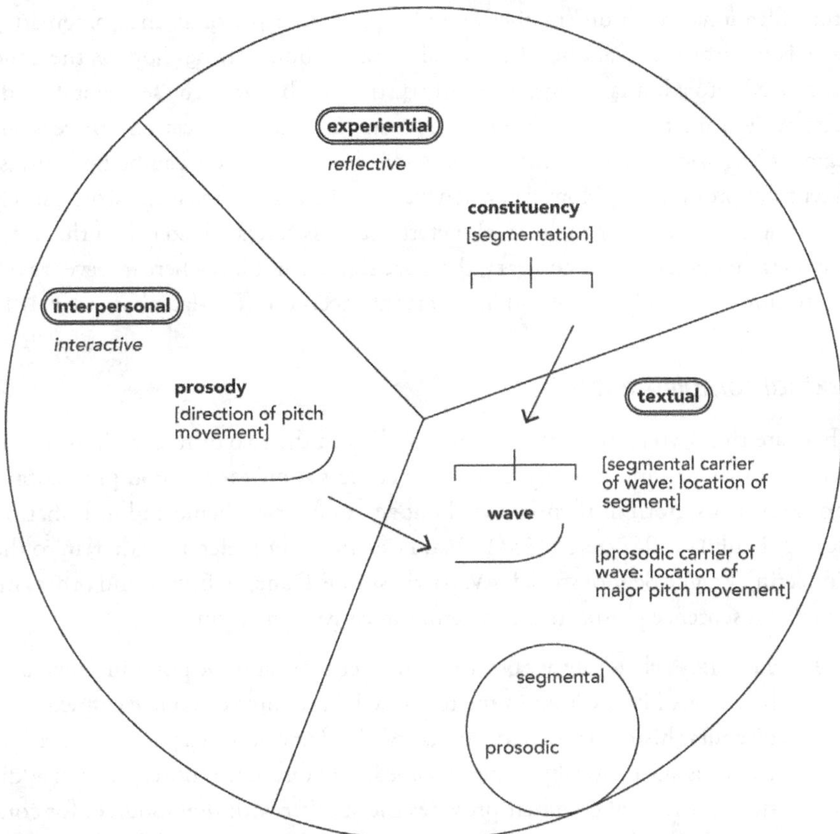

Figure 5.19 The carriers of textual waves

the experiential and interpersonal modes to create a wave-like mode of expression "carried" by constituency and prosody; the situation is diagrammed in Figure 5.19 (cf. Figure 5.1).

The textual metafunction coordinates the ideational and interpersonal metafunctions at an abstract level: it shows how both these metafunctions can be "carriers" of textual waves. This happens within the systemic part of the textual metafunction: the English voice system conflates the interpersonal Subject with one of the experiential participants.

What I have just said concerning the textual metafunction and its mode of expression might be read as a suggestion that the textual metafunction comes in later than the other two. Developmentally, as children make the transition into the mother tongue(s) spoken around them, this is probably the case: while there is a proto-ideational function (mathetic) and a proto-interpersonal one (pragmatic), there is no proto-textual one; the textual metafunction only develops as the child has moved into adult language. The early distinction between the segmental mode of expression and the prosodic one does not carry any wave implications: there is one segment (e.g. *ama*) which is also the prosodic domain, so there can be no contrast in terms of prominence. However, when we consider adult language, it would surely be wrong to suggest that the textual metafunction is activated later than the other two metafunctions; on the contrary, there are significant cases where it serves as the motivation behind ideational and interpersonal decisions (cf. Matthiessen 1991b).

Textual complementarities

There are thus two textual waves corresponding to the two different kinds of carriers, constituency and prosody. These two carriers allow for two **complementary** textual systems. Both of them are well known, of course: theme and information (see e.g. Halliday 1967/8; 1985b/1994a; Fries 1981; and references therein to the pioneering Prague School work by V. Mathesius, F. Daneš, J. Firbas, and others on functional sentence perspective and communicative dynamism).

1. THEME. A clause always occurs in some context at some point in a text; and by virtue of its location in the text it will have some discourse context – its discourse history (it may, of course, be the first clause of a particular text). It will thus automatically occur in some broad discourse context; but in addition, the textual grammar provides the speaker with the resources for contextualizing the ideational and interpersonal meanings of the clause with respect to the discoursal context in which the clause unfolds. The speaker contextualizes the clause by setting up part of the clause as its own local context or Theme.

2. INFORMATION. The textual metafunction is also concerned with what happens to the development of the clause once it has been "grounded" in the current discourse environment. More specifically, it gives the speaker the resources to direct the listener's attention to which part of the clause is **New** information rather than already given.[11] In the unmarked case (where clause and information unit are the same and New comes at the end of the information unit), the clause is characterized by two textual peaks of prominence: Theme (followed by non-prominence, Rheme) + New (preceded by non-prominence, Given) – see Halliday (1979a); *IFG* (*Introduction to functional grammar*): 316 (see *IFG*: appendix 1 for a discussion of the example in context); see Figure 5.20.

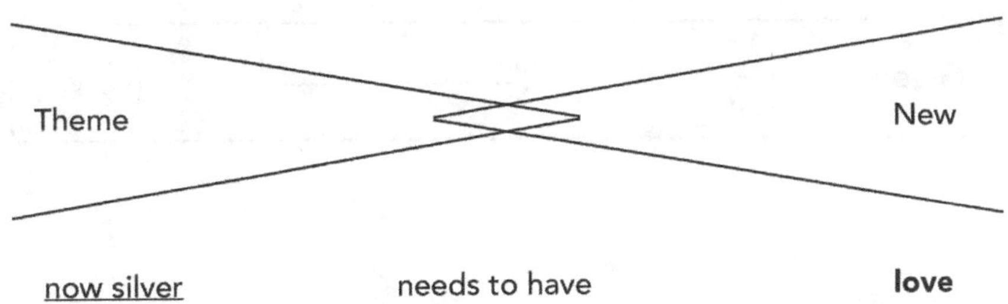

Figure 5.20 Interaction of textual waves through clause–information unit

Wavy constituency

Given a continuum between a textual peak of prominence and a trough of non-prominence, we can impose a discrete interpretation by drawing a boundary between the two at some point: we can posit two simultaneous constituency structures to interpret an example such as the one shown in Figure 5.20: Theme + Rheme and Given + New. In the case of thematic prominence, it is comparatively easy to draw the boundary, since the carrier of the wave is constituency (see Halliday 1985b/1994a: ch. 3, for the interpretation of English). In the case of new prominence, it is comparatively harder to draw the boundary between Given and New, since the carrier of the wave is not constituency but prosody. Consequently, the boundary between Given and New is more indeterminate (Halliday 1985b/1994a: 275).[12] (Identifying the end of the New is not a problem since it coincides with the end of the intonational or tonic prominence.) A constituency interpretation of the clause *now silver needs to have love* is given in Figure 5.21.

The leftward arrow pointing from New to Given is Halliday's way of indicating that the boundary between Given and New is indeterminate. In an example such as *now silver needs to have love*, the assignment of the thematic constituents Theme + Rheme may seem quite straightforward; but the picture is less clear when there are multiple elements as in *however, last week he decided to quit; however, last week, unfortunately, he decided to quit; last week, however, he decided to quit.*

The textual structures Theme + Rheme and Given + New **simulate** the wave mode in constituency terms. However, these structures are still separated as layers from the experiential transitivity structure of the clause. Consequently, the Theme + Rheme and Given + New structures are fundamentally different from any constituency analysis that locates textual constituents within the same constituency hierarchy as the experiential constituents. In particular, formal grammars often operate with a COMP element that may correspond to (part of) Theme, and this element is located within the overall formal constituency structure (for example

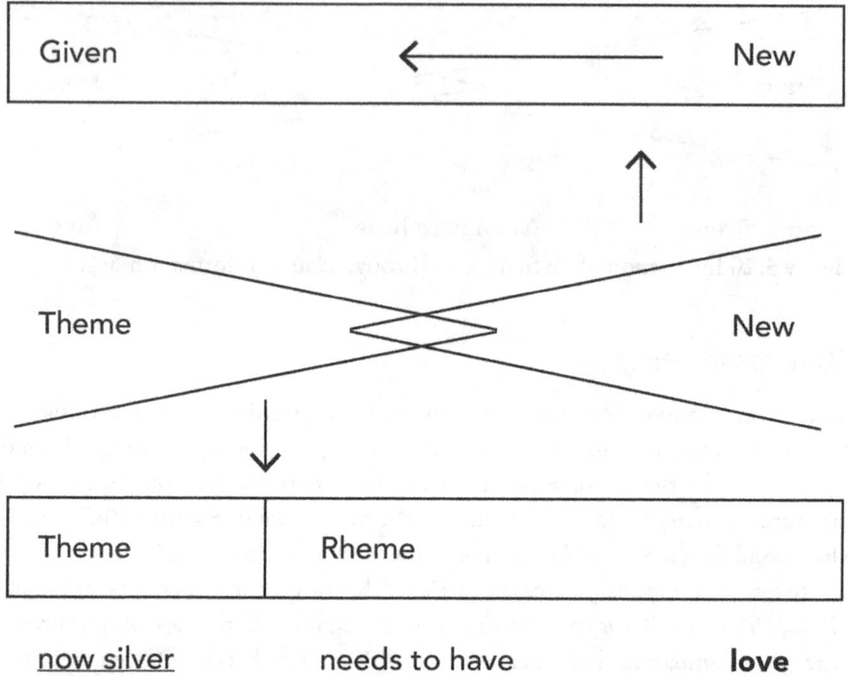

Figure 5.21 Wave continuum interpreted as constituency discreteness

as S-bar: COMP + S). This does not predict that the relationship between, say, COMP and S is radically different from the relationship between, say, V and NP; but the functionally different structures of, say, Theme + Rheme and Process + Goal show this difference.

5.4 Combining the metafunctional perspectives: complementarity and resonance

In the last section I reviewed and elaborated on Halliday's (1979a) presentation of his theory of metafunctional modes and tried to show that the metafunctions create different kinds of meaning and deploy different modes of expression. It is to a large extent because of this difference that they can be teased apart and maintained as separate but simultaneous resources within the linguistic system – separate and simultaneous, so largely independently variable. But having separated out the metafunctions *analytically*, we can then go on to ask first how they **complement** one another in the linguistic system by providing fundamentally different perspectives and second how they **resonate** with one another by showing the same picture in different metafunctional perspectives – or, at least, compatible pictures.

I will begin by looking at the complementarity and resonance of the textual and interpersonal metafunctions (Section 5.4.1) and then at the complementarity and resonance of the textual and experiential metafunctions (Section 5.4.2). I will explore resonance a bit further in Section 5.5.

5.4.1 Textual + interpersonal

Textual and interpersonal meanings are quite different. While the textual metafunction is concerned with creating differences within a clause (or other grammatical units) in terms of degrees of textual prominence, the interpersonal metafunction deals with meanings that pervade the whole domain they are assigned to. The difference between the textual wave and the interpersonal prosody is thus entirely motivated. It is manifested very clearly in the different ways in which the two metafunctions employ intonation and sequence in English.

1. Intonation. The interpersonal metafunction uses intonation as an overall contour, i.e. the direction of the pitch movement; that is, it uses intonation as a prosody. Although there is one major pitch movement, the movement within the tonic, the movement within the pretonic is also significant (Halliday 1967). In contrast, the textual metafunction uses only the salient or prominent part of the intonation contour, more specifically the location of the major pitch movement, and it is not concerned with the direction of the pitch movement. In other words, the textual metafunction uses intonation as a wave, with the major pitch movement as the peak of prominence.

2. Sequence. The interpersonal metafunction uses sequence very specifically in English: it contrasts the relative sequence of Subject and Finite, achieving the same kind of expressive potential as the basic opposition between falling and rising pitch (see Section 5.3.2). In other words, it employs sequence as a prosody. In contrast, the textual metafunction does not manipulate the relative sequence of two elements to create an opposition such as falling vs. rising; instead, it uses the linear unfolding of the clause as an expression of a move from textual prominence to textual non-prominence. In other words, it employs sequence as a wave (peak followed by trough). Once we have recognized the difference between sequence as prosody (interpersonal, realizing mood) and sequence as wave (textual, realizing theme), we can predict that alternative "codings" for mood and theme will be different across languages and that the differences will be precisely along the lines of prosody and wave. Thus, alternatives in languages other than English to the prosodic use of the relative sequence of Subject and Finite include pitch contour

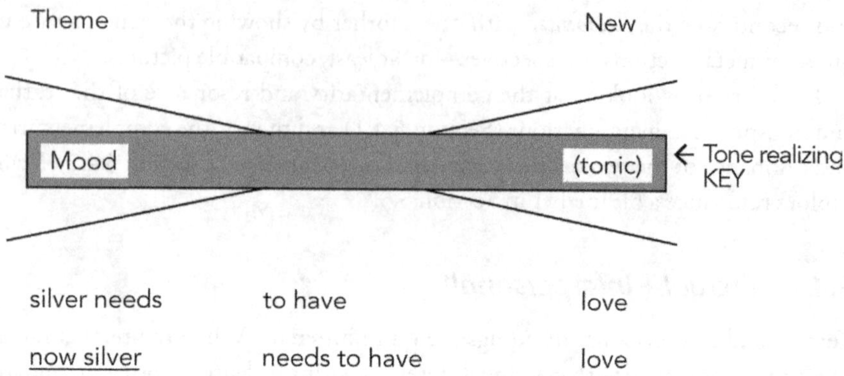

Figure 5.22 Interpersonal prosody and textual wave together

and clause-initial or final mood particles, both of which are prosodies, while alternatives to the wave use of sequence include markers of the thematic peak such as Japanese *wa* and Tagalog *ang*.

Now, while the textual and interpersonal modes complement one another as different modes of organization, they also **resonate**: they are mapped onto one another in a motivated way. In the English clause, the selection of unmarked Theme gives the key to the MOOD selection; the Theme is one or more elements of the Mood (see Halliday 1985b/1994a: section 3.3). There is a similar association between INFORMATION and the delicate MOOD systems known as KEY: the major pitch movement in the tone group realizes the "primary" key of the information unit, and as the tonic it is also the focus of the New within the information structure. In the unmarked case, this can be schematized as in Figure 5.22.

While THEME and INFORMATION are independent systems and create two different kinds of textual prominence, MOOD and KEY are really different aspects of the same system, KEY simply being the more delicate MOOD systems realized by intonation in spoken English, and together they create an interpersonal prosody throughout the clause/information unit. MOOD is realized through the Mood element (Subject, Finite), part of which falls within the first textual prominence, Theme; KEY is realized as an intonation contour, a tone, that extends throughout the information unit, but the major movement in pitch realizing the primary selection in KEY coincides with the focus of the second textual prominence, New. Consequently, interpersonal meaning in the clause is both the textual point of departure of the clause/information unit and its textual destination: as the speaker starts, they indicate their interpersonal angle on the information, and as they come to the end (where the addressee may take over as speaker), they indicate

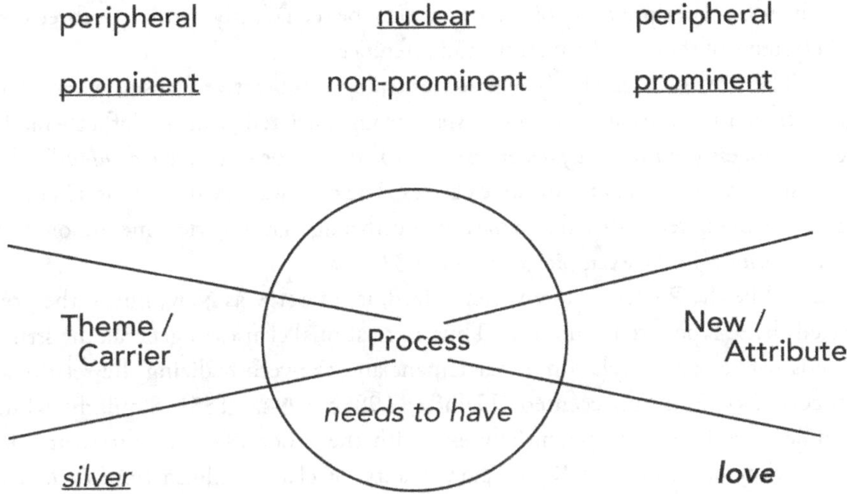

Figure 5.23 Experiential "centrality" (nuclearity) superimposed on textual "centrality" (prominence)

their interpersonal angle again. This may also happen through MOOD TAG, with a Moodtag right at the end of the clause, picking up the Mood from the beginning of the clause.

5.4.2 *Textual + experiential*

We have seen that there are two peaks of textual prominence in the unmarked mapping of clause to information unit, Theme (within Given) + New (within Rheme). In the experiential structure of the clause, its transitivity structure, the Process is typically taken as the nuclear part in which participants and circumstances are more or less centrally involved (see Figure 5.6 above); but in textual terms, it is very often background; it falls *between* the two peaks of textual prominence, between Theme and New. These two peaks are selected from the less nuclear elements of the transitivity structure, from participants and circumstances. The textual view of the clause is thus quite different from the experiential one: what looks "peripheral" from an experiential point of view is prominent from a textual point of view; and what is most nuclear from an experiential point of view, the Process, is often non-prominent. Thus, we can superimpose the two views of the clause to bring out the complementarity of textual and experiential centrality as shown in Figure 5.23.

The textual peripherality of the Process can be seen clearly within the three textual systems of theme, information, and reference.

1. The Process is rarely thematized outside of imperative clauses, where it is given thematic status as Predicator. Apart from restricted examples of a thematic verbal process (*Insisted the former Prime Minister: "The cases are ridiculous"*), the Process is not thematic in indicative clauses. The only way it can serve as Theme is in fact by being reconstrued as a participant through grammatical metaphor as in *his withdrawal* in the example given under 3 below.

2. While the Process is rarely thematized, it can serve as New; but in the preferred clause type it tends not to.[13] Thus, in relational clauses in general, the structure is participant + relation + participant and the verb realizing the relational process is typically unaccented (Halliday 1985b/1994a: 155). Similarly, while middle material clauses potentially end with the Process (as in *he showered, he erred*), they often develop Range participants for clausal culmination: *he took a shower* rather than *he showered, he made a mistake* rather than *he erred*. (Compare also the English model of ascription, where the quality being ascribed to a carrier is construed not as a Process but as a participant-like Attribute (Range): *one glass is enough* rather than the rather rare type *one glass suffices*, which is the norm in many other languages.)

3. Another indication of non-prominent status of the Process within the textual metafunction is that the verbal group realizing it has not evolved the kind of determination system the nominal group has evolved for "tracking" referents in (and around) a discourse. That can only be achieved by reconstruing the process as a participant through grammatical metaphor:

> *If it appears that Saddam will be forced out of Kuwait,*
> *his withdrawal – and his continuation in office – will have to be coupled*
> *with arrangements to guarantee the security of the region.* (Time)

It is important to emphasize the complementarity of the textual and experiential perspectives on the clause. The textual metafunction tends to get marginalized in linguistics (relegated to the experiential periphery, as it were) because of the experiential bias in much linguistic theorizing; thus, Themes are often said to be peripheral, marginal, or external to the (experiential) nucleus or centre of the clause. But from a textual point of view, they are anything but peripheral; they are central and it is the Process that is "peripheral" – a transition between the textual peaks of prominence. And we need this textual perspective to be able to explain many of the properties of the clause in English, and in other languages.

In the typical clause the experiential and textual metafunctions thus complement one another in their different centralities. But at the same time this

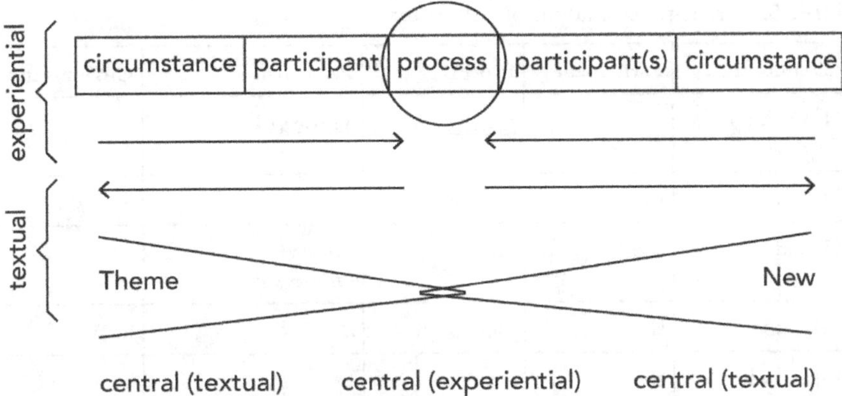

Figure 5.24 Centrality throughout the clause

complementarity is also a kind of harmony: the experiential and textual metafunctions alternate in centrality throughout the clause as diagrammed in Figure 5.24.[14]

Here are some examples (taken from CEC; Theme underlined and tonic constituent in bold):

||| <u>On the twentieth</u> I stayed up in Madison for **Christmas** // ||
   the **<u>twenty-fifth</u>** // I flew to San **Francisco.** // |||
||| <u>At AC</u> // I used to work, <u>I</u> wanted to work **on Sundays** // || to finish my **thesis** // || <u>and in bank **holidays**</u> // I used to borrow Mike
   Barrett's key // |||

That is, the experientially nuclear Process is likely to be textually non-prominent (not thematic, probably not the focus of newsworthiness [although it certainly can be the focus of the New information; see e.g. Halliday 1985b/1994a: 185–6], and not recoverable through reference) while the less nuclear participants and circumstances preceding and following it are likely to fall within the textual prominences of thematicity and newsworthiness.

So far we have considered the resonance between the experiential and the textual metafunctions in terms of the organization of a single clause. We can now add one more textual system, REFERENCE, and add the dimension of discourse time to see what happens in successive clauses. Let's start with a short text written by a child, taken from Hasan's discussion of cohesive harmony in Halliday and Hasan (1985). The experiential organization set out in Table 5.1 is the same as what we have already encountered: each clause consists of a nuclear process (double underlining), one or more participants involved in it (single underlining), and possibly

Table 5.1 Transitivity analysis of a short text

Circumstance	Participant	Process	Participant	Circumstance
[1] Once upon a time		<u>there was</u>	**<u>a little girl</u>**	
[2] and	<u>**she**</u>	went out		<u>for a walk</u>
[3] and	**she**	saw	*a lovely little teddybear*	
[4] and so	**she**	took	*it*	home
[5] and when	**she**	got		home
[6]	**she**	washed	*it*	
[7] and when	**she**	took	*it*	to bed with her
[8]	**she**	cuddled	*it*	
[9] and	**she**	fell	straight to sleep	
[10] and when	**she**	got up		
[11] and	**0**	combed	*it*	with a little wirebrush
[12]	*the teddybear*	opened	*his* eyes	
[13] and	0	started to speak	to **her**	
[14] and	**she**	had	*the teddybear*	for many weeks and years
[15] and so when	*the teddybear*	got	dirty	
[16]	**she**	used to wash	*it*	
[17] and every time	**she**	brushed	*it*	
[18]	**it**	used to say	some new words from a different country	
[19] and that's how	**she**	used to know how to speak	English, Scottish and all the rest	

associated circumstances (dotted underlining); elements that are not part of the experiential transitivity structure are not underlined:

From a textual point of view, reference resonates very clearly with the experiential organization. There are two reference chains running through the text, 'the girl' (in bold) and 'the teddy bear' (in italics). They run through the participants, but not, of course, the processes and not the circumstances either (with the exception of the Accompaniment *with her* in [7]). Circumstances are textually prominent as Theme (*Once upon a time* in [1]) or prominent as the last part of the New (*for a walk, home, to bed with her, with a little wirebrush, for many weeks and years*); but once they have been introduced to provide a thematic context or to give some new information, they do not tend to get picked up referentially. In other words, the participants construe referents that have a good deal of textual staying power, but the circumstances don't. That is, in addition to being stable through experiential time, participants are also stable through textual time: the two time perspectives resonate with one another. Furthermore, as Hasan (1984a) has shown, the participatory relationships construed by the experiential metafunction between the referents also tend to be stable through a text (segment). Thus, the favourite clause types in the little narrative above can be diagrammed as in Figure 5.25 in decreasing ordering of frequency (where each line connecting the constituents indicates one occurrence):

A single short text such as the one given above can of course only illustrate the resonance; but the general picture can be confirmed by more extensive text counts, which would also show that all participant types haven't got the same staying power in text.

We have seen, then, that participants tend to be textually prominent – thematically, as news or by virtue of textual staying power – whereas the process tends not to be. The textual prominence of participants and non-prominence of the process is particularly true of one of the favourite relational clause structures of English transitivity: Identified + Process + Identifier.[15] The experiential metafunction sets up a textually transparent structure, where the Identified is the Theme and the Identifier is the New (cf. Halliday 1985b/1994a: 41–4):

What the surgeon doesn't really consider	*is*	*the etiology of the cyst*
Identified	Proc.	Identifier
Theme		New

Here the Process is only a linking relation. The two participants, Identified and Identifier, illustrate how the experiential metafunction can harmonize with

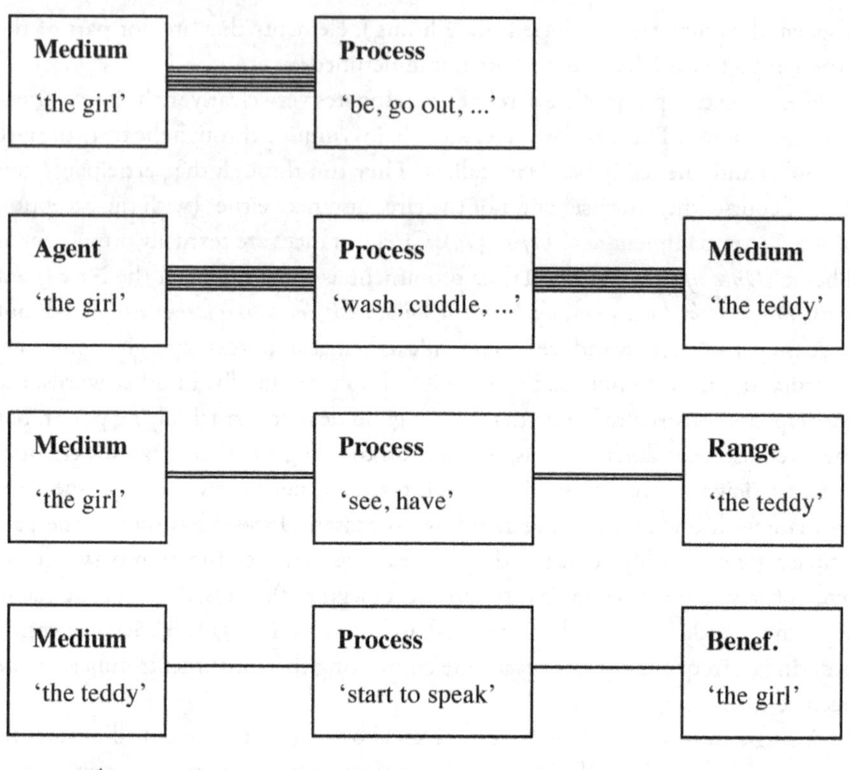

Figure 5.25 Favourite clause types (transitivity configurations) in terms of frequency

the textual one, creating a particular constituency structure, Identified + Process + Identifier, that can serve textual purposes. The example is, of course, a variant of *The surgeon doesn't really consider the etiology of the cyst*, which is different both experientially and textually from the first example. It is not structured as an identifying clause and the thematic element is different – *the surgeon* rather than *what he doesn't consider*. The experiential metafunction opens up the variation through clausal nominalization, *what the surgeon doesn't really consider*; and the textual metafunction motivates this experiential construction. In other words, to make *the surgeon doesn't really consider* thematic (textual), the grammar nominalizes it as a clause serving in an identifying clause (experiential). This illustrates both the way in which the two metafunctions harmonize within one another and how the textual metafunction can use one of the other metafunctions as a "carrier." This construction also allows us to return to the earlier point that the second-order nature of the textual metafunction does not mean that it is temporally or causally ordered

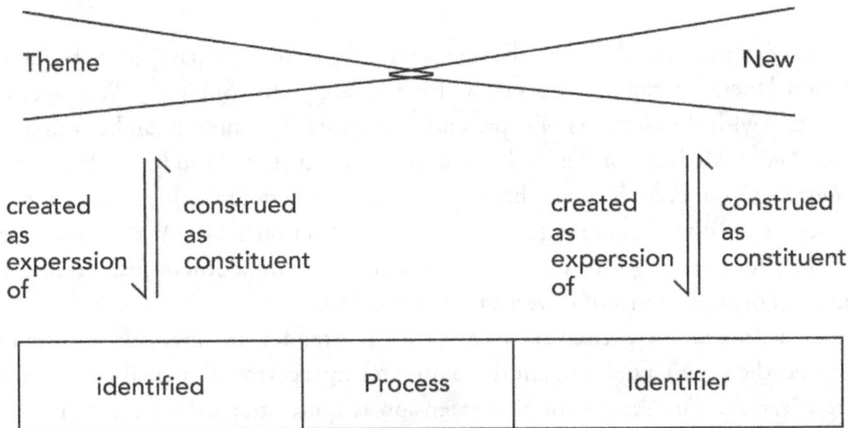

Figure 5.26 Textual wave motivating and construed by experiential constituency

after the other two metafunctions: they can be organized as means to serve textual ends. At the same time, the experiential metafunction construes both Theme and New as constituents, as Identified and Identifier: see Figure 5.26.

The clausal nominalization in this type of construction is one type of grammatical metaphor; nominalization may also occur at lower ranks, as illustrated in the example under 3. above: *his withdrawal – and his continuation in office – will have to be coupled with arrangements to guarantee the security of the region*. Halliday (1988b/2004c) has shown how this type of ideational metaphor has developed as powerful textual resource in scientific English; it makes it possible to group thematic and new information very clearly in written discourse.

Grammatical metaphor of the type just mentioned can be interpreted, then, as a resource for achieving experiential and textual resonance: there is a congruent experiential organization of the clause (*the surgeon doesn't really consider the etiology of the cyst; he withdrew and continued in office*) that does not achieve textual organization appropriate to the occasion; but alongside it there is another metaphorical experiential organization that embodies a constituent structure that resonates with the textual metafunction. It is this metaphorical structure that "carries" the textual values appropriate to the occasion. In other words, from the point of view of the textual metafunction, an alternative constituent carrier of the textual wave is created through grammatical metaphor.

5.5   Modes of expression extending across metafunctions

The fact that the different metafunctions favour different modes of expression does not mean, of course, that a given metafunction cannot possibly draw on a mode of expression other than the one it typically favours. In particular, the interpersonal metafunction may operate with a function such as Subject or Wh that can interface with the elements of experiential structure (i.e. Subject can be conflated with Agent, Medium, or Beneficiary) or "segments" like the Moodtag in Figure 5.7 (*don't they*), but even these may have a prosodic interpretation rather than a primarily segmental one as I have suggested for Subject (Section 5.3.2). At the same time, it is easy for us as linguists to misrepresent a given metafunction by interpreting its mode of organization as if it were of a different kind.

Constituency in particular is likely to be extended in linguistic theorizing beyond the experiential domain to be used for interpersonal, textual, and logical organization. The reason for this extension is quite straightforward. Since the experiential metafunction is the resource for construing our experience of the world, it stands to reason that we apply it as linguists also to the "reality" created by language, even to interpersonal and textual reality. Again, this is not to suggest that experiential constituency is extended to the other metafunctions only in our metalanguage, in our language about language. It happens in language as well; but there is a very significant property of such extensions: they essentially always seem to be metaphorical. Thus, as we have seen, experiential constituency bracketing such as Identified + Process + Identifier comes to stand for textual organization through grammatical metaphor. Let me give a few additional examples of this principle (thematic participant underlined; culmination of news in bold):

> (i) material: Actor + Process + **Range**
> *Poirot made **an unsuccessful attempt to look modest***
> (: *Poirot attempted unsuccessfully to look **modest***)
> (ii) mental: perceptive: Senser + Process + **Phenomenon**
> *The seventies saw **a massive outpouring of political sentiment on both the right and the left.***
> (: *In the seventies political sentiment on both the right and the left poured out **in great quantity***)

The agnate more congruent versions are given in parentheses; as can be seen very clearly, they have different textual structures. The second more congruent version is, of course, still metaphorical. These examples and the ones given in Section 5.3.2 illustrate how the experiential mode of organization comes to serve textually through grammatical metaphor. The same principle that grammatical metaphor expands the grammatical resources so that one metafunctional mode can come to express meanings from another metafunction applies to the interpersonal metafunction as well. However, here it is primarily the logical subtype of the ideational metafunction rather than the experiential one that is involved. More specifically, logical projection can come to express mood or modality; one clause projects an interpersonal value onto another clause:

> **Shouldn't think** → *he had much time left*
> (: *He **probably didn't** have much time left*)

This has the effect of assigning a prosody to the whole clause *he had much time left*: the modality and polarity are projected onto the clause as a whole. Indeed, the metaphorical realization of modality may work together with congruent realizations to form prosodies (cf. Section 5.3.2):

> **I think probably** *there **might** be lots of copies of texts.*

There is a crucial conclusion to be drawn from the observation that the grammar itself uses the ideational, segmental modes of organization for interpersonal and textual meanings primarily in the context of grammatical metaphor: if we adopt constituency (or interdependency, for that matter) as the only mode of interpretation in our metalanguages, this will obscure a very fundamental semogenic strategy of the linguistic system itself.

I have indicated a number of particular constituency analyses where I believe there is good reason to explore one or other of the non-constituency modes of organization (Sections 5.3 and 5.4). To sum up, Table 5.2 lists these examples of "over-extended" constituency and adds a few more.

5.6   Conclusion

We have seen that the metafunctions embody very different modes of meaning – very different principles of semantic organization, and that their modes of expression also differ quite fundamentally. Thus, while both the experiential and textual metafunctions embody a kind of "centrality," experiential centrality (nuclearity) and textual centrality (prominence) are quite distinct and organize the clause in complementary ways; and the interpersonal metafunction differs from both in that it operates with a continuity or colouring of meaning throughout the clause rather than centrality, expressed prosodically. At the same time there is a general sense in which the metafunctional complementarities also constitute a "conspiracy" to achieve a harmonious organization of the clause where one metafunctional perspective harmonizes or resonates with another. Thus, a constituency configuration such as Identified + Process + Identifier or Actor + Process + Range is a representation of experience, but it is also a potentiality for a textual distribution

Table 5.2 Constituency as "over-extended" default model vs. multifunctional model with different modes of expression

Constituency (typically formal) and afunctional	Pluri-modal (functional) and plurifunctional
NP+VP (traditionally: Subject + Predicative); S-bar: COMPL + S	textual: Theme + Rheme (simulated wave) and interpersonal: Mood + Residue (simulated prosodic)
hierarchic depth in constituency (as in modification)	logical: interdependency ordering (as in modification)
X-bar	logical: interdependency (particulate)
S-Adverbial vs. VP-adverbial	interpersonal Adjunct as prosody vs. experiential Adjunct (particulate)
higher verb/predicate (as with modality and polarity)	interpersonal: modality and polarity as prosody
dominate; command; c-command; etc.	–
nucleus – periphery	experiential: nucleus – periphery (particulate) interpersonal: prosodic textual: peak – trough – peak (wave)

of information into Theme + New (see Section 5.4.2). Or, to take another example of such a metafunctional conspiracy, experiential agency-volitionality, interpersonal modal responsibility, and textual thematicity (or topicality in this environment) may harmonize with one another within the same element of the clause. It is precisely because the metafunctions are separate principles that such resonance is meaningful and worth exploring. Similarly, when we consider the relationship between the textual and interpersonal metafunctions, we find that they are coordinated in such a way that the textual metafunction makes interpersonal selections prominent in two ways in the typical clause (see Section 5.4.1).

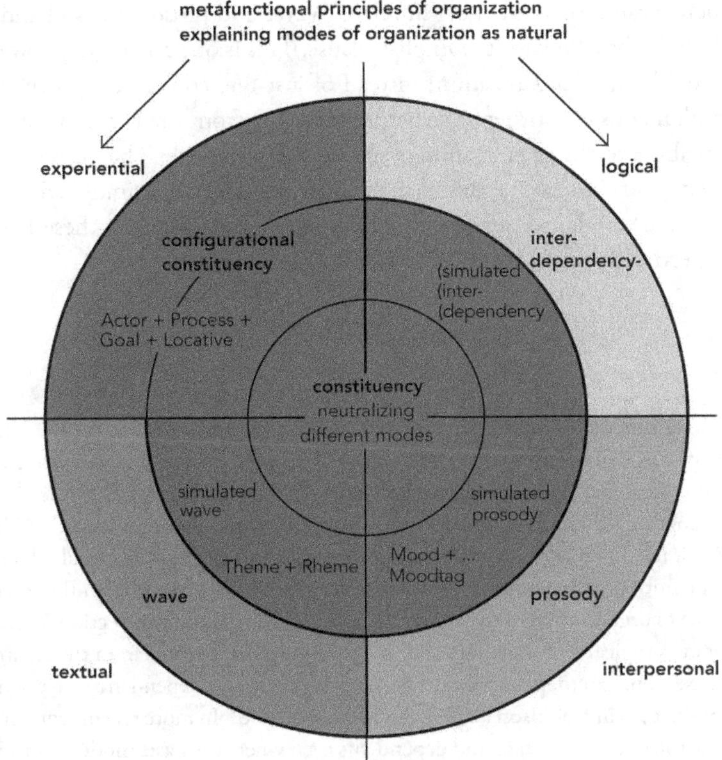

Figure 5.27 Cline between neutralizing constituency and diversified metafunctional modes

I began by identifying the thesis that syntagmatic organization in grammar is mono-modal – constituency. This mode neutralizes the different modes of meaning; it is not possible to derive the different metafunctional contributions to the organization of the clause from a single constituency structure. I contrasted this thesis with its antithesis: there are different modes of meaning, each of which engenders a different mode of expression. This antithesis differs from the thesis not only in that it assumes different modes of syntagmatic organization; it also expands the conception of grammatical organization up to the point where it makes contact with the metafunctions as explanatory principles – grammatical structure is no longer insulated from its semiotic environment as an autonomous construct. I have tried to diagram this difference in the scope of grammar between the thesis and the antithesis in Figure 5.27.

The semantically based functionality of the linguistic system "collapses" in the innermost circle of constituency as the only mode of syntagmatic organization; but constituency can be extended to "simulate" waves and prosodies, as Halliday (e.g. 1985b/1994a) has done for the English clause. This is one crucial step towards the multimodal kind of organization; instead of just one constituency structure, we find simultaneous constituency structures deriving from the three metafunctions that contribute to the organization of the clause in English. The non-experiential constituency structures are simulated waves (textual) and simulated prosodies (interpersonal), and, as I suggested in Sections 5.3.2 and 5.3.3, these have their own properties as constituency representations.

Notes

1   Any given theory that operates with constituency may not, of course, emphasize the diversification of meaning into different modes; and if it does not, the single mode of syntagmatic organization may indeed seem more plausible. But nowadays it is fairly common to recognize different modes of meaning, whether this account is based on Halliday's (1967/8) pioneering work on metafunctions or some more recent functional scheme.

2   The notion of dependency in dependency theory is different from the interdependency mode of organization of the logical metafunction mentioned in Section 5.2.2. Briefly, dependency is typically multivariate and valency bound (in particular, in the environment of the clause), but interdependency is not. Constituency and dependency have sometimes been combined, as in Robinson (1970) and Hudson (1976). In more recent work, it is common to use the notions of heads and dependents even where the basic mode of organization is constituency; they have, for instance, often been used in typological "word order" studies.

3   This is not to suggest that children stop gesturing in a meaningful way. Rather, vocalization was taken up as the specifically linguistic mode of expression, freeing gestures for another semiotic system. The limiting case of different modes of meaning and expression within one semiotic system can be said to be the bifurcation into two distinct but coordinated semiotic systems.

4   Drawing on Halliday (1979a), McGregor (1990) has proposed a set of correlations that is related but different in certain significant ways. I still prefer the position taken in Matthiessen (1989), first presented at the Systemic Workshop in Ann Arbor, Michigan 1985; but it will not be possible to compare the different proposals here.

5   It is not possible to compare Halliday's metafunctions with other functional frameworks here; for some brief comparisons see e.g. Halliday and Hasan (1985); Matthiessen (1991a). The characterizations given below are not definitions of the metafunctions: as theoretical constructs, they can only be defined in terms of their location in the overall theory of language in context (cf. Halliday 1978, in particular p. 131) – by reference to stratification, internal organization as system, modes of realization, and so on. This multiple accountability of the metafunctions (or any other theoretical construct for that matter) is absolutely crucial in a theory of language in context as a multidimensional semiotic space.

6　Both participants and circumstances have been discussed extensively in terms of (deep) cases in linguistics and computational linguistics, but usually without a distinction between the two. The process is typically not given a deep case.

7　Except that the difference between the experiential and logical modes is not brought out as clearly as when constituency is used to interpret experiential organization; but experiential dependency would still contrast with logical interdependency (in particular in the environment of the clause).

8　Though it may still have prosodic characteristics relative to the phonological system as a whole.

9　If we take the notion of prosody as the point of departure in reasoning about the expression of interpersonal meanings, we can see that a construction such as *I don't think —> he's coming* is the ideational metafunction's way of achieving a prosodic effect. Positioned like a juncture prosody, a clause projects an interpersonal value (modality, polarity) onto another clause as a whole. Indeed, we find this strategy taken up regularly in certain languages – for modality in Tagalog (Martin 1990) and for negative polarity in Tongan (what Payne 1986 calls higher negative verbs and notes is typical of languages in the Polynesian area).

10　The prosody affects elements of the clause. There are certain conditions under which it may go "beyond" the clause and affect subelements such as the Qualifier of a nominal group (*Henry keeps pictures of himself all around the house*); but these are motivated departure from the general principle that the clause is the relevant unit. For a discussion of comparable textual departures from this principle, see Matthiessen (1991b). In addition, nominal groups may also be the domain of reflexive prosodies; for instance: *Henry's picture of himself.*

11　To be more accurate, this should be stated in terms of the information unit; it is coextensive with the clause in the unmarked case but only in the unmarked case.

12　Even here constituency does play a role. The intonational prominence achieved through the major pitch movement takes place within one syllable, the tonic syllable, but as we move up one stratum from phonology to lexicogrammar, this translates into a grammatical constituent: in the unmarked case, the New includes at least that grammatical constituent within which the tonic syllable falls.

13　In spoken English in particular, though, the Process is often realized by a phrasal verb, which makes it possible for part of the Process to come in the unmarked position of new information after a non-subject participant (see Halliday 1985b/1994a), as with *note down* in *well, I have noted him **down***.

14　If a circumstance is thematic, the clause is in fact likely to be chunked into two units of information, one corresponding to the thematic circumstance and one to the rest.

15　It is a particular subtype of the relational clause type. One property of relational clauses in general is that the verb realizing the Process tends to be unaccented (see Halliday 1985b/1994a: 155), i.e. phonologically non-prominent. The limiting case is a clause without a Process, which is quite common in relational clauses across languages.

Chapter 6

Fuzziness construed in language: a linguistic perspective

6.1   The pervasiveness of fuzzy classes

Zadeh (1972/1987: 467–8) has suggested that fuzziness is a central property of human cognition:

> Fuzziness plays an essential role in human cognition because most of the classes encountered in the real world are fuzzy – some only slightly and some markedly so. The pervasiveness of fuzziness in human thought processes suggests that much of the logic behind human reasoning is not the traditional two-valued or even multi-valued logic, but a logic with fuzzy truths, fuzzy connectives and fuzzy roles of inference. Indeed, it may be argued that it is the ability of the human brain to manipulate fuzzy concepts that distinguishes human intelligence from machine intelligence.

If we take a constructivist view of the role of language in relation to human thinking, we can interpret Zadeh's insight as follows (cf. Halliday and Matthiessen 1999). Human beings experience the world around them and inside them as non-discrete. This experience does not come in the form of ready-made classes (or categories) to be named by language; rather, the experience is construed by language as meaning organized into networks of fuzzy classes.[1] These networks of fuzzy classes of meaning construe our experience of a non-discrete world. What Zadeh calls "human thought" is thus essentially experience construed as meaning, and processes of cognition are semantic processes. Fuzziness is thus constructed by language as an essential property of how we construe – how we interpret and represent – our experience of the world.

Now, if we view language in the way that generative linguistics has done since the 1950s as a set of rules for defining linguistic structures, then the insight that language construes our experience of a non-discrete world as fuzzy classes of meaning does not seem very central to the organization of language itself. Our attention is likely to be restricted to those aspects of language that are concerned with the category of fuzziness itself – "hedges" (*very, more or less, essentially, slightly* etc.), "scalar adjectives" (*tall, fat, jolly* etc.) "fuzzy quantifiers" (*all, few, a few, lots of, many* etc.), and the like (cf. again Zadeh 1972, McCawley 1993: ch. 13, esp. pp. 468–78[2] and the work derived from generative semantics in the late 1960s and early 1970s) or to classes of entities (such as birds and cups) in the work by Rosch, Labov, and others. Even in more recent work on "categorization" (e.g. Lakoff 1987; Taylor 1989), categorization has tended to remain a special concern rather than a primary principle of linguistic organization.

However, if we take a broader view of language, we will be able to see that the structures that generative linguistics has focussed on are in fact a "secondary" kind of organization. Together with other tactic resources (e.g. intonation) they serve to realize the classes and combinations of classes of meaning that constitute the primary mode of organization of language. Indeed, language is centrally concerned with construing classes. This point has recently been argued very persuasively by Ellis (1993: 27–44), particularly in the chapter "The heart of language: categorization":

> Categorization, not syntax, is the most basic aspect of language, and it is a process that must be understood correctly if anything else (including syntax) is to be understood; and categorization, not communication, is the most important function of language, one that is prior to all others ... Every language is a particular system of categorization ... If situations themselves present a limitless variety, a language can only have a finite set of categories. It follows that language functions as the instrument of human knowledge and communication only because it simplifies the complexity of experience by reducing an infinite variety to a finite set of categories. This simplification is the central fact and process of categorization, and thus the central fact of language and the knowledge it affords us of our world. For communication to be possible, then, there must have been a considerable degree of processing of experience – of analyzing it, abstracting from it, focusing and shaping it. It is in this complex process that the essence of language is to be found, not in communication per se. ... what is communicated is not the facts of the situation merely in itself (again, that is an impossible notion) but the place of that situation within the set of categories of the language.

Why should language be centrally concerned with classification? The reason is that language is, among other things, a **resource** for construing human experience, and as a resource its fundamental organization is that of a network of options in construing experience, where each option constitutes a class. That is, a central aspect of construing experience as meaning in language is to impose a classificatory order, where phenomena that are not alike can be construed as alike by being assigned to a class in the network of classes.

Since the primary mode of linguistic organization is that of a network of options – a network for imposing classificatory order on our experience, it follows that fuzziness is also a central property of the primary mode of organization. That is, it is not confined to those systems of language that are explicitly concerned with fuzziness as an aspect of our experience nor to taxonomies of entities, but rather it is inherent in the primary mode of organization that has evolved as a resource for construing all experience – that is, in the network of options.

Why should the classes of meaning construed by language be inherently fuzzy? There appear to be several reasons. One is that this is the central way of construing our experience of a non-discrete world. The world does not present itself to us as a set of ready-made classes; rather, we have to impose order by means of construing our experience of the world. Another reason is that languages are natural systems rather than artificial ones: they have evolved over the millennia in an unconscious way; they have not been the target of conscious design (unlike artificial semiotic systems such as symbolic logic, Boolean algebra, graphs, etc.). Yet another reason is that meaning is fundamentally intersubjective and classes of meaning are always being negotiated between people. Here fuzziness leaves room for, and is the result of, innumerable acts of negotiation.

All experience is thus construed into a network of fuzzy classes of meaning. This has been obscured because when logic was derived from natural language by design, fuzziness was also removed from it by design. Thus, everyday reasoning is fuzzy reasoning and it is only in those restricted contexts which demand crispness that designed formal logic is applicable.

6.2   Networks of classes as primary mode of organization – the system network

If we accept Ellis's (1993) argument that language is centrally concerned with classification (as I have interpreted that insight here: that is, with construing experience into networks of fuzzy classes of meaning), it might seem that we have to start from scratch since generative linguistics has not focussed on classification. (Indeed, taxonomic tendencies in pre-generative linguistics have been condemned.) However, the European structuralist tradition in linguistics was much more balanced in this respect: throughout most of this century, two fundamental modes of organization were recognized (building on Saussure 1916) – the paradigmatic mode (options of choice) and the syntagmatic mode (structural realizations of choices) – as in Firth's (e.g. 1957c) system and structure theory. And within the Firthian strand of this broadly structuralist tradition, a further step was taken by Halliday (e.g. 1966b): he proposed as a theoretical base for the interpretation of language that the ***paradigmatic mode is primary*** – that language is essentially a network of options. The options in this primary mode of organization are realized (expressed, coded) in the secondary, syntagmatic mode of organization (including structures but also other modes of realization such as intonation). In addition, he invented a form of representation for this mode of organization – the **system network**.

The system network makes it possible to map out the primary, paradigmatic mode of organization of language as a network of interlocking options or classes. Specifications of how these options are realized (expressed, coded) in structure are given in terms of partial structural specifications associated with options in the network. (If we think of these options as classes, we can think of the realization statements as specifications of the properties that characterize the classes.) Figure 6.1 is an example of a system network. It is taken from that part of the grammar of English that provides the resources for construing our experience of flux – of quanta of change in the flow of events. (For a detailed description of the grammar of English using system networks, see Matthiessen 1995a; for more detailed discussion of system networks, see e.g. Halliday 1976a; Matthiessen and Bateman 1991; Matthiessen and Halliday 1999.)

The system network says that there are two primary simultaneous sets of options, **systems**, available for simple clauses: "middle/effective" (known as agency) and "material/mental/verbal/relational" (process type). (If we think in terms of classification, we can say that simple clauses are classified along two dimensions – those of agency and process type. In contrast to e.g. strict taxonomies, discrimination networks, and decision trees, system networks thus allow for co-classification.)

A system thus consists of an **entry condition** (the condition under which the contrasting options are available, or in terms of classification, the class being further subclassified), and an **exclusive disjunction** of two or more terms (representing the contrasting options, i.e. contrasting classes). In addition, a term may have one or more **realization statements** associated with it (the realization in structure of that term, or [from the point of view of classification] the specification of characteristic properties). For example, the term "material" has associated with it the realization statements + Actor (which means: the function Actor is present in the structure of

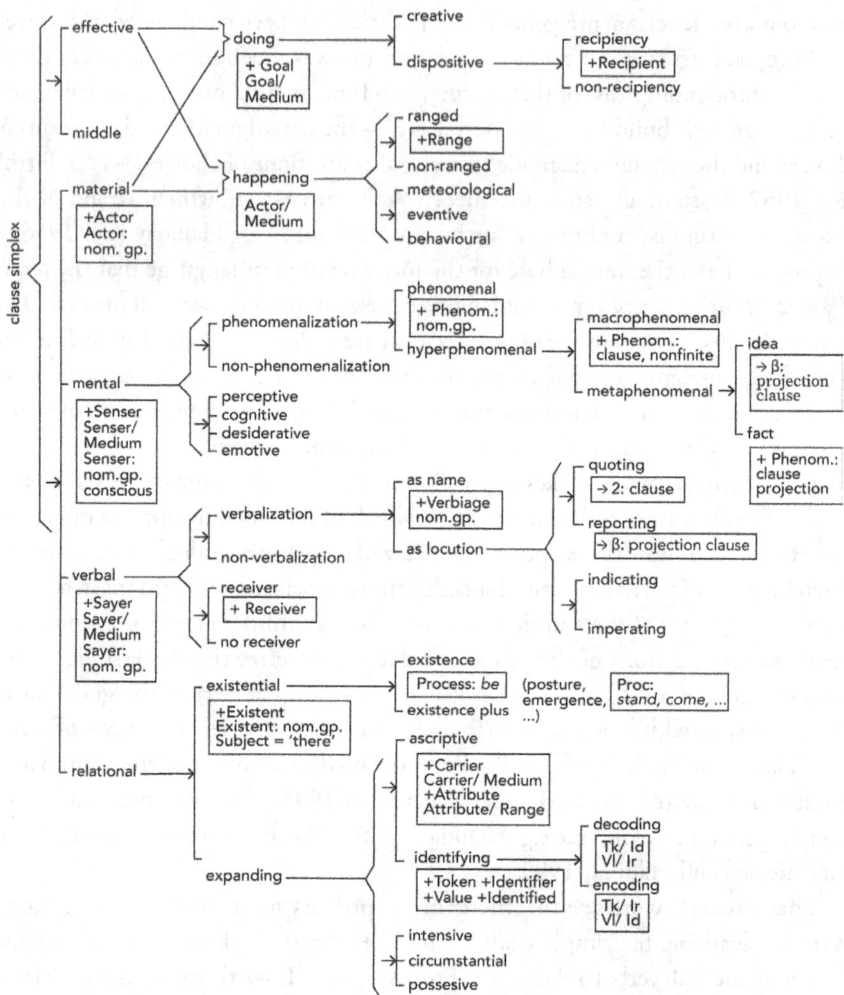

Figure 6.1 Grammatical options in construing change

the clause) and Actor: nominal group (which means: the function Actor is realized by ["value restricted to"] a grammatical unit of the class "nominal group").

Any term or complex of terms may lead to more **delicate** (more specific) systems: the systems of the network are ordered in delicacy from least delicate (the far left) to most delicate (the far right). (Delicacy was the name given to this ordering of systems by Michael Halliday over thirty years ago. In later work on networks within other traditions, this ordering has been called "subsumption"; and the general notion has also been discussed in terms of "granularity.") For example, the term "verbal" is the entry condition to two simultaneous systems, "verbalization/non-verbalization" and "receiver/non-receiver"; and the terms "material" and "effective" are the conjunctive entry condition to the system "doing" (which happens to be a system with a single term, the so-called **gate**).

As this example illustrates, the system network represents both the inherent organization of inter-related options (in this case options in how to construe a quantum of change by means of some type of clause) and an ordering over structural specifications (by means of the realization statements associated with systemic terms). It is in this sense that language is centrally concerned with classification.

Formally, the system network is a kind of graph or network; more specifically, it is a directed acyclic graph.[3] The systems are partially ordered (partially, since systems can be simultaneous). The illustration I have just given would seem to suggest that the system network is only another formal resource for representing classification of the classical ("Aristotelian") kind, more or less equivalent to other such resources; and it has been investigated from this point of view (e.g. by Mellish 1988). However, what is really of interest in the present context is rather what systemic theory says about paradigmatic organization represented by system networks and how the system network is implemented to express the theory as faithfully as possible. I will start with the theory that lies behind system networks (Section 6.3) and then turn to the challenge of faithful implementation (Section 6.4).

6.3   The theory of systemic organization represented by system network

Systemic theory has always held the view that options (classes) may be indeterminate or fuzzy. Thus, the terms of a system are intended to represent fuzzy classes rather than crisp ones. Halliday (1961) introduced the notion of a **cline** (scale): the terms of a system may represent regions on a cline rather than clear-cut classes in classical taxonomy. The descriptive importance of this theoretical notion was very clear also in his early work on intonation (e.g. Halliday 1967), where pitch movements form a cline from high fall to high rise with intermediate values between the two, represented "discretely" as a system of a fixed number of tones in a system network. Later systemic theoreticians explored the notion of topology to be able to construe the fuzziness of terms in systems: see e.g. Lemke (nd) and Martin and Matthiessen (1991). I will discuss this theoretical orientation by referring to one of the systems of Figure 6.1 – PROCESS TYPE.

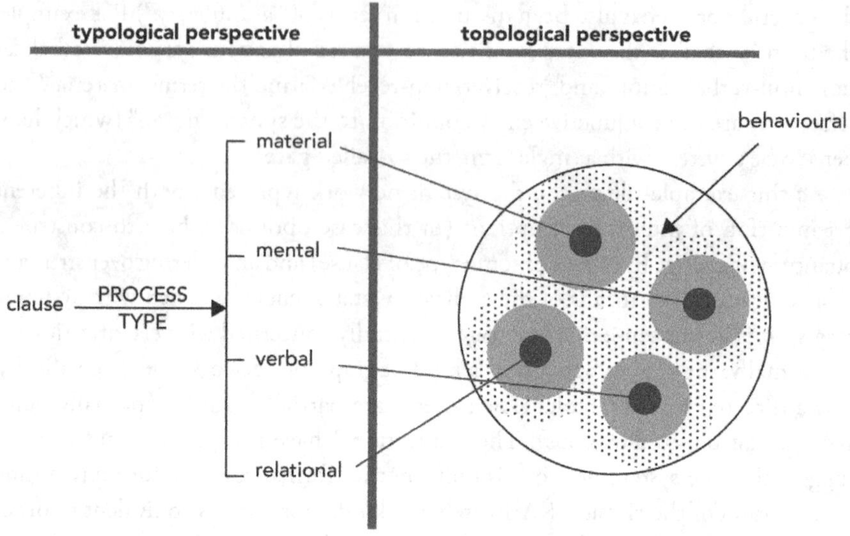

Figure 6.2 The PROCESS TYPE system viewed topologically

PROCESS TYPE is a clause system for construing of experience of quanta of change into different domains of experience – material (the domain of doing and happening), mental (the domain of sensing, i.e. conscious processing), verbal (the domain of saying), and relational (the domain of being and having). These different options (classes) are distinguished by a variety of grammatical criteria (see Halliday 1985b/1994a: ch. 5; Matthiessen 1995a: ch. 4); these criteria do not yield categorically different options (classes), but rather a set of options whose more delicate subtypes are more or less different. We can interpret this situation theoretically in terms of topology (see Martin and Matthiessen 1991). Topologically, these types correspond to regions in a continuous space: see Figure 6.2.

The situation is described in Halliday and Matthiessen (1999: 135–6) as follows:

> As with all systems in language, any given subtype or any given instance will be more or less like **prototypical** material, mental, verbal or relational clauses according to the reactances noted above. The grammar construes the **non-discreteness** of our experience of the world by creating borderline cases and blends. One such area is that of behavioural processes (Halliday 1994a: 139) – "processes of physiological and psychological behaviour, like breathing, dreaming, smiling, coughing." These can be interpreted as a subtype of material processes or as a borderline category between material and mental. They include

Table 6.1 Material and mental "separated" by behavioural

Criteria	Material	(Behavioural)	Mental
	wait	*listen*	*hear*
1. tense	unmarked present: present-in-present *be ... ing* *I'm waiting*	*I'm listening*	unmarked present: simple *I hear*
2. projection	[can't project] **I'm waiting that they're away*	[can't project] **I'm listening that they're away*	can project *I hear that they're away*
3. Consciousness	[does not impute consciousness] *It (the bus) waited*	does impute consciousness *it listened = the cat*	does impute consciousness *it heard = the cat*
4. Pro-verb	Is probed by *do* *Waiting is the best thing to do*	Is probed by *do* to some extent *listening is the best thing to do* but hardly *sneezing is the best thing to do*	[is not probed by *do*] **hearing is the best thing to do*

conscious processing construed as active behaviour (watching, listening, pondering, meditating) rather than as inert sensing (seeing, hearing, believing). Like the Senser in a mental clause, the "Behaver" in a behavioural one is endowed with consciousness; whereas in other respects behavioural clauses are more like material ones. Like material clauses (but unlike mental ones), behavioural clauses can be probed with *do*: *What are you doing? – I'm meditating* but not *I'm believing*. Furthermore, behavioural clauses normally do not project, or project only in highly restricted ways (contrast mental: cognitive *David believed → the moon was a balloon* with behavioural: *David was meditating → the moon was a balloon*);[4] nor can they accept a "fact" serving as Phenomenon (mental: *David saw that the others had already left* but not behavioural: *David watched that the others had already left*). In these respects, behavioural processes are essentially part of the material world rather than the mental one. Many of them are in fact further removed from mental processes, being physiological rather than psychological in orientation.

Thus, if we consider some criteria distinguishing material and mental clauses, we find a topological cline with behavioural as an intermediate region on the cline (as shown diagrammatically in Figure 6.2). These criteria are given in Table 6.1.

What this means is that if we construe our experience of some quantum of change as *he was watching the children play in the park* (*when the stranger appeared*), we have selected to construe it as "sort of like" a material process and "sort of like" a mental process – we have construed it as a behavioural process that has features of both. This kind of gradation is inherent in the system of PROCESS TYPE – as in most other systems of the lexicogrammar.

6.4   Realizing fuzzily interpreted system networks

Theoretically, networks of options (classes) are thus networks of fuzzy types rather than crisp ones: experience is construed fuzzily. This has been discussed by reference to topology since the spatial metaphor allows us to map classes onto regions related to one another in proximity. But how do we represent this theoretical interpretation of networks of classes? The traditional systems of representation used in linguistics and computational linguistics force us to impose discrete cut-off points between terms in systems. Thus, to represent the theory of systemic organization, we use subsumption lattices of various kinds (system networks interpreted in this way, frame-based inheritance networks, conceptual graphs); they all operate with discrete types. However, we can now explore fuzzy representations to enable us to realize our theoretical conceptions more faithfully.

In the systemic representation of system networks, a term in a system can be interpreted as the name of a fuzzy set (cf. McCawley 1993: 476, on fuzzy predicates having fuzzy sets as their extensions); and together the terms of that system name fuzzy sets that shade into one another. The fuzzy implementation of the system network would thus correspond to the topological perspective: see Figure 6.3. This line of enquiry raises many questions, of course. The most critical one is the question of how to characterize degrees of membership – how to specify the characteristic function assigning membership.

Specifying a fuzzy implementation of system networks is an important research task. Here the research can be guided by Ralescu's work on fuzzy conceptual graphs, where properties characterizing conceptual nodes are given weights (see

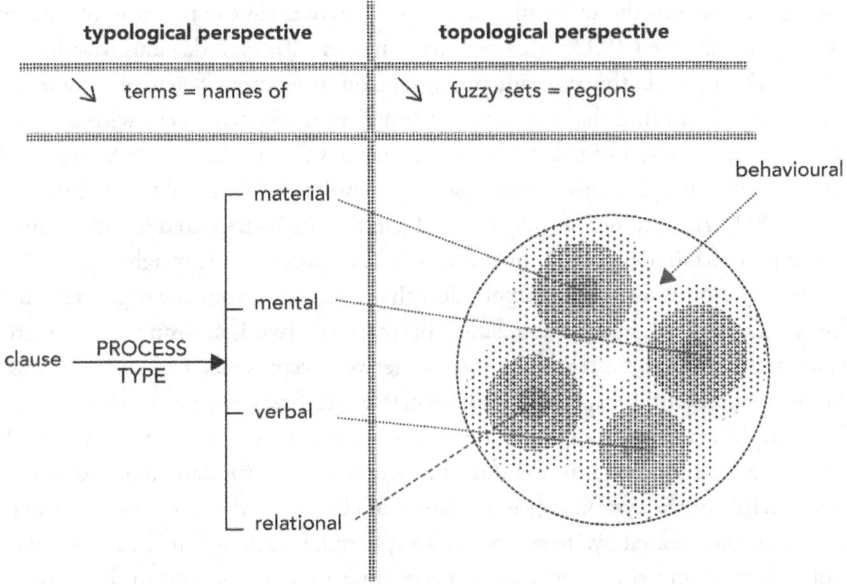

Figure 6.3 Fuzzy implementation of system networks

e.g. Ralescu and Baldwin 1989). For example, for mental processes (cf. Figure 6.1 and Table 6.1), the property of the Senser being conscious might be given more weight than the property of having simple present tense (to refer to present time). Such weightings of properties would be quite typical of how classes are construed in the network of classes represented by the system network.

6.5   Fuzzy construal and instantiation

Ralescu and Baldwin (1989) discuss how classes can be learned from examples and counter examples. This issue is fundamental to the fuzzy nature of networks of fuzzy classes of meaning for construing human experience. The illustrative example of a system network given in Figure 6.1 represents the overall potential of the grammar of English for construing a quantum of change. This overall potential constitutes one end-point of the **cline of instantiation**. The other end-point on this cline is that of instances – examples of classes selected to construe phenomena in particular situations. The overall potential is instantiated whenever options are selected, but each selection in the course of instantiation changes the overall potential. The potential represents the accumulation of instances over time in the form of a system (see e.g. Matthiessen 1993c [this volume, Chapter 10]; Halliday and Matthiessen 1999). We can study this systemic potential from the point of view of instances in text. Here we will find that the various features of the system occur with different relative frequencies; and these relative frequencies accumulate to form probabilities in the overall systemic potential (see e.g. Nesbitt and Plum 1988; Halliday and James 1993). Any feature of this potential will thus be instantiated in a given situation with a certain degree of probability – it has a probabilistic weighting.

Instantiation is a temporal dimension that is distinct from the organization of the system network itself. The relation between the two is an important research issue in the present context. The system network represents a network of fuzzy classes for construing experience. These classes are fuzzy relative to one another; for example, material processes shade into relational ones (as shown in Figure 6.2). This systemic fuzziness is internal to the system – it is a fundamental property of the principle of the systemic differentiation of classes. At the same time, it is manifested in, and created by, instantiation, so systemic fuzziness is related to systemic probability. To put this very crudely: every time a mental process in the system is instantiated with a conscious Senser, the systemic probability of the Senser of a mental process being conscious is reinforced; at the same time, the fuzzy class of mental processes is being construed again and again as one where the consciousness of the Senser is a central property.

6.6   Conclusion: construing the construal of fuzzy classes

In Section 6.1, I suggested that all experience can be construed as meaning organized into networks of classes. This includes our experience of the abstract relation of classification – the relation of being a member of a class. Class membership is itself construed as a class in the network of classes; more specifically, it is construed by the intersection of "intensive" and "ascriptive" in the system network shown in Figure 6.1. Thus, clauses such as *this is a circle*; *a platypus is an animal*; *she is tall* construe class membership. Not surprisingly, class membership is construed as a fuzzy class, with indeterminate borders to other classes, such as those construing identity and analogy. Figure 6.4 illustrates the dimensions of indeterminacy construed by the grammar of relational clauses.

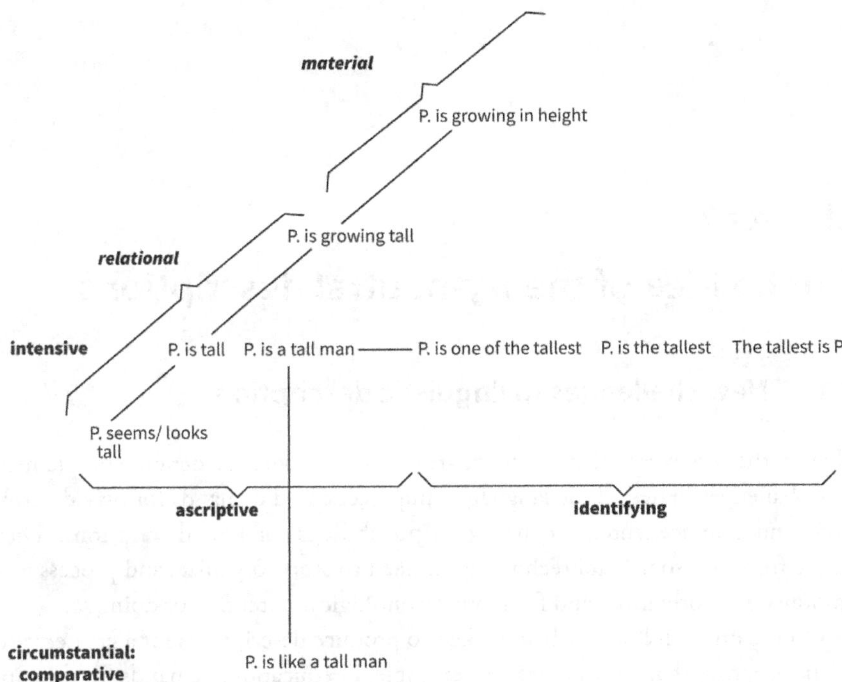

Figure 6.4 Class membership construed as a fuzzy class

Notes

1   Here **construe** means "actively interpret and represent as meaning": that is, using language we can construct our experience as meaning. The nature of the process of constructing experience as meaning emerges very clearly in language-based studies of how a young child learns about the world: see Painter (1993, 1996) in particular. Such studies also show how once experience is being constructed as meaning, it can be constructed cooperatively in dialogue, it can be shared, and it can be negotiated. Experience as meaning is thus intersubjective experience.

2   See also Channell's (1994) valuable study of "vague language," with case studies of: approximating quantities with numbers and approximators, approximating quantities with round numbers, approximating quantities with non-numerical vague quantifiers, and vague reference to categories.

3   There is one special kind of system that defines cycles. This is the logical type of system which allows for the option of choosing from the same set of options again. See e.g. Matthiessen and Bateman (1991: ch. 11).

4   For the special case of quoting by a behavioural process, as in *"You're late again," she frowned.*

Chapter 7

On the idea of theory-neutral descriptions

7.1   New challenges to linguistic description

Now, in the late twentieth century, we are faced with two considerable complementary challenges in describing languages: unprecedented demands for new descriptions and unprecedented technological possibilities for new descriptions. They derive from our social and technological need to store, organize, and process vast amounts of information, and from our technological potential for doing so.

On the one hand, we are being asked to produce descriptions for a greater variety of purposes than ever before. For example, in education, demands for description now go far beyond traditional demands for language teaching materials, and in artificial intelligence, computational modelling has introduced an entirely new kind of demand for description. The descriptions being demanded are also far more extensive than ever before. Internally, linguistics has finally extended its domain from words in sentences to include text in context, and as a result, descriptions need to cover more levels and take on the awesome resources of discourse semantics in context. But outside linguistics, consumers are also demanding far more comprehensive descriptions for their various needs. Such demands are part of what is commonly recognized as the information society – a form of socio-economic organization where information has become the primary commodity in many contexts.

On the other hand, the same technologies that create new demands for descriptions of language also challenge us by enabling us to extend our descriptions considerably. The tape recorder has made it possible to store spoken language systematically for the first time, and the computer is making it possible to engage in the description of vast corpora (far beyond the one-million-word standard set by the Brown Corpus in the 1960s: twenty-million- and even two-hundred-million-word corpora are entirely possible, as are open-ended corpora – cf. Sinclair 1991). Combined with new statistical techniques, such corpora constitute not only a quantitative change in descriptive potential but also a qualitative one: we can explore the probabilistic nature of the linguistic system in a way that has never before been possible in the history of thinking about language. The computer has also made it possible to develop descriptive models of a kind never available before – models of understanding, production, translation, and other linguistic processes.

These changes in the descriptive potential arguably form part of the real "revolution" in linguistics in the second half of the twentieth century. They do not merely constitute a more sophisticated version of what has been done for many previous generations, such as a more sophisticated account of linguistic universals, a more sophisticated account of linguistic types, a more sophisticated account of innate ideas, a more sophisticated account of psychological subject or language and the mind. Rather, they constitute a qualitative change in the phenomenological domain of linguistic description. The domain is coming to include phenomena that go far beyond what falls within the domain of commonsense – to include patterns that are not overtly observable. In this respect, the change is similar to the move in physical sciences from the bandwidth of everyday human experience to the microscopic and the macroscopic.

This dual challenge to description makes it particularly relevant to ask what possible significance theory may have in organizing the wealth of descriptive information we have to cope with – the kind of wealth we will get, for example, in reference grammars of the twenty-first century that are linked to flow-through corpora and exist as online hyper-documents instead of being bound between covers by the technology of the book. We know from other domains of human experience that technological advances have paved the way for crucial shifts in theory.

In most twentieth-century linguistics, there has been an uneasy disjunction between descriptive linguistics and theoretical linguistics existing as alternatives. In theoretical linguistics, description has often been pursued only within a very narrow domain, or merely illustrative, or even entirely lacking. In linguistic descriptive work, linguists sometimes characterize their descriptions as "purely descriptive," "theory neutral," or "theoretically eclectic" – often in the case of reference grammars. Such characterizations are sometimes offered with apologies by linguists who feel that theoretical advances have left them behind in an earlier tradition in which they were trained but which is supposedly of no current interest, and sometimes they are presented as positive features of the descriptions. These characterizations usually leave the relationship between theory and description fairly implicit – although they in fact depend crucially on how this relationship is theorized. Unless it is clear what the nature of this relationship is, it makes no sense to say that a description is free of, neutral with respect to, or eclectic with respect to theory. And freedom from theory, theoretical neutrality, and theoretical eclecticism most certainly do not put us in a good position to meet the challenges to description sketched above.

In this chapter, we will explore the disjunction between theory and description, and will consider characterizations of descriptions that downplay the role of particular theories (Section 7.2). Having problematized the role of theory and its relationship to description, we will examine the construal of theory description as semiotic resources and the relationship between them in Section 7.3. Using the construal proposed in Section 7.3, we will then examine the positions of Section 7.2 in Section 7.4. Then we return to the general issue of the dual challenge to description in the transition to the twenty-first century in Section 7.5.

7.2   The disjunction between theory and description

The relative prominence of theory and description in linguistics in this century has been varied across time periods and traditions, but it seems always to have been linked to **consumer considerations**. That is, not only is the nature of theory related to the consumer (see Halliday's [1964] discussion of syntax and the consumer), but so is its role in description. These consumer considerations include audience and basic research questions. In general, if the audience is outside linguistics, the response in descriptive work has often been to avoid theory rather than to try to popularize it, as has happened within the natural sciences. The basic research questions have often been opposed as descriptive, theoretical, or applied.

7.2.1   The break between theory and description

At the beginning of the twentieth century, American work on language had a descriptive orientation, whereas the new European work was more theoretical. Sampson (1980: 58–9) characterizes the contrast as follows:

> The nature of the languages dealt with was one of the chief differences between the Boasian and Saussurean traditions. Saussure had seized the attention of the scholarly world by inventing a new way of looking at phenomena which had been so familiar for so long that it seemed impossible for them still to hold any surprises ... Boas and his colleagues, on the other hand, were faced with the severely practical problem of working out what the current structure of various utterly alien languages was like ... it was so difficult to get to grips with the brute facts of these exotic languages that the Descriptivists had little time

to spare for drawing elegant logical distinctions between *langue* and *parole* or the like. Hence the name "Descriptivist": for this school, in a way that is true of no other group discussed in this book, the description of individual language was an end in itself, or a necessary first step towards understanding the wider culture of a particular community. The Descriptivists tended to think of abstract linguistic theorizing as a means to the end of successful practical description of particular languages, rather than (as Chomsky does, for instance) thinking of individual languages as sources of data for the construction of a general theory of language.

By the 1980s, the situation had changed dramatically in the US. One of us remembers a lecture given by Chomsky sometime in the mid-eighties at UCLA to a general audience where he claimed that it used to be possible to get a PhD in linguistics by submitting a description of some language, but that the discipline had advanced so much that now such a description was background for a more theoretical piece of PhD work. Chomsky's claim is of course only the generativist perspective on the discipline. The "descriptivist" tradition has survived, and dissertations with a descriptive focus are still being submitted. But in the meantime, a highly theoretical orientation had emerged within American structuralism, first with the "post-Bloomfieldians" and later with the "generativists."[1] The "post-Bloomfieldian" focus still had a descriptive orientation in that it was concerned with discovery procedures. The generativists were also concerned with procedures to a considerable extent, but these procedures had shifted to a theoretical orientation in that they dealt with argumentation based in theory. The introduction to Soames and Perlmutter (1979: xi–xii) is a representative example:

> The best way to learn syntax is not simply to study it, but to do it. The purpose of this book is to bring readers to the point where they can "do syntax" themselves. This ability is essential for understanding the field and reading its burgeoning literature.
>
> We have designed the book for students in linguistics, for those in related fields, and for those studying linguistics for what it can contribute to their general education. We have found that focusing on syntactic argumentation is the key to meeting the needs of each of these groups.
>
> The student who learns how to use linguistic data to argue for one hypothesis over another learns the essence of scientific method. An important advantage of linguistics in this respect is that its data is

generally much more accessible than data in other sciences and typically can be obtained without time-consuming experiments. In the course of constructing syntactic arguments, the student discovers that each time a set of data leads to the rejection of one hypothesis, another must be formulated and tested against further data. In this way, one is led to investigate language in greater and greater depth and to discover the surprising intricacy of what may initially have seemed to be a familiar and ordinary phenomenon.

Syntactic argumentation is also crucial for the student who wishes to go further in linguistics. For this student, it is as important to learn the reasons for a theory as it is to learn the theory itself. Particular theories and proposals will give way to others in time. What remains most stable are the standards of argumentation and the criteria for choosing among competing hypotheses. In addition, as new theories replace old, each new one is expected to account for the data covered by its predecessors. Thus, in constructing arguments the student not only learns why some hypotheses have been rejected in favor of others, but also becomes familiar with data that has shaped the direction of the field.

"Doing syntax" had thus come to mean syntactic argumentation rather than discovery procedures for description. But there is a continuity in the orientation towards rules or procedures. The theory being argued about was now based on a narrow descriptive focus elaborated in considerable detail – Postal's (1974) work on raising is a classic example. The only attempt to create a fairly comprehensive description at the time, the "UCLA grammar," was arguably a failure. Thus, Stockwell, Schachter, and Partee (1973: iii) describe their project as follows:

> This work was originally undertaken under the title "Integration of Transformational Theories of English Syntax" in the naive expectation that most of the information about the analysis of the grammar of English that was available up through the summer of 1968 could be brought together and integrated in a single format. Now, quite a bit later than we intended, and considerably less integrated than we had hoped ...

The difficulty the UCLA team faced was a reflection of the prestige activity of "doing theory" on small descriptive samples. This problem was certainly recognized by leading theoretical linguists of the time. In his foreword to Levi (1978: xi), James McCawley wrote: "Existing textbooks in transformational grammar provide students with extensive training in the grinding of axes but little training in the use of already ground axes in the felling of trees."

And in his well-known critical assessment of the failure of generative grammar, Gross (1979: 859) comments:

> one may wonder why no linguist has been able to construct a transformational grammar with the type of coverage that traditional grammars used to provide ... The only recent attempt in this direction (Stockwell et al. 1973) is not a grammar; it is an attempt to integrate partial data of heterogeneous origins, and a study in consistency of rules. It is the only compilation of transformational constraints ever attempted, and is now obsolete – mainly because new theoretical developments have, it seems, entirely modified the situation.

Theory was thus not being produced to support comprehensive description but rather to answer Chomsky's philosophical questions about language. The theory that was produced was oriented towards rules – towards ruling in and out. This made very good sense since one issue high on the agenda was formulating constraints on what constituted a possible language as a step towards explaining how language could be learned. Consequently, theory was not really concerned with construing overall linguistic subsystems in comprehensive descriptions. It makes sense that the 1970s saw the rise of a kind of lexicalism that embodies a view of lexicogrammar as fairly unrelated lexical fragments, as in Becker's (1975) conception of the phrasal dictionary. In addition, there was little sympathy for the view that there could be different theories for different consumer needs – Halliday's (1964) plea for this view, intended to open up the field, was not at all well received in general. The so-called linguistic wars of the late sixties and early seventies revolved around the choice of the correct theory – although generative semanticists had really developed new research questions and thus needed a different kind of theory, as later developments in the direction of cognition and metaphorical systems have clearly shown. This is Lakoff's (1987: 181) assessment:

> Generative linguistics (in the Chomskyan tradition) takes for granted that there is an autonomous language faculty that makes no use at all of general cognitive capacities. This is not an idle assumption on the part of generative linguistics. It is an assumption that is necessary in order to maintain the basic metaphor on which generative linguistics is based, namely, A GRAMMAR IS A FORMAL SYSTEM. A *formal system* is a collection of rewriting rules that can mimic an algorithmic

computation. The theory of generative linguistics is mathematically characterized in terms of such algorithmic systems, which manipulate symbols without regard to their meaning. By definition, an algorithmic system is one in which no algorithm can be sensitive to the way a symbol is semantically interpreted. If a generative grammar is such a system, then it is by definition required that no interpretation of the symbols – no meaning, no understanding of them – can be made use of in any rule of grammar. To do so would be to abandon the theory of generative linguistics – to give up on the basic metaphor that a grammar is a formal system in the technical sense.

It is not surprising that there was a very strong reaction against the prevailing theory in the late 1970s and early 1980s in the move towards "West-Coast Functionalism" (by Givón, Thompson, DuBois, and others) and also in the move towards cognitive linguistics (by Lakoff, Langacker, and others). Givón (1979) has been quite polemical, but his stance is symptomatic of the reaction:

> For over 50 years now linguistics has been in a state of siege, in a seemingly endless crisis of its philosophy and methodology. Initially, the crisis may have been ascribed to the impact of mechanistic views of the physical sciences on Saussure, on the one hand, and of behaviorist psychology on Bloomfield on the other. The structuralist dogma which followed has three major characteristics:
>
> 1.   The a priori and arbitrary curtailment of the database relevant to the investigation
> 2.   The rise of the formalism as "theory"
> 3.   The neglect or devaluation of the notion of evaluation
>
> At its onset, transformational-generative grammar brought a tide of rising hopes on all three counts. However, the cumulative experience of the past twenty years in linguistics suggests that in all fundamental ways the transformational-generative revolution has remained at the dead center of structuralist methodology. (pp. 2–3)

Givón's characterization of "structuralist dogma" foregrounds the role of description and the conception of theory. Matthiessen's impression of the situation based on observing the scene from UCLA from 1979 to 1988 is that many scholars who grew up linguistically in the 1960s and 1970s in the US reacted against theory as a straightjacket since their primary experience with theory was generativist. They felt that by adopting a particular theory they were prevented from achieving both descriptive and explanatory insights rather than being enabled to achieve them by the theory. They still had an interest in theory, but to avoid the straightjacket they embraced eclecticism and sought accounts outside of language, mainly in cognition and perception. The fact that the immediate reference point was the generative theory they reacted against goes some way towards explaining the relative lack of reference to European functionalism. The American functionalist reaction against generative style theory was combined with the continuing descriptivist tradition.

7.2.2　*View of theory in reference grammars*

While mainstream theory developed in such a way that a disjunction between descriptive linguistics and theoretical linguistics was created and "being theoretically oriented" came to mean not having a commitment to comprehensive unified descriptions, descriptive work continued both in what Sampson refers to as the descriptivist tradition in the quote above and in American and European work outside this tradition, e.g. concerned with producing reference grammars and other comprehensive accounts. But the view of the relationship to theoretical concerns changed. Since the 1960s at least, linguists have often felt obliged to say that their descriptions are not theoretical: there is a cline from being "free" of theory to being "neutral" and then to being "eclectic." Let us quote from a few introductions to major descriptions and then discuss the motifs that are illustrated (our bolding throughout).

Cantarino's (1974) three-volume syntax of Modern Arabic prose:

> I have mentioned my purpose, but perhaps I should define it more closely: my goal is to present a humanistic study of the Arabic language which will enable its prospective users to become aware of the intricate syntactical pattern of the linguistic system and, even more, of its logical and semantic content and the language's potential for literary expression. Thus, I decided to avoid **experimental application of any particular theory that might obscure** the special attention I wished to focus on the semantic and literary aspects of the language. An exclusive concentration of the language structure might have increased the interest of this presentation in certain linguistic circles, but at the same time it would certainly have **excluded** many prospective **users** with an interest in Arabic other than purely linguistic. Therefore, I have in general used a meaning-based theory of grammar as a basis for my syntactical analysis. This gives the study a greater internal unity than would have been possible had I tried to combine descriptive and logical

notions of grammar. I have also used traditional terminology as have all my predecessors in analogous studies. ... (pp. ix–x)

Quirk et al.'s (1972) introduction to their reference grammar of English:

It will be obvious that our grammatical framework has drawn heavily both on the long-established tradition and on the insights of several contemporary schools of linguistics. But while we have taken account of modern linguistic theory to the extent that we think justifiable in a grammar of this kind, we have not felt that this was the occasion for detailed discussion of theoretical issues. Nor do we see the need to justify the fact that we **subscribe to no specific one** of the current or recently formulated linguistic theories. Each of those propounded from the time of de Saussure and Jespersen onwards has its undoubted merits, and several (notably transformational-generative approaches) have contributed very great stimulus to us as to other grammarians. **None**, however, seems yet **adequate to account for all linguistic phenomena**, and recent trends suggest that our own **compromise position** is a fair reflection of the way in which the major theories are responding to influence from others. (p. vi)

Huddleston's (1984) introduction to the grammar of English:

I have likewise made minimal assumptions about the reader's familiarity with "traditional grammar" – all terms borrowed from the traditional repertoire, such as "noun", "transitive verb", "relative clause", and so on, are fully explained. Although the book covers a fair amount of the grammar, it is not simply a short grammar of English, inasmuch as it devotes a good deal of attention to the problem of justifying the analysis proposed (where, for example, it differs from the traditional analysis) or of choosing between alternative analyses – it is in this sense that it is directed towards the student of linguistics. It does not, however, attempt to formalise the grammar: it is not "generative" – and it is **not written within the framework or model of any particular contemporary school** of linguistics such as "transformational grammar", "systemic grammar", "functional grammar" or the like. It follows, rather, a **"structural" approach** in a very broad understanding of that term, one where the grammatical categories postulated derive from a study of the combinatorial and contrastive relationships the words and other forms enter into. (p. xi)

Dixon's (1972) description of Dyirbal:

The grammar is written at two distinct "levels". The "facts" of the grammar – affixes, their syntactic effect, types of construction, and so on – are described in chapters 3, 4 and 6. Chapter 5 interprets some of these facts, setting up explanatory generalisations and describing the "deep" grammar of Dyirbal in terms of a number of syntactic relations and a number of transformational rules. It has seemed desirable to (at least partially) **separate facts from interpretations** in the case of a language like Dyirbal that has not previously been described in any way. **The correctness of chapters 3, 4 and 6 cannot seriously be in dispute**. Chapter 5, however, is far more open to argument. A quite different set of generalisations, with greater explanatory power, might well be providable instead of those given here. As linguistic theory progresses chapter 5 is rather likely to stand in need of revision; this is unlikely to be true for chapters 3, 4 and 6. (p. xix)

Dixon's (1991) grammar of English:

I work in terms of the broad theoretical apparatus of linguistics that has been built up over the past two thousand years (word classes, main and subordinate clauses, underlying and derived forms, structures and systems, etc.), utilising the insights of Dionysius Thrax, Edward Sapir, Leonard Bloomfield, Kenneth Pike, Michael Halliday, Noam Chomsky and Bernard Comrie, among others. Theoretical ideas are brought in as they assist the central task, of describing the syntactic and semantic organisation of English. I have not chosen to restrict myself by casting the description in terms of any of the systems of **nomenclature** that are currently referred to as "linguistic theories" and which have, in the past few decades, grown, flourished and perished with such rapidity.

The use of **jargon** and symbolisation has been kept to a minimum on the principle that, in a subject such as linguistics, if something can be explained it should be explainable in **simple, everyday language**, which any intelligent person can understand. That is not to say that this book can be read through quickly, like a novel. It is a serious, scientific attempt to explain the interrelations of grammar and meaning. (pp. 3–4)

Given the disjunction between theory and description that had emerged, scholars such as these with a substantial descriptive commitment are in a real dilemma. The motifs that emerge from their remarks can be interpreted as follows:

1. Contrasts

- Facts vs. theoretical interpretation: descriptive facts are uninterpreted and correct; they can be established independently of theoretical interpretation, the latter being a separate step.
- Commonsensical clarity vs. theoretical obscurity: scientific accounts of grammar can be put in everyday, commonsensical terms to achieve clarity, whereas theory obscures this clarity.
- Comprehensive description vs. deployment of particular theory: there is a trade-off between descriptive comprehensiveness and theoretical consistency. Either we achieve comprehensiveness by being theoretically eclectic or we achieve theoretical consistency by giving up on comprehensiveness.

2. View of theory

- Theory as transient fashion: theories develop on a growth model, are fashionable for a while but have built-in obsolescence – only descriptive facts are permanent.
- Theory as jargon: theory is embodied in jargon/nomenclature/technical vocabulary, which makes it obscure.
- Theory as representation: theory is embodied in symbolizations or representations, which are of no help in description.
- Theory as straightjacket: theory is a constraint on what we can say descriptively and gets in the way of descriptive insights.
- Theory as impractical expert enterprise: theory addresses issues that are narrowly theory-internal, but are of no applied value.
- Theory as approach: theory is an approach for deriving grammatical categories.

This is not to say that all the linguists quoted above hold these views; clearly they do not. But they have all had to move away from explicit theory in their descriptive work, either entirely in the sense of being "free" of theory, adopting a commonsense position,[2] or adopting a compromise by means of theoretical neutrality or eclecticism. This is perfectly understandable given the dominant theoretical climate. However, the price is quite high: the amount and kind of information that can be achieved in description will be limited, and it is very hard to test the description for consistency and for comprehensiveness and explicitness. We will return to this point in Section 7.4, but first we would like to ask if the attitude towards theory in descriptive work is the only one possible at present. Even though it seems to dominate, it is, in fact, not the only solution to the problem of the disjunction between theory and description: another solution is ***to reconstrue theory and its role in description***. Let's turn to traditions construing theory as a resource for making meaning in description.

7.3   Construing theory description as a semiotic resource

7.3.1 *Theory as resource*

As the disjunction between theory and description developed in "mainstream" American linguistics, tagmemics developed in quite a different direction. Theory was developed to serve as a resource. It is worth quoting the greatest American descriptive-theoretical linguist of the twentieth century, K.L. Pike, at some length. This is his view after almost half a century of dialogue between theory and description, taken from Pike (1982):

> The list and kind of things men will find will vary radically if they adopt different theories as tools with which to search for these units. The theory is part of the observer; a different theory makes a different observer; a different observer sees different things, or sees the same things as structured differently; and the structure of the observer must, in some sense or to some degree, be part of the data of an adequate theory of language. A particular language, of a particular culture, in relation to a particular person with his particular history constitutes an implicit theory for that person.
>
> Tagmemic theory is, in this respect, a theory of theories which tells how the observer universally affects the data and becomes part of the data ...
>
> "Why study theory? Why not just be practical?" So speak those who fail to realize that the line between theory and practice is blurred – that in many situations only an approach to theory will allow practical results to be obtained in reaching one's goals. Today's practicality is often no more than the accepted form of yesterday's theory.
>
> A theory is like a window.
>
> The intellect, in order to get outside itself and to interpret the sense data impinging on the body, needs in advance some kind of idea of the way in which the data may turn out to be organized. Then it can search for pattern. A theory in this sense is *directional* ...
>
> A theory must be simpler than reality if it is to be helpful. It attempts to strip away from attention those items which are not important to the observer at the moment ...
>
> In trying to choose or build a theory we would seek an organized, systematic arrangement of general principles which help us to understand something about our physical or conceptual world. ... Since we

want a theory to help us, a theory may be viewed as a conceptual tool. A good theory is a useful one. Usefulness, in turn, is relevant to some purpose, some goal. This implies that theories may be good or bad, relative to the sociological setting in which they are found. (pp. 3, 5, 7)

In Pike's view, a linguistic theory is thus a tool or resource for construing what we observe. It determines what we see and it allows us to construe patterns. We develop theory to understand language and to address practical problems. The measure of the success of a theory is its usefulness. This way of looking at theory is fundamentally different from the view embodied in the disjunction between theory and description reviewed in the previous section. In this respect, the tagmemic view of theory is very similar to the systemic functional one: see Halliday (1980, 1985c).

7.3.2   Theory explicitly construed as semiotic resource

What kind of resource is theory? Following Firth and Hjelmslev, we can interpret **linguistic theory as a semiotic system**. Hjelmslev (1943: 105–6) characterizes linguistics as a metalanguage, which he defines as a language whose content plane is a language:[3]

> *Man er nemlig, efter den udvikling logistikken har taget i de polske logikeres undersøgelser, forberedt paa existensen af sprog hvis inholdsplan er sprog. Dette er de saakaldte metasprog, hvorved forstaas sprog der handler om sprog. Et saadant metasprog maa netop lingvistikken vaere. ... Saedvanlig vil et metasprog vaere (eller kunne vaere) helt eller delvis identisk med sit objektsprog. Saaledes vil lingvistikken, der beskriver et daglisprog, selv kunne betjene sig af dette daglisprog under beskrivelsen.*
>
> "One is, after the development logic has undergone in the Polish logicians' investigations, prepared for the existence of a language whose content plane is a language. This is so-called metalanguage, which is understood as language which deals with language. Linguistics may be precisely such a metalanguage. ... A metalanguage will customarily be (or able to be) completely or partially identical with its object-language. Consequently, linguistics, which describes an everyday language, will be able to deploy the everyday language being described." (Matthiessen's translation, see Hjelmslev (1953: 76–7) for an alternative translation by F.J. Whitfield.)

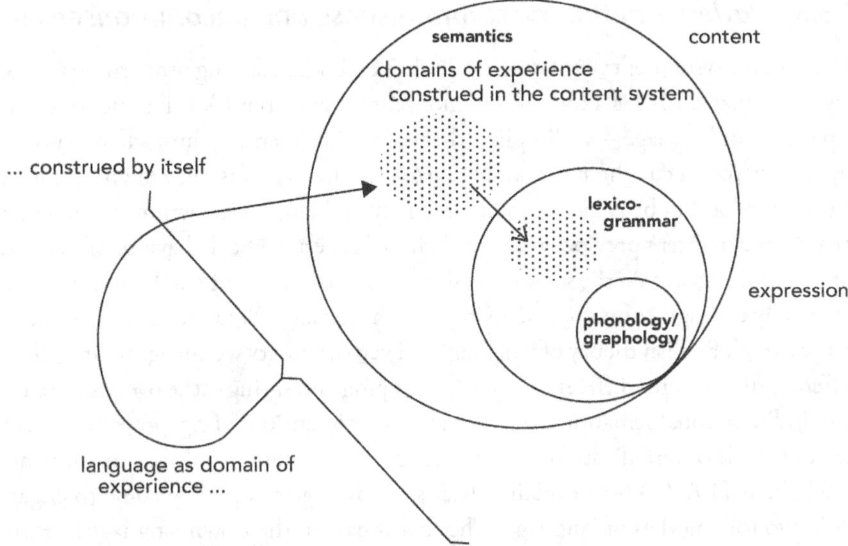

Figure 7.1 Language turned back on itself

Firth's work explains how language can become "meta-" with respect to itself in metalanguage; he drew attention to linguistics as language turned back on itself (our bolding):

> The constructs or schemata of linguistics enable us to handle isolates that may be called language events. These systematic constructs are neither immanent or transcendent, but just **language turned back on itself.** ... The disciplines and techniques of linguistics are directed to assist us in making statements of meaning. Indeed, the main concern of descriptive linguistics is to make statements of meaning. (Firth 1948b/1957c: 190)

Figure 7.1 shows language turned back on itself: from an ideational point of view, the content plane construes our experience of the world around us and inside us. Language is part of this experience, so it makes sense that aspects of language are also construed within the content plane. This is not to say that there is just one contiguous domain of content concerned with language (as the diagram seems to suggest); rather, it is dispersed through the content system in everyday language as complementary perspectives on itself.

7.3.3 *Varieties of theory: commonsense and uncommonsense*

The content system of everyday contexts thus embodies, among other things, a theory of language. This is a folk or commonsense theory, but it's still a theory of our experience of language – an "implicit theory" in Pike's terms. Thus, when a mother says to her young daughter *Jessica, don't whinge!*, this is an instance of an ideational theory of what can be achieved interpersonally in dialogic interaction: she has construed her daughter's previous move in their dialogue as verbal behaviour of a certain kind – as whingeing. At the same time, she is, of course, assessing this behaviour interpersonally through connotation, giving it negative value. Whingeing has a location in the overall English theory of what kinds of verbal activity we engage in; it is, along different dimensions, different from e.g. gossiping and saying – the overall system is a multidimensional semantic space that involves dimensions of e.g. projection, manner and mode of verbalization, receiver-hood, subject matter, and accompaniment.

Halliday (1977: 32–4) explains that as children grow up, they come to engage with two folk models of language. The first is part of their own language learning and learning about language, while the second is a school model:

> The earliest linguistic terms an English-speaking child learns to use are not terms like *noun* and *verb*, or even *word* and *sentence*; in fact they are not nouns at all – they are verbs, typically *say* and *mean*, and shortly afterwards *tell* ... A child must understand a good deal about the nature of language to be able to report speech ... He must have internalised the concept of an act of meaning – of speech as symbolic action, distinct from but interdependent with acts of a non-symbolic kind. And when we look more closely, we find that he can already report acts of meaning before he has an explicit verb *say* with which to do so. [At this point Halliday presents an example of a child reporting an act of meaning at one year seven months.] A kite had fallen and its string lay stretched along the ground; his father had warned him not to trip over it. [This child] recalled the incident later, saying:
>
> > qài ... "qài ... maiɲʰ tìng"
>
> Translated in adult, [the child's] sentence meant, '(there was a) kite, (and Daddy said "there's a kite, mind (the) string"'. Already for [the child] at a year and a half, saying is a part of experience; like other actions and events, it can be observed, recalled and narrated.
>
> ...
>
> He also has a clear concept of "naming", which is the converse of meaning. ...

By the time he is two years old, a child has a considerable awareness of the nature and functions of language. When he starts to talk, he is not only using language; he is also beginning to talk *about* it. He is constructing a folk linguistics, in which (i) saying, and (ii) naming-meaning, denote different aspects of the same symbolic act. ...

Soon, however, the child will go to school; and once he is there, his ideas about language will be superseded by the folk linguistics of the classroom, with its categories and classes, its rules and regulations, its do's and, above all, its don'ts. Here a fundamental ideological change takes place in the child's image of language – and, through this, in his image of reality. Up till now, language has been seen as a resource, a potential for thinking and doing; he has talked about it in verbs, verbs like *call* and *mean*, *say* and *tell*, and rhyme. From now on, language will be, not a set of resources but a set of rules. And the rules are categorical – they operate on things; so he must talk about language in nouns, like *word* and *sentence*, and *noun* and *verb*, and *letter*.

It would be wrong to suggest, however, that the image of language as resource is totally submerged and lost. Unlike the linguistics of the classroom, which is codified (organised as a cultural institution), and so conscious and explicit, the linguistics of the family and neighbourhood, though it is *coded* (organised semantically), it is not codified; it is partly implicit ("covert", in Whorf's terminology), and so below the level of conscious awareness. For this reason it has considerable staying power ...

Saying, telling on the one hand and meaning-calling on the other, falls within two of a larger set of content systems for construing aspects of language in everyday talk – verbal and relational clauses, respectively. These systems include the following in the adult ideational lexicogrammar of English:

- Clause complexing: (i) projection: linguistic activity construed as a duality of [1] saying or sensing + [2] the content of saying or sensing; (ii) elaboration: restatement construing near-synonymy or paraphrase.
- Clause: (i) a small subtype of material clauses construing creation of, or acts on, semiotic objects (writing a book; editing, revising a document, etc., paraphrasing a sentence etc., deleting, inserting, moving a word, letter etc.), (ii) behavioural clauses construing linguistic activity (gossiping, chatting, consulting) or activity that may be accompanied by saying (frowning, grimacing, snarling); (iii) verbal clauses construing saying and mental clauses

construing sensing, alike in their ability to project, but different in that the senser but not the sayer has to be endowed with consciousness and in that saying but not sensing can be addressed to somebody; (iv) relational clauses: construing semiotic relationships – construing taxonomic classes and qualities, construing constituency relations, construing realization (including meaning [mean, express, signify, symbolize, denote, connote, refer to] and naming [name, call, term]).

- Group, nominal: (i) type of thing construing semiotic things (word, letter, sound, paragraph, chapter; talk, speech, gossip, document, book, novel, story, fable, allegory; fact, idea, issue, point, question, claim, advice); (ii) facets construing semiotic perspective on things (word; symbol, expression, meaning, as in *a word of advice, the meaning of "kataba"*).

These are aspects of the organization of the overall lexicogrammatical system towards the grammatical end. They also have lexical implications, however; for example, in the more delicate systems of verbal and mental clauses, and types of thing and facet in the nominal group (see Hasan 1987, on the grammatical implications for lexical distinctions in the move in delicacy towards lexis).

These systems are all part of the congruent mode. In addition, there are lexicogrammatical metaphors where various aspects of the construal of language in the congruent system are reconstrued metaphorically. An example is shown in Table 7.1.

There are systematic motifs in these metaphors, such as meaning as the content of a container, talk as words which can be manipulated in space, communication as conveying words through a channel with obstacles. These motifs also show up in other areas of the lexicogrammar, e.g. *empty words/phrases, think before one speaks, the word is out, a word of advice, to drop names.*

The commonsense "conduit metaphor" identified by Reddy (1979) is one source of scholarly thinking about language and communication. But non-metaphorical modes of the ideational grammar have also influenced the development of theory in the academic context. The set of verbs that can serve in verbal clauses has formed the point of departure for a more scientific theory of verbal goings-on – speech act theory. Edmondson (1981: 25) makes the following illuminating observation about the domain of investigation in speech act theory after having noted the use of "performatives" in descriptions (our bolding):

If we accept then a descriptivist analysis of overt performative utterances, the question arises not as to whether terms which may appear in such performative utterances characterize all the basic things we

Table 7.1 Congruent and incongruent (metaphorical) construals of experience of "languaging"

Congruent domain	Metaphor
Process: speak	put thoughts into words
Process: speak + Manner: forcefully etc.	have a loose/sharp tongue; find one's tongue; snap somebody's head off; skate around the subject; not to mince words; have a heart to heart; spill the beans; let the cat out of the bag; get across; get thoughts/ideas ... into somebody's head; get a word in edgewise; eat one's words; echo somebody's words
Sayer: somebody + Process: say → projection	word/rumour/news spread that ... : the statement/question/... is [[projection]]

can do with language, but as to why some utterances may be described appropriately by the use of such performative formulae, while others may not. ... An investigation matching illocutionary terms with systematically-distinguished categories of events which may be referred to in an utterance that may be characterized by that matching illocutionary term reveals which types of illocutionary act are conceptually distinguished in the lexis of English ... The conclusion to be drawn from this discussion is that **illocutionary category's in Searle's theory are common-sense, not technical categories** ... Searle is a philosopher, not a discourse analyst. For the characterisation of verbal behaviour in spoken discourse **we require technical terms.**

The discussion above sketches the commonsense models of language; and they engender more uncommonsense versions. Based on work in ethnography, linguistics, and language-oriented histories of science, we now have a fairly clear picture of what happens in general in the move from the registers of daily life to the registers of science – from commonsense (folk) models to uncommonsense (scientific) ones. The changes can be summarized as in Table 7.2.[4]

These are systematically related shifts in the whole meaning-making potential. Together they can construct a considerable distance to daily experience, but they also tend to fragment it since the scientific focus on some domain of experience is usually much more clearly bounded than the commonsense one. While commonsense models are constituted as indeterminate regions within the overall semantic space, scientific ones are constituted in expert registers, framed as "knowledge" within institutionalized disciplines or subdisciplines.

7.3.4   *Construing theory as a semiotic resource*

We have seen that language is being turned back on itself in the construction of commonsense theories of language. A commonsense theory of language is constituted in language by deploying the resources of verbal clauses and projection, of relational clauses, and so on in a systematic way. Similarly, an uncommonsense theory of language is constituted in language by deploying these resources in a systematic way. But here the patterns of deployment are more open to conscious design – to theory construction. The boundary between the commonsense and the uncommonsense modes of deployment is not sharp; we have seen that commonsense constructs may form the base for theoretical edifices, and if theory is denied a place in descriptive work, it is likely that the boundary is further blurred so that description is left with a commonsense understanding that is far from adequate. At the same time, the resources deployed in an uncommonsense theory of language are different from those deployed in a commonsense theory. They are different in a registerial sense: covertly or cryptically and overtly. They are covertly different in that grammatical selections are constrained in particular ways, and they are overtly different in that such constraints may be codified lexically in technical lexis. The resources are also different in the sense that they may include semiotic systems other than language – in particular, systems of formal, symbolic representation (predicate logic, boolean algebra, fuzzy set theory, and so on) and systems of visualization by diagrams (the circle diagrams used here to represent stratification, box diagrams, system networks in graphic mode, and so on).

How can we construe the relationship between theory and linguistic resources or other semiotic resources in which it is constituted? Again, Firth (1948b/1957c: 141) provides a way in (our bolding):

Table 7.2 Commonsense and uncommonsense models of experience

	Commonsense models constituted in everyday registers	Uncommonsense models constituted in scientific registers	References
delicacy	folk taxonomies: –fairly few steps in delicacy with special status of basic level –evolved, so indeterminate –overt taxonomic criteria, often mixed	scientific taxonomies: –further steps in delicacy, codified as species, family etc. –designed determinacy –covert taxonomic criteria, observable by scientific means (genes, etc.)	Berlin, Breedlove, and Raven et al (1973): Wignell, Martin, and Eggins (1989)
delicacy of focus	folk scale: –objects and events at bandwidth of daily human experience	scientific scale: –including micro-scoping and macro-scoping relative to daily human experience	Unsworth (1995)
mode of construal	congruent: –congruent clauses of all process types with partic-ipants according to the domain, e.g. human Actors or Sensers	metaphorical: –phenomena reconstrued metaphorically, e.g. processes reconstrued as things. –metaphorical relational clauses with processes reconstrued as things serving as participants related causally, temporally, etc.; or metaphorical material clauses, often with processes of movement involving abstract and metaphorical things in an abstract space	Halliday and Martin (1993)

What I am emphasizing is not the need for a mere reform of terminology or a dabbling in agreed nomenclature when there is no agreed doctrine, but the necessity for turning the technique of semantics, historical and descriptive, **on to our own technical terms and the conceptual framework and system of ideas** within which they function or have functioned in our statements of fact and of theory. With such views in mind, most of us in the school of linguistics in London are increasingly aware of the problems of vocabulary and syntax in technical statements. We are experimenting with notation, tabulation, and the use of diagrams and other technical and even mechanical aids.

We can think of what Firth suggests as turning our metalanguage back on itself – turning our theory back on itself to understand how it is organized as a semiotic resource for making theoretical meanings. In recent work, we have begun to turn systemic functional theory back on itself as a semiotic system so as to characterize the theory itself as a resource for making meanings about language in context. We thus have at our disposal the fundamental dimensions along which systemic theory interprets language and other semiotic systems. For present purposes, we will focus on the stratification of metalanguage. Here Hasan's work on verbal art provides the central insight. We can construe the relationship between theory and the semiotic systems in which it is constituted as analogous to, and modelled on, the relationship between "theme" and "verbalization" in Hasan's theory of language and verbal art, begun in the 1960s and summarized in Hasan (1985a: 96–8) as follows:

... we need to recognize three strata in verbal art, amongst which the relationship is analogous to that amongst the strata of language. The strata in verbal art would be as follows:
Theme
Symbolic articulation
Verbalization
... [Verbalization] is the point of primary contact with the work. We can begin to know a piece of verbal art only if we know the language. (Note the important difference here between verbal art and painting or sculpture.) Knowing a language implies knowing the relations between the meanings, wordings, and the sounds. At this level the literature text is like any other text ... The stratum of theme is the deepest level of meaning in verbal art; it is what a text is about when dissociated from the particularities of that text. In its nature, the theme of verbal art is very close to a generalisation, which can be viewed as a

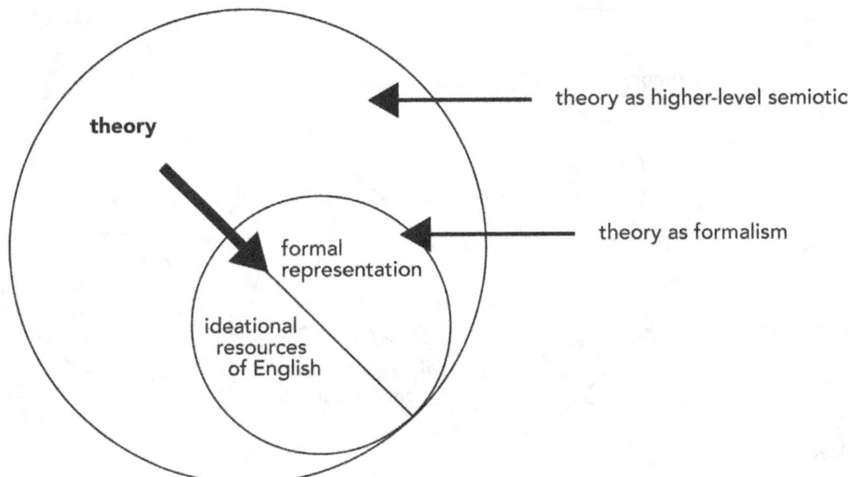

Figure 7.2 The stratification of metalanguage

> hypothesis about some aspect of the life of social man. ... [Theme and
> verbalisation] are brought into contact with each other through the
> stratum of SYMBOLIC ARTICULATION. This level is analogous
> to that of lexico-grammar in the semiotic system of human language.
> It consists of the system of signs that create the meanings of the highest
> stratum – theme.

Hasan goes on to characterize symbolic articulation further, but for present purposes we can stop here and turn from verbal art to linguistics seen as metalanguage. We can construe it as (at least) a two-stratal system, analogous to theme – verbalization: a stratum of the theoretical meaning-potential, and the stratum in which it is constituted or realized: see Figure 7.2. This second stratum encompasses the registers of linguistics in a particular language such as English and also complementary semiotic systems, in particular systems of formal representation and of visualization in diagrams.

7.3.5   *Theoretical value realized by descriptive tokens*

We now have an interpretation of theory as a semiotic resource for construing language. This interpretation will put us in a position to examine the role of theory in description – but we also need to determine the relationship between theory and description. Continuing the line of interpretation followed above, we can explore

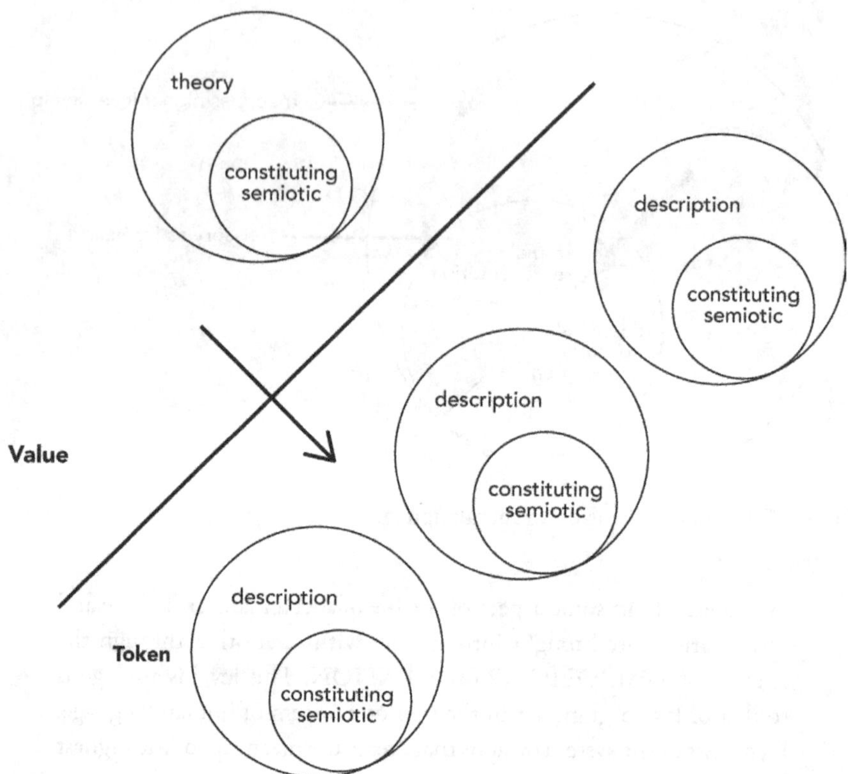

Figure 7.3 Descriptive tokens construing theoretical value

the relationship among theory and description in terms of the dimensions of systemic functional theory. For instance, theory and description might be related in delicacy at the same order of realization; they might be related in instantiation at the same order of realization; or they might be related in realization at different orders of abstraction. Different theories may quite possibly select different dimensions (e.g. if substantive universals are part of the theory in the form of "universal" primitive functions such as Subject or semantic primitives); but from a systemic functional point of view, the appropriate dimension is realization: theory is realized by description. In other words, particular descriptions of languages realize the general theory of language in a token–value relationship: see Figure 7.3. This does not mean that description is a passive reflection of theory; on the contrary, description **construes** theory. Theories are semiotic systems and they are created semiotically in acts of description, just as these descriptions realize the higher-level theoretical semiotic.

Table 7.3 General theory of language and particular descriptions, illustrated by English

General theory	Particular description of English
lexicogrammar × experiential × system × highest rank	TRANSITIVITY (=AGENCY and PROCESS TYPE and CIRCUMSTANTIATION)
lexicogrammar × experiential × term in system × highest rank	middle, effective; material, mental, verbal, relational; locative, non-locative; ...
lexicogrammar × experiential × structure: micro-function × highest rank	Actor, Goal, Recipient; Senser, Phenomenon; Location, Cause, Manner, ...
lexicogrammar × interpersonal × system × highest rank	MOOD
semantic × interpersonal × system × highest rank	SPEECH FUNCTION

Since the theory is itself a stratified semiotic resource, any particular description will also be stratified in this way. In general, it will be organized by the theoretical organization as well as by its own organization within the parameters set by the theory. Examples of theoretical categories realized in the description of English are given in Table 7.3.

Interpreting theory as a semiotic resource means saying that it is like language itself. It is a resource for making meanings in the first instance, not a set of rules for restricting possible descriptive statements. Halliday has emphasized this conception of theory in various contexts, for example:

> Describing a language is a work of interpretation; and interpretation is a theoretical pursuit. New descriptions, therefore, enforce new theories. But this, as I see it, is where the theory comes from. I am not really a theoretician; I have been interested in theoretical matters only because I had to be, because it was necessary to construct some new theoretical framework in order to accommodate certain aspects of the interpretation I wanted to suggest. But the resources of language are

extraordinarily rich, and the ways in which things can be related to each other are of an intricacy that we have hardly yet begun to conceive of. The theory should not restrict the kinds of interpretive statement we can make; it needs to be rich enough to allow for all kinds of elaborations and extensions – especially extension in delicacy, given that what we know about language today is only a fragment of what there is to be found out – without having to be patched up and mended all the time. For this reason my conceptual apparatus has always been extravagant rather than parsimonious. Since I was drawing no conclusions from the form of the theory, beyond the obvious one that language must be such-and-such if such-and-such a theory can account for it, there was no virtue in restricting its scope. (Halliday 1980: viii)

Systemic theory is explicitly constructed both for thinking with and for acting with. Hence – like language, again – it is rather elastic and rather extravagant. To be an effective tool for these purposes, a theory of language may have to share these properties with language itself: to be non-rigid, so that it can be stretched and squeezed into various shapes as required, and to be non-parsimonious, so that it has more power at its disposal than is actually needed in any one context. (Halliday 1985b/1994a: 11)

We are now in a position to examine the role of theory in description according to the positions already identified in Section 7.2.

7.4   The construction of theoretical meaning

Theory can be seen, then, as a semiotic resource for description – one that gives value to the description in the sense discussed in Section 7.3.5. If we adopt this view, downplaying theory in description does not mean that one is freed from a confining set of rules but rather that one is deprived of an enabling resource. Appeal to the resources of everyday lexicogrammar, with technical vocabulary being rejected, means that the resources for descriptive interpretation are restricted to commonsense theory, or that uncommonsense theory is being used and created covertly in cryptic patterns of the deployment of what is claimed to be everyday lexicogrammar. Let us start with this motif in Section 7.4.1 and then move onto theoretical neutrality and eclecticism.

7.4.1 *Appeal to commonsense – implicit construction of theory*

To assess the role theory can play in linguistic description, we need to appreciate the relationship between commonsense models constituted in everyday registers and scientific ones constituted in scientific registers. We need to develop the language-based understanding of theory sketched in Section 7.3.3. However, when theory is characterized in linguistic terms, it is often given a very narrow interpretation in language. One folk view of theory that is sometimes echoed even in discussions by professional linguists is that it is embodied in "jargon" – in scientific or technical vocabulary. Consequently, if it is possible to stay clear of "jargon," one has avoided the restrictive trap of theory. But this view betrays a lack of understanding of what is codified in lexical systems: lexical distinctions codify patterns of constraints on less delicate distinctions with the overall lexicogrammatical systems.

To take a very obvious example: if we use the wording "*x* is *a*" consistently in such a way that *x* and *a* are constrained to be related as expression and content (as in "green is go," "*kataba* is 'write'"), this is equally theoretical as "*x* denotes *a*." The only difference is that in "*x* denotes *a*" we have codified the pattern lexically in such a way that it is quite overt. It is not at all clear that there is any virtue in trying to hide such theoretical consistency by avoiding technical vocabulary.

Technical vocabulary is thus not an isolated component of the manifestation of theory in language that can be removed surgically to achieve greater clarity. In their study of scientific language, Halliday and Martin (1993: 4) emphasize that technical vocabulary is only part of lexicogrammar (our bolding): "Of course, **technical terms** are an **essential** part of scientific language; it would be impossible to create a discourse of organized knowledge without them. **But** they are **not the whole story**. The distinctive quality of scientific discourse lies in the **lexicogrammar** (the "wording") as a whole, and any response it engenders in the reader is a response to the **total patterns of discourse**."

Firth (1948b/1957c: 140) recognized a long time ago that language is turned back on itself in linguistics (see above), but that the language of everyday life cannot serve as the sole resource for linguistics (our bolding):

> Let it be borne in mind that language is often not very apt when used about itself, even in technical linguistic studies. If we pause to consider the stylistics **of the language of the common sensual life**, we can be sure it **will not serve as the language of linguistic science**. The technical language for the systematic statement of the facts of language cannot, any more than for mathematics, be the language of everyday

common sense. Professor Hjelmslev, fully realizing this, has endeavoured to frame a sort of linguistic calculus which might serve the linguistic sciences in the way mathematics has served the physical sciences. Even if the attempt be considered unsuccessful, it has not been sufficiently understood that the work of Professor Hjelmslev in general linguistics has been in the direction of our emancipation from the handicap of the common-sense idiom and "self-explanatory" nomenclature in half a dozen languages, and from the limitations of the technique of comparative grammar. However much we may disagree with it or dislike it, the terminology is necessitated by a system of thought, which is more than can be said of a certain type of work which adds little to knowledge, bristles with neologisms, and brings nothing but discredit on what some people misrepresent as modern linguistics.

7.4.2   *From freedom to eclecticism*

Freedom from theory in description is thus an illusion. Even if we avoid overt technical vocabulary, implicit theoretical value inheres in the patterns of deploying the resources of lexicogrammar in description. Apart from the likelihood that it will be harder for consumers to gain access to such an implicit theoretical code, there are ideological implications. Halliday (1993c: 223) characterizes these as follows:

> There is no such thing as theory-free engagement with language, whether one is actively intervening in the linguistic practices of a community or systematically describing the grammar of a particular language. The linguist who claims to be theory-free is like the conservative who claims to be non-political: they are both saying, to be impartial is to leave things as they are – only those who want to change them are taking sides.

Allegedly theory-free descriptions are thus a form of theoretical impartiality or neutrality. But "neutrality" is quite misleading since it really means the dominant theoretical status quo. In general, it would seem that **theoretical neutrality** means one of the following things:

1. Theoretical categories as seen from history (neutrality = common ancestor)
2. Theoretical categories as seen from mainstream (neutrality = dominance)
3. Theoretical categories as seen from intersection of all current theories (neutrality = smallest common denominator).

1. If neutrality is to be achieved by appeal to a common ancestor – say the Western tradition of linguistic theory, this means that descriptions will always have antiquated values; they will be confined to theory before the modern schools of linguistics. Thus, a reference grammar from the late twentieth century would not differ substantially in overall outline and interpretation from a grammar from, say, the seventeenth century (ignoring attitudes towards prescription and the role of Latin). And this is often the case, of course. Even descriptive interpretations may show similarity; for example, we might compare Dixon's (1991) new approach to English grammar on semantic principles, to the following extract from Robinson (1641):

> Nominative Case after the Verbe
>> Verbes Substantives, as …
>> Also Verbes that betoken bodily moving, going, resting, or doing, …
>> The Genitive Case after the Verbe.
>> This Verbe, *Sum*, I am, when it betokeneth or importeth possession, owing, or otherwise pertaining to a thing, as a token, property, duty, or guise: it causeth the Noune, Pronoune, or Participle following, to be put in the Genitive Case: …
>> Verbs that betoken to esteeme or regard, require a Genitive Case, betokening the value: …
>> Verbes of accusing, condemning, warning, purging, quitting, or assailing, and such like: will have a Genitive Case of the crime, or of the cause, of the thing, that one is accused, condemned, or warned of: …

This is the theoretical approach of traditional grammar: the verb is in construction with nouns showing different cases; and differences in case are accounted for by reference to different semantic types signified ("betokened") by verbs. There is a sense of formal word systems – the paradigms of traditional grammar; but there is no theory of a multidimensional semantic space construed by the grammar's transitivity system. Semantic types are simply given as lists with no further semantic organization revealed by the interpretation.

While it is quite understandable that linguists involved in descriptive work might try to achieve a kind of theoretical neutrality by returning to traditional grammar, it is rather like using Newtonian theory to describe physical systems because it is more accessible than e.g. quantum theory and because one can avoid choosing among modern competing theories. Furthermore, just as Newtonian theory was based on a certain bandwidth of the universe, traditional theory was construed in the description of Ancient Greek and Latin, so that they gave rise to supposedly theoretical distinctions such as the contrast between syntax and morphology and the categories of subject, predicate, and object. In any case, the tradition was never uniform; it always embodied the two theoretical conceptions of language as rule and language as resource (Halliday 1977).

2. Alternatively, theoretical neutrality may mean selecting theoretical categories from the modern manifestation of the theoretical conception of language as rule – i.e. from what is often referred to as mainstream linguistics, which is currently Standard Average American Metalanguages (SAAME). Any illusion that such a description is "neutral" vanishes rapidly if one compares it with a description deploying e.g. Gustave Guillaume's psycho-mechanic theory, tagmemic theory, or systemic functional theory.

3. A theory-neutral description might also be one which only draws on those theoretical categories that are shared by all theories. This would amount to the intersection of all current theoretical resources. If non-SAAMEs are taken into account, there would be a considerable diversity, and the intersection would be very small indeed. A theory-neutral description could not, for example, make use of theoretical categories such as constituency; (grammatical) rule; grammatical functions (such as Subject, Object, Predicate); system; or of any assumptions about the relationship between syntax and morphology, or between grammar and lexis. All these constitute domains of variation across metalanguages. Such theory neutrality would lead to very content-free description.

Instead of trying to achieve neutrality, many linguists adopt the much more plausible position of **theoretical eclecticism**. That is, the theoretical resource used in description is a kind of metalinguistic pidgin, maybe on the way to creolization. This is indeed one way in which new theoretical systems may develop, but development means a move away from eclecticism towards a resource that is recognizable as an integrated system. As it is typically used, the disadvantage with eclecticism is that it makes it very hard to reason with the theoretical resources across domains described in terms of different theoretical sources.

Eclecticism tends to arise along certain dimensions of the overall system of language in contexts so that we get different theories for different stratal domains, different theories for different metafunctional domains of meaning, different theories for the delicate (lexis) and the indelicate (grammar), and different theories for the system and the instantiation of the system. For example, one may combine a lexical functional grammar theory 1of syntax with an autosegmental theory of phonology. Then these two domains of language, syntax and phonology, are construed in terms of fairly different kinds of structures – syntactic c-structures and f-structures and phonological multi-tiered structures. They may simply continue to coexist in this way in one's theoretical understanding of language as the eclecticism invites them to do. Alternatively, one may ask whether the differences are really phenomenological or a property of the difference in theory. However, this is a very hard question to answer precisely because the theoretical resources used are different in kind. One might explore the question by trying out a c- and f- structure interpretation of phonological syntagms or a multi-tiered interpretation of syntactic ones, which is a very reasonable approach but a move away from eclecticism.

In contrast, since systemic functional theory is a resource for construing language in context, it can be used to construe both syntax and phonology. They are construed as different stratal domains manifesting the same general principles for organizing a stratal subsystem. For instance, they are both interpreted as ranked systems of options that are realized by different modes of structure. This approach will work to the extent that the theory is general, abstract, and flexible enough so as not to impose the organization of one (stratal) domain upon another e.g. by construing syntactic structure as if it was segmental phonemic structure.

7.4.3   *Increasing the meaning-making potential through theory*

The view taken here is, then, that theory is a semiotic resource for making meaning in description: description is given value through theory. Since theory is a system of meanings, it gives a higher-level organization to the meanings made in description. The richer the theory we have at our disposal, the richer we can make our description. Let us begin by illustrating this principle with respect to a simple example, and then suggest how certain areas of description might be explored further with the resources of systemic functional theory.

If we want to describe the example *The spy came in from the cold*, the theory at our disposal will determine how far we can take the description:

> With a theory of words, we might be able to posit a syntagm determiner + noun + verb + preposition + determiner + noun, assuming we could find criteria for word classes. These criteria would be likely to be some mix of appeals to meaning and form in paradigm (e.g., *spy* : *spies*, but *come(s)* : *came*), and combinability – though all of these already presuppose something beyond a theory recognizing words. The description would not be very informative.
>
> With an embryonic theory of rank, we might be able to begin to ask questions about, say, words in sentences. We could, for example, differentiate *the spy came in from the cold* from *did the spy come in from the cold* as instances of different sentence types – provided we had a theory of types.
>
> With an embryonic theory of structure, we could begin to answer questions about words in sentences by reference to structural functions. We could,

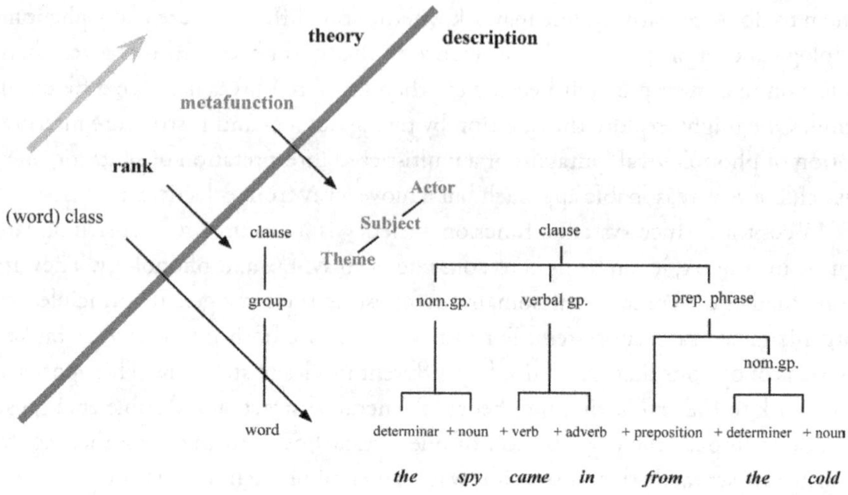

Figure 7.4 Expansion of theoretical potential

for example, recognize Subject (*the spy*) + Predicate (*came in from the cold*), and this might lead us to fill out the description of rank with an intermediate rank of groups/phrases.

With a metafunctional theory of structure, we could differentiate different modes of meaning in the sentence. We could, for example, recognize Subject (*the spy*) + Predicator (*came in*) + Adjunct (*from the cold*) alongside Actor (*the spy*) + Process (*came in*) + Location (*from the cold*) and Theme (*the spy*) + Rheme (*came in from the cold*). This would allow us to relate the example to a multidimensional account of sentence types on the one hand and to a multifunctional account of meaning on the other.

This list suggests a step-wise building up of the theoretical potential for descriptive interpretations that become more informative with each step: see Figure 7.4. Each step makes it possible to answer previous questions more systematically, but it also leads to new kinds of questions that will demand further theoretical development. Once the last step on the list above has been reached, the sentence can be related to discourse in a systematic way.

What we can say about particular domains of description depends, then, on what our theoretical potential provides us with. One of the domains of lexicogrammar that has received a good deal of attention in typological-functional descriptive work since the 1970s is "case marking systems." The classical notion of case as a word system was "up-ranked" so that not only overt morphological categories were taken into view but also more covert syntactic ones, often under the heading of "syntactic

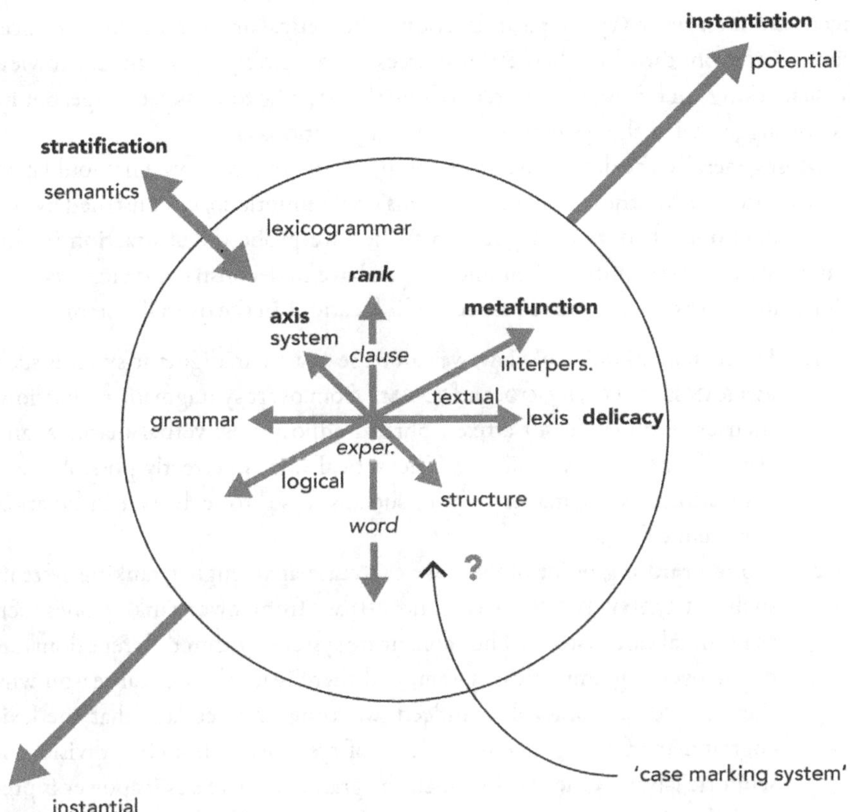

Figure 7.5 Probing "case marking system" theoretically

processes." The early distinction between the nominative-accusative, or transitive, model – familiar from traditional grammar – and the ergative (-absolutive) model was further elaborated, e.g. with the study of aspectual and other factors determining the domains of "split" systems such as are found in Hindi. These factors were related to the transitivity parameters identified in Hopper and Thompson's (1980) influential study of degrees of transitivity. Dixon (1979) constituted a valuable reference point for much of the work in the 1980s. Later, DuBois (1987) proposed an account of ergativity that related it to the flow of information in discourse.

There has thus been a steady progression in the expansion of the domain of "case marking," in the differentiation of different "case marking systems," in the identification of factors correlating with "splits" in such systems, and in understanding of the informational significance of a particular system in discourse. Theoretically, these descriptions have been eclectic. Loosely speaking, they have been cast in terms of a typological-functional theoretical orientation; but advances have come from different theoretical sources. Alternatively, we might try to view "case marking" in terms of the system of one theory. The topic is very large, but let us just suggest what the systemic functional implications are.

Most generally, the descriptive abstraction of "case marking system" would have to be located within the overall multidimensional semiotic space construed by systemic functional theory: see Figure 7.5. When we probe the abstraction in this way, it ceases to be a unified phenomenon: we have to deconstruct it along various dimensions, so as to give various aspects of it locations in the overall system.

1. From an **axial** point of view, we can tease apart paradigmatic systems such as TRANSITIVITY, MOOD, and THEME from overt syntagmatic realizations such as nominal (case) affixes, phrasal adpositions, verbal markers, and clausal constituency sequence. Theoretically, it is perfectly possible for a realizational syntagmatic category such as "case" to realize a combination of systemic features.

2. From a **ranking** point of view, we can tease apart higher-ranking systems such as TRANSITIVITY, MOOD, and THEME from lower-ranking ones such as nominal case systems. They constitute systems within different domains of the overall grammatical system, and there is no theoretical reason why they should be isomorphic. Indeed, we know theoretically that the lexicogrammar of a language is a system of systems, with a clear division of semiotic labour. One way in which the grammar increases its power is precisely by allowing the same lower-ranking system to serve to realize terms in different higher-ranking systems located in different environments at the higher rank.

3. From a **metafunctional** point of view, we can tease apart different metafunctional perspectives. A given realizational category such as a nominal case or a phrasal adposition may serve within one metafunction; or it may combine metafunctional contributions. Having teased apart the different metafunctional perspectives, we can then ask to what extent they harmonize with one another.

4. From a **delicacy** point of view, we can relate lexical patterns of transitivity to grammatical ones. Thus, if a language is discovered to have ergative pairs of lexical verbs, this suggests that the grammar of TRANSITIVITY also embodies an ergative system since lexis and grammar are related along the cline of delicacy.

5. From an **instantiation** point of view, we can relate instantial patterns in transitivity in text to the overall transitivity potential they instantiate. The

instantiation in text may create an instantial system that has significance against the background of the overall potential (see e.g. Halliday 1973, for instantial systems in Golding's *The Inheritors*). Intermediate between the instantial and the overall potential of a language, we find the repertoire of registers, or registerial subpotentials, of the overall potential that are located in particular situation types. These registerial subpotentials will foreground certain aspects of the transitivity system and background others. We can thus tease apart the transitivity system according to register variation; and we can evaluate textual evidence according to this variation. For example, we are likely to find the transitive model of transitivity foregrounded in traditional narrative, but the ergative model foregrounded in certain scientific English: see Caffarel (1997) for a discussion of this point with respect to French.

As noted above, accounts of "case marking systems" grew out of descriptions of word-rank nominal cases; generalizations were thus, in a sense, built up from below as the notion of "case marking" was extended to syntax. We have just suggested that case marking systems cease to appear to be single domains if we try to locate them systemic functionally in the overall lexicogrammatical system. Indeed, Comrie (1981: 108) notes, "it is misleading to classify a language as being either ergative or not, rather one must ask: to what extent, and in what particular constructions is the language ergative, i.e. where does its syntax operate on a nominative-accusative basis and where does its syntax operate on an ergative-absolutive basis." A rich theory should make us ask these and other questions, as we have shown.

7.5   Meeting new descriptive challenges

So far we have concentrated on the problem of the relationship between theory and description as it emerges from fairly traditional descriptive work, such as traditional reference grammars, and we have shown theory is a resource for enriching description, as in our example of how it can add dimensionality in descriptions of transitivity. In work on English, we have had the benefit of a string of reference grammars in this century by Jespersen, Poutsma, Kruisinga, Quirk et al., and others. While they have varied e.g. in their attitude towards diachrony, they have all been on a fairly traditional model: a linear sequence through the units of the grammar. The reference grammar of the twenty-first century will, we believe, be a very different kind of semiotic object; and it will constitute a challenge to the role of theory in description. To round off the discussion in this chapter, let's consider how new descriptive challenges in this context can be met.

After producing a substantial reference grammar on Quechua (cf. Weber 1989), David Weber gave a talk at UCLA in the first half of the eighties as an introduction to his thesis defence, outlining what he felt would be a more useful, new form of reference grammar – the grammar he would have liked to have written given what he now knew. Among its interesting features were a hypertext-like ability to go from illustrative text to description, and from description to illustration. As Matthiessen listened to his presentation, he thought to himself, "Aha! He'd like a reference grammar organized in terms of systemic functional theory."

Weber was reflecting on the need to have reference grammars that are linked in a systematic way to exemplifying continuous text and which can be accessed in different ways, not just by means of linear look-up. In addition, we can now recognize additional challenges for the reference grammar of the twenty-first century:

- It will have to support a variety of readings by a variety of readers, differing in their consumer needs – discourse description, educational linguistics, computational linguistics, clinical linguistics, and so on – and in their degree of expertise.
- It will have to support a variety of uses – not only traditional grammatical analysis and argumentation, but also discourse analysis and in addition discourse generation and revision.
- It will have to support links not just to exemplifying texts but also to a flow-through corpus where text can constantly be processed in terms of the categories of the grammar and provide evidence for refinements of the grammar.
- It will have to support arguments and alternatives by making it possible to trace through the description to find out what the implications are for locating the interpretation of a phenomenon relative to other systemic interpretations and by making it possible to project alternative interpretations.

Technologically, a reference grammar meeting these demands will have to be a computational resource. It will thus be freed from the traditional presentational limitation of a hard-copy book between covers. However, technology only serves to make this possible. It is well known from database design that the real challenge is a more theoretical one: it is to identify the dimensions for organizing the descriptive information encoded in the database.

Systemic functional theory both supports and demands a type of reference grammar that is technologically much more advanced than the traditional one. The theory is multidimensional (rank, delicacy, metafunction, axis, instantiation, and so on), and the way in which the dimensions relate to one another is quite explicit. The theory thus makes it possible to **shunt** along these dimensions (cf. Halliday

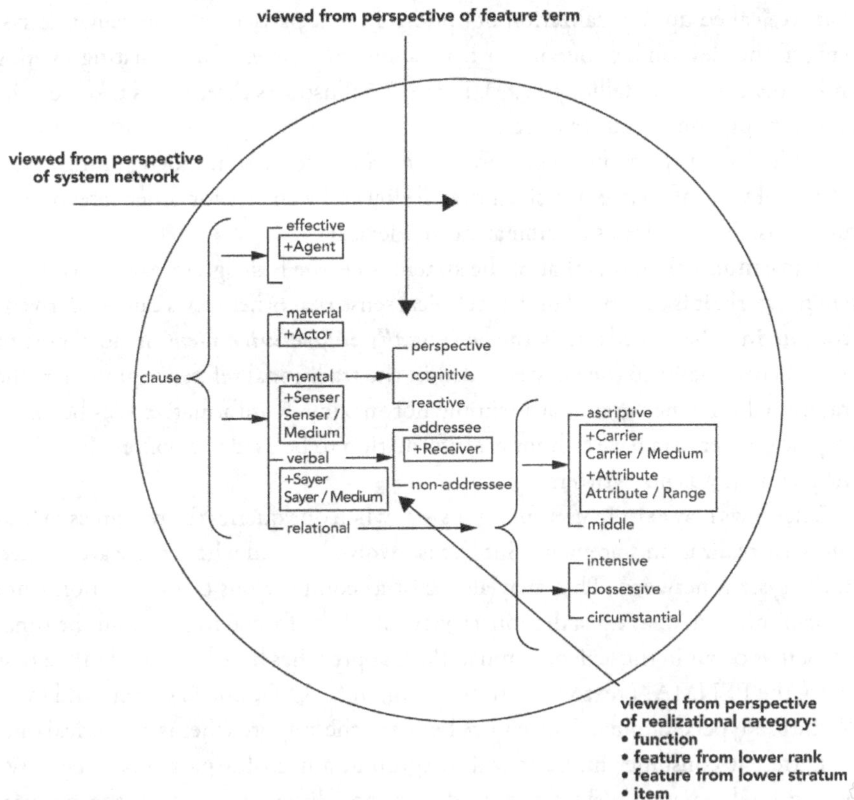

Figure 7.6 Different views on resources

1961: section 7.2) to adopt different **views** on the lexicogrammatical resources.[5] Thus, it is possible to adopt a logical view, an experiential view, an interpersonal view, or a textual view; these views constitute different "projections" of the map of the overall resources of the grammar. It is also possible to vary the view according to rank (e.g. from above or from below – a syntactic or morphological view in the specific sense of Halliday 1961: section 5.3), according to delicacy (e.g. a view up to tertiary degree of delicacy), according to system (a system-network-based view or a feature-based view), according to realization (e.g. a system-based view or a structure-and-item-based view), according to register variation (a general view or a register-specific one; cf. Matthiessen 1993a on register-specific partitions of resources). Finally, it should be possible to adopt views external to the lexicogrammar; in particular, it should be possible to adopt a view from a socio-semantic system specific to some situation type so that we see only those aspects of lexicogrammar that are "called up" by realization of options in that particular socio-semantic system (cf. the view on lexicogrammar from a semantic system for regulating a young child's behaviour in Halliday 1973). Figure 7.6 illustrates three views taken on the same lexicogrammatical resources.

Table 7.4 illustrates different views on the resources within lexicogrammar. The canonical view of a system is given first, followed by entries for other categories – functions, features, items (grammatical and lexical).

The **canonical view** is that of the system – i.e. the lexicogrammar as a vast system network. It is canonical in the technical sense that other views can be "derived" from it; in other words, it is the *maximally informative view*. It does not, of course, correspond to the view encoded in the traditional reference grammar: the traditional reference grammar is simply not maximally informative – as becomes very clear when you have to hunt for information to be used in a context for which the grammar was not written.

The views may exist in user functions – as when one queries the resources to find out what realization statements Subject is involved in and where these are located in the system network. They may also exist as compilations of information from the canonical view, as e.g. a dictionary view of all the formal items, or all the functions, that occur in the lexicogrammar. Both approaches have been used in the past in e.g. the PENMAN text-generation system, in M. O'Donnell's system, and in C. Nesbitt's HyperGrammar. The choice between these approaches is a practical one.

Different consumer interests will foreground a need for particular views. We have gained experience with the need to adopt different views on the resources in computational work; the processes of generation and parsing access the resources according to different views. In particular, O'Donnell's work on parsing with a grammar originally created for generation (the NIGEL grammar, see Matthiessen and Bateman 1991) has demonstrated the importance of creating views making information easily accessible to the parsing process in the form of look-up tables (see Matthiessen, O'Donnell, and Zeng 1991). But the need to adopt different views is not unique to computational work; it is quite general across all uses of lexicogrammar. For example, if one needs the lexicogrammar to diagnose second-language-learner problems in some system such as modality, the system-based view is needed to create a systemic profile of what learners are able to produce so as to be able to zoom in on problem areas (cf. Gibbons and Markwick-Smith 1992). If one needs the lexicogrammar in text analysis, a "dictionary" view will be very helpful for look-up of grammatical and lexical items, and a system view will be necessary to interpret the text against the background of the overall lexicogrammatical potential.

Table 7.4 Views on the lexicogrammatical resources of a language according to data type (derived from Figure 7.6)

Data type	Example entry	
system	mood tag	entry condition: "imperative/declarative" terms: "tagged" (+Moodtag; +Tagfinite; +Tagsubject; Tagfinite ^ Tagsubject; Moodtag (Tagfinite, Tagsubject); Tagfinite: auxiliary; Tagsubject: pronominal)/"untagged"
function	Subject	realizations with Subject as operand *insert:* MOOD TYPE: "indicative" *preselect:* INDICATIVE MOOD PERSON: "interactant-subject" Subject: interactant/"non-interactant-subject" Subject: other … *order:* INDICATIVE TYPE: "declarative" Subject ^ Finite INTERROGATIVE TYPE: "yes-no" Finite ^ Subject WH-SELECTION: "non-wh-subject" Finite ^ Subject
	Phenomenon	realizations with Phenomenon as operand *insert:* PHENOMENAL: "phenomenal" + Phenomenon *preselect:* PHENOMENALITY1: "simple-phenomenal" (Phenomenon: nominal group)/"complex-phenomenal" (Phenomenon: clause) PHENOMENALITY2: "expansion-phenomenal" (Phenomenon: non-finite)/"projection-phenomenal" (Phenomenon: projection-clause) ---

Continued

Table 7.4 Views on the lexicogrammatical resources of a language according to data type (derived from Figure 7.6) (Continued)

Data type	Example entry	
feature	nominal group	system: CLASS OF GROUP: "nominal group" realizations: *preselect:* PROCESS TYPE: "material" Actor: nominal group
	tagged	system: MOOD TAG realizations: *insert:* +Moodtag; +Tagfinite; +Tagsubject; *order:* Tagfinite ^ Tagsubject; *expand:* Moodtag (Tagfinite, Tagsubject); *preselect:* Tagfinite: auxiliary; Tagsubject: pronominal
item	the	lexify: SPECIFIC SELECTION: "non-selective" Deictic = *the*
	become	"feature set": 'become' preselect: TYPE OF INCHOATIVE: "unmarked inceptive" Process: 'become'

The reference grammar of the twenty-first century will thus be a multidimensional resource supporting multiple user views. However, it can be more than a reference source of the kind the traditional reference grammar is. It can also be a resource for automatic processing of text in parsing, generation, and translation. On the one hand, this means that it can be linked to programs for computational modelling of text processing. On the other hand, it means that the parser should be able to analyse text corpora for automatic analysis, for automatic exemplification of grammatical categories with respect to some text sample, and for computer-aided further development of the lexicogrammatical resources, either generally or with respect to some particular register.

How far away is the reference grammar of the twenty-first century? It is already supported by current systemic functional theory in pre-implementational form. Now we will have to try to move towards such a reference grammar in a dialogue between theory and implementation. Certain key aspects are already being tried out in implementations, e.g. Cummings' (1987) SYSPRO for graphing and testing system networks; COMMUNAL, developed by Robin Fawcett and his group; and Webster's (1993) Functional Grammar Processor. Let us exemplify from the PENMAN system and work taking place in our computational modelling group in Sydney.

In the PENMAN text-generation system, there is a set of user functions for accessing information about the lexicogrammatical resources from various points of view. It is also possible to graph the system network to various degrees of delicacy and, if desired, according to metafunctional slices. However, the PENMAN system remains a system for computational linguistic modelling. Both O'Donnell's Coder and Nesbitt's HyperGrammar go farther in exploring capabilities that an online reference grammar will need.

O'Donnell has developed a grammatical Coder for analysing text systemically by making selections from a system network. If delicate features are selected, less delicate ones are automatically inferred; and the Coder will select unmarked features unless these selections are overridden by the linguist in the coding process. To make it possible to test an analysis, O'Donnell has linked the Coder to a systemic generator so that the user can generate an example from a systemic analysis and compare the original example with the one automatically generated. O'Donnell has also developed an integrated system for parsing, generation, and resource exploration. The resource explorer enables the user to tour the lexicogrammatical resources. For example, it is possible to graph some part of the overall system network and then select systemic features to get further information about them.

Nesbitt's HyperGrammar is a tool for developing and referencing lexicogrammatical resources. It has been designed as a system to reflect in its organization as a

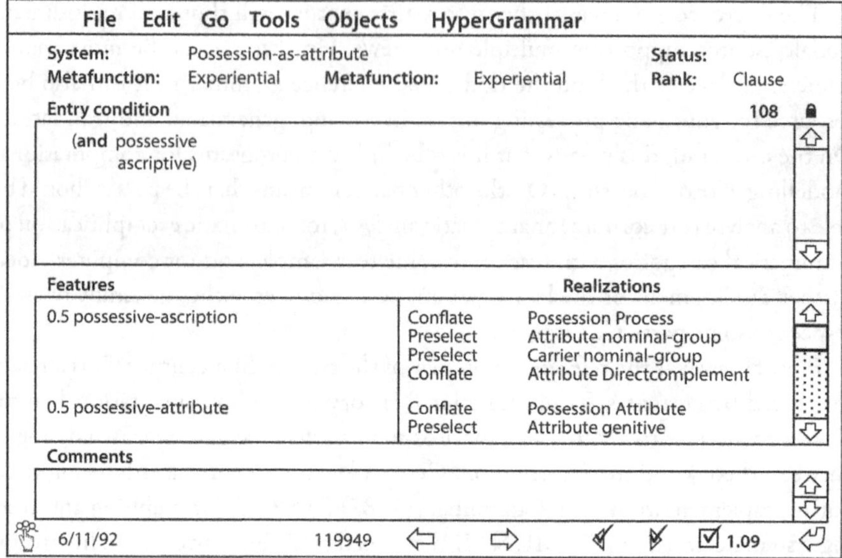

Figure 7.7 Card for system POSSESSION-AS-ATTRIBUTE

resource the organization of the resources of the linguistic system. It is at its heart a system for the writing and maintaining of system networks. What a word processor is to the production of text, HyperGrammar is to the development of system networks. But while a word processor has no connection with a text after it has been finished, HyperGrammar is in this sense more a linguistic information management system. The basic unit of information is a system in the system network; it is represented as a "card" (using the HyperCard™ organizational metaphor). Each card specifies the name of the system, its metafunctional address, its address within a systemic region such as transitivity or mood, its feature terms and their realizations, and comments, where examples, interpretations, and arguments for the analysis adopted can be given: see Figure 7.7.

Cards form a stack of cards, which represents the lexicogrammatical system network. Cards are linked in various ways. For example, it is possible to select a systemic term and move to the system(s) where it occurs as (part of) the entry condition. It is also possible to access all the features of the system network from a card to go to cards where they are used; Figure 7.8 shows the feature menu. HyperGrammar has been developed as a first step in an investigation of how we

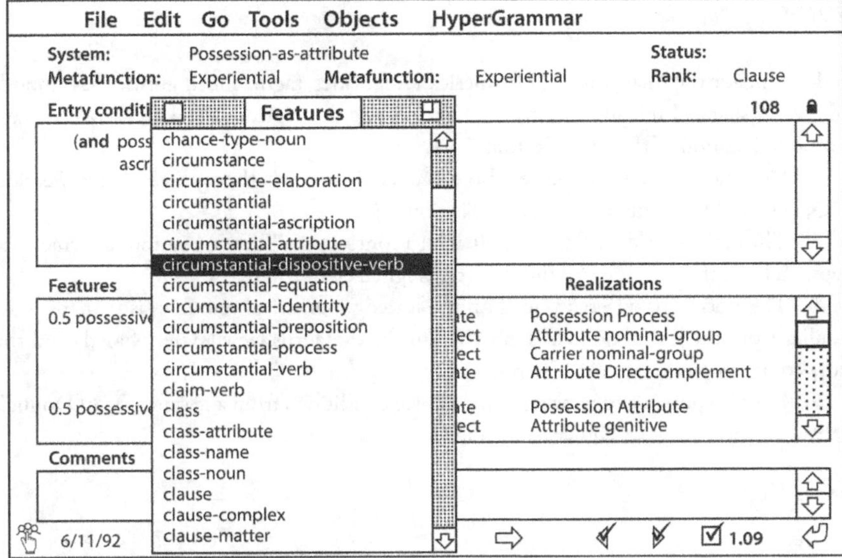

Figure 7.8 Window listing the features in the grammar

can address the need to rethink reference grammars for the twenty-first century (see Nesbitt 1994).

7.6   Conclusion

We have suggested how far a particular theory can take us in description, both in developing descriptions (Section 7.4) and in operating on descriptions as reference sources (Section 7.5) – but only if the theory is rich enough to meet the new descriptive challenges we have discussed. A rich theory is a flexible one; it is a theory that enables more than one descriptive interpretation of some phenomenological domain and that defines more than one perspective on that domain within a single description. This flexibility will ensure that we are not locked into one perspective in description. It thus meets the needs theoretical neutrality and eclecticism were designed to address. However, it does so without losing the power of a rich theory to determine the consequences of adopting one perspective or another since the theory clearly defines how the dimensions along which we can make perspectival shunts intersect with one another.

Notes

1   Outside the "mainstream" of American linguistics, tagmemic linguistics has embodied a very balanced relationship between theory and description. We will discuss the tagmemic conception of theory in Section 7.3.1.

2   Commonsense is, of course, also a theory; it is a *folk*-theory: see further Section 7.3.3; and cf. Pike's "implicit theory" in Section 7.3.1.

3   The table only identifies two points on a continuum. There are various intermediate steps, such as informed folk taxonomies (cf. Wignell et al. 1989).

4   The notion of different views on the lexicogrammatical resources is perhaps most familiar from the lexical domain, embodied in the thesaurus view (system-based) and the more common dictionary view (item-based).

5   It is also possible to view semantic choice conditions from a feature: see O'Donnell (1994) on compiling out choice conditions from choosers.

Chapter 8

Interview with Christian Matthiessen (Liverpool, 1998)

RCEI (Revista Canaria de Estudios Ingleses) After having listened to several lecturers discussing their own ideas concerning the use of different varieties in the analysis of language within SFL [systemic functional linguistics], may I ask you what your view on this issue is?

C.M. (Christian Matthiessen) Well, it seems to me, thinking about the different varieties of analysis, that there is an interesting theoretical challenge here – the question of how to conceptualize such variation. We have been thinking about this for quite some time now, since the eighties, trying to think explicitly about the systemic functional theory as a metalanguage – a resource for describing language that is itself like language (this line of thinking goes back to J.R. Firth, who characterized linguistics as language being turned back on itself). This conception of the theory has been helpful, you know, when thinking about what are the features of the organization of SFL, but also when thinking about the contexts in which it has been developed, or is being developed, and the contexts of application to a range of tasks, including educational, clinical, and computational ones. And so the notion of dialects of SFL, of course, follows directly from this metaphor of metalanguage. But in addition to dialectal variation, there is also the other kind of variation we find in language itself – variation according to context of use: functional variation, where we can recognize families of functional varieties or "registers." It's an interesting issue how to sort out this kind of variation within SFL – the registers of the systemic functional metalanguage. I mean, I think some of the variation we find within systemic functional linguistics has developed as functional variation because scholars have faced different research questions, different demands of application. Just as an example, a number of the features of the model that Jim Martin has developed – e.g. his development of additional strata within context – can be related to his concern with educational contexts. I think a number of the features of the model Robin Fawcett has presented – e.g. his reduction of the full axial organization within the strata of semantics and lexicogrammar – can be related to the computational context. That doesn't mean that if you are addressing educational issues the model has to be like Jim Martin's model, for instance, or if you are addressing computational concerns, it has to be like the Cardiff model; and it does not mean that their models cannot be applied to different contexts: they can be and they have been – for example, John Bateman has found Jim's work very significant in the computational context. Rather, it's a question of how different contexts of application will foreground different aspects of the total systemic functional metalanguage. I think one of the strengths of this metalanguage is that, as far as I know, it's the only theory of language that spans such a wide range of concerns and applications; other theories tend to be contextually more restricted, even to the point where they have essentially been designed for a single context of research (as has arguably been the case with the Chomskyan program of research). I can't think of any other theory that, for instance, would both have a strong engagement with educational concerns, with computational modelling of language, with clinical work, and then also with literary stylistics, multimodal semiotics, and so on. I think this is one of the fundamental strengths of systemic functional theory: it has this wide range of applications and they can enrich one another.

RCEI If scientific research in these fields is not based on strong backbones within SFL whereby things may begin to drift away and disappear, would we not be running an important risk?

C.M. Yes! I think that point is important. We must keep returning to the theoretical "backbone" – interpreting it all the time as a resource (rather than as a set of rules), i.e. as a meaning potential enabling us to construe language. The potential danger is that people working within particular research contexts continue to develop functional varieties specific to those contexts without considering other contexts and without feeding the work back into the general metalanguage of systemic functional theory; the result might be divergence and fragmentation, thus decreasing the power of the general theory. One thing I often argue we should be doing is to say, "Well, if we have this experience from the educational context, the computational context, and so on, let's make sure that this is part of the 'backbone,' so that these experiences available as resources also for other people." Since we can actually theorize the specialization within different contexts in systemic functional terms and since systemic functional theory is inherently holistic in orientation, I think we can avoid the danger of the fragmentation of knowledge that has concerned many twentieth-century scholars, such as the quantum physicist David Bohm. So far I don't think that the functional varieties of systemic functional theory have diverged much. Interestingly, Michael Halliday's own "backbone" of systemic functional theory has, in my opinion, been very successful in both being elastic enough to move into different contexts but also being thought through enough, systematic enough, to leave the general outlines of the theory clear. This seems to me to be a possible difference between the very highly elaborated model that Robin Fawcett presents, the Cardiff model, and the kind of model that Michael Halliday and other people in and around Sydney have been developing and elaborating. Halliday's model specifies a small number of general semiotic dimensions such as stratification, instantiation, axis, and rank, so anything that you put in the model must be placed relative to all of these dimensions; there are no ad hoc categories floating around in the account. Thus, any interpretation of a linguistic phenomenon will be located along one or more of these semiotic dimensions; in interpreting it, you say, "Okay, this is a matter of stratal organization; this is a matter of the cline of instantiation; this is a matter of metafunctional organization; and so on." So everything will be placed in this multidimensional semiotic space, and I think this kind of metaphor of the multidimensional space constructed in modelling language is helpful (just as the multidimensional thinking in physics has been) because it ensures that you are always asking where you are; if we are changing something, adding something, then the implications are always very clear. It's certainly pedagogically useful, helping our students build up clear, systematic maps of the dimensions of language.

RCEI And do you think that research on the series of system networks to make explicit the language potential is one of these backbones?

C.M. I think system networks will continue to play a very important role, certainly in our own work. Before Robin Fawcett and his group started their computational work here in Cardiff in the mid-1980s, some of us were involved in computational research at an institute in Los Angeles, the Information Sciences Institute. Our work was started by William C. Mann in 1980. The main focus was the development of a computational text-generation system (which came to be known as the PENMAN system) building on Michael Halliday's account of the grammar and of language in general. He was a consultant on the project and provided us with the first system network of the English clause. The system network was the "backbone" of our work right from the beginning: unlike the structure-oriented grammars that had been used in computational parsing in the 1960s and 1970s (e.g. so-called transition network grammars), the system network made explicit how the grammar is organized as a resource for making meanings, and therefore we were able to specify how grammatical choices could be controlled in a meaningful way in the course of the generation of a text. The system we developed is still in use around the world; John Bateman, Elke Teich, and others have taken it further in the form of the KPML (Komet-PENMAN, MultiLingual) system. John has developed a very user-friendly interface and made it available to researchers together with an excellent user manual. In Sydney, we have also built on the PENMAN foundations, developing a new generation of systemic functional system for producing text in various languages accompanied by contributions from other semiotic systems, such as maps and diagrams. The system network has been central in making this possible because it allows us to abstract away from structural differences among languages – and among different semiotic systems – and to specify the multilingual and multimodal meaning potential in an integrated way. The systemic functional approach to language (and to semiotic systems in general) is fairly unique in foregrounding the systemic, paradigmatic axis of organization, and the main resource for modelling this organization is the system network.

RCEI To explore another important characteristic of SFL, what distinguishes its functional approach to language from other approaches also called functional, like that in Simon Dik's grammar?

C.M. It has now been over ten years since I talked with Simon Dik before he passed away, and their work keeps developing; but from those discussions and from reading seminal work within his framework, I had a sense that one difference is that the Dikian functional grammar has focussed mainly on "lexicogrammar," to put it in systemic functional terms – that is, with the stratum of wording: lexis and grammar (including both "syntax" and "morphology" – "morpho-syntax," as it is sometimes called nowadays). What they call "semantics" corresponds most closely to ideational – more specifically, experiential – lexicogrammar, and what they call "pragmatics" corresponds most closely to textual lexicogrammar; the interpersonal metafunction has been backgrounded in their work on lexicogrammar, as it was in the Prague School. Like Daneš' work beginning with his proposals in the early 1960s, the Dikian framework equates stratification and metafunction; but in systemic functional theory, stratification and metafunction are two distinct dimensions, so that where the Dikian framework has three "components" – pragmatics, semantics, and syntax – we have a two-dimensional space of six regions: ideational (logical and experiential), interpersonal and textual semantics; and ideational, interpersonal, and textual lexicogrammar. This means, among other things, that the functional "components" in Dik's framework are ordered (pragmatics > semantics > syntax), like the strata of a stratal theory, whereas the metafunctions of systemic theory are simultaneous. They've not been concerned very much with the other content systems – discourse semantics and context, nor with the expression system of phonology (graphology or sign), so in that sense their focus is a narrower one, and from the systemic functional point of view that's significant, because a good deal of the functionalism in the systemic functional approach to lexicogrammar derives precisely from the fact that it's related to higher levels of organization – to semantics and context – and because the full range of lexicogrammatical systems can only be seen if the phonological system of intonation is taken into account as an expressive resource. The systemic functional approach is holistic in character (as opposed to "componential"); it is based on systems thinking (as opposed to Cartesian analysis). I think that's one difference.

Another difference is that Dik's grammar is oriented more towards the syntagmatic axis, focussing on function structure, whereas systemic functional theory is both systemic or paradigmatic and structural or syntagmatic and foregrounds systemic organization as the basis for interpreting language. The Dikian framework has nothing that is equivalent to the system networks of systemic functional theory.

A third difference, I think, is the sort of the range of things that people are looking at. I mean, all through the 1980s and early 1990s I think it's true to say that in Dik's functional grammar there's been a strong connection between functionalism and typology, so they have tended to look at particular areas of language in a typological perspective, thus cutting across languages, whereas in systemic functional work there's always been a very high priority on developing comprehensive accounts of particular languages first. This is tied up to the systemic functional view of how you would compare and contrast languages and do linguistic typology. In systemic functional work on typology there is, I think, a commitment to an approach that is based on very comprehensive descriptions of particular languages so that you don't export the description of English to other languages (as happened with descriptions of grammars of various languages before the twentieth century done by missionaries on the basis of Latin etc.). This systemic functional approach is illustrated by a new book on systemic functional typology being edited by Alice Caffarel, Jim Martin, and me; the book contains systemic functional descriptions of a range of languages (French, German, Telugu, Tagalog, Pitjantjatjara, Chinese, and Japanese) and these form part of the base for typological generalizations across languages.

RCEI In your opinion, what are the main lines of expansion within SFL?

C.M. I think existing areas such as educational linguistics, literary analysis, social semiotics, and computational work will continue to develop. Within the educational area, I would hope to see the development of systemic functional work on second-language teaching and learning as an alternative to non-systemic work on language "acquisition" (most of us avoid the metaphor of "acquisition" because of the unfortunate implication that language is a commodity to be acquired rather than a meaning potential to be constructed interactively by the learner). I think that the computational area – with the general development of the computational work and so on – will continue to expand. I hope myself to see much more interaction between, say, the computational and the educational lines of work, so that the computational work within SFL can provide resources for educational work, modelling in the classroom, helping in the construction of educational knowledge, and so on. I think there are many opportunities here. I also see that the computational work can make more contact with corpus-based work in linguistics and provide systemic functional tools for analysing corpora. We're trying to do this at Macquarie University; Wu Canzhong is developing tools for supporting linguistic description; and there is similar work in Hong Kong and Singapore. I think that this will be a very significant continued development. I think there are some new areas where important work is likely to develop further, for example, multimodal work, forensic linguistics, clinical work related to language disorders, language in the changing workplace, and what Jim Martin calls PDA – positive discourse analysis, which can be seen as part of a general program for construing all the institutions that make up a culture by analysing text against the background of the social diversification and distribution of the overall meaning potential; but also the interesting area of language evolution and the study of the semiotic systems of our close relatives, such as the bonobos.

RCEI Would you say that the so-called trinocular vision of language description may remain as definitive not only for the description of languages but also for the description of other semiotic systems?

C.M. Yes, I quite agree with you that the kind of approach that the trinocular vision represents will continue to play an important role for the interpretation of language but also for the interpretation of other semiotic systems. And I think that the trinocular vision relates to the whole attempt to view semiotic systems holistically, always construing them in terms of the multidimensional semiotic space that we were talking about earlier: instead of being locked into a "monocular" vision, we keep shunting along the various semiotic dimensions, so that you can take a view "from above," "from around," and "from below" – prototypically in relation to the dimension of stratification, but also in fact by reference to other dimensions such as instantiation and rank. If you have that as part of the methodology, if you keep shunting along semiotic dimensions to obtain a trinocular perspective, then you ensure that you are always getting a rounded picture of whatever you're looking at, and I think in particular when we began working on other semiotic systems in the 1980s, the trinocular approach was very important because we had much less experience with looking at semiotic systems other than language. So if you keep shunting and looking at them from different angles – trinocularly, as it were, I think that we will get a balanced rather than an unbalanced picture.

While a good deal of work on "multimodality" in the computational context has been concerned with the view "from below," trying to solve problems of digitizing different expression systems, the systemic functional work by Michael O'Toole,

Gunther Kress, Theo van Leeuwen, and others has foregrounded the views "from above" and "from around" by exploring the metafunctional spectrum of meaning and by trying to map out the systemic organization of the meaning potential of different semiotic systems. Another aspect of the concern with "ocularity" is to try out different dimensions in the interpretation of semiotic phenomena. For example, if we also have the dimension of instantiation as part of our overall semiotic space, then that dimension can actually do a lot of work for us, and then maybe we would need fewer strata than in e.g. the classical "genre model," where context is stratified into "register," "genre," and "ideology." We thus play the different semiotic dimensions off against one another. I think that's important, and it relates to the trinocular perspective.

RCEI One last question: at the moment, are you working on languages other than English in Australia?

C.M. Yes, one thing we've been trying to push very hard is work on languages other than English and also, based on this, translation studies and typological work. I mentioned already the new book on systemic functional typology that we are publishing, and two scholars who have guided work on translation, Erich Steiner and Colin Yallop, have just edited a book with systemic functional contributions to the study of translation. In our own context in Australia, we have ongoing work on French (undertaken and directed by Alice Caffarel), Tagalog (Jim Martin), Vietnamese (Van Van Hoang – now back in Vietnam; Minh Duc Thai), Chinese (M.A.K. Halliday, Ed McDonald – actually now at NUS in Singapore – and others as well), Japanese (Kazuhiro Teruya, who has produced a general account of the lexicogrammar of Japanese; Keizo Nanri, Midori Fukuhara, Elizabeth Thomson, and others as well), Pitjantjatjara (David Rose); and other descriptions of other languages are in progress (e.g. Korean, Indonesian). There is naturally an orientation towards the Australia-Pacific region, but we lack work on Spanish, Portuguese, etc., and it would be wonderful if scholars interested in these languages were to do research on them. There has been very valuable work on different aspects of Spanish, including the work reported on at the systemic congress here in Cardiff; but we do not yet have a general systemic functional overview of Spanish of the kind developed for the languages mentioned above. I hope that the new systemic functional typology book I mentioned earlier can serve as a guide for scholars developing systemic functional descriptions of Spanish and of many other languages as well. Such work will of course be of value in the context of general typological work – and this is of considerable interest and significance; but my point has always been that a systemic functional description can be so much more than material for consumption within linguistics – it can serve to answer central questions about language within education, literary studies, clinical work, and so on.

RCEI Thank you very much for your time. I hope this interview with you and the two that I have held with Michael Halliday and Jim Martin will lead to a better understanding of SFL as a very valuable tool for analysing language.

Chapter 9

Halliday's conception of language as a probabilistic system

9.1   Introduction

This chapter is concerned with Halliday's ideas about language in terms of probability, viz. his conception of **language as a probabilistic system**. It elaborates on section 4.4 in Matthiessen (2014d/2021b: ch. 5). I will not try to introduce the theory of probability as a branch of mathematics (developed originally with gambling as an application); nor will I discuss different interpretations of probability – objective vs. subjective (Bayesian): the focus is on the probability of choice in language, not on the observer's subjective view. While it would be relevant to relate the probabilistic conception of language to indeterminacy in language more generally, I will simply focus on probability: indeterminacy in general is discussed in part III of Halliday (2004d) and also in Halliday and Matthiessen (1999), and certain aspects of indeterminacy are explored in Martin and Matthiessen (1991) – system networks in relation to topological representations – and in Matthiessen (1995b) – system networks in relation to fuzzy theory.

Since his early descriptions of Chinese, Halliday (e.g. [1956] 2006, [1959] 2006) has kept both qualitative and quantitative aspects of language in view; Halliday ([1991d] 2004d: 45) comments on his early work: "A linguistic system is inherently probabilistic in nature. I tried to express this in my early work on Chinese grammar, using observed frequencies in the corpus and estimating probabilities for terms in grammatical systems."

Halliday conceived of terms (features, options) in systems as having probabilities attached, and this is also apparent in his early text-based descriptions of English (e.g. Halliday [1963a] 2005b, [1963b] 2005b) with systemic contrasts where one term is "neutral" or "unmarked" and the other term or terms non-neutral or "marked." When he presented aspects of early systemic functional work on grammar at the Fifteenth Annual (First International) Round Table Meeting on Linguistics and

Language Studies at Georgetown University, in a US academic context, he characterized the work by him and other researchers in Britain as follows (Halliday [1964] 2003: 40; my emphasis, CMIMM):

> If I were asked to characterize the work in which I have been engaged together with some of my colleagues, I would say that our aim is to show the **patterns inherent in the linguistic performance** of the native speaker: this is what we mean by "how the language works". This presupposes a general description of those patterns which the linguist considers to be primary in the language, a description which is then variably extended, on the "scale of delicacy", in depth of detail. It involves a characterization of the special features, **including statistical properties**, of varieties of the language used for different purposes ("registers"), and the comparison of individual texts, spoken and written, including literary texts. This in turn is seen as a linguistic contribution towards certain further aims, such as literary scholarship, native and foreign language teaching, educational research, sociological and anthropological studies and medical applications. The interest is focussed not on what the native speaker knows of his language but rather on what he does with it; one might perhaps say that **the orientation is primarily textual** and, in the widest sense, sociological.
>
> The **study of written and spoken texts** for such purposes requires an analysis of at least sentence, clause and group structures and systems, with extension where possible above the rank of sentence. The analysis needs to be simple in use and in notation, variable in delicacy and **easily processed for statistical studies**; it needs to provide a basis for semantic statements, and to handle with the minimum complexity grammatical contrasts such as those in English expounded by intonation and rhythm; and it should idealize as little as possible, in the sense of excluding the minimum as "deviant".

In referring to "the linguistic performance of the native speaker," Halliday was of course taking into account the audience's familiarity with the distinction between "competence" and "performance" that Chomsky had made, so he translated text as "performance." It was not a distinction that was in any way part of systemic functional theory as it was being developed, but the status of text in the overall engagement with language was, of course, critical to the exploration of "statistical properties": see Section 9.2. About a decade later, Halliday (1973: 25, 51–3) characterized language as a **meaning potential** so that text could now be characterized as "actualized potential," what a speaker **means** in some context of situation in reference to what he or she **can mean** within the context of culture.

The research conducted during the initial phases of systemic functional linguistics was largely text- and corpus-based, and thus provided material for quantitative information. This was true not only of Halliday's own work on phonology and lexicogrammar,[1] but also of the work by colleagues and research students, e.g. the work on scientific English by Huddleston et al. (1968), with many counts of different categories; El-Menoufy's (1969; cf. also 1988) account of the role of intonation in grammar (based on 4 hours of casual conversation, amounting to 7,012 tone groups); and of course the text-based research that led to the description of the system of cohesion (e.g. Hasan 1968), presented comprehensively by Halliday and Hasan (1976). But, unfortunately, it was hard to get corpus-based linguistic research published in the 1960s, and the studies from this period remain unpublished.

However, during the 1960s, systemic functional linguistics was developed in a direction that made it easier to accommodate quantitative information. Halliday's development of a system-based theory with system networks as the representation of paradigmatic relations (see Matthiessen 2014d/2021b) enabled him to reason about quantitative information in relation to both systems ordered in delicacy and systems simultaneous in delicacy. For example, Halliday ([1961] 2002c) draws attention to the value of "frequency counts" as the description is extended in delicacy:

> As the description increases in delicacy the network of grammatical relations becomes more complex. The interaction of criteria makes the relation between categories, and between category and exponent, increasingly one of "more/less" rather than "either/or". It becomes necessary to weight criteria and to make statements in terms of probabilities. With more delicate secondary structures, different combinations of elements, and their relation to groupings of the unit next below, have to be stated as more and less probable. [...] the "more/less" relation itself, far from being an unexpected complication in grammar, is in fact a basic feature of language and is treated as such by the theory. It is not simply that all grammar can be stated in probability terms, based on frequency counts in texts: this is due to the nature of a text as a sample. (pp. 48–9)
>
> The theoretical place of the move from grammar to lexis is therefore not a feature of rank but one of delicacy. It is defined theoretically as the place where increase in delicacy yields no further systems [...]

> No description has yet been made so delicate that we can test whether there really comes a place where increased delicacy yields no further systems: relations at this degree of delicacy can only be stated statistically, and serious statistical work in grammar has hardly begun. (p. 54)

And Halliday ([1964] 2003: 48–9) notes the possibility of accounting for "partial dependence" between terms in simultaneous systems in probabilistic terms: partial dependence may also be manifested statistically, where the selection in one system affects the relative probabilities of selection in another system.

Halliday's conception of language as a probabilistic system is directly related to his image of language as **resource** (Matthiessen 2014d/2021b). But what aspects of systemic functional theory enabled him to model language probabilistically – and how was probability viewed during the 1960s at the time when Halliday developed systemic functional theory out of scale-and-category theory?

9.2   Locating probability: theory and data

Leading up to the 1960s, there had been important contributions to the quantitative study of language that *could* have led to a general acceptance that language is a probabilistic system. These contributions included the work by George Zipf (e.g. 1935) and the seminal work on the quantification of information by Claude Shannon (1948) that led to the development of **Information Theory**. Shannon was concerned with information in a technical, engineering sense: "The fundamental problem of communication is that of reproducing at one point either exactly or approximately a message selected at another point. Frequently the messages have meaning; that is they refer to or are correlated according to some system with certain physical or conceptual entities. These semantic aspects of communication are irrelevant to the engineering problem. The significant aspect is that the actual message is one selected from a set of possible messages."

And in referring to information in this sense and certain key properties such as redundancy, Halliday has been careful to distinguish **information**, which is measurable, from **meaning**, which is not; information is in a sense meaning that can be measured, meaning being the more general category (e.g. Halliday [1991d] 2004d: 45). Information in this technical sense is inherent in systems of any stratum of language. In the early days, Information Theory was received with interest by some linguists (cf. the reviews by Goldsmith 2000; Manning 2003; Van de Walle 2009), including Hockett (1955), Jakobson ([1961] 1971) and Gleason (1961:

ch. 19); but as Chomsky's generative linguistics came to dominate in the 1960s, Chomsky's dismissal of probabilistic considerations and of the kind of evidence that can be derived from corpora steered linguistics away from such concerns. As Manning (2003: 289) puts it, "In the 1950s there were prospects for probabilistic methods taking hold in linguistics, in part owing to the influence of the new field of Information Theory (Shannon 1948). Chomsky's influential remarks had the effect of killing off interest in probabilistic methods for syntax." Similarly, Jurafsky (2003: 39) observes, "Much research in linguistics and psycholinguistics in the 1950s was statistical and probabilistic. But this research disappeared throughout the '60s, '70s, and '80s."

The negative attitude towards the probabilistic nature of language in "theoretical" linguistics was part of the same ideology according to which corpus studies had no theoretical value. After quoting Svartvik's (1966: vii) view that "corpus-studies will help to promote descriptively more adequate grammars," Halliday ([1991c] 2004d: 63) comments:

> This modest claim ran against the ideology prevailing at the time, according to which corpus studies had nothing to contribute towards an understanding of language. Chomsky's theory of competence and performance had driven a massive wedge between the system and the instance, making it impossible by definition that analysis of actual texts could play any part in explaining the grammar of a language – let alone in formulating a general linguistic theory.
>
> Explicitly rejected was the relevance of any kind of quantitative data. Chomsky's sarcastic observation that "I live in New York is more frequent than I live in Dayton Ohio" was designed to demolish the conception that relative frequency in text might have any theoretical significance. [Footnote: Made in the course of a denunciation of corpus studies in a lecture at the Linguistic Society of America Summer Institute, Bloomington, July 1964.]

The separation of the system and the instance was one of two theoretical obstacles getting in the way of investigations of language as a probabilistic system, in the context of Chomsky's form of generative linguistics. I will discuss it in Section 9.3 under the heading of the "cline of instantiation." The other theoretical obstacle was the focus on the syntagmatic axis to the exclusion of the paradigmatic one. I will discuss this obstacle in Section 9.4 under the heading of the "hierarchy of axis." Both theoretical obstacles meant that it was difficult to find a place for probability in the theory.

9.3   The cline of instantiation: frequency (instantial) and probability (potential)

If language is conceived of dichotomously as *langue* and *parole* along Saussurean lines or as "competence" and "performance" along Chomskyan (e.g. 1965) lines[2] (later "I-language" and "E-language," e.g. Chomsky 2000), then linguists face the challenge of locating the probabilistic conception of language in relation to these two domains. What happened was that competence was conceptualized and theorized in **categorical** terms, and represented by rule systems that were equally categorical in nature (see e.g. the critical discussion by Ellis 1993, and Halliday's [1995a] 2004a comments based on the different views in systemic functional theory). This was the domain of "theoretical linguistics." At the same time, performance was studied, with attention given to quantitative features such as frequency, latency, and duration; but such research was carried out mainly in psycholinguistics – see e.g. Jurafsky (2003), and there was no link to theoretical work on competence. In their introduction to *Probabilistic linguistics*, Bod, Hay, and Jannedy (2003: 1) characterize the view as follows:[3]

> One of the foundations of modern linguistics is the maxim of categoricity: language is categorical. Numbers play no role, or, where they do, they are artifacts of nonlinguistic performance factors. Thus, while it is widely recognized that real language can be highly variable, gradient, and rich in continua, many linguists would argue that the competence that underlies such "performance factors" consists of well-defined discrete categories and categorical grammaticality criteria. Performance may be full of fuzziness, gradience, and continua, but linguistic competence is not.

There was thus a fundamental disconnect between the **domain of data** (natural, elicited or experimental), "performance," and the **domain of theory**, "competence": theory and data couldn't be linked. This was the "massive wedge between the system and the instance" identified by Halliday ([1991d] 2004d: 63) in the passage quoted at the end of the last section. As long as the domain of theory and the domain of data are kept insulated from one another, it is difficult to see how observed frequencies in texts ("performance") can be theorized, i.e. incorporated within a theory of language.[4]

Halliday has developed a radically different alternative view – one that makes it possible to theorize observed **frequencies** in text as **probabilities** inherent in the

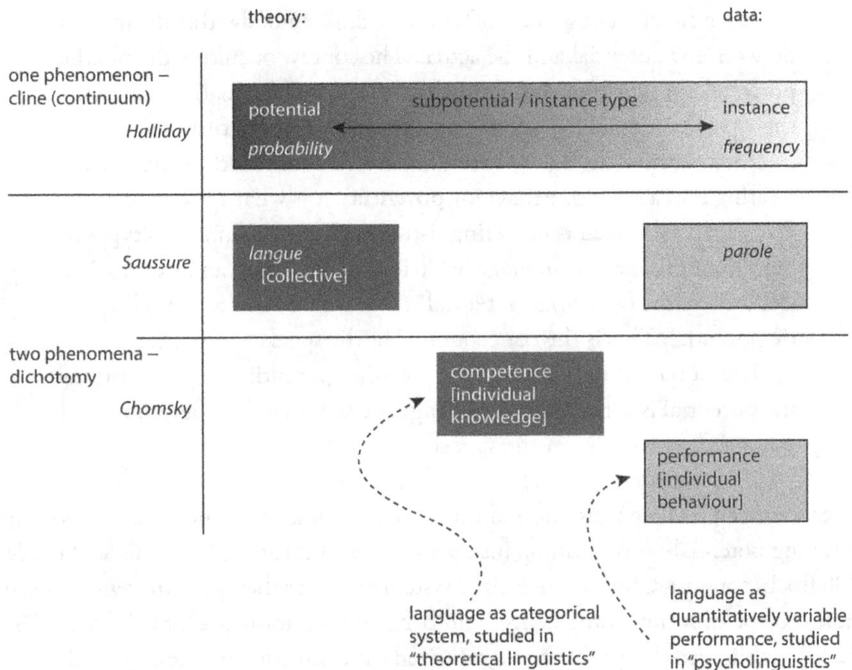

Figure 9.1 System and text – conceptualized as one continuous phenomenon extended along the cline of instantiation, or two distinct phenomena forming a dichotomy

system. The key point is that system and text are not two different phenomena but simply one phenomenon, language, seen from different observer vantage points: see Figure 9.1, where Halliday's theory (the top half of the figure) is contrasted with those of Saussure and Chomsky (the lower half of the figure). Let me introduce this in two steps.

1. First, system and text are related to one another simply as **potential to actual**, or instantial, thus being ***of the same phenomenal order***; this understanding was articulated by Halliday (1973a: 49–51), already referred to above:

> Language ... is a range of possibilities, an open-ended set of options in behaviour that are available to the individual in his existence as social man. The context of culture is the environment for the total set of these options, while the context of situation is the environment of any particular selection that is made from within them.

Malinowski's two types of context thus embody the distinction between the potential and the actual. The context of culture defines the potential, the range of possibilities that are open. The actual choice among these possibilities takes place within a given context of situation. [...]

If we regard language as social behaviour ..., this means that we are treating it as a form of behaviour **potential**. It is what speakers can do. But "can do" by itself is not a linguistic notion; it encompasses types of behaviour other than language behaviour. [...] we need an intermediate step, where the behaviour potential is as it were converted into linguistic potential. This is the concept of what the speaker "can mean".

The potential of language is a meaning potential. [...] The meaning potential is ... realized in the language system as lexicogrammatical potential, which is what the speaker "can say".

System and text are thus one and the same phenomenon, simply viewed as either meaning potential or as meaning instances – acts of meaning (cf. Halliday [1992e] 2003b). In contrast, Chomsky theorized system and text as being of *different phenomenal orders*, knowing (competence) and behaving (performance); Halliday (1973a: 52–3) highlighted this problem and criticized the distinction on these grounds:

> Meaning potential is defined not in terms of the mind [Chomsky's "competence," CMIMM] but in terms of the culture; not as what the speaker knows, but as what he can do – in the special sense of what he can do linguistically (what he "can mean", as we have expressed it). This distinction is important because "can do" is of the same order of abstraction as "does"; the two are related simply as potential to actualized potential, and can be used to illuminate each other. But "knows" is distinct and clearly insulated from "does"; the relation between the two is complex and oblique, and leads to the quest of a "theory of performance" to explain the "does".

In addition, Chomsky's "competence" is a feature of the *individual* speaker ("ideal speaker-listener"), whereas Halliday's "meaning potential" is a feature of the collective, of the **speech fellowship** operating in a particular context of culture. The meaning potential is thus a collective resource, and individual meaners are trustees in this resource. In this respect, Saussure's *langue* is significantly different from Chomsky's "competence"; like the meaning potential, langue is a feature of the collective. However, it is still insulated from *parole*.

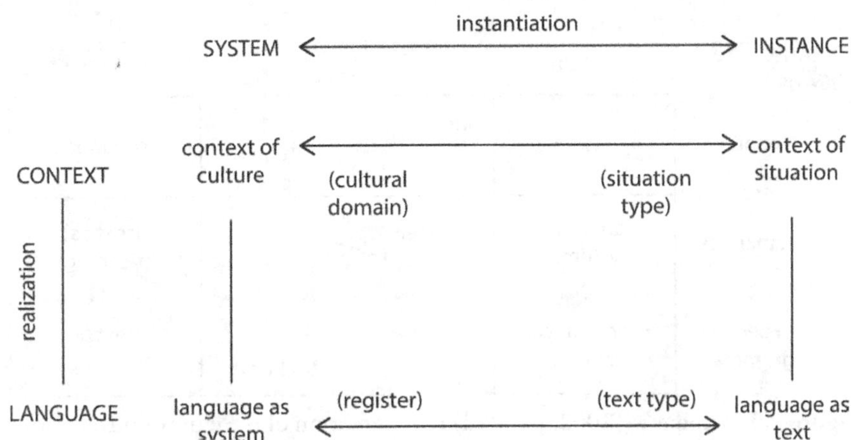

Figure 9.2 Halliday's ([1991a] 2007) representation of the cline of instantiation

2. Second, potential and actual, or potential and instance, are theorized as part of an extended continuum, the outer poles of the **cline of instantiation**; Halliday ([1991a] 2007) introduces a figure where he intersects "instantiation" with "realization," reproduced here as Figure 9.2. In this figure, he shows that instantiation is extended between "system" and "instance"; it is represented as a cline with intermediate regions: cultural domain/register and situation type/text type. These intermediate regions are specified further in Halliday ([2002a] 2004d), as shown in Figure 9.3. (Note that at the stratum of context, "cultural domain" in Figure 9.2 and "institution" in Figure 9.3 both refer to subsystems within the overall system of culture.)

Let me quote Halliday ([1992c] 2002c: 359) at some length as he introduces the cline of instantiation:

> Consider the notion of climate. A climate is a reasonably stable system; there are kinds of climate, such as tropical or polar, and these persist, and they differ in systematic ways. Yet we are all concerned about changes in the climate, and the consequences of global warming. What does it mean to say the climate is changing? Climate is instantiated in the form of weather: today's temperature, humidity, direction and speed of wind, etc., in central Scotland are **instances** of climatic phenomena. As such they may be more, or less, **typical**: today's maximum is so many degrees higher, or lower, than **average** – meaning the average at this place, at

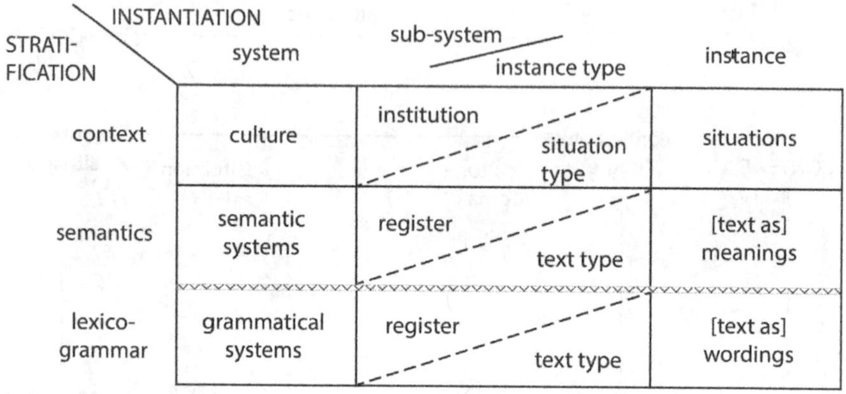

STRATI-FICATION \ INSTANTIATION	system	sub-system / instance type		instance
context	culture	institution	situation type	situations
semantics	semantic systems	register	text type	[text as] meanings
lexico-grammar	grammatical systems	register	text type	[text as] wordings

Figure 9.3 Halliday's ([2002a] 2004d) representation of the cline of instantiation

this time of year, and at this time of day. The average is a statement of the **probabilities**: there is a 70 per cent chance, let us say, that the temperature will fall within such a range. The probability is a feature of the system (the climate); but it is no more, and no less, than the pattern set up by instances (the weather), and each instance, no matter how minutely, perturbs these probabilities and so changes the system (or else keeps it as it is, which is just the limiting case of changing it).

The climate and the weather are not two different phenomena. They are the same phenomenon seen by two different observers, standing at different distances – different time depths. To the climate observer, the weather looks like random unpredictable ripples; to the weather observer, the climate is a vague and unreal outline. So it is also with language; language as system, and language as instance. They are not two different phenomena; they are the same phenomenon seen by different observers. The system is the pattern formed by the instances; and each instance represents an exchange with the environment – an incursion into the system in which every language is involved. The **system** is permeable because each **instance** redounds with the context of situation, and so perturbs the **system in interaction with the environment**. Thus both realization and instantiation are involved in the evolution of language as a dynamic open system.

Now the relation of system to instance is in fact a cline, a continuous zoom; and wherever we focus the zoom we can take a look into history. But to know what kind of history, we have to keep a record of which end we started from. To the system observer, history takes the form of evolution; the system changes by evolving, with selection (in the sense of "natural selection") by the material conditions of the environment. This is seen most clearly, perhaps, in the evolution of particular subsystems, or registers, where features that are functionally well adapted are positively selected for; but it appears also in the history of the system as a whole once we look beyond the superficial clutter of random fluctuations into the grammar's cryptotypic core. To the instance observer, on the other hand, history is individuation: each text has its own history, and its unique meaning unfolds progressively from the beginning. (Note that the probability of any instance is conditioned both systemically [a register is a resetting of the overall probabilities of the system] and instantially, by the transitional probabilities of the text as a Markoff chain.)

Halliday's theory of cline of instantiation is a fundamental contribution of the theoretical understanding of language. It provides the bridge between quantitative information as frequency and quantitative information as probability, and between the domains of data and of theory.

At the instance pole of the cline of instantiation, we can observe the **relative frequency** of the instantiation (occurrence) of terms in systems; and at the potential pole of the cline, we can interpret these relative frequencies as **systemic probabilities.** At the instance pole, we are analysing texts – the **data** constituting the basis for any generalizations we make, moving up the cline of instantiation towards the potential pole. At the potential pole, we **theorize** the system that we posit as the principles behind the instantial patterns that we can observe.

At the same time, we also recognize patterns that are intermediate between the outer poles of the cline of instantiation. We can interpret these intermediate patterns by approaching them from either pole. Looked at from the potential pole of the cline, they can be interpreted as **sub-potentials** – quantitatively, as resettings of the systemic probabilities of the potential pole (e.g. Halliday [1991c] 2004d: 65–6, 70; [1992b] 2004d: 84–6; 2013). Looked at from the instance pole of the line, they can be interpreted as **instance types** – quantitatively, as averages of relative frequencies observed in instances.

9.4   The hierarchy of axis: probabilities in systems

Quantitative information is thus extended along the cline of instantiation, from systemic probabilities to relative frequencies in texts. But probabilities of what, frequencies of what? In a sense, any category in language can be counted; researchers in many disciplines have been counting words for a wide range of purposes. However, the categories that we count are ***ultimately derived from contrasting options*** in the systems that make up a system network[5] – from choice. This is thus central to the probabilistic interpretation of language, as Halliday ([1991d] 2004d: 45) has emphasized:

> Obviously, to interpret language in probabilistic terms, the grammar (that is, the theory of grammar, the ***grammatics***) has to be paradigmatic: it has to be able to represent language as **choice**, since probability is the probability of "choosing" (not in any conscious sense, of course) one thing rather than another. Firth's concept of "system", in the "system/structure" framework, already modelled language as choice. Once you say "choose for polarity: positive or negative?", or "choose for tense: past or present or future?", then each of these options could have a probability value attached.

(The same remarks apply to any stratal subsystem of language in context; e.g. to interpret the sound system of a language in probabilistic terms, the theory of phonology has to be paradigmatic.) For example, we may count active and passive forms of the verb, or rather of the verbal group; but behind this is the systemic contrast in voice between "active" and "passive" verbal groups (cf. Halliday [1991c] 2004d; Halliday and James 1993 [reprinted in Halliday 2004d]). Thus, when Halliday ([1966b] 2002c) developed the theory of language on a paradigmatic base – foregrounding system over structure, he made it possible to locate probabilities within the overall account of language: in the description of the system of language, ***probabilities are attached to terms in systems***, e.g. 'active 0.9'/'passive 0.1,' and the system is thus the locus of probability (the distribution of probabilities, the probability profile of a system), of information and of redundancy (in the sense of Information Theory; see further below); and in the analysis of texts, we count the occurrences of terms in systems.

Thus, in the system of process type, we count each occurrence (selection) of one of its terms, 'material'/'behavioural'/'mental'/'verbal'/'relational'/'existential' so that we can establish a **frequency profile** for this system: see Figure 9.4. The process types range in frequency from 'material' to 'existential': 'material (39.2 per cent)'/'relational (36.1 per cent)'/'mental (10.8 per cent)'/'verbal (8.3 per cent)'/'behavioural (3.4 per cent)'/'existential (2.3 per cent).' Interpreted systemically, 'material' is the term that is the most likely to be selected and 'existential' the one least likely to be selected.

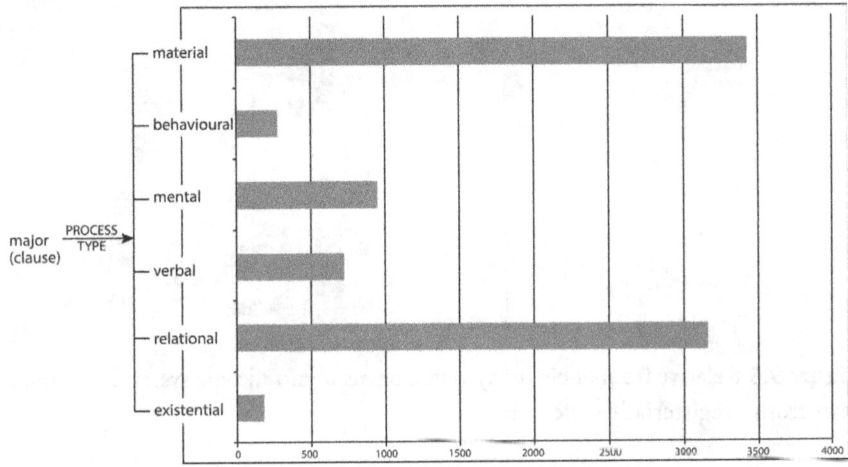

Figure 9.4 Relative frequencies of systemic terms in texts from a registerially varied sample

The system of process type is a low-delicacy system within the experiential clause grammar; its entry condition is 'major clause.' Consequently, a reasonably high number of clauses have been analysed to establish the frequency profile in Figure 9.4 – around 8,700, although this is still very much in the exploratory pilot study range (cf. Matthiessen 1999, 2006), However, as we explore systems ordered in delicacy, moving from less delicate (more general) systems to more delicate ones, the numbers will inevitably decrease.

The analysis of relative frequencies in a set of systems ordered in delicacy can be illustrated by reference to the interpersonal grammar of the clause in English: see Figure 9.5.

There are four systems ordered in delicacy: status (also called freedom), mood type, indicative type, and interrogative type. The number of clauses analysed for each step in delicacy is as follows:

- STATUS: 8,786 (out of 9,388 'major' clauses) – 'free' 6,821/'bound' 1,965
- MOOD TYPE: 6,330 (out of 6,821 'free' clauses) – 'indicative' 6,128/'imperative' 202
- INDICATIVE TYPE: 6,120 (out of 6,128 'indicative' clauses) – 'declarative' 5,679/'interrogative' 441
- INTERROGATIVE TYPE: 442 (out of 442 'interrogative' clauses) – 'wh-' 210/'yes/no' 232.

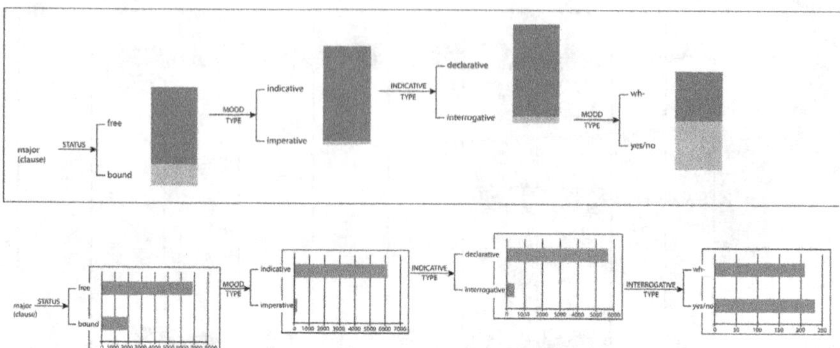

Figure 9.5 Relative frequencies of systemic terms in mood type systems ordered in texts from a registerially varied sample

While this is still very much work in progress, the general picture is clear: the population of units (clauses, in this case) decreases as delicacy increases (this being the general inverse relation between extension and intension); for systems that have low-frequency terms as their entry condition, the effect is of course magnified. Thus, interrogative type has 'interrogative' as its entry condition, and 'interrogative' is much less frequent than 'declarative' in the system of indicative type. Consequently, as we increase the delicacy of the systemic analysis, we have to increase the size of the sample of texts that we analyse if we want our counts to be reasonably representative and reliable – which raises the question of the extent to which the analysis can be automated (see Section 9.6; cf. also Halliday and James 1993 [reprinted in Halliday 2004d]; Halliday [1991c] 2004d: 67, and endnote 7, p. 74).

There is another consideration that is also important: while the systems of increasing delicacy shown in Figure 9.5 all have simple entry conditions (thus in a sense forming a strict taxonomy of modal options in the clause), more delicate systems often have complex entry conditions – for example, I could have included mood tagging, which has a disjunctive entry condition of 'declarative' and 'imperative.'

Discussing the corpus-based study of systemic probabilities by Halliday and James (1993 [reprinted in Halliday 2004d]) and their selection of systems to investigate, Halliday ([1993a] 2004d: 145) draws attention to these methodological considerations relating to the study of systems of increasing delicacy: "The systems to be counted had to be very general ones, not those of a more "delicate" kind; they should be systems that apply to a large number of instances. This is partly to ensure that each term occurs with sufficient frequency; but there is a more significant factor, which is this – that any general hypothesis about probabilities ceases to apply when one moves to more specific sets of options, because these tend to have complex entry conditions. A system network is not a strict taxonomy."

When he carried out exploratory counts in the mid-1960s, Halliday adopted a 2000/200 instance criterion (Halliday [1993a] 2004d: 134; cf. also Halliday [1992b] 2004d: 81):

> I collected a small sample of four different registers of English, just big enough to yield a total of 2,000 occurrences of whatever category provided the entry condition to the systems I wanted to study. For example, in order to count instances of indicative/imperative mood, I had to have 2,000 independent clauses, because it is here that the choice is made: each independent clause selects one or the other. But to compare declarative with interrogative I had to count 2,000 indicative clauses, because it is the indicative clause that is either declarative or interrogative. The reason for settling on a figure of 2,000 occurrences was the following: first, I estimated it needed about 200 occurrences of the less frequent term to ensure a reasonable degree of accuracy; and second, that the less frequent term in a binary system seemed to occur about 10 per cent of the time. So if I restricted the counting to binary systems, 2,000 instances tended to yield around 200 occurrences of the less frequent term in the system.

This gives a very clear sense of methodological considerations involved in analysing texts in terms of systems of varying degrees of delicacy. In my pilot investigation, interpersonal clause systems (Figure 9.5), equally exploratory as Halliday's work in the mid-1960s, the lowest number occurrences is of 'imperative': 202 instances (which of course partly reflects the registerial composition of my opportunistic sample of texts; cf. Matthiessen 2006).

9.5   Types of probability and probability profiles

9.5.1 *Types of probability*

In Halliday's characterization of probabilities in language, all probabilities are systemic: "probability is the probability of 'choosing' ... one thing rather than another" (Halliday, [1991d] 2004d: 45). As illustrated in Figure 9.4 and Figure 9.5, we can count the number of times terms in a given system are selected in a sample of

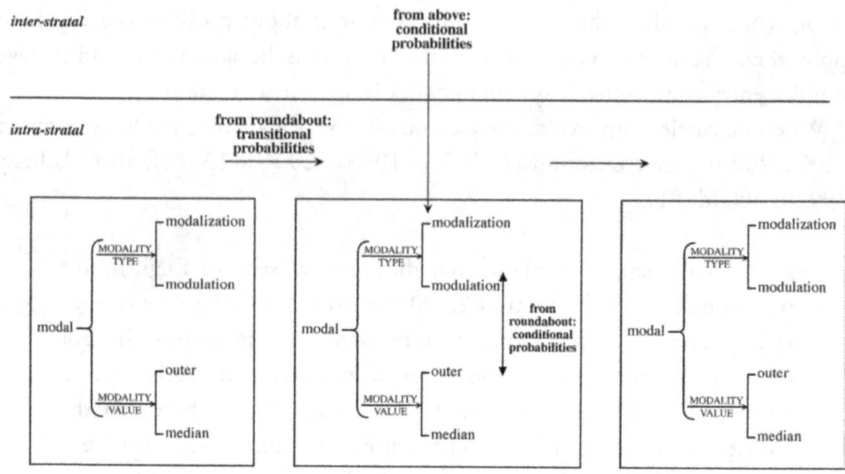

Figure 9.6 Schematic representation of conditioning effects on systemic probabilities

texts, and interpret these relative frequencies as systemic probabilities. For example, in the system indicative type (Figure 9.5), the relative frequencies are 92.8 per cent "declarative" choices and 7.2 per cent "interrogative" ones; so we can interpret this as approximating a probability ratio of "declarative 0.9" vs. "interrogative 0.1." In contrast, in the system interrogative type (Figure 9.5), the relative frequencies are 47 per cent "wh-" choices and 52.5 per cent "yes/no" ones; so we can interpret this as approximating a probability ratio of "wh- 0.5" vs. "yes/no 0.5." These two systems would thus have significantly different probability profiles: see Section 9.5.2. Of course, we need to analyse vastly larger samples of text from a wide range of dialogic registers to get more reliable results.

The probabilities associated with terms in a system are subject to "conditioning effects" deriving from the environment in which the system operates: see Table 9.1. Conditioning effects may be either intra-stratal, from roundabout the system whose probabilities are being conditioned, or inter-stratal, from above the system being conditioned. These are illustrated schematically for the system of modality in Figure 9.6.

1. Intra-stratal conditioning effect. Intra-stratal conditioning effects are systemic terms (with associated probabilities) located within the same stratum as the conditioned system.[6] They are either (i) simultaneous, **conditional** probabilities, or (ii) sequential (linear), **transitional** probabilities. The former have been investigated by systemic functional researchers; the latter remain less explored.

Table 9.1 Types of systemic probabilities

Type of probability		*Characterization*	*Reference*
probability		probability of choosing one term rather than another in a system	Halliday ([1991d] 2004d: 45)
probability due to conditioning effect: intra-stratal – "from roundabout"	transitional probability	repeated successive selections in the same system as a text unfolds	Halliday ([1992b] 2004d: 85)
	conditional probability	parallel selections in simultaneous systems within the same unit	Halliday ([1992b] 2004d: 87)
probability due to conditioning effect: inter-stratal – "from above"	(conditioned probability)	conditioning of probabilities "from above," due to code or register	Halliday ([1991d] 2004d: 48–52; [1991c] 2004a: 66)

(i) Conditional probabilities. Simultaneous systems are systems that are not ordered in delicacy in relation to one another but are of the same order of delicacy, having the same entry conditions like modality type and modality value in Figure 9.6. Halliday ([1992b] 2004d: 88) characterizes conditional probabilities as follows: "With conditional probabilities ... the two choices are being made simultaneously, and so either can be treated as the environment for the other; ... we could equally well ask, what is the effect on the probability of declarative/interrogative of choosing either active or passive in the same clause? The two effects may be reciprocal, but they may not ..."

Thus, in the example in Figure 9.6, each term in the two systems will have its own systemic probability; however, in addition, there may be **favoured** combinations and **disfavoured** ones. This was brought out for simultaneous systems in another grammatical domain, viz. that of the clause nexus, in a pioneering study by Nesbitt and Plum (1988). They analysed spoken texts – interviews with dog fanciers – in terms of the simultaneous systems of taxis and logico-semantic type. They found certain favoured combinations; for example, the combination "hypotaxis" and "enhancing" is favoured over "parataxis" and "enhancing," whereas "parataxis" and "extending" is favoured over "hypotaxis" and "extending." The significance of their study is highlighted by Halliday in a number of his papers on probability and grammar from the early 1990s, collected in Halliday (2005a). He raises the issue of the "direction" of conditioning. In Matthiessen (2002b), I examine the same set of simultaneous systems based on the analysis of a registerially varied sample of text. However, let me introduce another interesting example, one that will also be relevant to the discussion in Section 9.5.2 of probabilistic profiles of systems.

In the experiential grammar of the clause in English, the systems of PROCESS TYPE and of AGENCY are simultaneous; both have "major clause" as their entry condition, and are thus very general, low-delicacy systems. The system of PROCESS TYPE was represented in Figure 9.4. The system of agency is the choice between "middle" and "effective," with the following relative frequencies: "middle" 74.7 per cent/"effective" 25.3 per cent. The intersection of these two simultaneous systems is shown in Figure 9.7. The picture is quite striking. If we look at the intersection in terms of AGENCY, we can see that the distribution of "middle" and "effective" across the process types is quite uneven: most "effective" clauses are "material," with just a fairly small proportion of "relational" clauses. In fact, in "material" clauses, the ratio of "middle" to "effective" is roughly 50/50, but in all the other process types, it is 90 per cent or more/10 per cent or less. (For these different probability profiles, see the next subsection.)

In other words, if we view the interaction between terms in the systems of AGENCY and PROCESS TYPE from the point of view of AGENCY, we can compare the predicted ratio of "middle" to "effective" for each process type based on the overall ratio of "middle" 74.7 per cent/"effective" 25.3 per cent with the actual ratio; this comparison is graphed in Figure 9.8. For "material" clauses the predicted number of "middle" clauses is higher than the actual number, whereas the predicted number of "effective" clauses is lower than the actual number; but for all other process types, it is the reverse: they all have a higher proportion of "middle" selections over "effective" ones based on the systemic frequencies in the system of agency ("middle" 74.7 per cent/"effective" 25.3 per cent).

(ii) Transitional probabilities. As already noted, while conditional probabilities have been explored by systemic functional linguists, there has been less work (as far as I know) on transitional probabilities (probabilistic parsing would be one area where transitional probabilities are of interest). Like conditional probabilities, transitional probabilities are intra-stratal rather than inter-stratal: they operate within the same stratum as the system whose probabilities are being conditioned, but unlike conditional probabilities, they are not located within the same cycle of instantiation of the system, but rather within an earlier cycle. In other words,

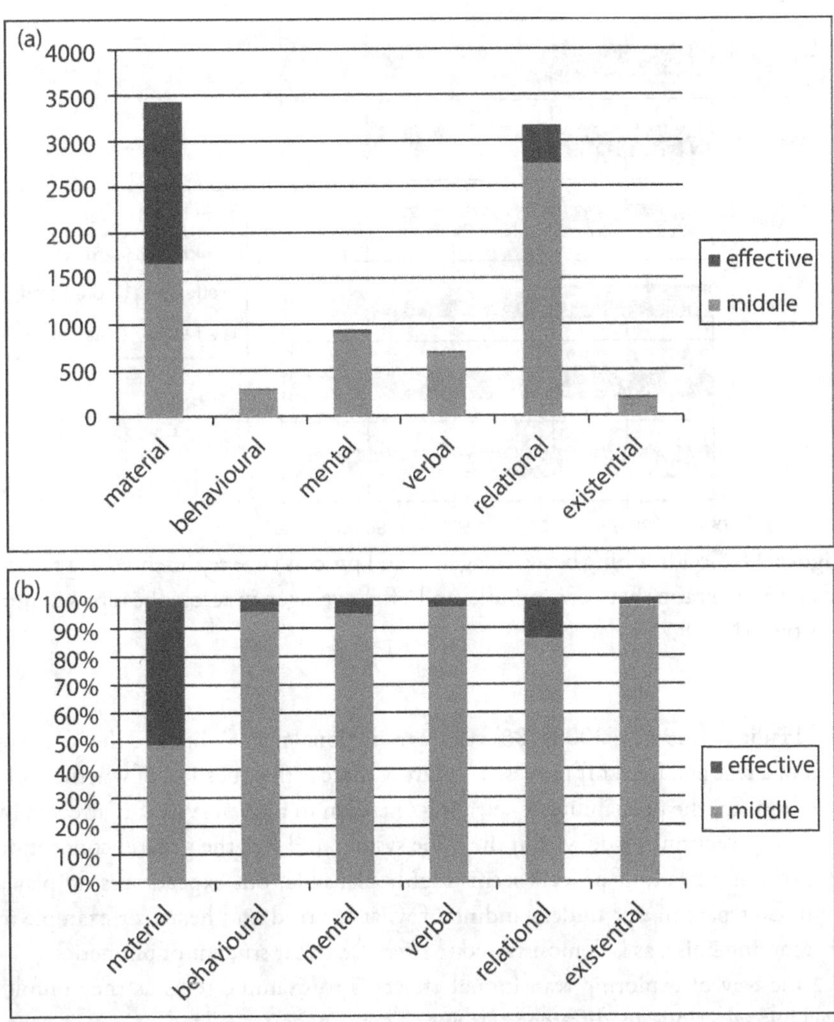

Figure 9.7 The intersection of the simultaneous systems agency ('middle'/'effective') and process type ('material'/'behavioural'/'mental'/'verbal'/'relational'/'existential') in terms of (a) absolute numbers and (b) percentages (N = 8,769 clauses)

transitional probabilities are linear in nature, being concerned with successive traversals of the same system. Halliday ([1992d] 2003b: 370) characterizes transitional probabilities in terms of **intratextual history**: "The other is that of transitional probabilities: if the grammar of a language is represented as a probabilistic system, as I would consider it to be, then the intratextual history of any sentence is the perturbation of its inherent probabilities by the selections made earlier in the text."

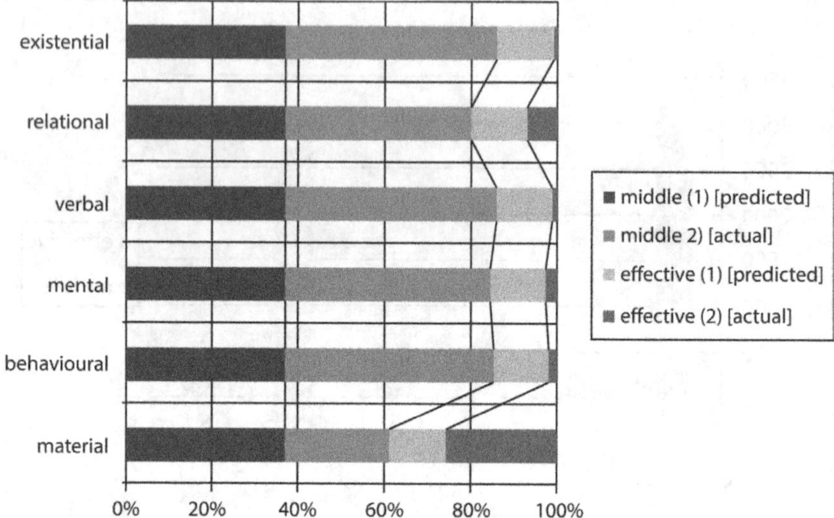

Figure 9.8 Conditioning between agency and process type represented as predicted and actual ratios between 'middle' and 'effective' agency across the terms in process type (N = 8,752 clauses)

and Halliday ([1992b] 2005a: 85) relates transitional probabilities to the "conception of a text as a Markoff process": "Thirdly there is the question of whether, and if so how far, the probability of selecting one term in a given system is affected by previous selections made within the same system. [...] But the general conception of a text as a Markoff process seems highly plausible; our expectances do play a significant part in our understanding of what we read and hear (for example in overcoming noise, as is demonstrated to every first-year student of phonetics.)"

One way of exploring transitional effects is to examine texts as they unfold, tracking selections in different systems. This can be visualized as a **text score** (e.g. Matthiessen 1995a, 2002a, using a term I have taken from Weinreich 1972 ['Textpartitur']). A text score thus shows successive selections in one or more systems, unit by unit (e.g. clause by clause), as a text unfolds, as is illustrated for major interpersonal clause systems (cf. Figure 9.5) in a passage of a telephonic service encounter in Figure 9.9. Looking at the text score from left to right, we can see how local frequency patterns emerge clause by clause: in the system of mood type, "indicative" is consistently chosen over "imperative"; and in the system of indicative type, "declarative" emerges over "interrogative" as the (locally) unmarked selection. It is thus possible to see how relative frequencies gradually emerge as texts

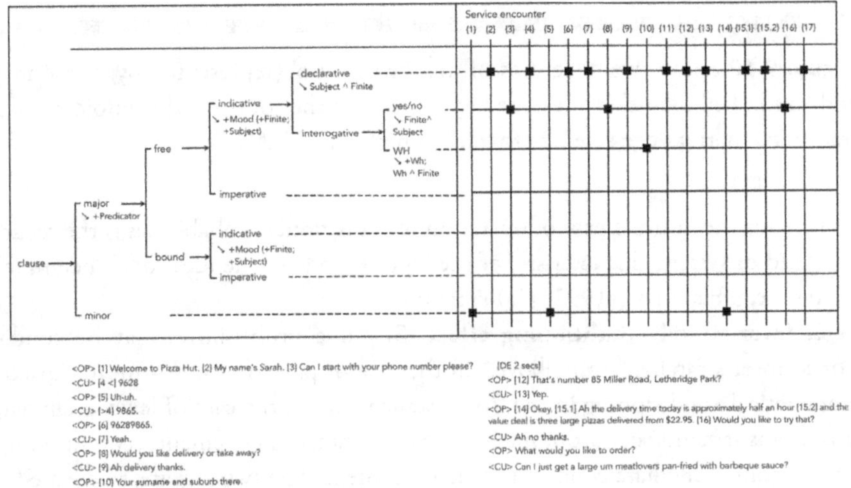

<OP> [1] Welcome to Pizza Hut. [2] My name's Sarah. [3] Can I start with your phone number please?
<CU> [4 <] 9628
<OP> [5] Uh-uh.
<CU> [>4] 9865.
<OP> [6] 96289865.
<CU> [7] Yeah.
<OP> [8] Would you like delivery or take away?
<CU> [9] Ah delivery thanks.
<OP> [10] Your surname and suburb there.
<CU> [11] Harding. Letheridge Park.

[DE 2 secs]
<OP> [12] That's number 85 Miller Road, Letheridge Park?
<CU> [13] Yep.
<OP> [14] Okey. [15.1] Ah the delivery time today is approximately half an hour [15.2] and the value deal is three large pizzas delivered from $22.95. [16] Would you like to try that?
<CU> Ah no thanks.
<OP> What would you like to order?
<CU> Can I just get a large um meatlovers pan-fried with barbeque sauce?

Figure 9.9 Text score showing selections (each selection being represented by a square) in interpersonal clause systems for a sequence of seventeen clauses (each clause being represented by a numbered vertical line) in a passage from a telephonic service encounter

unfold. The text score does not, of course, show any transitional effects from one selection to another; but it may be possible to identify passages where such effects appear to be in operation.

Selections in certain systems are likely to appear periodically in the course of the unfolding of a text. Thus, while most Theme selections in a (traditional) narrative are likely to be "unmarked," "marked" selections are likely to appear periodically, as shown in Figure 9.10. In terms of transitional conditioning, we can note that "marked" selections are very likely to be followed by "unmarked" ones – usually a whole sequence of "unmarked" Themes; there is only one exception in this text where "marked" is chosen twice in a sequence. (*This time the dove flew back to Noah with a green olive branch in its beak. Somewhere there was a bit of dry land.*) We can explore successive selections of this kind in terms of intra-stratal transitional probabilities; but it is of course also possible that larger-scale semantic patterns (and, mediated by semantics, also contextual patterns) condition the probability of selecting "marked" inter-stratally "from above": in narratives, "marked Theme" selections tend to occur as part of the Placement, and then to signal the start of new episodes (cf. Hoey 2006). There is of course no conflict between these two perspectives on the conditioning of the choice between "marked" and "unmarked" Theme.

Figure 9.10 Successive selections of 'marked theme' (represented by diamonds) and 'unmarked theme' (represented by squares) in the course of the unfolding of a traditional narrative (a retelling for children of "Noah's Ark")

Perhaps the limiting case of operation of transitional probabilities is the recursive kind of system characteristic of the logical mode of the ideational metafunction: see e.g. Halliday ([1992b] 2005a: 90–1).

2. Inter-stratal conditioning effect. Systemic probabilities may be conditioned inter-stratally, "from above." In the case of phonology, this means lexicogrammatical conditioning in the first instance; and in the case of lexicogrammar, this means semantic conditioning in the first instance. The semantic conditioning will, of course, mediate conditioning from context. The two key areas here are (i) coding orientation and (ii) register.

(i) Halliday ([1991d] 2005a: 48–52) discusses two studies that bring out differences in coding orientation in probabilistic terms, Plum and Cowling (1987) and Hasan's large-scale research project concerned with interaction between mothers and children (e.g. Hasan 1989, 2009; Hasan and Cloran 1990; see Matthiessen 2014d/2021b). For example, Plum and Cowling's (1987) study, based on interviews conducted for the Sydney Social Dialect Survey, shows that the relative frequencies of the selections in the system of primary tense of "past" vs. "present" vary according to social class: see Figure 9.11. In particular, selections by lower-working-class speakers are skewed towards the "present," whereas selections by middle-class speakers are skewed towards the "past." Commenting on this result, Halliday ([1991d] 2005a: 50) observes, "This is a classic manifestation of Bernstein's principle of code, or (to give it the more accurate term) 'coding orientation'. If the linguistic system was not inherently of a probabilistic kind it could not display these sociolinguistic effects. As it is, this kind of quantitative study can reveal important features relevant to the deeper social order."

(ii) As already noted above, Halliday (e.g. [1991c] 2005a: 65–6, 70; [1992b] 2005a: 84–6; 2013) has characterized registers as resettings of systemic probabilities. Here the variation in systemic probabilities can be fairly dramatic, reflecting the fact that registers are different ways of using language, i.e. functional varieties of language. Let me use the system of process type as an example: see Figure 9.12; average across a registerially mixed sample shown in Figure 9.4. While we need much larger samples, there are some interesting patterns shown in Figure 9.12 that are likely to reflect general tendencies. For example, "material" clauses are most dominant in narratives (traditional ones, like nursery tales, where they construe

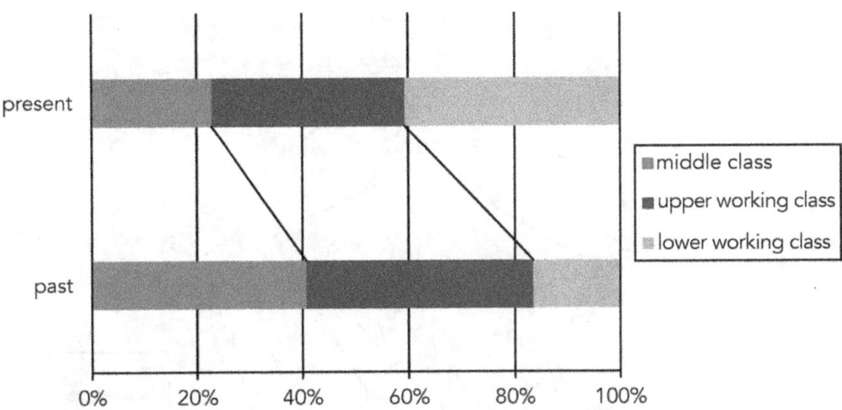

Figure 9.11 Variation in relative frequency in primary tense selections according to social class – graph of data from Plum and Cowling (1987)

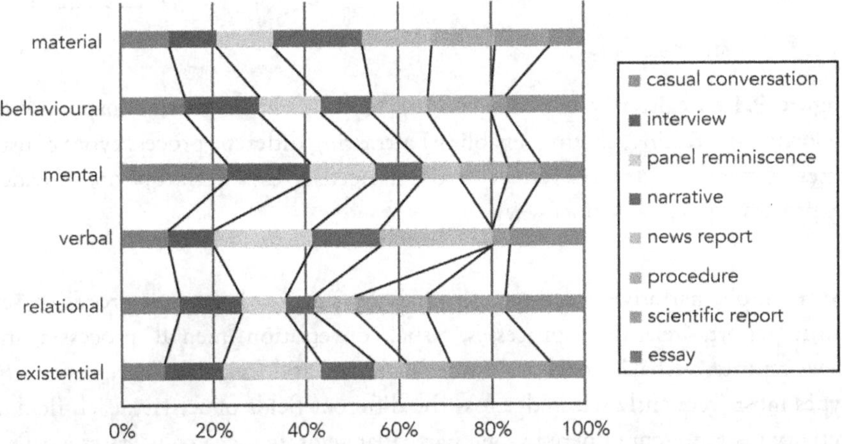

Figure 9.12 The relative frequency of terms in the system of process type in eight different registers

the event line of the narrative); "mental" clauses are more prominent in casual conversation than in any of the other registers; and "verbal" clauses are more common in news reports than in any of the other registers, whereas they are absent in procedures.

Figure 9.12 shows how the relative frequency of each process type varies from one register to another. We can also look at this variation from the point of view of the conditioning register; Figure 9.13 shows how registers grouped according to the field of activity (socio-semiotic process) tend to attract different process types.

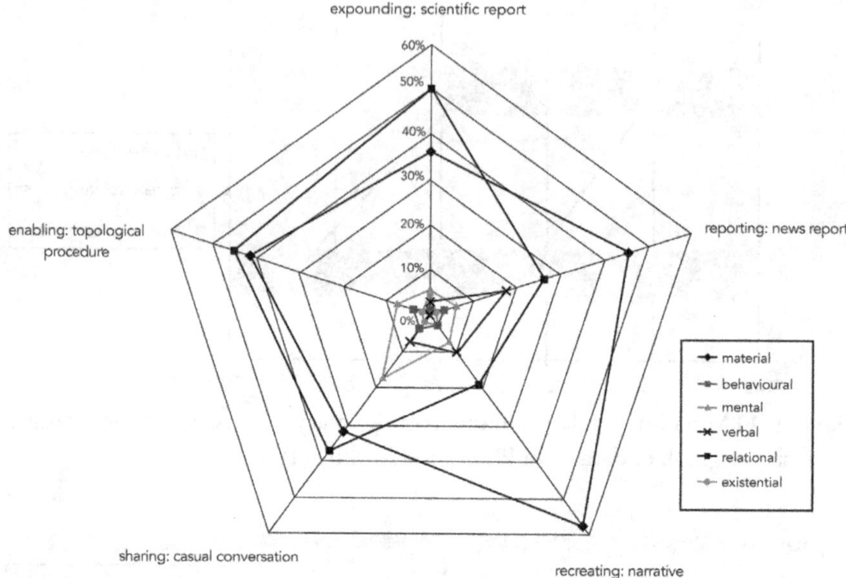

Figure 9.13 Registers grouped according to the field of activity (expounding, reporting, recreating, sharing, enabling) attracting different process types constitutes a different angle on experience and thus needs to exploit the options provided by process types in a distinct way

For example, narratives (of the traditional kind) attract "material" processes, scientific reports "relational" processes, casual conversation "mental" processes, and news reports "verbal" processes. While "material" and "relational" clauses are the types most frequently selected across the different fields of activity, each field of activity (as represented here by one particular register each) constitutes a different angle on experience and thus needs to exploit the options provided by process types in a distinct way.

9.5.2　Probability profiles

Once a system is theorized as contrasting terms with probabilities attached, the question arises what **probability profiles** systems turn out to have – that is, what the possible probability distributions across the terms of the system are. For example, in systems with two terms ("binary systems"), should we expect to find profiles ranging across all values from 0.5 : 0.5 to 0.99 : 0.01 – that is from equiprobable to the limiting case, bordering on categorical? In the example of interpersonal clause systems in Figure 9.6, there would appear to be two types of profile, roughly equiprobable (the system of interrogative type) and significantly skew (the other systems: status, mood type, and indicative type). This is not an accident. Halliday has shown both empirically and theoretically that these two probability profiles, **equi** and **skew**, are likely to be characteristic, at least of fairly general, indelicate systems. Discussing non-recursive systems, Halliday ([1991d] 2005a: 47–8) writes:

> In principle these should be able to range over all probability distribution from 0.5/0.5 to approximately 0/1. But this kind of spread seemed to me to be highly unlikely. It would be unlikely for all systems to be equiprobable, since this would not leave enough redundancy. [...] But it would be equally unlikely for systems to take up all possible distribution of probabilities along the whole continuum from equiprobable to maximally skew.
>
> On the basis of what little counting I had done [in the 1960s, CMMIM], I suggested a bimodal distribution. The hypothesis was that systems tended towards one or other of two types, (i) equiprobable and (ii) skew, with the skew tending toward a ratio of one order of magnitude (which I represented for obvious reasons as nine to one, i.e. 0.9/0.1). This corresponds to one interpretation of the concept of marking: type (i), the equiprobable, have no unmarked term, while type (ii), the skew, have one of their terms unmarked.

Working with a member of John Sinclair's research group at Birmingham University, Zoe James, in the early 1990s, Halliday tested the hypothesis based on two systems, polarity ('positive'/'negative') and primary tense ('past'/'present'[7]). Halliday and James (1993 [reprinted in Halliday 2005a]) examined these two systems in eighteen million words of the Birmingham Corpus (before it expanded into the hundreds of millions of words of the "Bank of English"). The findings were very clear (see also Halliday [1993a] 2005a: part II): the probability profile of polarity was skew, while that of primary tense was equi.

The study by Halliday and James (1993 [reprinted in Halliday 2005a]) was an important empirical investigation and, as Halliday (2013) notes, it needs to be followed up for other systems on a similar scale (or increased by another order of magnitude). As far as I know, it hasn't yet been followed up – we only have additional exploratory small-scale investigations such as Matthiessen (2006). One reason is, of course, practical: the amount of work involved is very considerable – well beyond lots of small-scale manual investigations (cf. Section 9.6 below).

At the same time, Halliday has also backed up his hypothesis about the probability profiles of systems based on **Information Theory** (Shannon 1948; Shannon and Weaver 1949). This theory is rather technical and mathematical, involving entropy, information, and redundancy (for a synopsis of Information Theory for linguists, see Goldsmith 2000). But the key issue that Halliday identifies is the trade-off between **information** and **redundancy**: see Table 9.2 (based on numbers in Halliday's [1991c] 2005a: 74, table in endnote 9).

Roughly, in equi systems, information (H) is above 0.9 and redundancy (R) below 0.1; in skew systems, information is below 0.7 and redundancy above 0.3. As I have indicated in the table (by means of the column and row headed "..."), there is thus a significant gap between equi systems and skew ones in terms of the relationship between information and redundancy. And this is the basis for Halliday's theoretical reasoning about the distinction between equi systems and skew ones. He has explained this in various places; for example, Halliday ([1991c] 2005a: 69) writes: "It is interesting to note that this skew profile of 0.9 : 0.1 is just at the point where, in Shannon and Weaver's theory of information, the redundancy measure works out at 50 per cent. (To be exact, $H = R = 0.5$ where the probabilities are 0.89 : 0.11.)"

A little later, he develops this point further (Halliday [1991c] 2005a: 69–70):

> it would be a matter of some significance if it turns out that grammatical systems tend towards a bimodal probability distribution where one mode is that of almost no redundancy and the other is that where redundancy is around 50 per cent. The actual values showing up in my own informal frequency counts would be defined by the following limits:

> (i) equiprobable
> p 0.5 : 0.5 ~ 0.65 : 0.35
> H 1 ~ 0.93
> (ii) skew
> p 0.8 : 0.2 ~ 0.89 : 0.11 ~ 0.95 : 0.05
> H 0.72 ~ 0.5 ~ 0.28

> In other words, the redundancy was either (i) less than 10 per cent or (ii) somewhere in the region of 30–70 per cent, and often towards the middle of that range, close to 50 per cent. If this is in fact a general pattern, it would suggest that the grammar of a natural language is

Table 9.2 The trade-off between information (H) and redundancy (R) for equiprobable (bold, dark shading) and skew (bold italics, light shading) system probability profiles (binary systems): the prototypical equi and skew profiles are shown in cells with heavy borders

	H = 1	H = 0.97	H = 0.91	...	H = 0.72	H = 0.47	H = 0.08
R = 0	0.5 : 0.5						
R = 0.03		0.6 : 0.4					
R = 0.09			0.67 : 0.33				
...							
R = 0.28					*0.8 : 0.2*		
R = 0.53						*0.9 : 0.1*	
R = 0.92							*0.99 : 0.01*

organized around the interaction between two modes of quantizing information: one where each act of choice – each instance – is maximally informative (it might equally well have been the opposite), and one where it is largely uninformative (since you could pretty well have guessed it already). Furthermore, it might be the case that these two kinds of system occur in roughly equal proportion.

As already noted, the two systems investigated by Halliday and James ([1993] 2005a), viz. primary tense and polarity, fall into the probability profiles of equi and skew, respectively; primary tense is very close to the "ideal" equi system in Table 9.2 (probability profile 0.5 : 0.5; information = 1, redundancy = 0), whereas polarity is very close to the "ideal" skew system (probability profile 0.9 : 0.1; information = approximately 0.5, redundancy = approximately 0.5).

But what about other systems? We will have to wait until researchers take on the (perhaps daunting!) task of replicating Halliday and James's ([1993] 2005) study for systems other than primary tense and polarity. While we are waiting, let me just report on my own small-scale exploratory investigation (an ongoing effort, based on manual analysis; see Matthiessen 2006, for an interim report).

Out of the wide range of systems that I have used in manual analysis of texts, I have chosen thirty-eight clause nexus and clause systems as a basis for exploring Halliday's bimodal probability profile of equi vs. skew systems. These thirty-eight systems are all binary ones (thus non-binary systems like process type are excluded): see Figure 9.14.

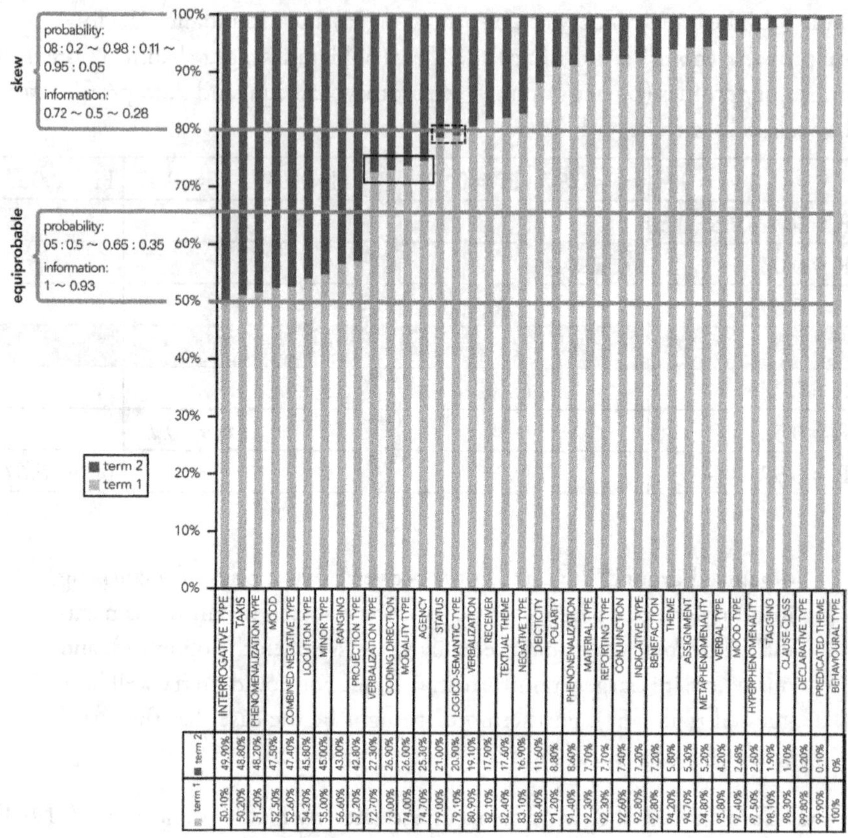

System	term 2	term 1
INTERROGATIVE TYPE	49.90%	50.10%
TAXIS	48.80%	50.20%
PHENOMENALIZATION TYPE	48.20%	51.20%
MOOD	47.50%	52.50%
COMBINED NEGATIVE TYPE	47.40%	52.60%
LOCUTION TYPE	45.80%	54.20%
MINOR TYPE	45.00%	55.00%
RANGING	43.00%	56.60%
PROJECTION TYPE	42.80%	57.20%
VERBALIZATION TYPE	27.30%	72.70%
CODING DIRECTION	26.90%	73.00%
MODALITY TYPE	26.00%	74.00%
AGENCY	25.30%	74.70%
STATUS	21.00%	79.00%
LOGICO-SEMANTIC TYPE	20.90%	79.10%
VERBALIZATION	19.10%	80.90%
RECEIVER	17.90%	82.10%
TEXTUAL THEME	17.60%	82.40%
NEGATIVE TYPE	16.90%	83.10%
DEICTICITY	11.60%	88.40%
POLARITY	8.80%	91.20%
PHENOMENALIZATION	8.60%	91.40%
MATERIAL TYPE	7.70%	92.30%
REPORTING TYPE	7.70%	92.30%
CONJUNCTION	7.40%	92.60%
INDICATIVE TYPE	7.20%	92.80%
BENEFACTION	7.20%	92.80%
THEME	5.80%	94.20%
ASSIGNMENT	5.30%	94.70%
METAPHENOMENALITY	5.20%	94.80%
VERBAL TYPE	4.20%	95.80%
MOOD TYPE	2.68%	97.40%
HYPERPHENOMENALITY	2.50%	97.50%
TAGGING	1.90%	98.10%
CLAUSE CLASS	1.70%	98.30%
DECLARATIVE TYPE	0.20%	99.80%
PREDICATED THEME	0.10%	99.90%
BEHAVIOURAL TYPE	0%	100%

Figure 9.14 Systemic probability profiles in relation to Halliday's distinction between skew and equiprobable systems

Out of these thirty-eight systems, thirty-four can fairly clearly be interpreted as either equi or skew systems.[8] Four systems have profiles that fall in-between the probability ranges of "skew" and "equiprobable"; they all have a profile of approximately 0.25 : 0.75:

- VERBALIZATION TYPE: "named" (+verbiage) 27.3 per cent, 'locuted' (+projection) 72.7 per cent
- CODING DIRECTION: "encoding" 27 per cent, "decoding" 73 per cent
- MODALITY TYPE: "modalization" 26 per cent, "modulation" 74 per cent
- AGENCY: "effective" 25.3 per cent, "middle" 74.7 per cent.

Of these, the results for the system of AGENCY are the most robust: it is the least delicate system (simultaneous with PROCESS TYPE) of the four, and the absolute number of clauses analysed in terms of this system is fairly high (around 9,000). The other systems are all more delicate, so the absolute numbers are much lower, and we should set them aside for the time being until we have reached much higher numbers in our counting.

The system of AGENCY would thus seem to be an exception to the bimodal probability distribution hypothesized by Halliday (for low-delicacy systems). However, it is interesting to note that when we intersect AGENCY with the simultaneous system of PROCESS TYPE, as shown in Figure 9.8, it splits into two domains: in the environment of "material" clauses, its probability profile is that of an equi system, but for the other process types, it is that of a skew system. This may be a general pattern with 0.25 : 0.75 system; but to assess the situation, we will have to wait for the results of extensive corpus-based studies.

9.5.3 Quantitative and qualitative correlations

As we have seen, in Halliday's account of the probabilistic nature of language, quantitative and qualitative aspects of choice are complementary ("probability is the probability of 'choosing' ... one thing rather than another"). But how is this complementarity manifested? This is of course in itself a major research question – and we could go back to Zipf (1935) to review findings in this area. Within the stratum of lexicogrammar, one manifestation of the complementarity is the cline between grammar and lexis. As is well known, if we count the frequency of occurrence of lexicogrammatical items, it turns out that the more frequent they are, the more likely they are to be grammatical rather than lexical – the highest-frequency items always being grammatical ("function words") rather than lexical ("content words"). As the frequency decreases, the proportion of lexical items increases: see Figure 9.15; and as we move towards grammatical items, the increase in frequency is exponential. And there is also, of course, a reflection of the frequency of wordings on the expression plane: the more frequent a lexicogrammatical item is, the "shorter" and more reduced its expression tends to be.

In addition to the general correlation between the distinction between grammatical and lexical items, and frequency in text illustrated in Figure 9.15, there may be more specific patterns. One area that I have explored is the frequency of the different process types (see Figure 9.4) and their qualitative elaboration in the lexicogrammar measured crudely in terms of the number of verbs (or really verb senses) belonging to each process type (see Matthiessen 1999, 2006, 2014a). In general, it turns out that relative frequency and systemic elaboration correlate. There is one exception, viz. "relational" clauses. Although they are almost as frequent as "material" ones, there are many fewer verbs devoted to them. However, this is not

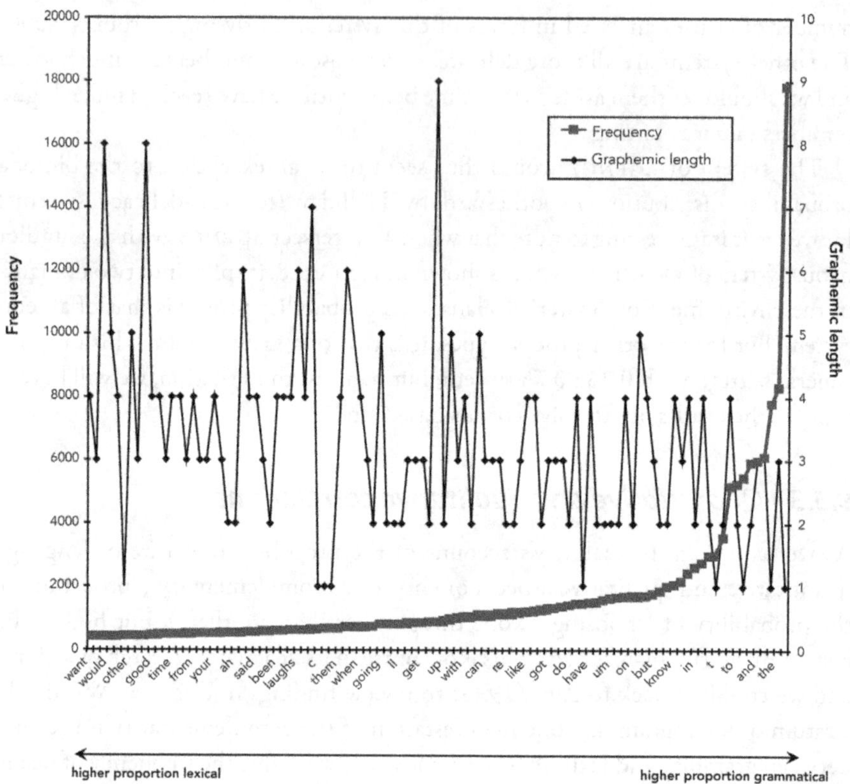

Figure 9.15 Frequency of lexicogrammatical items and the cline between lexis and grammar

surprising, given the nature of "relational" clauses: the systemic elaboration is in the participants rather than in the process.

9.6   Investigating the corpus

Any investigation of quantitative patterns in language depends on the existence of corpora and on tools for analysing them. In a sense, we are tantalizingly close to a real breakthrough based in terms of the analysis of massive volumes of text; but there are still severe constraints on what we can access as far as the grammar is concerned. Our access to the corpus is still fairly "superficial"; the way corpora are represented and the suite of corpus analysis tools are much more supportive of lexical analysis than of grammatical analysis. Manning (2003: 294) characterizes the situation as follows:

It's easy to search corpora for something like *as least* as constructions; it is far harder to search corpora for something like participial relative clauses or locative inversion constructions. Such technological limitations have meant that corpus linguistic research has been largely limited to phenomena that can be accessed via searches on particular words. The average corpus linguist's main research tool remains the word-concordancing program, which shows a searched-for keyword in context (perhaps with morphological stemming, sorting options, etc.). However, a (theoretical) syntactician is usually interested in more abstract structural properties that cannot be investigated easily in this way.

This is very similar to the assessment Halliday has expressed over the years; for example, Halliday ([2002b] 2005a: 171) notes:

In principle, as I think is generally accepted, the corpus is just as useful, and just as essential, for the study of grammar as it is for the study of lexis. Only, the grammar is very much harder to get at. In a language like English, where words may operate all the way along the continuum, there are grammatical items like *the* and *and* and *to* just as there are lexical items like *sun* and *moon* and *stars*, as well as those like *behind* and *already* and *therefore* which fall somewhere in the middle; occurrences of any of these are easily retrieved, counted, and contextualized. But whereas *sun* and *moon* and *stars* carry most of their meaning on their sleeves, as it were, *the* and *and* and *to* tell us very little about what is going on underneath; and what they do tell us, if we just observe them directly, tends to be comparatively trivial. It is an exasperating feature of patterns at the grammatical end of the continuum, that the easier they are to recognize the less they matter.

In corpus studies in linguistics, there have tended to be two approaches to the processing of corpora. One approach has been to represent corpora in standard orthography, and to analyse them directly using analysis tools – usually some kind of concordancing program. In the UK, this approach was taken by John Sinclair and his team at the University of Birmingham. Another approach has been to develop software such as word class ("part of speech," "POS") taggers and more full-fledged parsers to annotate corpora with additional information (a POS-tagged corpus, or a parsed corpus, a "treebank" or "treebanked" corpus), and then to analyse these annotated corpora using additional analysis tools to search annotated corpora. In the UK, this approach was taken by Geoffrey Leech and his team at the University of Lancaster.

Linguists adopting the first approach have argued that annotation introduces a theoretical or descriptive bias in the analysis of the corpus; but McEnery and Hardie (2011) address and (I think it is fair to say) demolish their argument. Even if a corpus has been annotated, it is of course perfectly possible to bypass the annotation; and whatever form of analysis we subject an unannotated corpus to will of course also embody a linguistic bias. By representing a corpus by means of standard orthography, we have of course already made various theoretically significant decisions, and introduced a bias.

For any given research task, researchers will have to consider what kind of corpus to use and what kinds of computational tools to use, including both annotation tools and search tools. When Halliday and James ([1993] 2005a) carried out their corpus analysis of polarity and primary tense, they had access to the unannotated Birmingham corpus of around twenty million words. They decided that annotation would, at that time, not have been of great help; instead, they searched the "raw" corpus. Their account of how to go about looking for grammatical features based on orthographic words is methodologically very helpful, and still relevant today, at least if one hasn't got access to an annotated corpus.

Even with an annotated corpus with good search tools such as COCA, the Corpus of Contemporary American English (http://corpus.byu.edu/coca/), it can be hard to carry out investigations into grammar. Assume that we want to explore the probabilistic nature of the system of modality in English (cf. Figure 9.6). This will include searching for orthographic words that potentially realize modal operators such as *can, may, will, must,* and modal adverbs such as *perhaps, maybe, probably, certainly.* One problem is of course that one and the same orthographic word can often realize different grammatical and lexical words. For example, the orthographic word *will* can be a temporal or modal operator (grammatical word) serving as Finite in the clause, a lexical verb serving as Event in the verbal group, or a lexical noun serving as Thing in the nominal group (unless it is used as a Classifier in the nominal group). These possibilities are represented schematically in Figure 9.16.

If we only have access to a "raw" corpus, we will have to search for instances of the orthographic word *will*; but all the instances that turn up will have to be examined manually in some way – for example drawing on the methods used by Halliday and James (1993 [reprinted in Halliday 2005a]). However, what would the situation be if we can search for *will* with tags representing different word classes? It will depend on what tags are available and on how reliable they are. As an

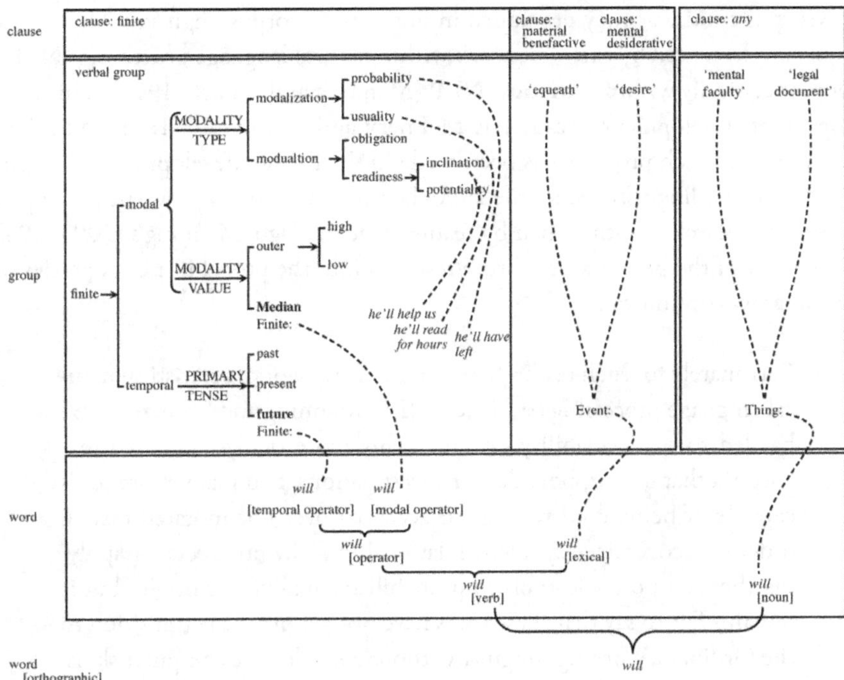

Figure 9.16 Lexicogrammatical differentiation of orthographic word *will*, first at word rank and then at group rank

illustration, I have tabulated tags in COCA that can be used in an attempt to pick out the right kind of *will*: see Table 9.3.

Searches for forms of the lexical verb *will* and for the lexical noun *will* turn up many instances of the operator *will*. However, the good news is that when one searches for the "modal auxiliary" *will* (i.e. will. [vm*]), the result seems reliable; I examined the first 100 occurrences, and they are all instances of the operator *will*. But that is as far as we can get at present: there are no tags to differentiate between modal and temporal *will*, nor between the different modal senses of *will*. This is not a criticism of COCA; it would indeed be quite hard to distinguish these types automatically. Therefore, to continue the analysis, we would have to examine 860,679 occurrences of the operator *will*, and analyse them manually (and we could, of course, reasonably ask how much we have actually gained from the tagging in this particular case – compare Halliday and James' (1993 [reprinted in Halliday 2005a]), decision not to try to produce a tagged version of the corpus they had access to).

Corpus studies as they developed in linguistics, "corpus linguistics," have now been supplemented by extensive work within natural language processing (NLP), more specifically within **statistical NLP** (Manning and Schütze 1999). This is an important development because, as McEnery and Hardie (2011: section 2.5.3) observe, not much progress has been made in the further development of corpus tools in corpus linguistics since the 1990s because these tools tend to be developed by single researchers rather than by teams. A decade ago, Manning's (2003: 294) assessment of the potential for future research into the probabilistic properties of grammar was optimistic:

> Fortunately for such research, recent intensive work in statistical natural language processing (statistical NLP; Manning and Schütze 1999) has led to the availability of both many more richly annotated text corpora that can support deeper investigations, and many more tools capable of being used with good accuracy over unannotated text in order to recover deep syntactic relationships. The prospects for applying these corpora and tools to probabilistic analysis are bright, but it remains fair to say that these tools have not yet made the transition to the Ordinary Working Linguist without considerable computer skills.

The Ordinary Working Linguist may be in a better position now than ten years ago; but many such linguists are still constrained in terms of how much of the power of statistical NLP they can tap into (cf. also McEnery and Hardie 2011: section 9.3, on the relative lack of interaction between "corpus linguistics" and "computational linguistics"). For discussions dealing specifically with corpus studies within SFL, see Teich (2009), Wu (2009), and cf. also Bateman and O'Donnell (2015).

The development of more powerful tools for corpus analysis will make it possible to extend the research into language as a probabilistic system based on Halliday's theoretical foundation. At the same time, his systemic functional linguistics has a great deal to offer in the further expansion of corpus studies. For example, in their review of criticisms of Biber's (1986, 1988, onwards) "multidimensional" ("MD") approach in corpus studies, McEnery and Hardie (2011: section 5.4.3) note that one problem is that his choice of features is not motivated, in addition to the fact that the features chosen are limited to only those that can be retrieved in the analysis of tagged corpora:

> So we might argue that the MD methodology could be more solidly founded if based on a selection of features which is both principled and exhaustive – a standard which Biber's feature-lists approach but

Table 9.3 Examples of tags in COCA that can be applied in searches for instances of *will* in order to try to refine these searchers

Class	COCA label	Tag	Occurrences	Comment
operator [temporal/ modal]	modal auxiliary	will.[vm*]	860,679	this seems reliable; the first 100 instance are all operators
lexical verb	base from of lexical verb	will. [wO*]	1,891	most of the hits are operator *will*
	infinitive	will.[v?i*]	128	
	third person singular	will.[v?z*]	0	
	past (v-ed)	will.[v?d*]	0	
	past participle (v-en)	will.[v?n*]	0	
	present partici-ple (v-ing)	will.[v?g*]	0	
	lexical verb	will.fvv*]	2,019	most of the hits are operator *will*
noun	noun	will.fn*]	50,060	this includes both common noun *will* and proper noun *Will*; operator *will* is also picked up, e.g. *Will thoroughbred racing have its historic moment?*

do not reach. How might such a motivated list of lexicogrammatical features be derived? At this point we move into the realm of hypothesis. However, one possible approach is to consider the functions of a language as a feature tree. This could start at the very high level of nominal components versus verbal components (since the noun–verb distinction is one of the most universal features of language structure), and then diversify from there, with attention to contrasting linguistic options and category alternatives at each branch in the tree.

They provide an example of part of such a tree. An alternative to what they propose would be not to reinvent the linguistic wheel, but instead to draw on the extensive systemic functional literature and to use systemic descriptions in the form of system networks to derive principled selections of features from comprehensive (exhaustive) descriptions. Their "tree" is simply a partial reflection of what would be covered by a comparable system network. Here corpus studies can benefit from Halliday's move to give the theory of language a paradigmatic base (see Martin and Matthiessen 1992) and to theorize the corpus in terms of the cline of instantiation, thereby relating the domain of data (the instance pole of the cline) to the domain of theory (the system pole), as shown in Figure 9.1.

9.7   Conclusion

When Halliday began exploring the probabilistic nature of language, first in his text-based work on Chinese in the 1950s and then, moving from the late 1950s into the 1960s, also in his text-based work on English, it was conceivable that more linguists would have joined him in taking an interest in the probabilistic nature of language, stimulated by the development of Information Theory. However, the history of linguistics took a different turn – a turn towards the categoricity of competence, and the insulation of competence from performance, so that it was left to those taking an interest in performance, initially mainly psycholinguists, to deal with quantitative issues. In spite of this turn towards the categoricity of competence, Halliday and other systemic functional linguists continued to explore the probabilistic nature of language, taking advantage of the development of the technology of the corpus (starting in particular in the second half of the 1980s).

However, the academic climate was changing rather dramatically. One reason was of course precisely the development of corpus studies in linguistics. Another was the development in computational linguistics of what came to be known as statistical NLP (and also, importantly, in work on speech recognition[9]). This was related to the construction of grammatical frameworks such as lexical functional grammar (LFG) and head-driven phrase structure grammar (HPSG) designed to be used in computational systems; in this way, formal grammarians came to appreciate the value of the corpus and of a probabilistic understanding of language (probabilistic parsers were part of the convincing evidence[10]). It is also important to note that probabilistic insights have been taken into consideration in models of cognition (see e.g. Charter, Tenenbaum, and Yuille 2006).

A number of these developments are brought together by Bod, Hay, and Jannedy (2003) under the heading of *Probabilistic linguistics*. Their own introduction and the various contributions to the book, including work on phonology, grammar (syntax and morphology), and semantics, make a very powerful case for a theoretical understanding of language as a probabilistic system. Thus, there is now an interesting opportunity to relate the kind of work reported on by the contributors to *Probabilistic linguistics* to Halliday's conception of language as a probabilistic system. In Bod, Hay, and Jannedy (2003), there is only one reference to Halliday, viz. to the second edition of his *Introduction to functional grammar*, but not to any of his empirical and theoretical work on language as a probabilistic system since the 1950s. The reference is provided by Manning (2003) in his chapter on "probabilistic syntax."

Discussing the goals of joint research with other scholars, Manning (2003: 340) writes, "We want to be able to predict the overall rate of the different systemic choices (Halliday 1994a) that can be made for certain input." This suggests that it would be possible to construct a bridge between these two communities of scholars concerned with the probabilistic properties of language. A number of the cases Manning discussed could certainly be interpreted and illuminated in systemic functional terms; some of his key examples (e.g. in reference to Optimality Theory) involve what I would interpret as competing motivations across metafunctions in the organization of the clause involving probabilistic considerations within the metafunctional systems that are in competition. In systemic functional research, one pioneering study that could serve as a model for future investigations informed by computational work is Munro (2004), who used the techniques of machine learning to "infer an accurate description of functional categories" of the nominal group in English.

Halliday's conception of language as a probabilistic system is, of course, an integral and natural part of his conception of language as a (complex) dynamic open system (with reference to the work by Jay Lemke, e.g. Lemke 1984). In this connection, it is interesting to consider Ball's (2004) comments on complexity; after a brief discussion of "catastrophe theory" and "chaos theory," he writes (pp. 4–5):

> The current vogue is for the third of these three C's: complexity. The buzzwords are now "emergence" and "self-organization", as complexity theory seeks to understand how order and stability arise from the interaction of many agents according to a few simple rules.

The physics I shall discuss in this book is not unrelated to the idea of complexity – indeed, the two often overlap. But very often what passes today for "complexity science" is really something much older, dressed up in fashionable apparel. The main themes in complexity theory have been studied by physicists for over a hundred years, and these scientists have evolved a toolkit of concepts and techniques to which complexity studies have added barely a handful of new items. At the root of this sort of physics is a phenomenon which immediately explains why the discipline may have something to say about society: it is a science of collective behaviour. At face value it is not obvious how the bulk properties of insensate particles of matter should bear any relation to how humans behave en masse. Yet physicists have discovered that systems whose component parts have a capacity to act collectively often show recurrent features, even though they might seem to have nothing in at all in common with one another.

The title of Ball's book is *Critical mass: How one thing leads to another*, and he has added an elaboration "being an enquiry into the interplay of chance and necessity in the way that human culture, customs, institutions, cooperation and conflict arise." Adding language to this mix would seem highly appropriate – language conceived of in probabilistic terms. When we conceive of language in probabilistic terms, we can examine the effect of "collective behaviour"; the system that embodies systemic probabilities is located at the potential pole of the cline of instantiation embedded in the context of culture of a speech fellowship, as shown in Figure 9.1. Systemic probabilities are always being shaped by collective behaviour. Let me end my chapter by linking this understanding to a point made by Halliday (2013) under the section heading of "probability and prediction"):

The concept of meaning as choice, or as choosing, whether or not it is being represented as a system network, may suggest a bias towards the individual meaner: the notion of an act of meaning, in particular, carries with it a suggestion of this kind. But choosing may be an activity of a whole population, as it is when they vote in an election or a referendum. Meaning as choice can likewise be thought of in the context of a population – in the statistical sense: it may be concerned with very large quantities of acts of meaning, within which large-scale patterns and tendencies may be observed.

The network makes no prediction about what a particular person is going to mean on some particular occasion. It makes predictions about the behaviour of a population. It defines the range of options that is available to them as meaners, their meaning potential as producers and receivers in the social semiotic universe of language.

Notes

1   On Halliday's early compilation and use of corpora, first of Chinese (Cantonese, in 1949; Mandarin, in the 1950s) and then of English (beginning, in the late 1950s, with one hour of 'natural conversation'), see Halliday ([1992b] 2005a: 76–8).

2   For example, Chomsky (1965: 4): "We thus make a fundamental distinction between competence (the speaker-hearer's knowledge of his language) and performance (the actual use of language in concrete situations). [...] linguistic theory is mentalistic, since it is concerned with discovering a mental reality underlying actual behavior."

3   Their characterizations of "modern linguistics" is of course of a particular brand of modern linguistics – the kind of modern linguistics associated with Chomsky. It is important to emphasize that while his kind of linguistics dominated the scene for quite a while, there were other significant kinds of "modern linguistics" around the world, including (but not restricted to) Pike's Tagmemic Linguistics (in the tradition of US anthropological linguistics), Lamb's Stratificational Linguistics (incorporating the European structuralist tradition as it had been developed by Hjelmslev), and the continuation of the Prague School – and of course the Firthian-Hallidayan tradition.

4   Lyons (1977: 29) suggested a distinction between "system sentence" – "the sentence as an abstract, theoretical model of the language-system" – and "text-sentence" – "the sentence as something that can be uttered (i.e. as the product of a bit of) language-behaviour"; but this distinction merely seems to emphasize the effect of the wedge Halliday ([1991c] 2004d: 63) refers to, and it was never taken up by linguists in general.

5   This "derivation" may involve one or more steps in a chain realization; but these steps are – or can be made – fully explicit, as is clear from computational models and implementations of systemic functional linguistics.

6   And also within the same ranked unit: in principle, there may be conditioning effects across units of different ranks. Qualitatively, such conditioning is represented by inter-rank preselection, but it seems very likely that there are also analogous quantitative effects.

7   This is of course really 'past'/'present'/'future'; but he excluded 'future' since it is much less common than 'past' and 'present.'

8   There are two systems that are on the borderline of skew systems (status [or freedom] and logico-semantic type); but they are very close to skew: 0.79 rather than 0.8.

9   See Goldsmith (2000), who makes a strong case for the value of Information Theory to phonological theory, noting the early interest by Roman Jakobson and other researchers concerned with phonology and phonetics.

10   In systemic functional linguistics, probabilistic parsing was explored by Robin Fawcett and his research team (e.g. Fawcett and Weerasinghe 1993; Weerasinghe 1994); cf. also Souter and Atwell (1992).

Chapter 10

Instantial systems and logogenesis*

10.1 Instantial systems seen logogenetically

In this chapter, I shall explore two key categories in the processing of text – **instantial systems**, i.e. systems of those selections that are made in the processing of a particular text, and **logogenesis**, the construction of meaning in the form of instantial systems as a text unfolds. Both of these have been on the agenda of systemic functional theory for a long time; they are, for example, part of the discussion in Halliday (1978), even though the technical terms are more recent. However, they have not yet been modelled in general terms. One central reason for this is no doubt that they presuppose accounts of processes – in particular, the process of instantiation and the process of modifying an instantial system in the unfolding of text – and linguistics does not have a tradition of explicit accounts of processes.

This is not to say that linguists have ignored processes. On the contrary, the nineteenth century was dominated by a thematic of another kind of genesis, evolution – so much so that Saussure had to create a sharp dichotomy between diachrony and synchrony, and between *langue* and *parole* to allow the new thematic of structuralism to focus on synchronic slices of *langue*. Although a number of linguists rejected the sharp distinction between diachrony and synchrony (see e.g. Otto Jespersen's 1917 review of Saussure's *Cours*), Gustave Guillaume (e.g. 1929) was one of the few linguists at the time to take the process of unfolding text into serious consideration, building it into his psychomechanic theory as a move from the potential to the actual, and later Louis Hjelmslev (1943) emphasized both system and process, although no process accounts grew out of this.[1] For European structuralists in general, issues of parole fell outside the domain of theorizing, just as Chomsky's later distinction between competence and performance meant that performance fell outside the domain of theorizing in generative linguistics. In the European context, Prague School linguists pioneered process-oriented metaphors such as Firbas's communicative dynamism

(CD; see Firbas 1992, for a recent review and overview) and Danes's (1974) themat-ic progression (interpreted systemic functionally in Fries 1981), and the metaphor of flow of information is used quite widely in functional, discourse-oriented linguis-tics nowadays; however, the accounts themselves do not involve processes but rather "traces" of processes such as sequences of numbers to indicate CD progression types, such as Theme to Theme, Rheme to Theme, and reference chains.

In contrast to linguistics, computational linguistics is centrally concerned with modelling processes, making use of constructs such as parsing algorithms, transi-tion networks, dynamically updated history lists, and stacks. It has indeed provided one environment for identifying the need to deal with instantial systems and logo-genesis. In my own experience, I became aware of this in the 1970s through research Bengt Sigurd carried out at the University of Lund, where he showed how reference could be handled in a computational model by continuously updating the set of (identifiable) referents in the processing of text, and how text generation could be thought of as a traversal of a semantic network (Sigurd 1977); and then again in the early 1980s, as I had become involved in the development of the PENMAN text-generation system at USC/Information Sciences Institute and we needed to consider issues such as traversing a system network by instantiating systemic features in the generation of text (see e.g. Matthiessen 1983a, 1983b; Mann and Matthiessen 1983). In the history of systemic theory, this kind of issue had already been raised and addressed in a computational setting by Henrici (1966). Thus, procedures for traversing a system network – traversal algorithms – have certainly become part of systemic modelling (see e.g. Matthiessen and Bateman 1991) even if they may have remained unconnected with the *general* theoretical discussion.

But in the meantime, the issue of the modelling of time has been raised by a number of systemic linguists: Martin's (1985) paper on the distinction between process and text as two *aspects* of human semiosis was seminal in bringing the issue of time into a theoretical focus. He reported, among other things, on Ventola's (e.g. 1987) use of flow chart to order choices temporally in dialogue. The use of the flowchart has also been explored by Fawcett, e.g. in Fawcett, van der Mije, and van Wissen (1988). Eggins (1990) and Slade (1996) have tackled the problem of how dialogue is developed dynamically; the question of how a casual conversation can continue to unfold was addressed by Eggins, who gives us an insight into a casu-al conversation as a potentially never-ending expansion. The process, or dynamic, perspective has been further developed as an approach to grammar by Ravelli (e.g. 1995). Hasan's (1983) notion of instantial lexical organization, developed in Fries (1982), is crucial to the understanding of logogenesis and instantial systems; and her work on cohesive harmony (1984b) points towards the power of the instantial system in representing patterns created in a text, as does Halliday's (1973) account of the different instantial systems in Golding's *The Inheritors*. Halliday introduced the notion of logogenesis and has used the logogenetic perspective in a number of papers, such as his discussion of the clause complex as a feature of "choreographic" spoken grammar and his "history of a sentence" (1988a); in particular, he has shown how it reveals the way in which meaning is built up in a text to allow for the move from the congruent to the metaphorical (Halliday 1988b/2004c; see also Halliday and Matthiessen 1999/2006: ch. 9).

Towards the end of the 1980s, two theoretically central papers drew on computational modelling to further our theoretical understanding of dynamic accounts. Bateman (1989) problematized logical, recursive systems and the division of labour between the systemic potential and specifications of how it is to be instantiated, and O'Donnell (1990) proposed a model of exchange that moved away from relying on exchange structures and towards a method of ordering exchange states in an unfolding dialogue. This logogenetic model of exchange has been further developed by O'Donnell and Sefton (1995) as part of the Dialogue project at the University of Sydney. Crucial to this model is the notion that as a text unfolds, different parts of the overall systemic potential become accessible. I will discuss this approach further in Section 10.3.2. Outside the computational context but within the exploration of logogenesis in Sydney, Fuller (1995) has developed the account of logogenesis in the investigation of "popular science" discourses, showing for example how H. Gould builds up his discourse by incorporating strands from various bodies of discourse. In contrast to the logogenetic model of exchange referred to above, Tsui (1989) posits logogenetically specialized systems: systemic potentials that are available at different points in an unfolding text.

It is clear, then, that a number of recent studies have indicated that logogenesis is an important dimension of the overall theory of language in context. Here I would like to explore it by explicitly relating it to instantial systems. Let me begin by referring to the characterization of logogenesis in Halliday and Matthiessen (1999/2006: 18): "there is the **unfolding** of the act of meaning itself: the instantial construction of meaning in the form of a text. This is a stochastic process in which the potential for creating meaning is continually modified in the light of what has gone before; certain options are restricted or disfavoured, while others are emprobabled or opened up. We shall refer to this as the **logogenetic** time frame, using logo(s) in its original sense of 'discourse.'"

I will interpret the changing potential for creating meaning instantially as the **instantial system** of a text. An instantial system is a partial "copy" of the system of the register that the text is an instance of: it represents the options available at any point in the unfolding text to speaker and listener and is being modified throughout the text until the text has come to a closure. In Section 10.2, I will explore the nature of instantial systems and modification. In Section 10.3, I will focus on the logogenetic ordering of modification in particular. Then, in Section 10.4, I will relate instantial systems and logogenesis to other aspects of the overall organization of the system-process of language in context. I will bring up issues such as the following. The extent to which the final version of the instantial system is retained beyond the life of the text as a modification of the more general registerial system can be assumed to be variable. From the point of view of a particular person, the question is to what extent they have changed as a result of processing the text – e.g. the extent to which an addressee has learned something from the text in the sense of expanding and revising their earlier systems. I will return to this issue towards the end of the chapter, including the important differentiation of the perspectives of the different interactants taking part in a text.

10.2   Modifying instantial systems in logogenesis

A text can be interpreted as an ongoing process of selection of features – an ongoing instantiation of a more permanent system (cf. Halliday 1978). Thus, we can interpret a recipe as, among other things, successive selections in the simultaneous systems of the clause. To get a sense of the way these selections unfold, we can view the text as a systemic "score": see Figure 10.1.

The leftmost columns represent clause systems that are part of the overall grammatical potential. If we track the instantiations of their features in the unfolding of the text – [1] through [12] – we see how an instantial system emerges in the sense of principled patterns of instantiation. For instance, the opposition between "imperative: jussive" and "declarative" emerges as the one that's operational in the text. An instantial system, then, is one that is created in the course of instantiation.

An instantial system can be thought of as a transient copy of a more permanent system – a registerial system in the first instance (for further discussion, see Section 10.4.2). But it is a partial copy. At first it shows only certain features of the registerial system, and then it is filled in as the text unfolds. Filling in the system means both opening up parts of it and closing off other parts, both of which are meaning-creating processes; it is a continuous process of modification taking place as a text unfolds. How is an instantial system modified logogenetically? The modification may involve the following types of change:

Expansion: terms in systems or whole systems may be added.
Subtraction: terms in systems or whole systems may be removed.

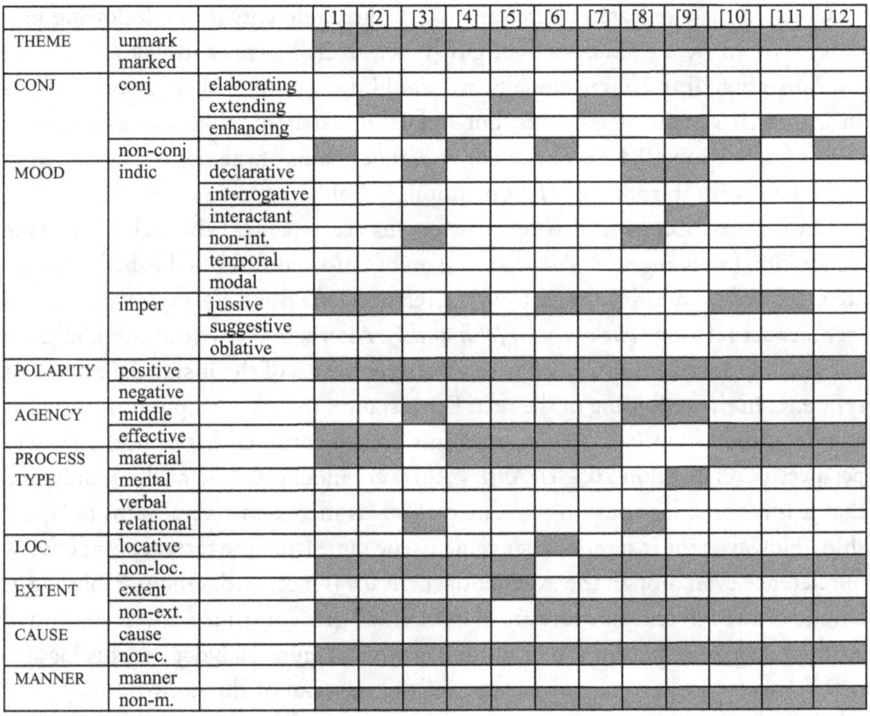

			[1]	[2]	[3]	[4]	[5]	[6]	[7]	[8]	[9]	[10]	[11]	[12]
THEME	unmark		■	■	■	■	■	■	■	■	■	■	■	■
	marked													
CONJ	conj	elaborating												
		extending		■			■		■					
		enhancing			■						■		■	
	non-conj		■			■		■				■		■
MOOD	indic	declarative			■					■				
		interrogative												
		interactant									■			
		non-int.			■					■				
		temporal												
		modal												
	imper	jussive	■			■		■	■			■	■	
		suggestive												
		oblative												
POLARITY	positive		■	■		■		■			■	■	■	■
	negative													
AGENCY	middle				■					■	■			
	effective		■	■		■	■	■	■			■	■	■
PROCESS TYPE	material		■	■		■		■	■			■		■
	mental										■			
	verbal													
	relational				■					■				
LOC.	locative							■						
	non-loc.		■		■		■		■	■		■	■	■
EXTENT	extent					■								
	non-ext.		■	■	■		■	■	■	■	■	■	■	■
CAUSE	cause													
	non-c.		■	■	■	■	■	■	■	■	■	■	■	■
MANNER	manner													
	non-m.		■	■	■	■	■	■	■	■	■	■	■	■

Figure 10.1 Systemic score of a recipe

Other revision: existing terms in systems or whole systems may be reorganized.

One of the descriptive tasks facing us now is to establish to what extent and under what conditions these types of modification occur. We may hypothesize that the metafunctional origin of systems will play a role in determining how it is modified in the course of logogenesis. Let us consider examples from each metafunction.

10.2.1 REFERENCE *as an example of logogenesis*

Like textual systems in general, REFERENCE is dynamic in nature (cf. Matthiessen 1989, 1992); more specifically, it is concerned, first, with introducing new discourse referents into the instantial system of referents shared by speaker and listener as identifiable and second, with keeping track of them once they have been introduced into the system.

Consider first repeated references to discourse referents in the following narrative written by a primary school girl [taken from Martin and Rothery 1980]: see Appendix, Text 1. Traditionally, we would not interpret these systemically as an instantial system of referents, but rather in a structure-like way as reference chains (cf. Section 10.4.3). The major reference chains of the text are tabulated in Table 10.1, with introductory first mentions in bold.

On most occasions in this text, the chains are expanded through identifying elaboration (*an orange thing, it, it, it,* ...); on occasion, already established referents are extended by means of a part–whole relation (*the front, the control room*) or a member-set relation (*one of them, John and I*). Alternatively, we can think of these not as **chain relations *but as* relations between states of the instantial system of referents** in the unfolding of the text. For instance, the space ship is introduced as a node in the instantial system of referents. Let us consider this from the reader's perspective (cf. Section 10.4.4). At first, it is very indelicate: the reader is only told that it is a non-conscious object. The delicacy is increased several steps to "space ship." However, the instantial node remains the same from the textual point of view of reference even though the experiential delicacy is increased. Once established as a node in the referent network, the "space ship" gets confirmed and reconfirmed again and again as part of the instantial network. Figure 10.2 depicts this logogenetic process in the form of snapshots of the traversal of the network, staggered relative to one another to give a sense of the passage of logogenetic time.[2]

In this first example, the instantial network is expanded simply through elaboration: it is elaborated in delicacy, and the same node is "restated" again and again as the text unfolds. This is the basic logogenetic principle of reference. However, the expansion of the referential network may also involve extension of various types: new nodes are created through addition (aggregation), through set membership (selection), and through the part–whole relationship (meronomy). Let's consider an example of expansion through additive extension first: see Figures 10.3 and 10.4.

In the extension of the root node "space ship," both set membership and meronymy are used: see Figure 10.5.

This short text thus illustrates expansion as a logogenetic principle. We have seen examples of both elaboration and extension. To these, we might add enhancement as the way in which "orange thing" is introduced relative to its location, the sky:

    elaboration: thing --> ship
    extension: ship --> control room
    enhancement: into sky --> orange thing

Table 10.1 The major reference chains of a narrative

clause	I	we	John	an orange things	part	ships	one of them	other
1								
2								
3				**an orange thing**				
4				it				
5.1	I							
5.2				it				
6				it				
7	I			it				
8				the thing				
9				it				
10	I							
11				it				
12					**the back of the capsule**			
13								
14.1	I		**the**					
14.2			**person**		**the front**			
14.3								
15			he					

Continued

Table 10.1 The major reference chains of a narrative (Continued)

clause	I	we	John	an orange things	part	ships	one of them	other
16.1	I		him					
16.2	I							
17				the entire ship				
18	I		him					
19			him					they
20			he					
21.1	I		him					
21.2	me		he	this gigantic vessel				
21.3			him					
22	me		he, his					
23.1	me		John					
23.2		we (+)						
24								
25.1		**we**						the
25.2		you						police
25.3								they
26								
27								

clause	I	we	John	an orange things	part	ships	one of them	other
28						ships		
29.1			John					
29.2						them		
30			his			them		
31		us				one of them		
32.1		we					it the hold of	
32.2							the ship	
33.1		John and I					the control	
33.2		our					room the ship	
34		we						this; the planet

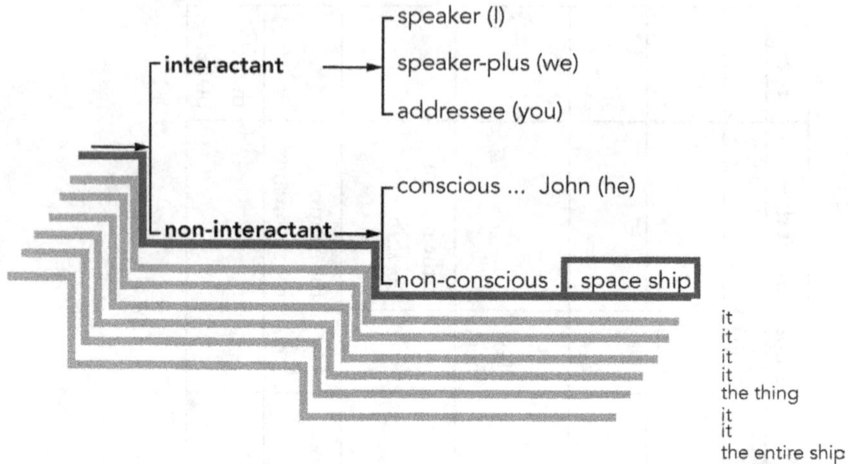

Figure 10.2 Introducing and confirming a referent node in the instantial network

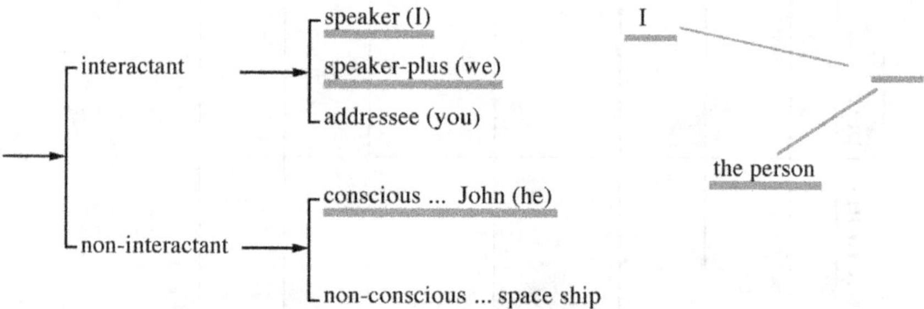

Figure 10.3 Expansion of instantial reference system (1)

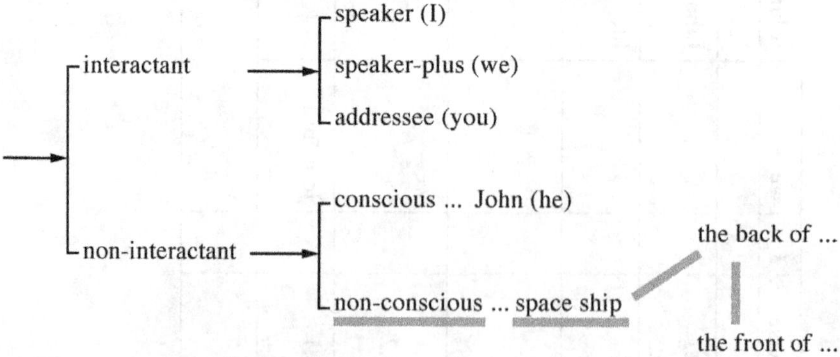

Figure 10.4 Expansion of instantial reference system (2)

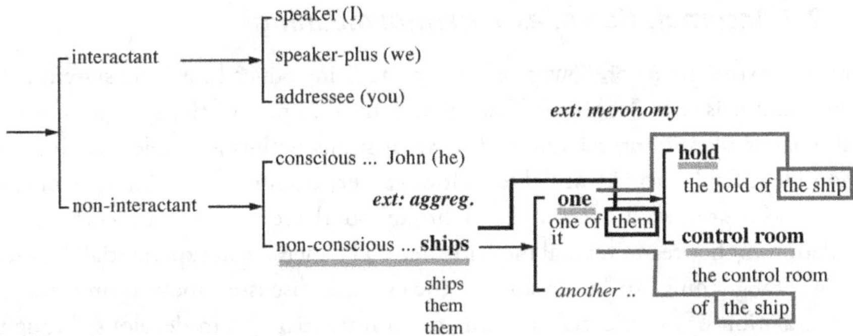

Figure 10.5 Expansion of instantial referent system (3)

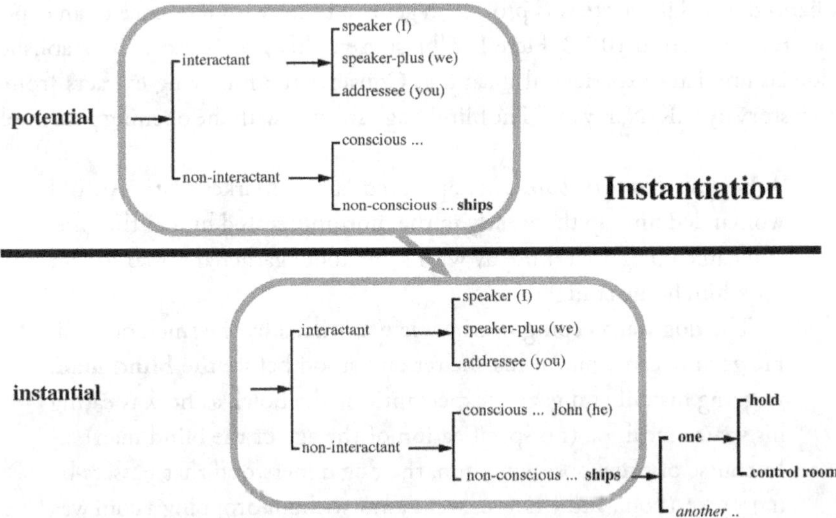

Figure 10.6 Instantial system after the text has unfolded

The instantial system is developed step by step. At the outset of the text, it is only a partial "copy" of the relevant potential. By relevant potential, I mean that part of the overall systemic potential that is conventionally available in the situation type in which the text is set to unfold; this is a registerial subpotential. As the text unfolds, the instantial system is continuously being modified, and, by the end of the text, it has reached the state shown in Figure 10.6.

10.2.2 Accumulation of experiential meaning

From a textual point of view, a referent node is introduced into the system net-work, and it is then "confirmed" again and again as part of the system on every subsequent identifying reference. Its textual status is thus a simple switch from "non-identifiable" to "identifiable." However, experientially and interpersonally, meanings continue to be accumulated throughout the text. Let's consider this accu-mulation in the area of textual meaning here. The increase in experiential delicacy from "orange thing" to "space ship" in the example discussed above is one kind of accumulation of experiential meaning as an instantial system develops through-out a text. But this is not the only way in which experiential meaning accumulates logogenetically. Given that a referent node has been established textually, experien-tial meaning can accrue to it through the various kinds of expansion.[3] In addition to being further elaborated in delicacy, it can also be experientially extended and enhanced. I will illustrate this process in general terms with reference to an expos-itory text in Section 10.2.3. Here I will just exemplify how a textually established node accumulates experiential meaning. Consider the following extracts from a short story by R.K. Narayan, "The blind dog," starting with the opening paragraph:

> **A beggar**, *blind in both eyes*, appeared at the Market Gate. An old woman led him up there early in the morning, seated him at the gate, and came up again at midday with some food, gathered his coins and took him home at night.
>
> The dog was sleeping nearby. He was stirred by the smell of food. He got up, came out of his shelter and stood before **the blind man**, wagging his tail and gazing expectantly at the bowl, as he was eating his sparse meal. [... (no specification of the age of the blind man) ...] In course of time, observing him, the dog understood that passers-by must give a coin, and whoever went away without dropping a coin was chased by the dog; he tugged the edge of their clothes by his teeth and pulled them back to **the old man** and let go only after something was dropped in his bowl. [...]
>
> Life for the dog took a new turn now. He came to take the place of the old woman. He lost his freedom completely. His world came to be circumscribed by the limits of the white cord which the ribbon-vendor had spared. He had to forget wholesale all his old life – all his old haunts. He simply had to stay on for ever at the end of that string. When he saw other dogs, friends or foes, instinctively he sprang up,

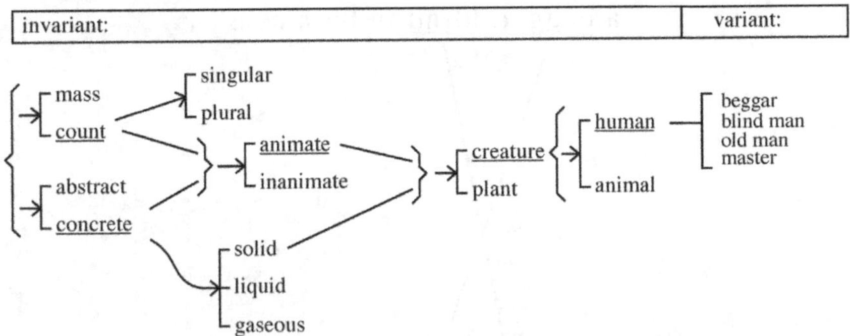

Figure 10.7 Invariable and variable part of experiential class in instantial system

tugging the string, and this invariably earned him a kick from **his master**. [...]

But as he slowed down even slightly **his master** goaded him on fiercely with his staff. The dog whined and groaned under this thrust. "Don't whine, you rascal. Don't I give you your food? You want to loaf, do you?" swore **the blind man**. The dog lumbered up and down and round and round the marketplace with slow steps, tied down **to the blind tyrant**.

There are two main characters in this story, the dog and the old man. As the story unfolds, their relationship changes dramatically; and this change is constructed step by step in the instantial system. From the point of view of explicit experiential classification,[4] the blind man is expanded to become the dog's master, and then his blind tyrant. The dog, however, remains invariant: it is classified as "dog" throughout. The instantial system thus comes to embody a contrast between the two characters in terms of the "systemic spread" constructed for them in the system:

animal: dog
human: beggar/old man/blind man/master/blind tyrant

This systemic spread is shown in Figure 10.7 as the variable systemic classification of the old man.

What makes it possible for experiential meanings to accumulate in this way? Still focussing on explicit experiential classification, we can note that a central logogenetic principle is what might be called "logogenetic distillation," using Martin's notion of distillation (see Halliday and Martin 1993: 30, 172, 276): meanings that are distributed over more than one nominal group are distilled into one nominal

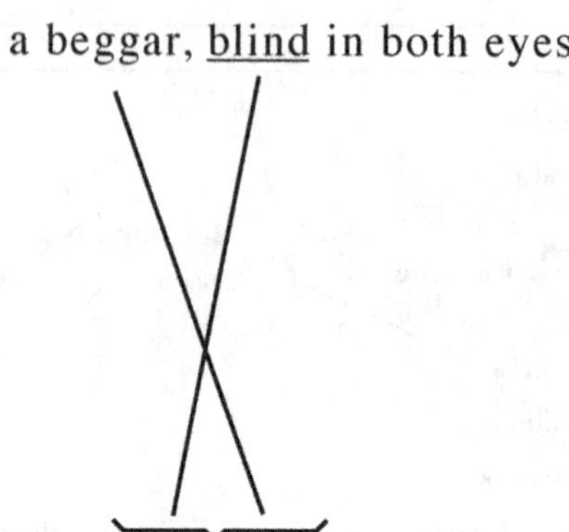

Figure 10.8 An example of logogenetic distillation

group so as to make explicit experiential classification possible. For example, the old man is explicitly classified as a "beggar" on first introductory mention, and his blindness is presented as a separate elaboration. Later, these two experiential motifs are distilled as "blind beggar" – experiential class + qualitative modification; see Figure 10.8:

In scientific or technical expository discourse, classification plays an important role in such logogenetic distillation. The combination of Classifier(s) + Thing can serve as a strategy for "distilling" meaning in unfolding discourse. Classifiers are often introduced in a discourse only after their implicit relation to the Thing has been represented. This kind of logogenetic build-up can ensure that the Classifier + Thing combination is interpretable in its discourse environment. For example, "Closely associated with sleep and wakefulness are cyclical variations that appear in all living organisms from plants to human beings. These cyclical changes take place about every twenty-four hours. They are called ***circadian rhythms*** from the Latin *circa*, meaning 'about', and *dies*, meaning 'day.'"

Here "cyclical variations that appear in all living organisms from plants to human beings ... cyclical changes" is distilled as "rhythm" and "take place about every twenty-four hours" as "circadian"; and the experiential meanings are codified as a technical term.

10.2.3 Expansion of ideational system

Expository genres are centrally concerned with the expansion of the ideational system available to the listener or reader: interpreting an expository text means

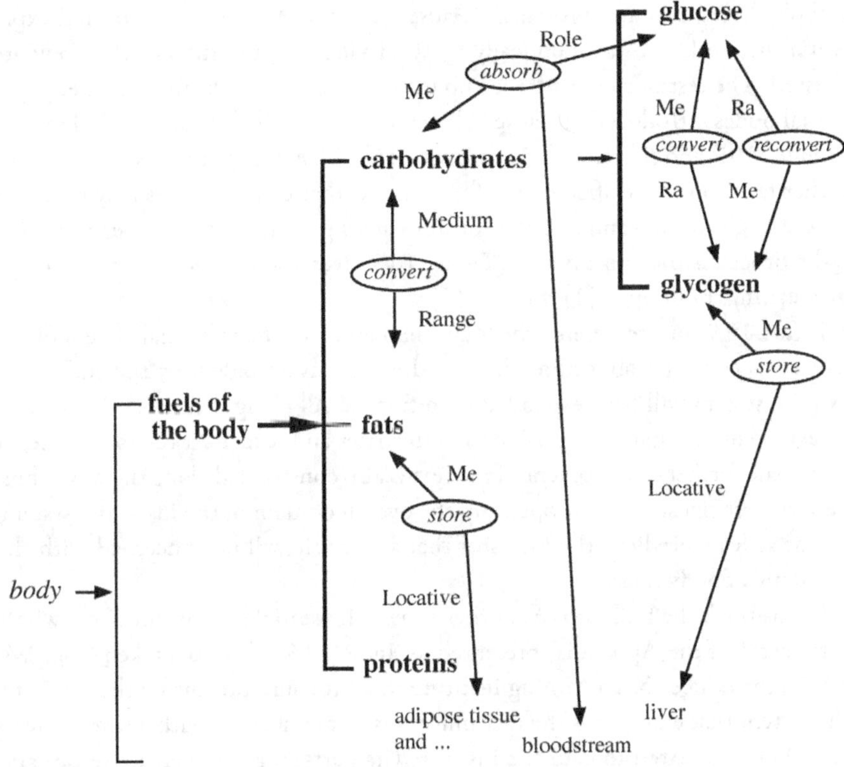

Figure 10.9 Logogenetic state of instantial experiential system

building up an instantial ideational system. From a cognitive perspective, it means "acquiring" knowledge through the text. What kinds of systems are built up? In the most general terms, they may be either logical or experiential. Instantial logical systems include centrally sequences of selections of logico-semantic relations. For example, "the blood sugar level goes down" is related instantially to "the liver reconverts some of its stored glycogen into glucose" through temporal enhancement in the body fuels text given as Text 2 in the Appendix, to be discussed presently. Experiential systems include centrally taxonomies of experiential classes related to one another in various process configurations. Let me illustrate such systems with respect to an expository text, concerned with the fuels of the body (the text is set out in two columns, Theme + Rheme; this information will be used in Section 10.3): see Appendix Text 2.

Clause [1] constructs the root of the experiential taxonomy that is built up as the text unfolds: "fuels of the body" is identified as the superordinate of "carbohydrates, fats and proteins." Clauses [2] and [3] expand the overall experiential network non-taxonomically by specifying how the fuels of the body are ingested. The rest of the text builds up instantial subnetworks for the three experiential nodes introduced in clause [1] – carbohydrates ([3] through [6]), fats ([7] through [10]) and proteins ([11] through [16]). These subnetworks include both further taxonomic specifications – for example, that carbohydrates may be either glucose or glycogen – and role relationships among the taxonomic types according to the processes they take part in. Figure 10.9 gives a schematic representation of the meanings built up in [1] through [6].[5]

Figure 10.9 thus represents the logogenetic state of the instantial system of the body fuels text after about one third of the text has unfolded. By the end of the text, the system will have expanded even further: all along there is an increase in the experiential instantial available to both writer and reader. At the same time, of course, the further development of the text is also constrained along the way. Thus, the very first clause, while it opens up the overall domain of the instantial system, sets, or at least predicts, the limits of that system: it will be concerned with the taxonomy of body fuels.

Let us track the build-up of another type of instantial system through a whole text, Text 3 of the Appendix, presented as Table 10.6. This text, taken from Wu (1992), introduces Xi'an Mining Institute in a brochure presenting the institute. The system that emerges as the text unfolds is not concerned with a taxonomy of types, but with extensions to the institute (its parts in a very general sense) and enhancements (its location and its temporal origin [not shown below]) once it has been given an academic identity through elaboration (one of the top ten). The root node of the instantial ideational semantic network being built up as the text unfolds is "Xi'an Mining Institute." Table 10.2 shows the expansions of this node and subsequent nodes in bold, with type of expansion marked as follows: = for elaboration, + for extension, and × for enhancement. The build-up is shown as a series of snapshots of the nodes of the system, with two such logogenetic states per paragraph. The table also indicates a distinction between nodes that become part of the system and are selected again and again throughout the text (italics) – Xi'an Mining Institute – and nodes that become part of the system but are not selected again (shaded), although they could have been so are still part of the system – all the expansions of the institute:

This table gives a sense of how the instantial system is expanded gradually as the text unfolds in terms of its nodes, with the changing status of these nodes. But it does not show the relationship among these nodes in the instantial system network. This system network is represented by a fragment containing the nodes is shown in Figure 10.10. The nodes named in the text are shown in bold; other

Table 10.2 Expansion of nodes in the Xi'an Mining Institute text, segment by segment

0	1		2		3		4		5	
Xi'an Mining Institute	*Xi'an Mining Institute*	*Xi'an Mining Institute*	*Xi'an Mining Institute*	*Xi'an Mining Institute*	*Xi'an Mining Institute*	*Xi'an Mining Institute*	*Xi'an Mining Institute*	*Xi'an Mining Institute*	*Xi'an Mining Institute*	*Xi'an Mining Institute*
	= one of the top ten	one of the top ten	one of the top ten	one of the top ten	one of the top ten	one of the top ten	one of the top ten	one of the top ten	one of the top ten	one of the top ten
	+ enrolment	enrolment	enrolment	enrolment	enrolment	enrolment	enrolment	enrolment	enrolment	enrolment
		= students	students	students	students	students	students	students	students	students
			× Xi'an	Xi'an	Xi'an	Xi'an	Xi'an	Xi'an	Xi'an	Xi'an
				+ heritage & facilities	heritage & facilities	heritage & facilities	heritage & facilities	heritage & facilities	heritage & facilities	heritage & facilities

Continued

Table 10.2 Expansion of nodes in the Xi'an Mining Institute text, segment by segment (Continued)

0	1		2		3		4		5	
					+ staff	staff	staff	staff	staff	staff
						= dedication	dedica-tion	dedica-tion	dedication	dedication
							+ degrees	degrees	degrees	degrees
								+ specialties & courses	+ library	library
										+ holdings & facilities

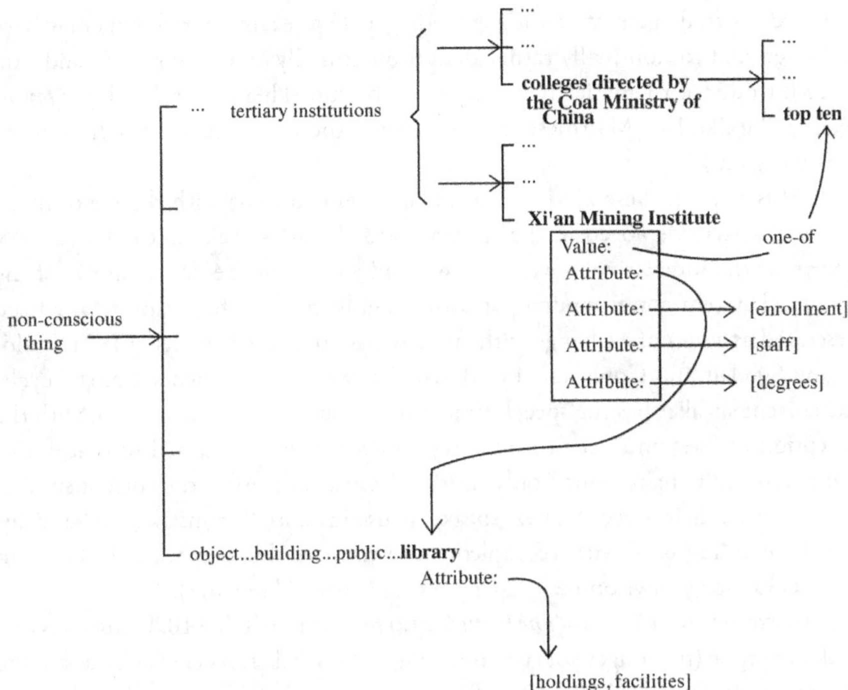

Figure 10.10 Fragment of final state of the instantial system of the Xi'an Mining Institute text

nodes are presupposed as part of the more generalized systems known to the reader. As already noted, the focus of this text is not the creation of further taxonomic organization. Rather, it is concerned with establishing links among Xi'an Mining Institute and nodes instantiating existing types (such as "enrolment," "staff," "library"). The accrual of meaning is thus essentially embodied in these links.

While Table 10.2 shows the order in which the set of nodes is expanded, Figure 10.10 only represents the final state. I will return to the issue of logogenetic order in Section 10.3.

10.2.4 Interpersonal negotiation

The instantial systems illustrated so far have a **linear** development: the textual reference nodes accumulate, as do the experiential types. They may, of course, cease to be confirmed in the instantial system in the sense that at some logogenetic point they are no longer selected (as happens in the Xi'an Mining Institute system). But they are still available even if they have to be given extra weight if they are selected again after a logogenetic gap. (For example, referents may have to be referred to nominally rather than pronominally and they may in addition be re-introduced thematically by means of absolute Themes marked by *as for*, *as to*, and the like [see Matthiessen 1992]; new experiential types may have to be glossed again.)

In this respect, these kinds of instantial system contrast with the major interpersonal system deployed in the creation of dialogue – the SPEECH FUNCTION system of the interactive move. Here we find a **cycle** in the development of the instantial system corresponding, at least roughly, to what has traditionally been described as a *unit* of exchange with an exchange structure (see Berry 1981, building on Sinclair and Coulthard 1975).[6] At the beginning of such a dialogic cycle, the current speaker has the speech functional resources available to them with the exception of "respond": the turn-taking is instantially constrained so that out of the system "initiate/respond," only "initiate" is available. After the current speaker has produced their move, the next speaker is also instantially constrained: basically, they have to "respond" with a complementary move (unless they want to change to another exchange environment, e.g. by asking *What did you say?*).

The extract from Pinter's *The birthday party* shown in Table 10.3 illustrates one exchange cycle (the longer passage from which this is taken is given as Text 4 in the Appendix, presented as Table 10.7). Systemic options that are not available because of logogenetic constraints are presented in strikethrough style, and options that are instantiated in the current move are shown in bold.

Let's consider the changing instantial system from the beginning of the extract, where Meg is about to make a dialogic move. Given the current state of the unfolding of the dialogue, there is no move to respond to, so only "initiate" is instantially available to Meg. She selects to initiate and further to "demand" "information" about an "element." Unless he wants to open up another dialogic environment, Petey has to "respond" in kind, which means that the "goods-&-services" and "demand" options are not instantially available. After Petey has made his move, there is a logogenetic opening up: Meg can choose either to follow up by responding or to initiate a new logogenetic cycle. She chooses to respond. Ignoring the possibility of another follow-up, we can assume that after her response, the logogenetic state of the instantial system of speech function is that only "initiate" is available: if the dialogue is to go on, a new exchange cycle has to be initiated.

The basic dialogic principle is thus a cycle of modification rather than a "linear" expansion of the instantial system throughout the dialogue.

Table 10.3 Selections in one exchange cycle

		Meg's moves:	**Petey's moves:**
Meg:	What **are you** reading?	**initiate**/~~respond~~ & (give/ **demand** & **informa-tion**/goods-&-services): polarity/**element**	
Petey:	**Someone's just** had a baby.		~~initiate~~/ **respond**: **direct**/indi-rect & **give**/ ~~demand~~ & **information**/ ~~goods-&-ser-vices~~
Meg:	Oh, **they haven't!**	initiate/**respond**: **direct**/indirect & **give**/ demand & **information**/ ~~goods-&-services~~	
Petey/ Meg:		**initiate**/~~respond~~ & give/ **demand** & **information**/ goods-&-services	**initiate**/ ~~respond~~ & give/**demand** & **informa-tion**/goods-&-services

10.3   Logogenetic ordering of instantiation

I have exemplified instantial systems from all three metafunctional perspectives and at different stages of logogenetic development. I have briefly referred to princi-ples for developing such systems, but I haven't discussed the central issue of how the development of instantial systems is ordered logogenetically. This is indeed a major descriptive research question: we need to undertake a good deal of textual studies to investigate the development of their instantial systems. At the same time, it is

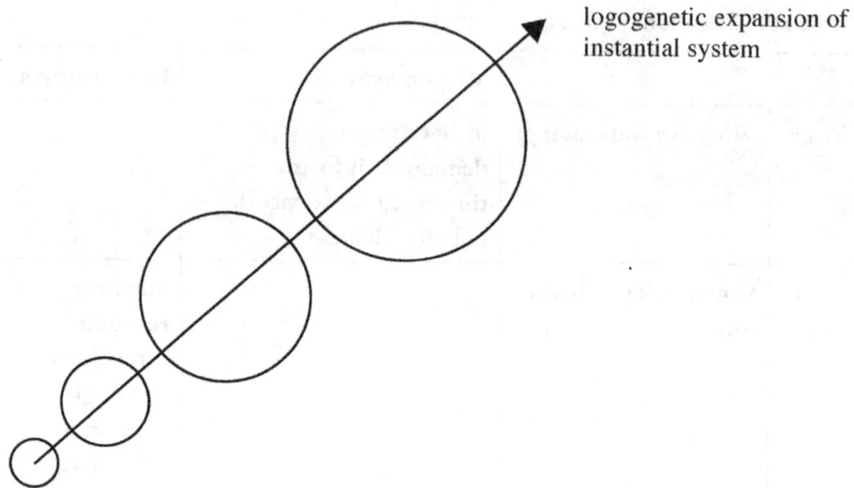

Figure 10.11 Logogenetic expansion of instantial system

also a major challenge to our theory and our representation: how do we model the orderly change of an instantial system? Here I can only make certain preliminary observations and summarize work in progress on dialogue modelling.

We have seen that *one* central aspect of the logogenetic development of the instantial system is expansion: the system is elaborated in delicacy, or new links are established. This situation is diagrammed in Figure 10.11 and was illustrated above for both the body fuels text and the Xi'an Mining Institute text.

Here the most central logogenetic question is how the increase in complexity is managed; how the expansion is ordered in such a way that it can be tracked by the listener or reader. I will explore this question in Section 10.3.1, identifying the guiding role the textual metafunction plays. At the same time, however, we also have to recognize that the system shrinks logogenetically. At the outset of a text, the whole (registerial) system is, in principle, available. Only a very small part of it is instantiated. As more subparts are instantiated, the instantial system is opened up, but it is also closed off in the sense that generalized options that are available are not taken up. This situation is shown in Figure 10.12.

With respect to both these aspects of logogenesis, we can clearly investigate analogies with other kinds of genesis – ones involving language at different time frames (ontogenesis and phylogenesis; see Section 10.4.1) but also ones involving other kinds of system, such as cosmogenesis.

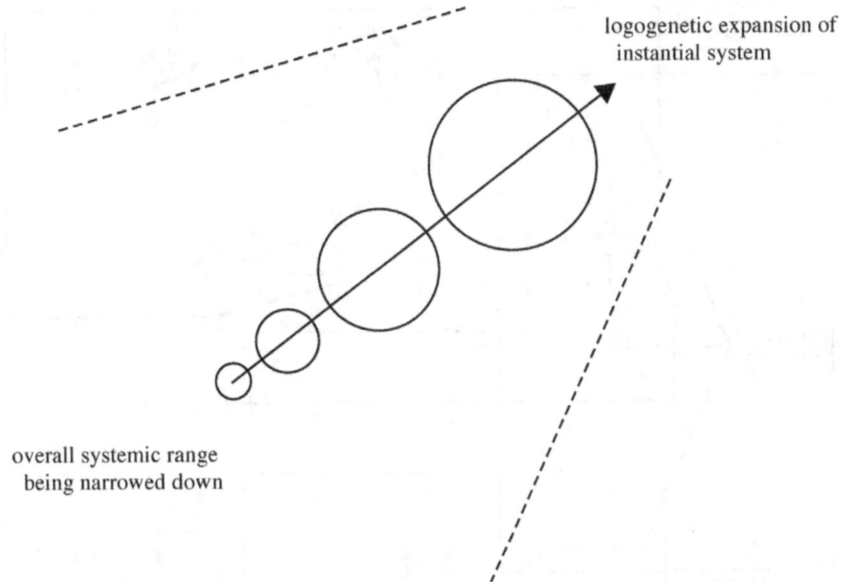

Figure 10.12 Logogenetic restriction of instantial system

10.3.1 Logogenetic ordering of development of instantial system

The primary logogenetic ordering of the body fuels text is ideational. More specifically, it is based on the delicacy of the instantial system to be developed in the text.
Figure 10.13 shows this step-wise build-up of the instantial system.

The diagram in Figure 10.14 brings out the organization of the text: the general
category of body fuels is thematic in units [1] and [2]. Then, subtypes of body
fuels, introduced rhematically in [1], are picked up thematically at the points of
major rhetorical shifts in the text ([3], [7], and [11]), relying on the lexical cohesive
relation of repetition. Globally, the flow of information is thus Rheme –> Theme
as far as the method of development is concerned (this is one of the patterns identified in Daneš 1974a).

The general principle that this example illustrates is this: the textual metafunction guides the logogenetic build-up of the instantial experiential system.
The Themes are selected in such a way that they present the current logogenetic
growth-point in the experiential system. For instance, when the selection of Theme
returns to "proteins," this is an indication that that part of the network is not to be
expanded. The situation is the same in the Xi'an Mining Institute text. The Themes

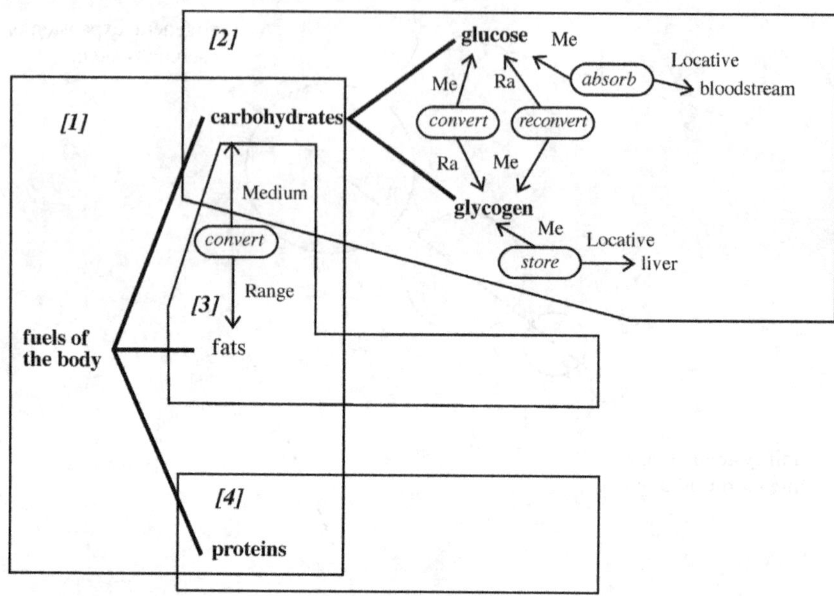

Figure 10.13 Step-wise build-up of instantial system

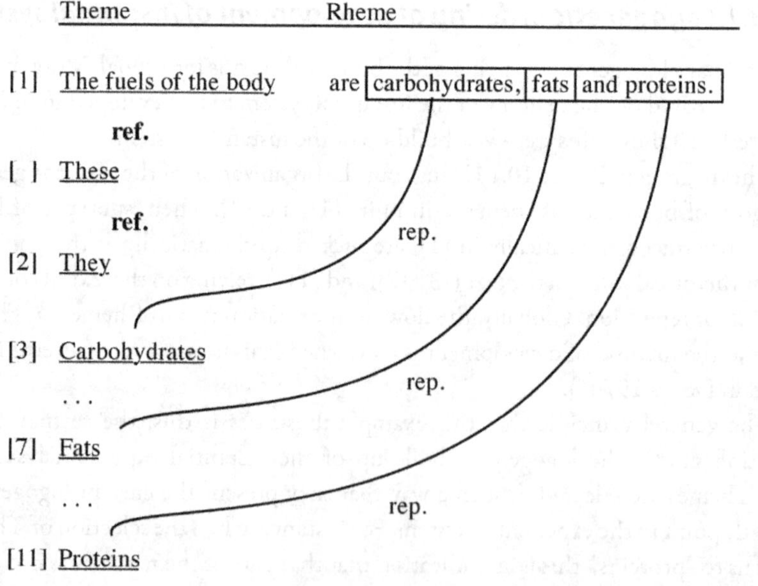

Figure 10.14 The textual ordering of the build-up of the instantial experiential system in the Body Fuels text

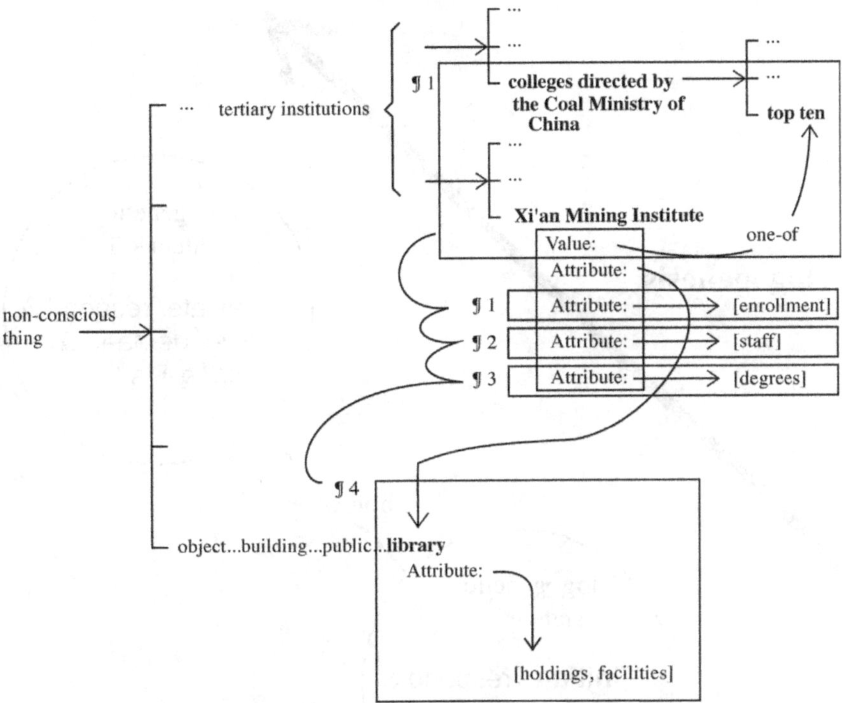

Figure 10.15 The textual ordering of the build-up of the instantial experiential system in the Xi'an Ming Institute text

selected as the text unfolds move successively from one experiential growth-point to another: see Figure 10.15.

10.3.2 O'Donnell and Sefton's model of logogenetic ordering

We have seen that there is a systematic ordering in the move from one instantial systemic state to another. We have also seen how the textual metafunction can serve to guide the genesis of meaning in the instantial system, e.g. by presenting the current expansion point. However, this still leaves open the question of how to model logogenetic ordering. In dealing with change, the standard AI approach would be to specify two states – the starting state (or condition) and the endstate (or effect) – and an operator defining the change between the two. For example, if one speaker initiates an exchange by asking a question (i.e. demanding information), this would be the input logogenetic state. The end state would be the set of speech functional options open to the intended next speaker – respond by giving information

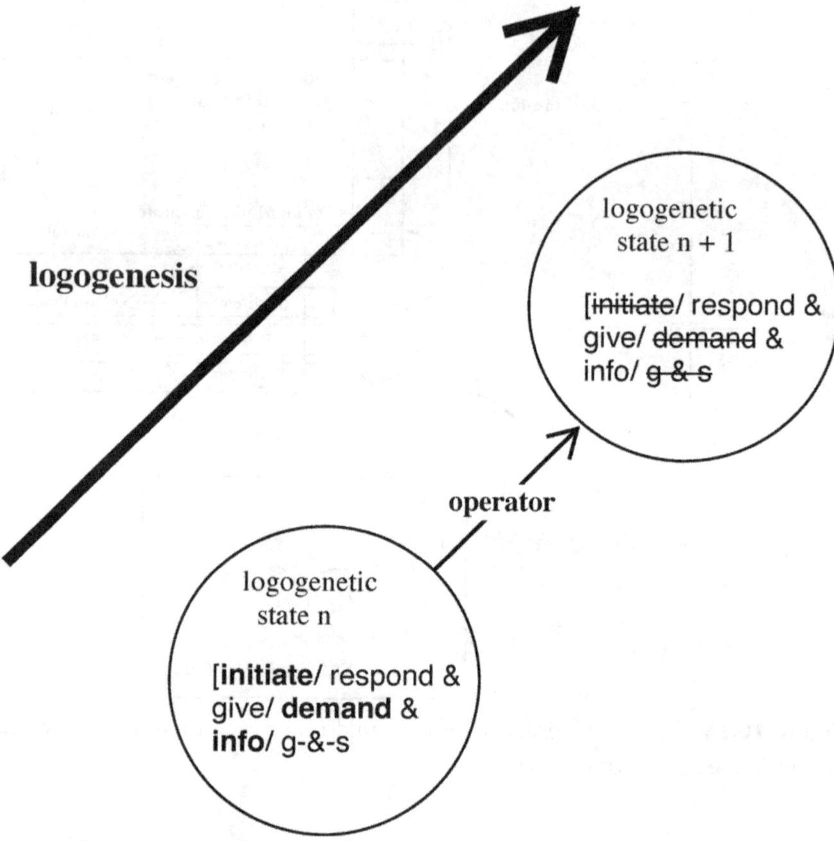

Figure 10.16 Logogenetic ordering as change operator

(ignoring discretionary options) – and the operator would be the change between these two dialogic states: see Figure 10.16.

In recent work on dialogue modelling, O'Donnell and Sefton (1995) have taken a more elaborated and sophisticated version of this approach, drawing on O'Donnell's (1990) earlier work on dialogue. At any point in an unfolding dialogue, the current speaker can choose among instantially active speech functional options. When one speaker makes a choice, this determines what options are instantially open to the next speaker. They capture this logogenetic ordering by defining a classification over all possible dialogic states. When the current speaker makes a speech functional selection, the classification of dialogic states changes – what we might call a logogenetic state potential – and the change is manifested in a specification of what speech functional options are instantially

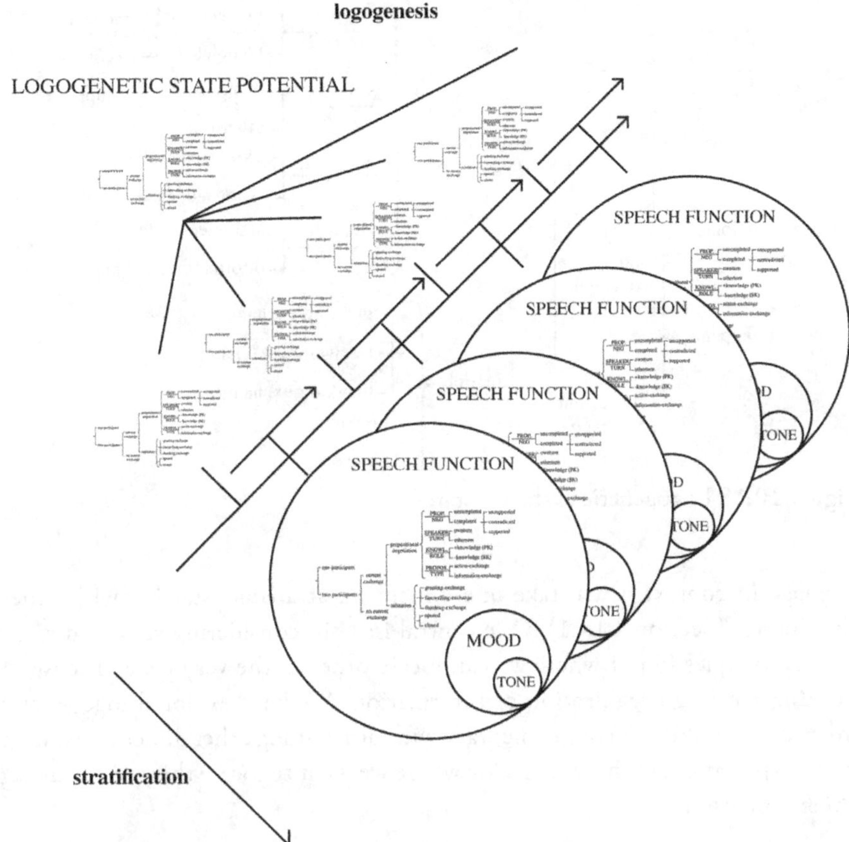

Figure 10.17 Logogenetic ordering

open to the next speaker: see Figure 10.17 (for the speech function system, see Figure 10.18).

The logogenetic state potential is represented as a system network: see Figure 10.17. In this approach, the temporal ordering of logogenesis is construed as a typological ordering.

10.4   Locating instantial systems and logogenesis in the overall system

So far I have focussed almost exclusively on instantial systems and their logogenetic creation. I will now consider them relative to the overall system of

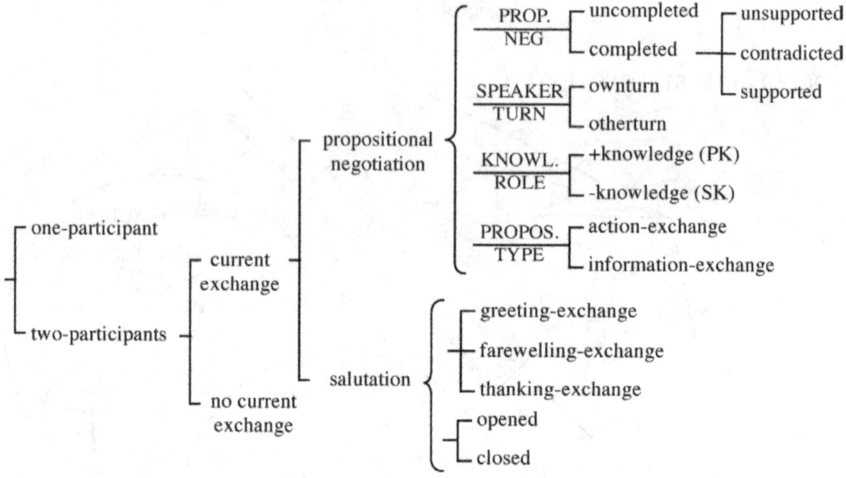

Figure 10.18 Logogenetic exchange states

language in context. I will take one dimension at a time, starting with other time frames (Section 10.4.1). One central issue in considering various dimensions is the question of where we can locate order in the very general sense of meaning-creating organization of information. We have explored logogenetic order; but that order is complementary with order along other dimensions, so in our interpretation, we have to decide where we want to locate this order – along which dimension.

10.4.1 Location relative to other time frames

The time frame of the instantial system is that of a single text – that is, the time over which the system is **instantiated** through **logogenesis**. However, this is only the shortest time frame over which meaning is created in a system. Innumerable instantial systems are created in the life of an individual person, each constituting an enactment of an instantial persona of that person. The person's meaning potential grows throughout this more extended time-scale of meaning-creation – **ontogenesis**. The person is part of more extended social organizations – multigenerational social groups. Through these social groups the time frame of the creation of meaning extends much further than the life of a person to the species.[7] This is the time frame of **phylogenesis**, where the overall system *evolves* over time. We thus have three different domains of semogenesis – the instantial personae of a person, the person, and the group extending into the species – and these are associated with

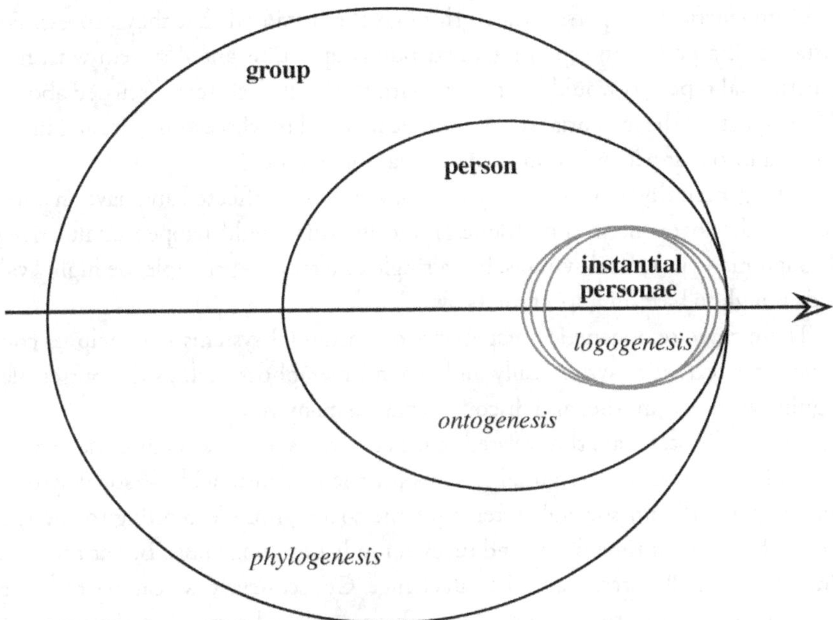

Figure 10.19 The three time frames of semogenesis and their domains

three different time frames – the logogenetic, the ontogenetic, and the phylogenetic time frames – and three different modes of genesis – instantiation, growth, and evolution. Figure 10.19 relates logogenesis to these other time frames and domains. This figure is also intended to show that each type of semogenesis takes place in the environment of another (logogenesis within ontogenesis, and ontogenesis within phylogenesis), and that, at the same time, logogenesis enables ontogenesis, which in turn enables phylogenesis (see Halliday and Matthiessen 1999/2006).

There is, obviously, a good deal of indeterminacy in what constitutes a single text; and texts are not isolated from one another, but often unfold in series. This last observation relates to the notion of inter-textuality (see Lemke 1985b, 1995b). We can now approach this phenomenon from the point of view of the instantial system, and we can recognize that it has histories along all three time scales. Logogenetically, the instantial system may be part of a logogenetic series, as in a series of lectures, a series of breakfast conversations, a series of gossip sessions in the workplace: when a system is instantiated for an individual text to create an instantial system, it may be instantiated against the background of previous "instalments"; and it may itself provide the background for future ones.

Ontogenetically, a person learns through the instantial that they process. For instance, if a person interpreting a text builds up an instantial system with new experiential types (as would be the case with the body fuels text discussed above), these aspects of the instantial system may be retained in whole or in part and incorporated into that person's more general meaning potential.

Phylogenetically, an instantial system may have been affected and have an effect beyond the logogenetic time frame. Typically, this would happen cumulatively through many instantial systems, but a single one may, in principle, be highly valued enough to have an impact on its own.

These three semogenetic perspectives on instantial systems may help us construe inter-textuality systemically and ground metaphors such as discourses dialoguing with one another and discourses having many voices.

Instantial systems are thus related to other systems in the ways discussed above. Each kind of system – instantial systems [of the text instance], personal systems [of the person], and societal systems [of the social group, extending to the species] – has its own time frame and its own mode of semogenesis. But at the same time, these are all systems; and they all change. Consequently, we can try to model instantial systems in the same way as we have modelled systems in the past; and we can explore whether logogenesis shares properties with ontogenesis and phylogenesis. For instance, we might expect to find general principles of **semogenetic ordering** in the build-up of information in systems. Halliday has found this to be the case for grammatical metaphor (see Halliday and Martin 1993): the congruent mode tends to precede the metaphorical mode in all three semogenetic orders: it evolves later in the general system; the child learns it later; and it is instantiated later in the text. It seems reasonable to assume that both systems and semogenesis are fractal along these lines.

10.4.2 Location along instantiation relative to the potential

The instantial system instantiates the overall systemic potential. The dimension of instantiation is a cline, with these two kinds of systems as poles. But there are intermediate types: we can recognize these either as the accumulation of instantial systems over time emerging as a potential (looking at them from the point of view of the instantial) or as patterns of instantiation (looking at them from the point of view of the potential). Within language we recognize such intermediate systems as **registerial systems** (see Halliday 1978, 1991a; Matthiessen 1993a). Within context – the socio-semiotic environment language is embedded in – we recognize these as situation *types*, intermediate between the situational instance (context of situation) and the cultural potential (context of culture). Figure 10.20

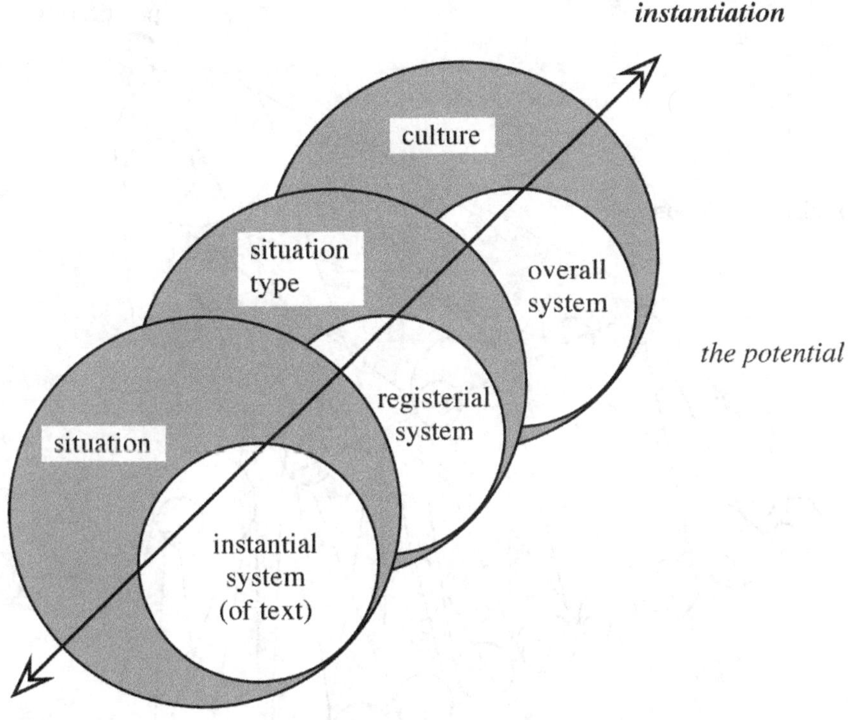

Figure 10.20 Context of culture and context of situation along dimension of long-term instantiation

shows the ordering of these three regions of language context along the dimension of instantiation.

Now, the instantiation move from the overall potential to an unfolding instantial system is a narrowing of the potential. More specifically, a registerial system is a subpotential located somewhere within the overall system, deploying only those aspects that are needed in its situation type, and an instantial system is, similarly, a subpotential located somewhere within its registerial system, deploying only those aspects that are needed in its context of situation. Consequently, **variation** is an inherent property of instantiation. Along the dimension of instantiation, there are always variants in instantiation. Here we recognize those variants that are fairly stable – registerial varieties of the overall potential, or registers in short – but instantial systems are, in a similar way, varieties of some registerial system. Instantiation and variation are shown together in Figure 10.21.

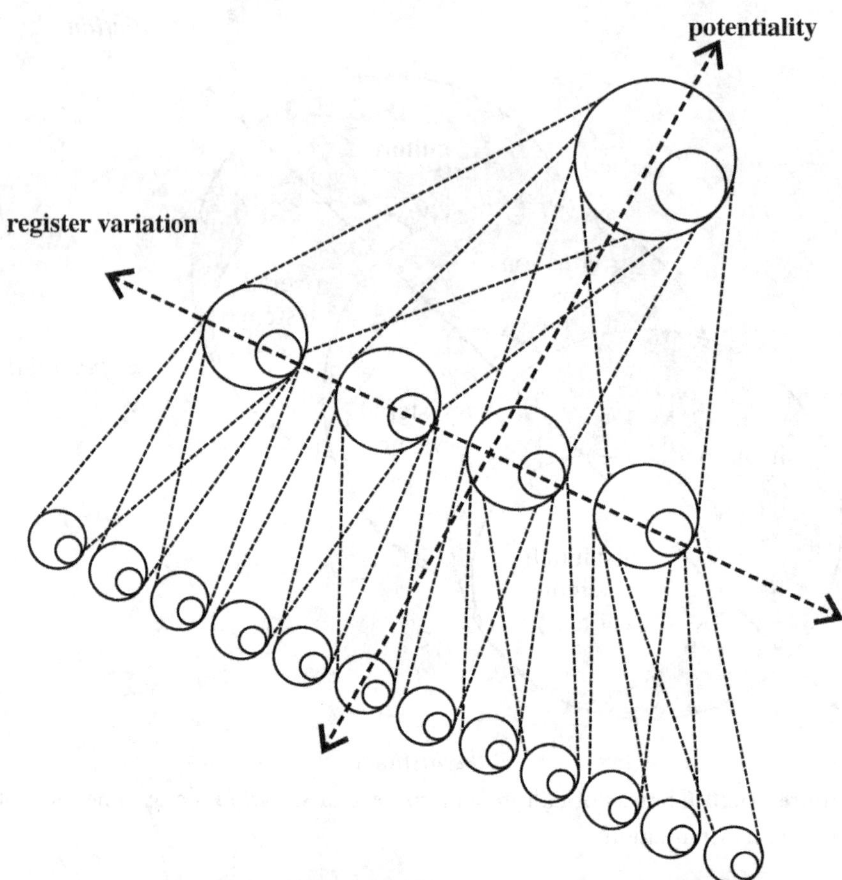

Figure 10.21 The intersection of potentiality and register variation

The instantial system is a selection along the dimension of instantiation; that is to say, it is a subpotential of a registerial potential (within which it falls), and, by another step, a subpotential of the overall meaning potential of the culture (within which the registerial potential it belongs to falls). It is thus **profiled** against the background of more generalized systems along the dimension of instantiation. Such a profile is meaningful and motivated. Thus, given a lexicogrammatical or semantic profile (i.e. a profile in the content plane), we can interpret its significance in contextual terms, by reference to field, tenor, and mode. I will illustrate this within the interpersonal metafunction, at the level of lexicogrammar. The contextual

Table 10.4 Meg's and Petey's interpersonal selections

SYSTEMS: terms selected			Meg	Petey
TOTAL # clauses			18	14
major clause	TOTAL		**17** 94%	**14** 100%
	ELLIPSIS: full		11 65%	7 50%
	ELLIPSIS: elliptical		6 35%	7 50%
	MOOD TYPE: indicative	INDICATIVE TYPE: declarative	7 41%	14 100%
		INDICATIVE TYPE: interrogative — wh-	6 35%	0 0%
		INDICATIVE TYPE: interrogative — yes/no	3 18%	0 0%
		MOOD PERSON: interactant — speaker	4 24%	2 14%
		MOOD PERSON: interactant — speaker-plus	0 0%	0 0%
		MOOD PERSON: interactant — addressee	3 18%	2 14%
		MOOD PERSON: non-interactant	11 65%	10 71%
		DEICTICITY: temporal	13 81%	13 93%
		DEICTICITY: modal	3 19%	1 7%

Continued

Table 10.4 Meg's and Petey's interpersonal selections (Continued)

SYSTEMS: terms selected		Meg	Petey
	MOOD TYPE: imperative	0 0%	0 0%
	VOCATION: non-vocative	16 89%	14 100%
	VOCATION: vocative	2 11%	0 0%
	POLARITY: positive	12 80%	11 79%
	POLARITY: negative	3 20%	3 21%
minor clause	TOTAL	1 6%	0 0%

significance of this instantial profile will thus be within tenor (rather than field or mode). More specifically, we will consider a passage of dramatic dialogue taken from Pinter's *The birthday party*. A married couple, Meg and Petey, are sitting at the breakfast table. Meg is making conversation. They are both in their sixties, so we can assume that the instantial system is one of thousands of systems enacting their relationship over the years. The text is given as Text 4 in the Appendix (Table 10.7), with the selections from interpersonal clause systems.

The passage is fairly short. In all, Meg contributes eighteen clauses and Petey fourteen. Since our focus is interpersonal, the central question is what the **instantial differential** between them is – how their profiles against the overall interpersonal clause potential differ from one another. Table 10.4 presents a summary of the interpersonal selections made by Meg and Petey.

If we consider mood type systems first, we see that the breakfast conversation is concerned with the exchange of information (rather than goods-&-services), realized (congruently) by "indicative" clauses. Within this type, there is a clear contrast between Meg and Petey. While Meg favours "interrogative" clauses over "declarative" ones (by a ratio of roughly 6:4), Petey is exclusively "declarative." This ties in with the textual system of clausal ellipsis: while Petey is just as likely to produce full clauses as elliptical ones, Meg is much more likely to produce full ones (the ratio is roughly 6:4). Semantically, this suggests that Meg take on more work initiating

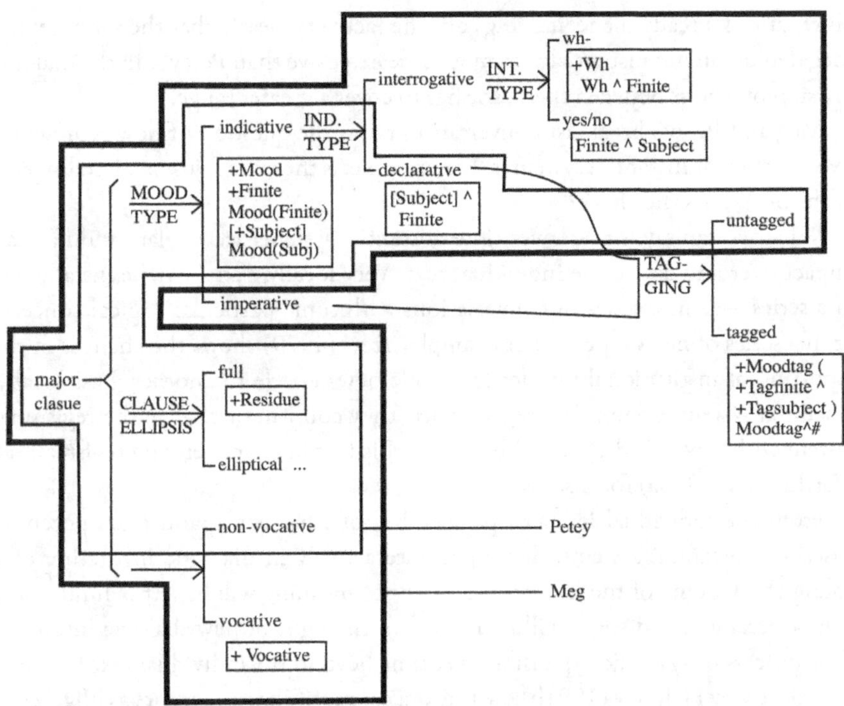

Figure 10.22 Meg's and Stanley's instantial profiles against the overall mood system

exchanges than Petey does, since initiating moves are typically "full" clauses and responding ones "elliptical." Together, these two observations point in the same tenor direction: in their relationship, Meg is the one who has to take the initiative by taking the interest to demand information from Petey. He responds by giving on demand; but he does not reciprocate. Other differences in their profiles might provide minor motifs in the tenor of their relationship: Meg uses Vocatives to identify Petey, and she uses minor clauses to express her emotive attitude. As with all the selections, these are just instances in the system built up during the particular breakfast conversation Pinter has chosen to present in the play. The instantial personae they enact may be transient perturbations in their long-term relationship; but they may also be confirmations of the roles they have settled into after a long married life.

Figure 10.22 shows the range of options of the instantial systems Meg and Petey have created as selections within the overall mood potential by the end of their breakfast conversation. Apart from representing in diagrammatic mode the observations already made, it brings out the fact very clearly that the subpotential Meg deploys in her instantial system is more extensive than Petey's; in the dialogic division of labour between them, she has to cover a greater range.

Meg and Petey's breakfast conversation raises the question of how representative a particular instantial system is. For example, is the extract just analysed typical of the breakfasts they have?

What we can say is that, over time, instantial systems accumulate and have an impact over and above the individual text. Very locally, texts may be instalments in a series – as in a series of conversations with some particular topical concern, or in a series of news reports. For example, Trew (1979) shows the changes in the reporting of institutional murder from one news article to another. Less locally, instantial systems accumulate registerially: they confirm or change the registerial system within which they fall. We can use this fact in characterizing registers: see Matthiessen (1993a) for discussion.

From the individual learner's perspective, one has to expand one's potential based on instantial systems, developed interactively in dialogue in the life of a young child. Some of the instantial patterns of meaning will be left behind, some will be retained, and some will be revised in the light of new dialogic instances. This process of systemic expansion over time beyond the individual text is shown very clearly by Halliday (1991b): he tracks a cat motif that re-appears as Nigel construes cats step by step in his own semantic network over a long period of time. Similarly, Painter (1993) shows how a young child construes his experience of the world through language as he learns language.

10.4.3 Location relative to axis

Order may obtain along any of the dimensions of language in context – ranked order, syntagmatic order, paradigmatic delicacy order, stratal order, logogenetic order, and so on. The order created through the logogenesis in the development of an instantial system thus stands in a relationship of complementarity with other kinds of order. These orders are of distinct kinds, but if we look across the overall system we find recurrent principles, and there are many examples in the history of linguistics of some phenomenal domain being interpreted first in terms of one kind of order and then, in the light of more information, in terms of another kind. From a theoretical point of view, we have to choose one or more among the various dimensions when we interpret order we observe in discourse (cf. Martin 1985). As discussed so far, logogenetic order obtains within the unfolding instantial system – as presented here, it is an ordering over instantial paradigmatic states. This immediately suggests that it stands in some form of complementarity with syntagmatic

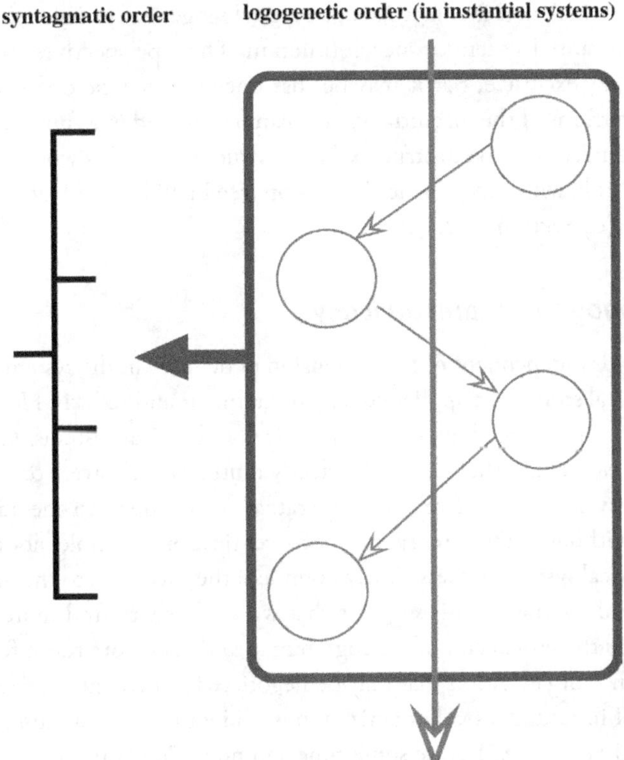

Figure 10.23 Two different kinds of order in discourse

order. If we examine past descriptions of generic organization, exchange organization, reference, and other discourse semantic domains, we find that the syntagmatic specification of the text (or part of the text) as a product dominates: we find syntagmatic order as the primary kind of interpretation deployed rather than logogenetic order in the instantial system. The complementary perspectives embodied in these two kinds of order are shown in Figure 10.23 as they apply to dialogic exchange. (The circles represent moves, characterized by systemic selections; the tree on the left-hand side represents the structure of a unit of exchange, such as dK1 ^ K2 ^ K1 ^ fK2.)

From a syntagmatic point of view, dialogic exchange is ordered as exchange structures such as dK1 ^ K2 ^ K1 (see e.g. Berry 1981; Martin 1992a: ch. 2). Here exchange is construed as a unit whole consisting of a configuration of moves in certain exchange roles. From a logogenetic point of view, dialogic exchange is ordered as successive instantial states of the speech functional options (see Section

10.3.2). Here, exchange is construed as a partial logogenetic order over states in the unfolding instantial system of speech function. These perspectives are not necessarily mutually exclusive; but it may be that once logogenetic order obtaining in successive versions of the instantial system can be handled in a fully general way, it is no longer necessary to construe exchange structurally. This would certainly be the case, I think, with componential cohesion (see Halliday and Hasan 1985) such as reference (cf. Section 10.2.1).[8]

10.4.4 Logogenesis and delicacy

Logogenesis is independent of the dimension of delicacy in the system; at the lexicogrammatical stratum, it applies equally to grammar and to lexis. However, there is a difference in degree between grammatical and lexical systems. Grammatical systems are closed and their terms are clearly mutually exclusive. For instance, the mood type system "indicative" vs. "imperative" is not open to the addition of a third term without a radical reorganization over time of the whole mood system. In contrast, lexical systems are less clearly bounded; they are open to the introduction of new lexical contrasts. This suggests that we are likely to find more indeterminacy towards the lexical end of lexicogrammar, and also more room for instantial organization – organization that may be negotiated in dialogue. Indeed, the phenomenon of instantial lexical organization was identified and discussed by Hasan (1985a) and Fries (1982) quite some time ago now. This is not to say that we do not find instantial grammatical systems: we certainly do. But they are probably more likely to develop as restrictions on the grammatical potential (as in Meg and Petey's breakfast conversation) rather than as expansions of the potential (such as the lexical expansions in the body fuel text).

The difference between grammar and lexis is only one of degree, of course; the overall potential of both evolves over time through instantial patterns. We see this perhaps most clearly when somebody plays with the system, as Michael Frayn does with the tense system in his novel *A very private life*. It opens in the following way:

> Once upon a time there **will** be a little girl called Uncumber.
>
> Uncumber **will** have a younger brother called Sulpice, and they **will** live with their parents in a house in the middle of the woods. There **will** be no windows in the house, because there **will** be nothing to see outside except the forest. While inside there **will** be all kinds of interesting things – strange animals, processions, jewels, battles, mazes, convolutions of pure shapes and pure colours – which *materialise* in the air at will, solid and brilliant and almost untouchable. For this **will** be in

the good new days a long, long while ahead, and it **will** be like that in people's houses then.

Here we see an instantial revision of the meaning of the tense system beginning to emerge. Primary future (in bold) can combine with *once upon a time, in the good new days, a long while ahead* where we would expect to find the primary past; and it contrasts with the primary present (in italics) in some instantially particular way that is different from the "past/present" contrast in narratives and that will only come into focus gradually for the reader.

10.4.5 Location relative to subjectivity: whose system is it anyway?

As long as we focus on the overall linguistic systemic potential of a culture, we can unify or merge different tenor perspectives for certain purposes: when we do so, we represent the collective resources of that culture. However, these collective resources are distributed across personal domains, partly as a manifestation of the division of labour. When we consider instantial systems, different tenor perspectives become critical. The tenor differential, measured e.g. in power, familiarity, and expertise (see Martin 1992a), is always being negotiated as a text unfolds. Logogenesis involves the perspectives of all the interactants taking part in this negotiation; and the ongoing negotiation is embodied in their respective instantial systems. The emerging impact of the text as it unfolds can be modelled in terms of changing relationship among the interactants' instantial systems. For example, if one speaker is trying to "gain the upper hand," this may be recorded in the increasing likelihood that they will select certain speech functions and the dominated dialogic partner(s) certain other complementary ones (cf. Burton 1980; Birch 1993). Or, to take an example from the ideational domain, if the addressee learns from the unfolding text by expanding one's ideational system (e.g. elaboration in taxonomic delicacy), the differential in expertise between speaker and addressee has been narrowed to some extent. Whether the interactants have established similarity or difference (cf. Eggins 1990, on the exploration of difference against the background of similarity in casual conversation among friends), they will certainly have learned more about one another instantially.

Instantial systems created logogenetically thus have to be modelled in terms of **intersubjectivity**. (This is also the perspective that has to be foregrounded when logogenesis is related to the ontogenetic time frame: see Halliday 1975; Trevarthen 1987; Painter 1993.) Instantial systems are created collaboratively; and they have meaning only relative to other instantial systems. We have to avoid getting trapped

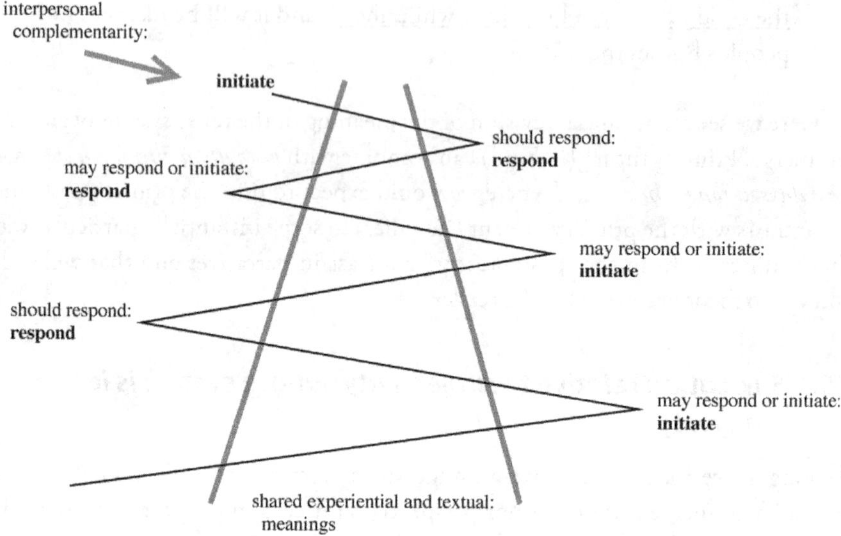

Figure 10.24 Interpersonal give and take in the expansion of instantial experiential and textual systems

in two other kinds of subjectivity – (**intra-**)**subjectivity** and **meta-subjectivity**. Subjectivity – or more explicitly, intra-subjectivity – is the perspective of the isolated individual as a container of cognitive processes. This perspective characterizes mainstream cognitive science (cf. Matthiessen 1993b). If this perspective is adopted, the addressee has to be construed in terms of hearer models or the like: the speaker's beliefs about the mental states of the addressee (cf. Halliday and Matthiessen 1999/2006: 111–12, on the nature of such models). Meta-subjectivity[9] is a non-interactant point of view – the perspective of the eavesdropping analyst who can view the text as a finished product.

Among the instantial systems illustrated here, both the instantial textual systems of reference and the experiential taxonomic ones are viewed from the perspective of the addressee as far as their logogenetic expansion is concerned. But, at the same time, the speaker has to track this expansion; in fact, one has to guide it in such a way that the addressee can manage the process. The interpersonal systems of speech function considered briefly above are different in that they seem to go through logogenetic cycles that are constructed interactively, with complementary selections made by the interactants; for instance: I initiate —> you should respond; I respond —> you may respond or initiate; I initiate —> ..., and so on. Figure 10.24 shows the interpersonal complementarity (but without the cycles represented diagrammatically) scaffolding the expansion of the instantial experiential

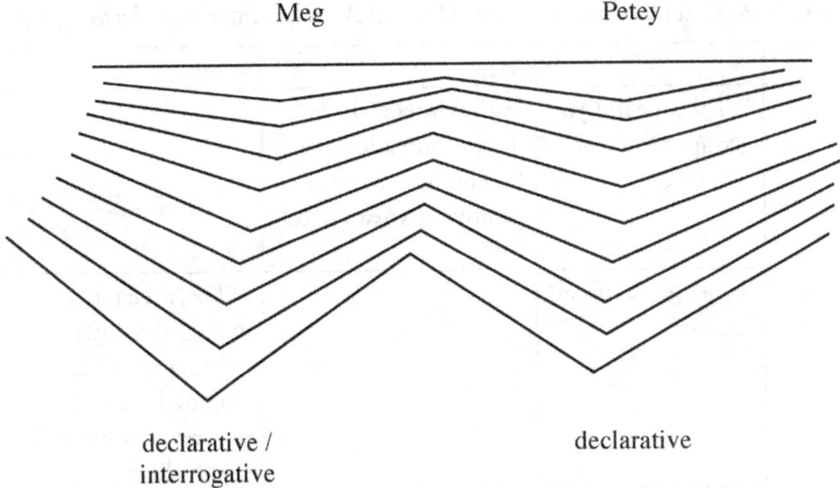

Figure 10.25 Emergent instantial system

and textual systems that the two interlocutors can assume are shared. This diagram is misleading in one crucial respect: from an interpersonal point of view, the experiential and textual expansions reduce the interpersonal distance, at least with respect to familiarity.

For example, in the breakfast conversation between Meg and Petey, there is a local decrease in "knowledge distance" between them as they share something Petey has read in the paper – Petey: *Someone's just had a baby.* – Meg: *Who?* – Petey: *Some girl.* – Meg: *Who?* – Petey: *Lady Mary Splatt.* Move by move they thus come to share "Lady Mary Splatt's just had a baby."

10.5 Conclusion

Logogenesis is the creation of meaning in the process of instantiation. We can try to interpret this process as change in instantial systems – change that is both expanding in the sense of adding new options and restricting in the sense of systematically not taking up options that could have been taken up: options are opened up and closed down. Both of these aspects of logogenetic change are meaning creating: expansion overtly, and restriction covertly. Restriction is meaningful against the background of the potential relative to which it is a restriction. And both emerge only gradually as the text unfolds. For instance, the longer their breakfast conversation lasts, the more the division of labour between Meg and Petey is confirmed

Table 10.5. First exchanges between Meg and Petey in Pinter's *The birthday party*

		Meg:	**Petey:**
Meg:	What time **did you** get up this morning, Petey?	indic: (inter.: wh- & interactant: addressee & temporal: past) & positive & **vocative** & full	
Petey:	Same time as usual.		indic: (declarative: untagged & interactant: speaker & temporal: past) & non-vocative & positive & elliptical
Meg:	**Was it** dark?	indic: (inter.: yes/no & non-interactant & temporal: past) & non-vocative & positive & full	
Petey:	No, **it was** light.		indic.: (declarative: untagged & non-interactant & temporal: past) & non-vocative & positive & full

in the differential between their instantial systems (e.g. Meg: declarative/interrogative; Petey: declarative): see Figure 10.25 (loosely based on the epigenetic landscape in Fishbein 1976: 36).

In their first exchanges, Meg and Petey set the parameters for the rest of their conversation, as shown in Table 10.5.

Similarly, when two middle-aged male academics interview a young woman applying to do English honours and the senior of the two academics says *Well, you are proposing taking on quite something, Mrs. Finney, aren't you?* and Mrs. Finney responds *Yes, I am; I should like to, anyhow,* they have in an abstract way sewn the logogenetic seed from which the rest of the interview grows. The interviewers demand information from Mrs. Finney quite freely and she responds, downgrading herself through modality (see Svartvik and Quirk 1980 for the transcript of this interview). We might think of this as a logogenetic fractal – a general pattern that is manifested again and again in new environments as the text unfolds. In the body fuels text, the first clause, *The fuels of the body are carbohydrates, fats and proteins*, defines the root of the instantial system to be developed and can be read as a forecast of the overall taxonomic organization of the text.

Through expansion, the instantial system gets more complex, and this complexity has to be managed logogenetically. If it is not, listeners or readers feel that the text is meandering randomly all over the place; they get lost in chaos. How this build-up in complexity is achieved is one of the central research questions we have to face if we adopt the perspective of the logogenesis of instantial systems.

Appendix: Texts

Text 1: Space ship narrative

[1] It was a beautiful Saturday night. [2] Looking up at the sky it was like hundreds of a Christmas tree's branches, each one with a thousand lights. [3] Then, as if from nowhere, **an orange thing** blurred into the sky with tremendous speed. [4] **It** looked like a meteorite with red and blue sparks. [5] I thought **it** would burn up, [6] **it** began to sink. [7] I watched **it** fall, [8] **the thing** seemed to slow down. [9] **It** hit the ground about 200 m. away. [10] I heard an explosion, then raced forwards. [11] **It** looked like the ... of a space capsule. [12] *The back of the capsule* was on fire [13] (the heat was unbearable). [14] I shielded my face, rushed up *the front* and dragged *the person* out [15] (*he* had cuts all over him). [16] I carried *him* about 20 m when I heard a deafening explosion, [17] **the entire ship** burst into flames. [18] I took *him* back to my house and called an ambulance. [19] *They* took *him* to intensive care. [20] After a week *he* was in a satisfactory condition. [21] Every time I visited *him* *he* told me this interesting story about *him* escaping from these aliens and back to Earth in **this gigantic vessel** which had burst up. [22] In the first visit *he* told me his name John Graves. [23] *John* also told me in two weeks {*we*} would have an invasion. [24] A fleet of 12 vessels shall converge upon the earth, there will be many deaths and terrible destruction. [25] *We* told **the police** but they said "you're Nuts". [26] During the two weeks there were lots of UFO sightings. [27] Then when the two weeks were over a rain of terror hit the earth. [28] **Ships** were firing this way and that way. [29] *John* knew there was only one way to stop them. [30] *His* plan was to guide **them** into each other. [31] One of **them** landed near *us*. [32] *We* reached *it* by dodging phaser fire and climbing into *the hold of the ship*. [33] *John and I* gradually made *our* way to *the control room*, flew **the ship** towards another one then escaped in a pad. [34] *We* did this with every ship and so saved the planet.

(From Martin and Rothery 1980.)

Text 2: The body fuels exposition

[1] <u>The **fuels** of the *body*</u>	are **carbohydrates, fats and proteins.**
<u>These</u>	are taken in the diet.
[2] <u>They</u>	are found mainly in cereal grains, vegetable oils, meat, fish and diary products.
[3] <u>**Carbohydrates**</u>	are the principal **source of energy** in most diet.
[4] <u>They</u>	are absorbed into the *bloodstream* in the form of **glucose.**
[5.1] <u>**Glucose**</u>	not needed for immediate use is converted into **glycogen**
[5.2] <u>and</u>	stored in the *liver*.
[6a] <u>When the *blood* sugar concentration</u>	goes down,
[6b] <u>the *liver*</u>	reconverts some of its stored **glycogen** into **glucose.**
[7] <u>**Fats**</u>	make up the second largest **source of energy** in most diets.
[8] <u>They</u>	are stored in *adipose tissue* and round the principal *internal organs*.
[9a] <u>If excess **carbohydrate**</u>	is taken in,
[9b] <u>this</u>	can be converted into **fat**
<u>and</u>	stored.
[10a] <u>The stored **fat**</u>	is utilized
[10b] <u>when the *liver*</u>	is empty of **glycogen.**
[11.1] <u>**Proteins**</u>	are essential for the growth and rebuilding of *tissue*,
[11.2] <u>but they</u>	can also be used as a **source of energy.**
[12] <u>In some diets, such as the diet of the Eskimo,</u>	they form the main **source of energy.**
[13] <u>Proteins</u>	are first broken down into **amino acids.**
[14.1] <u>Then they</u>	are absorbed into the *blood*
[14.2] <u>and</u>	pass round the *body*.
[15] <u>**Amino acids** not used in the *body*</u>	are eventually excreted in the *urine* in the form of urea.
[16] <u>**Proteins**, unlike **carbohydrates** and **fats**,</u>	cannot be stored for future use.

Text 3: Xi'an Mining Institute

Table 10.6 Thematic analysis of the Xi'an Mining Institute text

Theme	Rheme (in bold: Culminative)
	Founded in 1958
Xi'an Mining Institute	is consistently **ranked as one of the top ten colleges under the direction of twhe Ministry of the Coal Industry of China.**
The total **enrolment**	is currently 2,245, including 1,469 undergraduates, 51 specialized students, 55 postgraduates, and 490 correspondence students.
Most of the **students**	come from northwest China,
but there	are some from other areas.
Xi'an Mining Institute	is **located in the southern suburbs, three kilometres from the centre of Xi'an (population 2.8 million), the capital of Shaanxi Province in the Northwest of China.**
The Institute	is fortunate
in	having ready access to the **educational facilities** of the Xi'an area.
The ancient capital of China	has a rich cultural **heritage** in art, music, and history.
Its many museums, historical buildings, and great educational institutions	offer a magnificent resource to the students.
These and the many scenic spots and historical sites of the Xi'an area	are made easily accessible by public transportation.
The institute	offers a Bachelor's **degree** with seven majors and a Master's **degree** with five majors.

Table 10.6 Thematic analysis of the Xi'an Mining Institute text (Continued)

Theme	Rheme (in bold: Culminative)
It	has altogether eleven **specialities**, 31 **sections**, 193 various **courses**, and 59 laboratories and exhibition **rooms.**
Xi'an Mining Institute	has about 1,000 **faculty** members including 52 professors and associate professors, 212 lecturers.
The staff of the institute	displays dedication
in	shaping and guiding students' experiences.
One of the first of the newer generation of building on campus	is the Institute **library,**
which	currently **holds** about 430,000 **volumes** and approximately 1,000 periodical **files and journals.**
The 7,200 square-metre library	houses six reading **rooms** of different types with more than 700 seats for students.
It	also provides film-readers, duplicators, and some other excellent **facilities** for research and teaching.

(From Wu 1992.)

Text 4: Extract from Pinter's *The birthday party*

Table 10.7 Interpersonal selections by Meg and Petey in the first exchanges in the play

		Meg:	Petey:
Meg:	What time **did you** get up this morning, Petey?	indic: (interrogative: wh- & interactant: addressee & temporal: past) & positive & **vocative** & full	

Table 10.7 Interpersonal selections by Meg and Petey in the first exchanges in the play (Continued)

		Meg:	**Petey:**
Petey:	[**I got** up at the] same time as usual.		indic: (declarative: untagged & interactant: speaker & temporal: past) & non-vocative & positive & elliptical
Meg:	**Was it** dark?	indic: (interrogative: yes/no & non-interactant & temporal: past) & non-vocative & positive & full	
Petey:	No [~~it wasn't dark~~], **it was** light.		indic.: (declarative: untagged & non-interactant & temporal: past) & non-vocative & positive & full
Meg:	But **sometimes you go** out in the morning	indic.: (declarative: untagged & interactant: addressee & temporal: present) & non-vocative & positive & full	
	and **it's** dark		
Petey:	**That's** in winter.		indic.: (declarative: untagged & non-interactant & temporal: present) & non-vocative & positive & full

Continued

Table 10.7 Interpersonal selections by Meg and Petey in the first exchanges in the play (Continued)

		Meg:	**Petey:**
Meg:	Oh, [~~that's/is that~~] in winter	indic.: (declarative: untagged & non-interactant & temporal: present) & non-vocative & positive & elliptical	
Petey:	Yes, **it gets** light later in winter.		indic.: (declarative: untagged & non-interactant & temporal: present) & non-vocative & positive & full
Meg:	Oh.	minor clause/elliptical	
Meg:	What **are you** reading?	indic.: (interrogative: wh & interactant: addressee & temporal: present) & non-vocative & positive & full	
Petey:	**Someone's just** had a baby.		indic.: (declarative: untagged & non-interactant & temporal: present) & non-vocative & positive & full
Meg:	Oh, **they haven't** [**just** ~~had a baby~~]!	indic.: (declarative: untagged & non-interactant & temporal: present) & non-vocative & negative & elliptical	

Table 10.7 Interpersonal selections by Meg and Petey in the first exchanges in the play (Continued)

		Meg:	Petey:
	Who [~~has just had a baby~~]?	indic.: (interrogative: wh & interactant & temporal: present) & non-vocative & positive & elliptical	
Petey:	**Some girl** [~~has just had a baby~~].		indic.: (declarative: untagged & non-interactant & temporal: present) & non-vocative & positive & elliptical
Meg:	**Who** [~~has just had a baby~~], Petey, who?	indic.: (interrogative: wh- & non-interactant & temporal: present) & **vocative** & positive & elliptical	
Petey:	*I don't think* **you'd** know her. <As modality>		indic.: (declarative: untagged & interactant: addressee & temporal: present) & non-vocative & positive & full
Meg:	What's **her name?**	indic.: (interrogative: wh- & non-interactant & temporal: present) & non-vocative & negative & full	
Petey:	[~~Her name is~~] Lady Mary Splatt.		indic.: (declarative: untagged & non-interactant & temporal: present) & non-vocative & positive & elliptical

Continued

Table 10.7 Interpersonal selections by Meg and Petey in the first exchanges in the play (Continued)

		Meg:	Petey:
Meg:	**I don't** know her.	indic.: (declarative: untagged & non-interactant & temporal: present) & non-vocative & negative & full	
Petey:	No [~~you don't know her~~]		indic.: (declarative: untagged & inter-actant: addressee & temporal: present) & non-vocative & negative & full
Meg:	What **is it**?	indic.: (interrogative: wh- & non-interactant & temporal: present) & non-vocative & negative & full	
Petey:	Er – [**it's**] a girl.		indic.: (declarative: untagged & non-interactant & temporal: present) & non-vocative & positive & elliptical
Meg:	[~~Is it~~] **Not** a boy?	indic.: (interrogative: yes/no & non-interactant & temporal: present) & non-vocative & negative & elliptical	

Table 10.7 Interpersonal selections by Meg and Petey in the first exchanges in the play (Continued)

		Meg:	**Petey:**
Petey:	No [~~it's not a boy~~]		indic.: (declarative: untagged & non-interactant & temporal: present) & non-vocative & negative & elliptical
Meg:	Oh, what a shame.	minor clause: exclamation	
	I'd be sorry.	indic.: (declarative: untagged & interactant: speaker & modal) & non-vocative & positive & full	
	I'd much rather have a little boy.	indic.: (declarative: untagged & interactant: speaker & modal) & non-vocative & positive & full	
Petey:	**A girl's** all right.		indic.: (declarative: untagged & non-interactant & temporal: present) & non-vocative & positive & full
Meg:	**I'd** much rather have a little boy.	indic.: (declarative: untagged & interactant: speaker & modal) & non-vocative & positive & full	

Continued

Table 10.7 Interpersonal selections by Meg and Petey in the first exchanges in the play (Continued)

		Meg:	**Petey:**
Petey:	**I've** finished my cornflakes.		indic.: (declarative: untagged & inter-actant: speaker & temporal: present) & non-vocative & positive & full
Meg:	**Were they** nice?	indic.: (interrogative: yes/no & non-interactant & temporal: past) & non-interactant & positive & full	
Petey:	[~~They were~~] Very nice.		indic.: (declara-tive: untagged & non-interactant & temporal: present) & non-vocative & negative & elliptical

(From H. Pinter, *The birthday party*)

Notes

*   In preparing this chapter, I have benefited from comments by participants in the Third Chinese Systemic-Functional Symposium, held at the University of Hangzhou, June 17–20, 1993. I'm especially indebted to the organizer, Prof. Ren, whose plenary on tense selections in discourse at an earlier conference hosted by his university in October 1992, inspired me to give the present paper. I would also like to thank Gillian Fuller, Mary Macken, and Petie Sefton for input into my understanding of logogenesis during our collaboration on logogenesis for a systemic seminar series at Sydney University. I draw gratefully on the work by Michael O'Donnell and Petie Sefton in the context of our dialogue modelling project (in particular in Section 10.3.2).

1   In addition, processes have always been used as metaphors for what we now realize are better viewed as paradigmatic relationships — the transformations of traditional grammars (elaborated, e.g. in Sanctius' *Minerva* in the sixteenth century) and of transformational grammar.

2   This figure was created in a presentation program that allows for some simple animation: imagine the figure being built up one system-network traversal at a time.

3   This is indeed one powerful reason for reifying non-things as things through grammatical metaphor: they can be established as referents in an instantial system; they can be tracked; and they can accrue experiential meanings.

4   That is, experiential classification realized in nominal groups. The referents are also implicitly classified in terms of the roles they take on as participants in particular process types.

5   This figure was created in a presentation program that allows for some simple animation: to show the logogenetic expansion, it is built up one part at a time in this presentation.

6   This does not mean that there are no cumulative interpersonal effects. There clearly are; we find prosodic motifs, with an increase in volume (see Martin 1992b). We also find emerging patterns in the division of dialogic labour (cf. Section 10.4.2).

7   This extension is complex in that involves the move from dialects to the languages they are varieties of, to language — the general human potential (in the species) that these languages are manifestations of. Further, languages evolve, but not as monolithic systems, but as assemblages of dialectal and registerial varieties, and individual registers may change in a more cyclical way than languages do.

8   Relational structure such as we find in clause complexing and in conjunctive relations is different from constituency structure in that it does not presuppose a unit whole. It is, in a sense, a structural manifestation of logogenetic order, just as logical recursive systems embody a logogenetic ordering of instantiations of other parts of the system. I will not discuss these issues further here.

9   Sefton (1995) calls this super-subjectivity. I have used the term meta-subjectivity to emphasize that it is the perspective of the metalanguage, external to the interaction itself.

Chapter 11

Systemic functional morphology: The lexicogrammar of the word

11.1 Introduction

This chapter is concerned with the systemic functional approach to that area of lexicogrammar (the system of wording in a language, including both grammar and lexis) that has been studied under the heading of "morphology" in many frameworks and traditions in linguistics. The discussion is organized around the eight questions provided by the editors of this book, following their numbering. The questions are captured by the headings of the following eight sections, and under each heading I have quoted the question in full. Before I begin to address the questions, I will give a brief introduction to the chapter, and after answering the eight questions I will end with a short conclusion.

Systemic functional linguistics (SFL) originated with M.A.K. Halliday's work in the late 1950s and 1960s, and arguably constitutes the only theory of language from that period that is still developing and expanding. It represents a holistic and comprehensive engagement with language in context (e.g. Halliday 1976a, 1978, 1994a, 2002b, 2003b; Halliday and Martin 1981; Hasan, Matthiessen, and Webster 2005, 2007; Halliday and Webster 2009; Halliday and Matthiessen 2014); it includes:

- Systemic functional ***holistic*** **theory** of language as a higher-order human semiotic – and now also SF theory of other semiotic systems (e.g. Martinec 2005).
- Systemic functional ***comprehensive*** **descriptions** of an increasingly wide range of particular languages and comparisons and typological generalizations based on these descriptions (e.g. Caffarel, Martin, and Matthiessen 2004; Teruya et al. 2007; Teruya and Matthiessen 2015).

- Systemic functional ***extensive* analyses** of texts belonging to many registers (e.g. Eggins and Slade 2005 on the analysis of spoken discourse, and Martin and Rose 2007, on the analysis of written discourse), including both manual and automated analysis (cf. Wu 2009; Matthiessen 2014d).

These theoretical, descriptive (including comparative and typological), and analytical activities have been undertaken not only as ends in themselves but also in order to address a diverse spectrum of applications in e.g. education, healthcare, administration, or computation. Right from the start, SFL has been designed to have **the theoretical potential to be applied** to solve diverse problems in communities, and ultimately to improve the human condition; Halliday (e.g. 2002d) has characterized it as **appliable linguistics**, and a key part of appliable linguistics is **appliable discourse analysis** (Matthiessen 2014d; cf. Matthiessen 2012).

Systemic functional theory was developed by Halliday in the 1960s out of J.R. Firth's **system-structure theory**, one aspect of which was prosodic analysis (e.g. Catford 1969; Henderson 1987).[1] The first phase of development came to be known as **scale-and-category theory**; it was introduced by Halliday (1961), with a focus on grammar. In the next phases, he gradually developed this version into **systemic theory** (Halliday 1966b) and **systemic functional theory** (Halliday 1967/8, 1970a,b). This development was also informed by European functional linguistics – in particular, the Prague School, and US American anthropological linguistics; and it took place in dialogue with Sidney Lamb's stratificational linguistics.

Many of Halliday's theoretical positions were out of tune with "theoretical linguistics" in the increasingly dominant generative linguistic framework in the 1960s and 1970s, but have since then found resonances with subsequent developments in other linguistic traditions – it would be fair to say that the field has caught up with his ideas about language from the 1960s (Matthiessen 2015c). These positions include his theory of language as a probabilistic system, his theory of the functional organization of language, his model of grammar and lexis as a continuum rather than as separate modules, and his integration of syntax and morphology as grammar (or "morpho-syntax," to use a term that has come into use in linguistics[2]). Since these are directly relevant to the conceptualization of morphology, I will return to them at various points throughout this chapter.

11.2   The location of "morphology" in systemic functional theory

1. What is the place of morphology in the systemic functional theory?

In many linguistic theories, morphology is a distinct module or component – one that is separate from syntax; in this respect, modern theories have tended to follow traditional grammar with "accidence" as a separate component of the grammar. In contrast, in systemic functional *theory*, morphology and syntax are not separate modules but rather simply regions within lexicogrammar. This insight goes back to the proto-systemic theory presented by Halliday (1961: section 5.3):

> Traditionally these terms have usually referred to "grammar above the word" (syntax) and "grammar below the word" (morphology); but this distinction has no theoretical status. [Footnote: Cf. Firth (1957a): "It follows that the distinction between morphology and syntax is perhaps no longer useful or convenient in descriptive linguistics" (p. 14).] It has a place in the description of certain languages, "inflexional" languages [Footnote: i.e. languages in which inflexional systems are a regular feature of word structure. *Free* and *bound* are generalized class categories, linked to the generalized structure categories of *simple* and *compound* (above, 2.3): "free" is "able to stand as exponent of one-element structure of the unit next above", "bound" is "unable to stand, etc.". A member of a "free" class can thus be exponent of a "simple" structure, while a member of a bound class can operate only in "compound" structures.] which tend to display one kind of grammatical relation above the word ("free" items predominating) and another below the word ("bound" items predominating).

In other words, the distinction between syntax and morphology is not a theoretical one; it is not part of the general **theory** of language as a human semiotic, more specifically as a higher-order human semiotic (see e.g. Halliday 1996). In **descriptions** of particular languages, it may turn out that the subgrammars of units of different ranks have somewhat different characteristics, but this is not a general property of language.[3] Indeed, languages vary considerably in how they divide the lexicogrammatical labour between the units of different ranks such as clauses, groups, words, and morphemes,[4] and a given language is likely to vary in this respect over time, as has been highlighted in the last few decades by studies dealing with grammaticalization. Languages also vary in terms of the location of the gateway or interface between grammar and phonology. However, the general principle that emerges again and again in the description of different languages with a reasonably elaborate word grammar is that word grammar operates intimately together with clause and group grammar. For example, in Arabic (Classical and Modern Standard), the systems of tense and aspect have the verbal group as their systemic domain (i.e. group rank), and realizations of systemic options in these systems are located either at group rank (tense "particles" *sawfa* and *qad*, tense auxiliary *ka:na*) or at word rank (prefix *sa-*, which alternates with *sawfa* in the realization of 'future'; and the aspectual contrast in verb morphology between 'perfect' and 'imperfect' realized by "transfixes" (patterns of vowels and non-root consonants overlaying the consonantal root), e.g. (third person masculine singular form [which is the citation form] of the verb 'write,' with the consonantal root *k t b) kataba* vs. *yaktubu*.

According to systemic functional theory, descriptions of word grammar, or "morphology," are located within the overall "architecture" of language in terms of a number of **semiotic dimensions** as shown in Figure 11.1 (see e.g. Halliday and Matthiessen 2014: ch. 1; Matthiessen 2007a),[5] viz. the **hierarchy of stratification** [3], the **hierarchy of rank** [1], the **spectrum of metafunction** [5], the **cline of instantiation** [4], the **hierarchy of axis** (not shown in the figure) and the **cline of delicacy** [2]:

- In terms of the **hierarchy of stratification** [3], morphology is part of the content plane of language – semantics (meaning) and lexicogrammar (wording), more specifically the lower of the two content strata, viz. **lexicogrammar**. This means that there are two stratal relationships to take account of, both with important descriptive issues for any given language: semantics ~ lexicogrammar (what are the semantic correlates of words and morphemes?; what is the potential for non-congruent, metaphoric relations between these correlates and words/morphemes?), and lexicogrammar ~ phonology (or lexicogrammar ~ graphology, in written language; lexicogrammar ~ sign, in sign language) (what are the phonological realizations [markers, signals] of words and morphemes [e.g. vowel harmony, accent, phonotactic patterns e.g. in terms of boundaries]; are there phonological words?).

- Within lexicogrammar, morphology is located in terms of the **hierarchy of rank** [1] – the **rank scale** of grammar (Halliday 1961): it is the grammar of the lower-ranking units of words and morphemes, thus complementing the grammar of the higher-ranking units of clauses and groups/phrases.[6] But this is one area where languages vary considerably; as already noted, the division of grammatical labour varies around the languages of the world in terms of rank (see further below), and languages also vary over time, changing the location of grammatical labour along the rank scale. One type of change is grammaticalization, and this typically involves a move of items down the rank scale from the status of free words via clitics to bound morphemes.

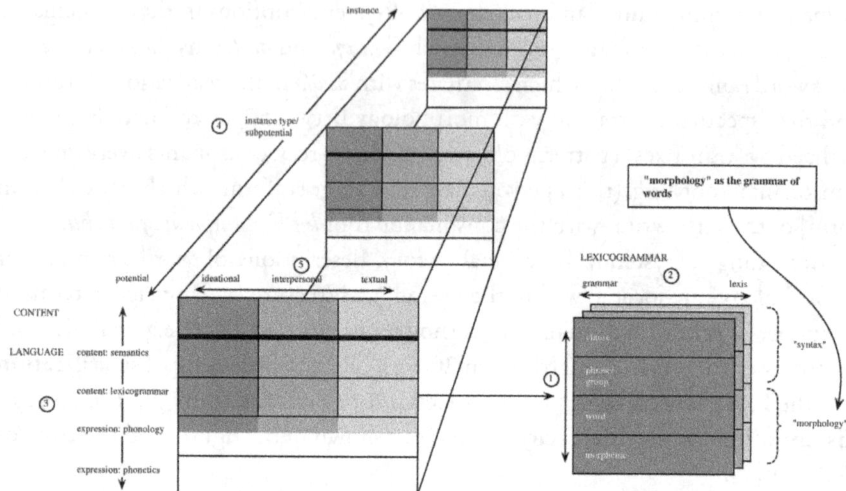

Figure 11.1 Morphology simply as the grammar of words within grammar ("morpho-syntax") rather than as a separate module – located in terms of the semiotic dimensions of rank, delicacy, stratification, and instantiation

- In terms of the **spectrum of metafunction** [5], morphology is multifunctional (like all of lexicogrammar), being organized by all the metafunctions – i.e. ideationally (logically and experientially), interpersonally, and textually. These make complementary contributions to the make-up of words.
- In terms of the **cline of instantiation** [4], morphology is part of the "wording potential" of language, i.e. the system of lexicogrammar, extending from the potential pole of the cline to the instance pole. This aspect of the location of morphology is crucial to the investigation of **systemic probabilities** through text frequencies[7] and to the modelling of grammaticalization – and, more generally, of both ontogenesis and phylogenesis.
- In terms of the **hierarchy of axis** (not shown in Figure 11.1), morphology is organized **paradigmatically** in the first instance, just like all other aspects of language: as part of lexicogrammar, morphology is organized as options in wording, represented by means of **system networks**, and morphological options are realized syntagmatically by morphological structures, represented by means of function structures.
- In terms of the **cline of delicacy** [2], morphology extends from the least delicate pole of the cline to the most delicate one; in other words, it extends along the lexicogrammar continuum from closed grammatical systems to

open lexical sets, thus ranging from grammatical words and morphemes to lexical ones.[8] Thus, morphology is accurately characterized as **word lexicogrammar** rather than just as word grammar. This aspect of the location of morphology is important in the investigation of grammaticalization as the move of items from lexical to grammatical environments (often also involving an ascent in rank).

The combination of the dimensions of stratification and rank enables us to show that the **word** is a *location* defined by these dimensions, as shown in Figure 11.2, not a thing in itself. Consequently, its nature depends on its relationship to other locations, other "units."[9] The dimensions define the views we can take on the location of the word: we can view it "from below," "from above," or "from roundabout" in terms of rank and in terms of stratification. Particular views may represent attempts at definitions of the word; for example, the stratal view "from below" has been the source of phonological characterizations of the word and the rank view "from above" the source of grammatical characterizations based on structural distribution, as with Bloomfield's (1933: 178) "a word is a minimum free form" (cf. the review of approaches by Dixon and Aikhenvald (2003) and their arguments in favour of differentiating grammatical words and phonological words – a differentiation that follows automatically from the stratal theory of SFL). However, to understand the word more holistically, more systemically, we must characterize them **trinocularly** (for trinocularity, see e.g. Halliday 1996). This means recognizing that while the different perspectives will agree in prototypical cases, there will be cases where they give conflicting results; but this is characteristic of all categories in language, not just of words (cf. the discussion of clauses in Halliday and Matthiessen 2014: 15–17) – a consequence of language being an **evolved**, or rather **evolving**, system instead of a **designed** one.

The dimensions represented in Figure 11.1 give the location of "morphology" within the total model of language in context. At the same time, it is also important to emphasize the **fractal nature** of local organization, i.e. of organization that is local to a subsystem of language. In many theories of language, different components or modules are organized according to different principles and are named accordingly, e.g. (different versions of) phrase structure grammar, categorial grammar, metrical phonology, autosegmental phonology, or lexical phonology. In contrast, in SFL, all areas of language are organized in the same way by systems whose options are realized by function structures. Thus, the **axial organization of language** is fractal in the sense that it is manifested in different local environments throughout the linguistic system. System networks with realization statements

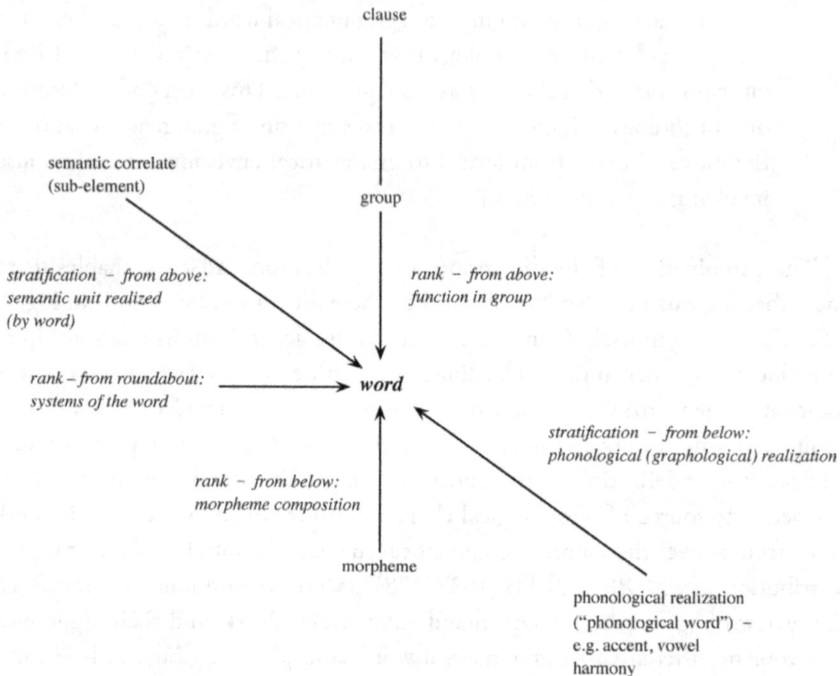

Figure 11.2 The basic unit of morphology, word, viewed trinocularly in terms of the hierarchies of rank and stratification

have been used in the description of semantics, lexicogrammar (both syntax and morphology), and phonology.

This fractal organization is part of the ***theoretical*** architecture of language in SFL. But in our descriptions of particular languages, we can also posit **descriptive fractals** in the sense of semantic categories that are manifested throughout the content systems of these languages (cf. Halliday's 1998/2005a: 321–9 demonstration of the foregrounding of ergative patterns in English grammar, manifested in both syntax and morphology). For example, in his description of English, Halliday has identified the logico-semantic types of **projection** and **expansion** as motifs that are manifested throughout semantics and lexicogrammar, as shown in e.g. Halliday and Matthiessen (1999/2006; 2014: ch. 10). This is important in descriptions of the morphological region of the lexicogrammar of a language. It is part of the task of the description to identify and reveal the manifestation of such fractal patterns. For example, relations of cause, manner, time, and space are manifested throughout ranked units of the lexicogrammar of English, including in the grammar of words

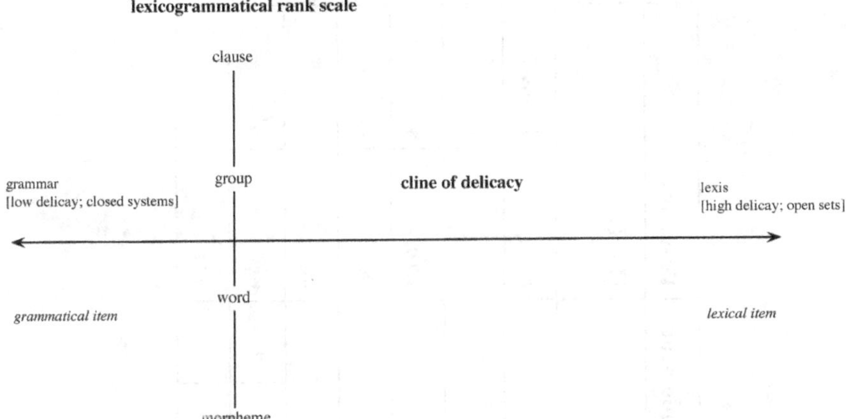

Figure 11.3 Word and lexical item as locations along the rank scale and the cline of delicacy, respectively

in the form of derivational affixes (e.g. *pre-* 'before'; *post-* 'after'; cf. *before they were unified* > *before unification* > *post-unification*). Such fractals are an important aspect of grammatical metaphor, and lower-ranking markers are often created through the process of grammaticalization (e.g. *free* > *–free*).

Let me round off this overview of the location and nature of morphology in SFL with a very brief example taken from my description of the personal pronominal system of Akan (Niger-Congo: Kwa) (cf. Fawcett's 1988, systemic description of personal pronouns in English). The system can be set out as a traditional paradigm in tabular form: see Table 11.1. The table includes both free and bound pronouns. Personal pronouns may serve as Subject in the clause, as Subject in the verb (in which case they are prefixes serving in word structure, but they are discussed here), as Complement in the clause, and as Possessor in the nominal group. These forms are presented together in Table 11.1. The possessive pronouns may have different forms (allomorphs) before a following vowel and before a following consonant. For example, 'your (sg.) hoe' is *wásɔ* (*w-* + *asɔ* 'hoe') but 'your (sg.) cloth' is *wó ntomá*. The complement form may be zero if it is third person singular inanimate.

The pronominals set out in Table 11.1 can be represented systemically as in Figure 11.4.[10] The realizations of the systemic options in the network are shown informally in the table to the right of the network. The maximal pronominal realization is the phonological template $V_1C_1V_2C_2$, which is further specified in the table. The realization statements will refer to the segments. The default tongue root value is neutral; and the default tone is L (low). Bound pronominals

Table 11.1 The personal pronouns of Akan

		Prefix		Emphatic		Complement		Possessive	
		[advanced/ neutral tongue root]		[H]				[L/H]	
								before C	*before V*
speaker [1st p.]	singular	*me*		*mé*		*me*		*me*	*m'*
	plural	*yɛ*		*yɛ́n*		*yɛn*		*yɛ(n)*	*y'*
addressee [2nd p.]	singular	*wó*		*wó*		*wo*		*wo*	*w'*
	plural	*mo*		*mó*		*mo*		*mo*	
non-interactant [3rd p.]	singular	*ɔ*	*ε*	*ɔnó*	*ɛnó*	*no*	*Ø*	*ne*	*n'*
	plural	*wɔ*		*wɔn*		*wɔn*		*wɔn*	

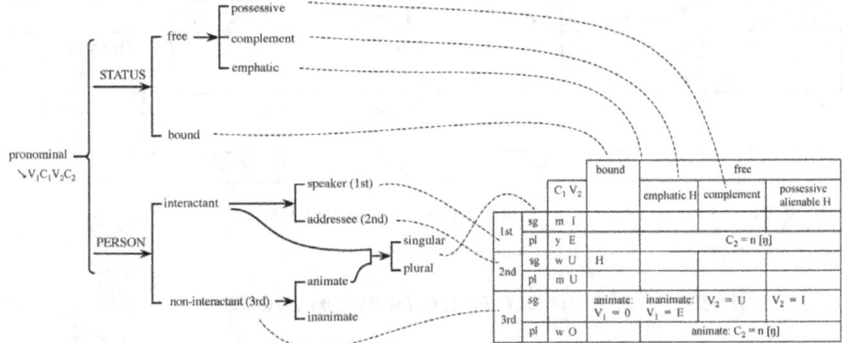

Figure 11.4 System network representing pronominal options in Akan

are verbal prefixes; they have advanced/neutral tongue root according to vowel harmony.

This sketchy description of the pronominal system of Akan illustrates a number of key features of the systemic functional approach to morphology:

- The primary description is **systemic** rather than **structural**. Systems are ordered in delicacy from most general (least delicate) to most delicate, but systems can also be simultaneous, like STATUS and PERSON, and thus unordered in delicacy.
- Syntagmatic specifications, both items like pronominals and structures, are given as **realizations** of systemic options (terms, features) or combinations of systemic options (like 'addressee' and 'singular' and 'bound' realized as a high tone [H]).
- Lexicogrammatical realizations may be **intra-stratal**, i.e. internal to lexicogrammar, or **inter-stratal**, i.e. external, referring to phonological (or graphological) patterns. In the example given here, all realization statements refer to phonological specifications of pronominals.

The description of Akan pronominals includes realization statements specifying their phonological shape. Realization statements elsewhere in the grammar of Akan refer to the system of pronominals. For example, in the description at word rank of the function structure of verbs, there are five functions, viz. Subject ^ Temporal$_1$ ^ Modal ^ Event ^ Temporal$_2$, as shown in Figure 11.5. The Subject function is realized by a preselection of (at least) the systemic feature 'bound' in the system network set out in Figure 11.4. In this way, morphological descriptions are related by upwards and downwards by realization statements.

Subject	Temporal₁	Modal	Event	Temporal₂	
ɔ-	*ré-*	*m-*	*fura*		'he won't put on'
ɔ-		*m-*	*furà*	*a*	'he hasn't put on'
3SG		NEG	put on		

Figure 11.5 The structure of Akan verbs with examples

11.3　Difference from other theoretical models

2. To what extent is the systemic functional theory different from the other theoretical models with respect to the description of morphological phenomena?

There are a number of differences that make systemic functional theory unique in its approach to the "description of morphological phenomena";[11] these include:

- **Integration:** morphology is not treated as a separate module in the SF architecture of language; it is simply the lexicogrammar of words, organized in the same way as the rest of lexicogrammar, and indeed the rest of language (the fractal principle referred to above).
- **Axial orientation:** as with all of language, the primary organizing principle is paradigmatic rather than syntagmatic – the systemic representation of morphology as a resource for creating meaning through "words," and syntagmatic specifications (items and structures) are specified as realizations of (combinations of) systemic options, as illustrated in Figure 11.4.
- **Metafunction:** as with all of lexicogrammar, morphology is organized metafunctionally, embodying different modes of meaning and their distinct modes of expression (univariate: serial/multivariate: configurational, prosodic, periodic; see Table 11.2, discussed below).

11.3.1 Axial orientation

Apart from the fact that morphology is treated as an integral part of lexicogrammar, the most fundamental difference between SFL and most, or even all, other theoretical models is arguably the **axial orientation** of systemic theory. The orientation is **paradigmatic** rather than syntagmatic; i.e. while virtually all theoretical models of morphology are essentially based on morphological **structure**, systemic functional theory is based on **system**. The mainstream structural conception is reflected in the characterization of "morphology" in introductory accounts.[12] For example:

Aronoff and Fudeman (2011: 1): "In linguistics *morphology* refers to the mental system involved in **word** formation or to the branch of linguistics that with words, their internal structure, and how they are formed."

Lieber (2013: 2): "morphology is the study of word formation, including the ways new words are coined in the languages of the world, and the way forms of words are varied depending on how they're used in sentences."

Haspelmath and Sims (2010: 1): "Morphology is the study of the internal structure of words."

Wikipedia: "In linguistics, morphology is the identification, analysis, and description of the structure of a given language's morphemes and other linguistic units, such as root words, affixes, parts of speech, intonations and stresses, or implied context."

Thus, the focus tends to be on a syntagmatic conception of morphology, or **morphotactics**. In contrast, in SFL morphology is viewed paradigmatically as the ***resource of making meaning with words*** – the lexicogrammatical options in wording available to language users at word rank.[13] The fundamental contrast in the conception of morphology between paradigmatic and syntagmatic approaches can be characterized with reference to the comparison of models in the 1950s initiated by Hockett's (1954) distinction between *item-and-arrangement* (IA), *item-and-process* (IP) and *word-and-paradigm* (WP) models, and supplemented by Robins' (1959) defence of WP.[14] IA and IP are concerned with structure in the first instance. In contrast, WP is concerned with paradigm in the first instance. It originated with traditional grammar – the familiar paradigms of nouns, adjectives, pronouns, verbs, and other word classes; and it is the closest to the systemic approach, which was brought out by Hudson's (1973) account of Beja morphology.[15] One key difference between WP and the systemic approach is that in SFL, the system behind paradigms is modelled – the system that defines or generates paradigms (as Halliday [1966a] put it during the period of the concept of "deep grammar" in generative linguistics, a system is a "deep paradigm"). Another is that **realization statements** are specified, thus making the relationship between system and structure fully explicit. Yet another is that WP is just a special case of "unit paradigms" – it's systems all the way, from clause to word or morpheme: a word paradigm is simply the paradigm of a unit at word rank, and like paradigms at other ranks, it is engendered by systems.

Table 11.2 Metafunctional organization of content plane – mode of meaning and mode of expression

Metafunction	Mode of meaning	Mode of expression	
ideational: logical	construing experience as meaning	univariate	serial
ideational: experiential		multivariate	configurational
interpersonal	enacting roles and relations as meaning		prosodic
textual	presenting meanings as salient ~ non-salient		periodic

The systemic approach to morphology – i.e. the approach of taking paradigmatic organization as primary – has a number of important consequences; for example, it makes it possible to do the following:

- Abstract away from **varied realizations** ("segmental" vs. "non-segmental" in many discussions, but see immediately below on modes of expression) in order to capture systemic generalizations.
- Avoid having to posit a layer of additional syntagmatic items (e.g. "underlying representation") to handle suppletive allomorphs and lexicogrammatically conditioned allomorphs since this variation turns out to be simply a matter of variation in realization of options in different systemic environments.
- Provide a location for **probabilities** as properties of systemic options.
- Bring out **parametric pressures** e.g. in terms of analogy (cf. Heller and Macris 1967).
- Represent **grammaticalization** as a gradual move along the cline of delicacy from open lexical sets to closed grammatical systems (as well as a descent along the rank scale).

11.3.2 Metafunction

While there are various functional theories of language in general and of grammar in particular, the **metafunctional theory** developed originally by Halliday (e.g. 1967/8, 1970a,b; 1979a) within SFL is unique in a number of respects, including the recognition of distinctive metafunctional modes of meaning and the correlation between these and modes of expression (e.g. Halliday 1979a; Matthiessen 1989; Martin 1996): see Table 11.2. It applies to the content plane of language, both semantics and lexicogrammar, and thus also to morphology.[16]

Halliday's metafunctional theory makes it possible to explore how the metafunctions are manifested in morphological systems, e.g.:

- **Logical**: systems of DERIVATION, in principle with the potential for linearly recursive word formation
- **Experiential**: grammatical systems of e.g. GENDER (CLASS), ASPECT, TENSE; lexical systems of DENOTATION
- **Interpersonal**: grammatical systems of e.g. PERSON, MODE; lexical systems of CONNOTATION
- **Textual**: grammatical systems of "PRESENTATION" (e.g. VOICE, REFERENCE).

What systems are manifested within the different metafunctions at word rank is, of course, subject to considerable cross-linguistic variation. For example, languages may have interpersonal systems with the verb and the noun as their domains – verbal systems of mode or evidentiality, or of "speech level" (some combination of formality and honorification), and nominal systems of attitude. One interesting open empirical issue is to what extent textual considerations are manifested in words, e.g. whether they correlate with preferences for prefixing, suffixing, a mixture, or some other type. Morphological "mechanisms" that have been described for many languages in the typological literature may serve one metafunction in one language but another metafunction in another language. For example, reduplication is likely to be experiential if it serves as a realization of 'plural' but interpersonal if it serves as a realization of 'amplification.' This relates to the issue of the correlation of modes of expression with modes of meaning, as summarized in Table 11.2.

As Figure 11.6 indicates, logical organization is distinct from the three other modes of organization in that it is **univariate** rather than multivariate (cf. Halliday 1965, 1979a). Structurally this means that logical organization is serial and involves internal nesting, which is reflected in the idea of "hierarchic structure" in syntagmatically-based accounts of morphology (see e.g. Haspelmath and Sims 2010: ch. 7 on "morphological trees"). For example, the adjective *unavoidable* can be analysed logically as shown in Figure 11.6.

The logical univariate organization involves internal nesting. To bring this out, the logical structure can be visualized by means of the graphic representation used in RST (Rhetorical Structure Theory), as illustrated in Halliday and Matthiessen (2014: ch. 7) for clause complexes; thus, the logical structure of *indecipherability* –

un-	*avoid*	*-able*
β	αα	αβ

tru(e)	*th*	*ful*	*ly*
α	βα	ββα	βββ

Figure 11.6 Logical analysis of words as morpheme complexes

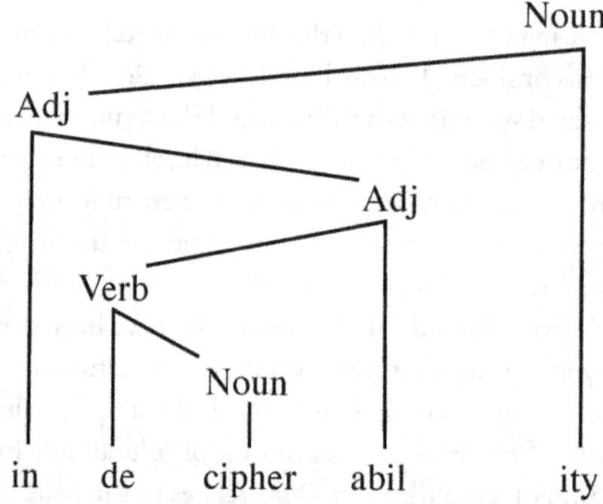

Figure 11.7 Spencer's (1994: 74) IC analysis of *indecipherability*

αβ [*in-*] αααβ [*de-*] αααα [*cipher*] ααβ [*-able*] β [*-ity*] – is visualized in this way in Figure 11.8. This can be compared with the IC (Immediate Constituent) analysis given by Spencer (1994: 74), from whom I've taken the example of *indecipherability*: see Figure 11.7.

Similarly, compounds also display internal nesting in their logical structure, as in the two contrasting examples from Halliday (1965/1981: 36) shown in Figure 11.9.

This analysis of morpheme complexes brings out the analogy between morpheme complexes and groups (which can be interpreted as word complexes up to a point; cf. Halliday and Matthiessen 2014: ch. 6), and also between morpheme complexes and complexes at other ranks. Using a tired old example,

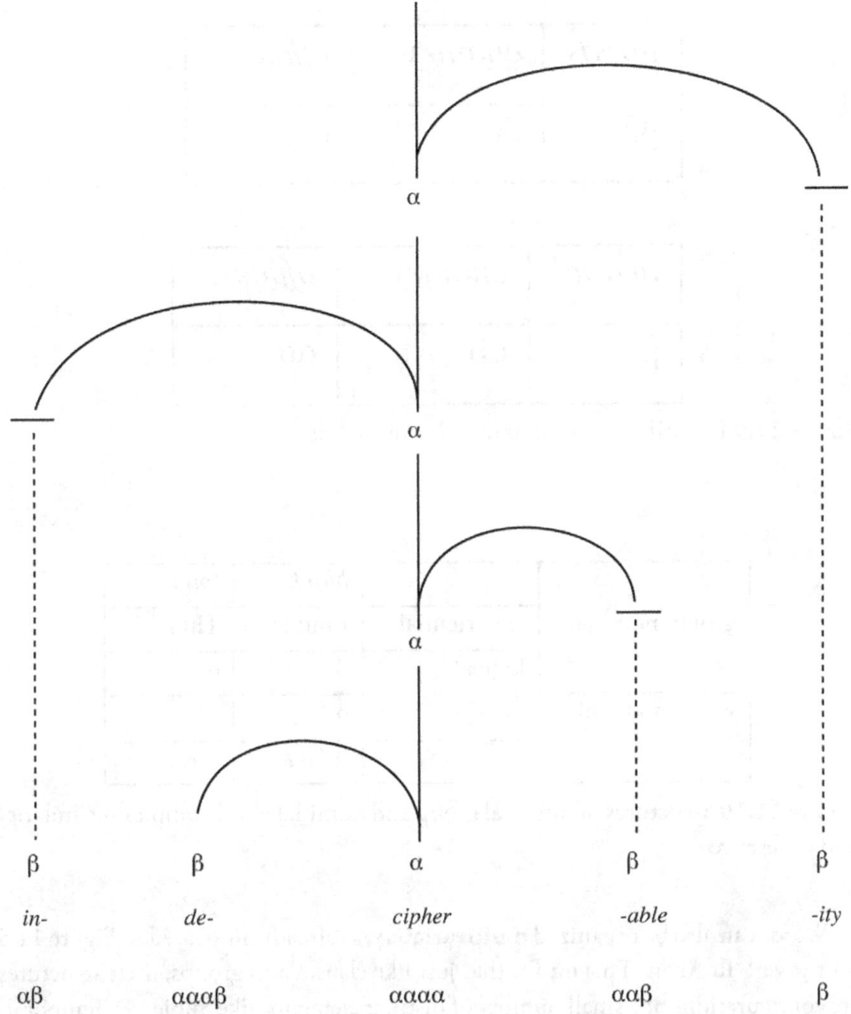

Figure 11.8 Visualization of the logical structure of *indecipherability* by means of the graphic conventions of RST

we can distinguish between two analyses of *black bird*, (i) as a nominal group fragment, in which case it has the accent pattern *black 'bird* and is spelt as two orthographic words, and (ii) as a nominal word complex, a compound, in which case it has the accent pattern *'blackbird* and is spelt as one orthographic word (Figure 11.10). They share the logical (univariate) structure β ^ α, but they differ in that the nominal group also has an experiential (multivariate) structure, Epithet ^ Thing.

goods	*enquiry*	*office*
ββ	βα	α

branch	*enquiry*	*office*
β	αβ	αα

Figure 11.9 Logical analysis of nominal compounds

		black	**'bird**
group: nominal	experiential	Epithet	Thing
	logical	β	α
word: nominal		β	α
		'black	*bird*

Figure 11.10 Structures of nominal group and nominal word complex – similarity and difference

Words can also be organized **multivariately**, as already illustrated in Figure 11.5 for the verb in Akan. This means that just like clauses and groups, their structures are configurations of a small number of distinct elements, like Subject ^ Temporal$_1$ ^ Modal ^ Event ^ Temporal$_2$ in the Akan verb. As in groups, such multivariate structures may be simultaneous with univariate structures: the two types of structure capture different generalizations about the structure of words. In polysynthetic languages, the structures of verbs are more extended and can be interpreted multivariately; their structures are configurations of elements that in non-polysynthetic languages would be likely to occur in the verbal group (e.g. Temporal and Modal elements) or in the clause (e.g. elements of the core transitivity structure, and of mood). For example, in her description of the grammar of Mapuche, Smeets (2008: 17–20, part V) identifies thirty-six elements, or "slots," that are "filled" by one of around a hundred verbal suffixes, the multivariate macro-structure being "(Root) – Valency modifiers – Aspect – Semantic modifiers – Truth value – Flection" (p. 149). Such extended verb morphology is, of course, common in indigenous languages spoken in the Americas.

Multivariate word structures may embody contributions from the different metafunctions; i.e. elements of multivariate structures may realize options in experiential, interpersonal, or textual word systems. For example, in the Akan verb (Figure 11.5), the Temporal elements realize options in experiential systems and the Modal element realizes options in interpersonal systems. In this respect, words in languages with elaborate word grammars are like groups in languages such as English, Chinese, Vietnamese, and Thai: multivariate structures of words and groups are multifunctional in nature, and they contrast with multivariate structures of clauses, where each metafunction engenders its own functional structure like the transitivity (experiential), mood (interpersonal) and theme (textual) structures of the clauses of many languages. But this is of course an area where we need many more comprehensive descriptions of large numbers of languages with different characteristics.

As I noted above and summarized in Table 11.2, the different metafunctional modes of meaning tend to be realized by different **modes of structure**. This is perhaps seen more clearly in the clause (as in Halliday 1979a), but these tendencies are also manifested in the structure of words. Thus, interpersonal structure is **prosodic** in nature, a prototypical example being an intonation contour extending over a clause in the unmarked case (see Halliday 1967; Halliday and Greaves 2008); but prosodic structures are also found at word rank, which is brought out by Poynton's (1984) study of interpersonal choices in the system of address in Australian English. She shows how iterations of suffixes can create interpersonal prosodies, e.g. of endearment in *Gregsypoodles*, made up of *Greg* + *-s* + *-y* + *-poo* + *-dle* + *-s* (p. 197), and intensified by the length of the prosody (in contrast with the nesting in derivations like "in-de-cipher-able-ity" above). Similarly, swearing can be expressed prosodically, and the placement of expletives in the structure of words can be interpreted as prosodic: in English, they can occur as infixes, as exemplified by Aronoff and Fudeman (2011): *fan* + *fucking* + *tastic*, *abso* + *effing* + *lutely*.

11.4   Word grammar and language typology

3. How does the systemic functional theory analyse and/or classify the different morphological types of languages?

From the start, the position in the SFL tradition has been that language typology is best carried out *in terms of particular systems* rather than of whole languages, as scholars tended to do in the nineteenth century when morphological types of language were first proposed. Thus Halliday (1959–60) writes:

> The first problem in linguistic typology is to decide what is being classified. Traditionally, the answer has been: languages. But this raises a difficulty. This is not primarily the difficulty of defining "a language", since within limits any definition would suffice provided it was adhered to rigorously. Rather the difficulty is that if we want to say that two languages are alike, that Lx resembles Ly, then we must presuppose that Lx resembles itself. (p. 166)
>
> Linguistic typology can thus perhaps be regarded as the typology of language features, rather than as the typology of languages. (p. 177)

There is now general consensus among linguists working on language typology that languages are far too complex to be classified as organic wholes, and the empirical work on language typology represented by the World Atlas of Language Structures (WALS) database (e.g. Dryer and Haspelmath 2013) as a great resource is geared towards features, many of which can be interpreted as systemic features in systems such as tense, aspect, number, and person. Databases of this kind provide a foundation for empirical work on morphologic typology, and make it possible to investigate syndromes of combinations of features.

The classic morphological typology developed in the nineteenth century was in a sense deconstructed already by Sapir (1921). Reviewing such contributions to morphological typology and continuing Sapir's approach of deconstructing the earlier typologies, Comrie (1981) suggests two different indices, the **index of synthesis** and the **index of fusion**. Such distinctions fall out naturally from the architecture of systemic functional accounts of morphology since they reflect different dimensions of organization (cf. Figures 11.1 and 11.2):

- **Rank:** The **index of synthesis** relates to the rank scale of lexicogrammar; it reflects the rank-based division of lexicogrammar labour of a language – the division of this labour across ranks.
- **Axis:** The **index of fusion** relates to the dimension of axis; it reflects the realization of systemic features by grammatical items at morpheme rank, i.e. by morphemes.

I will discuss each in turn, taking these two dimensions as illustrations of what can be brought out by SFL in the area of linguistic typology. There are certainly additional important considerations in relation to semiotic dimensions, including the cline of instantiation and the spectrum of metafunction. The former has begun to be illuminated in language typology in studies concerned with grammaticalization, since this, among other things, involves movements along the cline of instantiation as well as the hierarchy of rank. But the latter remains less well explored, although, again, studies of grammaticalization are revealing tendencies such as the move from ideational to interpersonal and textual (cf. Traugott 1997).

11.4.1 Rank

In terms of **rank**, languages vary, as I have put it, with respect to the **division of lexicogrammatical labour** across the ranking units of a language.[17] For example, lexicogrammatical work done at group rank in e.g. Chinese (Halliday and McDonald 2004), Vietnamese (Thai 2004), and Thai (Patpong 2005) is done at word rank in e.g. Japanese (Teruya 2007) and even more so in Mapuche (Smeets 2008), Amuesha (Aikhenvald 2012), and Panare (e.g. Payne 1997). Thus, "morphological types" must be explored in terms of patterns along the rank scale as a whole for grammatical units of different classes, keeping in mind the possibility of different tendencies for nominal and verbal units (e.g. allowing for the possibility of fairly expanded verbs and fairly simple nouns, as is the tendency in polysynthetic languages).

One aspect of this is the need to establish correspondences among languages across ranks in terms of the status and domain of operation of grammatical items, ranging from items operating as particles in the structure of the clause to bound affixes operating in the structure of the word, each type having different phonological properties reflecting the scale from "free" to "bound" grammatical items. Some key correspondences are shown in Figure 11.11. Such correspondences are also likely to constitute **paths of grammaticalization**, as with verb > auxiliary > verbal affix, pronoun > pronominal clitic > pronominal affix. Such paths are **rank descendant**: items move down the rank scale (and at the same time they are likely to move along the cline of delicacy from more delicate to less delicate, and to be gradually reduced phonologically).

As noted above, grammatical items operating at different ranks have different phonological statuses. In their typological overview of the phonological status of "formatives" ("grammatical markers"), Bickel and Nichols (2013a) differentiate three types: isolating formatives ("full-fledged phonological words"), concatenative formatives ("phonologically bound"), and non-linear formatives ("realized not in linear sequence but by direct modification of their host"), viz. ablaut and tone in their sample of languages.[18] Their isolating formatives are thus grammatical items that operate at clause (or group) rank; their concatenative formatives are

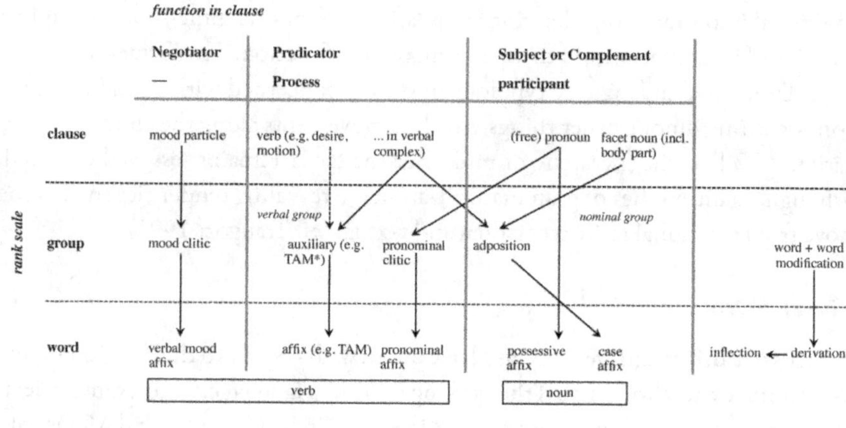

Figure 11.11 Examples of correspondences of grammatical items across the rank scale, e.g. from free modal particles serving in the clause to bound modal affixes serving in the verb

grammatical items that operate as clitics at group rank or as bound affixes at word rank; and their non-linear formatives operate at word rank.

Correspondences between grammatical items at different ranks of the kind illustrated in Figure 11.11 above are concerned with the ranks of the **domains of realization** of options in systems but not with the **location of the systems** themselves. This can be illustrated for the system of polarity, the contrast between 'positive' and 'negative' clauses: see Figure 11.12. It is perfectly possible that this system has the clause as its **systemic domain** of operation, interacting with other clausal systems such as mood (the grammar of speech function), regardless of whether the realization of the 'negative' option operates in the clause, the verbal group, or the verb.

The rank position of items of realization thus has to be separated from the question of where the relevant system is located, the systemic domain. But this question is of central interest in typological work relating to morphology. Since many typological investigations are concerned with the rank of *items* rather than with that of *systems*, we still know much less about the degree to which languages vary with respect to the location of systems that are comparable across languages. It is clear that items drift down the rank scale over time, but to what extent does this affect the systems whose terms they serve as realizations of? The terms of a given system may in a sense be realized at different ranks, as with the well-known case of tense systems where terms may be realized by tense auxiliaries and/or tense affixes (Table 11.3). And there may be even more variation in the nature of the realization

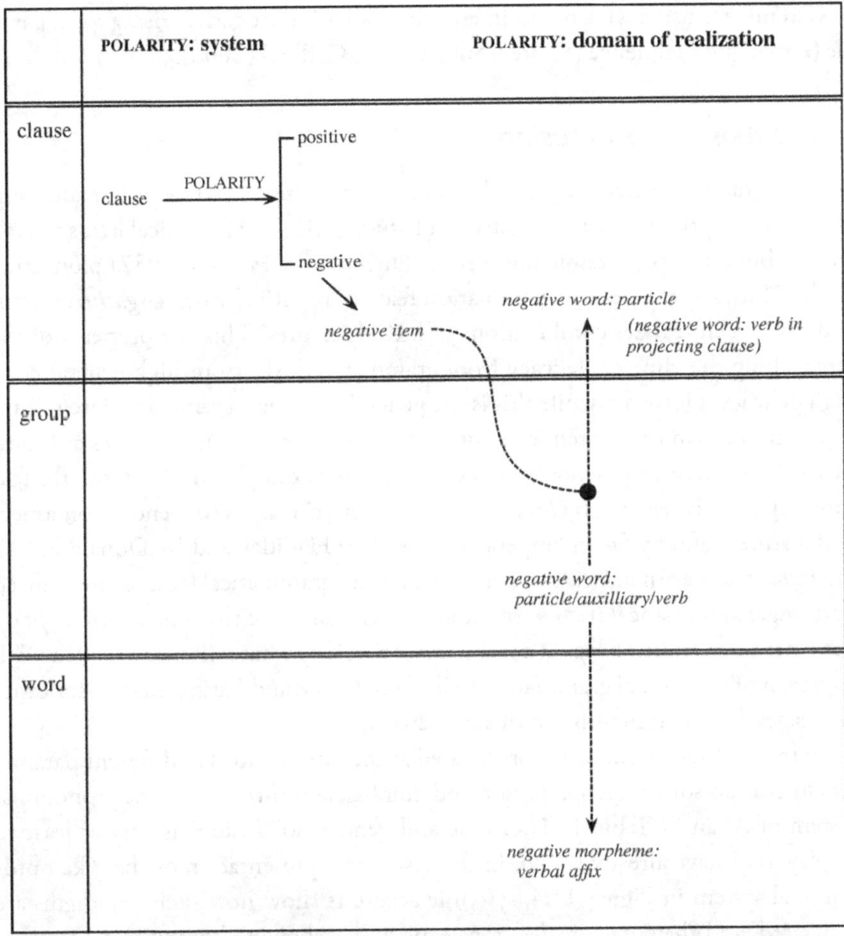

Figure 11.12 Segmental realizations of the 'negative' terms in the system of polarity – realizational spread of negative items in terms of rank around the languages of the world

Table 11.3 Rank of realizations of terms in the primary tense system of English

	Past	**Present**	**Future**
group rank: auxiliary	[*did*]	[*does*]	*will* (*shall*)
word rank: suffix	v-*ed*	Ø	–

of systemic terms, as with mood in French – polar interrogative: rising tone/particle (est-ce que)/sequence (Finite ^ Subject): see Caffarel (2006).

11.4.2 Axis: index of fusion

In lexicogrammar, there is a general tendency for **grammatical** items to realize single systemic options, as with 'negative' in Figure 11.12, and for lexical items to realize combinations of systemic options, as illustrated by Hasan's (1987) pioneering study. Thus, *not* realizes the grammatical feature 'negative,' whereas *gather*, *scatter*, and *strew* each realizes combinations of lexical features. This is a property of the move along the cline of delicacy from grammar to lexis, from high generality to high delicacy. However, while this is the general tendency, grammatical items may realize more than one systemic feature, although never as many features as lexical items. This can be represented as conditioning; for example, in Mandarin, the feature 'negative' is realized by *bu* or *mei* in 'indicative' clauses (depending on aspectual features) and by *bie* in 'imperative' ones (see Halliday and McDonald 2004). However, there are many cases where two or more grammatical features are realized by a single grammatical item without any particular sense that one is primary and the others are conditioning. In a sense, this is precisely what is illustrated by the WP approach of traditional grammar, initially from Greek and Latin and then for other languages described in terms of this framework.

In the WP approach, words are located at the intersections of different parameters such as person and tense, person and number, as illustrated for the pronominal system of Akan in Table 11.1, or case and gender, so "fusion" is easy at least to display. As I have already shown in the systemic representation of the Akan pronominal system in Figure 11.4, systemic accounts show how such paradigms are generated, and they make realizations explicit, i.e. showing how systemic features are realized by grammatical (or lexical) items. Consequently, the degree of fusion turns out to be simply **a measure of the number of systemic features realized by a single item**.[19] Let me illustrate this by means of a sketch of the system of specific (definite) determination in German: see Figure 11.13. In this systemic description, there are two primary systems, number and case. In the system of number, the feature 'singular' leads to the system of gender; i.e. 'singular' is the entry condition of that system. This is simply because in the system of determination, there are no gender contrasts in the plural.

The realizations in the system of determination in Figure 11.13 are shown in **gates**, "systems" with complex entry conditions and a single option or feature (e.g. Matthiessen 1985; these are not labelled here but they could be, e.g. 'nominative

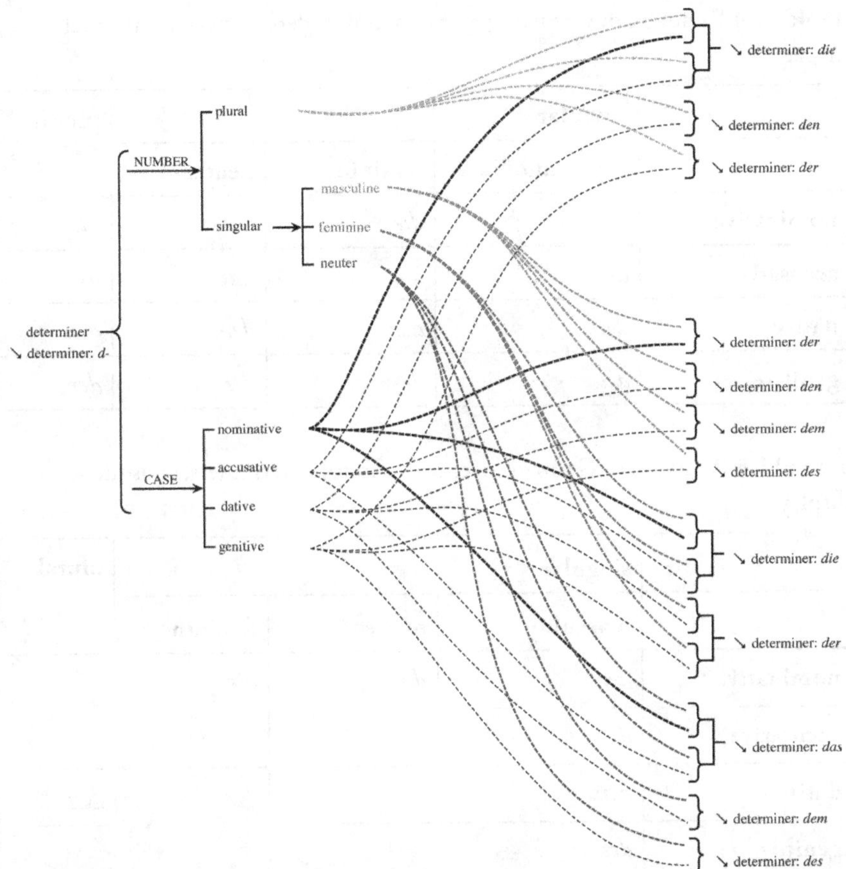

Figure 11.13 Sketch of system of specific (definite) determination in German, with complexes of features from systems of number and case realized by specific determiners

singular masculine determiner'). These gates represent the "fusion," the complex of features realized by a single item such as *der*. The realization statements are informal, but they serve to illustrate how the degree of fusion is reflected simply by the realization patterns. In German, all specific determiners are realized by one syllable with the phonotactic structure Onset: C_1 ^ Rhyme [Peak: V (^ Coda: C)] – the syntagm of phoneme classes thus being C_1VC_2. The consonant realizing the Onset, C_1, is always /d/, and the Rhyme is /ɛr/, /i:/, /e:m/, or /as/, the vowel realizing the Peak thus being either unrounded front or central, ranging from close to open.[20]

Table 11.4 Paradigm of German specific (definite) determiners, traditional display

	singular			plural
	masculine	feminine	neuter	
nominative	*der*	*die*	*das*	*die*
accusative	*den*	*die*	*das*	*die*
dative	*dem*	*der*	*dem*	*den*
genitive	*des*	*der*	*des*	*der*

Table 11.5 Paradigm of German specific (definite) determiners, consolidate display

	singular			plural
	masculine	neuter	feminine	
nominative	*der*	*das*	*die*	
accusative	*den*			
dative	*dem*		*der*	*den*
genitive	*des*			

In the traditional paradigms of specific determiners in German, the same phonological/orthographic "word" appears in different places, as shown in Table 11.4. Thus, in the traditional account, there are simply two different items *den*, one realizing 'masculine' and 'accusative' and the other realizing 'plural' and 'dative.' It is possible to bring out the distribution of each item by rearranging the tabular display, as in Table 11.5. This still leaves two locations for *der* and *den*. In the systemic representation capturing such generalizations would be easy; for example, we could introduce additional gates with disjunctive entry conditions for each distinct form of the specific determiner. However, the more interesting descriptive issue is whether systems could be revised to capture generalizations such as the neutralization of 'nominative' and 'accusative' except in the 'masculine' gender. Elsewhere in the description of case in German, it makes sense to begin by distinguishing 'nominative' and 'oblique,' and then 'oblique: accusative/dative/genitive.'[21] But these are issues specific to the description of German, and my point is simply that the systemic description makes it possible to raise such issues and explore different accounts.

11.4.3 Other considerations

I have used the dimensions of rank and axis to explore some central aspects of morphological typology. Another dimension that is important from the point of view of linguistic typology is the hierarchy of stratification. The interface between lexicogrammar and phonology (and secondarily, in languages with writing systems, graphology) is subject to cross-linguistic variation in terms of patterns of phonological (graphological) realization (cf. Figure 11.2; Dixon and Aikhenvald 2003: 13-18, on phonological words): is there a phonological (graphological) correlate of the word or morpheme (or of any other grammatical unit); what are the patterns of syllabification; what are patterns of realization relating to vowel harmony, accent patterns, and other prosodic features such as juncture prosodies (such as /ʔ/ in German before words beginning with a vowel)?

At the same time, it is clearly important not to isolate morphological typology from lexicogrammatical typology in general. There are likely to be descriptive fractals with patterns of manifestations across different ranks of lexicogrammars, e.g. pertaining to univariate patterns. And patterns of realization touched on in the previous subsection are relevant across ranks, not only at word rank. For example, the presence of *do* as Finite in English depends not on a single systemic feature but on a combination of features in the clausal systems of MOOD and POLARITY.

11.5   The lexis–grammar continuum

4. How does the systemic functional theory explain the lexical/grammatical distinction?

As noted above, lexis and grammar are treated as a **continuum** defined by the **cline of delicacy – lexicogrammar**, and not as separate modules. While generative linguistics originally took over Bloomfield's (1933: 269, 274) notion of the lexicon as a special component, a repository of items and irregularities, it is important to note that:

A complete description of language will list every form whose function is not determined by structure or by a marker; it will include,

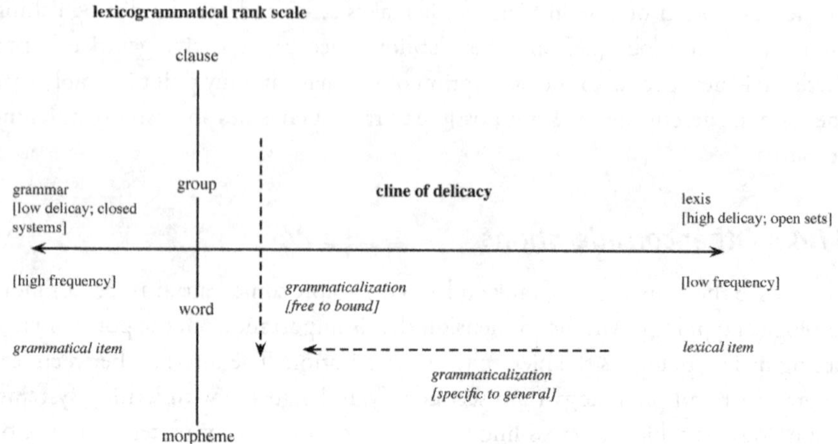

Figure 11.14 Word as location along rank scale and grammatical/lexical items as locations along cline of delicacy

accordingly, a *lexicon*, or list of morphemes, which indicates the form-class of each morpheme, as well as lists of all complex forms whose function is in any way irregular. (p. 269)

The lexicon is really an appendix of the grammar, a list of basic irregularities. This is all the more evident if meanings are taken into consideration, since the meaning of each morpheme belongs to it by an arbitrary tradition. (p. 274)

SF linguists never accepted Bloomfield's position,[22] but instead developed a **systemic conception of lexis**, thus foregrounding the paradigmatic axis while at the same time drawing on Firth's notion of **collocation** to characterize syntagmatic patterns. Within the content plane of language (i.e. semantics and lexicogrammar[23]), lexis is treated as most delicate grammar at the stratum of wording (see e.g. Halliday 1961; Hasan 1987; Matthiessen 1992; Tucker 1998) and as most delicate semantics at the stratum of meaning (see e.g. Halliday and Matthiessen 2006). Lexical items realize (combinations of) systemic features just as grammatical items do.[24] In turn, lexical items are realized by features within the phonological stratum.

Since lexis is modelled in terms of the cline of delicacy in the first instance, it follows that *lexical items are distinct from words*, i.e. from the unit of word on the rank scale between groups and morphemes. This was shown schematically in Figure 11.3 and is represented again as Figure 11.14 with details discussed here added. Lexical items can correspond to one word or one free morpheme (bound ones being grammatical rather than lexical items), or to more than one word or morpheme. **Multi-word lexical items** are quite common in languages; one kind in English discussed and analysed in some detail in Halliday and Matthiessen (2013: ch. 6) is phrasal verbs such as *look up*, *put up with*. Beyond such examples we find the kind of lexical pattern that has become well-known by the name J.R. Firth gave it: **collocation**, or the company that words keep (for an early treatment, see Halliday 1966b; and for a recent exploration, see Tucker 2007).

One consequence of theorizing the relationship between grammar and lexis in terms of the cline of delicacy is that it becomes possible to investigate the **degree of fusion** of lexicogrammatical features in the realization by lexicogrammatical items. Here the general tendency is very clear: towards the grammatical pole of the cline, items tend to realize single or few features, but towards the lexical pole of the cline, items tend to realize complexes of several features. This is in fact the continuum between grammatical items and lexical items: grammatical items realize single or few features in closed grammatical systems, whereas lexical items realize several features in more open systems ("sets"). There is of course cross-linguistic variation; e.g. in English, the grammatical item *the* realizes the single feature 'non-selective' (see Halliday and Matthiessen 2014: 366), but variants of the German equivalent *der* etc. realize combinations of features, as shown in Figure 11.13.

Another consequence is that it becomes possible to produce comprehensive frequency profiles of lexicogrammatical items along the cline of instantiation. The general picture is clear: in the move along the cline of instantiation from most general to most delicate, items realizing features along this path decrease in frequency – first exponentially, then steadily. In other words, grammatical items are much more frequent than lexical ones, but there is an intermediate region of items that lie between grammar and lexis – and this region is, of course, important in the process of the grammaticalization of lexical items.

11.6   Main challenges

5. What are the main challenges of the systemic functional theory concerning the analysis of issues of morphology and its relation to other levels of linguistic analysis?

In a way, at this point, the main challenge is descriptive rather than theoretical; it is to produce many more *descriptions* as part of the systemic functional descriptions of a growing number of languages. Such descriptions need to be:

- **Comprehensive:** they need to cover systems of all ranks and metafunctions up to a certain point in delicacy, thus representing morphology in its niche in the linguistic ecosystem.

- **Meaning-oriented**: they need to describe lexicogrammar as the lower of the two content plane strata standing in a natural (rather than conventional or arbitrary) relationship to the higher of the two content strata, i.e. semantics.
- **Text-based**: they need to be empirically grounded in extensive analysis of large volumes (archives or corpora) of registerially varied naturally occurring text, thereby also providing the basis for probabilistic description through the analysis of text frequencies.

Like all systemic functional descriptions, descriptions focussed on morphology in particular (within the overall comprehensive description of a language) are designed to be **appliable** (cf. Halliday 2002c; Matthiessen 2014d). This means, among other things, that morphological descriptions of particular languages are not only required to support linguistic comparison, typology, and theory development, but also various applications: they need to be resources in language-based education – e.g. helping the move into subject-specific knowledge in secondary schools and discipline-specific knowledge in universities (as in the teaching of medicine; cf. Chabner 2011, a work that helps medical students by making Greek and Latin morphology in English medical terminology somewhat more accessible), and they need to be resources in the computational modelling of language – explicit and comprehensive enough to support the key tasks of text analysis and text generation by computer (e.g. Matthiessen and Bateman 1991; O'Donnell and Bateman 2005; Teich 2009). From a theoretical point of view, such applications are like an engineering test of the accounts; and from a societal point of view, they relate to the challenge to academic disciplines that they need to take **social accountability** very seriously, building it into the centre of the academic vision and program (cf. Halliday 1984b; Matthiessen 2012).

As we move around the languages of the world, we find many descriptive challenges – i.e. challenges in the description of particular languages that may be purely descriptive or also have a theoretical component. One class of descriptive challenge we find in various languages has to do with related patterns at different ranks and the degree of naturalness in the relation between lexicogrammar and semantics – familiar e.g. from descriptions of gender and noun class systems (cf. Corbett 1991). Let me just give a brief example of such a descriptive challenge.

In Modern Standard Arabic (MSA; e.g. Badawi, Carter, and Gully 2004/2016; Ryding 2005; for a systemic functional description, see Bardi 2008), there are fifteen derivational morphological classes of triliteral verbs, ten of which are reasonably common and productive, but fewer classes of quadriliteral verbs. They are often exemplified in terms of the triliteral verb 'do,' with the basic pattern of consonantal template (radicals) of /f - ʕ - l/, in Arabic script فعل, or of the triliteral verb 'write,' with the basic pattern of consonantal template (radicals) of /k - t - b/, in Arabic script كتب. These are basic forms belonging to class I, and like class I stems in general, they can be "augmented" by transfixes according to regular patterns to form derived stems of other classes. For example, class II is characterized by a geminate second radical, as in *faʕʕala*; class III by a long version of the first syllable, as in *fa:ʕala*; class IV by the prefix *ʔa-* and absence of a vowel after the second radical, as in *ʔafʕala*; and class V by the prefix *ta-*, as in *tafaʕala*. The different verb classes have class meanings that are clearly related to the clausal system of TRANSITIVITY; they include causative, stative, reflexive, and reciprocal – a number of which relate to transitivity contrasts in valency (cf. Haspelmath and Sims 2010). For example, class II and IV verbs are causative variants of class I (or transitive, if class I is intransitive); class V verbs are middle variants of class II.

Thus, one central descriptive task is to work out the correspondences between options in the system of **transitivity** and options in the system of verb classes. However, on the one hand, there may be gaps in the derivation of particular verbs, and on the other hand, the meanings of derived forms may be different from the predictable meaning of a given class since particular verbs tend to evolve new meanings. The descriptive challenge is thus to identify all the correspondence between clausal **transitivity** options, e.g. in the system of **agency** ('middle'/'effective') and verb classes, and to find ways of dealing with gaps in the derivational classes of particular verbs and with meanings that are not predicted by the verb class meanings.

This kind of "tension" between higher-ranking grammar and lower-ranking grammar is a familiar one in the description of languages, and between highly general grammatical systems (such as the system of agency) and much more delicate lexical systems. Examples similar to the verb classes in MSA could be drawn from noun classes (gender) in various language, e.g. Bantu languages or various languages spoken in Australia.

11.7 Current research proposals

6. What are the current research proposals of the systemic functional theory for the study of lexical and morphological phenomena of natural languages?

Writing in the mid-1990s, Halliday (1994b/2004a: 437) points out that morphology has not been a focus of research: "in other respects systemic work is notably ill-balanced; there has been little study of morphology and phonology."

In the two decades since then, there have been few studies specifically focussed on word grammar; but the situation has still improved descriptively since systemic functional linguists have worked on various languages with a good deal of morphology, including Japanese, Korean, Finnish, Arabic, Western Desert (e.g. Shore 1992; Rose 2001; Teruya 2007; Bardi 2008; cf. Teruya and Matthiessen 2015). However, the empirical base of descriptions against which the theory is constantly being tested through applications needs to be expanded quite significantly. It is important to produce thematic publications that highlight the descriptive work on the word grammars of this growing range of languages in order to ensure that recurrent motifs will be documented and that this very valuable work will become more widely known.

At the same time, it is clearly essential to undertake new research into the lexicogrammar of words as part of the overall investigation of the lexicogrammars of different languages – research that is empirically grounded in large registerially varied corpora of texts, thus including the potential for quantitative analysis (cf. Baayen 2003), and research designed to shed light on the meaning-making potential of word grammar.

In future research, it would be very helpful if researchers can focus on the **systemic organization** of morphology in order to bring out the **implicate order** of paradigmatic organization that engenders the **explicate order** of syntagmatic organization,[25] thus showing the morphological potential of a language and complementing the syntagmatic concerns of most studies of morphology. This would mean both investigating phenomena that do not tend to come into focus in syntagmatically oriented investigations of morphology and reviewing well-known phenomena such as allomorphy, grammaticalization, and degrees of productivity in paradigmatic terms instead of mainly in syntagmatic terms.

11.8   Assessment of work on morphology

7 As an important researcher in linguistics, how do you assess the recent researches on morphology developed from the theoretical perspective of systemic functional linguistics? Are the results positive or is still there a lot for doing in this research area?

From the point of view of SFL, looking in from outside, as it were, at non-systemic functional work on morphology, there are certainly many positive results – in particular, the impressive body of descriptions of an increasing number of languages, covering different geographic areas, families, and linguistic types; and this descriptive body of work provides a more solid data source for linguistic comparison, typology, and theory. Here, the work on grammaticalization during the last couple of decades has been enormously important, also theoretically, showing for example the need for unified accounts of "morpho-syntax" – i.e. grammar in our (traditional) sense – and also of lexis.

There have also clearly been advances in theory covering the domain of morphology, including the probabilistic conception of morphology (e.g. Baayen 2003). Outside SFL, it is probably fair to say that there is as yet no consensus about the relationship between syntax and morphology – whether they are separate modules or a unified one (cf. e.g. Haspelmath and Sims 2010: section 7.4). In SFL, the position is quite clear: theoretically, they are simply regions within the stratum of lexicogrammar, and differences will depend on the nature of particular languages as they are revealed empirically in descriptions.

In terms of SFL, the "mainstream" theoretical conception of morphology still seems restricted in its theoretical and descriptive scope; it is focussed on the structure of words rather than on morphology as a subsystem of the system of language. In other words, the paradigmatic properties of morphology have still not been brought out sufficiently clearly or systematically, leaving key questions unanswered. Similarly, morphological theory could be illuminated by a metafunctional interpretation of the organization of morphological resources.

Personally, I think a good deal of work on morphology (and also on phonology) suffers from the lack of a clear distinction between high-level **theory** and lower-level **representation** of theory by means of some system of notation, whether this system is fairly informal or more formal with mathematically well-understood representation properties (such as typed feature structures). It is very important to be able to bring out leading theoretical ideas and key insights while at the same time allowing for the possibility of different forms of representation (and further down the hierarchy, in computational modelling, of different programming languages). Sometimes scholars may be seduced and distracted by the challenge and excitement of solving morphological jigsaw puzzles in terms of some semi-formal notation and lose sight of the fundamental theoretical questions.

11.9   Potential for research on word grammar

8. What kind of advice would you give to those readers who wish to start their studies in morphology from the theoretical perspective of systemic functional linguistics? And what publications or papers on this subject do you recommend for these readers?

The potential is very considerable – partly since the vast majority of work on morphology has been focussed on structure, in some version of IA or IP, rather than on system; so there are clearly important discoveries to be made by undertaking extensive systemic descriptions as part of the overall description of lexicogrammars of a wide variety of languages. Various issues have been examined in structural terms, like characterization of agglutinative structures, morphemes, and pattern structures, and it would be very valuable to re-examine these in systemic terms.

My advice would be to set out on a twenty-first-century investigation of morphology as part of the *system* of lexicogrammar, and as part of the *system* of language as a whole, drawing on the resources that have now become available, like the WALS database and corpora of various languages, and the technologies that have been developed in corpus linguistics and (more significantly at present) in natural language processing, like taggers and (morphological) parsers and machine learning techniques. In terms of data, the project would thus be like other current "usage-based theories," but in terms of theory, the project would be aligned with systems thinking, complexity studies (cf. Beckner et al. 2009), and relational modelling. Drawing out the implications of Halliday's "axial rethink" (Matthiessen 2014d/2021b) for morphology as part of lexicogrammar would be a valuable research project in its own right – *re-imagining morphology* not as simply the structure of words but as the system for creating meanings through words. This would, of course, go together with the *re-imagining of phonology* as the sounding potential of language, serving as the resource for realizing wordings (lexicogrammar) as sound.

11.10 Conclusion

The task assigned to me in writing this chapter has been to outline the SFL approach to morphology by addressing eight key questions. This is a challenge because, unlike many theories and frameworks, SFL does not theorize and model morphology as a separate component or module in the overall "architecture" of language. This means that it is really necessary to take a few steps back to the point where there are no assumptions about morphology as a separate entity. And there are related challenges such as the standard view of the "lexicon" as a separate module and the orientation towards the syntagmatic axis and the focus on structure. The way in which SFL differs from most current theories and approaches would be brought out clearly if one tried to adapt the framework devised by Stewart (2008) in his excellent "A consumer's guide to contemporary morphological theories." For example, the fundamental issue of axial orientation – paradigmatic or syntagmatic – isn't part of this framework; but it would need to be in order to expand the overview to include SFL since the paradigmatic orientation of SFL permeates the whole conception and modelling of language (cf. Matthiessen 2015c).

Organizing my account around the eight important questions posed by the editors of this volume, I have tried to produce a reasonably coherent account of the

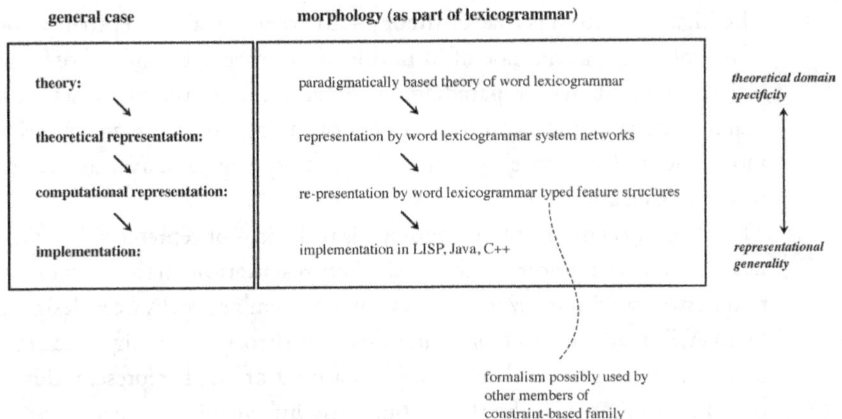

Figure 11.15 The stratification of metalanguage in the case of morphology (as part of lexicogrammar)

SFL account of that area of lexicogrammar that has been labelled "morphology" in linguistics. There are clearly many gaps in my account. By way of conclusion, let me mention just one that I have alluded to above: the **stratification of the metalanguage** that we use to give accounts of morphology.

The need to stratify descriptions of linguistic systems became very clear in computational linguistics and AI in the late 1970s in the area of knowledge representation – which can be seen as concern with the representation of meaning (cf. Halliday and Matthiessen 1999/2006). In a classic paper, Woods (1975) critiqued the free-for-all in the development and use of semantic networks, arguing for the need for explicit specifications of the interpretation of such networks. This was first addressed by Brachman (1979) in another classic and pioneering article where he articulated the "epistemological status" of the different abstractions in semantic networks. His proposal was to distinguish different levels of specification, distinguishing e.g. an epistemological level from an implementational one, and to ensure that graphic representations had clear algebraic interpretations. It influenced his own work on KR as a frame-based inheritance network, KL-ONE, and on other contributions since the early 1980s – now also very relevant to the work on "ontologies" (cf. Guarino 2009). Brachman's notion of levels can be interpreted more generally as **strata in the metalanguages** we use in describing languages (see e.g. Matthiessen 1988a; Halliday and Matthiessen 1999/2006; Teich 1999; Matthiessen 2007a). Here the stratal range is from theory to computational model or implementation: see Figure 11.15.

1. The highest stratum is that of **theory** – the theoretical conceptualization of morphology; in the case of SFL, this means theoretical model of word lexicogrammar based on paradigmatic organization in the first instance – making the systemic organization of morphology primary, and treating morphological structures, patterns along the syntagmatic axis, as derived through realization.

2. This theoretical model of morphology is realized – or represented – at the next stratum, the stratum of **theoretical representation**, in the form of system networks with realization statements. System networks were designed by M.A.K. Halliday as a representation of his theory of paradigmatic organization. They can be characterized as a kind of graph representation – one that is tailored to the theory but fairly informal in character. System networks have less coverage than the theory of paradigmatic organization; e.g. the theory says that the terms of systems form the outer poles of clines rather than discrete categories, but in the systems of system networks, the features are treated as discrete. One might say that they describe crisp rather than fuzzy sets – if one were to interpret the representation in set theoretic terms (cf. Matthiessen 1995b).

3. System networks have been re-represented one metalinguistic stratum down by means of different more **computationally oriented formalisms**; examples of different approaches include Patten and Ritchie (1987), Mellish (1988), and Bateman, Emele, and Momma (1992). These re-representations gain in explicitness, moving (closer) to formalism that has been implemented computationally, with well-understood mathematical properties; but they have less expressive coverage than system networks with realization statements.

4. The lowest stratum in the metalanguage is thus the **implementation of the computational representation** in some programming language such as LISP, Prolog, Java, or C++; in principle, the same computational representation should be implementable, and re-implementable, in different programming languages – there should be a certain degree of arbitrariness between the two strata. The stratal ascent constitutes a step-by-step increase in formal **explicitness**, but a gradual loss in **coverage** of linguistic phenomena. In this sense, the theoretical stratum has the potential for the most comprehensive coverage of morphological phenomena. At the same time, as indicated in Figure 11.15, the stratal ascent is also a move from a specifically linguistic theory to programming languages that are quite general in terms of what they can represent. As we move to the stratum of computational representation, we are likely to bump into representations used

by other linguistic theories: this is the area discussed under the headings of unification-based grammars, feature-based grammars, and constraint-based grammars. This is thus where it is possible to borrow a formalism from another theory to deal with representational problems (cf. Teich 1999).

The point of this discussion of the stratification of our metalanguage for describing morphological phenomena in different languages is to bring out the need for stratal coverage, making sure that these phenomena are dealt with in terms of theory, theoretical representation, computational representation, and (ultimately) implementation in explicit computational models. As I suggested in Section 11.8, my personal view is that a good deal of work on morphological phenomena has neglected theory in favour of representation – or, to put it another way, treated forms of representation as if they were theory. By the same token, we cannot remain within the theoretical stratum; we must extend the coverage to the lower strata where representational issues are exposed and confronted and dealt with.

In the development of holistic accounts of morphology, work on the different metalinguistic strata must proceed in constant dialogue, informing one another. In this short chapter, I have only been able to sketch the systemic functional approach to morphological phenomena at the first two strata, theory and theoretical representation; we need to extend the account downward if we are to develop fully explicit models – and morphological generators, parsers, and translators.

Notes

1　Prosodic analysis was developed in the description of phonological systems, contrasting with the phonemic analysis that grew out of US American structuralist linguistics. It is also relevant to the exploration of morphology, as in Palmer's (1962) description of the broken plural nouns of Tigre. The insights of prosodic analysis have been incorporated in SFL, including in SF phonology (see Halliday 1992d, 2000).

2　With a dramatic increase since around 1980 according to Google's Ngram Viewer. The term appears to reflect the need for treating morphology and syntax as unified rather than separate, thus in a sense recapturing the insight embodied in the traditional use of the term "grammar."

3　For the fundamentally important distinction between the general **theory** of language and **descriptions** of particular languages, see e.g. Halliday (1993c), Matthiessen and Nesbitt (1996), and Matthiessen (2007a).

4　For example, languages may do more work at group rank or at word rank; and while many languages have phrases ("contracted clauses") operating alongside groups at the same rank, other languages appear to manage without phrases. Languages thus also vary in respect of the units of their rank scales, this being a descriptive matter; thus, in the description of prototypical cases of analytical and isolating languages such as Vietnamese, we may not need to distinguish between word and morpheme on the rank scale.

5   **Dimensional architecture** is fundamentally different from componential or **modular architecture**: language is theorized in terms of relations that obtain along semiotic dimensions rather than in terms of components. This relational conception of language in SFL draws on Hjelmslev and is similar to the work in Lamb's stratificational linguistics in certain key respects – but different from the modular conception that has been dominant in the US American structuralist and generative linguistics since the 1930s.

6   Compare Longacre's (1964: 101) definition of the word in terms of the tagmemic equivalent of the rank scale: "a class of syntagmemes of a comparatively low hierarchical order, ranking below such syntagmemes as the phrase and the clause and above such syntagmemes as the stem (as well as above roots which have no external structure and are therefore not syntagmemes)." This is comparable to locating words between groups and morphemes on the rank scale.

7   The theory of language as probabilistic system in SFL goes back to Halliday (1959); for an overview, see Matthiessen (2015b). In the 1960s, this notion ran counter to the prevailing generative metatheory; but the importance of investigating the probabilistic nature of language has now gained much more general acceptance, as in Bod, Hay, and Jannedy (2003), and this includes morphology (see e.g. Baayen 2003; Haspelmath and Sims 2010: ch. 10).

8   Note that **lexical items** are defined in reference to the cline of delicacy, not in reference to rank, as shown in Figure 11.3: lexical items can be morphemes, words, or multi-word expressions. Halliday (1961/2002c: 59) made this clear from the start: "Not only may the lexical item be coextensive with more than one different grammatical unit; it may not be coextensive with any grammatical unit at all, and may indeed cut right across the rank hierarchy." Thus, **word** and **lexical item** are distinct categories in the theory: word is defined in terms of the hierarchy of rank, whereas lexical item is defined in terms of the cline of delicacy.

9   There's a hint of relational characterization of the word in Sapir's (1921: 34) definition, "one of the smallest, completely satisfying bits of isolated 'meaning' into which the sentence resolves itself"; but on the whole linguists have defined the word as a "thing in itself" rather than as a unit defined by its relationship to other units, foregrounding one point of view rather than relying on trinocular vision.

10   According to this network, the distinction in animacy is common to all third person pronouns: this may not be correct. I have found examples for the bound ones and the emphatic free ones; the complement pronoun is omitted if the referent is inanimate.

11   Stewart (2008) surveys thirteen current theories of morphology (morphology, autolexical syntax, categorial morphology, distributed morphology, lexeme–morpheme base morphology, lexical morphology and phonology, natural morphology, network model, network morphology, paradigm function morphology, prosodic morphology, and word syntax) using five parameters, viz. morpheme-based ~ word/lexeme-based, formalist ~ functionalist, in grammar ~ in lexicon, phonological formalism ~ syntactic formalism,

and incremental ~ realizational. It would be possible to use his very helpful framework to profile the SF approach to morphology against the theories he surveys, but it would be necessary to take a step back to unpack some assumptions, e.g. the assumption that the "lexicon" is a module, and it would be valuable to add some parameters, e.g. system-based ~ structure-based.

12   Note incidentally that the Wikipedia entry slips in its characterization of "morphology" from the phenomenon to the study of the phenomenon, and this happens in other discussions of morphology as well – a problem pointed out and discussed by Halliday (1984c); but the emphasis is still on "structure."

13   This of course includes the resources for creating new words that may not yet have become part of the collective resource, as with *unjailbroken* in the following example from Macworld (macworld.co.uk): *We need the install file of the app, but we won't be allowed to install it directly on the iPad (at least, not if it's unjailbroken – is that a word?).*

14   In more recent discussions of approaches to morphology, it is the two that can be derived from the US American tradition, IA and IP, that tend to be discussed. For example, in their excellent introduction to morphology, Aronoff and Fudeman (2011: section 2.5) compare the pros and cons of IA and IP but leave WP out of the discussion entirely. This is, no doubt, because of the focus on the "item," the morpheme as an identifiable segment based on the syntagmatic orientation.

15   Compare his earlier proto-systemic description of Beja in terms of Halliday's scale-and-category theory (Hudson 1964).

16   Here it is important to emphasize again the significance of the paradigmatic orientation of SFL. Having distinguished the different metafunctional types of structure, Halliday (1979a: 79) notes: "Systemic theory takes the system, not the structure, as the basis of the description of a language, and so is able to show how these types of structure function as alternative modes of the realization of systemic options." Thus, while "non-segmental" morphemes have been a concern in US structuralist and subsequent approaches to morphology, they are not at all a problem for systemic accounts; as can be inferred from Halliday's comment just quoted, "segmental" and "non-segmental" morphemes are simply different modes of realization of systemic options – in fact, the modes of realization are more finely differentiated than simply "segmental" vs. "non-segmental," as shown in Table 11.2. (In Firthian prosodic analysis, so-called segments are in a sense simply the limiting case of prosodies – phonematic units where prosodic boundaries coincide.)

17   Bresnan (2001: 6) makes a similar point couched in terms of "competition" rather than "division of labour": "across languages, there often appears to be an inverse relation between the amount of grammatical information expressed by words and the amount expressed by phrases. [...] We can summarize this generalization with the slogan, 'Morphology competes with syntax.'" (In formal linguistics, "phrase" corresponds to both group and phrase in SFL.)

18   In their use of the term, "ablaut" includes the overlay pattern characteristic of Semitic languages.

19   There is variation in terminology here. For example, Bickel and Nichols (2013a,b) use the term "exponence" to refer to "the number of categories that cumulate into a single

formative" and the term "fusion" to refer to "the degree to which grammatical markers (called *formatives* in the following) are phonologically connected to a host word or stem."

20   In a full description, such realizations would be stated in terms of phonological features in phonological systems. This is important for various reasons including the important point that given a systemic description of the phonology of a language, it is possible to choose the delicacy of the specification of phonological properties, thereby avoiding the kind of overspecification in syntagmatic representations of phonological structure that leads to the need for something like rules such as the devoicing rule in German for word-final /-g, -d/ in words like *Krieg, Hund* (cf. the Prague School notion of **archiphoneme**).

21   The genitive is, of course, only a "marginal" case in the realization of elements of the clause (participants and circumstances); its domain is really that of the nominal group. Therefore 'oblique' is really 'accusative' vs. 'dative.'

22   See e.g. Matthiessen (1992), Wanner (1997). Lexicalist developments since the early 1970s within generative linguistics have moved it closer to SFL in certain respects, and work within different versions of construction grammar is closer still, but the conceptions tend to differ from SFL in that they are structural rather than systemic in orientation.

23   As opposed to the expression plane of language, phonology, and phonetics (or graphology and graphetics).

24   The systemic functional approach is thus ***different from*** "componential analysis," originally from anthropological linguistics (e.g. Goodenough 1956): see Halliday and Matthiessen (2006). In componential analysis, features interpreted syntagmatically; they are components of the senses of lexical items. In contrast, in systemic analysis, features are interpreted paradigmatically; they are parameter values, opening up the possibility of fuzzy modelling (cf. Matthiessen 1995).

25   Using these terms in the sense of Bohm (1980) as they have been taken up in linguistics.

Chapter 12

The architecture of language according to SFL: some reflections on implications for neurosemiotics

12.1   Introduction

This chapter originated in a series of exchanges with Adolfo García on the topic of SFL and the developing field of neurosemiotics, which he is a leading contributor to: see e.g. García, Franco-O'Byrne, and Ibáñez (2020) and García and Ibáñez (2023). I'm very grateful to him for his insights and his pioneering research into language and the brain guided by systemic functional linguistics and relational network theory.

I'll take "neurosemiotics" to refer to the relationship between systems operating in two distinct phenomenal realms, of different orders of complexity, viz. **biological systems** and **semiotic systems**.[1] Within biological systems, the focus is on the domain of neurobiology. In this respect neurosemiotics is comparable to another exploration of a bridge between systemic orders, viz. social neuroscience (e.g. Cacioppo and Decety 2011) and neurosociology (e.g. Franks 2010), mappings between the neurobiological and social orders (see Ibáñez, Sedeño, and García 2017). I'll explore the relationship between the neurobiological and semiotic orders from the point of view of systemic functional linguistics (SFL), discussing the relationship by reference to an ordered typology of systems of increasing complexity operating in different phenomenal realms.

But first let me make a few personal remarks about the occasions when I have been lucky enough to learn about this relationship from a distance. I write about neurosemiotics "from a distance" because I've been trained in linguistics and always worked as a linguist, lacking the background in neuroscience that would put me in a position of advancing proposals or models relevant to the development of neurosemiotics. The contributions we can make as linguists with my kind of background are to try to engage in dialogue and take the theory of language as far as we are able to in order to meet the needs of experts on the "neuro" part of neurosemiotics. In other words, we should try to develop "biologically implementable" accounts of language (see further below). I also note that contributions to research in neurolinguistics and neurosemiotics tend to be detailed, very specific studies based on sophisticated methods and tools, usually by teams of researchers.

12.1.1 1970s: first encounters with neurolinguistics

One of my first encounters with neurolinguistics was in Sweden around 1978, at a public defence of a PhD thesis written by a scholar exploring the innateness of universal grammar along the lines of Noam Chomsky and Eric Lenneberg (e.g. Lenneberg 1967). The opponent was Alvar Ellegård, a great Swedish linguist known for his work on English and also for his introduction of transformational linguistics of the generative semantics variety in Sweden (Ellegård 1953, 1971), and research based on corpora; he later published an introduction to language and the brain (Ellegård 1988).[2] He demolished the thesis by the hapless PhD candidate, who had actually already been awarded a PhD in biology many years earlier, during a session that lasted several hours. (In the Swedish system, this kind of adversarial tenor could permeate defences; in other countries, where I have been involved in the process myself as an examiner or as a supervisor, the assumption is generally that a thesis will not reach the examination stage unless it can be expected to pass without too much agony.)

One conclusion I drew from witnessing this prolonged defence was that the relationship between language and the brain is a very intricate, complex one, and one would need to ground any claims in real empirical evidence – abstract claims about universal grammar produced in the philosopher's armchair were not enough. This was a challenge at the time in view of the restricted ways of investigating the brain available to researchers. The focus on language universals in Chomskyan linguistics owed a great deal to Roman Jakobson's interest in universals formulated in the intellectual environment of the Prague School. He added the universalist component to the post-Bloomfieldian tradition Chomsky built on in the US. Like many others, I was of course aware of Jakobson's (1941) classic research monograph linking observations of language typology, learning of language by children, and loss of language by speakers suffering from aphasia, which I think was still accepted at the time as a grand hypothesis (although cf. Sampson's [1980] rather negative assessment of Jakobson's overall contribution to linguistics[3]).

A decade after the public defence referred to above, Ellegård (1988) published *Språket och hjärnan: språk och tal, minnet, höger-vänster, inlärning, tänkande* (*Language and the brain: language and speech, memory, left-right, learning, thinking*), which was a good introduction to neurolinguistics for me at the time, adding to what I had been able to glean from Luria's (1976) earlier general book about the brain. Ellegård's book appeared just as technological breakthroughs into brain scanning and imaging techniques were beginning to make a real difference in neuroscience, gradually shedding light on earlier ideas relevant to language and the brain, such as localistic and holographic interpretations, and more generally moving well beyond nineteenth-century dissection of deceased brains belonging to individuals who in life had suffered from language disorders or invasive studies of the living brain during brain surgery of the kind undertaken by Wilder Penfield in the 1950s (Penfield 1958). (I gather from the literature that many earlier notions are still around, like the idea that Broca's area is a privileged language region, even though more recent evidence supports quite different interpretations: e.g. Barrett 2017.)

12.1.2 1980s: UCLA

When I moved from Lund University to UCLA in 1979, I retained my outsider's interest in research into language and the brain, and luckily for me this was an intellectually rich environment. By the second half of the 1980s, I had audited a course at UCLA offered by Susan Curtiss (well-known for her study of Genie, a tragic case of a "wild child" [Curtiss [1977], noted in part because of the light it was thought it might shed on language "acquisition" and the critical period of language learning). She also invited an expert at UCLA on split brain phenomena, Eran Zaidel (e.g. 1983). I learned about the classification of different kinds of aphasia and other language deficits and disorders, and the brain regions they were associated with, like the language areas of the cortex; but it was clear that achieving standard categories across very varied cases was a considerable challenge.

In terms of the linguistic interpretation of problems, I found it helpful to be familiar with linguistic theories that were quite different from the current mainstream generative linguistic theory. (During the 1980s, I went to a number of LACUS (Linguistic Association of Canada and the United States) conferences, where non-Chomskyan linguists were able to present their work, one of the contributors being Michel Paradis, e.g. 2004.) At least, I realized that alternative interpretations were possible and depended critically on the nature of the theory, as did the scope of the theoretical conception of language – ranging from quite narrow in the case of generative theories to holistic in the case of SFL. For example, given a generative linguistic conception of language, anomia might be interpreted as difficulties in "retrieving" words of fairly high specificity from the "mental lexicon";[4] but in SFL, the semiotic dimension of the cline of delicacy would be relevant to the interpretation: speakers have difficulties in going beyond a certain point in delicacy, but listeners can still recognize delicate lexical items. (Cf. Barrett 2017: 121, on conceptual "granularity": "Preciseness leads to efficiency; this is a biological payoff of higher emotional granularity.") In addition, I had an opportunity to learn from Vicki Fromkin, who had been Harry Whitaker's thesis committee chair at UCLA (Whitaker 1969), how slips of the tongue and other speech errors were used as evidence for certain linguistic theories, like the theory of distinctive phonological features prevalent in generative phonology and taken over from Roman Jakobson. (I would of course interpret such phenomena systemically in terms of terms in systems rather than in terms of component parts of phonemes.)

This line of exploration can, of course, be said to go back to Jakobson's (1941) classic study mentioned above of child language development, aphasia, and language typology – a remarkable achievement also considering that he was fleeing increasingly Nazi-dominated Europe via Sweden, where he gained access to patients with aphasia, to the US. But in my view, he had made the fundamental theoretical mistake of reinterpreting paradigmatic values, as articulated within Prague School phonology by Trubetzkoy (1939), as syntagmatic components of phonemes (Matthiessen 2021a) – distinctive features (Jakobson 1949) – and that is how they have been treated in generative phonology. To me, this fundamental mistake was instructive in the sense that it helped me realize that physiological, neurological, and other biological data drawn from observation can be interpreted along different lines according to the theoretical framework adopted in linguistics. Thus, the data Jakobson used from aphasic patients and interpreted syntagmatically in terms of distinctive features could equally well, and in my view better, be interpreted paradigmatically in terms of terms in phonological systems. And the same applied to a number of later studies that used some version of Chomsky's theory to interpret phenomena observable in linguistic "performance" (as it was conceptualized at the time).

12.1.3 *1980s: need for cline rather than dichotomy*

I remember one occasion when Noam Chomsky came to UCLA to give a talk, and Vicki Fromkin (from our Department of Linguistics) asked him about the kind of research she was doing with colleagues. He replied, essentially dismissing it from the realm of linguistic theory and scientific investigation since it was concerned with performance in the first instance rather than with competence (cf. Whitaker 1969: 8–17; García, Sullivan, and Tsiang 2017: 159–60) – though as I recall he was fairly "nice" about it; I think he and Vicki Fromkin were friends, and she had probably, wisely, expected a dismissive answer along the lines he gave. Fromkin had, of course, worked towards a "performance model," visualized by flowchart-like diagrams (e.g.

Fromkin 1968), a task that was undertaken separately from the development of theories of competence because competence and performance had been theorized as distinct phenomena.

To me, it was a reminder of the importance of having a linguistic theory capable of reinterpreting dichotomies like competence and performance (as they were conceptualized at the time) or Saussure's *langue* and *parole* in such a way that the two parts could be related – which Halliday has done in his theory of language. I had read Halliday's (1973) conceptualization of potential and instance (or actual) in the 1970s, and also relevant work by Gustave Guillaume; and Halliday would later flesh out his theory of the **cline of instantiation** (e.g. Halliday 1991a, 2002a; Halliday and Matthiessen 1999). The theory of the cline of instantiation – or its possible analogue in other linguistic theories – is absolutely essential to the enterprise of neurosemiotics since it is necessary if we are to relate data (instantial patterns) to theory (generalizations about the potential), and since it provides us with an area within the architecture of language where we can locate processes of instantiation, including both generation and analysis.

During the 1980s, I also had a few valuable opportunities to listen to a number of representatives of stratificational linguistics and to meet and discuss with some of them, including Sydney Lamb, David Lockwood (e.g. 1972), Peter Reich (e.g. 1970), William Sullivan (e.g. 1980) and Ilah Fleming (e.g. 1988). One occasion was particularly informative: John Regan had invited Michael Halliday and Sydney Lamb to Claremont College in 1988 for a seminar where they presented their approaches and engaged in discussion. This was a very good opportunity to compare and contrast SFL and stratificational linguistics and the complementarity represented by these two linguists. For example, they discussed the correspondence between Halliday's probabilistic theory of language and Lamb's interpretation of strengthening and weakening of connections in relational network models of neural networks.[5] One conclusion I drew was that Halliday's social orientation did not mean that his contributions were not relevant to neurolinguistics – actually, quite the opposite, because he covered phenomena typically not within the purview of cognitive approaches, later explored under headings such as the social brain, dialogic cognition, dialogic mind, collective cognition, and group cognition (cf. also dialogic learning), influenced by Vygotsky's work (see Wells 1994; Byrnes 2006).

12.1.4 1980s: lessons from computational modelling

In fact, linguistic processes were central to my involvement in a series of related computational linguistic projects concerned with text generation by computer at the Information Sciences Institute/USC from 1980 through 1988 (cf. Matthiessen and Bateman 1991). The project leader was Bill Mann (cf. Matthiessen 2005), who had recruited Michael Halliday as an SFL consultant in addition to employing me as a research linguist with expertise in SFL.

Bill Mann had very good reasons for selecting SFL based on a systematic review of possible candidates in the late 1970s. One reason he chose SFL over other linguistic frameworks at the time was its orientation towards **choice** (treating the paradigmatic axis of organization as the primary kind of order in language – the "systemic" part of SFL). Another reason was its commitment to comprehensive descriptions. From the start, Halliday had placed high value on **comprehensiveness** – during a period when the dominant kind of theoretical linguistics did not – but tended to work with fairly small domain (cf. Gross 1979) to extract and test theoretical principle (an application of Cartesian analysis).

After working for a couple of years on the expansion of the computational systemic functional grammar of English that was part of the project (Matthiessen 1995a), I came to realize the true significance of developing and being able to view comprehensive systemic functional descriptions: one had to solve problems and could discern patterns that would not emerge in the "toy" examples theoretical linguists used to reason about and illustrate certain theoretical or representational points (cf. Lamb 2013: 156, on the value of system networks in language description). (See the discussion of descriptive fractal principles in Halliday and Matthiessen 1999 and 2014.)

Alongside his involvement in computational linguistics, Bill Mann had observed patients suffering from different kinds of aphasia, and he had read linguistic or linguistically informed characterizations of different kinds of aphasia. We discussed the work, and he commented that he didn't think such accounts would be successful until they added a **model of processes**, with buffers and working memory. This made excellent sense to me, since by then I had realized that linguists had not on the whole dealt with theoretical models of linguistics processes, instead focussing on accounts of the linguistic system and linguistic instances, i.e. texts. In systemic functional terms, theoretical accounts of processes of instantiation moving along the cline of instantiation between the potential and instance poles were needed, and we tried to provide them in our work on text generation (e.g. Matthiessen and Bateman 1991). Looking back to Bill's remarks around forty years ago, I would say that his general point has been well taken; for example, traditional "language areas" have now been problematized in the light of new insights into network connectivity and activation (e.g. Deacon 1997; Barrett 2017, 2021).

In this general context of AI and computational linguistics, I also learned about work involving processes in general in different domains, e.g. in models of **planning** and **goal pursuit**. For example, text generation could be thought of as a domain of application of goal pursuit models, and there were suggestions that a model of speech acts could be derived from a model of acts in general. (Later I realized that such suggestions could be viewed in relation to an account of systems in general, like the ordered typology of systems to be presented in Section 12.2.)

The systemic functional computational work at the Information Sciences Institute also meant that I learned about and worked with **network representations** in addition to systemic function system network, viz. members of the family of **frame-based inheritance networks**, a guiding early contribution being Brachman (1979). After a kind of free-for-all in the development of various semantic networks since the 1960s, which had been problematized by Woods (1975) in this thoughtful and provocative paper "What's in a link," he makes the crucial point that networks need to be conceptualized and represented at a number of distinct levels, each of which has certain functions and meets certain criteria (cf. the discussion of the stratification of our metalanguage and biological implementability in Section 12.6). Thus, among other points, he showed that graphic visualizations of networks must be underpinned by explicit mathematical specifications. The advances in KR also provided new insights into the contrast between procedural and declarative knowledge. In his systemic-informed SHRDLU system designed to understand text, Winograd (1972) had represented knowledge as procedures, and in Winograd (1975), he reviews the declarative and procedural approaches, and the complementarity between the two. This is relevant in approaching the relationship between linguistic semantics and sensorimotor ("bio-semiotic") systems, since motor representations have procedural implications.

I was also fortunate enough to be exposed to a parallel stream of research informed by network thinking, or **connectionism**. During the 1980s, research into (artificial) **neural networks** in AI was renewed after early interest in the 1960s had waned (Minsky and Papert 1969), drawing on ideas in neuropsychology and cybernetics going back to the 1940s (including Hebb's [1949] early insights into patterns of activation of neurons); see e.g. Rumelhart, McClelland, and The PDP Research Group (1986); Rumelhart, Widrow, and Lehr (1994). The new efforts had become possible thanks to increased computing power and were shown to be successful as an approach to machine learning. This network-based research involved artificial "neurons," including synapses with weights that could be increased or decreased, linked together in networks where signals could be propagated, and the neural network models contrasted fundamentally with the kind of "symbolic" modelling we were doing at the time, manually constructing computational specifications of the different parts of a computational text-generation system. In contrast, machine learning based on neural networks was automated, designed (in the systemic functional terms I introduced above) to move along the cline of instantiation from "data" at the instance pole towards generalizations about the system behind the data farther up towards the potential pole of the cline. This approach was thus radically different from the handcrafted models that had dominated in computational linguistics and in AI (as in expert systems); but this approach is not at all incompatible with systemic functional theory, according to which the linguistic system is "distilled" from innumerable instances of text, including quantitative information (i.e. systemic probabilities are distilled from relative frequencies in text, resonant with the notion of statistical learning; cf. Section 12.3.5).

12.1.5 1980s: advances in brain imaging

I left UCLA to take up a position as lecturer in the Department of Linguistics at Sydney University in 1988, at a time when new brain imaging techniques were becoming available and new findings were emerging – findings that would enable neurolinguists to move beyond the traditional model of the relationship between language and the brain. The effect on research has been dramatic, comparable to other technological advances that have increased the scientific power of observation like the telescope, the microscope, and the stethoscope.

I remember taking part in an invited workshop on language processing at Kyushu Institute of Technology in Fukuoka in the mid-1990s, and one of the presentations was by a neuroscientist who showed us the latest findings based on brain scanning techniques. The findings were impressive, but at the time, the temporal resolution was still not good enough to cope with the observation of speakers engaging in natural conversation. However, the situation was changing in very positive ways: after undertaking a systematic review and synthesis of "the first 20 years of PET and fMRI studies of heard speech, spoken language and reading," Price (2012: 838) comments:

> Indeed, our understanding of the functional anatomy of language has come a long way since the neurological model of Broca's and Wernicke's areas that dominated the field 20 years ago. For example, we now appreciate the importance of the cerebellum for word generation (Ackermann, Wildgruber, and Grodd 1997) and the involvement of the basal temporal language area, anterior cingulate and left inferior prefrontal cortex in a range of different language tasks [...]
>
> The next 20 years will need to focus on understanding how different regions interact with one another and how specialisation for language arises at the level of distinct patterns of activation in areas that participate in many different functions.

12.1.6 1990s onwards

Since the 1980s, I have continued to learn from work on computational modelling undertaken by us in Sydney Australia but also at the Brain Science Division of the RIKEN Institute in Tokyo, where Michio Sugeno led a large-scale five-year project that was informed by SFL and supported by fuzzy theory. After the completion of this project, Sugeno worked with a neuroscientist in Japan to investigate the metafunctional diversification of language in relation to the brain (Sugeno 2008). At the same time, I had opportunities to learn from scholars working in clinical linguistics, Beth Armstrong, and neuroscience, Michael Arbib and Terrence Deacon. Beth Armstrong (e.g. 1997, 2009) and I submitted a grant application to the Australian Research Council (ARC) to study the language of emotion in speakers suffering from certain kinds of aphasia, but we were unsuccessful – unfortunately, since I think it would have been a groundbreaking study at the time. One contribution would have been to draw on the insight in SFL that we must distinguish the ideational construal of our experience of emotion as feelings and the interpersonal enactment of it as attitudes and affects (Matthiessen 2007b). This would surely have related to more recent insights into how emotions are construed as meaning – how "emotions are made," as Barrett (2017) puts in in her paradigm-changing book.

From Michael Arbib, I learned about mirror neurons and the Mirror System Hypothesis in the evolution of language (e.g. Rizzolatti and Arbib 1998; Arbib 2012). This related to the centrality of language embodied as an integrative neural system, linking perception to production (I was reminded of Stetson's [1928] account of the perception of rhythm being related to production, discussed by Abercrombie 1967: 96–7 under the heading of "phonetic empathy" in his systemic functionally compatible overview of phonetics), to the work Michael Halliday and I were doing on the ordered typology of systems (Halliday and Matthiessen 1999; see further below), and to my attempt to sketch an account of the evolution of language (Matthiessen 2004a), drawing on the phases of increasing complexity identified by Halliday (1975, 2004a) in his study of language development (see Section 12.3.2). Centred around Michael Arbib and led by the University of New South Wales, we tried but failed to get funding for a major project, *The evolution of brain from action-oriented perception to language: a neuro-computational approach to action, vision and language*, consisting of six sub-projects and involving researchers from a number of different universities. I'm sure that this project would have led to major breakthroughs.

From Terrence Deacon, we received support for the notion that language and the brain have **co-evolved** (e.g. Deacon 1992, 1997) – i.e. they have evolved in a kind of dialectical movement towards greater complexity. He also argues for a different view of language in relation to the brain; for example, Deacon (1997: 287–8) notes:

> Though other primate brains have not evolved regions that are specifically used for language processes, those regions of the human brain that are did not arise *de novo*. The language areas are cortical regions that have been recruited for this new set of functions from among structures evolved for very different adaptations. They were selected during language evolution because what they were already doing offered the best fit to the new problems posed by language. Thus, we should stop thinking about Broca's and Wernicke's areas as "language areas". They are the areas that language most intensely utilizes. The question we should ask then is why? What is it about these areas that dictates the distribution of language functions that we observe?
>
> [...] Broca's and Wernicke's areas represent what might be visualized as bottlenecks for information flow during language processing; weak links in a chain of processes. Once we abandon the idealization that language is plugged into the brain in modules, and recognize it as merely a new use of existing structures, there is no reason to expect that language functions should map in any direct way onto the structural-functional divisions of cortex. It is far more reasonable to expect language processes to be broken up into subfunctions that have more to do with neural logic than with linguistic logic.

Deacon had started out on the East Coast of the US before moving to UC Berkeley, and being surrounded by linguists in the Chomskyan generative tradition, he found nothing compatible in Chomskyan linguistic theory, so had to develop his own framework for theorizing language, drawing on C.S. Peirce's work (see, in particular, Deacon 1997). The framework he developed seems very compatible with SFL (for the Peircean aspect, cf. Bateman 2018). On one occasion, I asked Deacon what characteristics linguistic accounts should have to be relevant to neurolinguistics and to neuroscience more generally. He answered that they should be "biologically implementable," which I interpreted in the light of the ordered typology of systems and my experience with working towards an understanding of computational implementability. This topic will come up in the concluding section of this chapter (Section 12.6).

In addition to the scholars just mentioned I've had the luck to meet, I have found deep insights compatible with SFL in the research led by Colwyn Trevarthen in the UK and by Patricia Kuhl, on statistical learning, and Lisa Feldman Barrett, on the construal of emotion, in the US. I'll return briefly to their contributions in these areas below, and just draw attention to a general contribution made by Barrett (2017).

Barrett (2017) is concerned with how "emotions are made," and in this course of developing her account, she shows that a number of received views about language and the brain need to be problematized or even replaced. Thus, she shows that the notion of the "triune brain" is wrong – our brains function as holistic systems, not simply as a series of additions to a "reptilian brain" (see also Barrett 2021: 3–28); and she also argues that although it has been assumed to be, Broca's area, or the "lateral prefrontal cortex," is not specific to language processing (p. 167):

> Today's textbooks in psychology and neurology still hold up Broca's area as the clearest example of localized brain function, even as neuroscience has shown that the region is neither necessary nor sufficient for language. [Footnote: A significant number of patients who suffer from Broca's aphasia have no damage in Broca's area, and conversely, about half the people with lesions in Broca's area do not have Broca's aphasia. Scientists continue to debate the function of Broca's area, which is better referred to as lateral prefrontal cortex, but few believe that it is specific to language production, grammatical abilities, or even general language processing. The current consensus is that it's part of several intrinsic networks, including the interoceptive and control networks. ...] Broca's area is actually a *failure* to localize a psychological function to a brain blob. Nevertheless, history was rewritten in Broca's favor, lending strength to the essentialist views of the mind.

Similarly, Steffen, Hedges, and Matheson (2022) argue that the widespread model of the triune brain is outdated; instead our brain is an adaptive brain: "In particular, the brain appears to work by integrating interoceptive and exteroceptive information to make predictions about future metabolic, energy, and other needs while it adapts to continually changing external and internal conditions to maintain homeostasis and to initiate allostasis as needed."

12.1.7 Insights gained

The various encounters on my personal journey as a linguist dilettantishly interested in neurolinguistics, and at the same time dedicated to contributing towards the development of a holistic theory of language over the years that I have mentioned in a fairly rambling fashion, helped me arrive at the insight that the neurologically most pervasive human system is language, serving to integrate a wide range of different areas of the brain because language relates to all sensorimotor systems as well as to other semiotic systems (cf. e.g. Bickerton 1995, on the linguistic cat being the "holistic" cat as an illustration of the pervasive connectedness of linguistic concepts; Christiansen and Chater 2008: 496, on the need to abandon "the vision of Universal Grammar as a language-specific innate faculty or language organ"). In this way, linguistic concepts or meanings are multivalent, serving as hubs in networks of connections to regions dedicated to different sensorimotor systems. But of course I know that this insight is neither unique nor original – and that before it can be called an insight, a huge number of additional empirical studies will have to be conducted; and I realize that this "insight" will need to be fleshed out in much more detail even to be given the status of a hypothesis.

Nevertheless, this "insight" suggests to me that a multidimensional relational theory of language in relation to other systems such as that offered by SFL can be very helpful precisely because:

1. It is a holistic theory of language, locating it in an ordered typology of systems, showing how language is enacted socially, embodied biologically, and manifested physically.
2. Such a theory can specify different ways in which language integrates a wide range of areas of the brain (say, from the amygdala to the frontal lobe, involving both hemispheres) – through the hierarchy of stratification, the spectrum of metafunction, the cline of instantiation, and processes of instantiation, to name just dimensions of the global organization of language.
3. These dimensions are all constituted in terms of relations; language itself and its interfaces to other systems are conceived of as a vast network of relations.
4. Such a theory can enable researchers to manage both "ecological validity" and "experimental control."

This last point comes from Trevisan and García (2019). They show that SFL can be a resource in achieving both. While the "ecological validity" of SFL research is probably generally accepted, SFL might have been thought of as too complex to give researchers a handle on "experimental control"; but they show that the "extravagance" of SFL theory (as Halliday has characterized it) can actually help us gain more control over experimental studies precisely because SFL identifies all the parameters researchers need to take into account.

12.1.8 Outline of the chapter

After these introductory observations based on my personal encounters as a linguist with works in neurolinguistics and with neurolinguists and neuroscientists, I will approach certain aspects of neurosemiotics in a few steps informed by SFL.

First, I will locate the potential phenomenal realms of study of neurosemiotics in terms of an ordered typology of systems of increasing complexity operating in different phenomenal realms (Section 12.2).

I will then identify some key properties of language brought out by the systemic functional "architecture" of language, properties that I think are particularly relevant to field of study of neurosemiotics (Section 12.3).

Next, I will focus on the implications of the stratification of language, with the distinction between internal strata and interface strata, paying particular attention to semantics as an interface stratum – a resource for transforming experience external to language into meaning (Section 12.4).

This characterization of semantics as an interface stratum is, in fact, oriented towards the ideational model of meaning, and in the next section, I will discuss the role ideational semantics resources play in construing categories of phenomena (Section 12.5).

By way of conclusion, I will concentrate on the key question of what it means for linguistic accounts to be biologically implementable, using the characterization suggested to me by Terrence Deacon (Section 12.6).

In filmic terms, the organization of the chapter is based on an initial establishing shot (my "macro-Theme") followed by views of certain details. Obviously, I can't elaborate on all the features of the overall picture shown in the establishing shot; rather, I will continue to narrow the focus section by section – from the ordered typology of systems, from all strata of language in context to interface strata, from interface strata to semantics, from semantics to ideational semantics (the "ideation base" interfacing with what lies outside language as far as content is concerned), essentially leaving interpersonal and textual semantics for other occasions.

12.2   Neurosemiotics located in terms of the ordered typology of systems

To explore neurosemiotics, elaborating on my interpretation stated above – that it is concerned with the study of the relationship between systems operating in two distinct phenomenal realms, viz. semiotic and biological systems – I will begin by sketching an ordered typology of systems operating in different phenomenal realms.

A number of such ordered typologies have been proposed by scholars from different disciplines over the years, including David Layzer (1990) from the point of view of astrophysics, Herbert Simon (1996) from the point of view of the "sciences of the artificia," Lotfi Zadeh from the point of view of fuzzy theory (cf. Yager and Zadeh 1992); and also from scholars dealing with varieties of some general systems theory (see e.g. Skyttner 1996, 2001). And of course contributions from a more philosophical vantage point, e.g. by Karl Popper and Pierre Teilhard de Chardin. The number of systemic orders will vary; and a recurrent debate about the assignment of phenomena to one order or another concerns the notion of reductionism. In general, reductionism would seem to involve attempts to characterize phenomena of one order only or largely in terms of an account of the order next below.

Here I will present a version developed with language and other semiotic systems in focus. Michael Halliday and I worked on it in the 1990s and introduced it in Halliday and Matthiessen (1999) (see also Halliday 1996), and produced further characterizations and elaborations of it (e.g. Halliday 2005a; Matthiessen 2007a, 2020, forthcoming b). I have represented it schematically in Figure 12.1. To us, this ordered typology was part of a general systems approach to language, where general principles are identified in the organization of different orders of system – including the move towards greater complexity in systems of different kinds (an early example being Halliday's [1961] analogy between grammatical units and units of a meal). Outside SFL, one manifestation in linguistics is the interpretation of language as a complex adaptive system (e.g. Steels 1998, in models of language evolution and later work on fluid construction grammar; Larsen-Freeman and Cameron 2008, in applied linguistics; Beckner et al. 2009; cf. Matthiessen 2009, where I try to make the connection with SFL).

12.2.1 The four orders of system

The systems in Figure 12.1 are represented in order of increasing complexity and will be presented in some detail: first-order systems – physical systems; second-order systems – physical systems + "life": biological systems; third-order systems – biological systems + value (social order): social systems; and fourth-order systems – social systems + meaning: semiotic systems. This can be hypothesized to reflect their appearance in the course of cosmogenesis, in the sense of Layzer (1990). Semiotic systems are of the highest order of complexity in that they are enacted in social systems, embodied in biological systems, and manifested in physical systems.

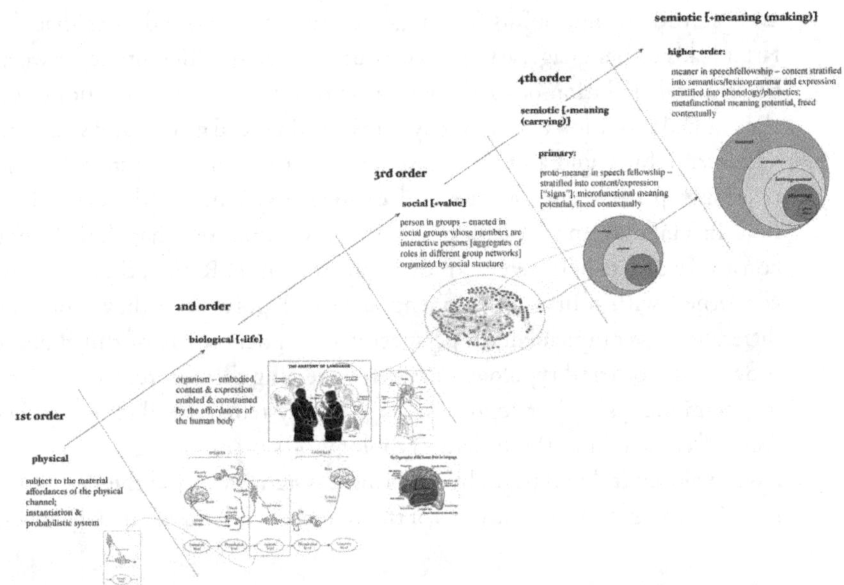

Figure 12.1 Schematic representation of the ordered typology of systems operating in different phenomenal realms

When we investigate different systemic orders, and the inter-relations between adjacent orders of system or non-adjacent orders of system mediated by an intermediate order of system, we can approach them from different starting points. More specifically, Halliday's notion of **trinocular vision** (e.g. Halliday 1978; Halliday and Matthiessen 2014) applies here just as in the study of language itself. For example, we can view neurobiological systems "from above," starting with language or another semiotic system or from social systems in order to frame them in terms of function and behaviour; "from below," approaching them from the vantage point of physical systems, examining e.g. the electrical and chemical properties of neurons and propagation of signals across synapses; or "from roundabout," viewing them from their own order of biological systems. (Thus, when we view the brain "from above," we can conceptualize it as a social brain [implying the notion of a social collective brain] or, by another step up, as a semiotic brain; see further below.)

Focussing on language and other semiotic systems, we needed to bring out two key points relevant to the model in Figure 12.1:

1. **Semiotic** and **social** systems need to be separated analytically so that their key properties can be differentiated. For example, in his "hierarchy of time-bound order," Layzer (1990) distinguishes between "biological evolution"

and "cultural evolution" as "cosmogenic processes" and indicates that the latter leads to "language, art, science"; but we need to differentiate between the gradual evolution of social systems within biological populations and the gradual evolution of semiotic systems within social groups and societies.

2.   The hierarchy would appear to have no place for cognitive systems, so the relationship between **semiotic** and **cognitive** systems needs to be clarified. In Halliday and Matthiessen (1999), we proposed that they do not constitute orders of different kinds of phenomenon. Rather, they are both concerned with fourth-order phenomena in Figure 12.1; they represent different but complementary perspectives on phenomena of this highest order in the ordered typology of systems, viewing them in terms of meaning (semiotic system) or cognition (cognitive systems). I will return to this issue after sketching the ordered typology of systems along the lines we have explored it. I will begin by adopting a system view, and then move on to a view foregrounding the users of the systems – individuals in collectives.

System view

The four orders of system operating in different phenomenal realms can be characterized briefly as follows, in order of increasing complexity.

> **First-order systems** are physical systems. As far as we know, they emerged on the order of 13.5 billion years ago, the emergence being the event known as the Big Bang. Throughout **cosmogenesis** (Layzer 1990), they have continued to increase in complexity, going through a number of phases. They are the most pervasive of all systems; their domain is the expanding cosmos itself, and they extend in scale from the minutest micro to the most mammoth macro – from the quantum world to the entire universe. Consequently, the study of them depends on many technologies, starting with the telescope and the microscope in the seventeenth century, methods of investigation (both experimental methods and non-experimental forms of observation – researchers can experiment with the micro-world using particle accelerators, but they have to be content with pure observation of the macro-world, lacking e.g. planet accelerators), and semiotic systems, including evolved varieties of language characterized as scientific language (e.g. Halliday 1988b) but also, centrally, designed semiotic systems such as branches of mathematics (like differential equations, trigonometry, probability theory), of painting and drawing (cf. the conscious design involved in introducing perspective, e.g. the work by Alfred Dührer).

Second-order systems are biological systems. They emerged out of physical systems under very special conditions – ones James Lovelock (e.g. 1991: 98) has called the "window for life" – in one little corner of the universe, our planet, around 3.5 billion years ago (as far as we know). The emergence was characteristic of the move from one order of systems to the next; systems of the lower order continue to increase in complexity until they reach a **tipping point** where the complexity gives rise to a new order: adding to the properties of physical systems, biological systems can individuate, self-replicate, and evolve from one generation to another (e.g. Maynard Smith and Szathmáry 1999). That is, cosmogenesis became **evolution**, subject to natural selection and inter-generational "memory" in the form of the genetic code. In Halliday and Matthiessen (1999) we summarized these properties as **+life**: biological systems are physical systems + life. That is, biological systems are still entirely physical – they are subject to the laws of physics – but they are +life: they are living physical systems. In terms of scale, their range is much narrower than that of physical systems. But once they had emerged, biological systems increased in complexity, including compositional complexity, now ranging from mono-cellular life forms to blue whales, and of course to whole ecosystems.

Third-order systems are social systems. They must have emerged out of biological systems on many separate occasions; that is, social groups and societies must have emerged out of biological systems many times under a wide range of conditions, increasing in complexity from eusociality along different paths (cf. Wilson 2019). The emergent property is that of **value** or social order. Unlike physical systems and biological systems, which are both material systems, social systems are **immaterial** systems; they are essentially constituted in order rather than in matter (whether inorganic or organic). In terms of individuals, this means that biological organisms have a new emergent property; they are no longer simply organisms within a biological population, they are **persons** in social groups – social groups that may form societies such as those of an anthill or a band of chimpanzees. Persons are multivalent; they are aggregates of the personae or **social roles** individuals take on in different **social role networks** (e.g. Firth 1950; Halliday 1978; Butt 1991; Lemke 1995a; Halliday and Matthiessen 1999; cf. also Matthiessen 2013, in relation to patients in healthcare). Importantly, this means that one and the same biological organism may play a wide range of roles in different role networks, even potentially apparently conflicting ones leading to tensions in personalities. Ontogenetically, individual human organisms emerge gradually as persons in interaction with members of social groups (Halliday 1978).

Fourth-order systems are semiotic systems. Like social systems, they are immaterial systems, so they are primarily constituted in order rather than in matter (though like social systems they are manifested in matter); and again like social systems, they must have evolved on many occasions, emerging in different social groups. The emergent property is that of **meaning**, and to carry or even create meaning, semiotic systems, unlike social systems, are stratified into two **stratal planes**, content and expression;[6] so a semiotic act is at the same time an observable expression (audible, visible, or within the realm of one of the other senses) and an act of meaning. Many – or most – semiotic systems are simply two-level systems of this kind, but language is of a higher order of complexity and has more semiotic power – power to mean. This is due to further stratification of both content and expression. In language, both the content plane and the expression plane are internally stratified. The content plane is stratified into semantics and lexicogram-mar, which among other things opens up the potential for metaphor. The expression plane is stratified into phonology and phonetics in spoken lan-guage, graphology, and graphetics in written language, or the analogues in sign languages of deaf communities. In fact, because of the conventional relationship between content and expression in language (Saussure's line of arbitrariness, Martinet's double articulation), linguistic expression is highly variable, e.g. writing can be tactile (Braille).

As far as we know, modern language has only emerged once, under special con-ditions in East Africa (which still leaves open the possibility of archaic languages in parallel lineages such as the Neanderthals). This is highly significant from the point of view of neurosemiotics, and of explorations of language and the brain more gen-erally, because it relates directly to the plausibility of the hypothesis put forward by Deacon (e.g. 1992, 1997) that language and the human brain evolved together – the **co-evolution** of language and the human brain. Under this interpretation, *Homo sapiens sapiens* were both anatomically modern humans (AMHs) and lin-guistically (or semiotically) modern humans (LMHs) when they emerged in the order of 150–250 thousand years ago. According to this account, modern language evolved out of archaic language, which in turn evolved out of protolanguage. In Matthiessen (2004a), I point to correlations between language and the brain in the phases of evolution, drawing on the literature at the time (see Table 12.3, to be discussed below).

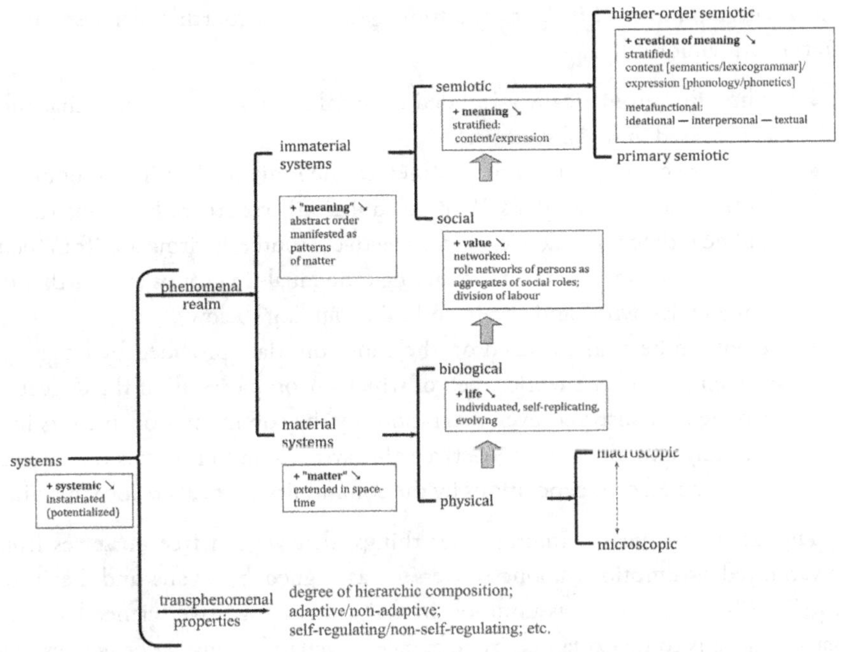

Figure 12.2 The ordered typology of systems operating in different phenomenal realms, with "inherited" and distinctive properties

Fourth-order systems have been approached from two different vantage points. As noted above, they have been interpreted as systems of **meaning** – as **semiotic systems.** This is the interpretation that has been developed within SFL, guided by Michael Halliday's (e.g. 1978) development of the conception of language as a social semiotic. However, starting already in the 1950s, the increasingly dominant conception of fourth-order systems has been that promoted by the macro-discipline of cognitive science: they have been conceived of as systems of **knowledge**, or **cognitive systems.** In Halliday and Matthiessen (1999), we discuss these alternative lines of interpretation of fourth-order phenomena and suggest that the two views can productively be treated as complementary (cf. also Matthiessen 2020; Matthiessen et al. 2022: ch. 6). This complementarity is supported by the continuing dialogue between SFL and stratificational linguistics, now relational network theory, since the 1960s, as noted by Halliday (2017) and also by Lamb (2013); see Section 12.6.

While I have said that the semiotic and cognitive interpretations are complementary, we have argued that the semiotic interpretation of fourth-order systems comes with a number of insights or advantages. Thus, if fourth-order systems are interpreted semiotically:

- They are automatically grounded in social systems, in the sense that they are enacted in social systems.
- They are consequently not confined to the individual "mind" ("bounded by the skin," in Halliday's 1978, formulation) but are, rather, constructed and negotiated interactively as a collective resource, inviting a shift in focus from single individuals to interacting individuals in groups (see further on "intersubjectivity" and "brain-to-brain coupling" below).
- They can be studied based on the enormous data provided by languages spoken around the world, each of which encompasses all of the collective experience construed over generations by the community of speakers into meaning and all of the collective value systems and protocols for interaction enacted over generations by the community of speakers into meaning.

The last point means, among other things, that we can free ourselves from unwarranted assumptions about universals, as argued by Evans and Levinson (2009). While a common assumption in mainstream cognitive science has been that language is to be explained by reference to general cognitive principles (e.g. "shaped by thought"), we would ask where such principles are supposed to come from (apart from being derived from biological sensorimotor systems), and we suggest instead that language (and other semiotic systems) will serve as the source in efforts to explain such general cognitive principles. This direction of explanation is supported by ontogenetic studies in SFL (as outlined by Halliday 1993b), Painter (1999) being a key contribution (and it is of course consistent with Vygotsky's insights into ontogenesis, e.g. Byrnes 2006). For example, Painter shows how mastering the resources needed for representing relations of identity towards the end of the third year of life creates the conditions for construing abstractions (as in *balance means that you hold it on your fingers and it doesn't go* ['fall']). Learning how to mean in interaction with others includes learning the resources for construing experience, e.g. for categorizing phenomena, for taxonomizing them, and for reasoning about sequences of events (cf. the discussion in Section 12.5.1 of the categorization of cats).

This Hallidayan SFL view is clearly resonant with many aspects of Vygotsky's work, which is brought out e.g. by Wells (1994) commenting on Halliday (1993b), and by Byrnes's (2006) edited volume on the complementarity of the two. It is also supported by studies of how speakers of different languages verbalize their experiences when they view video clips and are asked to report on what they see either in real time or after they have watched the clips. Studies include the work by Dan Slobin and his colleagues at UC Berkeley, which has led to what we can think of as an instantial version of the Sapir–Whorf Hypothesis – **thinking for speaking** (e.g. Slobin 1996, 2004a,b, 2008); and also the studies by Christiane von Stutterheim at Heidelberg University and her group and collaborators (e.g. Carroll and von Stutterheim 2011; Schmiedtová, von Stutterheim, and Carroll 2011; Flecken, von Stutterheim and Carroll 2014).

Von Stutterheim and her collaborators have found that the language spoken by the participants influences not only their conceptualization of the events but also their processes of perception: they will turn their gaze to details relevant to the resources of their language. For example, according to their account, one difference between English and German in the way they model experience of quanta of change is that German is oriented more towards the outcome, so in viewing representations of motion through space, speakers of German tend to report what they can see later than speakers of English since they need to see the outcome, and direct their gaze towards the area where they expect to outcome to show up.

Similarly, using various experimental methods, Boroditsky and collaborators have shown how languages with different systems construing different areas of experience – such as orientation in space-time, measure of quantities, differentiation of colours (clearly an old favourite in debates about "language and thought") – "shape thought" according to the particular models construed by the languages (e.g. Boroditsky 2001, 2011) and also guide perception (Lupyan et al. 2020) – in other words, a process we can call **perceiving for speaking**.

In a complementary line of research within neurolinguistics, Uri Hasson and his team have investigated story comprehension and storytelling using functional magnetic resonance imaging (fMRI) (e.g. Stephens, Silbert, and Hasson 2010; Hasson et al. 2012; Chen et al. 2016). They have shown that story comprehension and storytelling activate similar brain regions, and infer that this is based on semantic patterns since they seem to be comparable across languages (obviously allowing for differences, e.g. in the modelling of time). This is part of their notion of **brain-to-brain coupling**, which I will return to in the next subsection. Thus, psycholinguistic and neurolinguistic studies of the kind just referred to demonstrate the central role of language in discourse comprehension and production, also in guiding processes of perception and memory.

The brief sketch above of the ordered typology is couched in terms of systems; but starting with the biological order of system, individuation emerges as a property of systems, and **individuals** have different properties within different orders and form different kinds of **collective**: see Table 12.1.

Table 12.1 Individuals, collectives, and systemic orders

Systemic order		Individual	Collective
4th	semiotic	meaner (aggregate of meaning roles)	meaning groups – speech fellowships
3rd	social	person (aggregate of personae, social roles)	social group – society
2nd	biological	organism	biological population – species

The consideration of individuals is obviously important to the exploration and development of neurosemiotics since the brains of individual organisms come into focus not only as a domain of theory and modelling but also as a source of empirical evidence through increasingly sophisticated brain scanning and imaging techniques. From the point of view of SFL, it is interesting to note that conceptions of, and approaches to, the brain have increasingly come to be informed by both social and semiotic perspectives – thus becoming increasingly resonant with the systemic functional conception developed by Halliday and collaborators. Part of the challenge is to relate all three orders of humans set out in Table 12.1, both as individuals and as collectives. This is a motif in the work by Robin Dunbar and other scholars taking all three orders into consideration, e.g. Dunbar (1993, 1996, 2020), Gamble, Gowlett, and Dunbar (2014). Not surprisingly, the evidential base is still very uneven, involving both fairly direct evidence drawing on detailed studies of living brains in operation and inferences based on fragments of evidence such as records of fossils and dwellings, and involving different angles of vision, including the complementary insights from phylogenesis and ontogenesis but also semiotic, social, and neurological observation, recording, and analysis over short periods of people "languaging."

Neuroscientists have emphasized the point that our brains are both social and semiotic; i.e. our second-order biological brains are also third-order social brains and fourth-order semiotic brains. Thus, based on Deacon's (1992, 1997) hypothesis that language and the brain co-evolved and on evidence from brain imaging showing the pervasiveness of language in the brain, we can infer that our brains are **language brains** (cf. Halliday 2001), or more specifically grammar brains, since grammar can be interpreted as "the driving force" in the move from "primary to higher-order consciousness" (Halliday 2004b). Based on neurolinguistic research, Kuhl (e.g. 2007) has characterized our brains as **social brains.**[7] She suggests that phonological-phonetic learning is **gated by social factors**, including the increase in attention and arousal through social interaction, joint visual attention, and parental adaptation to the infant's need for processable input ("Motherese exaggerates acoustic cues for phonemes"). This view resonates with the systemic functional conception of early learning, related to Trevarthen's (e.g. 1979, 1987, 2011) work on empathy and **intersubjectivity**, and Bateson's (e.g. 1979) notion of **proto-conversation** (e.g. Halliday 1979c).

In her account of how "emotions are made," Barrett (2017) also highlights social considerations, devoting a whole chapter to "social reality." Here she shows how speakers of a language embedded in a culture understand (terms for) emotion concepts by consensus, negotiating them in everyday discourse; see also Section 12.5.2 on her account of "social reality." Once, when I picked up Michael Halliday at LAX on one of his visits from Sydney to our research project at the Information Sciences Institute, the first thing he said to me after we had greeted one another as he emerged from arrivals was: semantics is about consensus, not about truth. He had used his fifteen hours in the air productively! This **consensus view of meaning** is reinforced by Barrett's account of the social reality of emotions (as opposed to biologically universal emotions and essentialist accounts of emotions, the rejected classical view which she points out had been argued by Darwin 1872). This view of "social reality" has implications for the conception of human beings, not only as organisms (biological order), but also as persons (social order) and as meaners (semiotic order). Halliday (e.g. 1978) argues that we are not "bounded by the skin," and Barrett (2017) offers an interpretation along similar lines: "In the theory of constructed emotion, however, the dividing line between brain and world is permeable, perhaps nonexistent" (p. 153); "We don't know every detail about how the mind and brain work, but we know enough to say definitively that neither biological determinism nor cultural determinism is correct. The boundary of the skin is artificial and porous" (p. 170).

The inclusion of the social order of systems between biological and semiotic systems also resonates with Hasson et al.'s (2012) theory of **brain-to-brain coupling** (also e.g. Stephens, Silbert, and Hasson 2010). They observe that "despite the central role of other individuals in shaping our minds, most cognitive studies focus on processes that occur within a single individual" (p. 1). This has been the tendency in mainstream cognitive science and is one consequence, though not an inevitable one, of interpreting fourth-order systems as cognitive systems rather than as semiotic systems (enacted in social systems). They also "call for a shift from single-brain to a multiple-brain frame of reference," and they initiate this shift through their notion of brain-to-brain coupling, which they characterize as follows: "The premise of brain-to-brain coupling is that the perceptual system of one brain can be coupled to the motor system of another. This binding mechanism is similar to action-perception coupling within a single brain. Action-perception (or *stimulus-to-brain*) coupling relies on the ability of brains to actively interact with the physical world" (Hasson et al. 2012: 2).

Clearly, semiotic systems play a central role here, providing the resources for the exchange of meanings which underpin brain-to-brain coupling; and interactive social behaviours are also involved: "Many joint behaviors such as mating, group cohesion, and predator avoidance depend on accurate production and perceptions of social signals." (Hasson et al. 2012: 3) What Hasson et al. refer to as "social signals" are arguably always semiotic signals. In other words, it is language, together with other denotative semiotic systems, as a resource for exchanging meanings that underpins brain-to-brain coupling, enabling us to evolve virtual collective brains. (Cf. the role of gaze when semiotic acts emerge with protolanguage from material acts, described by Halliday 2003a: in performing a material act involving an object, e.g. grabbing it, infants will gaze at the object; but when they perform a semiotic act, an act of meaning, they will gaze at the addressee, the person addressed as the mediator of the act.)

12.2.2 Interpretations of the ordered typology

The ordered typology of systems operating in different phenomenal realms captures a number of fundamental features of the world of phenomena that we are currently able to engage with scientifically:

1. It represents an **ordering in complexity** from the simplest to the most complex systems in the sense that higher-order systems are also lower-order ones but with additional properties, so higher-order systems **inherit** the properties of lower-order ones, which means that, as a semiotic system, language inherits both the properties of the organism it is embodied in (cf. e.g. Delafield-Butt and Trevarthen 2015, on moving and meaning in the ontogenesis of narrative) and of the social groups it is enacted by (e.g. the interactive nature of the creation of meaning, meaning as based on consensus [negotiated in meaning groups], the social nature of learning).

2. It represents the **cosmogenesis of order** towards greater complexity since the Big Bang around 13.7 billion years ago, with each new order of system constituting a new cosmogenic phase (allowing for polygenesis among higher-order systems); as systems of new orders emerge, they develop

together with systems of lower orders – this co-development takes the form of **co-evolution** with the emergence of social systems out of biological ones and semiotic ones out of social ones, which is obviously of great interest in the investigation of the evolution of language in tandem with the evolution of social systems and biological ones (cf. Dunbar 1993, 1996, 2020; Gamble, Gowlett, and Dunbar 2014; Wilson 2019) – captured by Deacon's (1992, 1997) hypothesis about the co-evolution of language and the brain (cf. Table 12.3), such correlations across systems of different orders being of central interest to neurosemiotics.

3.   It involves **general systemic principles** operating within systems of all orders, including ones that emerge as systems within a given order increase in complexity (e.g. the formation of compositional hierarchies); these general principles can be interpreted as **systemic fractals** that are manifested within the domains that open up within systems of all orders – this being a central concern of the various manifestations of systems thinking (going back to Boulding 1956 and Bertalanffy 1968, and including more recent work on language as a **complex adaptive system**, e.g. Larsen-Freeman and Cameron 2008; Beckner et al. 2009), e.g. Skyttner (1996, 2001) (one possible example directly relevant to language being Steels' e.g. 1998 notion of level formation; cf. also Matthiessen 2009) and, related to this, **network science** (Barabási 2016).

4.   Starting with second-order systems (biological systems), systems in the ordered typology increase in complexity through evolutionary processes, which among other things involve **co-opting** existing forms of organization as new forms evolve – language being an important example of this principle, having an extended history of adapting earlier forms as in the case of the evolution of the vocal tract as a resource for the expression plane, e.g. the descent of the larynx increasing articulatory potential (e.g. P. Lieberman 1984, 2000; Deacon 1997; D. Lieberman 2013),[8] and as may be the case in the evolution of content plane resources drawing on our bio-semiotic systems, i.e. on our sensorimotor systems.[9]

5.   At a meta-level, i.e. at the level of the *study* of the different phenomenal realms, it is reflected in the **stages of the emergence of modern science** of a given order of phenomena, beginning with physical sciences around half a millennium ago (e.g. Halliday and Matthiessen 1999), the breakthrough to the modern science of each order of system depending on a combination of technology, methodology, theory, and semiotic resources.

The breakthrough to the modern science of systems of different orders – which we can gloss as "the cracking of their code" – depended on a number of "ingredients." These ingredients have been both material and immaterial in nature:

1. **Material components** have included the technology needed to extend the human senses so that we can perceive what is not accessible to us with only the naked eye, ear, and so on, preferably without intruding as observers, and so that we can record such observations to allow repeated investigation. In addition, in the study of certain realms, in particular of physical and biological phenomena, technology for experimentation has been essential, i.e. for investigations under controlled replicable conditions. For example, physical sciences depended for their early breakthroughs on the invention of the telescope and the microscope (in the seventeenth century), biological science – medicine in particular – on the invention of the stethoscope (in the early nineteenth century), and both social and semiotic sciences have depended on recording devices making it possible to "capture" processes of instantial behaviour and of instantial meaning (i.e. spoken texts in context).

2. **Immaterial components** have included new ways of organizing research, e.g. into teams operating in laboratories and societies for sharing findings, and of funding research, but also of new forms of semiotic resources, both the evolution of scientific registers (e.g.Bazerman 1988; Halliday 1988b; Swales 1990) and the design of new semiotic systems such as branches of mathematics like differential calculus, set theory, and probability theory – and in the representation of different aspects of accounts of language designed representational systems like Boolean algebra, predicate logic, production rules, transition networks, frame-based inheritance networks, and of course the relational networks of relational network theory (e.g. Lamb 1966, 1999, 2013; Lockwood 1972; García, Sullivan, and Tsiang 2017) and the system networks of SFL.

12.2.3 Language in relation to other systemic orders in the history of SFL

Using the ordered typology of systems as a frame of reference, we need to spell out the relationships between systems of different orders. In principle, this ought to build on accounts of immediately adjacent systems – semiotic to social, social to biological, and biological to physical. However, understandably, in view of the complexity of this research program, in linguistics we have tended to develop "hyphenated" branches that focus on the relationship between language and one order of system at a time, prototypical examples being sociolinguistics and neurolinguistics. In sociolinguistics, the focus has been on the relationship between language (at least implicitly treated as a semiotic system) and society within social systems, but usually without any reference to biological systems. In neurolinguistics, the focus has been on the relationship between language and the brain, but until recently usually bypassing considerations of the enactment of language in social systems and thus of social mediation (with important exceptions referred to above).

The engagement with lower-order manifestations of language, and also of other semiotic systems, obviously involves not only a focus on the relevant phenomena but also a dialogue with the relevant disciplines studying these phenomena – the fields of study concerned with social systems and with biological systems, and with the relationship to language. As far as SFL is concerned, social systems have been in view from the early stages, and the dialogue with social sciences goes back even to pre-systemic functional work by J.R. Firth and his colleagues, reflecting in part Firth's dialogue with Bronislaw Malinowski (e.g. Firth 1957a; Hasan 1985b) – the orientation towards ethnography rather than philosophy (cf. my remarks in the Introduction about Malinowski's earlier insights in relation to the later Wittgenstein).

And there is a long tradition of applications of SFL in **clinical linguistics** (e.g. Rochester and Martin 1979; Fine 1994, 2006; Armstrong 2009; Asp and de Villiers 2010, 2019; Ferguson, Spencer, and Armstrong 2017). Here the emphasis has, naturally, been on diagnosis and treatment rather than on basic research into the relationship between language and the brain. However, the systemic functional engagement with psycholinguistics and cognitive linguistics has been more challenging: while psycholinguistics pre-dates Chomskyan linguistics, the growth of psycholinguistics in the 1960s was heavily influenced by the development of Chomskyan linguistics, which was not conducive to a dialogue with SFL. (Kess 1992: 19, characterizes the 1960s as the "linguistic period" in the history of psycholinguistics, following the "formative period" and preceding the "cognitive period." But the "linguistic period" is really the Chomskyan linguistic period, as is clear from his introduction of this phase: "The rise of transformational generative grammar in linguistics is followed by its theoretical domination of psycholinguistic research, particularly from 1960 to 1969." This "linguistic period" could certainly have drawn on other, non-Chomskyan linguistic theories and frameworks being developed during the 1960s, such as tagmemic linguistics, stratificational linguistics, and SFL – traditions that would have helped foreground the need for "ecological validity" alongside "experimental validity." And this would have lead naturally to a socio-semiotic period complementing the "cognitive period.")

During the period when Halliday (e.g. 1978) explored the relationship between language and social systems, extending Firth's (e.g. 1950) social conception of speakers as persons defined by the social roles (personae) they play in social groups (cf. Table 12.1, and see Butt 1991), and developed the framing of this area in terms of social semiotics, the conditions were not yet ripe for engaging with language in relation to biological systems (apart from the established research in phonetics, like the British Abercrombie tradition, insightfully represented and extended by Catford 1977 – a contribution that gives an indication of what systemic phonetics could be like, as noted in Matthiessen 2021a). Brain science had yet to make the advances that began in the 1980s thanks to observational technology such as fMRI; nor were the conditions ideal at the time for engaging with cognitive interpretations of phenomena within fourth-order systems. While this was the period when psycholinguistics was being developed energetically as part of the general macro-discipline of cognitive science, together with early work that could be classified as cognitive linguistics, broadly conceived, in tandem with cognitive psychology, the contributions tended either to be based on experimental methodology (psycholinguistics) or not grounded in empirical evidence from neuroscience (early cognitive linguistics).

In fact, cognitive models tended to look quite similar to computational architectures (e.g. among many others, Fromkin's 1968 exploration of "performance models"; cf. Edelman's 1992, critique; and also Lamb 1999: 362, in reference to "flow-chart psycholinguistic models, which relate more easily to their metaphoric basis of computer software than to any neurological structures"), as can be seen in the linguistic analysis of samples of discourse from cognitive science (Matthiessen 1993b, 1998; Halliday and Matthiessen 1999: ch. 14). Halliday felt that experimental approaches were largely inappropriate since they tended to disrupt the phenomena being studied, preferring observation of authentic naturally occurring text in context (cf. Trevisan and García's 2019, discussion of "ecological validity" in SFL), such as in the work on language development (e.g. Halliday 1975, 2004b). As noted above, he also argued that humans are "not bounded by the skin": during this phase of cognitive science, the focus was typically on individual minds, and the recognition of the fundamental significance of social organization and interaction had not yet emerged very clearly.

When certain strands of research that were often brought together under the heading of cognitive science began to change, the conditions for dialogue initiated within SFL improved. One important change was the increasing awareness of and interest in cognitive science in Vygotsky's approach to ontogenesis and the conception and formation of the mind. While Vygotsky's work had been translated already as Vygotsky (1962), the more widespread engagement with it seems to have come only two decades later, significantly helped by Wertsch (1985); and it led to consideration of both social and semiotic factors (of the kind that were part of the Firthian-Hallidayan tradition, drawing on insights from Malinowski) in certain developments within cognitive science. This then paved the way for the recognition of resonances between Vygotsky's and Halliday's conceptualization of ontogenesis and the emphasis on the central role played by language in children's interaction with significant others: in response to Halliday's (1993b) steps towards a language-based theory of learning designed to add to theories of learning coming "from outside the study of language," Wells (1994) brought out the complementarity between Halliday and Vygotsky, an insight that has been followed up in a number of publications, e.g. Byrnes (2006), Han and Kellog (2019); and see also Hasan (1992, 2002, 2004) on **semiotic mediation** and related insights related to the Halliday–Vygotsky complementarity. By another step, we can relate this to Trevarthen's (e.g. 1987, 2011) theory of **intersubjectivity**, which he relates explicitly to Halliday's work, and to Hasson et al.'s (2012) notion of **brain-to-brain coupling**, mentioned in Section 12.2.1.

Another change was the highlighting by Gerald Edelman and a number of other scholars of the central role played by language in the evolution and development of "higher-order consciousness" out of "primary consciousness" (e.g. Edelman 1992, 2004; Edelman and Tononi 2000). Edelman (2004: 58–9) writes of what he calls higher-order consciousness that it "confers the ability to imagine the future, explicitly recall the past, and to be conscious of being conscious," and relates it to the emergence to language. Taking Edelman's work as his starting point, Halliday (1995b) reviews his interpretation of Edelman's account of "neural Darwinism," involving neuronal group selection, and he views higher-order consciousness as **linguistic consciousness**; he writes (2003b: 392), "Language, in Edelman's account, is an essential condition of higher order human consciousness. I cannot hope to do justice to the richness and breadth of his theory; but I would like to show, as much as I can, how closely it resonates with what we could observe in investigating language from the social-semiotic standpoint."

Halliday goes on to highlight points of contact between Edelman's account and SFL, both in terms of general theory and of particular empirical studies. The empirical work includes ontogenesis as a central concern, and Halliday (2004b) develops this further, expanding on the role of grammar within the stratified content plane in the move to higher-order consciousness. Rounding off his summary of Edelman's account, Halliday (2003b: 396) underlines the convergence in thinking:

It seems to me that Edelman's theory, far from "creating a gulf between linguistic theory and biology", resonates sweetly and powerfully with much that linguistic theory has to offer. This is obscured if we see only the dominant paradigm, the model of language first formulated by Chomsky on a Bloomfieldian base and subsequently held in place by two generations of his followers; but this is far from universally accepted, and is regarded by Ellis [1993, CMIMM], in the work referred to at the end of this paper, as fundamentally flawed. [Cf. Halliday's 1995a, review of Ellis 1993.]

Halliday's virtual dialogue with Edelman was very stimulating for a number of us in the SFL community.[10] There were a certain other neuroscientists whose work also seemed to resonate with systemic functional theory; in addition to Edelman, we read work by Terrence Deacon, Michael Arbib, and Suzanne Greenfield; and Deacon was invited to contribute to two SFL conferences, one in Sydney and one in Vancouver. (Edelman had also been invited on one occasion but was not able to come.) A fellow traveller in linguistics who did a great deal to support SFL, Fred Peng, encouraged us to learn more about neuroscience and get involved in neuro-linguistics. Coming from linguistics, he had made a great effort to learn about the brain, and he nudged me to do the same, which regretfully I was not in a position to do. One member of our community who followed this up with Fred was Paul Thibault, and he brought out important insights in Thibault (2004). A little later, Robin Melrose published two papers about language and the brain informed by SFL (Melrose 2005, 2006), which are noted and discussed by García and Ibáñez (2017: 307).

A good way of developing a sense of the significance of interpreting and the-orizing language as a fourth-order system in relation to systems of lower orders is to take some fundamental principle central to the organization of language and consider this organizational principle in terms not only of semiotic systems but also of systems of the lower orders. Since language is interpreted semiotically as a resource for making meaning and is modelled as a meaning potential, the orga-nization of this meaning potential as a network of options in meaning, options that language users choose among, it is productive to consider how the **mean-ing potential** of language is enacted as a **behaviour potential** within the social order and as an **action potential** within the biological order. Focussing on the contributions to part II of Fontaine, Bartlett, and O'Grady (2013) (cognitive and neurolinguistic views on choice) as particularly relevant to the development of neurosemiotics, I note Lamb's (2013) discussion of choice in relation to system networks and relational networks, Asp's (2013) chapter on choice in relation to neuroscience, and Gil's (2013) "neurocognitive interpretation of systemic functional choice." I'll return to Lamb's chapter at the end (Section 12.6) as part of a brief discussion of biological implementability and just refer very briefly to Asp's discussion here.

Asp is concerned with a neurologically informed interpretation of choice, in relation to degree of conscious awareness of choice and agency. She considers both the anatomy of choice and the physiology of choice, reviewing the literature that can shed light on these issues. She concludes (Asp 2013: 178):

> Through selective review of the literature on executive control processes, and the neuroimaging and lesion literature on choice in language and discourse, I have tried to set a frame in which it is possible to imagine a speaker who is an agent, not only capable of, but continuously making, conscious choices in discourse. This speaker-as-agent also carries out a great many activities with limited attention, relying on highly automated activations and selection-by-default for routine activities. S/he makes coffee in the morning without thinking about the sequences of actions necessary for the task. S/he talks without hesitating before each word to see if it fits the current syntactic frame or carries appropriate connotations. And this speaker-as-agent is certainly not consciously aware of the neurophysiological processes enabling this activity. However, if s/he is well, s/he is continuously monitoring these activities. S/he can inhibit an action, choose chocolate instead of coffee, plan to talk about an idea later and do so. The neural systems that support the ongoing monitoring, selection, inhibition and execution of action are the same ones that, in interaction with language, affect and memory networks, allow us to be agents of our discourse.

Thus, Asp also sheds light on individual speakers both as meaners (the semiotic order of system) and as organisms (the biological order). And by another step, what aspects of making choice meaners are aware of or can bring to consciousness. (On the consciousness of choice, see e.g. Soon et al. 2008, showing that what may be experienced as free choices, "decisions," may be determined by brain activity before the experience of the choice. This is related to Barrett's 2017 emphasis on the brain as always being involved in processes of prediction, producing predictions that are tested against sensory data.)

12.3 Properties of language ("architecture") important to biological implementability

In this section, I turn to the question of what properties that are characteristic of language, and of other semiotic systems, are particularly relevant to explorations of their relationship to the brain. In sketching the architecture of language, I will continue to draw on SFL.

12.3.1 Some key organizing principles in the architecture of language: hierarchies and clines

To avoid the potentially misleading connotations of the wording "architecture of language" – like rigid designed structure – we should perhaps replace it with the "anatomy of language," to be complemented by the "physiology of language"; but the metaphor of "architecture" to denote the organization of language has been used widely and is well established. In any case, here I would just like to highlight some of the central principles in the organization of language (in context) as a complex adaptive system in an ordered typology of systems. In SFL, this organization has been theorized **relationally** in terms of a number of **intersecting semiotic dimensions**. I will start with dimensions that are hierarchies or clines, and their properties, and then turn to a spectrum, the spectrum of metafunction.

Organizing principles: hierarchies and clines

The organization of language located in an ordered typology of systems is defined by a number of intersecting global and local semiotic dimensions, both hierarchies and clines. I'll also mention another type of dimension here, the spectrum of metafunction, and then return to it in some more detail in Section 12.3.2. I will elaborate on the hierarchy of stratification in Section 12.4. Here I'll review what I have said about organizing principles and add further information. The account is summarized in Table 12.2.

1. As already spelt out above, language is a **higher-order semiotic system** (e.g. Halliday 1995b) in the ordered typology of systems; it is a semiotic system (system of meaning) that is enacted as a social system, embodied as biological systems, and manifested as a physical system (Figure 12.1 and Figure 12.2). Therefore, in terms of neurobiology, our brains are both **social brains** and **semiotic brains** – more specifically, **language brains** (see Section 12.2.1 above). The embodiment of language in the human

brain (as well as other relevant parts of the body) is thus socially mediated (cf. the reference above to Kuhl, e.g. 2007, on language learning being "gated by social factors").

2. Internally, language is organized as a **system of systems** linked to one another in terms of different kinds of relation. While it can be modelled holistically, it is not monolithic, but these systems are not "modules" in the sense of modularity in generative linguistics[11] – they organize different domains within language but they are to a large extent organized in terms of **fractal principles**, i.e. principles of organization that are manifested throughout the different environments in which the systems of language operate. One of the fractal principles in language is the hierarchy of axiality, which is manifested within all stratal subsystems: all stratal subsystems are organized paradigmatically as resources within the overall resource of language – as potentials for meaning (semantics), wording (lexicogrammar), and sounding (phonology and phonetics); paradigmatic options are realized syntagmatically. Another is the rank scale, the compositional hierarchy also manifested within all stratal subsystems. Fractal principles of organization most likely also operate across systemic orders, emerging with increasing complexity. For example, compositional hierarchies operate in systems of all orders as they begin to increase in complexity. Thus, the "hierarchical coding hypothesis" in neurological object representation and recognition (Gazzaniga et al. 2019: 237–8) may be a manifestation of the same principle of systemic organization as the rank scale in language.

3. The systems that make up language can thus be differentiated and related to one another along a number of **semiotic dimensions**, including the dimensions of global organization – the hierarchy of stratification, the cline of instantiation and the spectrum of metafunction, and of local organization within each stratum – the rank scale (a compositional hierarchy) and the hierarchy of axiality (paradigmatic/syntagmatic axes); collectively these dimensions constitute the architecture of language (e.g. Halliday 2002a; Matthiessen 2007a, forthcoming a). Each semiotic dimension may be embodied neurobiologically in a distinct way. For example, the embodiment of **hierarchy of stratification** must involve a pathway from sensorimotor systems in general at the semantic interface to auditory-articulatory systems in general at the phonetic interface (cf. also Barrett's 2017 cascade model; see Section 12.4.3). The embodiment of **spectrum of metafunction** has implications in terms of the two hemispheres: the ideational metafunction can be interpreted as having been located in the neurolinguistic literature within the left hemisphere, while the interpersonal metafunction

has to a certain extent been linked to the right hemisphere; and the textual metafunction has been investigated mainly in terms of processing activity. The **cline of instantiation** has been studied in terms of the processes of instantiation, viz. studies of sentence and discourse comprehension and production (e.g. Kemmerer 2015: ch. 16).

4. Among the global semiotic dimensions, the **hierarchy of stratification** organizes language into **inner and outer stratal systems**, and the outer stratal systems, semantics and phonetics, serve as interfaces to other human systems, both fourth-order semiotic systems and bio-semiotic systems (sensorimotor systems). As already noted, this relates to studies of the pathway (or "cascade") from the semantic interface to the phonetic interface to sensorimotor systems and will be explored further in Section 12.4.1.

12.3.2 Some key organizing principles in the architecture of language: spectrum of metafunction

As a higher-order semiotic system, language is a resource not only for carrying meaning (as in primary semiotic systems) but also for **creating meaning within different metafunctional modes of meaning**, more specifically for construing our experience of the world around us and inside us as meaning (ideational); for enacting our roles, relations, and values as meaning (interpersonal); and for transforming these strands of meaning as a flow of text in context (textual). These different metafunctional modes of meaning appear, not surprisingly, to be embodied in different ways in the brain. In neurolinguistics, they have also been investigated using different methods, studies of the textual mode of meaning arguably standing apart as having been investigated primarily along the lines of processes of comprehension, whereas ideational and interpersonal meanings have been studied in terms of neurobiological correlates. It is important to note, however, that since researchers investigating the neurobiology of the different metafunctional modes of meaning do not frame their research in metafunctional terms, I have had to impose my interpretation of their research.

It is probably a fair assessment to say that in terms of metafunctional modes of meaning, the focus in neurolinguistic studies has been on **ideational meaning**, including logical sequences in discourse production and comprehension (e.g. neurolinguistic studies such as Ash et al. 2006, in a study of healthy speakers and patients with frontotemporal dementia; psycholinguistic studies such as Berman and Slobin 1994; ontogenetic studies such as Delafield-Butt and Trevarthen 2015; and also the work by Christiane von Stutterheim referred to in Section 12.2.1; for

Table 12.2 Systemic orders and global dimensions in the organization of language in relation to neurobiological implications

Systemic order	Global dimensions		Relation	Neurobiological implications
semiotic	stratification	[content:] semantics > lexico-grammar > [expression:] phonology > phonetics	realization	pathway from sensorimotor systems interfacing with semantics to auditory-articulatory systems interfacing with phonetics (Sections 12.3.4 and 12.4)
	instantiation	potential – subpotential/instance type – instance	instantiation (potential to instance; instance to potential)	activation in processes of production and comprehension, related to e.g. statistical learning
	metafunction	ideational [logical	experiential]	interpersonal	textual	conflation	modes of semantic interfacing with different extra-linguistic systems (Section 12.3.2)
		ideational		construing sensorimotor categories within different brain regions (including acts and activities) (Section 12.5)
		interpersonal		enacting sensorimotor categories: e.g. enacting proposals, enacting emotions, enacting intensions as acts (Section 12.3.2)
		textual		enabling production and comprehension, studied in terms of ERPs implicating N400, P600 (Section 12.3.2)
enacted as social				
embodied as biological				

an overview, see Kemmerer 2015: ch. 16) and experiential construal of (taxonomies of) categories, often in relation to sensorimotor systems and thus with connections to the relevant brain regions, discussed in Section 12.4.2 (e.g. Damasio 1989, 1990; Damasio and Damasio 1992; Martin 2007; Chatterjee 2008; Lambon Ralph et al. 2010; Wang et al. 2010; Watson et al. 2013; García and Ibáñez 2017, and cf. also Melrose 2005, on the ideation base in SFL; for an overview, see Kemmerer 2015: chs. 10–12).

However, relatively less research seems to have been done in neurolinguistics on neurological correlates of the **interpersonal and textual modes of meaning**. Thus, Egorova, Shtyrov, and Pulvermüller (2016) frame their study of the "brain basis" of the distinction in speech acts (speech functions) between naming and requesting speech acts by pointing to the focus of research: "The primary function of human language is to allow efficient communication in social interaction. Yet, the neurobiological mechanisms of this unique communication ability are still poorly understood. Most previous neuroimaging studies focused on structural aspects of language, including the brain basis of word and sentence processing" (p. 857).

While "efficient communication in social interaction" is only one of the two primary functions of language – the interpersonal function, the other being the ideational function,[12] providing us with the resources for construing our experience of the world as meaning – their assessment of the focus of neuroimaging studies is important.

Since the interpersonal and textual meanings are almost always mapped onto experiential ones, it is difficult to separate them out and to insulate them for observation or experimentation. Within the **interpersonal mode** of meaning, there has been some neuroscientific investigation of the semantic system of speech function ("speech acts"), which is realized by the grammatical system of mood, which in turn is realized by the phonological system of tone within prosodic phonology in English and many other languages, although not all (Figure 12.3). The system involved two primary systemic variables, viz. the orientation of the speech function, giving or demanding, and the nature of the commodity being exchanged, viz. information or goods-&-services (e.g. Halliday 1984b; Halliday and Matthiessen 2014: ch. 4). If the commodity is information (or "knowledge"), it is constituted in language itself (propositions); but if it is goods-&-services, the speech function serves to facilitate what is prototypically a non-linguistic act in order to effect the exchanges of goods-&-services (proposals). Thus, we would expect that they are different neurological implications. Egorova, Shtyrov, and Pulvermüller (2013, 2016) report on a study by means of fMRI where they compared the processing of naming an object (e.g. *What are these called?*) and requesting an object (e.g. *What can I get you?*[13]) – i.e. of the exchange of information (naming) and goods-&-services (requesting), and they found significant differences – as I would expect based on the basic difference in commodity between propositions and proposals. Thus Egorova, Shtyrov, and Pulvermüller (2016: 866) identified significant differences between the two; they found that in naming an object:

> the left angular gyrus, interfacing between visual and language areas tended to show relatively stronger activity during Naming compared with Requests. In contrast, Request understanding implies forming rich predictions on likely partner actions, which could follow this act in social communicative interaction (handing over the object, denying the Request etc.). Consistent with the relevance of predictive action knowledge for this speech act type, Requests activated the inferior frontal, premotor, parietal and temporo-occipital cortices most important for action and action sequence processing and for predicting future action performance and (auditory/visual) perception. The right TPJ [temporoparietal junction, CMIMM], known to be the main site for the processing of theory of mind and common ground knowledge, was found equally active for both speech acts. In sum, we show that the key human capacity of communicative use of language in social interaction context relies on a coordinated effort of a bilaterally distributed network unifying a range of multimodal neurocognitive systems.

Speech functions are, of course, mapped onto experiential figures (configurations of processes, participants, and circumstances; Halliday and Matthiessen 1999: ch 4), so even though Egorova, Shtyrov, and Pulvermüller (2016) tried to keep the experiential content constant across the speech functions (acts) of naming and requesting, it is hard to isolate the interpersonal contribution from the representation of experience. However, it may be possible to achieve this isolation of the interpersonal if we start with the interpersonal mode of expression, prosody, separated from experiential expressions (cf. Halliday 1979c, on prosody being the interpersonal mode of expression). Thus, researchers have investigated "affective," "emotive," or "attitudinal" uses of prosody, which realizes purely interpersonal choices in grammar, and by another step, semantics – the interaction base within the semantic system – and it is clear that in people with the normal lateralization, this involves the right hemisphere: see Section 12.3.6. In addition, Sugeno (2008: 1) refers to a study focussed on honorifics in Japanese, which fall within the interpersonal metafunction; but he does not provide any detailed results except to note that "the brain activities for understanding sentences with honorific expressions are different from those produced for understanding sentences without honorific expressions."

As for the **textual mode of meaning**, apart from aspects touched upon in studies of discourse production and comprehension such as reference (which is a textual system of cohesion; see Halliday and Hasan 1976; Halliday and Matthiessen 2014: ch. 9), perhaps the main focus has been on "information structure" (a term taken from Halliday but extended to include the system of theme in addition to the system of information; cf. Schwabe and Winkler 2007, and also Féry and Ishihara 2016).

Bornkessel-Schlesewsky and Schumacher (2016) provide an overview of studies of the "neurobiology of information structure," with the aim "to demonstrate that, rather than postulating neural correlates of specific IS [information structure, CMIMM] functions, a more promising approach is to consider IS affecting domain-general mechanisms by guiding predictive processing or providing cues for attention orientation" (p.18). In keeping with this, they view information structure in terms of studies of discourse comprehension in general and report on research based on event-related potentials (ERPs), identifying N400 and P600 as particularly significant. They suggest that information structure helps language users "update" their mental models and make "predictions," and go on to say of information structure notions that "their multidimensional contributions to the processing system – for example language-specific cues that generate predictions or the functions that trigger attention orientation – must be identified and used to improve our models of the language architecture" (p.19).

This interpretation is consistent with the conception of the "text base" in computational SFL (e.g. Bateman and Matthiessen 1993; Halliday and Matthiessen 1999) and more generally with the systemic functional interpretation of the textual metafunction as an enabling one (e.g. Halliday 1978; Matthiessen 1992) – a resource for speakers to guide their listeners in understanding text (and themselves in producing it). However, systemic functional accounts of the textual metafunction show that it is not only a kind of post-production unit in the production of discourse, but can actually guide both ideational and interpersonal choices; and this will also need to be taken account of.

12.3.3 Some key organizing principles in the architecture of language: variation among particular languages

These properties characterize language as a general human system – as it would have emerged in human evolution in the order of 150–250 thousand years ago as modern language emerged out of archaic language together with the evolution of

AMHs (*Homo sapiens sapiens*; see below). They represent the "architecture" of language according to systemic functional theory. However, we need to recognize that there is very rich variation among the particular languages that have been spoken throughout the history of linguistically modern humans and are still spoken today (very significant variation that may be downplayed or effaced in approaches based on universalist ideology).

In the second half of the twentieth century, the notion of language universals and of universal grammar, as conceived by Noam Chomsky and further developed within his strand of generative linguistics, came to dominate, marginalizing and devaluing the great descriptivist tradition pioneered in North America by Franz Boas, Edward Sapir, Mary Haas, Ken Pike, and others. However, in SFL, there has always been considerable emphasis on the pervasive and rich variation and diversity found among languages – informed by J.R. Firth's (e.g. 1957b) critical view of claims about universals, warning against the "universalist fallacy" (e.g. Teruya and Matthiessen 2015). And within the community of descriptive linguists and linguists exploring language typology, there is now a powerful, empirically well-informed pushback against premature claims about language universals, an important contribution being Evans and Levinson's (2009) arguments against "the myth of language universals" based on a systematic review of the various claims that have been made over the decades and of the collective findings emerging from major descriptions of a wide range of languages (cf. Matthiessen, forthcoming b). This is obviously very important in the context of neurosemiotics: we need to allow for this diversity in exploring the relationship between language and the brain, ensuring that over time the database of speakers is expanded to include users of many diverse languages (including "small languages" with very interesting features).

12.3.4 Language as a higher-order semiotic system

Neurosemiotics is concerned with the relation between all semiotic systems and the neural organization of biological systems, i.e. neurobiology. However, the fact that language is a higher-order semiotic system rather than a primary one (e.g. Halliday 1995b) is of fundamental significance when we consider its relation to the brain. Phylogenetically, this is at the heart of the hypothesis put forward by Deacon (1992, 1997) that language and the human brain evolved together. This **co-evolution** can be interpreted semiotically as the evolution of language as a higher-order semiotic, modern language out of archaic language, from a primary semiotic, and I have tentatively suggested certain correlations in between language and the brain in human evolution (Matthiessen 2004a), summarized in greatly simplified form in Table 12.3.

Modern humans – *Homo sapiens sapiens* – would have emerged in the order of 150–250 thousand years ago; they were both anatomically modern humans (AMHs) and what I have called **linguistically modern humans** (LMHs); to relate to neurosemiotics, we could call them semiotically modern humans, which makes excellent sense – except that it is important to take into account the nature of language as a higher-order semiotic system co-evolving with higher-order consciousness and with the brain (as noted above). In other words, among semiotic systems, it must have been the evolution of the increasing complexity and power of language that was the key factor.

While the record is fragmentary and the details are very complex,[14] my interpretation is focussed on the *relative* sequence of emerging properties, and the key point is simply that our brains are **language brains** and that major semiotic and biological transitions can be correlated. Obviously, brain imaging technology has now advanced to the stage where it is also possible to explore this relationship ontogenetically in terms of growth using minimally distracting brain imaging equipment (cf. Kuhl 2010a,b). (It is also important to note that while we are the only surviving lineage of hominins, there have been a range of others, ones that also migrated out of Africa, like *Homo erectus*; and their linguistic capacities are clearly of interest. For example, did Neanderthals, who disappeared as recently as forty thousand years ago, use a language of an archaic or modern kind? Studies have been conducted that investigated their capacity from the point of view of the expression plane, e.g. Conde-Valverde et al. 2021. However, Botha 2020, also considers behaviour such as collective hunting that can be interpreted as content-plane-oriented evidence for some kind of language.)

12.3.5 Language as inherently variable: probabilistic nature

The brain imaging technology referred to above has made it possible to shed light on the significance of language as a **probabilistic system**, particularly in language development, i.e. learning language as a probabilistic system – statistical learning (e.g. Erickson and Thiessen 2015). The conception in SFL of language as a probabilistic system goes back to Halliday (1959), including one that is learned as a probabilistic system (Halliday 2004), and it endured during the decades when the probabilistic nature of language was not recognized, and even dismissed, by Chomsky and generative linguists who followed him. It has now gained much wider acceptance in linguistics also outside in SFL, thanks in large measure to the development of big data in linguistics in the form of increasingly large corpora, and the tools and methods of analysis developed within (statistical) natural language processing (for an early overview, see Manning and Schütze 1999) and corpus

Table 12.3 Semogenic phases in ontogenesis and hypothesized in phylogenesis

Phase	Properties	Properties	Ontogenesis	Phylogenesis	
				period	Homo …
I – protolanguage	microfunctional	bistratal [content > expression]	around 5–8 months of age to middle of second year; starting to crawl	millions of years ago (far back in primate history)	
II – transition; archaic language in phylogenesis	macrofunctional	emergence of stratified content and expression	around middle of second year of life	around 2 million years ago	Homo habilis (c. 2.2 million years before present [BP]), Homo erectus (c. 1.8 million years BP) – first significant brain expansion
III – post-infancy adult language; modern language in phylogenesis	metafunctional	quadristratal [content: semantics > lexicogrammar; expression: phonology > phonetics]	starting to walk upright	around 150–250 thousand years ago	Homo sapiens sapiens (c. 200 thousand years ago): AMH (anatomically modern humans) and LMH (linguistically modern humans)

linguistics; and "deep analysis" techniques have been used in SFL (e.g. Teich et al. 2016). This in linguistics outside SFL is reflected in the publication of Bod, Hay, and Jannedy (2003), which includes contributions applying probabilistic modelling to different linguistic subsystems.

The probabilistic nature of language is based on the **cline of instantiation** (as a conceptual alternative in theories of language to the dichotomy between "competence" and "performance," as noted in Section 12.1.3). In the first instance, probability is the probability that terms in systems located at the potential pole of the cline of instantiation will be chosen in the processing of texts (that is, the probability that systemic terms will be instantiated in text during production or understanding). They are thus manifested as relative frequencies in texts; and in the course of innumerable instantiations in texts, they develop as probability distillations of relative frequencies in texts – a property that is also crucial in the gradual evolution of languages through changing patterns in texts within different registers (see e.g. Matthiessen 2015b).

The probabilistic nature of language is inherent in semogenesis – not only in phylogenesis, as just noted, but also in ontogenesis and in logogenesis (for the latter, see Chapter 10, this volume). According to Halliday (1975, 2004) this is an important characteristic of early language development: in interaction with caregivers and other speakers, young learners develop the system of language out of innumerable texts, constructing probabilistic profiles out of relative frequencies in texts. Halliday (2004a: 342) specifies this as one of the features he proposes in his contribution "toward a language-based theory of learning":

> Learning a semiotic system means learning its options **together with their relative probabilities,** and so building up a quantitative profile of the whole. This concept is familiar in linguistics with regard to word frequencies: it is accepted that speakers have a rather clear sense of the relative frequency of the words in their mother tongue; for example, in English, that *go* is more frequent than *walk,* and *walk,* in its turn, is more frequent than *stroll.* But remarkably little attention has been paid to probabilities in the grammar.
>
> Grammatical probabilities are no less part of the system of a language; and they are more powerful than lexical probabilities because of their greater generality. Children construe both kinds from the very rich evidence they have around them. By five years of age, a child is likely to have heard between half a million and a million clauses, so that, as an inherent aspect of learning the principal grammatical systems of the language, he has learnt the relative probabilities of each of their terms.

This insight into the nature of early language learning is, of course, based on socio-semiotic evidence, accumulated through case studies such as Halliday's own (1975) study and subsequent studies drawing on his framework (see e.g. Painter, Deewana, and Torr 2007; Torr 2015; Painter 2017).

However, the role of **statistical learning** (e.g. Erickson and Thiessen 2015) has been identified outside SFL in neuro-cognitive research, a seminal study being Saffran, Aslin, and Newport's (1996) investigation of word segmentation by infants. Characterizing their study, Saffran, Aslin, and Newport (1996: 1926) write: "The present study shows that a fundamental task of language acquisition, segmentation of words from fluent speech, can be accomplished by 8-month-old infants based solely on the statistical relationships between neighbouring speech sounds." The insights into "statistical learning" are clearly of fundamental importance; they make it possible to relate text as data to the system instantiated by text – along the cline of instantiation. Significantly, infants begin this process of statistical learning of aspects of the mother tongue(s) while they are still learning how to mean during the protolinguistic phase of language development, before they begin the transition into the mother tongue(s) spoken around them somewhere around the middle of their second year of life (for the ontogenetic phases, see Halliday 1975, 2004).

Reporting on research concerned with the expression plane into phonological-phonetic and word learning demonstrating that infants "take statistics," Kuhl (2010a: 717) writes, "A surprising new form of learning, referred to as "statistical learning" (Saffran et al. 1996), was discovered in the 1990s. Statistical learning is computational in nature, and reflects implicit rather than explicit learning. It relies on the ability to automatically pick up and learn from the statistical regularities that exist in the stream of sensory information we process, and strongly influences both phonetic learning and early word learning."

The research by Patricia Kuhl and her group has been enabled by new non-intrusive brain scanning technology (shown and discussed by Kuhl and Rivera-Gaxiola 2008, and demonstrated by Kuhl 2010b). Having reviewed studies of statistical language learning, Kuhl (2010a: 719) confirms the fundamental importance of this kind of learning:

> As reviewed, infants show robust learning effects in statistical learning studies when tested in the laboratory with very simple stimuli (Maye et al. 2002, 2008; Saffran et al. 1996). However, complex natural language learning may challenge infants in a way that these experiments do not. Are there constraints on statistical learning as an explanation for natural language learning? A series of later studies suggest that this

is the case. Laboratory studies testing infant phonetic and word learning from exposure to a complex natural language suggest limits on statistical learning, and provide new information suggesting that social brain systems are integrally involved, and, in fact, may be necessary to explain natural language learning.

The patterns of instantiation of the linguistic system at the potential pole of the cline of instantiation as texts at the instance pole of the cline depend on the contexts of use. Language has evolved to serve in an innumerable range of contexts, and each context represents specific distinct demands on the linguistic system. In other words, each context calls for some particular range of meanings, a subset of the overall meaning potential of a language – a **register**. A register is thus a functional variety of a language, one that has evolved as an adaptation of language used in a particular institutional setting. Registers can be characterized in qualitative terms as strategies of meaning adapting to particular institutional settings, and they can also be characterized quantitatively as particular settings of the overall systemic probabilities of a language – probabilities being probabilities of instantiation of systemic options, observed at the instantial pole of the cline of instantiation as relative frequencies (e.g. Halliday 1959, 2005a; Matthiessen 2006, 2015b).

In terms of the inherent variability of language, we need to take account of three kinds of variation, viz. **dialectal variation**, **registerial variation**, and **codal variation**. Here it is relevant to note that a great deal of psycholinguistic and neurolinguistic research concerned with discourse production and comprehension has been based on narratives, prominent examples being the pear stories and the frog stories (e.g. Chafe 1980; Berman and Slobin 1994; and cf. also Section 12.2.1 on psycholinguistic research based on reports and commentaries on video clips), partly because narrative discourse tends to be fairly congruent with concrete human activities involving sensorimotor systems (cf. Kemmerer 2015: ch. 16); but while this register, or register family, is central to all speech communities and is surely of ancient origin as a way of making sense of life and construing guidelines (cf. Halliday 2010), it is only one of the myriad of very varied registers that together constitute the meaning potential of a language, and it is thus a fairly narrow window on discourse processes.

12.3.6 Pathways in language across strata

The dimensional organization of language in context makes it possible to focus on a given region along one of the dimensions; for example, we can focus on the potential pole of the cline of instantiation, setting ourselves the task of describing

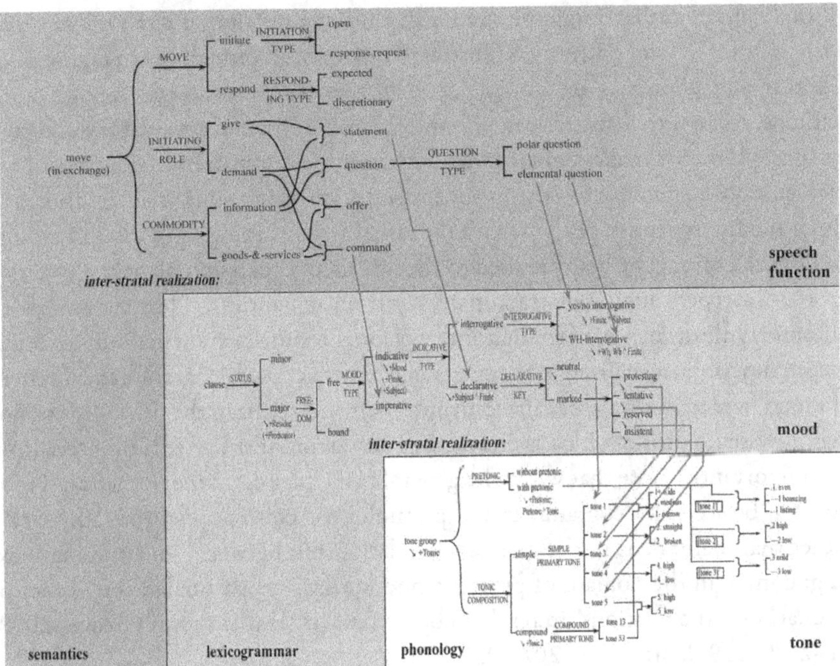

Figure 12.3 An interpersonal "slice" or pathway through semantics, lexicogrammar, and phonology

systems, or we can focus on one of the strata of the hierarchy of stratification, or one of the ranks of the hierarchy of rank (the rank scale). And this has been the tendency in a good deal of linguistics, with more occasional emphasis on interfaces between e.g. syntax and morphology or between morphosyntax and phonology.

However, it is absolutely necessary to take account of "inter" relations as well – inter-stratal relations, inter-rank relations, and inter-axial relations (cf. Matthiessen 1988a); in terms of representations of the brain, it is important to identify **pathways** that relate different domains within the architecture of language. One of the key pathways in the global organization of language is that which relates different strata to one another, e.g. within one and the same metafunction – what I have also called a "slice" through the system (cf. Barrett's 2017, notion of "concept cascades" referred to in Section 12.4). This can be illustrated in reference to the **interpersonal metafunction**; we can identify an interpersonal pathway through the overall system (cf. Matthiessen et al. 2005) – a pathway from tenor within context leading through interpersonal semantics (the system of speech function), interpersonal lexicogrammar (the system of mood), and interpersonal phonology (the system of tone) and its realization in phonetics (including direction of pitch movement). Such an **inter-stratal pathway** is illustrated in a very simplified way in Figure 12.3. Context and phonetics are not included in this figure, although they certainly could be. As an interface between phonology and the human articulatory-auditory systems, phonetics makes contact with bio-semiotic systems. Indeed, it must have evolved as an adaptation of existing motor and auditory systems (and also linked to visual and interoceptive systems, with the visual system aiding e.g. with lip-reading, while at the same time being related to the face as an expression plane).

This interpersonal inter-stratal pathway from semantics via lexicogrammar to phonology illustrates the fact that interpersonal terms in the semantic system of speech function are realized by interpersonal terms in the lexicogrammatical system of mood, which in turn are realized by interpersonal terms in the prosodic phonological system of tone, which is one of the subsystems of the system of intonation. It is important to note that while the general principle is that the inter-stratal relationship between lexicogrammar and phonology is conventional (or "arbitrary") rather than natural, as in the case of the relationship between semantics and lexicogrammar, in the domain of prosodic phonology – in particular, the system of intonation – the relationship tends to be natural (cf. Halliday and Greaves 2008: 71–2, 79, 169; Matthiessen 2021a).

This natural relationship has implications for the interpretation of neurolinguistic studies of intonation. The direction of pitch movement – the contour of the melody – serves to realize interpersonal content, so researchers have identified areas of the brain concerned with emotion, going back to Hughlings-Jackson's (1878 and 1879) pioneering observations about "affections of speech." He was helped by his insight that "The unit of speech is a proposition," and "Loss of speech is therefore the loss of power to propositionise" (1878: 312). Since his early observations, there have been a large number of studies of the perception of intonation and to a somewhat lesser degree of the production of intonation. Here we arguably need insights from rich functional linguistic accounts of intonation to relate what has been called "affective intonation (prosody)" or "emotive intonation (prosody)" to "syntactic intonation (prosody)" in the service of interpersonal systems, differentiating it from "syntactic intonation" in the service of textual and logical systems (for English, see Halliday and Greaves 2008 and references therein). Thus, while "affective intonation" has been seen as lateralized to the right hemisphere based on aphasic syndromes (e.g. Ross and Monnot 2008), the picture seems less clear for "syntactic intonation"; but this is hardly surprising given the fact that what has been called "syntactic intonation" is actually metafunctionally mixed, involving different facets of intonation (not only tone, [interpersonal] but also tonicity and tonality) [textual] and tone sequence, including concord [logical]).

As just noted, from a linguistic point of view, pitch contour is an interpersonal resource and needs to be separated from textual and logical uses of intonation. In English (and many other languages that deploy intonation grammatically), so-called "syntactic intonation" in interpersonal service involves the system of tone, a system of options among different tone contours. These options realize a wide range of different grammatical mood types, which in turn realize a wide range of semantic speech functions, as illustrated in Figure 12.3. Kemmerer (2015: 201) writes, "In the syntactic domain, intonation is often used to distinguish between declarative and interrogative sentences, and in some situations it is the only cue for this function"; but this is in fact only the tip of the prosodic iceberg: as just noted, the tone aspect of intonation covers the full range of mood types (not only the distinction between declarative and interrogative), and the more delicate options within these mood types shade into what has been characterized as attitudinal, affective, or emotive meanings of intonation (cf. Halliday and Greaves 2008: 49–50, 125–8). For example, a declarative with a degree of reservation is realized by a falling-rising tone (tone 4), with a low fall-rise, and an exclamation that indicates contempt or wonder is realized by a rising-falling tone (tone 5), with a low rise-fall and a breathy voice quality.

In terms of the stratal pathway shown in Figure 12.3, which needs to be extended to include both context and phonetics (both auditory and articulatory), we should expect the perception and production of intonation to involve different regions of the brain. (Indeed, in neurolinguistics, the contrasting acoustic attempts and functional ones to deal with explaining brain lateralization in the processing of intonation (e.g. Jia et al. 2013; Kemmerer 2015: 189–90) would seem to simply reflect the contrast between the view "from below" – acoustic – and the view "from above" – functional.) This seems quite clear from studies of "affective intonation"; in his survey of findings, Kemmerer (2015: 191) identifies parts of the temporal cortex (auditory representations of affective contours), the amygdala (relevance of affective contours), the right ventral frontoparietal cortex (simulation of affective states as a way of analysis), the basal ganglia (facilitating simulation and triggering responses), and the bilateral orbitofrontal and inferior frontal cortices (judging affective meanings). These would all seem to be interpretable in interpersonal terms, relating to the enactment of relations and values through the exchange of meanings. (However, note Barrett's [2017: ch. 1] critical review of attempts to find the "fingerprints" of emotions, showing that they do not exist; regarding the amygdala, she notes [p. 19]: "Brain regions like the amygdala are routinely important to emotion, but they are neither necessary nor sufficient for emotion.")

12.4   Language as a higher-order semiotic: stratification with interface strata

Being a higher-order semiotic system (Halliday 1995b), language is a **quadri-stratal system**: both the content plane and the expression plane, which are common to all semiotic systems, are further stratified in language, each into two strata. The content plane is stratified into semantics (meaning) and lexicogrammar (wording), and the expression plane (in spoken language) is stratified into phonology (sounding) and phonetics (sounding as manifested bodily activities). The relationship between the strata within each plane is **natural** rather than **conventional** (or "arbitrary," to use the term in English translations derived from Saussure's *arbitraire* – Michael Halliday once suggested to me that "conventional" would be a more appropriate English equivalent than "arbitrary"), but the relationship between content and expression is still largely conventional. (Exceptions to this principle of the conventional relationship between lexicogrammar and phonology include the prosodic domain within phonology and, within the articulatory domain, sound symbolism and onomatopoeia. But, while they may play a significant but limited role in ontogenesis and phylogenesis, we still need to recognize the extraordinary diversity among the roughly seven thousand languages still spoken around the world.) However, once the content plane has been stratified into semantics and lexicogrammar, the potential for **lexicogrammatical metaphor** has been created, and incongruent realizations of meaning can emerge alongside congruent ones (e.g. Halliday and Matthiessen 1999: ch. 6).

12.4.1 Stratification of language: internal and interface strata

The four strata of language are set out in Table 12.4, differentiated into internal strata (lexicogrammar and phonology) and interface strata (semantics and phonetics). (The distinction between the two corresponds to Hjelmslev's (1943) distinction between form and substance, which has influenced both stratificational linguists and systemic functional ones.) This differentiation is obviously of fundamental importance when we set out to explore the relationship between language and the brain, and the human body more generally. The interface strata relate to other human systems, more specifically to other semiotic systems, including both other socio-semiotic ones and bio-semiotic ones (i.e. sensorimotor systems). The internal strata are, from the point of view of the theoretical architecture of language as a semiotic system, insulated from other systems, being mediated by the interface strata.

Table 12.4 The stratification of language, with internal and interface strata differentiated and specification of other semiotic systems linked to interface strata

Plane	Language		Extra-linguistic systems	
	Form (internal)	Substance (interface)	Other semiotic systems	Bodily systems
Content		semantics	semiotic systems	bio-semiotic systems (sensorimotor systems)
	lexicogrammar			
Expression	phonology			
		phonetics		articulatory and auditory systems

According to the SFL architecture, the two interface strata are thus semantics and phonetics (or graphetics, in written language, or the analogue in sign languages); while lexicogrammar and phonology relate to their neighbouring stratal systems within language, semantics and phonetics also relate to systems that lie beyond language. Obviously, all stratal subsystems of language are embodied – they are manifested in neural patterns and processes; the issue here is simply the relationship to non-linguistic bodily systems.

The status of phonetics as an interface stratum has, of course, been generally established, and is reflected in the study of its embodied phases in the course of instantiation – articulatory and auditory phonetics (cf. Catford 1977: 4–8). The status of semantics as an interface stratum was emphasized early on in SFL by Halliday (1973: 63), e.g. "[Semantics] is the strategy that is available for entering the language system." Both of these interface strata relate to bio-semiotic systems (sensorimotor systems) and to other (social) semiotic systems, as illustrated in Figure 12.4.

As far as bio-semiotic systems are concerned, semantics can interface with all kinds of sensory system and all kinds of motor representation. In contrast,

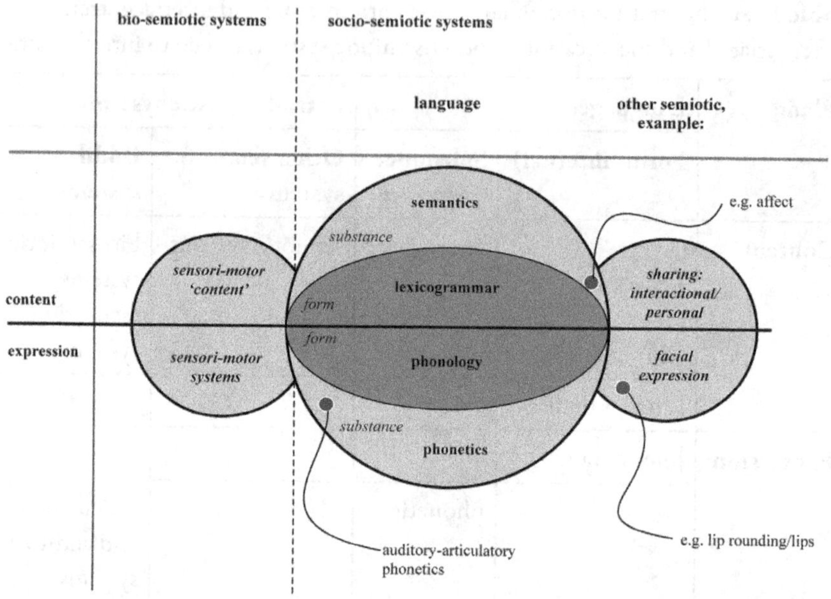

Figure 12.4 Semantics and phonetics as interface strata

phonetics is largely restricted to the auditory sensory system and to the motor control of articulation (although of course it is also related to the respiratory system and the control of the airstream mechanism). As an example of a social semiotic system other than language, I have selected facial expressions, i.e. the deployment of the face as an expressive resource in realizing a certain range of meanings that can be related to the interpersonal metafunction in language. There is also a connection on the expression plane since articulatory gestures, which are important in "lip-reading," relate to the shape of the lips and the facial region around them. Similarly, jaw clenching is likely to affect voice quality.

The semantic and phonetic interfaces are, arguably, dominated by different organizational principles, as indicated in Figure 12.5. Semantics is dominated by the metafunctional diversification of meaning – ideational (logical and experiential), interpersonal and textual (Section 12.3.2); but phonetics is dominated by the direction of instantiation associated with speaking vs. listening (though they are still relevant to one another through feedback). In other words, the semantic interface to external systems is, I would suggest, oriented towards the different metafunctional modes of meaning in the first instance, whereas the phonetic interface is oriented towards the distinct directions of instantiation. However, in phonetics,

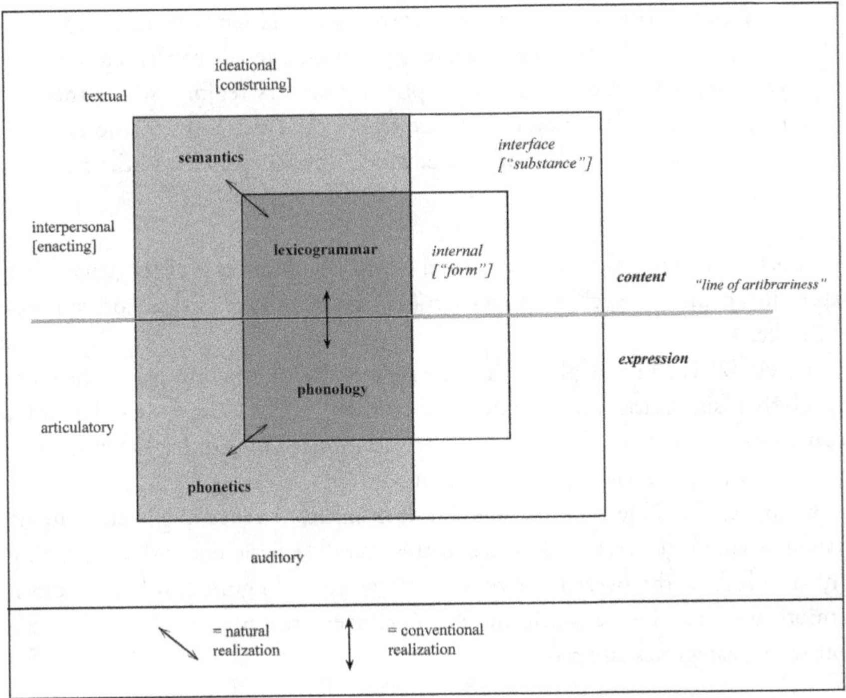

Figure 12.5 The stratal organization of language, with internal ("form") and interface ("substance") strata differentiated, and the interface modes of the interface strata indicated

we also need to take into account both the prosodic and articulatory domains. In what follows, I will focus on semantics as an interface stratum.

Descriptions in the neuroscientific literature of bio-semiotic systems suggest that they constitute a model for the stratification of semiotic systems (i.e. semiotic systems that are enacted socially, and thus inter-individual in orientation). Thus, Barrett's (2017: 120) **concept cascade model** suggests a stratal organization, stated succinctly in the caption of her Figure 6.1 (The concept cascade), reproduced here as Figure 12.6:

> When you develop a concept (right to left), sensory input is compressed into efficient, multisensory summaries. When you construct an instance of a concept by prediction (left to right), those efficient summaries unpack into ever more detailed predictions, which are checked against actual sensory input at each stage. [...]

Cascades begin – of all places – within our old friend the interoceptive network. That's where multisensory summaries are constructed in your brain. Cascades end in your primary sensory regions, where the tiniest details of your experience are represented, not just for vision as in our example but also for sound, touch, interoception, and the rest of your senses.

This organization has, of course, been "coopted" in the case of language for the expression plane – speech, writing, sign (in sign languages of deaf communites), or Braille.

Barrett (2017: 114) explains that the representation of concepts in the cortex is such that "similarities are separated from differences," leading to an efficient representation of concepts, "tremendous optimization." This can be interpreted as a systemic principle in the representation of concepts.

A "concept" is a bio-semiotic one; but it is linked to a meaning in the semantic system of language, a semantic sense in the overall sematic network of meanings. This is a hub in the overall network of categories – linguistic, other denotative semiotic ones, and bio-semantic ones; it is a convergence zone: see Section 12.5 on construing categories and cats.

12.4.2 Semantics

In discussions of semantics in linguistics outside SFL, there used to be a debate between two positions on the interpretation of semantics. According to one position, the interpretation of semantics was based on patterns internal to semantics, couched in terms of semantic features (or "components," as in componential analysis, originating in anthropological linguistics) and/or semantic structures (as in both generative semantics and interpretive semantics). This position tended to exclude "world knowledge" or "encyclopaedic knowledge." In terms of the systemic functional account sketched here, this debate can be viewed as a classic case of a thesis and antithesis opposition. And there is a systemic functional synthesis position: semantics is internally organized as a meaning potential, represented by means of system networks in many SFL publications (for a partial overview, see Hasan et al. 2007; cf. also Taverniers 2019), but it is at the same time also an interface to systems that lie beyond language, providing strategies for transforming their patterns into (linguistic) meaning. In other words, nodes (or "hubs") in semantic networks may also be linked to nodes in extra-linguistic networks (Halliday 1973; Halliday and Matthiessen 1999; and, with reference to the construal of our experience of space, in the ideation base part of semantics, Bateman et al. 2010; Matthiessen

2015a). At the same time, the semantic system is located at the potential pole of the cline of instantiation, so it is related to registerial domains of meaning mid-way between this pole and the instantial pole, where "encyclopaedic knowledge" may be located, and to the instantial meanings embodied in texts operating in contexts of situation. Such registerial domain models and instantial texts are, of course, part of the resources of a community, and may be remembered by individual members and "transmitted" from one generation to another as part of semiotic learning (complementing social learning and genetic transmission).

In the literature concerned with cognitive and neurological interpretations of meaning, there is also a contrast between two positions, the "**Amodal Symbolic Model**" and the "**Grounded Cognition Model**," corresponding to the two positions in linguistics mentioned above (for an overview, see e.g. Barsalou 2008; Kemmerer 2015). But there is also a position based on evidence from neuroscientific studies that is similar to what I called the synthesis position developed in SFL (cf. Michel 2020). Here the idea is that **hubs** in networks of relationship formed by links to representation of our experience of phenomena that we sense and interact with are linked by spokes to modality-specified representations, i.e. grounded in sensorimotor experience.[15] Thus, Lambon Ralph et al. (2010: 2720) write:

> Both classical and contemporary models of semantic memory ([...]) have advanced the intuitively appealing notion that semantic representations are constructed from the joint action of multiple, modality-specific association cortical regions, each of which codes the structure of information arising in a specific sensory, motor, or verbal domain. In this study, we tested and confirmed the hypothesis that, in addition to these modality-specific information sources, the formation of coherent concepts requires a set of modality-invariant representations and that these are underpinned by the anterior temporal lobes.
>
> This idea comes from philosophical, cognitive, and computational considerations of how modality-specific information can be combined to form semantic representations.

They call this the **hub-and-spoke model** of conceptualization (see also Lambon Ralph 2014) and represent it visually in a diagram reproduced here as Figure 12.6. I interpret this model systemic functionally as follows. The hub corresponds to a term or node in the semantic system – or a combination of terms, and it is part of the internal organization of the semantic system; we might call this the **endo-semantic organization** of meaning. The spokes that relate it to "modality-specific association areas" in the brain correspond to relations between semantics as an interlevel

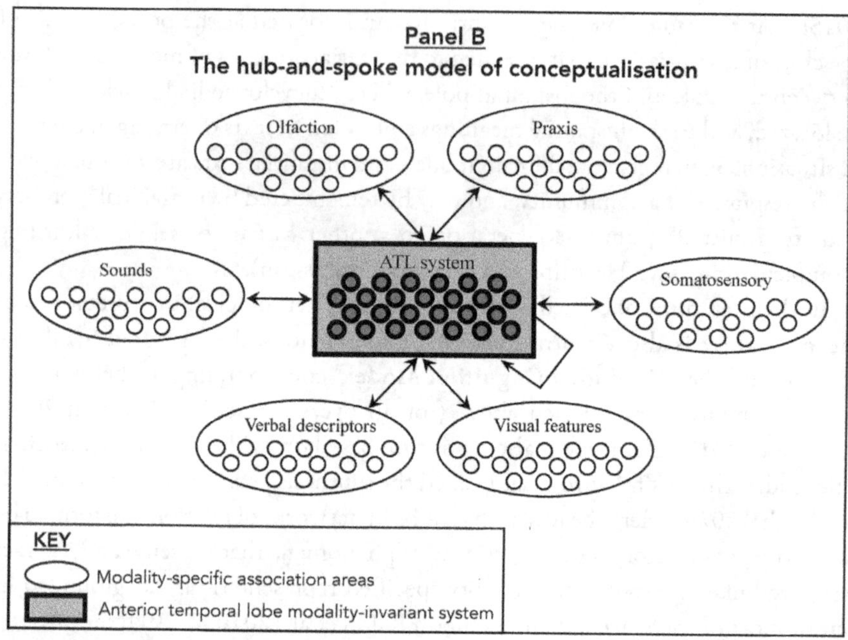

Figure 12.6 Lambon Ralph et al.'s (2010: 2718) "hub-and-spoke model" (ATL = anterior temporal lobe)

(interface to systems outside language) and nodes in bio-semiotic systems, i.e. sensorimotor systems. This is the **exo-semantic organization** of meaning.

As noted above, the "hub-and-spoke" model can be interpreted in terms of the systemic functional theory of the stratal organization of language, and the status of semantics as an interface between language and extra-linguistic systems, as visualized in Figure 12.7. According to this interpretation, the system of semantics provides the "hubs" in the form of nodes or semantic terms. These nodes are organized internally within semantics along the lines sketched in Halliday and Matthiessen (1999); the relations they enter into are internal to semantics, or **endo-semantic**. At the same time, they are realized lexicogrammatically[16] – cf. Lambon Ralph et al.'s (2010: 2718) "verbal descriptors," and by another stratal step either phonologically or graphologically (the form stratum within the expression plane of language); and they are related exo-semantically to areas outside language. The areas shown in Figure 12.7 are from the same range as those in Figure 12.6, i.e. from sensorimotor systems. In Halliday and Matthiessen (1999) we called them **bio-semiotic systems** to highlight the fact that they involve an embryonic content-expression pairing. Thus, our sensory systems construe perceptual input (expression), even when it

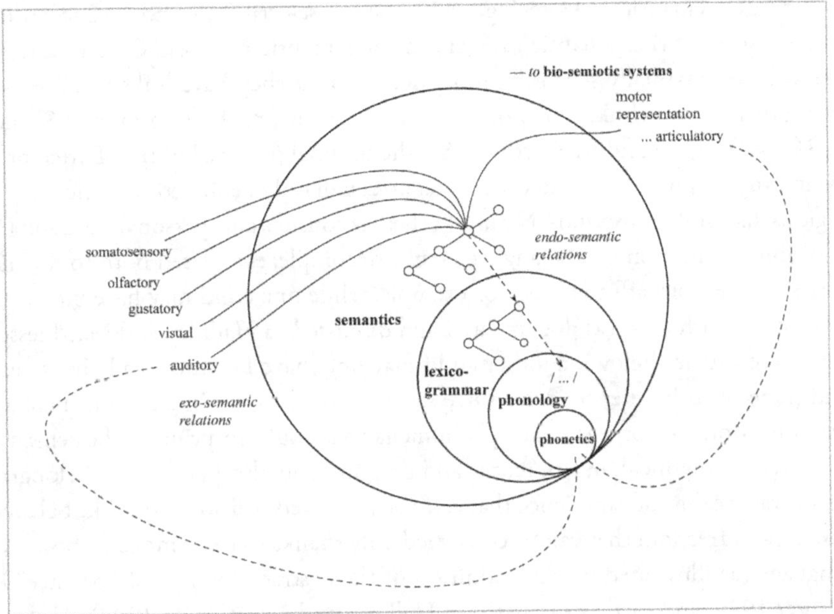

Figure 12.7 The system of semantics – as a stratal subsystem of language with endo-semantic and inter-stratal relations and as an interlevel with exo-semantic relations (note: only relations to bio-semiotic systems shown, not relations to other semiotic systems, which are indicated in Figure 12.4)

is partial, and they impose interpretations on this input (content) – cf. Rohrer (2004) on image schemata, and Gazzaniga, Ivry, and Mangun (2019: ch. 6) on object recognition; and similarly in the other direction, our motor system enacts plans (content) as motor programs (expression).

While Figure 12.7 is concerned with the stratal interface of the content plane – i.e. semantics, it represents one link from the stratal interface of the expression plane – i.e. phonetics, to auditory representation. Speech sounds are, of course, distinct from other sounds (cf. Halliday and Greaves 2008), but on the one hand they overlap in terms of our auditory experience (cf. Kemmerer 2015: 282), and on the other hand we also have to take account of onomatopoeia and phonaesthesia (Halliday and Greaves 2008: 168–9). There are other sensory connections as well, as indicated in Figure 12.4. In addition, we need to take account of lip-reading and the connection between visible pronunciation and facial expression (cf. expressions in various languages analogous to English *Say cheese!* used to invite people to smile by spreading their lips as they are to be photographed).

The exo-semantic links in Figure 12.7 apply selectively, of course, according to the nature of the semantic category in the semantic network. Certain categories will be maximally sensorily "grounded" in that they have links to all sensory regions, but the links may not have equal weight (cf. Warrington and Shalice 1984; Warrington and McCarthy 1987, the original proposal of the "Differential Weighting Hypothesis"), and other categories will only be linked to a selection of regions, like ambient sounds. Naturally, there is considerable personal variation (in addition to variation across language–culture complexes) related both to life histories and sensory affordances. For example, while one child may have grown up interacting with a cat (as documented and discussed in Halliday and Matthiessen 1999; see further below), another child may only have heard or read about cats; and none of us have encountered live sabre-toothed tigers. In addition there are extensive domains of imaginary phenomena that could in principle be sensed if they weren't mythical, like unicorns and dragons, and also phenomena belonging to abstract realms of experience that can't be perceived – abstractions like balance, justice, and freedom that can be construed only thanks to the semogenic power of language (as illustrated by the definition of the abstract concept of "balance" in Painter 1999, and further discussed in Halliday and Matthiessen 1999). Abstract realms of experience construed by language are, of course, often modelled on concrete realms of experience – our model of concrete space being a powerful source for other realms of experience – and more generally our model of the material world enables us to construe our experience of non-physical realms.

The interpretation of semantics as an interface with exo-semantic links to sensorimotor regions reflects the same position as in Halliday and Matthiessen (1999) and in Matthiessen (2015a) in a discussion of the construal of our experience of space. García and Ibáñez (2017: 324) propose a related but interestingly different model as an extension of stratification in SFL:

> Our contention is that such networks constitute an additional stratum which is naturally related to the semantics of the ideation base, and which may be termed sensorimotor level (Figure 4 [reproduced here as Figure 12.8]).
>
> What Figure 4 implies is that well-established semantic differentiations in the ideation base follow naturally from lower-level sensorimotor distinctions. The conical shape of the sensorimotor stratum indicates that whereas most of the cognitive space it represents greatly overlaps with the semantic system, it may also feature less extensive areas of overlap with hierarchically lower strata. This contemplates the possibility of direct interactions between the sensorimotor stratum

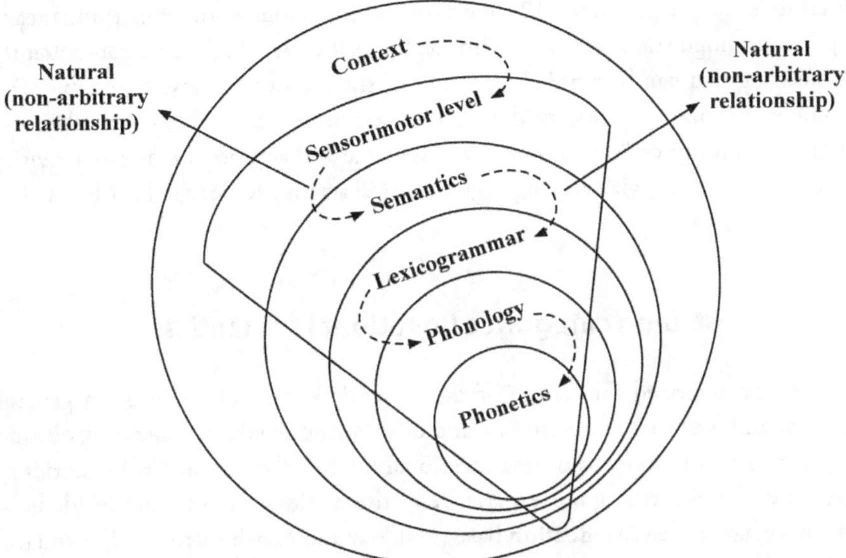

Figure 12.8 García and Ibáñez's (2017) Figure 4: Expanding the stratified SFL model via an additional stratum (the sensorimotor level)

and the lexicogrammar, phonology, and phonetics. Moreover, since the evidence reviewed includes both productive and receptive tasks, this new stratum would operate in a bidirectional fashion, as is the case with the others.

According to García and Ibáñez's (2017) stratally expanded model, the "sensorimotor level" is represented as an overlay "level." In contrast, according to the model I have sketched here, bio-semiotic systems or sensorimotor systems are stratally parallel to semantics, just as social semiotic systems other than language are. In other words, unlike context, they are not more abstract or more comprehensive than the semantic system of language; in fact, they are more partial in that they only include our experience of and engagement with the concrete world while semantics also includes the virtual world of abstractions (and of course interpersonal and textual meanings as well).

Bio-semiotic systems constitute the experiential environment that is construed in semantics (the "signified body") – or (in the case of motor systems) enacted, but I have focussed on ideational construal here, setting interpersonal enactment aside (cf. Section 12.3.2 for brief remarks). The bio-semiotic or sensorimotor systems are also related to semiotic systems other than language, as here semantics is again the interface to language (Figure 12.4): it provides the resources for construing meaning in non-linguistic semiotic systems as linguistic meaning – and consequently as meaning that can be worded by means of the resources of lexicogrammar. For example, if a person is told to draw a cat, he or she will be able to translate the linguistic concept of "cat" into a pictorial image and activate the motor activities needed to depict it (with varying degrees of skill across people who have learned to draw, of course).

12.5   Construing categories (ideational semantics)

Having characterized the nature of the semantic system of language in general terms as an interface to bio-semiotic and other semiotic systems operating outside language, I will now focus on the ideational model of meaning, i.e. semantics as a resource for construing our experience of the world around us and inside us – which we have called the **ideation base** (Halliday and Matthiessen 1999). I will use our construal of cats as an example, for reasons that will become clear; but one can compare it with other helpful illustrations, like Damasio's (1989: 26) evocation of the experience of engaging with a violin or Feldman and Narayanan's (2004: 385) illustration of what's involved in interpreting a request to pass the salt and then complying.

12.5.1 Construing cats

In work that is resonant with the SFL account sketched above, Bickerton (1995) suggests that linguistic concepts are holistic ones in terms of the different systems of the brain in the sense of something akin to the hub-and-spokes model and my representation in Figure 12.7. Bickerton (1995: 24) uses the category of cat as an illustration (cf. also Pulvermüller 2002: 224–5):

> There are, presumably, ensembles of neurons whose firing represents concepts. Recent work (e.g. Ojemann and Creutzfeld 1987, Damasio 1990, Hart and Gordon 1992) suggests that several such ensembles representing the same concept may be scattered through the brain: there may be, for instance, an auditory cat and a visual cat as well as a linguistic cat. Note that the linguistic cat is a different kettle of fish from the other mental cats. The linguistic cat is also a holistic cat. Ask me about the word *cat* and I can tap my auditory knowledge ("It purrs,

it miaows"), my visual knowledge ("It's usually black, brown, or gray – seldom if ever puce or scarlet"), and so forth. The word ties together aspects of catness that may well be stored in other areas of the brain, suggesting that its neural representation may serve as what has been called a **convergence zone** (Damasio and Damasio 1992).

If we view this ontogenetically, it is possible to track how young children construe linguistic categories over time, aggregating knowledge about them e.g. by observing or interacting with the phenomena being construed. As an illustration, in Halliday and Matthiessen (1999), we analysed excerpts of Halliday's (1975, 1984c) case study of one young child, Nigel, learning how to mean dialoguing about cats over a period of time of around 8 months (from 2 years, 10 months, and 22 days to 3 years, 6 months, and 12 days).

Text 1 Nigel at 2:10:22

Nigel	And you (= I) saw a cat in Chania Falls.
Mother	Yes, you saw a cat in Chania Falls.
Nigel	And you picked the cat up. Mummy, do cats like meat?
Mother	Yes, they do.
Nigel	Do cats like bones? Do cats like marrow?

Text 2 Nigel at 2:10:26

Nigel	Can I stroke the cat? You (= I) want to stroke the cat ... you want to scratch it ... it's drinking its milk ... it's moving its tail out ... it's moving its tail outside ... it's scratching ... it's putting its tail up ... what's this?
Mother	I don't know; I suppose it's its elbow.
Nigel	It's waggling its tail ... it's lapping it with its tongue ... you can go near its elbow ... you *can* go near its elbow ... but you can't go too near its face ... because it thinks you might take away its milk ... it was just a bit frightened ... it thinked[17] that you might take away its milk ... has it finished its milk?

Text 3 Nigel at 2:11:5

Nigel	(thinking about "The house that Jack built") What is a rat?
Father	It's a sort of big mouse.
Nigel	Does the rat go when the cat has killed it?
Father	No, it doesn't go any more then.
Nigel	Why did the cat kill the rat?
Father	Cats do kill rats.
Nigel	Why do they?
Father	(formula) You'll have to wait to understand that till you're a bit bigger.
Nigel	No I can understand it now.
Father	Well, cats just like to eat rats and mice.
Nigel	Why do they like to eat them?
Father	They just do.

Text 4 Nigel at 2:11:15

Nigel	Why did the cat go out? Mummy, why did the cat go out?
Mother	It gets fed up, having its tail squashed.

Text 5 Nigel at 3:0:26

Nigel	How do the cat's claws come out?
Father	They come out from inside its paws. Look, I'll show you.
Nigel	Does it go with its claws?
Father	Not if it's going along the ground.
Nigel	And not if it's climbing up a tree.
Father	Yes; if it's climbing up a tree it does go with its claws.

Text 6 Nigel at 3:2:7

Nigel	Will the cat eat the grape?
Father	I don't think so. Cats like things that go, not things that grow.

Text 7 Nigel at 3:5:12

Nigel	Cats have no else to stop you from trossing them ... cats have no other way to stop children from hitting them ... so they bite. Cat, don't go away! -- when I come back I'll tell you a story. (He does so.)

Text 8 Nigel at 3:6:12

Nigel	Can I give the cat some artichoke?
Mother	Well she won't like it.
Nigel	Cats like things that go; they don't like things that grow.

The cat that Nigel studies is construed (semantics) as figures of doing-&-happening (actions, activities, events), realized by (lexicogrammar) material clauses. This is the domain of doing, reviewed by García and Ibáñez (2017) in relation to the brain. Nigel construes the cat as Actor in figures of happening and also in figures of doing, where the process of doing it extends to impact another participant, a Goal – either one of its body parts that it manipulates or something potentially edible. In the latter case, he construes cats as killers and establishes a class of victims: rats and mice. He uses these figures to represent what he has observed or is observing the cat doing, and also to elicit 'why' or 'how' the cat does something.

(1) figure of doing-&-happening ↘ material clause

cat (body part) as Actor in process of happening: motion

why	*did*	*the cat*		*go out*	
how	*do*	*the cat's claws*		*come out*	
does	*it*	*go*		*with its claws*	
if	*it*	*'s climbing up*		*a tree*	
Reason	Pro-	Actor	-cess	Means	Scope

Cf. also (Nigel) *Cat, don't go away!*

cat as Actor in process of doing, configured with a Goal, either a body part or something edible

Reason	Actor	Process	Goal	Place	Means
	it	*'s drinking*	*its milk*		
	it '	*s lapping*	*it* [its milk]		*with its tongue*
	it	*'s moving*	*its tail*	*out(side)*	
	it	*'s putting*	*its tail*	*up*	
	it	*'s waggling*	*its tail*		
when	*the cat*	*has killed*	*it*		
why	*the cat*	*did ... kill*	*it* [the rat]		

Cf. also (Nigel) *has it finished its milk?*; *Will the cat eat the grape?*; (Father) *Cats do kill rats* – (Nigel) *Why do they?*; (Father) *Well, cats just like to eat rats and mice.* – (Nigel) *Why do they like to eat them?* – (Father) *They just do.* Note also: *Cats have no else to stop you from trossing them ... cats have no other way to stop children from hitting them ... so they bite.* Cf. Nigel's mother telling him in response to his question *Mummy, why did the cat go out?*: *It gets fed up, having its tail squashed.*

In addition, Nigel also construes himself as Actor in processes of doing, with the cat as 'done-to,' the Goal. Thus, cats can be acted upon; for example, he can handle them by picking them up. In other words, he is sampling instances 'pick up' + 'entity,' with the cat as a kind of entity. He construes his own experience of picking up the cat and would certainly be able to perform the act if told to pick it up. Here he is exploring possible interaction with the cat, and this also includes one instance where he construes the cat as Recipient, asking for permission to give it some artichoke.

cat as Goal

	Actor	Pro-	Goal	-cess
and	*you*	*picked*	*the cat*	*up*

Cf. also: (Nigel) *Can I stroke the cat? You (= I) want to stroke the cat .... you want to scratch it; that you might take away its milk*

cat as Recipient

Pro-Actor	-cess	Recipient	Goal
Can I	*give*	*the cat*	*some artichoke?*

(2) figure of sensing ⟍ mental clause

Cats are also construed by Nigel in (semantics) figures of sensing (thinking, perceiving, feeling, wanting), either as a Phenomenon with Nigel as Senser – more specifically, as an observer, or as Senser capable of projecting ideas into existence and with preferences for different food items. In other words, he imbues cats with consciousness; he uses figures of sensing to construe his own perceptual awareness of cats but also to model their processes of consciousness.

cat as Phenomenon

And	*you (= I)*		*saw*	*a cat*	*in Chania Falls.*
	Senser		Process	Phenomenon	Place

cat as Senser

it	*thinked*	*that you might take away its milk*
it	*thinks*	*you might take away its milk*
α		'β (idea)
Senser		Process
do	*cats*	*like* *meat/bones/marrow?*
Pro-Senser		-cess Phenomenon

Also: (Father) *Cats like things that go, not things that grow.* (Mother) *Well she won't like it* [artichoke]. – (Nigel) *Cats like things that go; they don't like things that grow.*

While Nigel does not construe cats as Sayers (in this particular sample), he does construe them, or rather the cat he lives with, as Receiver in a figure of saying:

(3) figure of saying ↘ verbal clause

cat as Receiver

(when I come back)	*I*	*'ll tell*	*you*	*a story*
	Sayer	Process	Receiver	Verbiage

There are also some instances of figures of being-&-having, realized by "relational" clauses; but they are used to characterize rats: (Nigel) *What is a rat?* – (Father) *It's a sort of big mouse.*

Over this period of around eight months, Nigel thus construes the category of cat in a number of different configurations or "frames" that are clearly grounded in his everyday life experiences (cf. the reference to the "Grounded Cognition Model" above). The excerpts illustrate how he construes the category of cat through a process of progressive refinement, developing an increasingly holistic sense of 'cat' as a semantic category, as a hub related to other experiential facets of cats – his sensorimotor experience.

The example of the construal of cats can also be taken as an illustration of the crucial point that "concepts" are not only labelled by words but are rather construed lexicogrammatically. This applies to all domains of experience, including the domain of emotion, discussed at the end of the next subsection in reference to Barrett's (2017) paradigm-changing research.

12.5.2 Construing figures

In discussing the example of Nigel construing his experience of cats linguistically, I've referred to different types of figure in the ideation base part of the semantic systems (doing-&-happening, sensing, saying, and so on; see Halliday and Matthiessen 1999: ch. 3). As indicated above, they are realized by clauses of different process types (material, mental, verbal, and so on). Figures serve as models of quanta of change in our experience of the flow of events around us and inside us. The different types of figure construed in the semantic systems of languages thus serve as theories of our experience of flux, or goings-on, sorted into different domains. These clearly have exo-semantic significance as well as constituting a coherent endo-semantic theory. For example, some figures model our experience of actions, activities and events "out there" in the world around us, implicating our sensorimotor engagement with them, while other types model our experience of the inner world of consciousness (cf. Edelman's 1989: 24, notion of higher-order consciousness: "Higher-order consciousness [including self-consciousness] is based on direct awareness in a human having language and a reportable subjective life").

There is clearly considerable variation around the languages of the world in how they construe models of quanta of change (cf. Section 12.3.3), reflected, among other things, in the fact that grammatically languages vary between just over one hundred quite general verbs and thousands of taxonomically quite specialized verbs; this variation is related to the complementarity of the experiential and logical modes of construing experience – as series and as configuration, respectively (cf. Matthiessen 2004b; Halliday and Matthiessen 1999: ch. 7; Matthiessen 2015a in reference to space, forthcoming b).

English draws heavily on the experiential mode of construing quanta of change in our experience of the flow of events. We can see this lexicogrammatically: semantic figures are realized (congruently) by grammatical clauses, and the different types of figuration in the semantics are realized by different terms in the lexicogrammatical system of process type. The description of this system in English is by now fairly well elaborated (e.g. Matthiessen 1995a: ch. 4; Halliday and Matthiessen 2014: ch. 5), giving us an account that can be used in the neurolinguistic studies, as shown by García and Ibáñez (2017) in their survey of research into figures of doing in relation to the brain (see also Kemmerer 2015: ch. 11); and the grammatical description has been extended considerably in delicacy by categorizing Levin's (1993) "verb classes" according to the process types in the description of the system (for details, see

Matthiessen 2014a; cf. also Neale 2002 on similar work based on the Collins verb dictionary). Here "verb classes" are really more than classes of verbs; they actually reflect nuclear transitivity configurations in the clause involving transitivity roles such as Process, Medium, Agent, Range, and Beneficiary, and certain circumstantial roles.

This descriptive elaboration of the options in ***process type*** gives us a "map" of the domains of our experience of "flux" construed by English. I have stored this description in a database, and to try to give a sense of the considerable elaboration of the system of ***process type*** represented in this database, I have visualized it by means of a radial chart (since charts that look more like pre-systemic taxonomic representation lack even the resolution of the radial chart when scaled down): see Figure 12.9. Each oval in the chart represents a "verb class," taken either from Levin (1993) or, where there is a gap in her description, from Matthiessen (1995a). The steps towards the periphery of the chart are steps in delicacy; the outmost ovals are the most delicately specified verb classes. Their members range from a small handful to well over one hundred; there are over 4,400 verbs in my database, or (more accurately) verbs with different senses classifiable in terms of the system of ***process type***.

Having introduced the chart, I can now return briefly to the categorization of cats. To relate the display to the analysis of Nigel's categorization of cats and to give a sense of what aspects of the overall collective resources of the lexicogrammar of English he deploys, I have annotated the chart with examples from the cat dialogues representing the different types he deploys in construing cats. Most of them involve material process type clauses, as we have already seen; here he construes cats as Actor, Goal, or Recipient. The resources of this part of the lexicogrammar enable him to construe his material engagement with cats and also their acts and activities that he has observed or heard about. The English lexicogrammar of English clearly provides many additional resources for construing our experience of cats; Nigel has not exhausted the possibilities, but he has used the resources to model cats in different participant roles and to locate them in his view of the world, including a sense of their potential to act or to be acted upon (see Halliday and Matthiessen 1999: 81 for a representation of the networking of cats in the ideation base of English semantics). Nigel also uses the resources of mental process clauses, modelling cats as phenomena he can observe but also as conscious beings, capable of liking and thinking – and even of construing ideas.

The lexicogrammatical resources visualized in Figure 12.9 provide language users with distinct but agnate models for construing a given quantum of change in the flow of events – what might be thought of as the same experience represented in different ways. However, it would be more insightful to say that they provide language users with the resources empowering them to develop multifaceted models of experience, models that are related ultimately in the semantic system of the language, reflected in domains of experience that are difficult to interpret, such

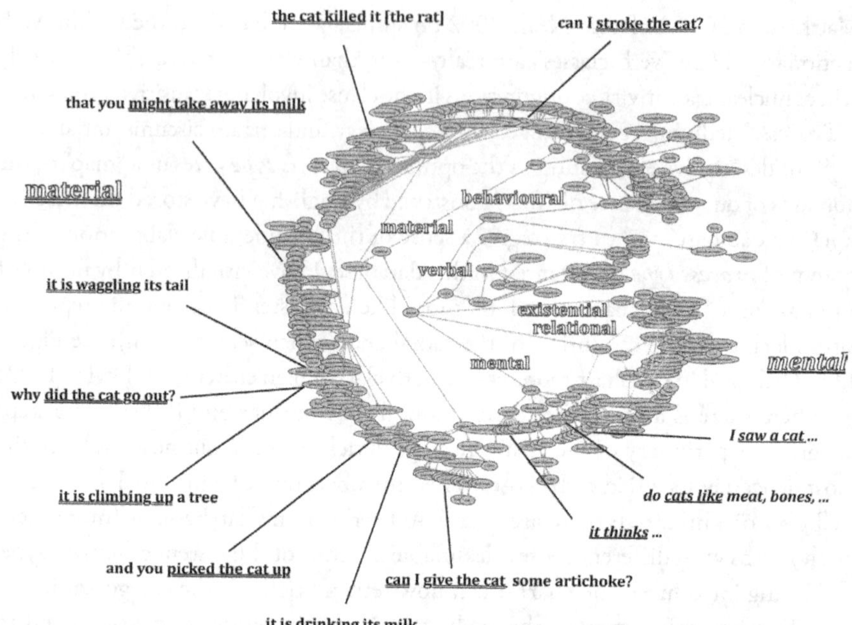

Figure 12.9 The extension of the grammatical system of process type in delicacy (Matthiessen 2014a), based on a classification of Levin's (1993) primary, secondary, and tertiary "verb classes" and supplemented by subtypes of process types taken from Matthiessen (1995a) where there are gaps in her coverage

as pain (Halliday 1998), emotion (Matthiessen 2007b), and even taste (Zhong, Huang and Dong 2020).

Here Barrett's (2017) research into emotions, "how emotions are made," is highly relevant and lends strong support to the constructivist account of how languages construe our experience of the world around us and inside us (e.g. Halliday and Matthiessen 1999). She shows that the common view that emotions are universal is a "myth," and she demonstrates that emotions are "constructed" in different ways by speakers of different languages embedded in different cultures. Her **construction theory of emotion** thus highlights the role of immaterial systems (i.e. social and semiotic systems), e.g. Barrett (2017: 145):

> Social reality is a driving force behind human culture. It's perfectly plausible for emotion concepts, as elements of social reality, to be learned from others during infancy, or even much later when someone moves from one culture to another (more on this shortly). Social

reality is therefore one conduit for transmitting behaviors, preferences, and meanings from ancestors to descendants via natural selection. Concepts are not merely a social veneer on top of biology. They are a biological reality that is wired into your brain by culture. People who live in cultures with certain concepts, or more diverse concepts, may be more fit to reproduce.

It follows that the lexicogrammatical resources for construing emotions vary from one language to another, resonating with the cultures they're "embedded" in. Barrett (2017: 146–7) provides a number of examples (footnotes omitted):

> scientists have documented numerous emotion concepts around the world that don't exist in English. Norwegians have a concept for an intense joy of falling in love, calling it "*Forelsket.*" The Danes have the concept "*Hygge*" for a certain feeling of close friendship. The Russian "*Tocka*" is a spiritual anguish, and the Portuguese "*Saudade*" is a strong, spiritual longing. [...] Here are a few more I find compelling:
>
> - *Gigil* (Filipino): The urge to hug or squeeze something that is unbearably adorable.
> - *Voorpret* (Dutch): Pleasure felt about an event before the event takes place.
> - *Age-otori* (Japanese): The feeling of looking worse after a haircut.
>
> Some emotion concepts from other cultures are incredibly complicated, perhaps impossible to translate into English, yet natives experience them as a matter of course.

She also gives examples of "some cherished Western emotion concepts" that are "completely absent in other cultures," including "anger" and "sadness." She goes on to point out that the notion of emotion is in fact not universal (p. 148):

> Beyond individual emotion concepts, different cultures don't even agree on what "emotion" is. Westerners think of emotion as an experience inside an individual, in the body. Many other cultures, however, characterize emotions as interpersonal events that require two or more people. This includes the Ifaluk of Micronesia, the Balinese, the Fula, the Ilongot of the Philippines, the Kaluli of Papua New Guinea, the

Minangkabau of Indonesia, the Pintupi Aborigines of Australia, and the Samoans. More intriguingly, some cultures don't even have a unified concept of "Emotion" for the experiences that Westerners lump together as emotional. The Tahitians, the Gidjingali Aborigines of Australia, the Fante and Dagbani of Ghana, the Chewong of Malaysia, and our friends the Himba from chapter 3 are a few well-studied examples.

In her account of emotions, Barrett includes a chapter on "how the brain makes emotions," illuminating it through developmental accounts, starting with the point that "a newborn is experientially blind to a great extent." She then shows how infant brains separate similarities from differences, summarize statistical relationships, and distill generalizations (p. 116): "an infant's brain distills widely dispersed firing patterns for individual senses into one multisensory summary. This process reduces redundancy and represents the information in a minimal, efficient form for future use." I can imagine how this line of explanation can also be applied to Halliday's (2004a) regarding how young children learn how to mean in interaction with others, distilling systemic patterns from innumerable instances of texts in context.

As part of her discussion of emotion and illness, Barrett (2017: 205–9) also illuminates our experience of pain, based on the same model as the one used for emotion, i.e. how the brain makes pain; and this could be further explored productively in the light of Halliday's (1998) account of the grammar of pain. And while Barrett focusses on the important role played by words for emotion concepts, and emphasizes that they vary across languages, we can take one step further and highlight the lexicogrammar of emotion, or of pain: it's not only lexical items ("words") that are significant within the lexical zone of lexicogrammar but rather the whole lexicogrammatical continuum from grammar to lexis, as Halliday's (1998) investigation of the grammar of pain shows very clearly (cf. Matthiessen 2007b on the lexicogrammar of emotion). The contrast in the English grammar of emotion between emotions being construed as 'impinging' on the senser (e.g. [from COCA] *This **infuriated** the Ustez and he looked at me as though I were feeble minded; I remember when it **grieved** me intensely; I'm **grieved** that we as a nation didn't take a decisive stand for righteousness.*) vs. emotions being construed as 'emanating' from the senser (e.g. [from COCA] *However, as I **grieved** the loss of my young nephew*) is centrally relevant to how we model and experience emotions, see Halliday and Matthiessen (2014) (as are various strategies involving lexicogrammatical metaphor, e.g. [from COCA] ***Anger seized** me, my fingers refused to move, I sat rigid for one long moment ...; but great **fear seized** the men who were with me; they fled and hid themselves ...; Mailer's **anger boiled over** and he sent Vidal to the ground with a punch.*).

The nature of language as a resource for making meaning, organized as a meaning potential with ranges of options, becomes very clear when we examine the choices translators make, especially when we study multiple translations of one source text (cf. Matthiessen 2014b on choice in translation). We also see this when we analyse texts produced by speakers reporting on the "same" experience as represented by video clips (cf. Section 12.2.1). However, to illustrate this point, let me draw on a dramatized example, taken from Matthiessen (2023: 2–3):

> We also find examples of speakers exploring choices in construing some aspect of experience, trying out different options in experiential systems. The following example is a constructed one in the sense that it comes from a drama, but it serves as a relevant illustration:
>
> [4] A Talent for Murder: author trying out different wordings [03:20]
>
> [Murder mystery writer played by Angela Lansbury, dictating to tape-recorder.] Where was I? Oh yeah. It was murder. There was a sharp audible gasp, Gabrielle's eyes *swept* the room ... *swept* ... *sweeping* the room. Uhm, her eyes **fastened on** Maxwell ... **fastened** Oh my God, **narrowed on, held, pinned** – Christ, maybe I should retire – Gabrielle's eyes (I'll clean that up later) her eyes **fastened on** Maxwell ....
>
> Here, after construing the activity of Gabrielle looking around the room as a movement configured as
>
> participant: 'Gabrielle's eyes' + process: 'swept' + participant: 'the room'
>
> the writer is searching for an appropriate lexical verb to serve as the process in the configuration
>
> participant: 'Gabrielle's eyes' + process + participant: 'Maxwell'
>
> and being dissatisfied with *fasten on*, she tries out other related options in the lexical field. [...] this illustrates clearly that she operates with a system of choice – in this case, choice in how to construe experience, evoking this imaginary experience for her readers.

Thus, while the experience the mystery writer is trying to evoke could have been represented by a 'behavioural' clause, with visual perception as activity (e.g.

Gabrielle looking around the room), she turns to the resources of 'material' clauses, thereby enriching the representation with additional specifications. This involves metaphor, more specifically metaphor within the lexical zone of lexicogrammar: the domain of perception as activity is mapped onto the domains of movement around a place and of grasping, with Gabrielle's eyes as Actor. This is then another step in developing an account of semantic relations, both endo-semantic ones (the mapping of one semantic domain onto another) and exo-semantic ones (accessing additional domains of sensorimotor experience).

12.6   Conclusion

In this chapter, I have noted some aspects of SFL in relation to changes in the macro-discipline of cognitive science and, more generally, in relation to an ordered typology of systems operating in different phenomenal realm, suggesting that neurosemiotics can shed light on the relationship between fourth-order systems (semiotic systems), and second-order systems (biological systems) – but mediated by third-order systems (social systems). I raised the issue of the interpretation of fourth-order phenomena either in cognitive terms as knowledge or in semiotic terms as meaning, indicating the insights that can be gained if we also view them semiotically as meaning – insights that come automatically with the language-based approach to cognition proposed within SFL (Halliday and Matthiessen 1999), e.g. socially gated brains, collective cognition, brain-to-brain coupling, intersubjectivity, and negotiation of experience in dialogue.

I then went on to focus on SFL as a resource helping us conceptualize and think about the relationship between semiotic and biological systems "from above" – i.e. from the vantage point of semiotic systems, and more specifically about the relationship between language and the brain. I suggested that one reason SFL can be helpful is the character of its architecture of language (and also of other semiotic systems) – an architecture that is relational in nature, based on multiple intersecting semiotic dimensions (the hierarchy of stratification, the spectrum of metafunction, the cline of instantiation, and so on) and the relations that have them as their domain. This lies at the heart of the conception of language as an extended relational network, organized as a system of systems. I suggested that this gives language an integrative role in relation to the brain – as the one human system that is extended in its embodiment across many regions of the brain, say from the amygdala to the neocortex. One aspect of this is what Lamb (2013: 145) calls the "great cognitive arch" (see also Lamb 1999; García, Sullivan, and Tsiang 2017: 42–7). This arch can be interpreted as foregrounding the dimension of stratification, relating "linguistic subsystems" via "conceptual subsystems" to "perceptual/motor systems." (But note

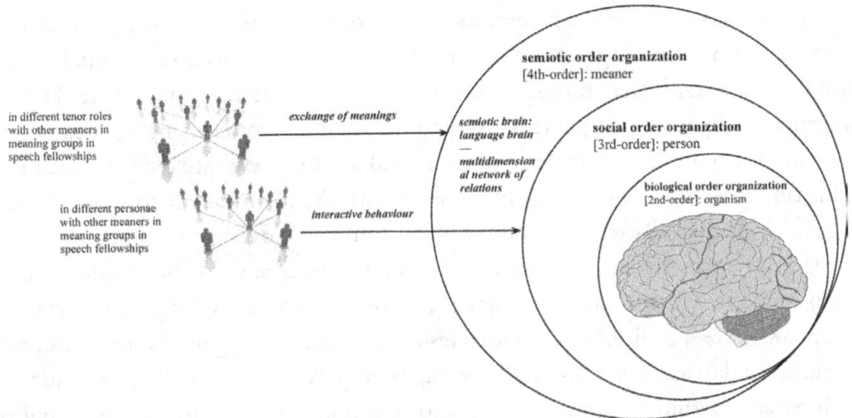

Figure 12.10 Systemic orders and the brain – biological: brain < social: social brain of person interacting with other people in different roles in social groups forming societies < semiotic: language brain of meaner exchanging meaning with other meaners in meaning groups forming speech fellowships

that both semantics and phonetics interface with sensorimotor systems, characterized here as bio-semiotic systems.) At the same time, we can explore other "arches," like the semiotic dimension of the metafunctional spectrum, implicating connections between the two hemispheres, and the moves along the cline of instantiation in the complementary directions of generation and analysis.

As part of the discussion of the ordered typology of systems, I also pointed to different conceptions of the brain that have emerged, the neurobiological conception of the brain being complemented by two views "from above": from the vantage point of social systems – the social brain – and from the vantage point of semiotic systems – the semiotic brain, or more specifically the language brain or even the grammar brain. These ordered views of the brain are visualized in Figure 12.10. I've referred to insights conceptualized in terms of intersubjectivity, brain-to-brain coupling, and social gating. These notions shed light on the systemic "layering" of the brain and pave the way for a neurosemiotics research that can be very resonant with Halliday's (e.g. 1978) semiotically informed conception of persons.

The "layering" also helps us locate breakthroughs in our deep history, like the rapid acceleration in our evolution thanks to social and collective learning (involving transmission across generations that does not depend on the relatively slow processes of biological evolution), and in collective knowledge and cognition – which depend on the modern language brain (cf. Christian 2004: 146, and his characterization of humans as "highly networked creatures," referring to Mears 2001). After the emergence of modern language and the modern language brain 150–250 thousand years ago, the neurosemiotic conditions were in place for a gradual and then rapidly accelerating pattern of human socio-cultural evolution – much more rapid and adaptable than biological evolution (e.g. Christiansen and Chater 2008). Interpersonally, language provides us with the resources for exchanging meaning – for coupling brains in "dialogic cognition," and linking them into collectives; at the same time, ideationally language provides us with the resources for collective learning and collective, distributed knowledge, accumulated over generations.

After characterizing semantics as a stratal interface to bio-semiotic and socio-semiotic systems outside language, I then focussed on ideational semantic resources, more specifically experiential resources for construing our experience of the world around us and inside us, emphasizing the importance of modelling semantics as an interface stratum and thus of taking exo-semantic relations into account, using as examples the categorization of cats in different participant roles involved in different processes and the categorization of figures according to the nature of processes. In the course of this, I referred to the hub-and-spoke model put forward in neurolinguistics.

In conclusion, let me return to the relationship between semiotic and biological systems, noting that Kuhl (e.g. 2007) has shown that phonetic-phonological learning is gated by social factors. Since I'm a linguist without a background in neuroscience, I have been wondering over the years what kinds of account I could produce that would be of use in neurolinguistics. I had an opportunity to ask Terrence Deacon when he was visiting us in Sydney, and his answer was very clear: he said that linguistic accounts must be **biologically implementable**. I thought that I understood what he meant, since working as a linguist in computational linguistics, I had learned what it means for a linguistic model to be computationally implementable.

But the next step of actually achieving biological implementability in linguistic models is, of course, harder. One fundamental aspect is clearly what exactly embodiment means, what the nature of the relationship between semiotic systems and biological ones is (mediated by social systems). For example, is it a natural one like the relationship between semantics and lexicogrammar or a conventional one like the relationship between lexicogrammar and phonology? It would seem to be more like the latter, i.e. conventional rather than natural, in at least one respect: individual neurons are not individually involved in the embodiment or realization of components of semiotic patterns but rather aggregates, assemblies, or ensembles of neurons functioning together (e.g. Hebb 1949; Edelman 1989, 1992; Pulvermüller 2002: 22ff.). Ideas such as single neurons representing particular memories had already had to be abandoned by the end of the 1920s. It is clear that the biological implementation must be robust and fault tolerant up to a point, so it must involve **redundancy** (as between lexicogrammar and phonology), **degeneracy**, and **plasticity**, and also the possibility of brain regions being repurposed (cf. Kemmerer 2015: 262, on cross-modal plasticity: "There is now abundant evidence that when congenitally deaf individuals acquire a sign language, superior temporal regions that would normally process linguistic information from auditory input become reconfigured to process it from visual input."; Barrett 2021: 38). (Regarding "cross-modal plasticity," unlike many other semiotic systems which have a fixed expression plane, language has a **variable expression plane** thanks to "double articulation": it can involve speech, sign, gesture and also touch [Braille].[18]) For example, Barrett (2017: 23) explains the nature of degeneracy in the processing of emotions: "Brain circuitry operates by the many-to-one principle of degeneracy: instances of a single emotion category, such as fear, are handled by different brain patterns at different times and in different people. Conversely, the same neurons can participate in creating different mental states (one-to-many)."

In his long-term research program, Sydney Lamb has addressed the relationship between linguistic and neural representations by developing a relational model of language that is, unlike Halliday's SFL, explicitly designed to be biologically implementable, or at least to be oriented towards biological implementability: see e.g. Lamb (1999, 2013) and García, Sullivan, and Tsiang (2017). Lamb (2013) suggests that system networks in SFL and relational networks are complementary, and that relational networks can help relate system networks to neural networks. He makes an important distinction between "abstract notation" of relational networks and "narrow notation" of relational networks, the second being closer to neural networks e.g. by capturing significant details having to do with degree of incoming and outgoing activation (cf. Henry Sweet's broad and narrow phonetic transcription). Based on this distinction, Lamb (2013) is in a position to outline the complementarity of the different kinds of network (p. 156):

> Levels of precision in description
> And so we have several different levels of notation available for different levels of precision. Systemic networks occupy a high level, which makes them suitable for describing linguistic phenomena of importance to language teachers, translators, grammarians and others. At lower levels we have the purely relational notations, the lower of which can be directly related to the still lower level of neural structures. [...]
> Systemic networks are especially useful for understanding the various types and subtleties of meaning conveyed in texts. RN notation is suited to describing (portions of) the cognitive systems of individuals. And the narrow RN notation is useful for helping to understand how the brain works. As all of these areas of application are valuable, all of the levels of notation are useful, each in its own way.

In certain respects, this is comparable to the approach we arrived at when we explored the computational implementability of system networks; see e.g. Matthiessen (1988b, 2007a, forthcoming a), Matthiessen and Bateman (1991), Matthiessen and Halliday (2009); and cf. Teich (1999). I interpreted the steps towards computational implementation as the **stratification of the systemic functional metalanguage**, ranging from **theory** via **theoretical representation** and **computational representation** to **implementation**, as set out in Table 12.5 in the two columns to the left under the heading of "stratification of metalanguage".

Focussing on how we account for the paradigmatic axis of language within the different metalinguistic strata, we can see that the theoretical stratum is concerned with the theory of paradigmatic organization (as part of the theory of axiality), which is theorized as primary in relation to syntagmatic organization (originally presented by Halliday 1966b). It includes not only aspects that can be realized at the level of theoretical representation but also aspects that cannot yet be realized at that level because we have not found or designed the representational resources needed (cf. Matthiessen 1988a), e.g. systemic continua, systemic interaction through marking and intersection of probabilities, logical systems (with systemic recursion), and textual systems conditionally dependent on terms in experiential and interpersonal systems. We have experimented with ways of complementary representations such as fuzzy set theory or at least complementary views – topologies (cf. Chapter 6, this volume).

In computational applications, system networks get realized, or re-represented, by means of some form of computational representation such as frame-based inheritance networks or typed feature structures. This entails an increase in explicitness of the kind needed for computational implementation, but the explicitness is at the expense of coverage e.g. of the (informal) marking conventions used in system networks. Finally, computational representations are realized, or re-presented, at the level of implementation by means of some programming language – LISP, Prolog, C++, Java, Python: there are various alternatives, a number of which have been used. Between theory and implementation, there is certainly a high degree of conventionality, reflected in the possible variation in programming languages but also in computational representations.

As we descend the hierarchy of metalinguistic stratification, we find that the coverage of phenomena decreases but the explicitness of specification increases; there is a clear trade-off between the two. We also find that the degree of domain specialization decreases: the theory of paradigmatic organization is specific to language (and other semiotic systems), but programming languages are used for a wide variety of tasks – hence the increasing range of options as we descend the hierarchy of metalinguistic stratification.

Table 12.5 Stratification of systemic functional metalanguage and Lamb's degrees of precision: one possible alignment

Stratification of systemic functional metalanguage		Lamb's (2013) levels of precision
theory	theory of paradigmatic (systemic) organization	
theoretical representation	system networks	abstract relational networks
computational representation	e.g. typed feature structures, frame-based inheritance networks	narrow relational networks
implementation	e.g. LISP, Prolog, C++, Java, Python	neural networks

When Terrence Deacon told me of the need for "biological implementability" in linguistic accounts developed to be relevant to neurolinguistics, I thought of the stratification of our metalanguage in computational linguistic work. This is one way of interpreting what Lamb (2013) says about levels of precision, and I have suggested one possible alignment with the strata or levels of the stratal organization of our metalanguage in the rightmost column of Table 12.5. According to my interpretation, abstract relational networks (his "RN notation") correspond approximately to system networks, although we should keep in mind that Lamb indicates that the level of specification is higher than that of system networks. Narrow relational networks (his "narrow RN notation") are analogous to computational representation, serving, respectively, as an interface between abstract representation and neural networks, and between theoretical representation and implementation. Finally, neural networks correspond to implementation. Like the stratum of implementation, neural networks are actually highly generalized in the sense that they represent many different kinds of system besides language, in fact all kinds of human system that are neurologically embodied. (But their nature qua neural networks is central to the whole organization; cf. Edelman's 1992: 211–52, critique of models of "the mind" that do not take the nature of the brain seriously, ones based on computer models, which he characterizes as the "false analogue" – "Mind without biology: a critical postscript," where he writes, "My goal is to dispel the notion that the mind can be understood in the absence of biology.")

The version of the stratification of the systemic functional metalanguage that I have sketched here is, of course, tailored to computational modelling. But Lamb's levels of precision are tailored to biological modelling, and within SFL I hope that the earlier experience with computational modelling can be helpful in progressing with the engagement with neurosemiotics – of course recognizing that neural networks are not programmed implementations in traditional computational linguistic systems. Rather, we can benefit by approaching our conception of language in relational terms by drawing on insights from the study of neural networks, and insights from networks science in general (Barabási 2016).

Here something like the ordered typology of systems sketched above will surely be central. It will, I'm sure, help us see and investigate language as the human system that is central in integrating the brain and at the same time central in making possible the collective brain. This is possible when we see fourth-order systems as systems of meaning – as semiotic systems, enacted in social systems (as argued in Halliday and Matthiessen 1999). In my view, the major advances in the interpretation of fourth-order systems as cognitive systems – reflected in important notions such as embodied cognition, the social brain, the collective brain, collective cognition, dialogic cognition – actually follow automatically if we view fourth-order systems as semiotic systems rather than as (only) cognitive systems.

Notes

1   In this respect, neurosemiotics is like neurolinguistics, but on the one hand I take it that it foregrounds meaning as a key property of semiotic systems, and on the other hand it is concerned not only with language but also with other semiotic systems such as gesture and pictorial semiotics, and thus explicitly with language as one kind of semiotic system – a higher-order semiotic system, in the sense discussed below.

2   Alvar Ellegård (e.g. https://en.wikipedia.org/wiki/Alvar_Ellegård) was an important scholar in Sweden, and would probably have been more internationally influential if he had been based at a top university in an English-speaking country. His contributions ranged over various areas in linguistics, and fairly late in life he conducted text-based research into Jesus as a character, partly based on the Dead Sea Scrolls, putting forward his interpretation of the myth of Jesus (e.g. Ellegård 1999).

3   And dealing specifically with the neurobiology of language, Whitaker (1969: 4-6) writes: "R. Jakobson … has long been interested in aphasia, as is well-known, but for all intents and purposes his studies have been neither empirical nor particularly explanatory. His major concern seems to be in providing aphasiologists with a linguistically-oriented descriptive nomenclature for the types of phasic disturbances." I would hope and argue that clinical linguistics informed by SFL goes far beyond this concern (cf. Armstrong 2009; Asp and de Villiers 2010, 2019; Ferguson, Spencer, and Armstrong 2017).

4   This was the period when accounts of lexis in language began to be conceived of as the "mental lexicon." According to Google's Ngram Viewer, the "mental lexicon" began to appear in books around 1970, and then the frequency increased exponentially.

5   One can explore details; for example Halliday's (2004d) theory of probabilistically associated and independent systemic terms in different systems can be interpreted in terms of insights going back to Hebb (1949). The nature of language as a probabilistic system has now received much more attention in research engaging with language, including research into language development based on statistical learning (see further below, e.g. references to Patricia Kuhl and to Lisa Feldman Barrett). Thus, Halliday's conception of language as a probabilistic system and the significance of relative frequencies in text as children process very large quantities of text have actually been reinforced in neurolinguistic work in the last couple of decades.

6   Cf. the two halves of the classic Stoic Saussurean sign, "signified" and "signifier" in the English translation of Saussure's terms. However, we foreground the systemic interpretation, so our focus shifts from separate signs to systems of meaning, organized as content plus expression.

7   Gazzaniga (1985: x) uses the term "social brain" in a different but ultimately related sense: "The data suggest that our mental lives amount to a reconstruction of the independent activities of the many brain systems we all possess. A confederation of mental systems resides within us. Metaphorically, we humans are more of a sociological entity than a single unified psychological entity. We have a social brain." This can be read in the context of the orders of individuals set out in Table 12.1.

8   This can be seen also in ontogenesis, as infants adopt bodily acts (gestures and vocalizations) as expressive resources in their protolanguages (e.g. Halliday 1975, 2004a). The expressive nature of the body is a general principle: Abercrombie (1968: 55) puts it succinctly as follows: "We speak with our vocal organs, but we converse with our entire bodies" – cf. Thibault's (2004) notion of the **signifying body**. And this notion of the signifying body can be complemented by the notion of the **signified body**, in the sense the content plane resources of language have evolved to construe our experience of our bodies (ideational) and to enact affective and empathic processes (interpersonal).

9   For example, both ideational content systems (semantics and lexicogrammar) and visual perception, a bio-semiotic system, involve actively construing meaning out of incomplete fragments, imposing patterns to make sense of them. Thus, image analysis seems to me to be similar to linguistic parsing and semantic interpretation in certain central respects. This struck me initially when I was invited by Michio Sugeno to spend some time at LIFE, the Laboratory for International Fuzzy Engineering, in Yokohama, and was introduced to, among other projects, a research project concerned with image analysis. This reminded me of an insight I had gained from Neisser's (1967) book on cognitive psychology, which I probably read in the late 1970s; he writes, "The burden of the argument will be that perception is not a passive taking-in of stimuli, but an active process of synthesizing or constructing a visual figure" (p. 16). This is certainly an important aspect of our notion of "construing our experience of the world," related to our conception of perceptual systems as bio-semiotic systems in Halliday and Matthiessen 1999. And since Neisser (1967),

this new insight into the brain has continued to be developed; Barrett (2017) emphasizes that the brain is not "reactive" but rather "predictive." In this way, linguistic construal of experience and visual perception are similar in that they are active processes of modelling experience rather than simply reflecting it; and there is a connection, as shown by studies by Christiane von Stutterheim and her team (e.g. Carroll and von Stutterheim 2011; Schmiedtová, von Stutterheim, and Carroll 2011).

10   When Halliday returned from the Nobel Symposium in Sweden that he had been invited to give his paper to, I was very keen to find out from him how his contribution had been received. When, after his return, I asked him during one of our weekly meetings, he smiled, saying he felt the linguists had been puzzled by his presentation, perhaps in particular the one who'd been given the task of commenting on his paper. The theme of the symposium was "The relation between language and mind." Michael told me jokingly that he'd first thought of including "never mind" in the title of his paper. In one of our many discussions about this area, we agreed that we found Susan Greenfield's characterization of the mind quite helpful; she says something like, "if you have to talk about the mind, think of it as a personalized brain" – personalized through cumulative experience, engagement with the world. This is, of course, an insightful way of transcending the old mind–brain dualism (boosted by Cartesian philosophy), one that accords well with Halliday's (1995b, 2004b) ontogenetic perspective.

11   Cf. Lieberman (2000) on the organization of the brain: "The correct model for the functional organization of the human brain is not that offered by 'modular' theorists such as Steven Pinker (1994, 1998) – a set of petty bureaucrats each of which controls a behavior and won't have anything to do with one another. The neural bases of human language are intertwined with other aspects of cognition, motor control, and emotion" (p. 2). And "The neural architecture of the functional language system differs profoundly from that implied by current 'modular' theories of mind (Chomsky 1980a,b, 1986; Fodor 1983)" (p. 7).

12   The textual metafunction is equally significant, but it is an enabling function, concerned with the creation of ideational and interpersonal meanings as a flow of text adapted to its context. In contrast, the ideational and interpersonal metafunction are strongly grounded also outside language through exo-semantic relations.

13   These are examples of prompts from Egorova, Shtyrov, and Pulvermüller (2016). The first, *What are these called?*, is clearly a demand for information (a question), realized grammatically by a wh-interrogative; but while the second example, *What can I get you?*, is grammatically also a wh-interrogative, semantically it would appear to be an offer (i.e. an offer to give the addressee an item of goods, an object) – one metaphorically realized as if it were a question. Nevertheless, the contrast between an exchange of information (*What are these called?*) and of goods-&-services (*What can I get you?*) applies.

14   For example, they include evidence from the fossil record of changes to the vocal tract (e.g. P. Lieberman 1984, 2000; D. Lieberman 2013), changes that may imply an expansion of the human articulatory potential, and of changes to the cranium, for example changes that may indicate an expansion of any area that has been found to be centrally involved in the neural representation of language. (Broca's area has been cited as an example

in the literature; but note the reference in this chapter to Barrett's [2017] deconstruction of long-standing assumptions about this area as a centre for linguistic processing.)

15   Cf. Damasio and Damasio's (1992: 91) characterization of "convergence zones": "Where can the records that bind together all these fragmented activities be held? We believe they are embodied in ensembles of neurons within the brain's many 'convergence' regions. At these sites the axons of feedforward projecting neurons from one part of the brain converge and join with reciprocally diverging feedback projections from other regions. When reactivation within the convergence zones stimulates the feedback projections, many anatomically separate and widely distributed neuron ensembles fire simultaneously and reconstruct previous patterns of mental activity." Thus, semantic terms, or nodes, may serve as convergence zones.

16   Here it is important to note the phenomenon within the content plane of **lexicogrammatical metaphor**. Seen from the point of view of semantics, this means that a given meaning is realized congruently by a given wording within lexicogrammar but that it may also be realized incongruently (metaphorically) as if it were a different meaning. Lexicogrammatical metaphor is highly relevant to the status of semantics as an interface and opens up the possibility that certain semantic domains are related to systems outside language through domains to which they are mapped through lexicogrammatical metaphor. Traditionally, most attention has been given to lexical metaphor, e.g. in philosophy and literary studies, and it has been illuminated in cognitive linguistics under the heading of "conceptual metaphor," introduced by Lakoff and Johnson (1980). Studies of "conceptual metaphor" have been very productive, but they have focussed mainly on lexical metaphor, which needs to be complemented by grammatical metaphor. And as noted above, metaphor is an expansion of the realizational relationship between meaning and wording, i.e. between semantics and lexicogrammar, so it is properly theorized as lexicogrammatical metaphor. In SFL, a great deal of research has been devoted to the study of grammatical metaphor, including also phylogenetic and ontogenetic studies. Both facets of lexicogrammatical metaphor, i.e. lexical ("conceptual") and grammatical metaphor, create new mappings between domains of meaning, which must be reflected in neural networks.

17   Nigel's version of *thought*.

18   While language is expression-plane variable in this way, individual language users may have different orientations. Halliday (2014) writes about his experience with language learners, saying that they may tend to be ear learners or eye learners. And Golestani, Price, and Scott (2011 : 4213) report on a study that shows that expert phoneticians with years of training in phonetic analaysis and transcription "found a positive correlation between the size of left pars opercularis and years of phonetic transcription training experience, illustrating how learning may affect brain structure." They speculate that some differences may already exist in uterus. As far as development due to training is concerned, expert phoneticians turn out to be like the famous case of London taxi drivers, who have a larger hippocampus than ordinary commuters (Maguire et al. 2000).

References

Abercrombie, David. 1967. *Elements of general phonetics.* Edinburgh: Edinburgh University Press. https://doi.org/10.3138/cmlr.23.4.56a

Abercrombie, David. 1968. Paralanguage. *British Journal of Disorders of Communication* 3(1): 55–9. https://doi.org/10.3109/13682826809011441

Ackermann, Hermann, Dirk Wildgruber, and Wolfgang Grodd. 1997. Neuroradiologic activation studies of cerebral organization of language capacities: A review of the literature. *Fortschritte der Neurologie, Psychiatrie.* 65: 182–94. https://doi.org/10.1055/s-2007-996321

Aikhenvald, Alexandra. 2012. *The languages of the Amazon.* Oxford: Oxford University Press. https://doi.org/10.1093/acprof:oso/9780199593569.001.0001

Arbib, Michael A. 2012. *How the brain got language: The mirror system hypothesis.* Oxford: Oxford University Press. https://doi.org/10.1093/acprof:osobl/9780199896684.001.0001

Armstrong, Elizabeth M. 1997. A grammatical analysis of aphasic discourse: Changes in meaning-making over time. PhD thesis. Sydney: Macquarie University.

Armstrong, Elizabeth M. 2009. Clinical applications. In Halliday and Webster (eds.), 143–53.

Aronoff, Mark, and Kirsten Fudeman. 2011. *What is morphology?* Second edition. Oxford: Wiley Blackwell.

Ash, Sharon, Peachie Moore, Shweta Antani, George McCawley, Michael Work, and Murray Grossman. 2006. Trying to tell a tale: Discourse impairments in progressive aphasia and frontotemporal dementia. *Neurology* 66: 1405–13. https://doi.org/10.1212/01.wnl.0000210435.72614.38

Asp, Elissa. 2013. The twin paradoxes of unconscious choice and unintentional agents: What neurosciences say about choice and agency in action. In Fontaine, Bartlett and O'Grady (eds.), 160–78. https://doi.org/10.1017/CBO9781139583077.011

Asp, Elissa, and Jessica de Villiers. 2010. *When language breaks down: Analysing discourse in clinical contexts.* Cambridge: Cambridge University Press. https://doi.org/10.1017/CBO9780511845352

Asp, Elissa, and Jessica de Villiers. 2019. Clinical linguistics. In Geoff Thompson, Wendy Bowcher, Lisa Fontaine, and David Schönthal (eds.), *The Cambridge handbook of systemic functional linguistics.* Cambridge: Cambridge University Press. 587–619. https://doi.org/10.1017/CBO9780511845352

Baayen, Harald. 2003. Probabilistic approaches to morphology. In Bod, Hay, and Jannedy (eds.), 229–87. https://doi.org/10.7551/mitpress/5582.003.0010

Bach, Emmon W. 1989. *Informal lectures on formal semantics.* Albany, NY: State University of New York Press.

Badawi, Elsaid, Michael G. Carter, and Adrian Gully. 2004. *Modern written Arabic: A comprehensive grammar.* London and New York: Routledge. Revised edition, 2016. Revised by Maher Awad. London and New York: Routledge. https://doi .org/10.4324/9781315856155

Ball, Philip. 2004. *Critical mass: How one thing leads to another.* London: Heinemann.

Barabási, Albert László. 2016. *Network science.* Cambridge: Cambridge University Press.

Barsalou, Lawrence W. 2008. Grounded cognition. *Annual Review of Psychology* 59: 617–45. https://doi.org/10.1146/annurev.psych.59.103006.093639

Bardi, Mohamed Ali. 2008. *A systemic functional description of the grammar of Arabic.* PhD thesis. Sydney: Macquarie University.

Barrett, Lisa Feldman. 2017. *How emotions are made: The secret life of the brain.* Boston: Houghton Mifflin Harcourt.

Barrett, Lisa Feldman. 2021. *7½ lessons about the brain.* Boston and New York: Mariner Books.

Bateman, John A. 1988. Aspects of clause politeness in Japanese: An inquiry semantic treatment. *The 26th Annual Meeting of the Association for Computational Linguistics.* 147–54. https://doi.org/10.3115/982023.982041

Bateman, John A. 1989. Dynamic systemic-functional grammar: A new frontier. *Word* 40(1–2): Systems, structure and discourse: Selected papers from the Fifteenth International Systemic Congress: 263–86. https://doi.org/10.1080/00437956.1989.11435808

Bateman, John A. 2008. Systemic functional linguistics and the notion of linguistic structure: Unanswered questions, new possibilities. In Jonathan J. Webster (ed.), *Meaning in context: Implementing intelligent applications of language studies.* London and New York: Continuum. 24–58. https://doi.org/10.1075/bct.1.04bat

Bateman, John A. 2018. Peircean semiotics and multimodality: Towards a new synthesis. *Multimodal Communication,* 7(1): 20170021. https://doi.org/10.1515/mc-2017-0021

Bateman, John A., Martin Emele, and Stefan Momma. 1992. The nondirectional representation of systemic functional grammars and semantics as typed feature structures. *Proceedings of COLING 92.* Nantes: COLING. 916–20. https://doi .org/10.3115/992383.992401

Bateman, John A., Joana Hois, Robert Ross, and Thora Tenbrink. 2010. A linguistic ontology of space for natural language processing. *Artificial Intelligence* 174: 1027–71. https://doi.org/10.1016/j.artint.2010.05.008

Bateman, John A., Kikui Gen'ichirou, and Atsuchi Tabuchi. 1987. *Designing a computational systemic grammar for text generation: A progress report.* Kyoto: Department of Electrical Engineering, Kyoto University.

Bateman, John, Daniel McDonald, Tuomo Hiippala, Daniel Couto-Vale, and Eugeniu Costetchi. 2019. Systemic functional linguistics and computation: New directions, new challenges. In Geoff Thompson, Wendy Bowcher, Lisa Fontaine, and David Schöntal (eds.), *The Cambridge handbook of systemic functional linguistics.* Cambridge: Cambridge University Press. 561–86. https://doi.org/10.1017/9781316337936.024

Bateman, John, and Christian Matthiessen. 1989. The text-base uncovered. In H. Bluhme (ed.), *Selected papers from the International Conference on Language and Text Research,*

Xi'an Jiaotong University, Xi'an, P.R.C., March 1989. Published as Bateman and Matthiessen, 1993.

Bateman, John, and Christian M.I.M. Matthiessen. 1991. *Systemic linguistics and text generation: Experiences from Japanese and English*. London: Pinter.

Bateman, John A., and Christian M.I.M. Matthiessen. 1993. The text base in generation. In Keqi Hao, Keqi Hao, Hermann Bluhme, and Renzhi Li (eds.), *Proceedings of the International Conference on Texts and Language Research*, Xi'an, 29–31 March, 1989. Xi'an: Xi'an Jiaotong University Press. 3–45.

Bateman, John, Christian Matthiessen, Keizo Nanri, and Licheng Zeng. 1991. The rapid prototyping of natural language generation components: An application of functional typology. *Proceedings of the 12th International Conference on Artificial Intelligence*, Sydney, 24–30 August 1991. Sydney. San Mateo, CA: Morgan Kaufman. 966–71. https://doi.org/10.5555/1625031.1625116

Bateman, John A., Christian M.I.M. Matthiessen, and Licheng Zeng. 1999. Multilingual language generation for multilingual software: A functional linguistic approach. *Applied Artificial Intelligence: An International Journal* 13(6): 607–39. https://doi.org/10.1080/088395199117289

Bateman, John A., and Michael O'Donnell. 2015. Computational linguistics: The Halliday connection. In Jonathan J. Webster (ed.), *The Bloomsbury companion to M.A.K. Halliday*. London: Bloomsbury. 453–66. https://doi.org/10.5040/9781472541888.ch-019

Bateman, John, and Cecile L. Paris. 2011. Constraining the deployment of lexicogrammatical resources during text generation: Towards a computational instantiation of register theory. In Eija Ventola (ed.), *Functional and systemic linguistics: Approaches and uses*. Berlin and New York: De Gruyter Mouton. 81–106. https://doi.org/10.1515/9783110883527.81

Bateman, John, and Michael Zock. 2022. Natural language generation. In Ruslan Mitkov (ed.), *The Oxford handbook of computational linguistics*. Second edition. Oxford: Oxford University Press. 747–69. https://doi.org.10.1093/oxford-hb/9780199276349.013.0015

Bateson, M. Catherine. 1979. The epigenesis of conversational interaction: A personal account of research development. In Margaret Bullowa (ed.), *Before speech: The beginning of human communication*. London: Cambridge University Press. 63–77.

Bazerman, Charles. 1988. *Shaping written knowledge: The genre and activity of the experimental article in science*. Madison, WI: The University of Wisconsin Press.

Becker, Joseph D. 1975. The phrasal lexicon. In Bonnie Nash-Webber and Roger Schank (eds.), *Theoretical issues in natural language processing*. Cambridge, MA 60–63. https://doi.org/10.3115/980190.980212

Beckner, Clay, Richard Blythe, Morten H. Christiansen, William Croft, Nick C. Ellis, John Holland, Jinyun Ke, Diane Larsen-Freeman, and Tom Shoenemann. 2009. Language is a complex adaptive system: Position paper. *Language Learning* 59(Suppl 1), *Language as a complex adaptive system*, edited by Nick C. Ellis and Diane Larsen-Freeman: 1–26. https://doi.org/10.1111/j.1467-9922.2009.00533.x

Bednarek, Monika, and Martin, J.R. 2010. *New discourse on language: Functional perspectives on multimodality, identity, and affiliation*. London: Continuum.

Bejarano, Virgilio, and Rolf Jörnving, 1967. *Spansk grammatik.* Uppsala: Almqvist and Wiksell.

Berlin, Brent, Dennis E. Breedlove, and Peter H. Raven. 1973. General principles of classification and nomenclature in folk biology. *American Anthropologist* 75: 214–42. https://doi.org/10.1525/aa.1973.75.1.02a00140

Berman, Ruth A., and Dan I. Slobin. 1994. *Relating events in narrative: A crosslinguistic development study.* Hillsdale, NJ: Erlbaum.

Bertalanffy, Ludwig von. 1968. *General system theory: Foundations, development, applications.* New York: George Braziller.

Berry, Margaret. 1977. *Introduction to systemic linguistics.* London: Batsford.

Berry, Margaret. 1981. Systemic linguistics and discourse analysis: A multi-layered approach to exchange structure. In Malcolm Coulthard and Martin Montgomery (eds.), *Studies in discourse analysis.* London: Routledge. 120–45.

Biber, Douglas. 1986. Spoken and written textual dimensions in English: Resolving the contradictory findings. *Language* 62(2): 384–414. https://doi.org/10.2307/414678

Biber, Douglas. 1988. *Variation across speech and writing.* Cambridge: Cambridge University Press. https://doi.org/10.1017/CBO9780511621024

Bickel, Balthasar, and Johanna Nichols. 2013a. Fusion of selected inflectional formatives. In Matthew S. Dryer and Martin Haspelmath (eds.), *The world atlas of language structures online.* Leipzig: Max Planck Institute for Evolutionary Anthropology. https://doi.org/10.5281/zenodo.13950591 (Available online at http://wals.info/chapter/20, Accessed on 2014-08-24.)

Bickel, Balthasar, and Johanna Nichols. 2013b. Exponence of selected inflectional formatives. Matthew S. Dryer and Martin Haspelmath (eds.), *The world atlas of language structures online.* Leipzig: Max Planck Institute for Evolutionary Anthropology. https://doi.org/10.5281/zenodo.13950591 (Available online at http://wals.info/chapter/21, Accessed on 2014-08-24.)

Bickerton, Derek. 1995. *Language and human behaviour.* London: UCL Press.

Birch, David. 1993. Drama praxis and the dialogic imperative. In Mohsen Ghassy (ed.), *Register analysis: Theory and practice.* London: Pinter. 43–56.

Bloomfield, Leonard. 1933. *Language.* London: Allen and Unwin.

Bod, Rens, Jennifer Hay, and Stefanie Jannedy (eds.). 2003. *Probabilistic linguistics.* Cambridge, Mass: MIT Press. https://doi.org/10.7551/mitpress/5582.001.0001

Bohm, David. 1980. *Wholeness and the implicate order.* London: Routledge. https://doi.org/10.4324/9780203995150

Bornkessel-Schlesewsky, Ina, and Petra B. Schumacher. 2016. Towards a neurobiology of information structure. In Caroline Féry and Shinichiro Ishihara (eds.), *The Oxford handbook of information structure.* Oxford: Oxford University Press. 581–98. https://doi.org/10.1093/oxfordhb/9780199642670.013.22

Boroditsky, Lera. 2001. Does language shape thought?: Mandarin and English speakers' conceptions of time. *Cognitive Psychology* 43:1–22. https://doi.org/10.1006/cogp.2001.0748

Boroditsky, Lera. 2011. How language shapes thought: The languages we speak affect our perceptions of the world. *Scientific American* February 2011, 63–65. https://doi.org/10.1038/scientificamerican0211-62

Botha, Rudolf. 2020. *Neanderthal language: Demystifying the linguistic powers of our extinct cousins.* Cambridge: Cambridge University Press. https://doi.org /10.1017/9781108868167

Boulding, Kenneth. 1956. General systems theory: The skeleton of a science. *Management Science* 2(3): 197–208. Reprinted in *E:CO* Vol. 6 Nos. 1–2, Fall 2004, 127–39. https://doi.org/10.1287/mnsc.2.3.197

Brachman, Ronald. 1978. *A structural paradigm for representing knowledge.* Bolt, Beranek, and Newman, Inc., Technical Report.

Brachman, Ronald J. 1979. On the epistemological status of semantic networks. In N.V. Findler (ed.), *Associative networks: Representation and use of knowledge by computers.* New York: Academic Press. 3–50.

Brachman, Ron J., and Hector J. Levesque (eds.) 1985. *Readings in knowledge representation.* Los Altos, CA: Morgan Kaufman.

Bresnan, Joan. 1980. Polyadicity: Part I of a theory of lexical rules and representation. In Teun Hoekstra, Harry van der Hulst, and Michael Moortgat (eds.), *Lexical grammar.* Berlin and Boston: De Gruyter Mouton. https://doi. org/10.1515/9783111711225005

Bresnan, Joan. 2001. *Lexical-functional syntax.* Oxford: Blackwell.

Brown, Roger, and Albert Gilman. 1960. The pronouns of power and solidarity. In Thomas A. Sebeok (ed.), *Style in language.* Cambridge, MA: MIT Press. 253–76. https: //doi.org/10.1515/9783110805376.252

Burton, Deirdre. 1980. *Dialogue and discourse: A sociolinguistic approach to modern drama and naturally occurring conversation.* London: Routledge.

Butler, Christopher. 1982. *The directive function of the English modals.* PhD thesis. Nottingham: University of Nottingham.

Butler, Christopher. 1985. Discourse systems and structures and their place within an overall systemic model. In James D. Benson and William S. Greaves (eds.), *Systemic functional approaches to discourse: Selected papers from the 12th International Systemic Workshop.* Norwood, NJ: Ablex. 213–28.

Butt, David G. 1991. Some basic tools in a linguistic approach to personality: A Firthian concept of social process. In Fran Christie (ed.), *Literacy in social processes: Papers from the Inaugural Australian Systemic Functional Linguistics Conference, Deakin University, January 1990.* Darwin: Northern Territory University. 23–44.

Byrnes, Heidi (ed.). 2006. *Advanced instructed language learning: The complementary contribution of Halliday and Vygotsky.* London and New York: Continuum.

Cacioppo, John T., and Jean Decety. 2011. Social neuroscience: Challenges and opportunities in the study of complex behavior. *Annals of the New York Academy of Sciences* 1224: 162–73. https://doi.org/10.1111/j.1749-6632.2010.05858.x

Caffarel, Alice. 1997. Models of transitivity in French: A systemic functional interpretation. In Anne-Marie Simon-Vandenbergen, Kristin Davidse, and Dirk Noël (eds.), *Reconnecting language: Morphology and syntax in functional perspectives.* Amsterdam and Philadelphia: John Benjamins. 249–96.

Caffarel, Alice. 2006. *A systemic functional grammar of French: From grammar to discourse.* London and New York: Continuum.

Caffarel, Alice, J.R. Martin, and Christian M.I.M. Matthiessen (eds.). 2004. *Language typology: A functional perspective.* (Current Issues in Linguistic Theory 253.) Amsterdam: Benjamins. https://doi.org/10.1075/cilt.253

Caldwell, David, and Zappavigna, Michele. 2011. Visualizing multimodal patterning. In Shoshana Dreyfus, Susan Hood, and Maree Stenglin (eds.), *Semiotic margins: Meaning in multimodalities.* London and New York: Continuum. 229–42.

Cantarino, V. 1974. *Syntax of modern Arabic prose: The simple sentence.* Bloomington: Indiana University Press.

Carroll, Mary, and Christiane von Stutterheim. 2011. Event representation, time event relations, and clause structure: A crosslinguistic study of English and German. In Jürgen Bohnemeyer and Eric Pedersen (eds.), *Event representation in language and cognition.* Cambridge: Cambridge University Press. 68–83. https://doi.org/10.1017/CBO9780511782039.004

Catford, J.C. 1969. J.R. Firth and British Linguistics. In Archibald A. Hill (ed.), *Linguistics today.* New York and London: Basic Books, Inc. 218–28.

Catford, J.C. 1977. *Fundamental problems in phonetics.* Indiana: Indiana University Pres.

Chabner, Davi-Ellen. 2011. *The language of medicine.* 9th edition. Saint Louis, MI: Saunders Elsevier.

Chafe, Wallace L. (ed.). 1980. *The pear stories: Cognitive, cultural, and linguistic aspects of narrative production.* (Advances in Discourse Processes, vol. III). Norwood, NJ: Ablex.

Channell, Joanna. 1994. *Vague language.* Oxford: Oxford University Press.

Charniak, Eugene, and Yorik Wilks (eds.). 1976. *Computational semantics.* Amsterdam: North-Holland

Charter, Nick, Joshua B. Tenenbaum, and Alan Yuille. 2006. Probabilistic models of cognition: Conceptual foundations. *TRENDS in Cognitive Sciences* 10(7): 287–91. https://doi.org/10.1016/j.tics.2006.05.007

Chater, Nick, and Mike Oaksford (eds.). 2008. *The probabilistic mind: Prospects for Bayesian cognitive science.* Oxford: Oxford University Press. https://doi.org/10.1093/acprof:oso/9780199216093.001.0001

Chatterjee, Anjan. 2008. The neural organization of spatial thought and language. *Seminars in Speech and Language* 29: 226–38. https://doi.org/10.1055/s-0028-1082886

Chen, Janice, Yuan Chang Leong, Christopher J. Honey, Chung H. Yong, Kenneth A. Norman, and Uri Hasson. 2016. Shared memories reveal shared structure in neural activity across individuals. *Nature Neuroscience* 20: 115–25. https://doi.org/10.1038/nn.4450

Chomsky, Noam A. 1965. *Aspects of the theory of syntax.* Cambridge, MA: MIT Press.

Chomsky, Noam A. 1980a. Rules and representations. *Behavioral and Brain Sciences* 3: 1–61. https://doi.org/10.1017/S0140525X00001515

Chomsky, Noam A. 1980b. Initial states and steady states. In Massimo Piattelli-Palmarini (ed.), *Language and learning: The debate between Jean Piaget and Noam Chomsky.* Cambridge, MA: Harvard University Press. 107–30.

Chomsky, Noam A. 1986. *Knowledge of language: Its nature, origin, and use.* New York: Praeger.

Chomsky, Noam A. 2000. *New horizons in the study of language and mind.* Cambridge: Cambridge University Press. https://doi.org/10.1017/CBO9780511811937

Christian, David. 2004. *Maps of time: An introduction to big history*. Berkeley, Los Angeles and London: University of California Press. https://doi.org/10.1525/9780520950672

Christiansen, Morten H., and Nick Chater. 2008. Language as shaped by the brain. *Behavioral and Brain Sciences*. Oct; 31(5): 489–508; discussion: 509–58. https://doi.org/10.1017/S0140525X08004998

Colby, Benjamin N. 1966. Cultural patterns in narrative. *Science* 151: 793–8. https://doi.org/10.1126/science.151.3712.793

Comrie, Bernard. 1981. *Language universals and linguistic typology*. Oxford: Blackwell.

Comrie, Bernard. 1985. *Tense*. Cambridge: Cambridge University Press.

Conde-Valverde, Mercedes, Ignacio Martínez, Rolf M. Quam, Manuel Rosa, Alex D. Velez, Carlos Lorenzo, Pilar Jarabo, José María Bermúdez de Castro, Eudald Carbonell, and Juan Luis Arsuaga. 2021. Neanderthals and Homo sapiens had similar auditory and speech capacities. *Nature Ecology and Evolution* 5: 609–15. https://doi.org/10.1038/s41559-021-01391-6

Corbett, Greville G. 1991. *Gender*. Cambridge: Cambridge University Press. https://doi.org/10.1017/CBO9781139166119

Cross, Marilyn, and Christian M.I.M. Matthiessen. 1997. Integrating and managing multimodal information sources: A problem for defence. In *Proceedings of the Artificial Intelligence in Defence Workshop AI '95*, edited by Simon Goss, Eighth Australian Joint Conference on Artificial Intelligence, Canberra 14 November 1995. 83–91.

Cross, Marilyn, Christian Matthiessen, Licheng Zeng, and Ichiro Kobayashi. 1998. Building multimodal systems: Compromise between theory and practice. *AAAI Technical Report* WS-98-09. https://aaai.org/Papers/Workshops/1998/WS-98-09/WS98-09-003.pdf

Cummings, Michael J. 1987. Syspro: A computerized method for writing system networks and deriving selection expressions. In Ross Steele and Terry Threadgold (eds.), *Language topics: Essays in honour of Michael Halliday*. Amsterdam: Benjamins.

Curtiss, Susan. 1977. *Genie: A psycholinguistic study of a modern-day "wild child"*. New York: Academic.

Damasio, Antonio R. 1989. Concepts in the brain. *Mind and Language* 4(3): 24–28. https://doi.org/10.1111/j.1468-0017.1989.tb00236.x

Damasio, Antonio R. 1990. Category-related recognition defects as a clue to the neural substrates of language. *Trends in Neuroscience* 13: 95–98. https://doi.org/10.1016/0166-2236(90)90184-C

Damasio, Antonio, and Hanna Damasio. 1992. Brain and language. *Scientific American* 267: 88–95. https://doi.org/10.1038/scientificamerican0992-88

Daneš, František. 1964. A three-level approach to syntax. *Travaux Linguistiques de Prague* 1: 225–40.

Daneš, František. 1974a. Functional sentence perspective and the organisation of the text. Danes František (ed.), *Papers on functional sentence perspective*. The Hague: Mouton. 106–28.

Daneš, František (ed.). 1974b. *Papers on functional sentence perspective*. Academia, Publishing House of the Czechoslovak Academy of Sciences. https://doi.org/10.1515/9783111676524

Darwin, Charles. 1872. *The expression of the emotions in man and animals*. London: John Murray.

Davey, Anthony. 1979. *Discourse production: A computer model of some aspects of a speaker.* Edinburgh: Edinburgh University Press.

Deacon, Terrence. 1992. Brain-language coevolution. In John A. Hawkins and Murray Gell-Mann (eds.), *The evolution of human languages.* Redwood City, CA: Addison-Wesley. (Proceedings Volume XI, Santa Fe Institute Studies in the Sciences of Complexity.) 49–85.

Deacon, Terrence. 1997. *The symbolic species: The co-evolution of language and the human brain.* Harmondsworth: Penguin Books.

Delafield-Butt, Jonathan, and Colwyn Trevarthen. 2015. The ontogenesis of narrative: From moving to meaning. *Frontiers in Psychology* 6: 1157. https://doi.org/10.3389/fpsyg.2015.01157

Dik, Simon C. 1978. *Functional grammar.* New York and North-Holland: Elsevier.

Dixon, R.M.W. 1972. *The Dyirbal language of North Queensland.* Cambridge: Cambridge University Press. https://doi.org/10.1017/CBO9781139084987

Dixon, R.M.W. 1979. Ergativity. *Language* 55(1): 59–138. https://doi.org/10.2307/412519

Dixon, R.M.W. 1991. *A new approach to English grammar, on semantic principles.* Oxford: Clarendon Press. https://doi.org/10.1093/oso/9780198242727.001.0001

Dixon, R.M.W., and Alexandra Y. Aikhenvald. 2003. Word: A typological framework. In R.M.W. Dixon, and Alexandra Y. Aikhenvald (eds.), *Word: A cross-linguistic typology.* Cambridge: Cambridge University Press. 1–41. https://doi.org/10.1017/CBO9780511486241.002

DuBois, J.W. 1987. The discourse basis of ergativity. *Language* 63(4): 805–53. https://doi.org/10.2307/415719

Dunbar, Robin I.M. 1993. Coevolution of neocortical size, group size and language in humans. *Behavioral and Brain Sciences* 16 (4): 681–735. https://doi.org/10.1017/S0140525X00032325

Dunbar, Robin. 1996. *Grooming, gossip, and the evolution of language.* London: Faber and Faber.

Dunbar, Robin. 2020. *Evolution: What everyone needs to know.* Oxford: Oxford University Press. https://doi.org/10.1093/wentk/9780190922894.001.0001

Dryer, Matthew S., and Martin Haspelmath (eds.). 2013. *The world atlas of language structures online.* Munich: Max Planck Digital Library. https://doi.org/10.5281/zenodo.3607047 Available online at http://wals.info/

Edelman, Gerald M. 1989. *The remembered present: A biological theory of consciousness.* New York: Basic Books.

Edelman, Gerald. 1992. *Bright air, brilliant fire: On the matter of the mind.* New York: Basic Books.

Edelman, Gerald. 2004. *Wider than the sky: The phenomenal gift of consciousness.* New Haven and London: Yale University Press.

Edelman, Gerald, and Giulio Tononi. 2000. *A universe of consciousness: How matter becomes imagination.* New York: Basic Books.

Edmondson, Willis. 1981. *Spoken discourse: A model for analysis.* London: Longman.

Eggins, Suzanne. 1990. *Conversational structure: A systemic-functional analysis of interpersonal and logical meaning in multiparty sustained talk.* PhD thesis. Sydney: University of Sydney.

Eggins, Suzanne and Diana Slade. 2005. *Analysing casual conversation*. London: Equinox.

Egorova, Natalia, Yuri Shtyrov, and Friedmann Pulvermüller, 2013. Early and parallel processing of pragmatic and semantic information in speech acts: Neurophysiological evidence. *Frontiers in Human Neuroscience* 7(86): 86. https://doi.org/10.3389/fnhum.2013.00086

Egorova, Natalia, Yury Shtyrov, and Friedemann Pulvermüller. 2016. Brain basis of communicative actions in language. *Neuroimage* 125: 857–67. https://doi.org/10.1016/j.neuroimage.2015.10.055

Ellegård, Alvar. 1953. *The auxiliary "do": The establishment and regulation of its use in English*. Stockholm: Almqvist och Wiksell.

Ellegård, Alvar. 1971. *Transformationell svensk-engelsk satslära*. Lund: Gleerup.

Ellegård, Alvar. 1988. *Språket och hjärnan: Språk och tal, minnet, höger-vänster, inlärning, tänkande*. Stockholm: Prisma.

Ellegård, Alvar. 1999. *Jesus: One hundred years before Christ; a study in creative mythology*. London: Century.

Ellis, John M. 1993. *Language, thought and logic*. Chicago: Northwestern University Press.

El-Menoufy, Afaf. 1969. *A study of the role of intonation in the grammar of English. Volume 1: Theory and description. Volume 2: Texts*. PhD thesis. London: University of London.

El-Menoufy, Afaf. 1988. Intonation and meaning in spontaneous discourse. In James D. Benson, Michael J. Cummings, and William S. Greaves (eds.), *Linguistics in a systemic perspective*. Amsterdam: Benjamins. 1–27. https://doi.org/10.1075/cilt.39.02elm

Erickson, Lucy C., and Erik D. Thiessen. 2015. Statistical learning of language: Theory, validity, and predictions of statistical learning account of language acquisition. *Developmental Review*: 66–108. https://doi.org/10.1016/j.dr.2015.05.002

Evans, Nicholas, and Stephen C. Levinson. 2009. The myth of language universals: Language diversity and its importance for cognitive science. *Behavioral and Brain Sciences* 32: 429–492. https://doi.org/10.1017/S0140525X0999094X

Fawcett, Robin P. 1973. *Systemic functional grammar in a cognitive model of language*. London: University College London. Mimeo.

Fawcett, Robin P. 1980. *Cognitive linguistics and social interaction: Towards and integrated model of a systemic functional grammar and the other components of a communicating mind*. London: Julius Groos Verlag, and Exeter University.

Fawcett, Robin P. 1983. Language as a semiological system: A re-interpretation of Saussure. In J. Morreali (ed.), *The Ninth LACUS Forum 1982*. Columbia, SC: Hornbeam Press. 59–125.

Fawcett, Robin P. 1988. What makes a 'good' system network good? In James D. Benson and William S. Greaves (eds.), *Systemic functional approaches to discourse: Selected papers from the 12th International Systemic Workshop*. Norwood, NJ: Ablex.

Fawcett, Robin P. 1984. System networks, codes, and knowledge of the universe. In Robin Fawcett, M.A.K. Halliday, S. Lamb, and A Makkai (eds.), *The semiotic of language and culture. Volume 2: Language and other semiotic systems of culture*. London: Frances Pinter. 135–79.

Fawcett, Robin, and Gordon Tucker. 1989. Prototype Generators 1 and 2. COMMUNAL Report Number 10, Computational Linguistics Unit, University of Wales College of Cardiff.

Fawcett, Robin P., A. van der Mije, and C. van Wissen. 1988. Towards a systemic flow-chart model for discourse structure. In Robin P. Fawcett and D. Young (eds.), *New developments in systemic linguistics. Volume 2: Theory and application*. London: Pinter. 116–43.

Fawcett, Robin P., and A. Ruvan. Weerasinghe. 1993. Probabilistic incremental parsing in systemic functional grammar. In Harry Bunt and Masaru Tomita (eds.), *Proceedings of the Third Workshop on Parsing Technologies*. Tilburg: Institute for Language Technology and Artificial Intelligence. 349–67.

Feldman, Jerome, and Srinivas Narayanan. 2004. Embodied meaning in a neural theory of language. *Brain and Language* 89: 385–92. https://doi.org/10.1016/S0093-934X(03)00355-9

Ferguson, Alison, Elizabeth Spencer, and Elizabeth Armstrong. 2017. Systemic functional linguistics and clinical linguistics. In Tom Bartlett and Gerard O'Grady (eds.), *The Routledge handbook of systemic functional grammar*. London: Routledge. 491–505. https://doi.org/10.4324/9781315413891-43

Féry, Caroline, and Shinichiro Ishihara. 2016. *The Oxford handbook of information structure*. Oxford: Oxford University Press. https://doi.org/10.1093/oxford-hb/9780199642670.001.0001

Fine, Jonathan. 1994. *How language works: Cohesion in normal and nonstandard communication*. Norwood, NJ: Ablex.

Fine, Jonathan. 2006. *Language in psychiatry: A handbook of clinical practice*. London: Equinox.

Firbas, Jan. 1959. Thoughts on the communicative function of the verb in English, German and Czech. I: *Brno studies in English* 1.

Firbas, Jan. 1987. On two starting points of communication. In Ross Steele and Terry Threadgold (eds.), *Language topics. Essays in honour of Michael Halliday*. Volume 1. Amsterdam: Benjamins. 23–47.

Firbas, Jan. 1992. *Functional sentence perspective in written and spoken communication*. Cambridge: Cambridge University Press. (Studies in English Language.)

Firth, J.R. 1948a. Sounds and prosodies. *Transactions of the Philological Society*: 127–52. Reprinted in J.R. Firth, 1959, *Papers in linguistics 1934–1951*. London: Oxford University Press. 121–38. Also in Frank Palmer (ed.), 1968, *Prosodic analysis*. London: Oxford University Press. 1–27. https://doi.org/10.1111/j.1467-968X.1948.tb00556.x

Firth, J.R. 1948b. The semantics of linguistic science. *Lingua* i.4. Reprinted in Firth, 1957c.

Firth, J.R. 1950. Personality and language in society. *Sociological Review* 42(1): 37–52. Reprinted in J.R. Firth, 1957, Papers in linguistics 1934–1951. London: Oxford University Press. 177–89. https://doi.org/10.1111/j.1467-954X.1950.tb02460.x

Firth, J.R. 1957a. Ethnographic analysis and language with reference to Malinowski's views. In Raymond Firth (ed.), *Man and culture: An evaluation of the work of Bronislaw Malinowski*. London: Routledge and Kegan Paul. 93–118.

Firth, J.R. 1957b. A synopsis of linguistic theory, 1930–55. In *Studies in linguistic analysis*. Special volume of the Philological Society. Oxford: Blackwell. 1–32. Reprinted in Frank Palmer (ed.), 1968, *Selected papers of J.R. Firth 1952–59*. London and Harlow: Longman.

Firth, J.R. 1957c. *Papers in linguistics 1934–1951*. London: Oxford University Press.

Fishbein, H. 1976. *Evolution, development, and children's learning.* Santa Monica, CA: Goodyear Publishing Company Inc.

Flecken, Monique, Christiane von Stutterheim, and Mary Carroll. 2014. Grammatical aspect influences motion event perception: Findings from a cross-linguistic non-verbal recognition task. *Language and Cognition* 6(1): 45–78. https://doi.org/10.1017/langcog.2013.2

Fleming, Ilah. 1988. *Communication analysis: A stratificational approach. A field guide for communication situation, semantic, and morphemic analysis.* Volume 2. Dallas, TX: Summer Institute of Linguistics.

Fodor, Jerry A. 1983. *The modularity of mind.* Cambridge, MA: MIT Press. https://doi.org/10.7551/mitpress/4737.001.0001

Fontaine, Lise M., Tom A.M. Bartlett, and Gerard N. O'Grady (eds.). 2013. *Systemic functional linguistics: Exploring choice.* Cambridge: Cambridge University Press. https://doi.org/10.1017/CBO9781139583077

Franks, David D. (ed.). 2010. *Neurosociology: The nexus between neuroscience and social psychology.* New York: Springer. https://doi.org/10.1007/978-1-4419-5531-9

Fries, Peter H. 1981. On the status of theme in English: Arguments from discourse. *Forum Linguisticum,* 6: 1–38. Reprinted in Janos S. Petöfi and Emel Sözer (eds.), 1983, *Micro and macro connexity of discourse.* Hamburg: Buske (Papers in Text Linguistics 45).

Fries, Peter H. 1982. On Repetition and Interpretation. *Forum Linguisticum* 7(1): 50–64.

Fromkin, Victoria. 1968. Speculations on performance models. *Journal of Linguistics* 4: 467–8. https://doi.org/10.1017/S002222670000164X

Fuller, Gillian. 1995. *Engaging cultures: Negotiating discourse in popular science.* PhD thesis. Sydney: University of Sydney.

Gamble, Clive, John Gowlett, and Robin Dunbar. 2014. *Thinking big: How the evolution of social life shaped the human mind.* London: Thames and Hudson.

García, Adolfo M., Daniel Franco-O'Byrne, and Agustín Ibáñez. 2020. Neurosemiotics: Blurbing a field beyond the "two cultures divide". In Ludmila Lacková, Claudio J. Rodríguez, and Kalevi Kull (eds.), *Gatherings in biosemiotics XX.* Tartu: University of Tartu Press. 92–7.

García, Adolfo M., and Augustín Ibáñez. 2017. Processes and verbs of doing, in the brain: Theoretical implications for systemic functional linguistics. *Functions of Language* 23(3): 305–35. https://doi.org/10.1075/fol.23.3.02gar

García, Adolfo M., and Agustín Ibáñez (eds.). 2023. *The Routledge handbook of semiosis and the brain.* London: Routledge. https://doi.org/10.4324/9781003051817

García, Adolfo M., William Sullivan, and Sarah Tsiang. 2017. *An introduction to relational network theory: History, principles, and descriptive applications.* London: Equinox.

Garvin, Paul. 1964. *A Prague School reader on esthetics, literary structure and style.* Washington, DC: Georgetown University Press.

Gazdar, Gerald, Ewan Klein, Geoffrey K. Pullum, and Ivan A. Sag. 1985. *Generalized phrase structure grammar.* Cambridge, MA: Harvard University Press.

Gazzaniga, Michael S. 1985. *The social brain: Discovering the networks of the mind.* New York: Basic Books.

Gazzaniga, Michael S., Richard B. Ivry, and George R. Mangun. 2019. *Cognitive neuroscience: The biology of the mind.* 5th edition. New York and London: W.W. Norton.

434   *References*

Gibbons, John, and Victoria Markwick-Smith. 1992. Exploring the use of a systemic semantic description. *International Journal of Applied Linguistics* 2(1): 36–50. https://doi.org/10.1111/j.1473-4192.1992.tb00022.x

Gil, José María. 2013. A neurocognitive interpretation of systemic functional choice. In Fontaine, Bartlett, and O'Grady (eds.), 179–204. https://doi.org/10.1017/CBO9781139583077.012

Givón, Talmy. 1979. *On understanding grammar.* New York: Academic Press. https://doi.org/10.1016/C2013-0-10728-3

Givón, Talmy. 2001. *Syntax: An introduction. Volume 1.* Revised edition. Amsterdam: Benjamins.

Gleason, Henry A. 1961. *An introduction to descriptive linguistics.* New York: Holt, Rinehart and Winston.

Goldsmith, John. 2000. On information theory, entropy, and phonology in the 20th century. *Folia Linguistica* XXXIV(1-2): 85–100. https://doi.org/10.1515/flin.2000.34.1-2.85

Golestani, Narly, Cathy J. Price, and Sophie K Scott. 2011. Born with an ear for dialects? Structural plasticity in the expert phonetician brain. *The Journal of Neuroscience* 31(11): 4213–20. https://doi.org/10.1523/JNEUROSCI.3891-10.2011

Goodenough, Ward H. 1956. Componential analysis and the study of meaning. *Language* 32(1): 195–216. https://doi.org/10.2307/410665

Gross, Maurice. 1979. On the failure of generative grammar. *Language* 55(4): 859–85. https://doi.org/10.2307/412748

Guerra-Lyons, Jesús. 2021. *Making meaning throughout writing trajectories: Towards a social semiotic account of language change in scholars' theory construction.* PhD thesis. Hong Kong: The Hong Kong Polytechnic University.

Guillaume, Gustave M. 1929. *Temps et verbe.* Paris: Champion.

Halliday, M.A.K. 1956. Grammatical categories in Modern Chinese. *Transactions of the Philological Society*: 177–224. Reprinted in Halliday, 2006, 209–48. https://doi.org/10.1111/j.1467-968X.1956.tb00567.x

Halliday, M.A.K. 1959. *The language of the Chinese "Secret history of the Mongols".* Oxford: Blackwell. (Publications of the Philological Society 17.) Reprinted in Halliday, 2006, 3–171.

Halliday, M.A.K. 1959–60. Typology and the exotic. Combination of two lectures, one delivered at the Linguistics Association Conference, Hull, in May 1959, the other to the St. Andrews Linguistic Society, in May 1960. In M.A.K. Halliday and Angus McIntosh (eds.), 1966, *Patterns of language: Papers in general, descriptive and applied linguistics.* London: Longman. 165–82.

Halliday, M.A.K. 1961. Categories of the theory of grammar. *Word* 17(3): 242–92. Reprinted in Halliday, 2002c, 37–94.

Halliday, M.A.K. 1963a. Intonation in English grammar. *Transactions of the Philological Society* 62(1): 143–69. https://doi.org/10.1111/j.1467-968X.1963.tb01003.x

Halliday, M.A.K. 1963b. The tones of English. *Archivum Linguisticum* 15(1): 1–28.

Halliday, M.A.K. 1964. Syntax and the consumer. In C.I.J.M. Stuart (ed.), *Report of the Fifteenth Annual (First International) Round Table Meeting on Linguistics and Language.* Washington, DC: Georgetown University Press. 11–24. Reprinted in Halliday, 2003, 36–49.

Halliday, M.A.K. 1965. Types of structure. *Working Paper for the O.S.T.I. Programme in the Linguistic Properties of Scientific English*. Reprinted in Halliday and Martin (eds.), 1981, 29–41.

Halliday, M.A.K. 1966a. Lexis as a linguistic level. In C.E. Bazell, J.C. Catford, M.A.K. Halliday, and R.H. Robins (eds.), *In memory of J.R. Firth*. London: Longmans. 148–62.

Halliday, M.A.K. 1966b. Some notes on 'deep' grammar. *Journal of Linguistics* 2(1): 57–67. Reprinted in Halliday, 2002c, 106–17. https://doi.org/10.1017/S0022226700001328

Halliday, M.A.K. 1967. *Intonation and grammar in British English*. The Hague: Mouton. https://doi.org/ 10.1515/9783111357447

Halliday, M.A.K. 1967/8. Notes on transitivity and theme in English 1–3. *Journal of Linguistics* 3–4. https://doi.org/ 10.1017/S0022226700012949; https://doi.org / 10.1017/S0022226700016613; https://doi.org/ 10.1017/S0022226700001882

Halliday, M.A.K. 1969. Options and functions in the English clause. *Brno Studies in English* 8: 81–88.

Halliday, M.A.K. 1970a. Language structure and language function. In John Lyons (ed.), *New horizons in linguistics*. Harmondsworth: Penguin Books. 140–65.

Halliday, M.A.K. 1970b. Functional diversity in language, as seen from a consideration of modality and mood in English. *Foundations of Language* 6.3: 327–51.

Halliday, M.A.K. 1973. *Explorations in the functions of language*. London: Edward Arnold.

Halliday, M.A.K. 1974. The place of "Functional sentence perspective" in the system of linguistic description. In František Daneš (ed.), *Papers on functional sentence perspective*. Berlin and Boston: Academia. 43–53. https://doi.org/10.1515/9783111676524.43

Halliday, M.A.K. 1975. *Learning how to mean: Explorations in the development of language*. London: Edward Arnold (Explorations in Language Study).

Halliday, M.A. K. 1976a. *System and function in language*. Edited by Gunther Kress. London: Oxford University Press.

Halliday, M.A.K. 1976b. The English verbal group. In Halliday, 1976a, 124–30.

Halliday, M.A.K. 1977. Ideas about language: Aims and perspectives in linguistics. Occasional papers. Number 1. *Applied Linguistic Association of Australia*. 32–49.

Halliday, M.A.K. 1978. *Language as social semiotic: The social interpretation of language and meaning*. London: Edward Arnold.

Halliday, M.A.K. 1979a. Modes of meaning and modes of expression: Types of grammatical structure and their determination by different semantic functions. In D.J. Allerton, David Holdcroft, and Edward Carney (eds.), *Function and context in linguistic analysis: A festschrift for William Haas*. Cambridge: Cambridge University Press. 57–79. https://doi.org/10.1515/9783111676524.57

Halliday, M.A.K. 1979b. One child's protolanguage. In Margaret Bullowa (ed.), *Before speech the beginnings of interpersonal communication*. Cambridge: Cambridge University Press.

Halliday, M.A.K. 1979c. The ontogenesis of dialogue. In Wolfgang U. Dressler (ed.), *Proceedings of the Twelfth International Congress of Linguistics*. Innsbruck: Innsbrucker Beiträge zur Sprachwissenschaft. 539–44. Reprinted in Halliday, 2004a, 144–52.

Halliday, M.A.K. 1980. Foreword. In Alex De Joia and Adrian Stenton (eds.), *Terms in systemic linguistics: A guide to Halliday*. London: Batsford.

Halliday, M.A.K. 1981. Text semantics and clause grammar: Some patterns of realization. *Seventh LACUS Forum*. Columbia: Hornbeam Press. 31–59. Reprinted as Text semantics and clause grammar: How is a text like a clause? in Halliday, 2002, 219–60.

Halliday, M.A.K. 1984a. On the ineffability of grammatical categories. In Alan Manning, Pierre Martin, and Kim McCalla (eds.), *The Tenth LACUS Forum*. Columbia, SC: Hornbeam Press. 3–18. Reprinted in Halliday, 2002c, 291–321. https://doi .org/10.1075/cilt.39.03hal

Halliday, M.A.K. 1984b. Language as code and language as behaviour: A systemic-functional interpretation of the nature and ontogenesis of dialogue. In M.A.K. Halliday, Robin P. Fawcett, Sydney Lamb, and Adam Makkai (eds.), *The semiotics of language and culture*. London: Frances Pinter. 3–35. Reprinted in Halliday, 2003, 226–50.

Halliday, M.A.K. 1984c. *Listening to Nigel*. Mimeo. Sydney University Linguistics Department. Published as part of Halliday, 2004a.

Halliday, M.A.K. 1985a. *Spoken and written language*. Geelong: Deakin University.

Halliday, M.A.K. 1985b. *An introduction to functional grammar*. London: Edward Arnold.

Halliday, M.A.K. 1985c. Systemic background. In James D. Benson and William S. Greaves (eds.), *Systemic functional approaches to discourse: Selected papers from the 12th International Systemic Workshop*. Norwood, NJ: Ablex. 1–15. Reprinted in Halliday, 2003, 185–98.

Halliday, M.A.K. 1988a. The history of a sentence: An essay in social semiotics. In Rosa Maria Bollettieri Bosinelli (ed.), *Language systems and cultural systems: Proceedings of the International Symposium on Bologna, Italian Culture and Modern Literature*. University of Bologna, October 1988. Reprinted in Halliday, 2003b, 355–74.

Halliday, M.A.K. 1988b. On the language of physical science. In Mohsen Ghadessy (ed.), *Registers of written English: Situational factors and linguistic features*. London and New York: Pinter Publishers. 162–78. Reprinted in Halliday, 2004c, 140–58.

Halliday, M.A.K. 1991a. The notion of 'context' in language education. In Thao Le and Mike McCausland (eds.), *Interaction and development: Proceedings of the international conference, Vietnam, 30 March–1 April 1991*. University of Tasmania: Language Education. 1–26. Reprinted in Halliday, 2007, 269–90. https://doi.org/10.1075/cilt.169.04hal

Halliday, M.A.K. 1991b. The place of dialogue in children's construction of meaning. In Sorin Stati, Edda Weigand, and Franz Hundsnurscher (eds.), Dialoganalyse III: Referate der 3. Arbeitstagung, Bologna 1990. Berlin and Boston: Max Niemeyer Verlag. 417–30. Reprinted in Halliday, 2004a, 373-381. https://doi.org /10.1515/9783111678504-034

Halliday, M.A.K. 1991c. Corpus studies and probabilistic grammar. In Karin Aijmer and Bengt Altenberg (eds.), *English corpus linguistics: Studies in honour of Jan Svartvik*. London: Longman. 30–43. Reprinted in Halliday, 2005a, 63–75.

Halliday, M.A.K. 1991d. Towards probabilistic interpretations. In Eija Ventola (ed.), *Trends in linguistics: Functional and systemic linguistics: Approaches and uses*. Berlin and New York: Mouton de Gruyter. Reprinted in Halliday, 2005a, 42–62.

Halliday, M.A.K. 1992a. *Language in a changing world*. Occasional Paper 13. Canberra: Applied Linguistics Association of Australia.

Halliday, M.A.K. 1992b. Language as system and language as instance: The corpus as a theoretical construct. In Jan Svartvik (ed.), *Directions in corpus linguistics: Proceedings of Nobel Symposium 82*, Stockholm, 4–8 August 1991. Berlin: Mouton de Gruyter. 61–77. Reprinted in Halliday, 2005a, 76–92. https://doi.org/10.1515/9783110867275.61

Halliday, M.A.K. 1992c. How do you mean? In Martin Davies and Louise Ravelli (eds.), *Advances in systemic linguistics: Recent theory and practice*. London: Pinter. 20–35. Reprinted in Halliday, 2002c, 352–68.

Halliday, M.A.K. 1992d. The history of a sentence: An essay in social semiotics. In Vita Fortunait (ed.), *La cultura italiana e le letterature straniere moderne*. Bologna: Longo Editore [for University of Bologna]. 29–45. Reprinted in Halliday, 2003b, 355–74.

Halliday, M.A.K. 1992e. The act of meaning. In James E. Alatis (ed.), *Georgetown University round table on languages and linguistics 1992: Language, communication and social meaning*. Washington, DC: Georgetown University Press. 7–21. Reprinted in Halliday, 2003b, 375–89.

Halliday, M.A.K. 1993a. Quantitative studies and probabilities in grammar. In Michael Hoey (ed.), *Data, description, discourse: Papers on the English language in honour of John McH. Sinclair*. London: Harper Collins. 1–25. Reprinted in Halliday, 2005a, 130–56.

Halliday, M.A.K. 1993b. Towards a language-based theory of learning. *Linguistics and Education* 5(2): 93–116. Reprinted in Halliday, 2004a, 327–52. https://doi.org/10.1016/0898-5898(93)90026-7

Halliday, M.A.K. 1993c. *Language in a changing world*. Occasional Paper 13. Canberra: Applied Linguistics Association of Australia. Reprinted in Halliday, 2003b, 213–31.

Halliday, M.A.K. 1994a. *An introduction to functional grammar*. 2nd edition. London: Edward Arnold.

Halliday, M.A.K. 1994b. Systemic theory. Ronald E. Asher (ed.), *The encyclopedia of language and linguistics*. Oxford: Pergamon Press. Volume 8. 4505–8. Reprinted in Halliday, 2004a, 433–41.

Halliday, M.A.K. 1995a. A recent view of "missteps" in linguistic theory (Review article of John M. Ellis, Language, thought and logic). *Functions of Language* 2(2): 249–67. https://doi.org/10.1075/fol.2.2.07hal

Halliday, M.A.K. 1995b. On language in relation to the evolution of human consciousness. In. Sture Allén (ed.), *Of thoughts and words: Proceedings of Nobel Symposium 92: The relation between language and mind*, Stockholm, 8–12 August 1994. Singapore, River Edge, NJ, and London: Imperial College Press. 45–84. Reprinted in Halliday 2003b, 390–432. https://doi.org/10.1142/9781908979681_0008

Halliday, M.A.K. 1995c. Fuzzy grammatics: A systemic functional approach to fuzziness in natural language. *Proceeding of 1995 IEEE International Conference on Fuzzy Systems*, Yokohama, Japan, vol. 1: 9–26.

Halliday, M.A.K. 1996. On grammar and grammatics. In Hasan, Cloran and Butt (eds.), 1–38. Reprinted in Halliday, 2002c, 384–417. https://doi.org/10.1075/cilt.121.03hal

Halliday, M.A.K. 1998. On the grammar of pain. *Functions of Language* 5(1): 1–32. Reprinted in Halliday, 2005b, 306–37. https://doi.org/10.1075/fol.5.1.02hal

Halliday, M.A.K. 2000. Phonology past and present: A personal retrospect. Folia Linguistica XXXIV. 1–2: 101–11. https://doi.org/10.1515/flin.2000.34.1-2.101

Halliday, M. A. K. 2001. Meanings, wordings and context: Modelling the language brain. Paper presented at RIKEN Brain Science Institute, Suzuki Hall, Wako, Japan, 5 October 2001.

Halliday, M.A.K. 2002a. Computing meanings: Some reflections on past experience and present prospects. In Guowen Huang and Zongyan Wang (eds.), *Discourse and language functions*. Shanghai: Foreign Language Teaching and Research Press. 3–25. Reprinted in Halliday, 2005a, 239–67.

Halliday, M.A.K. 2002b. The spoken language corpus: A foundation for grammatical theory. In Karin Aijmer and Bengt Altenberg (eds.), *Proceedings of ICAME 2002: The theory and use of corpora*, Göteborg, 22–26 May 2002. Amsterdam: Editions Rodopi. Reprinted in Halliday, 2005a, 157–89. https://doi.org/10.1163/9789004333710_003

Halliday, M.A.K. 2002c. *On grammar. Volume 1 in the Collected works of M.A.K. Halliday*. Edited by Jonathan J. Webster. London and New York: Continuum.

Halliday, M.A.K. 2002d. Applied linguistics as an evolving theme. Presented at AILA 2002, Singapore. Published in M.A.K. Halliday, 2007, *Language and education. Volume 9 in the Collected Works of M.A.K. Halliday*, edited by Jonathan Webster. London and New York: Continuum. 1–19.

Halliday, M.A.K. 2003a. *Linguistic studies of text and discourse*. Volume 2 in the *Collected works of M.A.K. Halliday*. Edited by Jonathan Webster. London and New York: Continuum.

Halliday, M.A.K. 2003b. *On language and linguistics*. Volume 3 in the *Collected works of M.A.K. Halliday*. Edited by Jonathan Webster. London and New York: Continuum.

Halliday, M.A.K. 2004a. *The language of early childhood*. Volume 4 in the *Collected works of M.A.K. Halliday*. Edited by Jonathan Webster. London and New York: Continuum.

Halliday, M.A.K. 2004b. On grammar as the driving force from primary to higher-order consciousness. In Geoff Williams and Annabelle Lukin (eds.), *The development of language: Functional perspectives on species and individuals*. London and New York: Continuum. 15–44. https://doi.org/10.1075/fol.5.1.02hal

Halliday, M.A.K. 2004c. *The language of science*. Volume 5 in the *Collected works of M.A.K. Halliday*. Edited by Jonathan J. Webster. London and New York: Continuum.

Halliday, M.A.K. 2004d. *Computational and quantitative studies*. Volume 6 in the *Collected works of M.A.K. Halliday*. Edited by Jonathan J. Webster. London and New York: Continuum.

Halliday, M.A.K. 2005a. On matter and meaning: The two realms of human experience. *Linguistics and the Human Sciences* 1.1: 59–82. https://doi.org/10.1558/lhs.2005.1.1.59

Halliday, M.A.K. 2005b. *Studies in English language*. Volume 7 in the *Collected works of M.A.K. Halliday*. Edited by Jonathan J. Webster. London and New York: Continuum.

Halliday, M.A.K. 2006. *Studies in the Chinese language*. Volume 8 in the *Collected Works of M.A.K. Halliday*. Edited by Jonathan J. Webster. London and New York: Continuum.

Halliday, M.A.K. 2007. *Language and education*. Volume 9 in the *Collected works of M.A.K. Halliday*. Edited by Jonathan Webster. London and New York: Continuum.

Halliday, M.A.K. 2010. Language evolving: Some systemic functional reflections on the history of meaning. Manuscript of plenary given at ISFC 37, UBC Vancouver, Canada, July 2010. https://doi.org/ 10.14288/1.0076567. Published in Halliday, M.A.K.,

2013, *Halliday in the 21st century*. Volume 11 in the *Collected works of M.A.K. Halliday*, edited by Jonathan J. Webster. London: Bloomsbury Academic.

Halliday, M.A.K. 2013. Meaning as choice. In Fontaine, Bartlett, and O'Grady (eds.), 15–36. https://doi.org/10.1017/CBO9781139583077.003

Halliday, M.A.K. 2014. Notes on teaching Chinese to foreign learners. *Journal of World Languages* 1(1): 1–6. https://doi.org/10.1080/21698252.2014.893675

Halliday, M.A.K. 2017. Foreword: On the creation, and creator, of RNT. In Adolfo M. García, William Sullivan, and Sarah Tsiang (eds.), 2017. *An introduction to relational network theory: History, principles, and descriptive applications*. London: Equinox. xv–xviii.

Halliday, M.A.K., and William S. Greaves. 2008. *Intonation in the grammar of English*. London: Equinox.

Halliday, M.A.K., and Ruqaiya Hasan. 1976. *Cohesion in English*. London: Longman.

Halliday, M.A.K., and Ruqaiya Hasan. 1980. *Text and context: Aspects of language in a social-semiotic perspective*. Tokyo: Sophia Linguistica.

Halliday, M.A.K., and Ruqaiya Hasan. 1985. *Language, context and text: Aspects of language in a social-semiotic perspective*. Geelong, Victoria: Deakin University Press.

Halliday, M.A.K., and Zoe L. James. 1993. A quantitative study of polarity and primary tense in the English finite clause. In John M. Sinclair, Michael Hoey, and Gwyneth Fox (eds.), *Techniques of description: Spoken and written discourse (A Festschrift for Malcolm Coulthard)*. London and New York: Routledge. 32–66. Reprinted in Halliday, 2005a, 93–129.

Halliday, M.A.K. and J.R. Martin (eds.) 1981. *Readings in systemic linguistics*. London: Batsford.

Halliday, M.A.K. and J.R. Martin. 1993. *Writing science: Literacy and discursive power*. London: Falmer.

Halliday, M.A.K., and Christian M.I.M. Matthiessen. 1999. *Construing experience through meaning: A language-based approach to cognition*. London: Cassell. Re-issued as: Halliday and Matthiessen, 2006, *Construing experience through meaning: A language-based approach to cognition*. London and New York: Continuum.

Halliday, M.A.K., and Christian M.I.M. Matthiessen. 2014. *Halliday's introduction to functional grammar*. 4th edition. London: Routledge.

Halliday, M.A.K. and Edward McDonald. 2004. Metafunctional profile of the grammar of Chinese. In Caffarel, Martin, and Matthiessen (eds.), 305–96. https://doi.org/10.1075/cilt.253.08hal

Halliday, M.A.K., and Jonathan J. Webster (eds.). 2009. *Continuum companion to systemic functional linguistics*. London and New York: Continuum.

Han, Hee Jeung, and David Kellog. 2019. A story without SELF: Vygotsky's pedology, Bruner's constructivism and Halliday's construalism in understanding narratives by Korean children. *Language and Education* 33(6): 506–20.

Hart, John, and Barry Gordon. 1992. Neural subsystems for object knowledge. *Nature* 359: 60–64. https://doi.org/10.1038/359060a0

Hasan, Ruqaiya. 1968. *Grammatical cohesion in written and spoken English, Part 1*. Programme in Linguistics and English Teaching, paper no. 7. London: University College London.

Hasan, Ruqaiya. 1979. On the notion of text. In Janos S. Petoefi (ed.), *Text vs. sentence: Basic questions of text linguistics*. Hamburg: Buske Verlag.

Hasan, Ruqaiya. 1983. A semantic network for the analysis of messages in everyday talk between mothers and their children. Mimeograph, Department of Linguistics, Macquarie University.

Hasan, Ruqaiya. 1984a. The nursery tale as a genre. *Nottingham Linguistic Circular 13*. Reprinted in Ruqaiya Hasan, 1996, *Ways of saying: Ways of meaning: Selected papers of Ruqaiya Hasan,* edited by Carmel Cloran, David Butt, and Geoffrey Williams. London: Cassell. 51–72.

Hasan, Ruqaiya. 1984b. Coherence and cohesive harmony. In James Flood (ed.), *Understanding reading comprehension*. Newark: International Reading Association. 181–219.

Hasan, Ruqaiya. 1985a. *Linguistics, language and verbal art*. Geelong, Victoria: Deakin University Press.

Hasan, Ruqaiya. 1985b. Meaning, context and text: Fifty years after Malinowski. In James D. Benson and William S. Greaves (eds.), *Systemic functional approaches to discourse: Selected papers from the 12th International Systemic Workshop*. Norwood, NJ: Ablex. 16–50.

Hasan, Ruqaiya. 1987. The grammarian's dream: Lexis as most delicate grammar. In Halliday, M.A.K., and Robin P. Fawcett (eds.), *New developments in systemic linguistics: Theory and description*. London: Pinter. 184–211.

Hasan, Ruqaiya. 1989. Semantic variation and sociolinguistics. *Australian Journal of Linguistics* 9: 221–75. https://doi.org/10.1080/07268608908599422

Hasan, Ruqaiya. 1992. Speech genre, semiotic mediation and the development of higher mental functions. *Language Sciences* 14(4): 489–528. https://doi.org/10.1016/0388-0001(92)90027-C

Hasan, Ruqaiya. 2002. Semiotic mediation and mental development in pluralistic societies: Some implications for tomorrow's schooling. In Gordon Wells and Guy Claxton (eds.), *Learning for life in the 21st century*. Oxford: Blackwell. Reprinted in Ruqaiya Hasan 2011, *Selected works of Ruqaiya Hasan on applied linguistics*. Beijing: Foreign Language Teaching and Research Press. 213–39.

Hasan, Ruqaiya. 2004. The world in words: Semiotic mediation, tenor and ideology. In Geoff Williams and Annabelle Lukin (eds.), *The development of language: Functional perspectives on species and individuals*. London and New York: Continuum. 158–81.

Hasan, Ruqaiya. 2009. *Semantic variation: Meaning in society and sociolinguistics*. Volume 2 in the *Collected works of RuqaiyaHasan*. Edited by Jonathan J. Webster. London and Oakville: Equinox.

Hasan, Ruqaiya. 2014. Text in the systemic-functional model. In Wolfgang U. Dressier (ed.), *Current trends in text linguistics,* Berlin and Boston: De Gruyter. 228–46.

Hasan, Ruqaiya, and Carmel Cloran. 1990. A sociolinguistic interpretation of everyday talk between mothers and children. In M.A.K. Halliday, John Gibbons, and Howard Nichols (eds.), *Learning, keeping and using language: Selected papers from the 8th World Congress of Applied Linguistics*, Sydney, 16–21 August 1987. Amsterdam: Benjamins. 67–99.

Hasan, Ruqaiya, Carmel Cloran, and David Butt (eds.). 1996. *Functional descriptions: Language form and linguistic theory*. Current Issues in Linguistic Theory, No. 121. Amsterdam and Philadelphia: Benjamins.

Hasan, Ruqaiya, Carmel Cloran, Geoff Williams, and Annabelle Lukin. 2007. Semantic networks: The description of linguistic meaning in SFL. In Hasan, Matthiessen, and Webster (eds.), 697–738. https://doi.org/10.1558/equinox.25350

Hasan, Ruqaiya, Christian M.I.M. Matthiessen, and Jonathan Webster (eds.). 2005. *Continuing discourse on language: A functional perspective.* Volume 1. London: Equinox.

Hasan, Ruqaiya, Christian M.I.M. Matthiessen, and Jonathan Webster (eds.). 2007. *Continuing discourse on language: A functional perspective.* Volume 2. London: Equinox.

Haspelmath, Martin, and Andrea D. Sims. 2010. *Understanding morphology.* 2nd edition. London and New York: Routledge. https://doi.org/10.4324/9780203776506

Hasson, Uri, Asif A. Ghazanfar, Bruno Galantucci, Simon Garrod, and Christian Keysers. 2012. Brain-to-Brain coupling: A mechanism for creating and sharing a social world. *Trends in Cognitive Sciences,* 16(2): 114–21. https://doi.org/10.1016/j.tics.2011.12.007

Hebb, Donald O. 1949. *The organization of behavior: A neuropsychological theory.* New York: Wiley.

Heller, Louis G., and James Macris. 1967. *Parametric Linguistics.* The Hague: Mouton.

Henderson, Eugénie J.A. 1987. J.R. Firth in retrospect: A view from the eighties. In Ross Steele and Terry Threadgold (eds.), *Language topics.* Amsterdam: Benjamins. 57–69.

Hengeveld, Kees, and J. Lachlan Mackenzie. 2008. *Functional discourse grammar: A typologically-based theory of language structure.* Oxford: Oxford University Press. https://doi.org/10.1093/acprof:oso/9780199278107.001.0001

Henrici, A. 1966. Some notes on the systemic generation of a paradigm of the English clause. *Working Paper for the O.S.T.I. Programme in the linguistic properties of scientific English.* Reprinted in Halliday and Martin (eds.), 1981, 74–98.

Hjelmslev, Louis. 1943. *Omkring sprogteoriens grundlæggelse.* Copenhagen: Akademisk Forlag.

Hjelmslev, Louis. 1953. *Prolegomena to a theory of language.* Translated by F.J. Whitfield. *Indiana University Publications in Anthropology and Linguistics (Memoir 7 of the International Journal of American Linguistics).* Baltimore, MD: Waverly Press.

Hockett, Charles. 1954. Two models of grammatical description. *Word* 10(2–3): 210–34. https://doi.org/10.1080/00437956.1954.11659524

Hockett, Charles. 1955. *A manual of phonology.* Indiana University Publications in Anthropology and Linguistics, Memoir 11. Baltimore: Waverly Press.

Hoey, Michael. 2006. Language as choice: What is chosen? In Susan Hunston and Geoff Thompson (eds.), *System and corpus: Exploring connections.* London: Equinox. 37–54.

Honnibal, Matthew. 2004. *Adapting the Penn Treebank to systemic functional grammar: Design, creation and use of a metafunctionally annotated corpus.* BA honours thesis. Sydney: Macquarie University.

Honnibal, Matthew, and J. R. Curran. 2007. Creating a systemic functional grammar corpus from the Penn Treebank. In *Proceedings of the ACL 2007 Workshop on Deep Linguistic Processing.* Prague: Association for Computational Linguistics. 89–96.

Hopper, Paul J., and Sandra A. Thompson. 1980. Transitivity in grammar and discourse. *Language* 56: 251–99. https://doi.org/10.1353/lan.1980.0017

Huddleston, Rodney D. 1984. *Introduction to the grammar of English.* Cambridge Textbooks in Linguistics. Cambridge: Cambridge University Press. https://doi.org /10.1017/CBO9781139165785

Huddleston, Rodney D., Richard A. Hudson, Eugene Winter, and A. Henrici. 1968. *Sentence and clause in Scientific English: Final report of O.S.T.I. Programme.* London: University College London: Communication Research Centre.

Hudson, Richard A. 1964. *The grammatical study of Beja.* PhD thesis. London: London University.

Hudson, Richard A. 1971. *English complex sentences.* Amsterdam: North Holland.

Hudson, Richard A. 1973. An item-and-paradigm approach to Beja syntax and morphology. *Foundations of Language* 9: 504–48.

Hudson, Richard A. 1976. *Arguments for a non-transformational grammar.* Chicago: University of Chicago Press.

Hudson, Richard. 1984. *Word grammar.* Oxford: Blackwell.

Hughlings-Jackson, John. 1878. On affections of speech from disease of the brain. *Brain,* 1: 304–30. https://doi.org/10.1093/brain/1.3.304

Hughlings-Jackson, John. 1879. On affections of speech from disease of the brain. *Brain,* 2: 202–22. https://doi.org/10.1093/brain/2.3.323

Ibáñez, Agustín, Lucas Sedeño, and Adolfo M. García (eds.). 2017. *Neuroscience and social science: The missing link.* Switzerland: Springer. https://doi.org/10.1007/978-3-319-68421-5

Jacobs, Paul S. 1985. PHRED: A generator for natural language interfaces. *Computational Linguistics* 11(4): 219–42. https://doi.org/10.3115/984305.984307

Jakobson, Roman. 1941. *Kindersprache, Aphasie und allgemeine Lautgesetze. Uppsala: Uppsala Universitets* Årsskrift. Translated in 1968 as *Child language, aphasia and phonological universals.* The Hague: Mouton.

Jakobson, Roman. 1949. On the identification of phonemic entities. Travaux du Cercle Linguistique de Copenhague V: 205–213. Reprinted in 1962, Roman Jakobson: *Selected writings I.* The Hague: Mouton. 418–25.

Jakobson, Roman. 1961. Linguistics and communication theory. Presented in the Symposium on Structure of Language and its Mathematical Aspects, New York, 15 April 1960. Published in *Proceedings of Symposia in Applied Mathematics XII.* Reprinted in Roman Jakobson, 1971, *Selected writings II.* The Hague: Mouton. 570–9. https://doi.org/10.1515/9783110873269.570

Jespersen, Otto. 1917. Review of Cours de linguistique générale de F. de Saussure. Edited by Charles Bally and Albert Sechehaye, assisted by Albert Riedlinger (Lausanne and Paris: Payot, 1916). Nordisk Tidsskrift for Filologi 6: 37–41.

Jia, Shiwei, Yiu-Kei Tsang, Jian Huang, and Hsuan-Chih Chen. 2013. Right hemisphere advantage in processing Cantonese level and contour tones: Evidence from dichotic listening. *Neuroscience Letters* 556: 135–139. https://doi.org/10.1016 /j.neulet.2013.10.014

Jurafsky, Dan. 2003. Probabilistic modeling in psycholinguistics: Linguistic comprehension and production. In Bod, Hay, and Jannedy (eds.), 39–95. https://doi .org/10.7551/mitpress/5582.003.0006

Kaplan, Ronald M., and Hans Uszkoreit. 2022. Obituary: Martin Kay. *Computational Linguistics* 48(1): 1–3. https://doi.org/10.1162/coli_a_00424

Kasper, Robert. 1988a. An experimental parser for systemic grammars. *The 12th International Conference on Computational Linguistics.* Budapest: COLING. 309–12. https://doi.org/10.3115/991635.991698

Kasper, Robert. 1988b. Systemic grammar and functional unification grammar. In James D. Benson and William S. Greaves (eds.), *Systemic functional approaches to discourse.* Norwood: Ablex. 176–99.

Kay, Martin. 1979. Functional grammar. *Proceedings of the Berkeley Linguistics Society.* 142–58. https://doi.org/10.3765/bls.v5i0.3262

Kemmerer, David. 2015. *Cognitive neuroscience of language.* New York and London: Psychology Press. https://doi.org/10.4324/9781138318427

Kempen, Gerard. (ed.). 1987. *Natural language generation.* Dordrecht: Martinus Nijhoff. https://doi.org/10.1007/978-94-009-3645-4

Kempen, Gerard. 1989. Language generation systems. In István S. Bátori, Winfried Lenders, and Wolfgang Putschke (eds.), *Computational linguistics: An international handbook on computer oriented language research and applications.* Berlin and New York: Walter de Gruyter. 471–80. https://doi.org/10.1515/9783110097924.8.471

Kess, Joseph E. 1992. *Psycholinguistics: Psychology, linguistics, and the study of natural language.* Amsterdam: Benjamins. https://doi.org/10.1017/S0008413100016212

Kobayashi, Ichiro. 1995. *A social system simulation based on human information processing.* PhD thesis. Tokyo: Tokyo Institute of Technology.

Kosko, Bart. 1993. *Fuzzy thinking: The new science of fuzzy logic.* New York: Hyperion.

Kuhl, Patricia K. 2007. Is speech learning 'gated' by the social brain? *Developmental Science* 10(1): 110–20. https://doi.org/10.1111/j.1467-7687.2007.00572.x

Kuhl, Patricia K. 2010a. Brain mechanism in early language acquisition. *Neuron* 67(5): 713–27. https://doi.org/10.1016/j.neuron.2010.08.038

Kuhl, Patricia. 2010b. The linguistic genius of babies. TEDxRainier, October 2010. https://www.ted.com/talks/patricia_kuhl_the_linguistic_genius_of_babies

Kuhl, Patricia K., and Maritza Rivera-Gaxiola. 2008. Neural substrates of language acquisition. *Annual Review Neuroscience* 31: 511–534. https://doi.org/10.1146/annurev.neuro.30.051606.094321

Lakoff, George. 1987. *Women, fire and dangerous things: What categories reveal about the mind.* Chicago: Chicago University Press.

Lakoff, George, and Mark Johnson. 1980. *Metaphors we live by.* Chicago: University of Chicago Press.

Lamb, Sydney M. 1966. *Outline of stratificational grammar.* Washington DC: Georgetown University Press.

Lamb, Sydney M. 1971. The crooked path of progress in cognitive linguistics. In Richard J. O'Brien (ed.), *Monograph series on languages and linguistics 24.* washington, DC: Georgetown University Press. 99–123.

Lamb, Sydney M. 1999. *Pathways of the brain: The neurocognitive basis of language.* Amsterdam: Benjamins. https://doi.org/10.1075/cilt.170

Lamb, Sydney M. 2013. Systemic networks, relational networks, and choice. In Fontaine, Bartlett, and O'Grady (eds.), 137–60. https://doi.org/10.1017/CBO9781139583077.010

Lambon Ralph, Matthew A. 2014. Neurocognitive insights on conceptual knowledge and its breakdown. *Philosophical Transactions of the Royal Society: Biological Sciences* 369 (1634), 20120392. https://doi.org/10.1098/rstb.2012.0392

Lambon Ralph, Matthew A., Karen Sage, Roy W. Jones, and Emily J. Mayberry. 2010. Coherent concepts are computed in the anterior temporal lobes. *PNAS* 107(6): 2717–22. https://doi.org/10.1073/pnas.0907307107

Larsen-Freeman, Diane, and Lynne Cameron. 2008. *Complex systems and applied linguistics.* Oxford: Oxford University Press.

Layzer, David. 1990. *Cosmogenesis: The growth of order in the universe.* New York and Oxford: Oxford University Press.

Lee, Jackson L., and John A. Goldsmith. 2016. Linguistica 5: Unsupervised Learning of Linguistic Structure. *Proceedings of NAACL-HLT 2016 (Demonstrations).* 22–26. https://doi.org/10.18653/v1/N16-3005

Lemke, Jay L. nd. The topology of genre: Text structure and text types. MS. Revised version to appear in Network 22.

Lemke, Jay L. 1984. *Semiotics and education.* Toronto: Victoria University. (Toronto Semiotic Circle Monographs, No. 2.)

Lemke, Jay L. 1985. Ideology, intertextuality and the notion of register. In James D. Benson and William S. Greaves (eds.), *Systemic functional approaches to discourse: Selected papers from the 12th International Systemic Workshop.* Norwood, NJ: Ablex. 275–94.

Lemke, Jay L. 1991. Text production and dynamic text semantics. In Eija Ventola (ed.), *Functional and systemic linguistics: Approaches and uses.* Berlin: Mouton de Gruyter: 23–38. https://doi.org/10.1515/9783110883527.23

Lemke, Jay L. 1995a. *Textual politics: Discourse and social dynamics.* London and Bristol, PA: Taylor and Francis.

Lemke, Jay L. 1995b. Intertextuality and text semantics. In Michael Gregory and Peter H. Fries (eds.), *Discourse and society: Functional perspectives.* Norwood, NJ: Ablex. 85–114.

Lenneberg, Eric H. 1967. *Biological foundations of language.* New York: Wiley.

Levi, Jay L. 1978. *The syntax and semantics of complex nominals.* New York: Academic Press.

Levin, Beth. 1993. *English verb classes and alternations: A preliminary investigation.* Chicago and London: The University of Chicago Press.

Li, Charles N., and Sandra A. Thompson. 1980. *Mandarin Chinese: A functional reference grammar.* Berkeley: University of California Press. https://doi.org/10.1525/9780520352858

Lieber, Rochelle. 2013. *Introducing morphology.* Cambridge: Cambridge University Press. https://doi.org/10.1017/CBO9780511808845

Lieberman, Daniel E. 2013. *The story of the human body: Evolution, health, and disease.* New York: Pantheon Books.

Lieberman, Philip. 1984. *The biology and evolution of language.* Cambridge, MA: Harvard University Press.

Lieberman, Philip. 2000. *Human language and our reptilian brain: The subcortical bases of speech, syntax, and thought.* Cambridge, MA: Harvard University Press.

Lockwood, David G. 1972. *Introduction to stratificational linguistics.* New York: Harcourt Brace Jovanovich.

Longacre, Robert E. 1964. *Grammar discovery procedures: A field manual.* The Hague: Mouton. https://doi.org.10.1515/9783110811636

Lovelock, James. 1991. *Gaia: The practical science of planetary medicine.* Sydney: Allen and Unwin.

Lupyan, Gary, Rasha Abdel Rahman, Lera Boroditsky, and Andy Clark. 2020. Effects on language on visual perception. *Trends in Cognitive Sciences* 24(11): 930–44. https://doi.org/10.1016/j.tics.2020.08.005

Luria, Aleksander R. 1976. *The working brain: An introduction to neuropsychology.* New York: Basic Books.

Lyons, John. 1977. *Semantics.* Volume 1. Cambridge: Cambridge University Press. https://doi.org/10.1017/CBO9781139165693

Maguire, Eleanor A., David G. Gadian, Ingrid S. Johnsrude, Catriona D. Good, John Ashburner, Richard S.J. Frackowiak, and Christopher D. Frith. 2000. Navigation-related structural change in the hippocampi of taxi drivers. *Proceedings of the National Academy of Sciences* 97: 4398–4403. https://doi.org/10.1073/pnas.070039597

Mann, William C. 1982. *The anatomy of a systemic choice.* Marina del Rey, CA: Information Sciences Institute, University of Southern California (ISI/RR-82-104). Also in *Discourse Processes* 8(1): 53–74. https://doi.org/10.1080/01638538509544607

Mann, William C. 1983a. An overview of the Penman text generation system. In Proceedings of the National Conference on Artificial Intelligence. *American Association for Artificial Intelligence.* 261–5. Also appears as Marina del Rey, CA: Information Sciences Institute, University of Southern California. ISI/RR-83-114.

Mann, William C. 1983b. An introduction to the Nigel text generation grammar. In *Nigel: A systemic grammar for text generation.* Marina del Rey, CA: Information Sciences Institute, University of Southern California (ISI/RR-83-105). Also in James D. Benson and William S. Greaves (eds.), *Systemic functional approaches to discourse: Selected papers from the 12th International Systemic Workshop.* Norwood, NJ: Ablex. 84–95.

Mann, William C. 1983c. Inquiry semantics: A functional semantics of natural language grammar. In *Proceedings of the First Conference of the European Chapter of the Association for Computational Linguistics.* 165–75. https://doi.org/10.3115/980092.980120

Mann, William C. 1984. A linguistic overview of the Nigel text generation grammar. In A. Manning, P. Martin, and K. McCalla (eds.), The Tenth LACUS Forum, 1983. Columbia, SC: Hornbeam Press. 255–65.

Mann, William C., Madeline Bates, Barbara J. Grosz, David D. McDonald, and Kathleen R. McKeown. 1982. Text generation: The state of the art and the literature. *American Journal of Computational Linguistics* 8.2: 62–70. http//doi.org/10.1145/358523.358553

Mann, William C., and Christian Matthiessen. 1983. *Nigel: A systemic grammar for text generation.* Marina del Rey, CA: USC/Information Sciences Institute (RR-83-105).

Mann, William C., and Christian Matthiessen. 1985. Demonstration of the Nigel text generation computer program. In James D. Benson and William S. Greaves (eds.),

Systemic functional approaches to discourse: Selected papers from the 12th International Systemic Workshop. Norwood, NJ: Ablex. 50–83.

Mann, William C., Christian Matthiessen, and Sandra Thompson. 1992. Rhetorical structure theory and text analysis. In William C. Mann and Sandra Thompson (eds.), *Discourse description: Diverse linguistic analyses of a fund-raising text*. Amsterdam: Benjamins. https://doi.org/10.1075/pbns.16.04man

Mann, William C., and James A. Moore. 1980. *Computer as author: Results and prospects*. USC/Information Sciences Institute, Research report 79–82.

Mann, William C., and James A. Moore. 1981. Computer generation of multiparagraph English text. *Computational Linguistics* 1(1): 17–29. https://doi.org/10.1145/358523.358553

Mann, William C., and Sandra Thompson. 1987. *Rhetorical structure theory: A theory of text organization*. Marina del Rey, Cal.: Information Sciences Institute, University of Southern California (ISI/RR-87-190). https://doi.org/10.1515/text.1.1988.8.3.24

Manning, Christopher D. 2003. Probabilistic syntax. In Bod, Hay, and Jannedy, 289–341. https://doi.org/10.7551/mitpress/5582.003.0011

Manning, Christopher D., and Hinrich Schütze. 1999. *Foundations of statistical natural language processing*. Cambridge, MA: MIT Press.

Martin, Alex. 2007. The representation of the object concepts in the brain. *Annual Review of Psychology*. 58: 25–45. https://doi.org/10.1146/annurev.psych.57.102904.190143

Martin, J.R. 1985. Process and text: Two aspects of human semiosis. In James D. Benson and William S. Greaves (eds.), *Systemic functional approaches to discourse: Selected papers from the 12th International Systemic Workshop*. Norwood, NJ: Ablex. 248–74.

Martin, J.R. 1988. Hypotactic recursive systems in English: Towards a functional interpretation. In James D. Benson and William S. Greaves (eds.), *Systemic functional approaches to discourse: Selected papers from the 12th International Systemic Workshop*. Norwood, NJ: Ablex. 240–70.

Martin, J.R. 1990. Interpersonal grammaticalisation: Mood and modality in Tagalog. *Philippine Journal of Linguistics* (Special monograph issue celebrating the 25th anniversary of the Language Study Centre, Philippine Normal College): 2–50.

Martin, J.R. 1991. Intrinsic functionality: Implications for contextual theory. *Social Semiotics* 1.1: 99–162. https://doi.org/10.1080/10350339109360331

Martin, J.R. 1992a. *English text: System and structure*. Amsterdam: Benjamins. https://doi.org/10.1075/z.59

Martin, J.R. 1992b. Macro-proposals: Meaning by degree. In William C. Mann and Sandra A. Thompson (eds.), *Text description: Diverse analyses of a fund-raising text*. Amsterdam: Benjamins. 359–95. https://doi.org/10.1075/pbns.16.14mar

Martin, J.R. 1996. Types of structure: Deconstructing notions of constituency in clause and text. In Eduard Hovy and Donia Scott (eds.) *Burning issues in discourse: A multidisciplinary perspective*. Heidelberg: Springer. 39–66. https://doi.org/10.1007/978-3-662-03293-0_2

Martin, J.R. (ed.). 2013. *Interviews with M.A.K. Halliday*. London: Bloomsbury Academic.

Martin, J.R., and Christian M.I.M. Matthiessen. 1991. Systemic typology and topology. In Frances Christie (ed.), *Literacy in social processes: Papers from the Inaugural Australian Systemic Functional Linguistics Conference*, Deakin University, January 1990. Darwin:

Centre for Studies of Language in Education, Northern Territory University. 345–83. Reprinted in J.R. Martin, 2010, *SFL theory, Volume 1* in the *Collected works of J.R. Martin*, edited by Wang Zhenhua. Shanghai: Shanghai Jiao Tong University Press. 167–215.

Martin, J.R. and P. Peters. 1985. On the analysis of exposition. In Ruqaiya Hasan (ed.), *Discourse on discourse*. Workshop reports from the Macquarie Workshop on Discourse Analysis. Applied Linguistics Association of Australia, Occasional Papers Number 7.

Martin, J.R. and Joan Rothery. 1980. *Writing Project Report*. Working Papers in Linguistics, No. 1. Sydney: Department of Linguistics, University of Sydney.

Martin, Samuel E. 1988. *A reference grammar of Japanese*. Tokyo, Rutland, and Vermont: Charles E. Tuttle Company. https://doi.org/ 10.1515/9780824843861

Martinec, Radan. 2005. Topics in Multimodality. In Ruqaiya Hasan, Christian M.I.M. Matthiessen, and Jonathan J. Webster (eds.), *Continuing discourse on language: A functional perspective, volume 1*, London: Equinox. 157–81.

Matthiessen, Christian M.I.M. 1981. A grammar and a lexicon for a text-production system. *Proceedings of the 19th annual meeting of the Association for Computational Linguistics*, Sperry UNIVAC. 49–55. https://doi.org/10.3115/981923.981939

Matthiessen, Christian. 1983a. The systemic framework in text generation: Nigel. In James D. Benson and William S. Greaves (eds.), *Systemic functional approaches to discourse: Selected papers from the 12th International Systemic Workshop*. Norwood, NJ: Ablex. 96–118. https://doi.org/10.3115/980092.980119

Matthiessen, Christian M.I.M. 1983b. Systemic grammar in computation: The Nigel case. In *Proceedings of the 1st annual conference of the Association for Computational Linguistics*, European Chapter. 155–65. https://doi.org/10.3115/980092.980119

Matthiessen, Christian M.I.M. 1983c. Choosing primary tense in English. *Studies in Language* 7(3): 369–430. https://doi.org/10.1075/sl.7.3.03mat

Matthiessen, Christian M.I.M. 1983d. How to make grammatical choices in text generation. In Alan Manning, Pierre Martin, and Kim McCalla (eds.), *The 10th LACUS Forum 1983*. Columbia, SC: Hornbeam Press. 266–84. https://doi.org /10.3115/981923.981939

Matthiessen, Christian M.I.M. 1984. Choosing tense in English. In *USC/ISI Report: ISI /RR*: 84–143. https://doi.org/ 10.1075/sl.7.3.03mat

Matthiessen, Christian M.I.M. 1985. The systemic framework in text generation: Nigel. In James D. Benson and William S. Greaves (eds.), *Systemic functional approaches to discourse: Selected papers from the 12th International Systemic Workshop*. Norwood, NJ: Ablex. 96–118.

Matthiessen, Christian M.I.M. 1987a. Notes on the organization of the environment of a text generation grammar. In Gerard Kempen (ed.), *Natural language generation: Recent advances in artificial intelligence, psychology and linguistics*. Dordrecht: Martinus Nijhoff. Also as USC ISI/RS-87-177. https://doi.org/10.1007/978-94-009-3645-4_17

Matthiessen, Christian M.I.M. 1987b. Systemic perspective on tense in English. In Margaret Berry, Christopher Butler, Robin Fawcett, and Guowen Huang (eds.), 1996, *Meaning and form: Systemic functional interpretations. Vol. 2 of Meaning and choice in language: Studies for Michael Halliday*. Norwood, NJ: Ablex.

Matthiessen, Christian M.I.M. 1988a. Representational issues in systemic functional grammar. In James D. Benson and William S. Greaves (eds.), *Systemic functional* approaches to discourse: Selected papers from the Twelfth International Systemic Work-shop*. Norwood, NJ.: Ablex. 136–75. Also as ISI/RS-87-179.

Matthiessen, Christian M.I.M. 1988b. A systemic semantics: The chooser and inquiry framework. In James D. Benson and William S. Greaves (eds.), *Systemic functional approaches to discourse: Selected papers from the Twelfth International Systemic Workshop*. Norwood, N.J.: Ablex. 221–42. Also as USC ISI/RS-87-189. https://doi.org /10.1075/cilt.39.10mat

Matthiessen, Christian M.I.M. 1989. Systemic theory and text generation: Some central design considerations. In *Proceedings of Australia-Japan Joint Symposium on Natural Language processing*, Melbourne University, November 27–29, 1989.

Matthiessen, Christian M.I.M. 1991a. Lexico(grammatical) choice in text-generation. In Cécile L. Paris, William R. Swartout, and William C. Mann (eds.), *Natural language generation in artificial intelligence and computational linguistics*. Dordrecht: Kluwer. 229–47. https://doi.org/10.1007/978-1-4757-5945-7_10

Matthiessen, Christian M.I.M. 1991b. Language on language: The grammar of semiosis. *Social Semiotics* 1(2): 69–111. https://doi.org/10.1080/10350339109360339

Matthiessen, Christian M.I.M. 1992. Interpreting the textual metafunction. In Martin Davies and Louise Ravelli (eds.), *Advances in systemic linguistics: Recent theory and practice*. London and New York: Pinter. 37–82. https://doi.org/10.1515/9783110260328

Matthiessen, Christian M.I.M. 1993a. Register in the round: Diversity in a unified theory of register analysis. In Mohsen Ghadessy (ed.), *Register analysis: Theory and practice*. London: Pinter. 221–92. https://doi.org/ 10.1075/rs.18010.mat

Matthiessen, Christian M.I.M. 1993b. The object of study in cognitive science. *Language as Cultural Dynamic* VI.1- 2: 187–243 (Special issue of *Cultural Dynamics*, edited by M.A.K. Halliday). https://doi.org/10.1177/092137409300600106

Matthiessen, Christian M.I.M. 1993c. Instantial systems and logogenesis. MS.

Matthiessen, Christian M.I.M. 1995a. *Lexicogrammatical cartography: English systems*. Tokyo, Taipei, and Dallas: International Language Sciences Publishers.

Matthiessen, Christian M.I.M. 1995b. Fuzziness construed in language: A linguistic perspective. *Proceedings of FUZZ/IEEE*, Yokohama, March 1995. 1871–8.

Matthiessen, Christian M.I.M. 1996. Tense in English seen through systemic-functional theory. In Christopher Butler, Margaret Berry, Robin Fawcett, and Guowen Huang (eds.), *Meaning and form: Systemic functional interpretations*. Norwood, NJ: Ablex. 431–98.

Matthiessen, Christian M.I.M. 1998. Construing processes of consciousness: From the commonsense model to the uncommonsense model of cognitive science. In J.R. Martin and Robert Veel (eds.), *Reading science: Critical and functional perspectives on discourses of science*. London: Routledge. 327–57.

Matthiessen, Christian M.I.M. 1999. The system of transitivity: An exploratory study of text-based profiles. *Functions of Language* 6(1): 1–51. https://doi.org/10.1075 /fol.6.1.02mat

Matthiessen, Christian M.I.M. 2002a. Lexicogrammar in discourse development: Logogenetic patterns of wording. In Guowen Huang and Zongyan Wang (eds.), *Discourse and language functions*. Shanghai: Foreign Language Teaching and Research Press. 91–127.

Matthiessen, Christian M.I.M. 2002b. Combining clauses into clause complexes: A multi-faceted view. In Joan Bybee and Michael Noonan (eds.), *Complex sentences in grammar and discourse: Essays in honor of Sandra A. Thompson.* Amsterdam: Benjamins. 237–322. https://doi.org/10.1075/z.110.13mat

Matthiessen, Christian M.I.M. 2004a. The evolution of language: A systemic functional exploration of phylogenetic phases. In Geoff Williams and Annabelle Lukin (eds.), *Language development: Functional perspectives on evolution and ontogenesis.* London: Continuum. 45–90.

Matthiessen, Christian M.I.M. 2004b. Descriptive motifs and generalizations. In Caffarel, Martin, and Matthiessen (eds.), 537–673. https://doi.org/10.1075/cilt.253.12mat

Matthiessen, Christian M.I.M. 2005. Remembering Bill Mann. *Journal of Computational Linguistics* 31(2): 161–71. https://doi.org/10.1162/0891201054224002

Matthiessen, Christian M.I.M. 2006. Frequency profiles of some basic grammatical systems: An interim report. In Susan Hunston and Geoff Thompson (eds.), *System and corpus: exploring connections.* London: Equinox. 103–42.

Matthiessen, Christian M.I.M. 2007a. The "architecture" of language according to systemic functional theory: Developments since the 1970s. In Hasan, Matthiessen, and Webster (eds.), 505–61.

Matthiessen, Christian M.I.M. 2007b. The lexicogrammar of emotion and attitude in English. Published in electronic proceedings based on contributions to the Third International Congress on English Grammar (ICEG 3), Sona College, Salem, Tamil Nadu, India, January 23–27, 2006.

Matthiessen, Christian M.I.M. 2009. Meaning in the making: Meaning potential emerging from acts of meaning. In anniversary issue of *Language Learning* 59 (Supplement 1): 211–35. https://doi.org/10.1111/j.1467-9922.2009.00541.x

Matthiessen, Christian M.I.M. 2012. Systemic functional linguistics as appliable linguistics: Social accountability and critical approaches. D.E.L.T.A. (Revista de Documentação de Estudos em Lingüística Teórica e Aplicada) 28: 437–71. https://doi.org/10.1590/S0102-44502012000300002

Matthiessen, Christian M.I.M. 2013. Applying systemic functional linguistics in healthcare contexts. *Text and Talk* 33(4–5): 437–66. https://doi.org/10.1515/text-2013-0021

Matthiessen, Christian M.I.M. 2014a. Extending the description of process type within the system of transitivity in delicacy based on Levinian verb classes. *Functions of Language* 21(2): 139–75. https://doi.org/10.1075/fol.21.2.01mat

Matthiessen, Christian M.I.M. 2014b. Choice in translation: Metafunctional consideration. In Kerstin Kunz, Elke Teich, Silvia Hansen-Schirra, Stella Neumann, and Peggy Daut (eds.), *Caught in the middle – language use and translation: A festschrift for Erich Steiner on the occasion of his 60th birthday.* Saarbrücken: Universaar, Saarland University Press. 271–333. https://doi.org/10.1515/9783110866193.41

Matthiessen, Christian M.I.M. 2014c. Appliable discourse analysis. In Fang Yan and Jonathan J. Webster (eds.), *Developing systemic functional linguistics: Theory and application.* London: Equinox. 135–205.

Matthiessen, Christian M.I.M. 2014d. Halliday on language. In Jonathan Webster (ed.), *The Bloomsbury companion to M.A.K. Halliday.* London and New York: Bloomsbury Academic. 137–202. Reprinted in Matthiessen, 2021b, 222–87. https://doi.org/10.1075/langct.00015.wan

Matthiessen, Christian M.I.M. 2015a. The language of space: Semiotic resources for construing our experience of space. *Japanese Journal of Systemic Functional Linguistics* Vol. 8: 1–64.

Matthiessen, Christian M.I.M. 2015b. Halliday's probabilistic theory of language. In Jonathan J. Webster (ed.), *The Bloomsbury companion to M.A.K. Halliday*. London and New York: Bloomsbury Academic. 203–41.

Matthiessen, Christian M.I.M. 2015c. Halliday on language. In Jonathan J. Webster (ed.), *The Bloomsbury companion to M.A.K. Halliday*. London and New York: Bloomsbury Academic. 137–202.

Matthiessen, Christian M.I.M. 2020. Translation, multilingual text production and cognition: A systemic functional approach. In Arnt Jakobsen and Fabio Alves (eds.), *The Routledge handbook of translation and cognition*. London: Routledge. [Ebook published 31 May 2020.] 517–44. https://doi.org/10.4324/9781315178127-34

Matthiessen, Christian M.I.M. 2021a. The architecture of phonology according to systemic functional linguistics. In Matthiessen, 2021b, 288–338.

Matthiessen, Christian M.I.M. 2021b. *Systemic functional linguistics, Part 1*. Edited by Kazuhiro Teruya, Canzhong Wu, and Diana Slade. Sheffield and Bristol: Equinox.

Matthiessen, Christian M.I.M. 2023. *System in systemic functional linguistics: A system-based theory of language*. Sheffield: Equinox.

Matthiessen, Christian M.I.M. forthcoming a. *The architecture of language according to systemic functional linguistics*. Book MS.

Matthiessen, Christian M.I.M. forthcoming b. Systemic functional linguistics – language description, comparison and typology: Key characteristics. In Bo Wang and Ma Yuanyi (eds.), forthcoming, *Theorizing and applying systemic functional linguistics: Developments by Christian M.I.M. Matthiessen*. London: Routledge.

Matthiessen, Christian M.I.M., and John Bateman. 1991. *Text generation and systemic linguistics: Experiences from English and Japanese*. London: Pinter.

Matthiessen, Christian M.I.M., Marilyn Cross, Ichiro Kobayashi, and Licheng Zeng. 1997. Generating multimodal presentations: Resources and processes. In *Proceedings of the Artificial Intelligence in Defence Workshop AI '95*. Edited by S. Goss, Eighth Australian Joint Conference on Artificial Intelligence, Canberra, November 14, 1995. 91–109.

Matthiessen, Christian M.I.M., and M.A.K. Halliday. 2009. *Systemic functional grammar: A first step into the theory. Bilingual edition, with introduction by Huang Guowen*. Beijing: Higher Education Press.

Matthiessen, Christian M.I.M., Ichiro Kobayashi, and Licheng Zeng. 1995. *Generating multimodal presentations: Resources and processes*. MS. Macquarie University.

Matthiessen, Christian M.I.M., Annabelle Lukin, David G. Butt, Chris Cleirigh, and Christopher Nesbitt. 2005. A case study of multistratal analysis. *Australian Review of Applied Linguistics* 19: 123–50. https://doi.org/10.1075/aralss.19.08mat

Matthiessen, Christian M.I.M., and Christopher Nesbitt. 1996. On the idea of theory-neutral descriptions. In Hasan, Cloran, and Butt (eds.), 39–85. https://doi.org/10.1075/cilt.121.04mat

Matthiessen, Christian M.I.M., Michael O'Donnell, and Licheng Zeng. 1991. Discourse analysis and the need for functionally complex grammars in parsing. In *Proceedings of the 2nd Japan-Australia Symposium on Natural Language Processing*, October 2–5, 1991, Kyushu Institute of Technology, Iizuka City, Japan.

Matthiessen, Christian M.I.M., and Sandra A. Thompson. 1988. The structure of discourse and "subordination". USC ISIIRS-87. Also in John Haiman and Sandra A. Thompson (eds.), 1988, *Clause combining in grammar and discourse*. Amsterdam: Benjamins. https://doi.org/10.1075/tsl.18.12mat

Matthiessen, Christian M.I.M., Bo Wang, Yuanyi Ma, and Isaac N. Mwinlaaru. 2022. *Systemic functional insights on language and linguistics*. Berlin: Springer.

Matthiessen, Christian M.I.M., Licheng Zeng, Marilyn Cross, Ichiro Kobayashi, Kazuhiro Teruya, and Canzhong Wu. 1998. The Multex generator and its environment: Application and development. *Proceedings of the International Generation Workshop '98*, August '98, Niagara-on-the-Lake. 228–37.

Maye, Jessica, Daniel J. Weiss, and Richard N. Aslin. 2008. Statistical phonetic learning in infants: Facilitation and feature generalization. *Developmental Science* 11: 122–34. https://doi.org/10.1111/j.1467-7687.2007.00653.x

Maye, Jessica, Janet F. Werker, and LouAnn Gerken. 2002. Infant sensitivity to distributional information can affect phonetic discrimination. *Cognition* 82(3): B101–B111. https://doi.org/10.1016/S0010-0277(01)00157-3

Maynard Smith, John, and Eörs Szathmáry. 1999. *The origins of life: From the birth of life to the origin of language*. Oxford: Oxford University Press.

McCawley, James D. 1993. *Everything that linguists have always wanted to know about logic but were ashamed to ask*. 2nd edition. Chicago: Chicago University Press.

McCord, Michael C. 1975. On the form of a systemic grammar. *Journal of Linguistics* 11: 195–212. https://doi.org/10.1017/S0022226700004539

McCoy, Horace. 1935. *They shoot horses, don't they?* New York: Simon and Schuster.

McDonald, David. 1980. *Language production as a process of decision-making under constraints*. PhD thesis. Cambridge, MA: MIT Report.

McDonald, David. 1983. Natural language generation as a computational problem: An introduction. In Michael Brady and Robert C. Berwick (eds.), *Computational models of discourse*. Cambridge, MA: MIT Press. 209–66.

McEnery, Tony, and Andrew Hardie. 2011. *Corpus linguistics: Method, theory and practice*. Cambridge: Cambridge University Press.https://doi.org/ https://doi.org/10.1017/CBO9780511981395

McGregor, William. 1990. The metafunctional hypothesis and syntagmatic relations. MS.

McKeown, Kathleen R. 1982. *Generating natural language text in response to questions about database structure*. PhD thesis. Philadelphia, PA: University of Pennsylvania.

McKeown, Kathleen R., and William R. Swartout. 1987. Language generation and explanation. *Annual Review of Computer Science*, 2: 401–49. https://doi.org/10.1146/annurev.cs.02.060187.002153

Mears, John. 2001. Agricultural origins in global perspective. In Michael Adas (ed.), *Agricultural and pastoral societies in ancient and classical history*. Philadelphia, PA: Temple University Press. 36–70.

Mellish, Chris. 1988. Implementing systemic classification by unification. *Journal of Computational Linguistics*, 14.1: 40–51.

Melrose, Robin. 2005. How a neurological account of language can be reconciled with a linguist's account of language: The case of systemic-functional linguistics. *Journal Neurolinguistics* 18(5): 401–21. https://doi.org/10.1016/j.jneuroling.2005.02.002

Melrose, Robin. 2006. Protolanguage, mirror neurons, and the "front-heavy" brain: Explorations in the evolution and functional organization of language. *Linguistics and the Human Sciences* 2(1): 89–109. https://doi.org/10.1558/lhs.v2i1.89

Michel, Christian. 2020. Overcoming the modal/amodal dichotomy of concepts. *Phenomenology and the Cognitive Sciences*, 20: 655–77. https://doi.org/10.1007/s11097-020-09678-y

Minsky, Marvin L., and Seymor A. Papert. 1969. *Perceptrons: An introduction to computational geometry*. Cambridge, MA: MIT Press. https://doi.org/10.7551/mitpress/11301.001.0001

Mitkov, Ruslan (ed.). 2022. *The Oxford handbook of computational linguistics*. Second edition. Oxford: Oxford University Press. https://doi.org/9780199573691.001.0001

Monk, Ray. 1991. *Ludwig Wittgenstein: The duty of genius*. London: Vintage.

Moore, James A., and William C. Mann. 1979. A snapshot of KDS: A knowledge delivery system. In *Proceedings of the 17th Annual Meeting of the Association for Computational Linguistics*, August 1979. 51–52. https://doi.org/982163.982177

Moravcsik, Edith A., and Jessica R. Wirth (eds.). 1980. *Syntax and semantics, volume 13: Current approaches to syntax*. Cambridge, MA: Academic Press. https://doi.org/10.1163/9789004373105

Munro, Robert. 2004. A probabilistic representation of systemic functional grammar. *The 31st International Systemic Functional Congress (ISFC31)*. Kyoto, Doshisha University. Available at: https://robertmunro.com/research/munro04probabilistic.pdf

Neale, Amy. 2002. *More delicatetransitivity: Extending theprocess typesystem networks for English to include full semantic classifications*. PhD thesis. Cardiff: Cardiff University.

Nebel, Bernhard, and Norman Sondheimer. 1986. A logical-form and knowledge-based design for natural language generation. *HLT '86: Proceedings of the workshop on strategic computing natural language*. 231–41.

Neisser, Ulric. 1967. *Cognitive psychology*. Des Moines, IA: Meredith Publishing Company.

Nesbitt, Christopher. 1994. *Construing linguistic resources: Consumer perspectives*. PhD thesis. Sydney: University of Sydney.

Nesbitt, Christopher N., and Gunther Plum. 1988. Probabilities in a systemic grammar: The clause complex in English. In Robin P. Fawcett and David Young (eds.), *New developments in systemic linguistics, vol. 2: Theory and application*. London: Frances Pinter. 6–39.

O'Donnell, Michael, and John A. Bateman. 2005. SFL in computational contexts. In Hasan, Matthiessen, and Webster (eds.), 343–82.

O'Donnell, Michael, and Peter Sefton. 1995. Modelling telephonic interaction: A dynamic approach. *Journal of Applied Linguistics* 10.1: 63–78.

O'Donnell, Mick. 1990. A dynamic model of exchange. *Word* 41(3): 293–328. https://doi.org/10.1080/00437956.1990.11435825

O'Donnell, Mick. 1994. *Sentence analysis and generation: A systemic perspective*. PhD thesis. Sydney: University of Sydney.

Ojemann, George A., and Otto D. Creutzfeld. 1987. Language in humans and animals: Contribution of brain simulation and recording. In Fred Plum (ed.), *Handbook of physiology, Section 1: The nervous system, Volume 5: Higher functions of the brain*. Bethesda: American Physiological Society. 675–99.

Painter, Clare. 1984. *Into the mother tongue. A case study in early child language development*. London: Pinter.

Painter, Clare. 1993. *Learning through language: A case study in the development of language as a resource for learning from 2 1/2 to 5 years*. PhD thesis. Sydney: University of Sydney.

Painter, Clare. 1996. The development of language as a resource for thinking: A linguistic view of learning. In Ruqaiya Hasan and Geoffrey Williams (eds.), *Literacy in society*. London: Longman. 50–85.

Painter, Clare. 1999. *Learning through language in early childhood*. London: Cassell.

Painter, Clare. 2017. Learning how to mean: Parent-child interaction. In Tom Bartlett and Gerard O'Grady (eds.), *The Routledge handbook of systemic functional grammar*. London: Routledge. (eds.), 619–33.

Painter, Clare, Beverly Derewianka, and Jane Torr. 2007. From microfunctions to metaphor: Learning language and learning through language. In Hasan, Matthiessen, and Webster (eds.), 563–88.

Palmer, F.R. 1962. *The morphology of the Tigre noun*. London: Oxford University Press.

Palmer, F.R. 1968. *Prosodic analysis*. London: Oxford University Press.

Paradis, Michel. 2004. *A neurolinguistic theory of bilingualism*. Amsterdam: Benjamins. https://doi.org/10.1075/sibil.18

Paris, Cécile, and Kathleen McKeown. 1987. Discourse strategies for describing complex physical objects. *Natural Language Generation* 135: 97–115. https://doi.org/10.1007/978-94-009-3645-4_8

Parret, Herman (ed.). 1974. *Discussing Language*. The Hague: Mouton.

Patpong, Pattama. 2005. *A systemic functional interpretation of Thai grammar: An exploration of Thai narrative discourse*. PhD thesis. Sydney: Macquarie University.

Patrick, Jon. 2008. The Scamseek Project – using systemic functional grammar for text categorization. In Jonathan J. Webster (ed.), *Meaning in context: Implementing intelligent applications of language studies*. London and New York: Continuum. 221–33.

Patten, Terry. 1986. *Interpreting systemic grammar as a computational representation: A problem solving approach to text generation*. PhD thesis. Edinburgh: Edinburgh University.

Patten, Terry. 1988. *Systemic text generation as problem solving*. Cambridge: Cambridge University Press. https://doi.org/10.1017/CBO9780511665646

Patten, Terry, and Graeme Ritchie. 1987. A formal model of systemic grammar. In Gerard Kempen (ed.), *Natural language generation*. Dordrecht: Martinus Nijhof. 279–99. https://doi.org/10.1007/978-94-009-3645-4_18

Payne, John R. 1986. Negation. In Timothy Shopen (ed.), *Language typology and syntactic description: Clause structure*. Cambridge: Cambridge University Press. 197–243.

Payne, Thomas E. 1997. *Describing morphosyntax: A guide for field linguistics*. Cambridge: Cambridge University Press. https://doi.org/10.1017/CBO9780511805066

Penfield, Wilder. 1958. *The excitable cortex in conscious man.* Liverpool: Liverpool University Press.

Pike, Kenneth. 1959. Language as particle, wave and field. Reprinted in Ruth M. Brend (ed.), 1972, *Kenneth L. Pike. Selected writings.* The Hague: Mouton. https://doi.org/10.1515/9783110812213-010

Pike, Kenneth. 1967. Grammar as wave. In Edward L. Blansitt, Jr. (ed.), Monograph series on language and linguistics 20 (18th Annual Round Table). Washington DC: Georgetown University Press. 1–14. Reprinted in Ruth M. Brend (ed.), 1972, *Kenneth L. Pike. Selected writings.* The Hague: Mouton. https://doi.org/10.1515/9783110812213-018

Pike, Kenneth. 1982. *Linguistic concepts: An introduction to Tagmemics.* Lincoln, NE, and London: University of Nebraska Press.

Pinker, Steven. 1994. *The language instinct: How the mind creates language.* New York: William Morrow.

Pinker, Steven. 1998. *How the mind works.* New York: W.W. Norton.

Plum, Guenter A., and Anne Cowling. 1987. Social constraints on grammatical variables: Tense choice in English. In Ross Steele and Terry Threadgold (eds.), *Language topics: Essays in honour of Michael Halliday.* Amsterdam: Benjamins. 281–305.

Pollard, Carl, and Ivan A. Sag. 1993. *Head-driven phrase structure grammar.* Chicago and London: University of Chicago Press.

Postal, Paul M. 1974. *On raising: One rule of English grammar and its theoretical implications.* Cambridge, MA: MIT Press.

Poynton, Cate. 1984. Forms and functions: Names as vocatives. *Nottingham Linguistic Circular* 13: 1–34.

Poynton, Cate. 1996. Amplification as a mode of realisation: Attitudinal modification in the nominal group. In Margaret Berry, Christopher Butler, Robin Fawcett, and Guowen Huang (eds.), *Meaning and form: Systemic functional interpretations, meaning and choice in language: Studies for Michael Halliday. Volume 2: Grammatical Structure: A functional interpretation.* Norwood, NJ: Ablex. 211–28.

Price, Cathy J. 2012. A review and synthesis of the first 20 years of PET and fMRI studies of heard speech, spoken language and reading. *NeuroImage* 62(2): 816–47. https://doi.org/10.1016/j.neuroimage.2012.04.062

Pulvermüller, Friedemann. 2002. *The neuroscience of language: On brain circuits of words and serial order.* Cambridge: Cambridge University Press.

Quirk, de Randolph, Sidney Greenbaum, Geoffrey Leech, and Jan Svartvik. 1972. *A grammar of contemporary English.* London: Longman.

Ralescu, Anca, and James Baldwin. 1989. Concept learning from examples and counter examples. *International Journal of Man-Machine Studies* 30(3): 329–54. https://doi.org/10.1016/S0020-7373(89)80006-9

Ravelli, Louise J. 1995. A dynamic perspective: Implications for metafunctional interaction and an understanding of Theme. In Ruqaiya Hasan and Peter H. Fries (eds.), *On Subject and Theme: A discourse functional perspective.* Amsterdam: Benjamins. 187–235. https://doi.org/10.1075/cilt.118.07rav

Reddy, Michael J. 1979. The conduit metaphor: A case of frame conflict in our language about language. In Andrew Ortony (ed.), *Metaphor and thought*. Cambridge: Cambridge University Press. https://doi.org/10.1017/CBO9781139173865.012

Reich, Peter A. 1970. Relational networks. *Canadian Journal of Linguistics/Revue canadienne de linguistique* 15(2): 95–110. https://doi.org/10.1017/S0008413100026347

Rizzolatti, Giacomo, and Michael A. Arbib. 1998. Language within our grasp. *Trends in Neurosciences* 21(5): 188–94. https://doi.org/10.1016/S0166-2236(98)01260-0

Robins, Robert H. 1957. Aspects of prosodic analysis. In *Proceedings of the University of Durham Philosophical Society* I, Series B (Arts), No. 1: 1–12. Reprinted in Frank R. Palmer (ed.), 1968, *Prosodic analysis*. London: Oxford University Press. 188–201.

Robins, Robert H. 1959. In defence of WP. *Transactions of the Philological Society* 1: 116–44. https://doi.org/10.1111/j.1467-968X.1959.tb00301.x

Robinson, Jane J. 1970. Dependency structures and transformational rules. *Language* 46: 259–85. https://doi.org/10.2307/412278

Robinson, Ralph. 1641. *An English grammar: Or, a plain exposition of Lilies Grammar. In English, with ease and profitable rules for parsing and making Latina: Very useful for young scholars, and others, that would in a short time learn the Latine tongue, which may serve as a comment for them that learn Lillie's Grammar*. London, Printed by Felix Kyngston for Mathew Walbank and Laurence Chapman.

Rochester, Sherry, and J.R. Martin. 1979. *Crazy talk: A study of the discourse of schizophrenic speakers*. New York: Plenum. https://doi.org/10.1007/978-1-4615-9119-1

Rohrer, Tim. 2004. Image schemata in the brain. In Beate Hampe (ed.), 2005, *From perception to meaning: Image schemas in cognitive linguistics*. Berlin and New York: Mouton de Gruyter. 165–93. https://doi.org/10.1515/9783110197532.2.165

Rosch, Eleanor H. 1973. Natural categories. *Cognitive Psychology* 4(3): 328–50. https://doi.org/10.1016/0010-0285(73)90017-0

Rose, David. 2001. *The western desert code: An Australian cryptogrammar*. Canberra: Pacific Linguistics. https://doi.org/10.15144/PL-513

Ross, Elliott D., and Marilee Monnot. 2008. Neurology of affective prosody and its functional–anatomic organization in right hemisphere. *Brain and Language* 104(1): 51–74. https://doi.org/10.1016/j.bandl.2007.04.007

Rumelhart, David E., James L. McClelland, and The PDP Research Group. 1986. *Parallel distributed processing, Volume 2: Explorations in the microstructure of cognition*. Cambridge, MA: MIT Press. https://doi.org/10.7551/mitpress/5237.001.0001

Rumelhart, David E., Bernard Widrow, and Michael E. Lehr. 1994. The basic ideas in neural networks. *Communication of The ACM* 37(3): 87–92. https://doi.org/10.1145/175247.175256

Ryding, Karin C. 2005. *A reference grammar of Modern Standard Arabic*. Cambridge: Cambridge University Press. https://doi.org/10.1017/CBO9780511486975

Sadock, Jerrold M., and Arnold M. Zwicky. 1986. Speech act distinctions in syntax. In Timothy Shopen (ed.), *Language typology and syntactic description: Clause structure*. Cambridge: Cambridge University Press. 155–97. https://doi.org/10.1017/CBO9780511619427.005

Saffran, Jenny R., Richard N. Aslin, and Elissa L. Newport. 1996. Statistical learning by 8-month-old infants. *Science* 274: 1926–8. https://doi.org/10.1126/science.274.5294.1926

Sampson, Geoffrey. 1980. *Schools of linguistics*. Stanford, CA: Stanford University Press. https://doi.org/10.1515/9781503621282

Sapir, Edward. 1921. *Language: An introduction to the study of speech*. New York: Harcourt, Brace, Jovanovich.

Saussure, Ferdinand de. 1916. *Cours de linguistique générale*. Paris: Payot.

Schank, Roger C., and Robert P. Abelson. 1977. *Scripts, plans, goals and understanding: An inquiry into human knowledge structures*. Hillsdale, NJ: Lawrence Erlbaum.

Schmiedtová, Barbara, Christiane von Stutterheim, and Mary Carroll. 2011. Language-specific patterns in event construal of advanced second language speakers. In Aneta Pavlenko (ed.), *Thinking and speaking in two languages*. Bristol: Multilingual Matters. 66–107. https://doi.org/10.21832/9781847693389-005

Schulz, Anke and Lise Fontaine. 2019. The Cardiff model of functional syntax. In Geoff Thompson, Wendy Bowcher, Lisa Fontaine, and David Schönthal (eds.), *The Cambridge handbook of systemic functional linguistics*. Cambridge: Cambridge University Press. 230–58. https://doi.org/10.1017/9781316337936.011

Schwabe, Kerstin, and Susanne Winkler (eds.). 2007. *On information structure, meaning and form*. Amsterdam and Philadelphia: Benjamins. https://doi.org/10.1075/la.100

Sefton, Peter. 1990. *Making plans for Nigel or defining interfaces between computational representations of linguistic structure and output systems: Adding intonation, punctuation and typography systems to the Penman system*. BA honours thesis. Sydney: University of Sydney.

Sefton, Peter. 1995. *State-potentials and social subjects in systemic-functional theory: Towards a computational socio-semiotics*. PhD thesis. Sydney: University of Sydney.

Sejnowski, Terrence J. 2018. *The deep learning revolution: Machine intelligence meets human intelligence*. Cambridge, MA: MIT Press. https://doi.org/10.7551/mitpress/11474.001.0001

Shannon, Claude E. 1948. A mathematical theory of communication. *The Bell System Technical Journal* 27: 379–423. https://doi.org/10.1002/j.1538-7305.1948.tb01338.x

Shannon, Claude E., and Warren Weaver. 1949. *The mathematical theory of communication*. Urbana, IL: University of Illinois Press.

Shieber, Stuart M. 1986. *An introduction to unification-based approaches to grammar*. Stanford: CSLI Publications.

Shore, Susanna. 1992. *Aspects of a systemic functional grammar of Finnish*. PhD thesis. Sydney: Macquarie University.

Sigurd, Bengt. 1977. Om textens dynamik. *Papers from the Institute of Linguistics*, University of Stockholm. Publication 34, September 1977.

Simon, Herbert A. 1996. *The sciences of the artificial*. 3rd edition. Cambridge, MA: MIT Press. https://doi.org/10.7551/mitpress/12107.001.0001

Sinclair, John M. 1991. *Corpus, concordance, collocation*. Oxford: Oxford University Press.

Sinclair, John M. 1992. Trust the text. In Martin Davies and Louise Ravelli (eds.), *Advances in systemic linguistics: Recent theory and practice*. London: Pinter. https://doi.org/10.4324/9780203594070

Sinclair, John M. and Malcolm Coulthard. 1975. *Towards an analysis of discourse: The English used by teachers and pupils.* London: Oxford University Press.

Skyttner, Lars. 1996. *General systems theory: An introduction.* Houndsmills: Macmillan.

Skyttner, Lars. 2001. *General systems theory: Ideas and applications.* Singapore, London, and Hong Kong: World Scientific.

Slade, Diana. 1996. *The texture of casual conversation.* PhD thesis. Sydney: University of Sydney.

Slobin, Dan I. 1996. Two ways to travel: Verbs of motion in English and Spanish. In Masayoshi Shibatani and Sandra A. Thompson (eds.), *Grammatical constructions: Their form and meaning.* Oxford: Clarendon Press. 195–219. https://doi.org /10.1093/oso/9780198235392.003.0008

Slobin, Dan I. 2004a. The many ways to search for a frog: linguistic typology and the expression of motion events. In Sven Strömqvist and Ludo Verhoeven (eds.), *Relating events in narrative: Typological and contextual perspective.* Mahwah, NJ: Lawrence Erlbaum Associates. 219–57. https://doi.org/10.7551/mitpress/4117.003.0013

Slobin, Dan I. 2004b. Relating narrative events in translation. In Dorit Diskin Ravid and Hava Bat-Zeev Shyldkrot (eds.), *Perspectives on language and language development: Essays in honor of Ruth A. Berman.* Dordrecht, Boston, and London: Kluwer Academic Publishers. 115–29. https://doi.org/10.1007/1-4020-7911-7_10

Slobin, Dan I. 2008. Relations between paths of motion and paths of vision: A crosslinguistic and developmental exploration. In Virginia C. Mueller Gathercole (ed.), *Routes to language: Studies in honor of Melissa Bowerman.* Mahwah, NJ: Lawrence Erlbaum Associates. 197–221.

Smeets, Ineke. 2008. *A grammar of Mapuche.* Berlin and New York: Mouton de Gruyter. https://doi.org/10.1515/9783110211795

Soames, Scott, and David M. Perlmutter. 1979. *Syntactic argumentation and the structure of English.* Berkley, Los Angeles, and London: University of California Press.

Soon, Chun Siong, Marcel Brass, Hans-Jochen Heinze, and John-Dylan Haynes. 2008. Unconscious determinants of free decisions in the human brain. *Nature Neuroscience* 11(5): 543–5. https://doi.org/10.1038/nn.2112

Souter, Clive, and Eric Atwell. 1992. A richly annotated corpus for probabilistic parsing. *AAAI Technical Report* WS-92-01. 22 32.

Sowa, John F. 1983. Generating language from conceptual graphs. *Computers and Mathematics with Applications* 9(1): 29–43. https://doi.org/10.1016/0898-1221(83)90005-6

Spencer, Andrew. 1994. Morphological theory and English. *Links and Letters* I: 71–84.

Steels, Luc. 1998. Synthesizing the origins of language and meaning using coevolution, self-organization and level formation. In James R. Hurford, Michael Studdert-Kennedy, and Chris Knight (eds.), *Approaches to the evolution of language: Social and cognitive bases.* Cambridge: Cambridge University Press. 384–404.

Steffen, Patrick R., Dawson Hedges, and Rebekka Matheson. 2022. The brain is adaptive not triune: How the brain responds to threat, challenge, and change. *Frontiers in Psychiatry* 13: Article 802606. https://doi.org/10.3389/fpsyt.2022.802606

Stephens, Greg J., Lauren J. Silbert, and Uri Hasson. 2010. Speaker–listener neural coupling underlies successful communication. *Proceedings of the National Academy of*

Sciences of the United States of America 107(32): 14425–30. https://doi.org/10.1073/pnas.1008662107

Stetson, Raymond Herbert. 1928. *Motor phonetics: A study of speech movements in action.* The Hague: Vol. III of Archives néerlandaises de phonétique expérimentale. https://doi.org/10.1007/978-94-015-3356-0

Stewart, Tom. 2008. A consumer's guide to contemporary morphological theories. *OSU-WPL* Volume 58, Fall 2008: 138–230.

Stockwell, Robert P., Paul Schachter, and Barbara Hall Partee. 1973. *The major structures of English.* New York: Holt, Rinehart and Winston.

Sugeno, Michio. 2008. Toward elucidating language functions in the brain. In Vicenç Torra and Yasuo Narukawa (eds.), *Modeling decisions for artificial intelligence: Proceeding of 5th international conference*, MDAI 2008 Sabadell, Spain, October 30–31, 2008. Berlin and Heidelberg: Springer. 1–2. https://doi.org/10.1007/978-3-540-88269-5_1

Sullivan, William J. 1980. Syntax and linguistic semantics in stratificational theory. In Moravcsik and Wirth (eds.), 301–27. https://doi.org/10.1163/9789004373105_013

Svartvik, Jan. 1966. *On voice in the English verb.* The Hague: Mouton. https://doi.org/10.1515/9783110801699

Svartvik, Jan and Randolph Quirk (eds.). 1980. *A corpus of English conversation.* Lund: Gleerup.

Swales, John. 1990. *Genre analysis: English in an academic research setting.* Cambridge: Cambridge University Press. https://doi.org/10.1075/z.184.513swa

Taverniers, Miriam. 2019. Semantics. In Geoff Thompson, Wendy Bowcher, Lisa Fontaine, and David Schöntal (eds.), *The Cambridge handbook of systemic functional linguistics.* Cambridge: Cambridge University Press. 55–91. http:/doi.org/10.1017/9781316337936.005

Taylor, John R. 1989. *Linguistic categorization: Prototypes in linguistic theory.* Oxford: Clarendon Press.

Teich, Elke. 1999. *Systemic functional grammar in natural language generation: Linguistic description and computational representation.* London: Cassell.

Teich, Elke. 2009. Computational linguistics. In Halliday and Webster (eds.), 113–27.

Teich, Elke, Stefania Degaetano-Ortlieb, Peter Fankhauser, Hannah Kermes, and Ekaterina Lapshinova-Koltunski. 2016. The linguistic construal of disciplinarity: A data-mining approach using register features. *Journal of the Association for Information Science and Technology* 67(7): 1668–1678. https://doi.org/10.1002/asi.23457

Teruya, Kazuhiro. 2007. *A systemic functional grammar of Japanese.* 2 volumes. London: Continuum.

Teruya, Kazuhiro, Ernest Akerejola, Thomas H. Andersen, Alice Caffarel, Julia Lavid, Christian M.I.M. Matthiessen, Uwe Helm Petersen, Pattama Patpong, and Flemming Smedegaard. 2007. Typology of MOOD: A text-based and system-based functional view. In Hasan, Matthiessen, and Webster (eds.), 859–920.

Teruya, Kazuhiro, and Christian M.I.M. Matthiessen. 2015. Halliday in relation to language comparison and typology. In Jonathan J. Webster (ed.), *The Bloomsbury companion to M.A.K. Halliday.* London: Bloomsbury Academic. 427–52.

Tesnière, Lucien. 1959. *Éléments de syntaxe structurale.* Paris: Librairie C. Klincksieck.

Thai, Minh Duc. 2004. Metafunctional profile: Vietnamese. In Caffarel, Martin, and Matthiessen (eds.), 397–431. https://doi.org/10.1075/cilt.253.09tha

Thibault, Paul J. 2004. *Brain, mind and the signifying body: An ecosocial semiotic theory.* London and New York: Continuum.

Tognini-Bonelli, Elena. 2001. *Corpus linguistics at work.* Amsterdam: Benjamins. https://doi.org/10.1075/scl.6

Torr, Jane. 2015. Language development in early childhood: Learning how to mean. In Jonathan J. Webster, (ed.), *The Bloomsbury companion to M.A.K. Halliday.* London: Bloomsbury Academic. 242–56.

Traugott, Elizabeth C. 1997. The role of the development of discourse markers in a theory of grammaticalization. Paper presented at ICHL XII, Manchester 1995 Version of 11/97. Published as "Le rôle de l'évolution des marqueurs discursifs dans une théorie de la grammaticalization". In M.M. Jocelyne Fernandez-Vest and Shirley Carter-Thomas (eds.), 2004, *Structure informationallée et particules énonciatives: Essai de typologie.* Paris: L'Harmattan. 295–333.

Trevarthen, Colwyn. 1979. Communication and cooperation in early infancy: A description of primary intersubjectivity. In Margaret Bullowa (ed.), *Before speech: The beginnings of human communication.* London: Cambridge University Press. 321–47.

Trevarthen, Colwyn. 1987. Sharing making sense: Intersubjectivity and the making of an infant's meaning. In Ross Steele and Terry Threadgold (eds.), *Language topics: Essays in honour of Michael Halliday, Volume 1*. Amsterdam: Benjamins. 177–99. https://doi.org/10.1075/z.lt1.17tre

Trevarthen, Colwyn. 2011. What is it like to be a person who knows nothing? Defining the active intersubjective mind of a newborn human being. *Infant and Child Development* 20(1): Special Issue: *The intersubjective newborn:* 119–35. https://doi.org/10.1002/icd.689

Trevisan, Piergiorgio, and Adolfo M. García. 2019. Systemic functional grammar as a tool for experimental stimulus design: New appliable horizons in psycholinguistics and neurolinguistics. *Language Sciences* 75: 35–46. https://doi.org/10.1016/j.langsci.2019.101237

Trew, Tony. 1979. "What the papers say": Linguistic variation and ideological difference. In Roger Fowler, Bob Hodge, Gunther Kress, and Tony Trew, *Language and control.* London: Routledge and Kegan Paul.

Trubetzkoy, N.S. 1939. *Grundzüge der Phonologie. Travaux au Cercle Linguistique de Prague 7. Prague.* Translated by Christiane A. M. Baltaxe, 1969, as *Principles of phonology.* Berkeley: University of California Press.

Tsui, Amy. 1989. Systemic choices and discourse processes. *Word* 40: 1–2. https://doi.org/10.1080/00437956.1989.11435802

Tucker, Gordon H. 1998. *The lexicogrammar of adjectives: A systemic functional approach to lexis.* London: Cassell.

Tucker, Gordon. 2007. Between grammar and lexis: Towards a systemic functional account of phraseology. In Hasan, Matthiessen, and Webster (eds.), 953–77.

Tung, Yu-Wen, Christian Matthiessen, and Norm Sondheimer. 1988. On parallelism and the Penman natural language generation system. USC, ISI/RR-98-195.

Turner, Geoffrey J. 1973. Social class and children's language of control at age five and age seven. In Basil Bernstein (ed.), *Class, codes and control: Applied studies towards a sociology of language*. London: Routledge and Kegan Paul. 135–201.

Ultan, Russell. 1978. Some general characteristics of interrogative systems. In Joseph H. Greenberg (ed.), *Universals of human language, Volume 4: Syntax*. Stanford, CA: Stanford University Press.

Unsworth, Len. 1995. *How and why: Recontextualizing science explanations in school science books*. PhD thesis. Sydney: University of Sydney.

Van de Walle, Jürgen. 2009. Roman Jakobson, cybernetics and information theory: A critical assessment. *Folia Linguistica Historica* 29(1): 87–123.

Van Valin, Robert, Jr., and William Foley. 1980. Role and Reference Grammar. In Moravcsik and Wirth (eds.), 329–52. https://doi.org/10.1163/9789004373105_014

Ventola, Eija. 1987. *The structure of social interaction: A systemic approach to the semiotics of service encounters*. London: Frances Pinter.

Vygotsky, Lev Semenovich. 1962. *Thought and language*. Edited and translated by Eugenia Hanfmann and Gertrude Vakar. Cambridge, MA: MIT Press. https://doi.org/10.1037/11193-000

Wang, Jing, Julie A. Conder, David N. Blitzer, and Svetlana V. Shinkareva. 2010. Neural representation of abstract and concrete concepts: A meta-analysis of neuroimaging studies. *Human Brain Mapping* 31: 1459–68. https://doi.org/10.1002/hbm.20950

Wanner, Leo. 1997. *Exploring lexical resources for text generation in a systemic functional language model*. (Dissertation zur Erlangung des akademischen Grades eines Doktors der Philosophie der Philosophischen Fakultät der Universität des Saarlandes.) PhD thesis. Saarlandes: Universität des Saarlandes.

Warrington, Elizabeth K., and Rosaleen A. McCarthy. 1987. Categories of knowledge: Further fractionations and attempted integration. *Brain* 110(5): 1273–96. https://doi.org/10.1093/brain/110.5.1273

Warrington, Elizabeth K., and Tim Shalice. 1984. Category specific semantic impairments. *Brain* 107(3): 829–54. https://doi.org/10.1093/brain/107.3.829

Watson, Catherine E., Eileen R. Cardillo, Geena R. Ianni, and Anjan Chatterjee. 2013. Action concepts in the brain: An activation likelihood estimation meta-analysis. *Journal of Cognitive Neuroscience* 25(8): 1191–1205. https://doi.org/10.1162/jocn_a_00401

Weber, David J. 1989. *A grammar of Huallaga (Huánuco) Quechua*. Berkeley and Los Angeles: University of California Press.

Webster, Jonathan. 1993. Text processing using the functional grammar processor (FGP). In Mohsen Ghadessy (ed.), *Register analysis: Theory and practice*. London: Pinter. 181–95.

Weerasinghe, A. Ruvan. 1994. *Probabilistic parsing in systemic functional grammar*. PhD thesis. Cardiff: University of Wales College of Cardiff.

Weinreich, Harald. 1972. Die Textpartitur als heuristische Methode. *Der Deutschunterricht* 24(4): 43–60.

Wells, Gordon. 1994. The complementary contributions of Halliday and Vygotsky to a "language-based theory of learning". *Linguistics and Learning* 6: 41–90. https://doi.org/10.1016/0898-5898(94)90021-3

Wertsch, James V. 1985. *Vygotsky and the social formation of mind.* Cambridge, MA: Harvard University Press. https://doi.org/10.2307/j.ctv26071b0

Whitaker, Harry A. 1969. On the representation of language in the human brain: Problems in the neurology of language and the linguistic aphasia. *UCLA Working Papers in Phonetics* 12.

Whitelaw, Casey, Maria Herke-Couchman, and Jon Patrick. 2005. Identifying interpersonal distance using systemic features. In James G. Shanahan, Yan Qu, and Janyce Wiebe (eds.), *Computing attitude and affect in text.* Springer. 199–214.

Wignell, Peter, J.R. Martin, and Suzanne Eggins. 1989. The discourse of geography: Ordering and explaining the experiential world. *Linguistics and Education* 1(4): 359–91. https://doi.org/10.1016/S0898-5898(89)80007-5

Wilson, Edward O. 2019. *Genesis: The deep origin of societies.* New York and London: Liveright Publishing Corporation.

Winograd, Terry. 1972. *Understanding natural language.* Edinburgh: Academic Press. https://doi.org/10.1016/0010-0285(72)90002-3

Winograd, Terry. 1975. Frame representations and the declarative/procedural controversy. In Daniel G. Bobrow and Allan Collins (eds.), *Representation and understanding: Studies in cognitive sciences.* New York: Academic Press. 185–210. https://doi.org/10.1016/B978-0-12-108550-6.50012-4

Winograd, Terry. 1983. *Language as a cognitive process: Syntax.* Reading, MA: Addison Wesley Longman Publishing.

Woods, William. 1975. What's in a link: Foundations for semantic networks. In Daniel G. Bobrow and Allan Collins (eds.), *Representation and understanding: Studies in cognitive science.* New York: Academic Press. 35–82. https://doi.org/10.1016/B978-0-12-108550-6.50007-0

Wu, Canzhong. 1992. *A functional approach to the problem of translating university introductions.* MA thesis. Xi'an: Xi'an Jiaotong University.

Wu, Canzhong. 2000. *Modelling linguistic resources.* PhD thesis. Sydney: Macquarie University.

Wu, Canzhong. 2009. Corpus-based research. In Halliday and Webster (eds.), 128–42.

Yager, Ronald R., and Lotfi A. Zadeh (eds.). 1992. *An introduction to fuzzy logic applications in intelligent systems.* New York: Springer. https://doi.org/10.1007/978-1-4615-3640-6

Zadeh, Lotfi A. 1965. Fuzzy sets. *Information and Control* 8(3): 338–53. https://doi.org/10.1016/S0019-9958(65)90241-X

Zadeh, Lotfi. 1972. A fuzzy-set theoretic interpretation of linguistic hedges. *Journal of Cybernetics,* 2(2): 4–34. Reprinted in Richard M. Tong, Hung T. Nguyen, Ronald R. Yager, and S. Ovchinnikov (eds.), 1987, *Fuzzy sets and applications: Selected papers by L.A. Zadeh.* New York: John Wiley and Sons. https://doi.org/10.1080/01969727208542910

Zaidel, Eran. 1983. A response to Gazzaniga: Language in the right hemisphere, convergent perspectives. *American Psychologist* 38(5): 542–6. https://doi.org/10.1037/0003-066X.38.5.542

Zappavigna, Michele. 2011. Visualizing logogenesis: Preserving the dynamics of meaning. In Shoshana Dreyfus, Susan Hood, and Maree Stenglin (eds.), *Semiotic margins: Meaning in multimodalities.* London and New York: Continuum. 211–29.

Zhong Yin, Chu-Ren Huang, and Sicong Dong. 2020. Bodily sensation and embodiment: A corpus-based study of gustatory vocabulary in Mandarin Chinese. *The Journal of Chinese Linguistics*: 1–36. https://doi.org/10.1353/jcl.2022.0008

Zipf, George K. 1935. *The psychobiology of language*. Boston: Houghton Mifflin.

Index